AF895914

LIVING LITURGY™

LIVING LITURGY™

Spirituality, Celebration, and Catechesis for Sundays and Solemnities

Year B • 2027

Katharine E. Harmon
Orin E. Johnson
Rámond Mitchell
Matthew Sherman

LITURGICAL PRESS
Collegeville, Minnesota

litpress.org

Cover design by Monica Bokinskie. Art by Br. Martin Erspamer, OSB, a monk of Saint Meinrad Archabbey, Indiana.

Published with the approval of the Committee on Divine Worship, United States Conference of Catholic Bishops.

Printed in the United States of America.

ISSN 1547-089X
ISBN 979-8-4008-0213-3

CONTENTS

Introduction vii

Season of Advent 1

Season of Christmas 23

Ordinary Time I 45

Season of Lent 63

Easter Triduum 93

Season of Easter 103

Ordinary Time II 141

Appendix A: *Readings (continued)* 261

Appendix B: *Lectionary Pronunciation Guide* 324

Contributors 328

INTRODUCTION

As a premier Catholic publisher, Liturgical Press remains committed to offering liturgical, spiritual, and scriptural resources rooted in the Benedictine tradition with a desire to deepen the faith and knowledge of today's richly diverse church. While these resources have changed and developed over the years, the commitment to sound theology and best pastoral practice remain hallmarks of our mission and ministry. *Living Liturgy*™ is one of our most loved and widely used incarnations of this commitment.

Living Liturgy helps people prepare for liturgy and live a liturgical spirituality—a way of living that is rooted in liturgy. The paschal mystery is the central focus of liturgy, of the gospels, and of this volume. As Pope Francis reminded us in his apostolic letter on liturgical formation, in the liturgy the paschal mystery is "rendered present and active by means of signs addressed to the senses (water, oil, bread, wine, gestures, words), so that the Spirit, plunging us into the paschal mystery, might transform every dimension of our life, conforming us more and more to Christ" (*Desiderio desideravi* 21). *Living Liturgy* is therefore more than a title. Rather, "living liturgy" is a commitment to a relationship with Jesus Christ, embodied in our everyday actions and interactions.

From its beginnings over 25 years ago, *Living Liturgy* has supported liturgical spirituality in distinctive ways, and with *Living Liturgy* 2027 we have streamlined this classic resource in order to highlight its unique features and pathways: centering each Sunday or solemnity by reflecting on the gospel; making connections between the gospel, readings, and psalm; making connections to our lived experience and how we grow deeper in the paschal mystery through our participation in the liturgy each week; offering insights into liturgical spirituality for particular liturgical ministries; and offering practical ideas for preparing the liturgy and its prayers.

At its heart, *Living Liturgy* is a resource for spiritual reflection, for presiders, preachers, lectors, music ministers, extraordinary ministers of Holy Communion, ministers of hospitality, members of the assembly, environment and catechumenal teams, liturgists, liturgy committees, and more. Now in a portable but substantial format, we hope this edition of *Living Liturgy* will continue to help foster liturgical participation and make liturgical spirituality a lived reality.

SEASON OF ADVENT

SPIRITUALITY

GOSPEL ACCLAMATION
Ps 85:8

℟. Alleluia, alleluia.
Show us, Lord, your love;
and grant us your salvation.
℟. Alleluia, alleluia.

Gospel

Mark 13:33-37; L2B

Jesus said to his disciples:
"Be watchful! Be alert!
You do not know when the time will come.
It is like a man traveling abroad.
He leaves home and places his servants in charge, each with his own work,
and orders the gatekeeper to be on the watch.
Watch, therefore;
you do not know when the lord of the house is coming,
whether in the evening, or at midnight,
or at cockcrow, or in the morning.
May he not come suddenly and find you sleeping.
What I say to you, I say to all: 'Watch!'"

Praying with Gospel Words and Phrases

Be alert . . . Watch . . . You do not know . . .

Reflecting on the Gospel

Advent is perhaps the most difficult season for the liturgy to feel like it meshes well with everything else going on in life. Lent coincides with the darkest coldest days of winter. Easter aligns with warming days and the earth itself springing back to life. In Advent, though, no matter how well the liturgy and music are crafted and executed, it can feel that these efforts, while working against the pervasive, secular "Christmas spirit" that imbues almost everything outside the church doors at this time of year, are nearly meaningless.

The mismatch is more than this dichotomy, however. Perhaps you've heard in a variety of circumstances the expression, "Participate, don't anticipate." Or perhaps while anxiously waiting for a hospital test result, you've realized that not knowing is the worst part of that waiting. The human condition is one of always wanting what it wants right away; of always wanting to know what is happening right now and what will be happening next; of always wanting power and influence over all these things and more. So indeed, Advent can be a time of fruitful opposition to quite a lot of the human existence—if we let it be so. And we should!

The gospel that begins our new liturgical year admonishes us, the faithful, to watch and be alert. Why? Because, simply, we do not know. In this pericope what is unknown is "when the lord of the house is coming." But for each of us today, this gospel calls us to embrace the unknown, as another expression goes, and to participate, actively, in our lives of faith instead of anticipating. So in fact, the gospel is calling us, really, to not know—and to be okay with not knowing.

We don't need all the things we want, our faith teaches us. We don't need to know—we can't even understand—the mind of God, and everything that is happing now or what is coming next. We don't need power and influence; Jesus taught us by washing feet and by dying on the cross. We need only God, God who is love, hope, joy, life, and salvation. Advent teaches us this if we let it, and that all the faithful truly need is to keep faithful watch.

To the Point

Advent as a season stands in opposition to some natural human tendencies. In broad strokes: we dislike waiting, we dislike not knowing, we dislike having no power. Further, Advent calls us to replace these desires with joyful hope and eager anticipation.

Preparing to Proclaim, Preach, and Pray

Making Connections Between the Readings: While the gospel passage seems to leave little room for interpretation, the passage from Isaiah paired with it fires the imagination with each passing sentence. In your mind's eye, picture the omnipotent divine Creator literally ripping a hole in the sky and clouds to visit us on earth, and the mountains and hills trembling before God's mighty deeds. And these apocalyptic sights are ones we have asked for! The passage itself is vague, about how the faithful have wondered away from God, our sinful deeds, how we have made ourselves unclean. What is the current, modern context that informs our sharing and our hearing of these words?

If we are clay in the hands of the divine potter, into what shall our God remake us? Far too often we believe ourselves to know the answer to this question, instead of letting God form and mold us into vessels for God's own purpose and dwelling place. When seeking to align our will with God's, some self-examination may be in order: Have we ever been guilty of making God in our own image? We are probably lying if we try to answer "no."

The epistle describes the power and vitality that the grace of Jesus Christ gives to each of his disciples: enriching speech, all knowledge, and ultimately, any spiritual gift. These are given to help each of us remain faithful, stay alert, and, as the gospel bids us, keep watch in our time of waiting and unknowing.

Making Connections to the Responsorial Psalm: It seems nearly invariable that, when reflecting on the Scriptures for a given liturgy, the psalm fulfills a certain role between at least the first reading and the gospel reading, and occasionally all the Scriptures. Sometimes that function might be imagined as a bridge; sometimes as a lynchpin; sometimes as a key, unlocking new and welcome insights. Focusing in more tightly, the psalm refrain is a lens through which we see not only the rest of the psalm verses but the readings as a whole.

Recall those frightful images from the Isaiah reading, and the reproach in the gospel to keep watch. These could be seen, without the psalm, as alarming and dire. We keep watch for the divine power that rends the skies and shakes mountains not for such literal destruction, but rather for salvation: "let us see your face and we shall be saved." God comes to care for, protect, make strong, and help us, and ultimately to give us new life.

CONNECTING TO EXPERIENCE: LIVING THE PASCHAL MYSTERY

It is easy to be lazy. It is easy to "fall asleep"—to become distracted, picking up our tasks or our telephone, quietly numbing our senses, calcifying our hearts and drowning out our ability even to hear the blaring cockcrow of the Word of God. We are called to more than this. The disciples who Jesus had gathered around him had the untold blessing of beholding the living God in Christ Jesus. Through the mystery of our faith, we are Jesus's disciples. And Jesus is with us now. When we see pained faces, hurting hearts, aching bodies, or wounded spirits, we see Christ, hear him. Do we believe this? We hear in the gospel today, "Be watchful! Be alert!" Advent calls us to remember who we are. We have the grace of God bestowed on us. We can choose to be focused. We can choose to watch, to see those in front of us. We never know when we might behold the face of Christ.

PROMPTS FOR FAITH-SHARING

- How can you watch for Christ today? This Advent? Where have you forgotten to look for him?
- Where, in your life, are you "asleep" to the needs of Christ and neighbor? How can you "wake up" to a new life of being attentive?
- Which gifts has Christ given you to stay alert and to take care of his household until he returns? Which of these gifts have you been reluctant to acknowledge and why?

Model Penitential Act

Presider: In today's gospel, Jesus calls his disciples to "stay awake" and "keep watch" for the coming of the Son of Man. Preparing our hearts for his coming, let us ask for his mercy and forgiveness . . . *[pause]*

Lord Jesus, you call us out of sin and darkness: Lord, have mercy.
Christ Jesus, you offer your sinful people compassion and love: Christ, have mercy.
Lord Jesus, you are the light of life: Lord, have mercy.

Model Universal Prayer (Prayer of the Faithful)

Presider: Awake and ready to follow God's will, we turn to him with our prayers and petitions.

Response: Lord, hear our prayer.

For the church throughout the world: may the faithful await with joy the light of Christ and find freedom from the darkness of sin, loneliness, and suffering, we pray . . .

For greater peace in our hearts, in our communities, and among those who lead us: may we choose the mercy of Christ as we seek fellowship with our neighbors, we pray . . .

For hearts open to the suffering of those near us and those far away: may our watchfulness this Advent season open our hearts as well as our eyes, we pray . . .

For deepening of our attention and our focus: may we reject distractions and self-absorption to be truly present to those around us, we pray . . .

Presider: Almighty and ever-living God, you are the Alpha and the Omega. As we begin this Advent season, may we remember the wonder of your love through our mercy and compassion to all the world. We ask this through Christ our Lord. **Amen.**

Liturgy and Music

It is wise to mark the changing of seasons with noticeable changes throughout the liturgy. Many of these are obvious and prescribed by the *General Instruction of the Roman Missal*, or other guiding documents. Advent brings violet hues to vestments, the progression of the Advent wreath, the absence of the Gloria on Sundays. Beyond the omission of the Gloria, other changes in the music of the liturgy are likely more subtle. Surely, there are hymns specific to the season. Further, we can help distinguish Advent as a unique time of year by how they and all the liturgical pieces of music are presented. Changes in use of unisons and harmonies, tempos, and use of (or resting of) certain instruments can be very effective in helping our assemblies mark the passing of time, and the different character of each liturgical season.

(continued on next page)

COLLECT

Let us pray.

Pause for silent prayer

Grant your faithful, we pray, almighty God,
the resolve to run forth to meet your Christ
with righteous deeds at his coming,
so that, gathered at his right hand,
they may be worthy to possess the
heavenly Kingdom.
Through our Lord Jesus Christ, your Son,
who lives and reigns with you in the unity
of the Holy Spirit,
God, for ever and ever. **Amen.**

FIRST READING

Isa 63:16b-17, 19b; 64:2-7

You, Lord, are our father,
our redeemer you are named forever.
Why do you let us wander, O Lord, from
your ways,
and harden our hearts so that we fear
you not?
Return for the sake of your servants,
the tribes of your heritage.
Oh, that you would rend the heavens and
come down,
with the mountains quaking before you,
while you wrought awesome deeds we
could not hope for,
such as they had not heard of from of
old.
No ear has ever heard, no eye ever seen,
any God but you
doing such deeds for those who wait for
him.
Would that you might meet us doing right,
that we were mindful of you in our
ways!
Behold, you are angry, and we are sinful;
all of us have become like unclean
people,
all our good deeds are like polluted rags;
we have all withered like leaves,
and our guilt carries us away like the
wind.
There is none who calls upon your name,
who rouses himself to cling to you;
for you have hidden your face from us
and have delivered us up to our guilt.
Yet, O Lord, you are our father;
we are the clay and you the potter:
we are all the work of your hands.

RESPONSORIAL PSALM
Ps 80:2-3, 15-16, 18-19

℟. (4) Lord, make us turn to you; let us see your face and we shall be saved.

O shepherd of Israel, hearken,
from your throne upon the cherubim, shine forth.
Rouse your power,
and come to save us.

℟. Lord, make us turn to you; let us see your face and we shall be saved.

Once again, O Lord of hosts,
look down from heaven, and see;
take care of this vine,
and protect what your right hand has planted,
the son of man whom you yourself made strong.

℟. Lord, make us turn to you; let us see your face and we shall be saved.

May your help be with the man of your right hand,
with the son of man whom you yourself made strong.
Then we will no more withdraw from you;
give us new life, and we will call upon your name.

℟. Lord, make us turn to you; let us see your face and we shall be saved.

SECOND READING
1 Cor 1:3-9

Brothers and sisters:
Grace to you and peace from God our Father
and the Lord Jesus Christ.

I give thanks to my God always on your account
for the grace of God bestowed on you in Christ Jesus,
that in him you were enriched in every way,
with all discourse and all knowledge,
as the testimony to Christ was confirmed among you,
so that you are not lacking in any spiritual gift
as you wait for the revelation of our Lord Jesus Christ.
He will keep you firm to the end,
irreproachable on the day of our Lord Jesus Christ.
God is faithful,
and by him you were called to fellowship with his Son,
Jesus Christ our Lord.

We should be mindful that, even though it is sometimes nicknamed "Little Lent," Advent should have "joyful, anxious anticipation" as a primary effect, not penitence. Still, it may be a good time to include a sung *Kyrie* if that is not already a regular practice. Consider using one hymn as a common gathering, communion, or sending hymn for the entire season. Not only will that help unify the season, but it will give your music ministers that much more time each week to prepare for Christmas!

Liturgical Ministers: Environment Ministers

The First Sunday of Advent shapes the church's posture for the entire season. Environment ministers are called to cultivate a space that embodies watchfulness, expectation, and restraint. The sanctuary should not appear festive but convey the quiet longing of a community awaiting the Lord. The Advent wreath with its first candle serves as a focal sign, drawing the assembly into attentive prayer. Violet vestments, evergreens, and modest arrangements communicate anticipation rather than celebration. Environment ministers are formed in their ministry by practicing patience and discernment, resisting the temptation to rush the season with Christmas decorations. Each subtle change in the worship space week by week invites the assembly to enter the rhythm of Advent, teaching the value of waiting, reflection, and spiritual attentiveness. Through this ministry, environment ministers help the community encounter the mystery of Christ's coming in a measured, prayerful way, shaping both the assembly's experience and their own capacity to minister with care and reverence.

Living Liturgy: Liturgy and Community

The gospel's call to "Be watchful! Be alert!" reminds us that Christian waiting is never complacent. To watch for Christ is to cultivate awareness of God's presence in daily life and to prepare to meet Christ in those who are most in need. In our communities, this might take the form of renewed attentiveness to the lonely, the grieving, or the poor. Advent waiting is a communal act. When we support one another, carry each other's hopes, and remain faithful in prayer, we live the reality of hope together. This First Sunday of Advent invites us to see waiting not as wasted time but as holy preparation.

SPIRITUALITY

GOSPEL ACCLAMATION
Luke 3:4, 6

℟. Alleluia, alleluia.
Prepare the way of the Lord, make straight his paths:
all flesh shall see the salvation of God.
℟. Alleluia, alleluia.

Gospel

Mark 1:1-8; L5B

The beginning of the gospel of Jesus Christ the Son of God.

As it is written in Isaiah the prophet:
Behold, I am sending my messenger ahead of you;
he will prepare your way.
A voice of one crying out in the desert:
"Prepare the way of the Lord, make straight his paths."
John the Baptist appeared in the desert proclaiming a baptism of repentance for the forgiveness of sins.
People of the whole Judean countryside and all the inhabitants of Jerusalem were going out to him
and were being baptized by him in the Jordan River
as they acknowledged their sins.
John was clothed in camel's hair, with a leather belt around his waist.
He fed on locusts and wild honey.
And this is what he proclaimed:
"One mightier than I is coming after me.
I am not worthy to stoop and loosen the thongs of his sandals.
I have baptized you with water;
he will baptize you with the Holy Spirit."

Praying with Gospel Words and Phrases
Crying out . . . proclaiming . . . forgiveness of sins . . .

Reflecting on the Gospel
Mark is the shortest canonical gospel, and it is generally acknowledged as the earliest one written. It is succinct if not abrupt, and essentially gives us only and exactly the good news we need to know. The very first words in Mark's Gospel introduce us to John the Baptist, in vivid ways that not many other figures in his Gospel receive. We hear about his ministry, what he looked like, what he ate, and many of the things he said while proclaiming the coming messiah. John is obviously important in Mark's otherwise brusque Gospel. Why might that be?

John's preaching can be seen as an overture before the main event: the salvific mission of his cousin, Jesus. The way of the Lord that is to be prepared links the historical end of the Babylonian exile to the current-day coming of Jesus; John the Baptist is on hand to prepare the way for Christ and for his freeing salvation.

More than that, John exists in this gospel to not only teach us by his words but by his example: how does one—how do we—today prepare for the coming of the Lord? Christmas, we will recall, exists as a celebration of not only the eternal Word taking on human flesh, but of that second coming at the end of human time. Taking John's example, we might today choose to live more simply than we currently do, in our attire and diets. We might choose to more freely share with those we encounter the way our lives have been impacted by our faith and our relationship with Jesus. We might more readily acknowledge our own lowliness and point, by our words and deeds, instead to the mighty God of heaven and earth.

To the Point
We too are called to make ready a straight path for God, into the hearts and minds of all the faithful, and into our own souls as well. This cannot be a passive experience, and it isn't always a quiet and inward-looking process. How do we balance the quiet stillness of the Advent season alongside the energetic needs of preparation and proclamation?

Preparing to Proclaim, Preach, and Pray

Making Connections Between the Readings: Isaiah, the prevailing prophet of Advent, rejoices this weekend as the Babylonian exile nears its end. This is what Mark's Gospel hearkens back to as it begins its proclamation of the good news. The captives are to return home, and that pathway home is to be made as direct and expedient as possible.

While often the expression is that one's faith must be more than words and must also be lived, here the prophet impels us to not only take faithful actions but to announce and proclaim the coming of the Lord. Here is the power and might of God, the care and guidance of the divine shepherd.

This godly power extends even over time itself, Peter warns us. Last week we were advised to be alert and to be ready, and even to not know what to be ready for. This week? The Lord is coming soon, whatever "soon" might mean to God. To God, a thousand years are like an evening come and gone. What might seem far off to our human senses might very well be as soon as you take your next breath. Yet the timing, on its own, is not really the point.

Rather, this unknown timing impels us not only to fervent action but to bold proclamation. At the end of the Babylonian exile all those who were displaced were gathered and returned home. It's just not enough to make sure we ourselves, individually, are prepared. No, we must make sure as many people as we can know the saving power of God and are brought into the Christian community of hope, salvation, and eternal life.

Making Connections to the Responsorial Psalm: Whereas last week we prayed by the psalm to see God's face and therefore salvation, this week the psalm seeks salvation not in a divine image but in divine kindness. Put another way, we pray this week to see God's image in action, to hear God's voice.

While our liturgical year leads us through the paschal mystery, and it might do so somewhat chronologically, it's not like we don't know the end of the story—at least thus far. Advent is both about the incarnation and about the second coming, which means we pray and live now as people in this paradoxical time sometimes called "already, not yet." Salvation has already been won but not yet attained in its fullest form. Christ, ascended, has no body, no hands nor feet nor voice, but ours. If others on earth are to know of God's mercy and salvation, that almost invariably will need to be by God's working in and through each of us.

CONNECTING TO EXPERIENCE: LIVING THE PASCHAL MYSTERY

Mark's Gospel tells us that baptism prepares us for the coming of Jesus. But for those of us who are already baptized, how do we prepare for Christ who is once *again* approaching this Advent? Baptism does not end with one day of washing. Baptism initiates us into Christ's paschal mystery. As the second letter of Peter tells us, God's arrival is marked by a fiery dissolution of all that has been, in order to clear the way for his fullness. For those of us who have been baptized, this is the fire of the Holy Spirit. This Advent, we can ask the Spirit to dissolve our struggles, our fears, and our distractions which keep us from receiving him anew at Christmas. We can focus on Christ and his coming. We come to the sacraments for his grace. His presence among us in incarnate strength is a fire that creates a new heaven and a new earth, both within us and without us!

PROMPTS FOR FAITH-SHARING

- How can you renew your baptismal commitment to Christ this Advent? What practice, habit, or prayer can you take on, that will help you to grow in the life of Christ?
- What can you wash away from your life this Advent, in order to make way for Christ?
- In this time of waiting, how can you become the presence of Christ to someone who needs you, so that you can make Christ's incarnation more complete?

Model Penitential Act

Presider: Today's reading from Isaiah enjoins us to prepare the way of the Lord! As we prepare our hearts, minds, and bodies for his coming, we ask for God's mercy . . . *[pause]*

Lord Jesus, you are the Shepherd of souls: Lord, have mercy.
Christ Jesus, you usher in a new day of pardon and peace: Christ, have mercy.
Lord Jesus, you offer us repentance and forgiveness: Lord, have mercy.

Model Universal Prayer (Prayer of the Faithful)

Presider: In Christ, we seek to create a new heaven and a new earth by the power of our baptism. In the hope of this renewal, we bring our petitions to the Lord.

Response: Lord, hear our prayer.

For the church: that it may renew the earth by its faith-filled witness in the world, we pray . . .

For those who hold public office in this country and across the globe: that they may transform their civic systems to best serve God's people, we pray . . .

For those who are in need of God's mercy: that all who yearn for mercy might find courage to reach out to the God of kindness and salvation, we pray . . .

For the members of this community: that we might seek God's way with repentance, striving, and joy, we pray . . .

Presider: God of mercy, your Son, Jesus Christ, came among us in order to renew both heaven and earth in the power of his light. Hear our petitions this day and, from your merciful heart, grant us the grace to receive your forgiveness, renewal, and strength. We ask this through Christ our Lord. **Amen.**

Liturgy and Stillness

It would be wise to be attuned to how the various senses of those in the assembly perceive what is happening in our liturgies, especially against the backdrop of what their presumed experiences are the other six days and twenty-three hours of the week. Notably, it can be quite challenging for any of us to recognize simple, quiet waiting as something active and preparatory, but so it is! In fact, in contrast to our Scriptures this weekend, sometimes stillness is the only and best thing we can do. While the Advent wreath helps us mark time, it also bids us "be patient," as for each week only certain candles may be lit while the remaining candles too must patiently wait. This can also be echoed in other pieces of the art and environment: a set of four banners, with one more revealed each passing Sunday, or indeed in the pacing of the prayers and music of the liturgy itself.

(continued on next page)

COLLECT

Let us pray.

Pause for silent prayer

Almighty and merciful God,
may no earthly undertaking hinder those
who set out in haste to meet your Son,
but may our learning of heavenly wisdom
gain us admittance to his company.
Who lives and reigns with you in the unity
of the Holy Spirit,
God, for ever and ever. **Amen.**

FIRST READING

Isa 40:1-5, 9-11

Comfort, give comfort to my people,
says your God.
Speak tenderly to Jerusalem, and proclaim
to her
that her service is at an end,
her guilt is expiated;
indeed, she has received from the hand of
the LORD
double for all her sins.

A voice cries out:
In the desert prepare the way of the LORD!
Make straight in the wasteland a
highway for our God!
Every valley shall be filled in,
every mountain and hill shall be made
low;
the rugged land shall be made a plain,
the rough country, a broad valley.
Then the glory of the LORD shall be
revealed,
and all people shall see it together;
for the mouth of the LORD has spoken.

Go up onto a high mountain,
Zion, herald of glad tidings;
cry out at the top of your voice,
Jerusalem, herald of good news!
Fear not to cry out
and say to the cities of Judah:
Here is your God!
Here comes with power
the Lord GOD,
who rules by his strong arm;
here is his reward with him,
his recompense before him.
Like a shepherd he feeds his flock;
in his arms he gathers the lambs,
carrying them in his bosom,
and leading the ewes with care.

RESPONSORIAL PSALM
Ps 85:9-10, 11-12, 13-14

℟. (8) Lord, let us see your kindness, and
grant us your salvation.

I will hear what God proclaims;
the LORD—for he proclaims peace to his
people.
Near indeed is his salvation to those who
fear him,
glory dwelling in our land.

℟. Lord, let us see your kindness, and
grant us your salvation.

Kindness and truth shall meet;
justice and peace shall kiss.
Truth shall spring out of the earth,
and justice shall look down from heaven.

℟. Lord, let us see your kindness, and
grant us your salvation.

The LORD himself will give his benefits;
our land shall yield its increase.
Justice shall walk before him,
and prepare the way of his steps.

℟. Lord, let us see your kindness, and
grant us your salvation.

SECOND READING
2 Pet 3:8-14

Do not ignore this one fact, beloved,
that with the Lord one day is like a
thousand years
and a thousand years like one day.
The Lord does not delay his promise, as
some regard "delay,"
but he is patient with you,
not wishing that any should perish
but that all should come to repentance.
But the day of the Lord will come like a
thief,
and then the heavens will pass away
with a mighty roar
and the elements will be dissolved by
fire,
and the earth and everything done on it
will be found out.

Continued in Appendix A, p. 261.

The *General Instruction of the Roman Missal* instructs that there should be several moments of silence during the liturgy: during the penitential act, after the presider's invitation "let us pray," following each Scripture passage, after the homily, and following the distribution of Holy Communion. If these moments are not intentional at our liturgies, Advent is the perfect time to be more aware of how silence is a necessary component of prayerful liturgies. Elijah, we must remember, recognized the voice of God not in powerful winds, earthquakes, or fires, but in a gentle whisper.

Liturgical Ministers: Music Ministers

On the Second Sunday of Advent, music ministers participate in a ministry that forms both the assembly and themselves. Isaiah's words, "Comfort, give comfort to my people," sets a tone of consolation and preparation. Music ministers are called to embody God's mercy and nearness while echoing John the Baptist's call to readiness. Music becomes a vehicle for the assembly to internalize Scripture while shaping prayer and reflection. In their ministry, musicians learn to balance pastoral sensitivity with liturgical fidelity, choosing melodies that invite participation and pacing that allows texts to resonate rather than rush. The church reminds us that sacred music is "a necessary or integral part of the solemn liturgy," and its purpose is "the glory of God and the sanctification of the faithful" (*Sacrosanctum Concilium* 112). Through careful, prayerful attention to their ministry, music ministers form the assembly's hearts in hope, peace, and repentance. At the same time, they themselves are formed in attentiveness, discernment, and theological understanding of the interplay between music and liturgical action. This Sunday, music ministers help the community encounter a God who consoles and calls us to conversion, guiding both their own and the assembly's participation in Advent's prayerful journey.

Living Liturgy: Liturgy and Justice

John the Baptist's voice challenges us to prepare the Lord's way by straightening what is crooked and leveling what is unjust. In Peter's letter, believers are urged to live in "holiness and devotion" as they wait for the Lord's coming. For the church today, this means that Advent cannot remain only interior or private. Our preparation is lived in public witness through acts of mercy, care for the vulnerable, and persistent advocacy for justice in our communities and society at large. Valleys of poverty must be lifted, mountains of arrogance leveled, rough ways of exclusion made smooth, and systems of oppression confronted with courage. Our readiness in Advent is authentic when it reshapes our communities to reflect the justice, mercy, and peace of Christ's kingdom.

SPIRITUALITY

GOSPEL ACCLAMATION
cf. Luke 1:28

℟. Alleluia, alleluia.
Hail, Mary, full of grace, the Lord is with you;
blessed are you among women.
℟. Alleluia, alleluia.

Gospel

Luke 1:26-38; L689

The angel Gabriel was sent from God
to a town of Galilee called Nazareth,
to a virgin betrothed to a man named Joseph,
of the house of David,
and the virgin's name was Mary.
And coming to her, he said,
"Hail, full of grace! The Lord is with you."
But she was greatly troubled at what was said
and pondered what sort of greeting this might be.
Then the angel said to her,
"Do not be afraid, Mary,
for you have found favor with God.
Behold, you will conceive in your womb and bear a son,
and you shall name him Jesus.

Continued in Appendix A, p. 261.

See Appendix A, p. 262 for the other readings.

Praying with Gospel Words and Phrases

How can this be . . . May it be done to me . . .

Reflecting on the Gospel

Though many of us could recite this gospel from memory, we do well to remember that each time we come upon it, we receive it with different eyes and ears, and in this moment, another year's worth of life experiences. Ponder for a moment how your life is different now than it was one year ago. Perhaps you live somewhere different—or very different! Perhaps some of your relationships have ended or are just beginning. You may be differently employed, you may look physically very different, you likely have experienced many things in ways no other human ever has or will.

Yet God comes to each of us not only knowing that but speaking to us as did the angel to Mary: do not be afraid. Why might we be afraid? Because so often God's call to us is shrouded in the unknown. Have you ever had that itch, that mysterious prod in your side that makes you feel called to something else, somewhere else, someone else—but you can't quite put your finger on it? If you're like me, that has happened so often you've lost count. And yet each time it's been God, again calling not to personal desires, knowledge, or power but to faith in the divine mystery and mission. "How can this be?" indeed.

And the question itself is evidence of faith, is evidence of a healthy relationship with God. We can note that Gabriel gives what one might call a non-answer in reply. It's a bit like the moment an exasperated parent is asked what's for dinner, and having not thought that far ahead yet, abruptly if not comically answers, "food." Gabriel explains to Mary that it's the power of God that will make what is asked of her a holy reality. And just as Advent today calls us to faithfulness, Mary becomes the example of that *par excellence*: May it be done to me, just like you've said.

What is that itch, that holy prod in your side today? How does the annunciation speak to it, and what is your Christian response to God's ever-present invitation?

To the Point

Mary's example makes real for us that God does not call us to fulfillment of our own desires, nor to knowledge or power, but only to faithfulness. God's words are spirit and life; God's will for us is only goodness, holiness, and unity with the Holy Trinity and all the faithful.

Model Penitential Act

Presider: All the ends of the earth have seen the salvation by our God. Coming before the Lord, we ask for his pardon and peace . . . *[pause]*

Lord Jesus, you are Son of God and son of Mary: Lord, have mercy.
Christ Jesus, you are the paschal lamb who takes away our sin: Christ, have mercy.
Lord Jesus, you are the Savior of the world: Lord, have mercy.

Model Universal Prayer (Prayer of the Faithful)

Presider: Like our mother, Mary, the Lord invites us to come to him with trust and hope. We turn to him with our prayers and petitions.

Response: Lord, hear our prayer.

For Pope N.: may he be filled with the wisdom of the Spirit in leading the faithful and promoting peace in the world, we pray . . .

For the lawmakers around the world: may they boldly defend vulnerable people from conception to natural death, we pray . . .

For all who hope for safety and stability in their lives: may they be freed from fear, escape violence, and find refuge, we pray . . .

For friends and loved ones suffering from anxiety, depression, and mental illness: may they find comfort, and may we support them with patience, we pray . . .

Presider: Lord our God, your servant Mary is mother of the church and mother of our Lord. Grant us courage to have faith as Mary did, and trust in your goodness. We ask this through Christ our Lord. **Amen.**

COLLECT

Let us pray.

Pause for silent prayer

O God, who by the Immaculate Conception of the Blessed Virgin
prepared a worthy dwelling for your Son,
grant, we pray,
that, as you preserved her from every stain
by virtue of the Death of your Son, which you foresaw,
so, through her intercession,
we, too, may be cleansed and admitted to your presence.
Through our Lord Jesus Christ, your Son,
who lives and reigns with you in the unity of the Holy Spirit,
God, for ever and ever. **Amen.**

Liturgy and Spirituality

The solemnity of the Immaculate Conception invites the church to reflect on Mary's unique role in salvation history. The *Catechism of the Catholic Church* states: "To become the mother of the Savior, Mary 'was enriched by God with gifts appropriate to such a role'" (CCC 490). Preserved from sin from the moment of her conception, Mary's life models total openness to God's will. In celebrating this feast, the liturgy calls the assembly to recognize God's grace at work in human life and to cultivate hearts receptive to divine love. Our prayers, hymns, and gestures during this celebration become opportunities to imitate Mary's humility and trust. Participating fully in the Mass encourages believers to seek holiness in everyday life, nurturing a spirituality that is both contemplative and active. In this way, the liturgical celebration deepens our awareness of God's transforming presence in our own lives and in the wider community.

SPIRITUALITY

GOSPEL ACCLAMATION
cf. Luke 1:28

℟. Alleluia, alleluia.
Blessed are you, holy Virgin Mary, deserving of all praise;
from you rose the sun of justice, Christ our God.
℟. Alleluia, alleluia.

Gospel

Luke 1:26-38; L690A

The angel Gabriel was sent from God
to a town of Galilee called Nazareth,
to a virgin betrothed to a man named Joseph,
of the house of David,
and the virgin's name was Mary.
And coming to her, he said,
"Hail, full of grace! The Lord is with you."
But she was greatly troubled at what was said
and pondered what sort of greeting this might be.
Then the angel said to her,
"Do not be afraid, Mary,
for you have found favor with God.
Behold, you will conceive in your womb and bear a son,
and you shall name him Jesus.

Continued in Appendix A, p. 263.

See Appendix A, p. 263, for the other readings.

Praying with Gospel Words and Phrases
Behold . . . Behold . . . Behold . . .

Reflecting on the Gospel
No, you're not experiencing déjà vu, this Marian solemnity indeed shares a gospel passage with the solemnity celebrated just four days ago. You might, in fact, be tempted to pick the other offered gospel passage today to avoid that repetition, especially considering it will be heard again on the Fourth Sunday of Advent(!)—and no one would blame you. There is a lot more to explore in the annunciation gospel, of course, than on the preceding pages. But it may be nice to place this same Mary—young, inquisitive, and faithful—in front of your assemblies one more time.

In the realm of marketing and public relations, it's a common rule of thumb that a customer needs to see a brand's marketing message at least seven times before making a purchase decision. This "rule of seven" emphasizes the power of repetition in a person's ability to recall something and make choices as a result of such messaging. Perhaps the church could learn a thing or two here!

One of the details that might be lifted from this passage is in fact the repetition of the word "Behold." Three times it appears: when Gabriel begins the specifics of God's calling to Mary; when Gabriel lifts Elizabeth and her pregnancy as an example of God's powerful love; and finally, when Mary replies with her sacred *fiat*. The word "behold" in English is generally equated to "see" or "observe," but has Old English roots that infer not just seeing but holding the thing, presumably with your hands. Similar Germanic words retain some of that meaning too, in fact.

Very few of us will experience the divine presence the way that Mary did, nor experience Mary in the way that Juan Diego did, he who literally held a miracle of roses in his tilma. Yet we are called to recognize, when faith powers our senses, that every human being is made in the image and likeness of God. Every human being, as Paul writes to the Corinthians, is "a temple of the holy Spirit" (1 Cor 6:19). In these ways, the activity, the voice, and the love of God is closer to us than we may dare imagine—even within our own mortal shells.

To the Point
The power and faithfulness of God is not something only transcendent, distant, and detached. It is immanent and real, close enough to hold in our hands, if we perceive the world with eyes, ears, and hearts of faith.

Model Penitential Act

Presider: Placing our hearts before the Lord who calls us to himself, we ask for his pardon and peace . . . *[pause]*

Lord Jesus, you hear the cries of poor: Lord, have mercy.

Christ Jesus, you have mercy on the powerful and the weak: Christ, have mercy.

Lord Jesus, you call all peoples to yourself: Lord, have mercy.

Model Universal Prayer (Prayer of the Faithful)

Presider: Joining Mary in unceasing prayer and hopefulness, we offer our petitions.

Response: Lord, hear our prayer.

For the church: that it may shelter refugees, migrants, and all who must find safety this day, we pray . . .

For leaders of nations: that they might be especially mindful of the women who work each day to care for, feed, and protect their families, we pray . . .

For all Indigenous peoples: may they preserve and embrace their heritage while thriving in the present, we pray . . .

For the poor: especially those within our parish boundaries who live in the shadow of violence, we pray . . .

Presider: Lord God, you anoint the poor and the lowly as your beloved servants. Hear our prayers this day, and allow us to be filled with praise so that we might always rejoice in you. **Amen.**

COLLECT

Let us pray.

Pause for silent prayer

O God, Father of mercies,
who placed your people under the singular protection
of your Son's most holy Mother,
grant that all who invoke the Blessed Virgin of Guadalupe,
may seek with ever more lively faith
the progress of peoples in the ways of justice and of peace.
Through our Lord Jesus Christ, your Son,
who lives and reigns with you in the unity of the Holy Spirit,
God, for ever and ever. **Amen.**

Liturgy and Diversity: Mary's Embrace of God's People

The feast of Our Lady of Guadalupe calls the church to celebrate the universal embrace of God's love. In appearing to St. Juan Diego, Mary affirmed her care for all people, especially those on the margins, and united communities through her maternal presence. In the liturgy, this feast invites the assembly to recognize the bonds that connect us as one church and as one family of God. Through the celebration of the liturgy, the faithful are drawn into deeper solidarity with one another. Participating fully in the Mass encourages believers to build inclusive communities that reflect Mary's compassion and welcome. Mary's witness encourages us to listen attentively to the needs of others and foster inclusion in both local and global contexts. This feast inspires us to live as a church that listens, welcomes, and stands in solidarity with all God's people, building bridges of understanding and hope wherever we are called to serve.

SPIRITUALITY

GOSPEL ACCLAMATION
Isa 61:1 (cited in Luke 4:18)

℟. Alleluia, alleluia.
The Spirit of the Lord is upon me,
because he has anointed me
to bring glad tidings to the poor.
℟. Alleluia, alleluia.

Gospel

John 1:6-8, 19-28; L8B

A man named John was sent from God.
He came for testimony, to testify to the light,
so that all might believe through him.
He was not the light,
but came to testify to the light.

And this is the testimony of John.
When the Jews from Jerusalem sent priests and Levites to him
to ask him, "Who are you?"
he admitted and did not deny it,
but admitted, "I am not the Christ."
So they asked him,
"What are you then? Are you Elijah?"
And he said, "I am not."
"Are you the Prophet?"
He answered, "No."
So they said to him,
"Who are you, so we can give an answer to those who sent us?
What do you have to say for yourself?"
He said:
"I am *the voice of one crying out in the desert,*
'make straight the way of the Lord,'
as Isaiah the prophet said."
Some Pharisees were also sent.
They asked him,
"Why then do you baptize
if you are not the Christ or Elijah or the Prophet?"

Continued in Appendix A, p. 264.

Praying with Gospel Words and Phrases
Testify to the light . . . I am not . . .

Reflecting on the Gospel
Our attention this Advent, beginning last week and continuing into this week, turns to John the Baptist. This Sunday is also called "Gaudete Sunday"—"Rejoice Sunday"—acknowledging the prescribed entrance antiphon of the day, with its text from the letter to the Philippians: "Rejoice in the Lord always. I shall say it again: rejoice! . . . The Lord is near" (4:4). The collect of the liturgy also refers to "the joys of so great a salvation," and the Old Testament, the psalm, and the epistle readings each call us to rejoicing as well—more on that in a moment. The rose candle on the wreath, lighter and perhaps cheerier than the violet ones, is lit today, and the presider has the option to wear rose colored vestments if desired.

Yet John the Baptist is not a figure one might describe, generally, as cheerful or joyful. There is a natural tension here: the precursor of the Messiah, a man who wore burlap, ate insects, and with fiery language rebuked Pharisees is the dominant figure on a weekend of joy and glad tidings. Today's gospel, at first hearing, seems at best to be a mismatch.

On closer inspection, though, our faith and our celebrations of it are filled with paradox. Christian paradox is perhaps best expressed in mystery—God's truth beyond all human understanding. Said more simply, it is the word "and." In our Scriptures, these paradoxes abound: both greatness and lowliness, both strength and weakness, both light and darkness, both first and last, both humanity and divinity, both life and death, both one and many. One does not replace the other nor become the other: both exist side by side, in mystery—the paschal mystery.

Within the liturgy, we've already explored how patience and prayerful silence might also be the most intensely active thing one can do this season. Today, John the Baptist, while decidedly unjoyful, calls each of us to a most joyful pursuit: following the one true light in the darkness, which the darkness could not overcome.

To the Point
Christian faith is, by definition, one of healthy paradox and mystery. Instead of seeking resolution and explanation, Christ calls us to embrace these enigmas, and to live them in word and deed. The critical concept in doing so is the simple word, "and."

Preparing to Proclaim, Preach, and Pray

Making Connections Between the Readings: As noted above, each of the readings today speaks of rejoicing. It's rare that the epistle matches so well the connective tissue that the first reading and gospel share. Most often the second reading is following its own track, a continuation of what was heard the previous Sunday, which will then be continued the following week. In the seasons of Advent, Christmas, Lent, and Easter, however, the full set of readings can often speak to a particular facet of the faith, as do our readings for this Sunday.

The verses from Isaiah urge us to rejoice because the spirit has anointed us for mission: evangelistic glad tidings, words and deeds of healing and freedom, and proclamation of our victory in and by our God. Further, this rejoicing is because of the justice that such a ministry can bring to birth; in Advent we of course recall the justice that the literal birth of the Messiah made manifest among us.

This messianic presence is perhaps the only reason that Paul can instruct the Thessalonians, and us, to rejoice always. You likely know some Christians who seem to perpetually exude joy, who always seem so hopeful and at peace. Such followers are by no means the norm, but are always a strong, living example of what a true Christian ought strive to be—perfectly holy as Paul names it.

Making Connections to the Responsorial Psalm: It's no surprise that our psalm today, with verses from Mary's *Magnificat*, speaks—sings, in fact—of rejoicing as well. We of course often hear of and from the Mother of God on the Fourth Sunday of Advent; this year her voice "sneaks in" a week early. Mary's joy, while visiting her cousin, is so great that she must sing it, as we often see in Luke's Gospel.

Mary, her visit with her cousin, and her song of praise create a web of connections: from the prophecy of Isaiah paired here with her song, which of course was sung in the presence not only of Elizabeth, but of John the Baptist, who would be born three months later and six months before Jesus's birth.

The *Magnificat* is sung in joyful praise, but it is also a strong hymn of justice, mercy, and the greatness of God—the concepts also embedded in the other Scriptures of the day.

CONNECTING TO EXPERIENCE: LIVING THE PASCHAL MYSTERY

How can we possibly proclaim liberty to captives? Healing hearts sounds equally impossible. But Jesus, though one of us, is not bound by human limits on his imagination. Jesus is the Christ, the one who came into the world, just as the prophet Isaiah describes. We also have been anointed with the Spirit of the Lord. How can we, baptized in Christ Jesus and transformed by the Spirit, cultivate justice and peace in the gardens and vineyards before us? We can bring joy. We who have been baptized are called to rejoice always, pray without ceasing, and in all circumstances give thanks. A spirit of joy can lighten the darkness, bring hope to the hopeless, and invite healing to hearts that are lonely, sad, afraid, or lost. We are to treasure this gift of joy and celebrate it each Sunday and every day of our lives of faith. Let us share our rejoicing and testify to the light who is Christ Jesus.

PROMPTS FOR FAITH-SHARING

- How does the gospel shed light upon your need for freedom? What is it in your life that keeps you captive?
- How can you help to free those near to you—family, friends, coworkers—from those things that make them captive? In what ways are you holding your neighbors captive?
- In what ways can you allow Christ to bring joy into your life more fully, so that your joy is a source of light and conversion for those around you?

Model Penitential Act

Presider: The psalm today comes from the mouth of Mary, mother of Jesus and mother of the church. With Mary, may we rejoice in God and remember his mercy as we prepare our hearts for the coming of the Lord . . . *[pause]*

Lord Jesus, you came to heal the brokenhearted: Lord, have mercy.

Christ Jesus, you offer refuge to sinners: Christ, have mercy.

Lord Jesus, you are the light which dispels our darkness: Lord, have mercy.

Model Universal Prayer (Prayer of the Faithful)

Presider: We come with hope before the Lord who offers us salvation, bringing our prayers for ourselves and all the world.

Response: Lord, hear our prayer.

For an increase in faith throughout the church, drawing the faithful to greater mercy and joy, we pray . . .

For courage among our leaders to remain steadfast in love for God and care for our neighbors, we pray . . .

For the poor, the hungry, and the brokenhearted among us and among the most vulnerable of the world, we pray . . .

For patience and peace with ourselves and with those who hate us, we pray . . .

Presider: God our Father, you have filled the hungry with good things and sent the rich away empty. Hear our prayers and petitions this day and fill us with your light so that we might go out to all the world to share the richness of Christ Jesus. We ask this through Christ our Lord. **Amen.**

Liturgy and the Altar

The document, *Built of Living Stones*, issued by the USCCB in 2000, tells us this about the altar of sacrifice one finds in every church building: "At the Eucharist, the liturgical assembly celebrates the ritual sacrificial meal that recalls and makes present Christ's life, death, and resurrection, proclaiming 'the death of the Lord until he comes.' The altar is 'the center of thanksgiving that the Eucharist accomplishes' and the point around which the other rites are in some manner arrayed. Since the Church teaches that 'the altar is Christ,' its composition should reflect the nobility, beauty, strength, and simplicity of the One it represents" (56).

The altar, then, embodies the whole of the mystery and paradox that is the liturgical celebration of our faith: the Eucharist is both sacrifice and meal, the sacrificial altar is simultaneously a dinner table, and within the celebration of Eucharist is past, present, and future in a single moment. It is the place where we, though many, are all one in Christ Jesus.

(continued on next page)

COLLECT

Let us pray.

Pause for silent prayer

O God, who see how your people
faithfully await the feast of the Lord's
Nativity,
enable us, we pray,
to attain the joys of so great a salvation
and to celebrate them always
with solemn worship and glad rejoicing.
Through our Lord Jesus Christ, your Son,
who lives and reigns with you in the unity
of the Holy Spirit,
God, for ever and ever. **Amen.**

FIRST READING

Isa 61:1-2a, 10-11

The spirit of the Lord GOD is upon me,
because the LORD has anointed me;
he has sent me to bring glad tidings to the
poor,
to heal the brokenhearted,
to proclaim liberty to the captives
and release to the prisoners,
to announce a year of favor from the LORD
and a day of vindication by our God.

I rejoice heartily in the LORD,
in my God is the joy of my soul;
for he has clothed me with a robe of
salvation
and wrapped me in a mantle of justice,
like a bridegroom adorned with a diadem,
like a bride bedecked with her jewels.
As the earth brings forth its plants,
and a garden makes its growth spring
up,
so will the Lord GOD make justice and
praise
spring up before all the nations.

RESPONSORIAL PSALM
Luke 1:46-48, 49-50, 53-54

℟. (Isa 61:10b) My soul rejoices in my God.

My soul proclaims the greatness of the Lord;
my spirit rejoices in God my Savior,
for he has looked upon his lowly servant.
From this day all generations will call me blessed:

℟. My soul rejoices in my God.

The Almighty has done great things for me,
and holy is his Name.
He has mercy on those who fear him
in every generation.

℟. My soul rejoices in my God.

He has filled the hungry with good things,
and the rich he has sent away empty.
He has come to the help of his servant Israel
for he has remembered his promise of mercy.

℟. My soul rejoices in my God.

SECOND READING
1 Thess 5:16-24

Brothers and sisters:
Rejoice always. Pray without ceasing.
In all circumstances give thanks,
for this is the will of God for you in Christ Jesus.
Do not quench the Spirit.
Do not despise prophetic utterances.
Test everything; retain what is good.
Refrain from every kind of evil.

May the God of peace make you perfectly holy
and may you entirely, spirit, soul, and body,
be preserved blameless for the coming of our Lord Jesus Christ.
The one who calls you is faithful,
and he will also accomplish it.

Further, not only is the altar Christ's cross on Calvary, but the church also teaches us that it is Christ himself. This is why we take care to adorn the altar carefully and appropriately, and offer it reverence, especially within the liturgy itself. Even though typical Advent art and environment is spare, Gaudete Sunday would be an appropriate celebration to adorn the altar with rose-colored flowers and fabrics.

Liturgical Ministers: Ushers and Greeters

Gaudete Sunday invites the church to celebrate the nearness of Christ's coming with hope and gladness. Ushers and greeters serve as the first point of encounter for the assembly, shaping the community's experience of worship through their attentiveness and warmth. Their presence fosters a sense of welcome and belonging, helping all who enter feel seen and valued. By offering assistance and a friendly demeanor, they communicate that in the liturgy, we wait in anticipation through joy-filled celebration. Ushers and greeters help the assembly enter more fully into the liturgical season, reminding the assembly that Advent is a journey of hope and expectation, not only a preparation for the feast of Christmas but also a call to attentive presence to God and neighbor. Their ministry quietly models the hospitality and attentiveness that reflect Christ's own care for humanity.

Living Liturgy: Liturgy and Prayer

Paul's words, "Rejoice always. Pray without ceasing. In all circumstances give thanks," capture the spiritual heart of Gaudete Sunday. Christian joy is rooted not in circumstances but in trust in God's presence and promises. During Advent, the faithful are invited to cultivate this joy through daily prayer, reflection, and attentiveness to God's work in the world. Prayer prepares hearts to recognize Christ's coming and strengthens the assembly's shared life of faith. When the community approaches worship with intentional prayerfulness by offering gratitude, petitions, and intercessions, it becomes a living witness to God's faithfulness. Gaudete Sunday calls the church to rejoice in anticipation of Christ's arrival, nurturing hope-filled hearts and fostering a deep spiritual attentiveness that sustains believers in both celebration and service.

SPIRITUALITY

GOSPEL ACCLAMATION
Luke 1:38

℟. Alleluia, alleluia.
Behold, I am the handmaid of the Lord.
May it be done to me according to your word.
℟. Alleluia, alleluia.

Gospel

Luke 1:26-38; L11B

The angel Gabriel was sent from God
to a town of Galilee called Nazareth,
to a virgin betrothed to a man named Joseph,
of the house of David,
and the virgin's name was Mary.
And coming to her, he said,
"Hail, full of grace! The Lord is with you."
But she was greatly troubled at what was said
and pondered what sort of greeting this might be.
Then the angel said to her,
"Do not be afraid, Mary,
for you have found favor with God.

"Behold, you will conceive in your womb and bear a son,
and you shall name him Jesus.
He will be great and will be called Son of the Most High,
and the Lord God will give him the throne of David his father,
and he will rule over the house of Jacob forever,
and of his kingdom there will be no end."
But Mary said to the angel,
"How can this be,
since I have no relations with a man?"
And the angel said to her in reply,
"The Holy Spirit will come upon you,
and the power of the Most High will overshadow you.

Continued in Appendix A, p. 264.

Praying with Gospel Words and Phrases
The Lord is with you . . . the throne of David his father . . .

Reflecting on the Gospel
We have arrived at the third possible hearing of this gospel in less than two weeks' time! What else might there be to say about these words, about this moment in salvation history?

The end of the Advent season always brings the faithful to reflect on Mary and her role in the birth of Christ. Mary, in this year's gospel passage, is described as someone who, when visited by the angel Gabriel, is troubled and pensive, who has questions about what she is being told, and who, after careful consideration, is able to say "Yes" to the Lord's calling to her and her life.

Mary is often called "the First Disciple" because of her relationship to Christ, her son. The words "disciple" and "discipline" have the same etymological root, referring to someone who learns, who studies, who follows a certain teacher or set of teachings. Often today when we hear the word "discipline," it refers to a punishment following some wrong or disobedient act. Yet we might more accurately view discipline, correctly applied and enacted, as a moment of learning and even formation.

It seems that even before Mary knew of her calling to become the mother of God incarnate that she must have already learned her faith well: from her parents, from rabbis and other holy men and women, and perhaps even from the ritual practices of her faith. Just as this gospel passage has been repetitive, the consistent presence of loved ones and faith-filled teachers, and the regular and unfailing practice of the rituals of her faith, surely embedded in Mary all that we know her to be.

Some occasionally complain that the liturgy is boring, in part because of its repetitive structures. This seems to come largely from those who attend Mass as spectators, as receivers only. Of course, we do watch and receive at Mass, but if we also give of ourselves and participate fully, not only will our corporate prayer cease to be boring, but it will help to form us into the believers God wishes us to be.

To the Point
Mary is our model of faith in ways both obvious and less evident. The people who consistently surrounded her and formed her, along with the practices of her faith, can teach us to seek out role models and regular prayer experienced today.

Preparing to Proclaim, Preach, and Pray

Making Connections Between the Readings: The Messiah was expected to be from the line of King David, and the Gospel of Matthew places Mary, the mother of Christ, in that line. David, in a time of peace, decides to honor the ark of God with some more permanent and apparently splendid structure. Nathan receives a divine message in a dream, to tell David that, rather than the king building a house for the ark, God will make the house of David a firm and enduring kingdom. The prophecy describes David resting (upon death) with his ancestors, and that David's heir will be God's own Son, forever ruling from a lasting throne.

That heir we, of course, believe to be Jesus Christ, son of Mary and, by the power of the Spirit, truly the Son of God, and therefore divine himself. In today's second reading, Paul writes to the Romans of the prophecy now made manifest and the glory due to God for sending us the divine Word incarnate, Jesus Christ. The Pauline writings can have, from time to time, run on sentences with many clauses, colons, commas, and such. This seventy-three-word pericope begins with a seventy-two-word sentence! When proclaiming this reading, take good care to ensure you understand it well, and speak slowly with relevant pauses to ensure a chance of comprehension from the assembly! The phrase "manifested through the prophetic writings" is key for this last Sunday of Advent.

Making Connections to the Responsorial Psalm: Psalm 89 this weekend picks up where the first reading concludes, which ought not be too surprising. David, the psalmist, sings with words we hear in the other Scriptures of the liturgy, some of which he heard Nathan tell him in the first reading. One word, "covenant," is not one that has come before us this Advent, but perhaps is the most succinct summary of this year's Advent journey.

We have prayed about replacing earthly desires with holy hope and trust; we have strived to balance stillness and sacred action; we have pondered other Christian paradoxes. And as we draw close to Christmas itself these all come together in King David, in Mary, and in Christ himself—the everlasting covenant made once and for all in his passion, death, and resurrection. Once, as a child about six years old, I tried to persuade my parents that Christmas must be more important than Easter: how could Jesus die for our sins without first being born? Being older and wiser now, of course, the two are inextricably linked and imbue one another with meaning and significance.

CONNECTING TO EXPERIENCE: LIVING THE PASCHAL MYSTERY

When we are overwhelmed by life, for good or for ill, the angel's counsel to Mary is worth heeding: "Do not be afraid . . . for you have found favor with God." Gabriel speaks these words to us, too. Because Christ has united himself to us through Mary, we, too, have favor with God. This is a great reason to temper our fears. When we face hardship, extreme burden, or overwhelming joy, we can turn to God with the confidence of knowing that we do not need to seek his favor; we already have it! Yet to receive the fullness of God's blessing, we do need to approach him with the same openness to his will that we see in Mary. Perhaps our prayer should be: "Lord, I am overwhelmed, but I know that you have favored me beyond my understanding. Let your will be done; I am your servant. Come to me, comfort me, and send me forth!"

PROMPTS FOR FAITH-SHARING

- Where, in your life, do you need to abandon fear and trust in the favor of God?
- How can you be more willing to do God's will? What plans do you have that are impeding your ability to accept God's plans for you?
- Is there something, somewhere, or someone toward which God is trying to send you? What is keeping you from seeing it?

CELEBRATION and CATECHESIS

Model Penitential Act

Presider: Today's gospel reminds us that the will of God can only be accomplished when we accept him fully, as Mary did. Aware of those times we have refused or pushed aside God's will for our lives, we ask for his pardon and peace . . . *[pause]*

Lord Jesus, you are the Son of God and the very sign of compassion: Lord, have mercy.

Christ Jesus, you are son of Mary, born miraculously for our sake: Christ, have mercy.

Lord Jesus, you are Son of the Most High, yet choose to dwell among us: Lord, have mercy.

Model Universal Prayer (Prayer of the Faithful)

Presider: By Mary's openness to God's will, we have found a place in our Lord's house forever. As his favored children, we now ask God for what we need.

Response: Lord, hear our prayer.

For the church, as it finishes its preparations for Christ's coming: may it never fail to find him in the poor and the afflicted, we pray . . .

For those in office: may they minister to those in their care with the generosity of God, and that they, too, may favor those on the margins, we pray . . .

For those who are homeless: may they, like the Holy Family, find God's care and protection in their hour of need, we pray . . .

For all gathered here: may the coming of the Lord be an experience of generosity and community, we pray . . .

Presider: God of power and compassion, your humble birth brought about a kingdom of true power and joy. Grant that we, like Mary, open ourselves to God's will. We ask this through Christ our Lord. **Amen.**

Liturgy and Catechesis

Liturgy is meant to be catechetical, though not explicitly. But that is only half the work of forming disciples. To fully be a disciple, one must be in relationship with the teacher, not solely a student. Our liturgies fall short if—through the prescribed texts, the music, and the preaching—they only strive to be catechetical and do not give space for the faithful, like Mary, to be at times troubled and pensive, and even to have questions about what the liturgy is expressing of our shared faith. If a person is given no room for this, we can't truly expect them to be or become the fullest expression of what it means to be a disciple.

(continued on next page)

COLLECT

Let us pray.

Pause for silent prayer

Pour forth, we beseech you, O Lord,
your grace into our hearts,
that we, to whom the Incarnation of Christ your Son
was made known by the message of an Angel,
may by his Passion and Cross
be brought to the glory of his Resurrection.
Who lives and reigns with you in the unity of the Holy Spirit,
God, for ever and ever. **Amen.**

FIRST READING

2 Sam 7:1-5, 8b-12, 14a, 16

When King David was settled in his palace,
and the LORD had given him rest from his enemies on every side,
he said to Nathan the prophet,
"Here I am living in a house of cedar,
while the ark of God dwells in a tent!"
Nathan answered the king,
"Go, do whatever you have in mind,
for the LORD is with you."
But that night the LORD spoke to Nathan and said:
"Go, tell my servant David, 'Thus says the LORD:
Should you build me a house to dwell in?

"'It was I who took you from the pasture
and from the care of the flock
to be commander of my people Israel.
I have been with you wherever you went,
and I have destroyed all your enemies before you.
And I will make you famous like the great ones of the earth.
I will fix a place for my people Israel;
I will plant them so that they may dwell in their place
without further disturbance.
Neither shall the wicked continue to afflict them as they did of old,
since the time I first appointed judges over my people Israel.
I will give you rest from all your enemies.
The LORD also reveals to you
that he will establish a house for you.
And when your time comes and you rest with your ancestors,
I will raise up your heir after you,
sprung from your loins,
and I will make his kingdom firm.

I will be a father to him,
 and he shall be a son to me.
Your house and your kingdom shall endure
 forever before me;
 your throne shall stand firm forever.' "

RESPONSORIAL PSALM
Ps 89:2-3, 4-5, 27, 29

℟. (2a) For ever I will sing the goodness of the Lord.

The promises of the LORD I will sing forever;
 through all generations my mouth shall proclaim your faithfulness.
For you have said, "My kindness is established forever";
 in heaven you have confirmed your faithfulness.

℟. For ever I will sing the goodness of the Lord.

"I have made a covenant with my chosen one,
 I have sworn to David my servant:
forever will I confirm your posterity
 and establish your throne for all generations."

℟. For ever I will sing the goodness of the Lord.

"He shall say of me, 'You are my father,
 my God, the Rock, my savior.'
Forever I will maintain my kindness toward him,
 and my covenant with him stands firm."

℟. For ever I will sing the goodness of the Lord.

SECOND READING
Rom 16:25-27

Brothers and sisters:
To him who can strengthen you,
 according to my gospel and the proclamation of Jesus Christ,
 according to the revelation of the mystery kept secret for long ages
 but now manifested through the prophetic writings and,
 according to the command of the eternal God,
 made known to all nations to bring about the obedience of faith,
 to the only wise God, through Jesus Christ
 be glory forever and ever. Amen.

We have already reminded ourselves that Advent as a season doesn't so much prepare us for a celebration of Christ's historical birth but rather the second and final coming of Christ, returning in glory to bring to completion the fullness of the reign of God. To that end, Advent and the days to come are opportunities to share with the faithful, especially though preaching and music, that Christ is still speaking through a church built of living stones in which each soul is, to quote Marty Haugen, "as words within the Word" ("All Are Welcome," GIA [GIA Publications]).

Liturgical Ministers: Altar Servers

The Fourth Sunday of Advent draws the church's attention to the nearness of Christ's birth and the mystery revealed through Mary's faithful "yes." Altar servers participate in a ministry that forms both themselves and the assembly. Their presence in the sanctuary helps the liturgy unfold with dignity, reverence, and joy. By moving attentively and participating prayerfully, servers embody the order of the Mass and the sacredness of the liturgical celebration. In doing so, they model devotion and attentiveness, helping the assembly focus on God's presence and the expectation of the Lord's coming. Serving in this way cultivates interior discipline and spiritual mindfulness, teaching ministers to unite practical service with prayerful attention. The ministry of the altar servers thus forms both the server and the assembly, creating a worship space that mirrors the sacred mystery of Advent and fosters hearts ready to receive Christ at Christmas.

Living Liturgy: Liturgy and Scripture

The Scripture readings for this Sunday highlight God's promise fulfilled in the birth of the Messiah and Mary's obedient "yes." In the liturgical context, the proclamation of the word shapes the assembly's hearts and minds, inviting their reflection, listening, and active participation in the sacred mysteries. Hearing the narrative of salvation within the Mass forms the assembly in hope and trust, reminding the assembly of God's constant presence and faithful love throughout history. Engaging Scripture liturgically cultivates a living encounter with God's plan, guiding believers to recognize God's presence in daily life, to discern God's will, and to respond in faithful action. The liturgy, grounded in God's word, calls the assembly to anticipate Christ's coming with hearts open to wonder and service, deepening their understanding of mercy and preparing the faithful to celebrate the mystery of the incarnation with both reverence and gratitude.

DECEMBER 20, 2026

FOURTH SUNDAY OF ADVENT

SEASON OF CHRISTMAS

It is fitting that humanity should be saved by one such as ourselves, and that we were—and are—redeemed in this way is a profound testament to human dignity.

SPIRITUALITY

The Vigil Mass

GOSPEL ACCLAMATION

℟. Alleluia, alleluia.
Tomorrow the wickedness of the earth will be destroyed:
the Savior of the world will reign over us.
℟. Alleluia, alleluia.

Gospel

Matt 1:1-25; L13ABC

The book of the genealogy of Jesus Christ,
the son of David, the son of Abraham.

Abraham became the father of Isaac,
Isaac the father of Jacob,
Jacob the father of Judah and his brothers.
Judah became the father of Perez and Zerah,
whose mother was Tamar.
Perez became the father of Hezron,
Hezron the father of Ram,
Ram the father of Amminadab.
Amminadab became the father of Nahshon,
Nahshon the father of Salmon,
Salmon the father of Boaz,
whose mother was Rahab.
Boaz became the father of Obed,
whose mother was Ruth.
Obed became the father of Jesse,
Jesse the father of David the king.

David became the father of Solomon,
whose mother had been the wife of Uriah.
Solomon became the father of Rehoboam,
Rehoboam the father of Abijah,
Abijah the father of Asaph.

Continued in Appendix A, p. 264, or Matt 1:18-25 *in Appendix A, pp. 264–265.*

See Appendix A, p. 265, for the other readings.

Praying with Gospel Words and Phrases

Genealogy . . . generations . . . "God is with us" . . .

Reflecting on the Gospel

Often this gospel—this whole vigil liturgy, in fact—gets overlooked, and is replaced by the "During the Night" prayers and readings. That gospel passage, after all, is the one that congregations expect to hear: the Lucan telling of the nativity straight out of the annual Charlie Brown special. It is vivid and descriptive, whereas the gospel for this liturgy is—well, long and not especially vivid or descriptive. Pair that with a Mass time often attended by families with young children, and there is potential for restlessness, inattentiveness, and a liturgy not well prayed.

Yet there are opportunities here! Because the gospel is so concerned with the generations of Jesus's ancestors, this makes it excellent fodder for preaching to exactly such an assembly. Invite children to imagine their parents as children, and their grandparents too, and how the faith and the wisdom of God was handed down time and time again, all the way to them, just as it was from Abraham to David to Mary. Even though it may be omitted, consider retaining this portion of the vigil gospel.

There are many varieties of families who will be in our pews on Christmas: those spanning multiple generations, those with any manner of "step" relations—stepsiblings, stepparents, and so on—and perhaps even quite modern mingling of family units and "chosen" relatives. This is the gospel of Christmas that details Joseph's response to learning of Mary's pregnancy before their marriage and consummation. At first, with at least some compassion, he does not want to shame Mary as would have been common. Yet after his dream and the divine message of the angel, he welcomes the quite untraditional family experience.

Joseph goes through this experience, and each experience recorded of his in the gospels, apparently, without uttering a single word. Of course that must not be true; rather, it's just a quirk of our gospels. Yet this quirk can also teach us the value of leading by example, of "walking the walk, not just talking the talk." This liturgy may be a good time to invite families to ponder the value in one another and what we can learn from one another—and not just our fathers. How does each member of the family help the others grow in holiness and faith?

To the Point

Don't just gloss over this gospel and this liturgy! Approached well, preached well, prayed well, this can truly become a meaningful experience reflecting on the birth of the Messiah and how this event can shape our daily lives, most especially within our families.

SPIRITUALITY

Mass during the Night

GOSPEL ACCLAMATION
Luke 2:10-11

℟. Alleluia, alleluia.
I proclaim to you good news of great joy:
today a Savior is born for us,
Christ the Lord.
℟. Alleluia, alleluia.

Gospel

Luke 2:1-14; L14ABC

In those days a decree went out from Caesar Augustus
that the whole world should be enrolled.
This was the first enrollment,
when Quirinius was governor of Syria.
So all went to be enrolled, each to his own town.
And Joseph too went up from Galilee from the town of Nazareth
to Judea, to the city of David that is called Bethlehem,
because he was of the house and family of David,
to be enrolled with Mary, his betrothed, who was with child.
While they were there,
the time came for her to have her child,
and she gave birth to her firstborn son.
She wrapped him in swaddling clothes and laid him in a manger,
because there was no room for them in the inn.

Continued in Appendix A, p. 266.

See Appendix A, p. 266, for the other readings.

Praying with Gospel Words and Phrases
No room . . . manger . . . Do not be afraid . . .

Reflecting on the Gospel
There is one person, or perhaps a couple, who doesn't even get a mention, let alone a name, in this familiar gospel passage of the nativity. Yet he or she or they play a crucial role in the birth narrative and can be such strong examples to us in our faith, if we allow ourselves to notice.

It's almost just a passing phrase, "there was no room for them in the inn." But like quite a lot of Scripture, it seems there are some details missing, ones that perhaps our imagination can productively fill. Imagine Mary and Joseph, approaching their last chance for lodging that night, tired and worn, desperation perhaps obvious on their faces. Mary's feelings too would likely have been obvious in any number of ways, given the impending birth of her child: anxious, excited, and a thousand other things. Who would have noticed all this? The innkeeper(s), of course. Imagine, with the census going on, their place would have been full for some time. Probably steeling their resolve to turn away visitor after visitor seeking shelter, they are greeted by a weary couple, about to give birth.

We can further imagine their hard hearts melting, and having an almost unthinkable idea, something that probably sounded like a mistake the moment it passed their lips: "Well . . . I could offer you . . . well, what about the animal pen around the back?" We don't know, but it's not hard to imagine Mary and Joseph now exuding immense gratefulness for such a strange offering. How would the innkeeper have reacted to this whole exchange?

Have you ever offered what little it is you have, even though it seems so poor and lacking? Perhaps there have been times where it seems you have truly nothing to offer—to a person in need, to a situation or context that seems so vast, so distant that what you have is less than a drop of water offered to an ocean of trouble and crisis. Have you been concerned that the gift you can offer is lacking, is flawed, is imperfect and even messy?

Do you think you have nothing to give? You have more to give than you know.

To the Point
God asks each of us, imperfect as we are, to share the gifts we have, as best we can, with a waiting world in need.

SPIRITUALITY

Mass at Dawn

GOSPEL ACCLAMATION
Luke 2:14

℟. Alleluia, alleluia.
Glory to God in the highest,
and on earth peace to those
on whom his favor rests.
℟. Alleluia, alleluia.

Gospel Luke 2:15-20; L15ABC

When the angels went away from them to heaven,
the shepherds said to one another,
"Let us go, then, to Bethlehem
to see this thing that has taken place,
which the Lord has made known to us."
So they went in haste and found Mary and Joseph,
and the infant lying in the manger.
When they saw this,
they made known the message
that had been told them about this child.
All who heard it were amazed
by what had been told them by the shepherds.
And Mary kept all these things,
reflecting on them in her heart.
Then the shepherds returned,
glorifying and praising God
for all they had heard and seen,
just as it had been told to them.

See Appendix A, p. 267, for the other readings.

Praying with Gospel Words and Phrases

"Let us go" . . . they went in haste . . . glorifying and praising God . . .

Reflecting on the Gospel

We have already, during Advent, spent a brief time examining Christian paradox and mystery, those seemingly oppositional facets of our faith that ought not be able to exist side by side. Yet not only may we not let one of these facets prevail over the other, they must exist simultaneously, not even side by side, but together as one. Christ, the "God-man," isn't one or the other, isn't divinity masked as humanity, isn't half one and half the other. Christ is fully God and, apart from sin, fully human, period, full stop.

There is Christian paradox hiding, embedded within this morning's gospel. The stillness of nighttime has been disrupted by the singing of the angels to the shepherds as this scene begins: a paradox of quietude and jubilation. The shepherds make haste to Bethlehem to visit a baby, lying still in the manger: more paradox. While the sleeping babe makes no cry, the shepherds go forth, offering praise and glory for what they've just experienced, and who they've just seen: yet another layer of paradox.

When we encounter such paradoxes in our day-to-day living, they can make us quite uncomfortable. "Cognitive dissonance" is one way to name these moments, things that just don't make sense, moments that our rational and even scientific minds can't resolve. Dissonance is a musical term, we likely know, two notes which, when heard together, simply don't sound good to most ears compared to consonant notes that do sound pleasing and resolved. Dissonance and consonance are, of course, subjective and relative terms, we should note—much like the old expression "one man's trash is another man's treasure."

It is in a person's darkest hour that they may most clearly see Christ's light; it is in our human weakness that we may come to know holy strength; it is our own mortality through which eventually we may receive heaven's eternal life. These opposites ought not be able to dwell peaceably side by side in harmony, yet our faith compels them to. Indeed, it is only through faith and the power of God that such opposites become paradox; not side by side any longer, these opposites are made one in Christ, as is all creation. This is divine mystery.

To the Point

Christians are called not only to understand Christian paradox and mystery; we are called to embrace it and find ways to live it and evangelize within and through it.

SPIRITUALITY

Mass during the Day

GOSPEL ACCLAMATION
℟. Alleluia, alleluia.
A holy day has dawned upon us.
Come, you nations, and adore the Lord.
For today a great light has come upon the earth.
℟. Alleluia, alleluia.

Gospel

John 1:1-18; L16ABC

In the beginning was the Word,
and the Word was with God,
and the Word was God.
He was in the beginning with God.
All things came to be through him,
and without him nothing came to be.
What came to be through him was life,
and this life was the light of the human race;
the light shines in the darkness,
and the darkness has not overcome it.

A man named John was sent from God.
He came for testimony, to testify to the light,
so that all might believe through him.
He was not the light,
but came to testify to the light.
The true light, which enlightens everyone,
was coming into the world.
He was in the world,
and the world came to be through him,
but the world did not know him.
He came to what was his own,
but his own people did not accept him.

Continued in Appendix A, p. 267, or
John 1:1-5, 9-14 *in Appendix A, p. 267.*

See Appendix A, p. 268, for the other readings.

Praying with Gospel Words and Phrases

Word . . . light of the human race . . . the Word became flesh . . .

Reflecting on the Gospel

The incarnation is the core mystery of our faith, and the nature of Christ as truly God and truly human was one of the foundational deliberations at the heart of many of the early church councils. It is fitting that humanity should be saved by one such as ourselves, and that we were—and are—redeemed in this way is a profound testament to human dignity. The prologue of the Gospel of John stands side by side with Genesis telling us we were created in God's image, and with Paul repeatedly reminding the Corinthians that they (in their bodies) are temples of the Holy Spirit.

This dignity, then, is not dependent on gender, race, ethnicity, class, education, accomplishments, or even belief: all of humanity and each human being has worth and dignity. Loving God with our whole hearts, minds, and souls, Jesus reminds us, is equivalent to loving our neighbor as we love ourselves. Further, Jesus instructs us that each and any human being is our neighbor, especially the ones we find most difficult to love.

Recognizing a divine presence in the hearts and souls of all around us cannot help but inform and transform our interactions with one another, and our very worship of the divine, especially on this solemnity of the incarnation. It is worth examining your Christmas preaching, prayers, and hymn texts—at least the ones that are more changeable year to year—to see if there is a unity in message regarding the importance of Mass celebrated today, with these particular and unique readings.

When "Word" is capitalized, it refers to the *Logos*, the Greek name for the eternal Word, existing from the beginning and forever, which broke into human time and space as Jesus Christ. We celebrate that inbreaking each Christmas with the nativity of the Lord—"Word of the Father, now in flesh appearing!," the last verse of "O Come, All Ye Faithful," typically reminds us at the beginning of the vast majority of Christmas liturgies throughout the English-speaking world.

To the Point

This liturgy, especially through the gospel, points us toward what the incarnation means in relation to human dignity and salvation. Make sure that preaching, intercessions, and music do the same!

Model Penitential Act

Presider: The Word was made flesh and dwells among us. With humbleness and joy, we come before the Lord who came to us, asking for pardon and peace . . . *[pause]*

Lord Jesus, you are the light of the human race: Lord, have mercy.
Christ Jesus, your light shines in the darkness and is not overcome: Christ, have mercy.
Lord Jesus, you made your dwelling among us and call us to yourself: Lord, have mercy.

Model Universal Prayer (Prayer of the Faithful)

Presider: The Lord Jesus comes to us to fill the world with light. Let us who are called to be God's children offer our prayers and petitions for ourselves and all the world.

Response: Lord, hear our prayer.

For the church: may all the faithful be filled with grace and truth this day, and the courage to share Christ's light with all the world, we pray . . .

For all who believe in God: may those who share a love for God be blessed with peace, we pray . . .

For family members who are absent or estranged: may our prayers for their well-being bring them grace and guidance in the Spirit, we pray . . .

For greater joy: may we look at our loved ones and our lives and be reminded of God's abundant blessings, we pray . . .

Presider: O God, you sent your only Son into the world so that we might be saved through him. Hear our prayers this day, guide us in your truth, and allow us to be the light to all the nations that you have called your children to be. We ask this through Christ our Lord. **Amen.**

Living Liturgy: Liturgy and Art

The preface of the nativity situates the assembly within the fullness of salvation history, proclaiming Christ's birth as the fulfillment of God's promise and the source of universal joy. This prayer of thanksgiving and praise not only introduces the eucharistic prayer but also shapes the assembly's perception of the liturgy as a living encounter with God's work in the world. Artistic expressions in the worship space echo the preface, making the narrative of salvation tangible. They highlight the wonder, dignity, and cosmic significance of the incarnation. By engaging with these forms, the faithful are drawn beyond observation to participation: they see, hear, and feel the story of God's plan embodied in the liturgy. Through these layered expressions, Christmas becomes a space where the faithful encounter the glory of God revealed in the human Christ and are formed to carry the beauty, meaning, and joy of this mystery into their daily lives.

COLLECT

(from the Mass during the Day)

Let us pray.

Pause for silent prayer

O God, who wonderfully created the dignity of human nature
and still more wonderfully restored it,
grant, we pray,
that we may share in the divinity of Christ,
who humbled himself to share in our humanity.
Who lives and reigns with you in the unity of the Holy Spirit,
God, for ever and ever. **Amen.**

SPIRITUALITY

GOSPEL ACCLAMATION
Heb 1:1-2

℟. Alleluia, alleluia.
In the past God spoke to our ancestors through the prophets;
in these last days, he has spoken to us through the Son.
℟. Alleluia, alleluia.

or:

Col 3:15a, 16a

℟. Alleluia, alleluia.
Let the peace of Christ control your hearts;
let the word of Christ dwell in you richly.
℟. Alleluia, alleluia.

Gospel

Luke 2:22-40; L17B

When the days were completed for their purification
according to the law of Moses,
they took him up to Jerusalem
to present him to the Lord,
just as it is written in the law of the Lord,
Every male that opens the womb shall be consecrated to the Lord,
and to offer the sacrifice of
a pair of turtledoves or two young pigeons,
in accordance with the dictate in the law of the Lord.

Now there was a man in Jerusalem whose name was Simeon.
This man was righteous and devout,
awaiting the consolation of Israel,
and the Holy Spirit was upon him.
It had been revealed to him by the Holy Spirit
that he should not see death
before he had seen the Christ of the Lord.

Continued in Appendix A, p. 269, or
Luke 2:22, 39-40 *in Appendix A, p. 269.*

Praying with Gospel Words and Phrases

According to your word . . . awaiting the redemption . . .

Reflecting on the Gospel

We all know the woman—there's at least one, or more sometimes, in each parish. She usually has some predictable attributes. She is the first to be a substitute in the eucharistic adoration chapel, helps launder the liturgical linens, and, most notably, is there at every single Mass the parish offers. Every. Single. One. Sometimes she is grumpy, sometimes joyful, but most importantly, she is there—always there.

Our parishes wouldn't survive without these modern-day versions of the Anna we hear about in today's gospel. And of course, frequently every parish "Anna" has a "Simeon" alongside. Anna "never left the temple, but worshiped night and day," we hear, and surely, Simeon too was in the temple each day while awaiting the promise of the Lord to be fulfilled. These sorts of souls sustain our parishes by presence, by prayer, by wisdom, by service, by example.

Luke doesn't tell us exactly what either of them saw in Jesus that helped them identify him as the chosen one, the Messiah. Simeon sees the Holy Family enter the temple for the consecration rituals, and *just knows*, apparently. Perhaps it was something to do with his advanced age, typically associated with the gift of wisdom, that allowed him to see what others that day apparently missed: that this child, Jesus, was someone special.

The elders of our faith communities, be that our parish, our ministries, or our families, have done and seen a lot of living. Along with holy wisdom, a long life grants to those blest with these years a certain perspective, sometimes optimistic, sometimes pessimistic, occasionally both at the same time! Simeon and Anna speak about the child to all who would hear it as the living embodiment of the hopes and expectations of all Jews awaiting the restoration of God's rule in Israel. The birth of Jesus brings these promises to fulfillment, but perhaps not in the earthly way that was hoped for and expected.

To the Point

Wisdom comes in many shapes and forms, even if hard to recognize at times. Often that wisdom is apparent more in presence and unassuming action than in speech or written word.

Preparing to Proclaim, Preach, and Pray

Making Connections Between the Readings: Many middle-aged (that is, Gen X) adults today feel a bit of a pinch: while still raising their children they also need to take care of their aging parents, who may need more help and attention at this point in their lives. This so-called "sandwich generation" can feel strained in a multiplicity of ways: time, and financial and mental health. A lot of this happens in part because few multigenerational families live together under a shared roof as they once did. Extended life spans, because of some successes of modern health care, are another reason.

This aspect of life today could make the reading from Sirach received quite differently from person to person in the pews. Some might hear it as a reminder of the stressors of their current life, or even as a "guilt trip" within their current circumstance. Lectors and preachers ought to be mindful of the variety of situations that comprise family life these days. The reading should be proclaimed with sensitivity and warmth, not sternness or severity, especially near the end. Preaching ought not shy away from describing the positive attributes of an ideal family life; similarly, the homily might want to avoid any definition of a family that is too specific. Many ears might tune out what is otherwise a helpful discourse.

The second reading enumerates those positive attributes, which lectors should proclaim slowly that all may ponder them well. Homilists should have no worry about repeating them verbatim: compassion, kindness, humility, gentleness, and patience. Paul tells us elsewhere in a different letter that these are all things that "Love is"; therefore, what God also is and what God desires of each of us.

Making Connections to the Responsorial Psalm: Psalm 128 is often sung at weddings, understandably, and the image of a family as a "fruitful vine" and "olive plants" is vibrant and evocative—but only if the faithful have some firsthand experiences with them! Especially in urban settings, quite a lot of the agricultural imagery of our Sacred Scriptures can sound nice, but lose impact and meaning.

Consider placing images of a grapevine or an olive tree in your bulletins or social media posts leading up to this Sunday. Grapevines have solid roots and cling to supports to grow well. What are these roots and supports of our faith? Olive trees do not grow quickly and take a lot of care and patience to cultivate. They begin life in a somewhat fragile state, eventually growing in strength and gaining the potential of bearing much fruit.

CONNECTING TO EXPERIENCE: LIVING THE PASCHAL MYSTERY

When families are beset by challenge and parents by stressful situations, anxiety, frustration, and anger are ready and waiting to enter our hearts. Once they have entered, love for our family easily becomes strained and choked with snapping and grudge-bearing. What about Mary and Joseph? They begin their lives together in some confusion, poverty, and fear. But instead of letting fear enter their hearts, they hear the voices of angels. They listen, and in faith and fortitude turn together to protect their child, moving to a place unknown. The model before us for family life is one of trust, companionship, and obedience to God's will. Mary and Joseph bore Christ in faith and made a home for him. Our own lives are beset by challenges: mistakes, misunderstandings, pain, and loss. But how do we respond? The parents of Jesus invite us to follow their example. Have faith. Choose strength. We are also called to welcome Christ Jesus into the home of our hearts.

PROMPTS FOR FAITH-SHARING

- Is your life full of conflict with family or friends? Do you know someone who struggles with such conflict? How can you help them? For what can you pray?
- When you feel that God is prompting you to be on the move, do you listen? How can you practice obedience to God in a new way?
- How can you, like Joseph, listen to your dreams? Is there some need or hope that you have not heeded, which you can act on today?

Model Penitential Act

Presider: Coming before the Lord who is the light of salvation, we ask for his mercy . . . *[pause]*

Lord Jesus, you fill us with your peace: Lord, have mercy.

Christ Jesus, you have prepared salvation for us: Christ, have mercy.

Lord Jesus, you call your people to be light for all the nations: Lord, have mercy.

Model Universal Prayer (Prayer of the Faithful)

Presider: Turning to the Lord who cares for his people from age to age, we offer our prayers and petitions.

Response: Lord, hear our prayer.

For Christian families: may we choose to love one another and invite Christ into our homes with prayer . . .

For our grandparents, elders, and senior friends: may we seek their wisdom and honor their lives, we pray . . .

For children who do not have families to care for them: may they be received into loving homes and find comfort, we pray . . .

For greater confidence in the Spirit: may we have the faith of Simeon and the gratitude of Anna, we pray . . .

Presider: O God, you call us to love one another, beginning with those closest to us. Heal hearts that are wounded and revive spirits in need of joy, so that we might follow in the footsteps of the Holy Family. We ask this through Christ our Lord. **Amen.**

Liturgy and Order

Several years ago, at my workplace, there was a photocopier dedicated to the ministries of the pastoral team I was part of. It was an incredible machine—collating, stapling, scanning—that did everything we needed. One day, however, I arrived to find an "out of order" sign on it. After asking around, I discovered that one of the small "feet" on the bottom had broken off. "What does that matter?" I wondered.

I soon learned that even this minor imbalance could cause serious issues. Without that one foot, the copier leaned ever so slightly. That subtle tilt could lead to a chain of problems: the motor that ran the scanning light could be strained, paper might misfeed from the drawers, and the toner might settle unevenly in the cartridge. Despite appearing almost fine, the machine couldn't function properly because of one small broken part.

Today's celebration speaks to the importance of order within a family—whether that's a household, a faith community, or other varying definitions. Our liturgies too are structured, are ordered to maintain reverence and unity across different places and contexts, while still allowing flexibility for true pastoral needs.

(continued on next page)

COLLECT

Let us pray.

Pause for silent prayer

O God, who were pleased to give us
the shining example of the Holy Family,
graciously grant that we may imitate them
in practicing the virtues of family life and
in the bonds of charity,
and so, in the joy of your house,
delight one day in eternal rewards.
Through our Lord Jesus Christ, your Son,
who lives and reigns with you in the unity
of the Holy Spirit,
God, for ever and ever. **Amen.**

FIRST READING

Sir 3:2-6, 12-14

God sets a father in honor over his
children;
a mother's authority he confirms over
her sons.
Whoever honors his father atones for sins,
and preserves himself from them.
When he prays, he is heard;
he stores up riches who reveres his
mother.
Whoever honors his father is gladdened by
children,
and, when he prays, is heard.
Whoever reveres his father will live a long
life;
he who obeys his father brings comfort
to his mother.

My son, take care of your father when he
is old;
grieve him not as long as he lives.
Even if his mind fail, be considerate of
him;
revile him not all the days of his life;
kindness to a father will not be forgotten,
firmly planted against the debt of your
sins
—a house raised in justice to you.

RESPONSORIAL PSALM

Ps 128:1-2, 3, 4-5

℟. (cf. 1) Blessed are those who fear the
Lord and walk in his ways.

Blessed is everyone who fears the LORD,
who walks in his ways!
For you shall eat the fruit of your
handiwork;
blessed shall you be, and favored.

℟. Blessed are those who fear the Lord and
walk in his ways.

Your wife shall be like a fruitful vine
in the recesses of your home;
your children like olive plants
around your table.

℟. Blessed are those who fear the Lord and walk in his ways.

Behold, thus is the man blessed
who fears the LORD.
The LORD bless you from Zion:
may you see the prosperity of Jerusalem
all the days of your life.

℟. Blessed are those who fear the Lord and walk in his ways.

SECOND READING
Col 3:12-21

Brothers and sisters:
Put on, as God's chosen ones, holy and beloved,
heartfelt compassion, kindness, humility, gentleness, and patience,
bearing with one another and forgiving one another,
if one has a grievance against another;
as the Lord has forgiven you, so must you also do.
And over all these put on love,
that is, the bond of perfection.
And let the peace of Christ control your hearts,
the peace into which you were also called in one body.
And be thankful.
Let the word of Christ dwell in you richly,
as in all wisdom you teach and admonish one another,
singing psalms, hymns, and spiritual songs
with gratitude in your hearts to God.
And whatever you do, in word or in deed,
do everything in the name of the Lord Jesus,
giving thanks to God the Father through him.

Wives, be subordinate to your husbands,
as is proper in the Lord.
Husbands, love your wives,
and avoid any bitterness toward them.
Children, obey your parents in everything,
for this is pleasing to the Lord.
Fathers, do not provoke your children,
so they may not become discouraged.

Continued in Appendix A, p. 270.
See Appendix A, pp. 269–270, for additional readings.

St. Paul reminds us in his letter to the Corinthians that though we are many parts, we are one body; when one part suffers, the whole body suffers. As we reflect on liturgical order, we might ask: Are certain elements in disrepair? Are lectors or altar servers poorly trained? Is the person responsible for liturgical environment well-formed? Identifying and addressing these "small feet" can strengthen the entire body of our worship.

Liturgical Ministers: Sacristans

On the solemnity of the Holy Family, the church honors the domestic church and roots the family as the first place of faith formation and holiness. Sacristans play a crucial role in supporting this celebration by preparing the sacred space where the community gathers to encounter God. The environment sacristans help create reflects the dignity and reverence due Christ's presence in the liturgy. Just as the Holy Family's life was marked by care, order, and devotion, their ministry embodies these virtues, making visible the respect and love for God's work in the assembly.
By attending carefully to every detail, sacristans help foster an atmosphere where families and all the faithful can enter more deeply into prayer and thanksgiving. Their ministry quietly supports the unfolding of salvation history within the liturgy, inviting all to experience the love, unity, and peace that the Holy Family models so perfectly.

Living Liturgy: Liturgy and Family Life (The Collect)

The collect for the solemnity of the Holy Family asks God to make us "imitate [the Holy Family] in practicing the virtues of family life." This liturgical prayer places the incarnation within the lived realities of home, showing that salvation unfolds not just in the temple or the sanctuary, but around the table, in obedience and in trust. The Holy Family reveals that God's grace sanctifies real relationships where love is tested, forgiveness is learned, and fidelity is formed. The liturgy invites us to see our homes as places where holiness takes root. It is where parents, children, and elders echo the mystery of Christ through patience, sacrifice, and shared joy. In this way, the family becomes the first place of discipleship and a living icon of the church.

SPIRITUALITY

GOSPEL ACCLAMATION
Heb 1:1-2

℟. Alleluia, alleluia.
In the past God spoke to our ancestors through the prophets;
in these last days, he has spoken to us through the Son.
℟. Alleluia, alleluia.

Gospel

Luke 2:16-21; L18ABC

The shepherds went in haste to Bethlehem and found Mary and Joseph,
and the infant lying in the manger.
When they saw this,
they made known the message
that had been told them about this child.
All who heard it were amazed
by what had been told them by the shepherds.
And Mary kept all these things,
reflecting on them in her heart.
Then the shepherds returned,
glorifying and praising God
for all they had heard and seen,
just as it had been told to them.

When eight days were completed for his circumcision,
he was named Jesus, the name given him by the angel
before he was conceived in the womb.

See Appendix A, p. 271, for the other readings.

Praying with Gospel Words and Phrases

Mary kept all these things, reflecting on them in her heart . . .

Reflecting on the Gospel

In addition to celebrating the *Theotokos*, the "God-Bearer" today, many hymnals and missalettes will still remind us that January 1 is also the World Day of Peace, as instituted by Pope Paul VI. We would be wise to recall on this day how Mary herself is a shining example of peace, justice, and dignity.

Like Mary, who took time to reflect of the events of the nativity in her heart, do we set aside times of stillness and peace to pray for and reflect on the coming of God's reign of justice? Do we allow for this at liturgy? Silence should follow each reading as well as the homily. When announcing, "Let us pray" before each collect, there should be copious silence to allow each member of the assembly to, you know, *pray*, so that the collect can indeed collect (different syllabic emphasis) all those prayers into one.

Like Mary, especially in her *Magnificat*, do we accept spoken prayers and lyrics of social justice as an integral part of our liturgical prayer? Mary is more than meek and mild, more than a lowly handmaid. Her *Magnificat* praises the God who casts down the mighty and raises the lowly.

Like Mary, who welcomed the lowly shepherds to witness the birth of the Messiah, do we truly welcome the lowly and outcast among us into our celebrations? Do we perhaps say we do but then offer nothing to such as these as a practical manifestation of that welcome?

As we celebrate Mary the God-Bearer today, let us also recommit ourselves and our liturgical ministries to the example given us by the Blessed Mother in prayer, in contemplation, and in action.

To the Point

We must be careful, especially by preaching and by choice of hymnody, not to depict the Blessed Mother too simply, too one-dimensionally. At times Scripture shows us Mary as gentle, pensive, and quiet, but other times presents Mary as fiery, commanding, and strong. Importantly, Mary isn't only ever just one or two of those things; what's important is that she is three-dimensional, human, and relatable!

Model Penitential Act

Presider: Coming with haste before the Lord, we ask for his pardon and peace . . . *[pause]*

Lord Jesus, you come from heaven to earth to greet us: Lord, have mercy.

Christ Jesus, you know our faults and our failings: Christ, have mercy.

Lord Jesus, you bring us to fullness of life: Lord, have mercy.

COLLECT

Let us pray.

Pause for silent prayer

O God, who through the fruitful
virginity of Blessed Mary
bestowed on the human race
the grace of eternal salvation,
grant, we pray,
that we may experience the intercession
of her,
through whom we were found worthy
to receive the author of life,
our Lord Jesus Christ, your Son.
Who lives and reigns with you in the
unity of the Holy Spirit,
God, for ever and ever. **Amen.**

Model Universal Prayer (Prayer of the Faithful)

Presider: Reflecting on the words we have heard in the gospel, we offer our prayers and petitions.

Response: Lord, hear our prayer.

That we, the church, might hear the word of God this day and choose to act with new conviction to love, we pray . . .

That our nation might seek goodness, truth, and beauty in the governing of its people, we pray . . .

That all who are without food, shelter, or safety this day might be encouraged and find refuge, we pray . . .

That this new year might bring justice to all nations, hope to all peoples, and peace to all homes, we pray . . .

Presider: Lord God, your servant, Mary, heard your word and responded with faith. Fill our hearts with the same constancy and courage, that we might make your presence known to all the world. We ask this through Christ our Lord. **Amen.**

Living Liturgy: Liturgy and Discipleship

The solemn blessing for this solemnity proclaims the heart of the Church's belief: "God, who through the childbearing of the Blessed Virgin Mary willed in his great kindness to redeem the human race" (Roman Missal, II. For Celebrations of the Saints 15). This prayer affirms what we believe, that Mary, by God's grace, participated in the work of redemption. Vatican II teaches that she cooperated "by her obedience, faith, hope and burning charity" (*Lumen Gentium* 61). Mary's motherhood is not only biological but is one that is spiritual and ecclesial. The liturgy forms us in this mystery that like Mary, we too are called to bear Christ into the world through faith-filled lives. As the year begins, this blessing becomes a commission. In her, we see discipleship lived fully: receiving God's word, trusting in divine mercy, and cooperating in the work of salvation.

SPIRITUALITY

GOSPEL ACCLAMATION
Matt 2:2

℟. Alleluia, alleluia.
We saw his star at its rising
and have come to do him homage.
℟. Alleluia, alleluia.

Gospel

Matt 2:1-12; L20ABC

When Jesus was born in Bethlehem of Judea,
in the days of King Herod,
behold, magi from the east arrived in Jerusalem, saying,
"Where is the newborn king of the Jews?
We saw his star at its rising
and have come to do him homage."
When King Herod heard this,
he was greatly troubled,
and all Jerusalem with him.
Assembling all the chief priests and the scribes of the people,
he inquired of them where the Christ was to be born.
They said to him, "In Bethlehem of Judea,
for thus it has been written through the prophet:
And you, Bethlehem, land of Judah,
are by no means least among the rulers of Judah;
since from you shall come a ruler,
who is to shepherd my people Israel."
Then Herod called the magi secretly
and ascertained from them the time of the star's appearance.
He sent them to Bethlehem and said,
"Go and search diligently for the child.
When you have found him, bring me word,
that I too may go and do him homage."

Continued in Appendix A, p. 271.

Praying with Gospel Words and Phrases

Magi from the east arrived . . . they departed for their country by another way. . .

Reflecting on the Gospel

On Epiphany in the Western church, we celebrate the visitation of the magi to the Christ Child. We hear very little about the journey they must have taken: we know not from where they came and to where they returned, for instance. But it is helpful to consider their journey as a procession.

At eucharistic liturgies, there are typically several processions: at the entrance, with the Book of the Gospels, the presentation of the gifts, the communion procession, and the recessional. There are others scattered throughout the year, like the Passion Sunday procession and the Holy Thursday procession to the altar of repose. Some teach that the first procession of Mass is each member of the assembly leaving their homes and journeying to the church.

Processions remind us that faith is a journey: like the Israelites through the desert, we too journey, escaping bondage and passing through waters of rebirth to new life. We recall that the ground we walk on is holy ground, and that the church to which we belong is rarely stationary but is a capital-C Church, active and in motion, from east to west, from sunrise to sunset, from birth to rebirth.

In other Christian traditions, especially the Eastern churches, the Epiphany isn't limited to the visit of the magi, but also includes Jesus's baptism as well as Jesus's first miracle at the wedding in Cana. These together are three important steps on Jesus's earthly journey and the beginning of his adult ministry. In Cycle A, we hear these three gospels on successive Sundays, in fact.

Returning to the magi's journey, there is practical reason that "they departed for their country by another way." There is also a theological reason: everyone in Scripture who encounters the divine has their life dramatically changed. The two common ways are by name change or by upending, literally, their life's path. Consider the disciples on the way to Emmaus: they never make it there, at least in Luke's Gospel. Their path turns 180 degrees around, back to Jerusalem to proclaim the resurrection. So it is, eventually if not every day, with all followers of the Way.

To the Point

One image of church that is not considered often enough is church—and each of us individually—as pilgrims, as travelers on a faithful journey. The pilgrimage of the magi is a perfect moment to remind us of this.

Preparing to Proclaim, Preach, and Pray

Making Connections Between the Readings: While we might choose to focus on journey in the gospel, the passages from Isaiah and Ephesians are much more concerned with the *what* and the *who* we journey toward: the splendorous light revealed in Jesus Christ. This illumination is so brilliant that all the world shall know it, all shall be guided by it, and all shall be brought to it, offering regal gifts and announcing the greatness of God.

The association is obvious, of course, but could bear a moment of explanation by homily or hymn. Especially poignant might be a connection to the innkeeper alluded to in Luke's nativity narrative and as considered earlier (Christmas Mass During the Night). The gifts desired are not precious and noble necessarily; indeed, in our perceived lowliness we have more to offer than we realize. The nineteenth-century Christina Rosetti poem often set to music, "In the Bleak Mid-Winter," would make a wise addition to the liturgy today, ending thus:

What can I give Him,
Poor as I am?
If I were a Shepherd
I would bring a lamb;
If I were a Wise Man
I would do my part,
Yet what I can I give Him,
Give my heart.

Making Connections to the Responsorial Psalm: No matter which setting of Psalm 72 is sung this weekend, verse three is a tongue twister! For that reason, it of course deserves attention and practice. What must not be overlooked, however, is the final verse. It's all well and good that the glorious light of Christ has been revealed, and that all nations shall bring him homage and tribute. Without diminishing this, what's perhaps more valuable is what the light of Christ really is, elaborated on at the end of today's excerpt from Psalm 72.

The light here is justice and mercy, directed as always to the lowly and poor. Those on the margins, those without resources, without power or influence: these are the ones who, Catholic social teaching reminds us, are always given the "preferential option." This is not only scriptural, it's coded in canon law: "[The Christian faithful] are also obliged to promote social justice and, mindful of the precept of the Lord, to assist the poor from their own resources" (c. 222).

CONNECTING TO EXPERIENCE: LIVING THE PASCHAL MYSTERY

Herod does not speak the truth today. He sits on his seat of power and should have little fear. Yet earthly power instills fear in him: jealousy, treachery, and licentiousness.

Perhaps Herod is right to be afraid. A king has been born who is unlike any power we have ever seen.

The birth of this child breaks all barriers between heaven and earth and the divisions of nation from nation. All peoples, from East to West, North to South, are called to come before him. Yet this baby's throne is not threaded with political maneuvering. His throne exists in the arms of his mother, Mary. His power is humility, peace, and justice. God's power is unlike any human power. When we confront God's power, do we speak the truth? Has the faith first promised to us in baptism anointed us to speak in the face of pride, deceit, and injustice? Or do we remain like Herod, afraid of the light and clinging to the darkness?

PROMPTS FOR FAITH-SHARING

- Like Herod, where in your life are you not being truthful to yourself or others?
- Like Herod, where in your life are you jealous of another person? How can you avoid interfering in their journey?
- Like the magi, how in your life can you be willing to travel "by another way"? How might this way be both a choice for safety and a risk?

Model Penitential Act

Presider: The light of Christ has dispelled the darkness that covered the earth. Coming before him, we ask him to fill our hearts with his light as we ask for his mercy and peace . . . *[pause]*

Lord Jesus, you gather your sons and daughters from afar: Lord, have mercy.
Christ Jesus, you govern your people with justice and comfort the afflicted: Christ, have mercy.
Lord Jesus, you are the light that dispels the darkness of sin and death: Lord, have mercy.

Model Universal Prayer (Prayer of the Faithful)

Presider: Coming before the Lord, we offer our hearts as we pray for all those in need of light and life.

Response: Lord, hear our prayer.

That the church throughout the world, along with our Orthodox brothers and sisters, might find light, restoration, and peace in our time, we pray . . .

That leaders of nations may learn from the magi who listened to the words of God's angel and not the commands of earthly powers, we pray . . .

That children suffering from neglect, discrimination, and violence will find protection in their communities and from advocates throughout the world, we pray . . .

That the faithful gathered here might find renewed strength in their baptismal call to be priests, prophets, and kings, we pray . . .

Presider: O God, you sent your Son into the world so that all nations might come to know your glory. Hear our prayers this day and fill us with your grace so that we might fulfill our baptismal call to be your faithful daughters and sons. We ask this through Christ our Lord. **Amen.**

Liturgy and Calendars

In this era of calendars on our personal digital devices synced to the cloud so as to be accessible to us in any given moment and place, some may not see the value in the sung proclamation, the "Announcement of Easter and the Moveable Feasts," which can be a part of the day's festivities. A quick internet search, if Easter is not already noted in our calendar, will tell us what most people would want to know, at least logistically.

This proclamation, though, tells us something more than just dates and holidays, if we choose to include it in our celebration. It reminds the faithful, as the days of Christmastide continue,

(continued on next page)

COLLECT

Let us pray.

Pause for silent prayer

O God, who on this day
revealed your Only Begotten Son to the nations
by the guidance of a star,
grant in your mercy
that we, who know you already by faith,
may be brought to behold the beauty of your sublime glory.
Through our Lord Jesus Christ, your Son,
who lives and reigns with you in the unity of the Holy Spirit,
God, for ever and ever. **Amen.**

FIRST READING

Isa 60:1-6

Rise up in splendor, Jerusalem! Your light has come,
the glory of the Lord shines upon you.
See, darkness covers the earth,
and thick clouds cover the peoples;
but upon you the LORD shines,
and over you appears his glory.
Nations shall walk by your light,
and kings by your shining radiance.
Raise your eyes and look about;
they all gather and come to you:
your sons come from afar,
and your daughters in the arms of their nurses.

Then you shall be radiant at what you see,
your heart shall throb and overflow,
for the riches of the sea shall be emptied out before you,
the wealth of nations shall be brought to you.
Caravans of camels shall fill you,
dromedaries from Midian and Ephah;
all from Sheba shall come
bearing gold and frankincense,
and proclaiming the praises of the LORD.

RESPONSORIAL PSALM

Ps 72:1-2, 7-8, 10-11, 12-13

℟. (cf. 11) Lord, every nation on earth will adore you.

O God, with your judgment endow the king,
and with your justice, the king's son;
he shall govern your people with justice
and your afflicted ones with judgment.

℟. Lord, every nation on earth will adore you.

Justice shall flower in his days,
and profound peace, till the moon be no more.
May he rule from sea to sea,
and from the River to the ends of the earth.

℟. Lord, every nation on earth will adore you.

The kings of Tarshish and the Isles shall offer gifts;
the kings of Arabia and Seba shall bring tribute.
All kings shall pay him homage,
all nations shall serve him.

℟. Lord, every nation on earth will adore you.

For he shall rescue the poor when he cries out,
and the afflicted when he has no one to help him.
He shall have pity for the lowly and the poor;
the lives of the poor he shall save.

℟. Lord, every nation on earth will adore you.

SECOND READING
Eph 3:2-3a, 5-6

Brothers and sisters:
You have heard of the stewardship of God's grace
that was given to me for your benefit,
namely, that the mystery was made known to me by revelation.
It was not made known to people in other generations
as it has now been revealed
to his holy apostles and prophets by the Spirit:
that the Gentiles are coheirs, members of the same body,
and copartners in the promise in Christ Jesus through the gospel.

that there is a connection between the nativity and the resurrection, and that the whole of the Christian year—the whole of our Christian lives—orbits the day of resurrection. Perhaps some in the pews this day also heard its "sister proclamation" on Christmas, "The Nativity of our Lord Jesus Christ," and it is well-suited then to place the resurrection event more completely in the context of salvation history.

Don't overlook this seemingly perfunctory and arcane bit of liturgy! It can have a powerful effect and communicate much when sung well (by a deacon or cantor) and approached with understanding and care.

Liturgical Ministers: Lectors

On Epiphany, the church celebrates Christ revealed to the nations as the light shining for all peoples. Lectors have a vital role in this feast, as the first epiphany in the liturgy happens through the word. Isaiah's bold vision, "Rise up in splendor, Jerusalem! Your light has come," and Paul's proclamation of the Gentiles as coheirs, set the stage for the gospel's climax: the magi encountering Christ. Lectors are not simply readers but heralds of this revelation. Through clear, prayerful proclamation, they allow the assembly to hear and receive God's unfolding mystery. This ministry demands preparation not only of voice but also of heart, which models a disposition open to being transformed by the very word one proclaims. Lectors must understand that their ministry is an extension of Christ's own mission: to bring light into darkness and lead the faithful into deeper communion with God through the living word.

Living Liturgy: Prayer Over the Offerings

The prayer over the offerings declares that the church now offers not gold, frankincense, or myrrh but "he who by them is proclaimed, sacrificed and received, Jesus Christ." This prayer reveals what we believe, that in the Eucharist, the Christ encountered by the magi is not symbolically present, but truly and substantially given (CCC 1376). Epiphany celebrates Christ's manifestation to the nations, and the liturgy makes that revelation immediate. In the Eucharist, the light to the Gentiles is both worshipped and received. This mystery forms the faithful to offer their own lives in return. Just as the magi laid down their treasures, we are called to lay down ourselves in worship and mission proclaiming by our lives the Christ we have encountered in sacrament.

SPIRITUALITY

GOSPEL ACCLAMATION
cf. John 1:29

℟. Alleluia, alleluia.
John saw Jesus approaching him, and said:
Behold the Lamb of God who takes away the sin of the world.
℟. Alleluia, alleluia.

or:

cf. Mark 9:7

℟. Alleluia, alleluia.
The heavens were opened and the voice of the Father thundered:
This is my beloved Son, listen to him.
℟. Alleluia, alleluia.

Gospel

Mark 1:7-11; L21B

This is what John the Baptist proclaimed:
"One mightier than I is coming after me.
I am not worthy to stoop and loosen the thongs of his sandals.
I have baptized you with water;
he will baptize you with the Holy Spirit."

It happened in those days that Jesus came from Nazareth of Galilee
and was baptized in the Jordan by John.
On coming up out of the water he saw the heavens being torn open
and the Spirit, like a dove, descending upon him.
And a voice came from the heavens,
"You are my beloved Son; with you I am well pleased."

Praying with Gospel Words and Phrases

One mightier than I is coming after me . . . You are my beloved Son . . .

Reflecting on the Gospel

In today's gospel, John the Baptist stands on the banks of the Jordan proclaiming, "One mightier than I is coming after me." John's ministry has drawn crowds, but he knows his task is not to point to himself—it is to prepare the way for another. His words remind us that authentic faith always turns the spotlight away from the self and toward Christ. Even in his humility, John's confidence lies not in what he can do, but in the One who comes to fulfill all righteousness.

When Jesus arrives and steps into the water, something extraordinary happens. The sinless Son of God joins the line of sinners waiting to be baptized. The One who has no need of cleansing identifies himself completely with our human condition. This moment is not about Jesus's repentance, but about his solidarity—with the broken, the weary, and the searching. In fact, he sanctifies the waters by entering them, making them a channel of grace for all who will follow.

As Jesus comes up from the water, the heavens are torn open and the Spirit descends upon him like a dove. Then a voice proclaims, "You are my beloved Son; with you I am well pleased." This Trinitarian moment—Father, Son, and Spirit—marks the beginning of Jesus's public mission. The Father's words do not confer something new upon Jesus; they reveal what has always been true. He is beloved. Before he performs any miracle, preaches any sermon, or calls any disciple, he is loved simply for who he is.

That same truth is spoken over each of us in baptism. Before our accomplishments or failures, before any title or task, God looks upon us and says, "You are my beloved." To live as a baptized Christian is to remember that this identity comes first and lasts forever. This means baptism is not merely a past event but an ongoing reality. Each day we are invited to live out our baptism—to die to sin, rise with Christ, and let the Spirit's presence renew the world through us.

To the Point

In Jesus's baptism, heaven meets earth, and divine love claims us as God's own.

May Jesus's baptism today remind each of us, charged with evangelizing the reign of God on earth, that the most missionary, evangelistic thing we can do as church is to let others know we care for them as God cares for us.

Preparing to Proclaim, Preach, and Pray

Making Connections Between the Readings: At first, it may feel incongruous that the first reading, from Isaiah, is text from the Suffering Servant, reminding us likely of Good Friday and Christ's passion. Our faith, by our ritual texts which echo Paul's epistle to the Romans, reveals that we who are baptized into Christ are baptized into Christ's death. So even Christ himself, his baptism one of the moments revealing him to be God's Son, is, even from the very beginning, set on a trajectory of service, suffering, death, and new life.

While our Christian lives are—or at least ought to be—lives of hope and joy, this is not to say that these things replace suffering and death; rather, we rejoice in them, through lives of service, encouraged by the promise of new and eternal life, united with each other in the Holy Trinity. This too is Christian paradox and mystery.

We should also note that while baptism begins our initiation into the church, Eucharist and confirmation complete it. The Bread of Life sustains us on our early journey of faith, and the Rite of Confirmation strengthens within us the gifts of the Holy Spirit given us at baptism, and seals them within us, for service to God and the church.

Peter's kerygma today is that what is given by baptism to Christ is given to all the baptized, universally, and that his mission is ours, to go about doing good and to heal those oppressed in any way by the devil, knowing, as Jesus did, that God is with us.

Making Connections to the Responsorial Psalm: The good works that we do, the healing that we are called to bring to all those in our midst: these are in the name of extending the blessings of peace—the peace not of this world but of the risen Christ, first given to us. At his final discourse at the Last Supper, Jesus offered this divine peace to the apostles, that their hearts not be troubled and that they have no fear—first during his passion and death, and then during coming days following his ascension.

The celebration of the baptism of Jesus is more than liturgical remembrance of an historical event: like all liturgy, it binds past, present, and future together as one. Psalm 29 today, rarely sung at liturgy, reminds us of this. The present tense language implies that, as it is sung, we are present at the Lord's baptism, at our own, and present to the eternal reign of God, where "The Lord is enthroned above the flood; the Lord is enthroned as king forever."

CONNECTING TO EXPERIENCE: LIVING THE PASCHAL MYSTERY

It's hard to change. It's hard to imagine how a hurting, painful life could be different. How do we stop being jealous. Angry. Depressed. Lost. It is hard to change. Alone. Today's gospel shows us a change. On this day, Jesus parts the waters of the Jordan and is baptized—and the heavens are torn open and the voice of God the Father tells us who he is. But when Jesus is baptized, does he change? Or does the voice of God announce who he is *so that we might know him*? Change for us sons and daughters of God is not so dramatic—the waters might not part and the heavens might not spill open with a thunderous voice. When we look for change in our difficult and painful lives, it is not that we need to be someone different. We need to remember *who we are.* We are daughters and sons of God. Grace-filled. And good.

PROMPTS FOR FAITH-SHARING

- Where do you need a kind of cleansing in your home, family, or work? How did it arrive at this point?
- Jesus reveals himself as the Son of God through his baptism. What does his baptism reveal to you that helps you to see him more accurately?
- Where in your life do you most need to remember that you are a child of God? What change might it bring to that part of your life?

Model Penitential Act

Presider: Coming before the Lord who fills us with his grace, we ask for his pardon and peace . . . *[pause]*

Lord, you call us to the waters of the Jordan: Lord, have mercy.

Christ Jesus, you have given us baptism to fill us with grace: Christ, have mercy.

Lord Jesus, you love us as sons and daughters of God: Lord, have mercy.

Model Universal Prayer (Prayer of the Faithful)

Presider: The Lord has gone before us, leading us in faith and baptism. Trusting in his promises, we offer our prayers and petitions.

Response: Lord, hear our prayer.

For the church: may all the baptized grow in faith and determination to live in Christ Jesus, we pray . . .

For leaders of nations: may they protect all people of faith, refusing discrimination and ending persecution, we pray . . .

For the suffering and downhearted: may we remind them of the love of Christ Jesus with our encouragement, we pray . . .

For all those gathered here: may we remember our baptism each day, recalling that we have the gift of God's grace to be God's daughters and sons, we pray . . .

Presider: O God, you call us always to yourself. Hear our prayers this day, and fill our hearts with the desire to always walk in your ways and to remember that you love us. We ask this through Christ our Lord. **Amen.**

Liturgy and Ritual

Water is one of the symbols of our faith steeped in paradox. It is, in a way, our first home in our mother's womb; for some of us it is our death and tomb. It cleans and purifies; it can be the bearer of illness and disease. In some places it is as common as rain or the seashore; in other places it is rarely seen in nature.

Water is, principally for the faithful, death and life simultaneously. If designed well, the font in our church reminds us of womb and tomb, with the water itself prominent and obvious (*Built of Living Stones* 68). Further, as baptism itself is the sacramental entry into the life of the church, it is desirable that the font and its water be near the entry doors to the church, and indeed set "on an axis with the altar" to "symbolize the relationship between the various sacraments as well as the importance of the Eucharist within the life and faith development of the members" (*Built of Living Stones* 69).

(continued on next page)

COLLECT

Let us pray

Pause for silent prayer

Almighty ever-living God,
who, when Christ had been baptized in the River Jordan
and as the Holy Spirit descended upon him,
solemnly declared him your beloved Son,
grant that your children by adoption,
reborn of water and the Holy Spirit,
may always be well pleasing to you.
Through our Lord Jesus Christ, your Son,
who lives and reigns with you in the unity of the Holy Spirit,
one God, for ever and ever. **Amen.**

or:

O God, whose Only Begotten Son
has appeared in our very flesh,
grant, we pray, that we may be inwardly transformed
through him whom we recognize as outwardly like ourselves.
Who lives and reigns with you in the unity of the Holy Spirit,
one God, for ever and ever. **Amen.**

FIRST READING

Isa 42:1-4, 6-7

Thus says the LORD:
Here is my servant whom I uphold,
my chosen one with whom I am pleased,
upon whom I have put my spirit;
he shall bring forth justice to the nations,
not crying out, not shouting,
not making his voice heard in the street.
A bruised reed he shall not break,
and a smoldering wick he shall not quench,
until he establishes justice on the earth;
the coastlands will wait for his teaching.

I, the LORD, have called you for the victory of justice,
I have grasped you by the hand;
I formed you, and set you
as a covenant of the people,
a light for the nations,
to open the eyes of the blind,
to bring out prisoners from confinement,
and from the dungeon, those who live in darkness.

RESPONSORIAL PSALM
Ps 29:1-2, 3-4, 3, 9-10

℟. (11b) The Lord will bless his people
with peace.

Give to the Lord, you sons of God,
give to the Lord glory and praise,
give to the Lord the glory due his name;
adore the Lord in holy attire.

℟. The Lord will bless his people with
peace.

The voice of the Lord is over the waters,
the Lord, over vast waters.
The voice of the Lord is mighty;
the voice of the Lord is majestic.

℟. The Lord will bless his people with
peace.

The God of glory thunders,
and in his temple all say, "Glory!"
The Lord is enthroned above the flood;
the Lord is enthroned as king forever.

℟. The Lord will bless his people with
peace.

SECOND READING
Acts 10:34-38

Peter proceeded to speak to those gathered
in the house of Cornelius, saying:
"In truth, I see that God shows no
partiality.
Rather, in every nation whoever fears him
and acts uprightly
is acceptable to him.
You know the word that he sent to the
Israelites
as he proclaimed peace through Jesus
Christ, who is Lord of all,
what has happened all over Judea,
beginning in Galilee after the baptism
that John preached,
how God anointed Jesus of Nazareth
with the Holy Spirit and power.
He went about doing good
and healing all those oppressed by the
devil,
for God was with him."

Other readings may also be used.
See Appendix A, p. 272.

This celebration must remind us of our own baptism and what that means as we go about our day-to-day lives. Consider including a sprinkling rite, supplanting the penitential act, and ensuring that the other variable parts of this liturgy strongly link Jesus's earthly mission (one description of which he once proclaimed himself from the prophecy of Isaiah) to our own.

We should also note that the church is still in Christmastide today, and therefore we should still include some music of the season.

Liturgical Ministry: Music Ministers

The ministry of music is integral to the church's prayer, especially on solemn occasions such as the Baptism of the Lord. Music ministers are not performers but liturgical ministers called to serve the assembly's active participation in the paschal mystery. Music ministers are called to a deepening appreciation of the relationship between music and liturgical texts, understanding that music both expresses and shapes the church's *lex orandi.* Through prayerful attention to the liturgical context, music ministers enable the assembly to enter more fully into the mystery celebrated. Their ministry unites voice and heart, fostering the church's communal offering of praise to the triune God. Proper formation grounds ministers in the theology and spirituality of the liturgy, helping them recognize that their role is to lead the assembly not only in song but in faithful and prayerful encounter with God's saving work.

Living Liturgy: The Gospel Acclamation

The gospel acclamation for the Baptism of the Lord (Mark 9:7) proclaims: "The heavens were opened and the voice of the Father thundered: This is my beloved Son, listen to him." This acclamation reveals the divine affirmation of Jesus as the Son of God, inaugurating his public mission and revealing the Father's love. As the assembly listens to these words, they participate in the revelation that forms the foundation of Christian identity. This moment invites the faithful to recognize Jesus not only as Savior but also as the beloved Son in whom they share by virtue of their own baptism. Through this sung proclamation, the community professes its faith in Christ and embraces its call to live as children of God, renewed and sent forth by the Spirit. Music ministers lead this proclamation, helping the assembly internalize the mystery of baptism and the call to discipleship rooted in God's love.

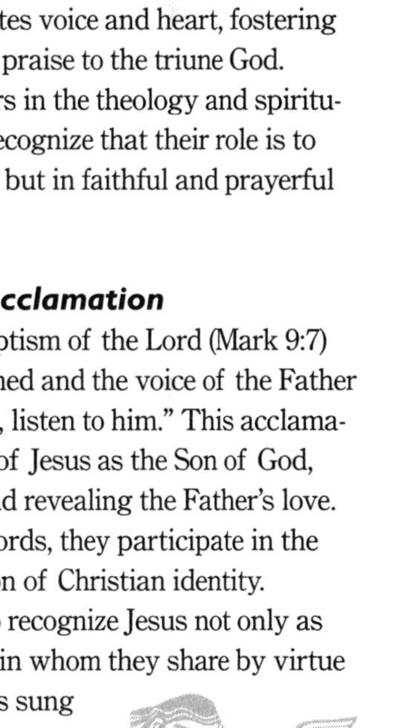

ORDINARY TIME I

SPIRITUALITY

GOSPEL ACCLAMATION
John 1:41, 17b

℟. Alleluia, alleluia.
We have found the Messiah:
Jesus Christ, who brings us truth and grace.
℟. Alleluia, alleluia.

Gospel

John 1:35-42; L65B

John was standing with two of his disciples,
and as he watched Jesus walk by, he said,
"Behold, the Lamb of God."
The two disciples heard what he said and followed Jesus.
Jesus turned and saw them following him and said to them,
"What are you looking for?"
They said to him, "Rabbi"—which translated means Teacher—,
"where are you staying?"
He said to them, "Come, and you will see."
So they went and saw where Jesus was staying,
and they stayed with him that day.
It was about four in the afternoon.
Andrew, the brother of Simon Peter,
was one of the two who heard John and followed Jesus.
He first found his own brother Simon and told him,
"We have found the Messiah"—which is translated Christ.
Then he brought him to Jesus.
Jesus looked at him and said,
"You are Simon the son of John;
you will be called Cephas"—which is translated Peter.

Praying with Gospel Words and Phrases

Behold . . . What are you looking for? . . . he brought him to Jesus . . .

Reflecting on the Gospel

In today's gospel (and the first reading as well), God's calls reach the ears, and indeed the very souls, of people not expecting it. Further, we also might not expect God's call to be given to ones such as these: an eleven-year-old, Samuel, apparently working as a sort of sacristan in the temple, and two men who are already disciples of another: John the Baptist.

In our liturgical work, there are elements of evangelization and catechesis. That is, we are charged with bringing people themselves to the liturgies and sharing the good news, as well as forming and educating them on matters of faith. More simply, we are charged with calling and fashioning new disciples. Over these few weeks of Ordinary Time, let us take a few moments each week to dig deeper into these facets of our ministries.

First, evangelization. How do we preach the good news to those who most need to hear it? Is that message of hope and salvation brought outside the church doors somehow? Are those fallen away from the faith invited to return? Many parishes have evangelization committees whose ministry is just that: for instance, reaching out to those who are registered in the parish but who have not been seen in the pews recently; spending time at public events being a faith-filled presence, ready for conversations about faith, community, and Christ; welcoming those who, by these efforts or others, have found their way again to the church building, curious about becoming "church" themselves.

Our Jewish brothers and sisters name this act of welcoming the stranger *Hachnasat or'chim*. Abraham is held as the pinnacle of such hospitality by his reception of wayfarers in Genesis 18. Some even note that his standing at the entrance of his tent is perhaps proactive, not waiting for others to come to him but eagerly seeking those who need welcome. It's worth noting that Scripture tells us, because of Abraham's *Hachnasat or'chim*, he and Sarah were in turn blessed with future generations (beginning with Isaac, father of Jacob, the patriarch of Israel), even though they were both advanced in age and had no reason to expect any new family members. Might our church families also be blessed by eagerly seeking out the lost and finding new ways to evangelize?

To the Point

As we enter this first brief stretch of Ordinary Time, we enter a period of learning to be disciples. Our first lesson, beyond following and intently listening, might be one of radical welcoming and inclusion as we evangelize the joy of the gospel.

Preparing to Proclaim, Preach, and Pray

Making Connections Between the Readings: In both the gospel and the first reading, not only is there connective tissue of people being called by God, but there is another commonality that might be easily overlooked. First, those who are called have with them a guiding presence, helping them more clearly hear and understand the divine calling, and gently directing them to an affirmative response. Samuel has Eli; Andrew and the unnamed disciple (traditionally John, son of Zebedee) have John the Baptist. Both Eli and John the Baptist have, it seems, more wisdom and understanding about what those called are experiencing and can help them discern and respond appropriately. They both immediately recognize the divine in their midst, and make sure that Samuel and the two disciples turn their attention completely to that calling.

That immediately bears fruit in the gospel, as Andrew quickly seeks out his brother Simon and brings him to Jesus as well. Not only has Jesus gained another follower but he has met the one who, some three years later, will become the cornerstone on which the whole church is built.

After the seasons of Advent and Christmas, here in Ordinary Time we encounter epistles that are not selected to align directly with the other Scripture passages. Yet there are often associations to be discovered. How is discipleship summarized, after all, if not "whoever is joined to the Lord becomes one Spirit with him"?

Making Connections to the Responsorial Psalm: It is noteworthy that in our psalm today, while the refrain is a presumed reply to God's call (echoing Samuel's reply), the text of the verses don't contain anything resembling a specific call from God. In fact, the verses begin not with a divine call but with our own voice, crying out from our apparently delayed anticipation.

We would do well to remember that our conversations with God—more commonly known simply as "prayer"—are two-way conversations. We not only speak to God but also need to listen to God. This is, by far, the harder portion. Allowing copious time for listening, eliminating distractions, allowing silence, and patiently waiting: none of these come naturally to the human condition.

Prayer aids—written booklets, online videos, smartphone apps—can certainly help, as can having a prayer partner. Such a person would not be so different than the guiding presences from our first reading and gospel today.

Lastly, we don't always need to know too much about the divine call to have an answer to it. Many times, the specifics of a calling don't go much beyond "follow me," relying on our trust and faith to reply as did Samuel, the apostles, and our psalmist today.

CONNECTING TO EXPERIENCE: LIVING THE PASCHAL MYSTERY

We might readily share a new book, a recipe, or a product we like; but what about the more difficult things to share? A place in line when we are in a hurry? A job opportunity that we might want as well? In the gospel today, Andrew shares. Could Andrew have had a more prominent place in the life of discipleship if he hadn't bothered to get his brother? Andrew was not the rock. Did Andrew know this would happen when he ran off to share the news with Simon? Did he ever find sharing the life of Christ difficult? Yet this is part of the call to discipleship: to call others to flourishing in the Christ-life. Andrew brought his brother to the Lord because he listened to the Lord. To listen means not only to hear but to respond: to try something new, to be transformed. May we listen and go forth, sharing the word of the Lord with all whom we meet.

PROMPTS FOR FAITH-SHARING

- Who in your life has shared Christ's invitation with you? How did their generosity change you?
- With whom in your life do you need to share Christ's invitation? What gifts do you have that would make you a more effective sharer of Christ's offer?
- When have you refused to share a gift—material or immaterial—with someone who needed it? What held you back?

Model Penitential Act

Presider: The Lord called Samuel out of his sleep to come before him. May we listen to the call of the Lord and begin by asking for his abundant mercy . . . *[pause]*

Lord Jesus, you call all sinners to yourself: Lord, have mercy.
Christ Jesus, you write your law upon our hearts: Christ, have mercy.
Lord Jesus, you have purchased us from sin and death: Lord, have mercy.

Model Universal Prayer (Prayer of the Faithful)

Presider: We come before the Lord as his gathered assembly, praying for our community here and for all the world.

Response: Lord, hear our prayer.

For the young people of the church discerning their vocations as lay faithful, as priests, or as members of religious communities: may they hear the Spirit's prompting in the midst of pressures from the world, we pray . . .

For those in power who have not yet let the word of God pierce their hearts: may the Lord put a new song within their mouths, we pray . . .

For the sick and the suffering in mind, body, and spirit: may the grace of God break through barriers of hardship in their lives, we pray . . .

For all here struggling to find community and friendship: may they find courage to continue seeking relationships and may those around them recognize their need, we pray . . .

Presider: Lord God, sacrifice and offering you want not, but instead you desire hearts inscribed by your law. Hear our prayers as we offer them to you and fill us with your Spirit so that we might proclaim your justice to all the world. We ask this through Christ our Lord. **Amen.**

Liturgy and Music

John the Baptist begins today's gospel passage with the iconic phrase, "Behold, the Lamb of God." These words we know well; they are a part of every eucharistic celebration, words of the priest celebrant just after the congregation sings of that same Lamb of God, who takes away the sins of the world.

Many of us are familiar with Martin Willett's "Behold the Lamb" (Oregon Catholic Press [OCP]), with its strong connection to Eucharist and eucharistic living. Even though we have just finished celebrating Christ's nativity, the phrase "Lamb of God" should call to mind that for which Christ was born—to be our paschal sacrifice. Bob Dufford's "Behold the Lamb of God" (OCP), may also spring instantly to mind and might not be as out of place as it initially seems, as we integrate our beliefs about the Messiah: the child of the cradle is also our Passover lamb.

COLLECT

Let us pray.

Pause for silent prayer

Almighty ever-living God,
who govern all things,
both in heaven and on earth,
mercifully hear the pleading of your people
and bestow your peace on our times.
Through our Lord Jesus Christ, your Son,
who lives and reigns with you in the unity of the Holy Spirit,
God, for ever and ever. **Amen.**

FIRST READING

1 Sam 3:3b-10, 19

Samuel was sleeping in the temple of the LORD
where the ark of God was.
The LORD called to Samuel, who answered, "Here I am."
Samuel ran to Eli and said, "Here I am. You called me."
"I did not call you," Eli said. "Go back to sleep."
So he went back to sleep.
Again the LORD called Samuel, who rose and went to Eli.
"Here I am," he said. "You called me."
But Eli answered, "I did not call you, my son. Go back to sleep."

At that time Samuel was not familiar with the LORD,
because the LORD had not revealed anything to him as yet.
The LORD called Samuel again, for the third time.
Getting up and going to Eli, he said, "Here I am. You called me."
Then Eli understood that the LORD was calling the youth.
So he said to Samuel, "Go to sleep, and if you are called, reply,
Speak, LORD, for your servant is listening."
When Samuel went to sleep in his place,
the LORD came and revealed his presence,
calling out as before, "Samuel, Samuel!"
Samuel answered, "Speak, for your servant is listening."

Samuel grew up, and the LORD was with him,
not permitting any word of his to be without effect.

RESPONSORIAL PSALM
Ps 40:2, 4, 7-8, 8-9, 10

℟. (8a and 9a) Here am I, Lord; I come to
do your will.

I have waited, waited for the LORD,
and he stooped toward me and heard
my cry.
And he put a new song into my mouth,
a hymn to our God.

℟. Here am I, Lord; I come to do your will.

Sacrifice or offering you wished not,
but ears open to obedience you gave me.
Holocausts or sin-offerings you sought not;
then said I, "Behold I come."

℟. Here am I, Lord; I come to do your will.

"In the written scroll it is prescribed for me,
to do your will, O my God, is my delight,
and your law is within my heart!"

℟. Here am I, Lord; I come to do your will.

I announced your justice in the vast
assembly;
I did not restrain my lips, as you, O
LORD, know.

℟. Here am I, Lord; I come to do your will.

SECOND READING
1 Cor 6:13c-15a, 17-20

Brothers and sisters:
The body is not for immorality, but for the
Lord,
and the Lord is for the body;
God raised the Lord and will also raise
us by his power.

Do you not know that your bodies are
members of Christ?
But whoever is joined to the Lord becomes
one Spirit with him.
Avoid immorality.
Every other sin a person commits is
outside the body,
but the immoral person sins against his
own body.
Do you not know that your body
is a temple of the Holy Spirit within
you,
whom you have from God, and that you
are not your own?
For you have been purchased at a price.
Therefore glorify God in your body.

Liturgical Ministry: Environment Ministers

As the church moves beyond the Christmas season into Ordinary Time, environment ministers guide the assembly through this transition. The environment of our worship space moves from the rich festivity of Christmas to a simpler, more reflective atmosphere that resists the mundane and invites renewed attentiveness to God's ongoing presence. This transition challenges environment ministers to move beyond the allure of lavish decoration and to embrace restraint as a form of sacred artistry. They must balance continuity and change, preserving the reverence of the season while preparing the assembly to engage with the ongoing journey of discipleship. Their task is to transform the space so that it speaks of quiet mystery and daily grace, inviting the faithful to recognize God's presence not only in grand celebrations but also in the rhythms of ordinary life.

Living Liturgy: Prayer after Communion

The prayer after Communion for the Second Sunday in Ordinary Time prays: "Pour on us, O Lord, the Spirit of your love, and in your kindness make those you have nourished by this one heavenly Bread one in mind and heart. Through Christ our Lord." This prayer encapsulates the ongoing transformation the Eucharist effects within the assembly. It expresses the deep longing and commitment the faithful carry beyond the liturgical celebration, desiring and loving Christ continually in their daily lives. The nourishment received in Communion is not only sustenance but a commissioning to live out discipleship with renewed zeal. The sacred space prepared by environment ministers supports this journey by fostering an atmosphere where the assembly can internalize the grace given and prepare to embody God's love in the world. This prayer invites the community to hold fast to Christ's presence, allowing that intimate encounter to shape their relationships, decisions, and mission.

SPIRITUALITY

GOSPEL ACCLAMATION
Mark 1:15

℟. Alleluia, alleluia.
The kingdom of God is at hand.
Repent and believe in the Gospel.
℟. Alleluia, alleluia.

Gospel

Mark 1:14-20; L68B

After John had been arrested,
Jesus came to Galilee proclaiming the gospel of God:
"This is the time of fulfillment.
The kingdom of God is at hand.
Repent, and believe in the gospel."

As he passed by the Sea of Galilee,
he saw Simon and his brother Andrew casting their nets into the sea;
they were fishermen.
Jesus said to them,
"Come after me, and I will make you fishers of men."
Then they abandoned their nets and followed him.
He walked along a little farther
and saw James, the son of Zebedee, and his brother John.
They too were in a boat mending their nets.
Then he called them.
So they left their father Zebedee in the boat
along with the hired men and followed him.

Praying with Gospel Words and Phrases

The kingdom of God is at hand . . . Come after me . . .

Reflecting on the Gospel

As we continue exploring the ways that liturgy encompasses welcoming and catechesis, we hear in today's gospel of Jesus's own evangelization of the reign of God. While Jesus invariably seems immediately effective with his calls, our experiences today are often more complicated.

Even if our evangelization and invitations have been effective, those who may be sitting in our pews on Sunday, for the first time or for the first time in a long time, could still have significant reservations and doubts about their presence in church. They might have feelings of unworthiness, they might feel like a fish out of water, and could perhaps be second-guessing why they even got out of bed that morning.

To break open that last point just a bit more: one need only do an internet search for recent Pew Research studies about religion to observe that many people, both those who call themselves still faithful and those who have left their faith, struggle greatly with many aspects of that faith. Our ministry, like Christ's, must be one that meets people where they are and offers loving invitations to form deeper relationships, both with God and with the Christian community. To try to do ministry in any other way is inauthentic and may not be the love that God is, and that God calls us to. Love can never force another person to a certain belief, a certain way of life, a certain holiness. Love is constant, love pursues, but ultimately love only offers, only invites: *Come, enter into the mystery. Journey with me; let us meet God together.*

Each time he encounters another human being, Jesus is always careful to meet each person where they are before inviting them into deeper holiness. Consider last week, where Jesus entered into some banter with Andrew and the other disciple, and spent the whole afternoon with them. Consider that, rather than spending many hours with him, immediately upon meeting Simon, Jesus gives him a new name. Then consider today's gospel, where Jesus's calling depends on analogizing the work of the fishermen to the ministry of evangelization and the saving of souls. Each apostle was met in a different way and brought into work of kingdom building on different terms. This is a guiding example for our similar Christian ministries, bringing all into relationship and holiness.

To the Point

Just as Jesus meets each of us where we are and only then invites us into transformative relationship, so too must our ministerial work be. Anything else cannot truly be called love.

Preparing to Proclaim, Preach, and Pray

Making Connections Between the Readings: We hear in the first reading this weekend about Jonah's testimony in Nineveh, a forerunner of Jesus's proclamation of the arrival of the reign of God. You remember Jonah, don't you? While we hear today of his successful preaching, Jonah was not always so keen on answering God's call affirmatively. Jonah did his best to run away from the Lord at first, only to be thrown into a stormy sea, swallowed by a whale, vomited up onto dry land, and called to a second time.

So too, in our efforts to expand the Christian community we must not grow disheartened if initial efforts seem unsuccessful. More often than not, Christian invitations must be offered many times over before they are accepted. Further, we mustn't let any repeated perceived failures dampen our joy and enthusiasm in the faith and in the gospels.

Preaching the reign of God, fundamentally, is preaching transformation and change, and so many are resistant to change, even if that change is visibly for the better. Inertia is not just a force to overcome in physics; it exists in human beliefs and behaviors as well. Look at the list of how the world is about to change which Paul offers us in the epistle. Everything is turned upside down! Is it any wonder that our evangelization efforts can appear fruitless at times?

It is so important then to recall that our own calling is not to success, at least as we perceive it. It's a call to holiness, which is something very different.

Making Connections to the Responsorial Psalm: This call to holiness is elaborated on in today's psalm, so make sure it is proclaimed well and not overlooked in the preaching this weekend. One might even describe it as an instruction manual for "evangelization by doing." God, teach us your compassion, your kindness. God, show me how to turn my own sinfulness into upright living, and teach me humility.

No Christian evangelist is perfect, but we are each called to work on our own discipleship while we evangelize and minister. We must be mindful, in these efforts, to never place ourselves above another, but only in relationship with others. We must be willing to not only teach and minister to, but to learn from and be ministered to by another, even if that "other" is unchurched, broken, and sinful—as we ourselves are sinful, after all.

These are ways of God, of fidelity, of a holy community that is united in Christ and faith in him.

CONNECTING TO EXPERIENCE: LIVING THE PASCHAL MYSTERY

We might *want* the world in its present form to pass away. We tire of our anxieties and stresses. Our hearts hurt over broken relationships and disappointed hopes. We don't know how to speak to our neighbor when political lines divide us into suspicion and even violence. When Paul speaks of the world passing away (second reading), he refers to Christ's coming at the end of time. How might we live as if the kingdom of God is already at hand? How can we place less priority on our fears and more on hope? How can we instill relationships and solidarity instead of stoking the fears of factions? Jesus calls us, just as he called Simon, Andrew, James, and John. These disciples turned from gleaning fish from the ocean to garnering souls for heaven. We are called to turn from our anxieties, fears, and brokenness. Will we allow Christ to transform us? How can we live as if Christ has come again?

PROMPTS FOR FAITH-SHARING

- What do you want to pass from your life, which perhaps you should keep? Is there anything that you are holding on to that should fade away so that Christ can be present?
- Like Jesus's first apostles, are you willing to drop what you are doing and follow with the same immediacy? If not, what's holding you back?
- If you could pick one aspect of your day that you could orient more toward the work of faith, what would it be?

Model Penitential Act

Presider: In the gospel today, Jesus begins proclaiming a gospel of repentance and finds his first followers. Let us hear his call to repentance and follow him, asking for his mercy . . . *[pause]*

Lord Jesus, you call us to repent and believe in the gospel: Lord have mercy.

Christ Jesus, you teach us your ways and guide us in your truth: Christ, have mercy.

Lord Jesus, you are our Savior who alone takes away the sins of the world: Lord, have mercy.

Model Universal Prayer (Prayer of the Faithful)

Presider: The Lord calls us to repent and believe in the gospel, for the kingdom of God is at hand. Preparing for his coming, we offer our prayers and petitions for ourselves and for all the world.

Response: Lord, hear our prayer.

For those discerning full initiation into the Catholic Church: may the faithful encourage them with joy and hospitality, we pray . . .

For nations undergoing elections and changes in power: may peace reign, we pray . . .

For those who suffer from displacement due to climate change and social unrest: may they be led to resources that sustain their lives while they await safe return to their homelands, we pray . . .

For all gathered here today: may we remember the grace first received in our baptism to become sons and daughters of God, through Christ Jesus, sealed with the Holy Spirit, we pray . . .

Presider: O God, your Son called his disciples to himself, offering them mercy and the forgiveness of their sins. May we remain steadfast in following his call, courageous in our rejection of sin, and constant in inviting all the world to love you more. We ask this through Christ our Lord. **Amen.**

Liturgy and Hospitality

Within the liturgy itself, there are many things that we who are responsible for the preparation and execution of our church's public prayer can be mindful of when ensuring we are welcoming of those who are joining us for the first time, or for the first time in a long time.

- Is there a greeting of the assembly from a lector or music minister prior to liturgy? Is it delivered in a clear, pleasing, and joy-filled tone?
- While asking those in the pews to greet those around them, particularly visitors, before Mass begins might seem wise, it can also feel to first-time congregants like they are being singled out, and any introverts in those ranks will perhaps want to curl up into a ball and hide under the kneelers for a few moments.

(continued on next page)

COLLECT

Let us pray.

Pause for silent prayer

Almighty ever-living God,
direct our actions according to your good pleasure,
that in the name of your beloved Son
we may abound in good works.
Through our Lord Jesus Christ, your Son,
who lives and reigns with you in the unity of the Holy Spirit,
God, for ever and ever. **Amen.**

FIRST READING

Jonah 3:1-5, 10

The word of the LORD came to Jonah, saying:
"Set out for the great city of Nineveh,
and announce to it the message that I will tell you."
So Jonah made ready and went to Nineveh,
according to the LORD's bidding.
Now Nineveh was an enormously large city;
it took three days to go through it.
Jonah began his journey through the city,
and had gone but a single day's walk announcing,
"Forty days more and Nineveh shall be destroyed,"
when the people of Nineveh believed God;
they proclaimed a fast
and all of them, great and small, put on sackcloth.

When God saw by their actions how they turned from their evil way,
he repented of the evil that he had threatened to do to them;
he did not carry it out.

RESPONSORIAL PSALM
Ps 25:4-5, 6-7, 8-9

℟. (4a) Teach me your ways, O Lord.

Your ways, O Lord, make known to me;
teach me your paths,
guide me in your truth and teach me,
for you are God my savior.

℟. Teach me your ways, O Lord.

Remember that your compassion, O Lord,
and your love are from of old.
In your kindness remember me,
because of your goodness, O Lord.

℟. Teach me your ways, O Lord.

Good and upright is the Lord;
thus he shows sinners the way.
He guides the humble to justice
and teaches the humble his way.

℟. Teach me your ways, O Lord.

SECOND READING
1 Cor 7:29-31

I tell you, brothers and sisters, the time is running out.
From now on, let those having wives act as not having them,
those weeping as not weeping,
those rejoicing as not rejoicing,
those buying as not owning,
those using the world as not using it fully.
For the world in its present form is passing away.

- Are hymn numbers visibly posted or clearly announced? What about the Gloria and other music of the ordinary of Mass? Is everything that someone sitting in the pews for the first time would need to fully participate in the liturgy readily and obviously available to them?
- More broadly, while there are many immutable texts of our liturgies, are we paying enough attention to the changeable ones: hymn texts, preaching, intercessions, and the like? Do our spoken and sung prayers of our own choosing leave room for mystery, for doubt, for questions?

Liturgical Ministry: Ushers and Greeters

Ushers and greeters serve not simply as welcoming faces, but as ministers who help the assembly cross the threshold into sacred time. Their quiet attentiveness helps foster a liturgical environment marked by order, reverence, and hospitality. By assisting with seating, attending to the needs of the assembly, and guiding the flow of movement during the liturgy, they allow others to enter more freely into prayer. Their role is particularly important at the beginning of Mass, as they help transition the community from arrival to worship, offering a form of stability and gentle structure. In this way, ushers and greeters are not on the margins of the liturgy but rather, they help hold the frame. Their ministry is a kind of liturgical hospitality, not only of welcome, but of presence and care for the gathered Body of Christ.

Living Liturgy: The Opening Procession

The opening procession is more than practical. The opening procession is a liturgical sign of who the church is. As the ministers move through the assembly toward the altar, the church enacts its identity as a pilgrim people, called and gathered by God. The movement from the door to the altar reflects the interior movement of each member of the assembly from the noise and distractions of the world into the silence and presence of Christ. Ordinary Time, beginning in these early weeks, is not about the "ordinary" in a casual sense but about ordered time, shaped by our response to Christ's call. This Sunday's gospel recounts the call of the first disciples. The procession, like their journey, begins with a response to rise, to follow, to gather, and to give. As the cross leads the ministers forward, the church follows not in symbol only, but in the lived discipleship the liturgy calls forth.

SPIRITUALITY

GOSPEL ACCLAMATION
Matt 4:16

℟. Alleluia, alleluia.
The people who sit in darkness have seen a great light;
on those dwelling in a land overshadowed by death,
light has arisen.
℟. Alleluia, alleluia.

Gospel

Mark 1:21-28; L71B

Then they came to Capernaum,
and on the sabbath Jesus entered the synagogue and taught.
The people were astonished at his teaching,
for he taught them as one having authority and not as the scribes.
In their synagogue was a man with an unclean spirit;
he cried out, "What have you to do with us, Jesus of Nazareth?
Have you come to destroy us?
I know who you are—the Holy One of God!"
Jesus rebuked him and said,
"Quiet! Come out of him!"
The unclean spirit convulsed him and with a loud cry came out of him.
All were amazed and asked one another,
"What is this?
A new teaching with authority.
He commands even the unclean spirits and they obey him."
His fame spread everywhere throughout the whole region of Galilee.

Praying with Gospel Words and Phrases

Authority . . . amazed . . . He commands even the unclean spirits . . .

Reflecting on the Gospel

Last week, these pages urged readers that any particular liturgical ministry we have must be one that "meets people where they are and offers loving invitations . . ." This and the rest of last week's writings could be seen, potentially, as oppositional to a faith and a liturgical practice of it that speaks and lives truth (or *Truth*, with a capital T). We hear of prophets this week in the Liturgy of the Word, beginning with Moses and continuing to Jesus, who teaches "with authority" while also commanding healing power over unclean spirits.

The love that was spoken of last week and the truth that is spoken of this week are of course not oppositional at all—God *is* love and God *is* truth, after all. Those who find contradictions here are perhaps concerned too much with content and not enough with the manner of delivery.

In 1964, Marshall McLuhan coined the phrase, "The medium is the message," and the world has been unpacking that ever since. While the deposit of faith left to us from our Scriptures and tradition is indeed vast and profound, it is a message sometimes not communicated well to the next generation of believers.

Here is a useful image from Mark Twain: "We should be careful to get out of an experience only the wisdom that is in it—and stop there; lest we be like the cat that sits down on a hot stove-lid. She will never sit down on a hot stove-lid again—and that is well; but also she will never sit down on a cold one any more" (*Following the Equator*). As we continue to ponder how our liturgical ministries invite, welcome, and begin to form disciples, let us be mindful that in our liturgies there could be, perhaps even unbeknownst to us, some moment which, though it only happens one time, may give someone the idea that it's not worth returning to the eucharistic table again. Most of the time, if there is that moment, it's not the message, it's the medium. Said another way, such a moment wouldn't be caused by the truth itself, but by the lack of love in passing on that truth to one another.

To the Point

The *Catechism of the Catholic Church* teaches that the ends do not justify the means (CCC 1749–61). More than that, the "how" we minister must be consonant with the message of the good news and the love that God is.

Preparing to Proclaim, Preach, and Pray

Making Connections Between the Readings: We don't hear much from Deuteronomy at liturgy. Perhaps this is because the book concerns itself largely with Mosaic Law, which Christians believe has been brought to fulfillment in Jesus Christ, and his life and teachings. Most of its exhortations and urgent language are worthy of further attention, however, especially when they come from Moses himself.

Moses tells of a coming prophet, seen from the Christian perspective as describing Christ, the Messiah. As if to teach the Israelites how to recognize this coming prophet, Moses explains in a long-winded way that the prophet will speak only what the one true God will command him to. Anything other than that, not only is such a man not a prophet of God, that man will die.

A prophet is sometimes defined as "one who speaks God's truth." To speak that truth, the message must also be of God's love, God's beauty, God's peace, and everything else that God is. The message must not only be about truth, love, beauty, and peace; it must itself recognizably *be* truth, love, beauty, and peace.

While Paul's message to the Corinthians must, on the whole, be seen as addressed to a particular community situated in a unique time and place, the broader message is for all times and places. God wishes, perhaps even needs, us all to be free from anxieties. Easier said than done, of course. The specific advice offered to the Corinthians seems largely inapplicable to most modern contexts but notice the general broad strokes message: focus entirely on the Lord, who teaches with authority and who is love incarnate.

Making Connections to the Responsorial Psalm: Moses, while leading the Israelites through the desert for forty years, dealt with the grumbles, the complaints, and even the unfaithful sinfulness of the community on many occasions. He refers to one of those times in the first reading, and Psalm 95 reminds us of another. The refrain, which is the lens that tints and colors our understanding of the rest of the text, urges us in all times to ensure our hearts are not hardened to hear God's voice.

If we are not careful, some of our day-to-day interactions in life can become little more than "stimulus-response," a consistent predictable reaction to some common, repetitive incitement. "There's John again, he always knows how to push my buttons . . ." "Gah, it's raining again today? I hate rain!" These are hardened hearts.

Softer hearts of faith instead leave room, between stimulus and response, for consideration, for kindness, for thoughtful responses, or even for no response at all. Sometimes not doing or not saying something is the most charitable and faith-filled response to someone or something that we can offer.

CONNECTING TO EXPERIENCE: LIVING THE PASCHAL MYSTERY

Would we ever ask the Lord *not* to speak to us? In our first reading, the people of Israel beg Moses not to let God come near lest God destroy them. Today's gospel describes this fear another way: an unclean spirit, a destructive force—or sin—drags our hearts away from God in terror. But God does not come to destroy us. Jesus hears the writhing tendrils of sin and says: "Quiet! Come out!" Jesus came to destroy the power of sin and death. Likewise, our love for our families, friends, or vocation should feed and be fed by our relationship with God—not detract from it. Our lives in the world cannot be separated from our life in Christ. How can we, as individuals and as the people of God, allow the city of God and the cities of the world to meet, serving as a leaven for human society and inviting all the world to transformation as God's children (*Gaudium et Spes* 40)?

PROMPTS FOR FAITH-SHARING

- Do you need Jesus to command anything of you? How can you be less afraid to ask him for help?
- Does your parish or community need Jesus to cleanse it? Is your community afraid to acknowledge this need?
- Do you have trouble believing that Jesus can work miracles? Are you, too, amazed to find out that he does? Where do you need to look more closely, to see what miracles are really happening?

Model Penitential Act

Presider: Our psalm today calls us not to harden our hearts when we hear the voice of God. Let us turn to God as we ask for pardon and peace . . . *[pause]*

Lord Jesus, you are the rock of our salvation: Lord, have mercy.

Christ Jesus, you are the shepherd who calls your people to repentance: Christ, have mercy.

Lord Jesus, you are the light which dispels the darkness: Lord, have mercy.

Model Universal Prayer (Prayer of the Faithful)

Presider: We come before the Lord who always listens, quieting our hearts and bearing our hopes as we offer our prayers and petitions.

Response: Lord, hear our prayer.

For those living married lives of faith and love: may they take time and space to listen to and to love one another, we pray . . .

For families whose members are suffering from addictions: may they seek and find health and healing, we pray . . .

For those who have fallen away from their faith: may they hear Christ's teaching anew, and desire to try again, we pray . . .

For those suffering in persecution, darkness, and fear: may they be rescued from their captors and brought to safety, we pray . . .

Presider: O God, you sent your Son to call us out of darkness and the shadow of death. Do not allow our hearts to be hardened, but fill us with your compassion and mercy as we pray for all the world. We ask this through Christ our Lord. **Amen.**

Liturgy and the Ambo

"The central focus of the area in which the word of God is proclaimed during the liturgy is the ambo," it says in *Built of Living Stones* (61), and that it is the place where "the Christian community encounters the living Lord in the word of God and prepares itself for the 'breaking of the bread' and the mission to live the word that will be proclaimed." It is the altar of the word, where Scripture is broken open and shared. The *General Instruction of the Roman Missal* tells us: "When the Sacred Scriptures are read in the Church, God himself speaks to his people, and Christ, present in his word, proclaims the Gospel" (29).

While many of us are hopefully aware of the sacred purpose of the ambo, it often becomes a place for many other verbal utterances, owing to its visibility and its microphone. Much like we wouldn't dream of celebrating "donut Sunday" from the consecrated altar, we should be careful to only use the ambo for its sacred purpose as well.

(continued on next page)

COLLECT

Let us pray.

Pause for silent prayer

Grant us, Lord our God,
that we may honor you with all our mind,
and love everyone in truth of heart.
Through our Lord Jesus Christ, your Son,
who lives and reigns with you in the unity
of the Holy Spirit,
God, for ever and ever. **Amen.**

FIRST READING

Deut 18:15-20

Moses spoke to all the people, saying:
"A prophet like me will the LORD, your God, raise up for you
from among your own kin;
to him you shall listen.
This is exactly what you requested of the LORD, your God, at Horeb
on the day of the assembly, when you said,
'Let us not again hear the voice of the LORD, our God,
nor see this great fire any more, lest we die.'
And the LORD said to me, 'This was well said.
I will raise up for them a prophet like you from among their kin,
and will put my words into his mouth;
he shall tell them all that I command him.
Whoever will not listen to my words which he speaks in my name,
I myself will make him answer for it.
But if a prophet presumes to speak in my name
an oracle that I have not commanded him to speak,
or speaks in the name of other gods, he shall die.'"

RESPONSORIAL PSALM
Ps 95:1-2, 6-7, 7-9

℟. (8) If today you hear his voice, harden
not your hearts.

Come, let us sing joyfully to the LORD;
let us acclaim the rock of our salvation.
Let us come into his presence with
thanksgiving;
let us joyfully sing psalms to him.

℟. If today you hear his voice, harden not
your hearts.

Come, let us bow down in worship;
let us kneel before the LORD who made
us.
For he is our God,
and we are the people he shepherds,
the flock he guides.

℟. If today you hear his voice, harden not
your hearts.

Oh, that today you would hear his voice:
"Harden not your hearts as at Meribah,
as in the day of Massah in the desert,
where your fathers tempted me;
they tested me though they had seen
my works."

℟. If today you hear his voice, harden not
your hearts.

SECOND READING
1 Cor 7:32-35

Brothers and sisters:
I should like you to be free of anxieties.
An unmarried man is anxious about the
things of the Lord,
how he may please the Lord.
But a married man is anxious about the
things of the world,
how he may please his wife, and he is
divided.
An unmarried woman or a virgin is
anxious about the things of the Lord,
so that she may be holy in both body
and spirit.
A married woman, on the other hand,
is anxious about the things of the world,
how she may please her husband.
I am telling you this for your own benefit,
not to impose a restraint upon you,
but for the sake of propriety
and adherence to the Lord without
distraction.

If there are logistical instructions or end-of-Mass announcements and the like, is there some other way or place to amplify these messages? When the church space is used for other purposes, for instance, concerts or a retreat or a parish mission, are we mindful to use the ambo appropriately and to avoid it when it's not fulfilling its prescribed functions?

Liturgical Ministry: Eucharistic Ministers

Extraordinary ministers of Holy Communion are entrusted with one of the church's most sacred responsibilities, which is distributing the body and blood of Christ to the faithful. This ministry is not just a task of distribution. It is a participation in the church's liturgical action and the mystery it serves. In their posture, Eucharistic ministers embody the reverence due to the Eucharist and help the assembly receive the sacrament with full awareness of its mystery. Their role is grounded in service, not status. They assist the presider in feeding the body of Christ to the Body of Christ, bridging the sacred table and the people of God. As ministers of Communion, they are called to a life of integrity, shaped by the very sacrament they offer. Their visible devotion and care deepen the assembly's own response of faith, awe, and thanksgiving.

Living Liturgy: The Penitential Act

The penitential act at the beginning of Mass is more than preparation. It is a liturgical expression of the church's deepest belief: that God is merciful, and we are in need of that mercy. This moment of communal confession is not private guilt but ecclesial faith. In proclaiming "Lord, have mercy," the assembly voices the truth at the heart of the gospel that salvation begins not with worthiness, but with God's initiative and love. The church prays as one in need, and in doing so, proclaims the God who forgives, heals, and restores. In this Sunday's gospel, Jesus's authority casts out unclean spirits; in the penitential act, the church entrusts itself to that same authority not in fear, but in trust. By beginning in mercy, the liturgy teaches the faithful how to live: dependent on grace, and always open to transformation.

JANUARY 31, 2027

FOURTH SUNDAY IN ORDINARY TIME

SPIRITUALITY

GOSPEL ACCLAMATION
Matt 8:17

℟. Alleluia, alleluia.
Christ took away our infirmities
and bore our diseases.
℟. Alleluia, alleluia.

Gospel

Mark 1:29-39; L74B

On leaving the synagogue
Jesus entered the house of Simon and Andrew with James and John.
Simon's mother-in-law lay sick with a fever.
They immediately told him about her.
He approached, grasped her hand, and helped her up.
Then the fever left her and she waited on them.

When it was evening, after sunset,
they brought to him all who were ill or possessed by demons.
The whole town was gathered at the door.
He cured many who were sick with various diseases,
and he drove out many demons,
not permitting them to speak because they knew him.

Rising very early before dawn, he left
and went off to a deserted place, where he prayed.
Simon and those who were with him pursued him
and on finding him said, "Everyone is looking for you."
He told them, "Let us go on to the nearby villages
that I may preach there also.
For this purpose have I come."
So he went into their synagogues,
preaching and driving out demons throughout the whole of Galilee.

Praying with Gospel Words and Phrases

He approached . . . The whole town was gathered . . . Let us go on . . .

Reflecting on the Gospel

Mark, in typical brusque style and in few words, tells his readers about the power of Jesus's presence. It heals physically, it cures spiritually, and because of this, even when Jesus wishes more private time, he yields to the desire of those who yearn to be near him.

Years ago, at a particular youth summer camp, the reconciliation service that took place during the week had become a bit distorted. To wit: participants would sometimes come to the service excited solely because it would be an opportunity to cry, and to cry hard. This experience of encountering Christ and the graces bestowed in the sacrament had given way to something much more human and, in most cases, quite far from the ideal. For many, the experience became merely a reason to let go of emotions in an unnecessary and unhealthy way.

Then there were always a couple of youth each year who worried that their experience of the sacrament was incomplete. "But I didn't cry . . ." became a familiar worry: both from those who really wanted to but for some reason didn't, and from those who were not moved by God's presence to do so. I have heard similar reactions from those who experience group adoration for the first time, especially in certain circumstances where many react to that presence of the Lord in emotional and profound ways.

Knowing what to do when in the presence of the Lord, be it sacramentally or otherwise, can be challenging—especially if it's our first time with a profound awareness of that presence. Further, even realizing that we are in the presence of the Lord can sometimes be even more of a challenge, particularly for those we have been considering here of late: those coming to church for the first time, or those returning after an extended absence. We should be especially aware of regular church attendees who may at times feel like Job in today's first reading, completely unaware of the sacred presence surrounding them.

To the Point

Concluding our brief time of reflection on invitation, welcome, and hospitality, we now consider presence: how to become more aware of God's presence, knowing what to do when in God's presence, and more concretely, how to be that holy presence for others.

Preparing to Proclaim, Preach, and Pray

Making Connections Between the Readings: The connection between the first reading and gospel today is one of disconnection, if such a thing is possible. Job, we will recall, is, in a way, Satan's guinea pig, testing his faith when Satan makes it appear to him that God has completely abandoned him, bringing his life and relationships to ruin and destruction. The pericope assigned for today is quite incomplete; we hear much of Job's complaints and lamentations, but little of the rest of the story. Job discusses his plight with three consoling friends, Elihu defends these friends and God as well, and Job even asks for—and receives—an audience with the Most High. Upon being in the presence of God, who details for Job the divine power and might that humankind dare not approach, Job repents and confesses once again obedience, trust, and faith. Job, then, is also an example to us of these very same attributes.

Was it not a blinding divine presence that put Saul, who persecuted the early Christian community, on the path of conversion? Paul describes himself, in what some younger people today would call a "humble brag," as "a slave to all so as to win over as many as possible" and that he has "become all things to all, to save at least some" (1 Cor 9:19, 22). Said another way, Paul meets the different communities he is evangelizing where they are, that he might show them some facet of the divine that leads them into faithfulness and holiness.

Making Connections to the Responsorial Psalm: Much like when God speaks with, or really *at*, Job near the end of that book of the Bible, this portion of Psalm 147 doesn't so much spend time on the justice and mercy of God as it does with the power and grandeur of God. This greatness, however, is made most manifest in works of justice and mercy; these indeed are the most visible signs of the God who is love.

For many of us, the presence of God can be so terribly difficult to discern in the times we'd think it most easy: praying in a quiet church, in a moment of peaceful adoration, even in the sacraments, which give us tangible outward signs of divine grace. Today's psalm gives us other places to look, listen, and sense: the rebuilding and reconstituting of broken communities, the healing of broken hearts, the providential support of the needy, and the casting down of the wicked, evil ones.

CONNECTING TO EXPERIENCE: LIVING THE PASCHAL MYSTERY

God's work happens at all hours of the day—but when evening has come with only the fire of lamps or stars to guide us, God reminds us how his presence pierces the darkness. Christ came in the night of the incarnation. Christ rose from the dead as the darkness passed across the earth. His paschal mystery spans the arc of everlasting night turning to everlasting day. In today's gospel, Jesus drives out demons in the dusk of sunset. Just when darkness seems to overwhelm us, God is present.

We might feel as if our problems, worries, pains, or sins are not worthy of Jesus's notice. They are. He has time unending for us—and compassion without bounds. Jesus is ready to drive out our darkness, too.

PROMPTS FOR FAITH-SHARING

- Jesus does not need a spotlight for his miracles, but do you? How can you grow in humility, to do God's work even if no one notices?
- Do you feel that Jesus is too busy to notice your pain? Knowing that he makes time for you, what healing do you want to ask of him?
- How can your church community go to "nearby villages," to bring the good news of God's healing? What is keeping your community from doing so?

Model Penitential Act

Presider: In today's gospel, the whole town gathers at the threshold where Jesus dwells, seeking healing. Following their example, let us ask for his healing as we call to mind our sins . . . *[pause]*

Lord Jesus, you took away our infirmities and bore our diseases: Lord, have mercy.

Christ Jesus, you heal the brokenhearted and bind up all our wounds: Christ, have mercy.

Lord Jesus, you came to bring all people to yourself: Lord, have mercy.

Model Universal Prayer (Prayer of the Faithful)

Presider: Coming before the Lord who hears us in our need, we offer our prayers and petitions.

Response: Lord, hear our prayer.

For the church: may the Holy Spirit fill the faithful with the fire of love and a thirst for justice and righteousness, we pray . . .

For nations whose leaders resort to intimidation and treachery to control their citizens: may God's justice call them to accountability, we pray . . .

For families who are suffering from economic instability: may they find solutions to sustain their loved ones, we pray . . .

For those gathered here today who are suffering in mind, body, or spirit: may the grace of God fill them with endurance and hope, we pray . . .

Presider: O God, you rebuild those who are broken and gather those who are scattered. Fill us with the hope of your healing and patience to know your wisdom. We ask this through Christ our Lord. **Amen.**

Liturgy and Change

Returning now to the youth camp and that devolved reconciliation service: After a few years of changing leadership and fruitful discussions on what to do with the celebration of the sacrament, we came to our decision on how to move forward productively. We had to "rip the Band-Aid off" so to speak and start again. The next year, the service was scheduled for both a new time and a new location, so that it might become a new way to encounter the Lord.

There were many not happy about that, and some who were. Even if it promises to be unpleasant for a moment, is there some Band-Aid you need to rip off your liturgical practices for a fresh start? Perhaps you are unaware of any, but someone, perhaps even an unexpected someone sitting in the pews, might be aware of some. How do we invite their voices in? How can we all help

(continued on next page)

COLLECT

Let us pray.

Pause for silent prayer

Keep your family safe, O Lord, with
unfailing care,
that, relying solely on the hope of
heavenly grace,
they may be defended always by your
protection.
Through our Lord Jesus Christ, your Son,
who lives and reigns with you in the unity
of the Holy Spirit,
God, for ever and ever. **Amen.**

FIRST READING

Job 7:1-4, 6-7

Job spoke, saying:
Is not man's life on earth a drudgery?
Are not his days those of hirelings?
He is a slave who longs for the shade,
a hireling who waits for his wages.
So I have been assigned months of
misery,
and troubled nights have been
allotted to me.
If in bed I say, "When shall I arise?"
then the night drags on;
I am filled with restlessness until the
dawn.
My days are swifter than a weaver's
shuttle;
they come to an end without hope.
Remember that my life is like the wind;
I shall not see happiness again.

RESPONSORIAL PSALM

Ps 147:1-2, 3-4, 5-6

℟. (cf. 3a) Praise the Lord, who heals the
brokenhearted.
or:
℟. Alleluia.

Praise the Lord, for he is good;
sing praise to our God, for he is
gracious;
it is fitting to praise him.
The Lord rebuilds Jerusalem;
the dispersed of Israel he gathers.

℟. Praise the Lord, who heals the
brokenhearted.
or:
℟. Alleluia.

He heals the brokenhearted
and binds up their wounds.
He tells the number of the stars;
he calls each by name.

℟. Praise the Lord, who heals the brokenhearted.
or:
℟. Alleluia.

Great is our Lord and mighty in power;
to his wisdom there is no limit.
The LORD sustains the lowly;
the wicked he casts to the ground.

℟. Praise the Lord, who heals the brokenhearted.
or:
℟. Alleluia.

SECOND READING
1 Cor 9:16-19, 22-23

Brothers and sisters:
If I preach the gospel, this is no reason for me to boast,
for an obligation has been imposed on me,
and woe to me if I do not preach it!
If I do so willingly, I have a recompense,
but if unwillingly, then I have been entrusted with a stewardship.
What then is my recompense?
That, when I preach,
I offer the gospel free of charge
so as not to make full use of my right in the gospel.

Although I am free in regard to all,
I have made myself a slave to all
so as to win over as many as possible.
To the weak I became weak, to win over the weak.
I have become all things to all, to save at least some.
All this I do for the sake of the gospel,
so that I too may have a share in it.

those in our pews be more aware of the presence of the Lord, right now, today?

Christ is present during Mass in four defined ways. The Constitution on the Sacred Liturgy (*Sacrosanctum Concilium*) teaches that he is present in the person of the priest who presides over the sacrifice of the Mass. Christ is present in his word "since it is he himself who speaks when the holy scriptures are read in church." He is also present in the assembly, "for he has promised 'where two or three are gathered together in my name there am I in the midst of them' (Mt 18:20)" (SC 7). He is uniquely present in the consecrated bread and wine: body, blood, soul, and divinity.

Liturgical Ministry: Altar Servers

Altar servers are often among the first to learn the physical grammar of the liturgy. They learn when to stand, bow, carry, and assist. But their ministry is not only about these movements that need to happen. Their ministry is about memory. Servers embody the liturgy's structure and sequence in visible ways. They become keepers of ritual memory, helping to ensure that what the church prays is enacted faithfully and gracefully. This task calls for interior discipline, not just external coordination. By attending to what comes next not with anxiety, but with quiet readiness, servers model a liturgical awareness that strengthens the community's prayer. Their ministry teaches the value of preparation, memory, and trust in the rhythm of the church's worship. In this way, altar servers help the whole assembly not just "get through" the Mass, but truly inhabit it.

Living Liturgy: The Gloria

The Gloria erupts early in the liturgy as a confession of faith from those who have just acknowledged their need for mercy. Coming after the penitential act, the Gloria is thanksgiving from the humbled. In this Sunday's gospel, Jesus is sought out by the sick, the weary, the burdened, and those who know their need. The Gloria reflects this same dynamic. It is the song of a people who, touched by mercy, can't help but praise. In praying, "you alone are the Holy One, . . . you alone are the Most High," the assembly proclaims a faith rooted in dependence, not in self-assurance. The church believes in a God whose glory is revealed not only in power, but in compassion and whose holiness makes room for human weakness.

SEASON OF LENT

SPIRITUALITY

GOSPEL ACCLAMATION
See Ps 95:8

If today you hear his voice,
harden not your hearts.

Gospel

Matt 6:1-6, 16-18; L219

Jesus said to his disciples:
"Take care not to perform righteous deeds
in order that people may see them;
otherwise, you will have no recompense from your heavenly Father.
When you give alms,
do not blow a trumpet before you,
as the hypocrites do in the synagogues and in the streets
to win the praise of others.
Amen, I say to you,
they have received their reward.
But when you give alms,
do not let your left hand know what your right is doing,
so that your almsgiving may be secret.
And your Father who sees in secret will repay you.

"When you pray,
do not be like the hypocrites,
who love to stand and pray in the synagogues and on street corners
so that others may see them.
Amen, I say to you,
they have received their reward.
But when you pray, go to your inner room,
close the door, and pray to your Father in secret.
And your Father who sees in secret will repay you.

Continued in Appendix A, p. 273.

See Appendix A, p. 273, for the other readings.

Praying with Gospel Words and Phrases

Do not blow a trumpet before you . . . anoint your head and wash your face . . .

Reflecting on the Gospel

We have reached the season of Lent, so now is the time for all things sad and repentant and morose and sackcloth and ashes and everything else depressing, right? No! Lent need not be those things, at least not overly so. We ought to be repentant for our sinfulness, yes; further, knowing our sinfulness led Jesus to his suffering and death on the cross can lead us to be sad and even grieve these things.

But to do so without also knowing there's more to the story is to, in a sense, make an idol out of only one tiny facet of our faith. It's not like during Lent we should remember only repentance, suffering, and death. While celebrating these things, we should also remember that there is new life that arises from these very same things—there is joy and even more celebrating to come.

Jesus instructs his followers not to make a performative show of their prayer, fasting, and almsgiving. These are, of course, done for devotion to God and for personal growth in holiness. At best, the performative exhibition of these practices is meant to bring earthly praise; at worst, such externals may be a complete mismatch for what resides in the heart and soul.

In current days, an analog might be "performative activism," sometimes called "slacktivism." Engaging whichever cause in this way—social media posts frequently, or other ostentatious offerings—emphasizes visibility over tangible results and completely lacks any sustained effort or meaningful impact. Actions speak louder than words, says the old maxim. While one could rightfully argue that social media posts can be interpreted as support or letting others know of your allyship, this is also easily argued to be a bare minimum of what Jesus calls us to, especially in Lent: works of justice and mercy, alongside our prayer and fasting.

To the Point

Lent is only one part of a broader story, a broader mystery, which as a whole, tells us where we've come from, who we are now, and who we should strive to be, and the future that awaits us all if we help each other grow in faith and holiness.

Model Universal Prayer (Prayer of the Faithful)

Presider: Let us bring our prayers and petitions before the Lord who hears us in our need.

Response: Lord, hear our prayer.

For the church: may we begin this Lenten season with fortitude and hope, desiring a renewal of our hearts, we pray . . .

For our leaders at home and in our nation: may they govern with justice and protect their people with mercy, we pray . . .

For those whose hearts are burdened by sadness: may they find the presence of the Lord walking with them as we journey toward Easter, we pray . . .

For all those gathered here today: may the ashes we have received remind us that we are made and loved by God, we pray . . .

Presider: Lord God, you call your people to enter into this holy season of Lent. May we remember we are dust, and remember our call to extend mercy to all that we meet. We ask this through Christ our Lord. **Amen.**

COLLECT

Let us pray.

Pause for silent prayer

Grant, O Lord, that we may begin with holy fasting
this campaign of Christian service,
so that, as we take up battle against spiritual evils,
we may be armed with weapons of self-restraint.
Through our Lord Jesus Christ, your Son,
who lives and reigns with you in the unity of the Holy Spirit,
God, for ever and ever. **Amen.**

Liturgical Ministry: Environment Ministers

Ash Wednesday marks a dramatic shift in the liturgical year. It is a moment when the sanctuary is intentionally stripped back to its bare essentials. Environment ministers are called to shape this starkness with care, removing excess decoration and embracing simplicity to reflect the penitential character of Lent. This minimalist space invites the assembly into a deeper interior conversion, free from distractions, focusing attention on God's mercy and the call to renewal. This deliberate austerity also challenges environment ministers. Just as the worship space is cleared of what is superfluous, ministers are invited to reflect on what might clutter their own lives. These may be habits, attachments, or distractions that keep them from fully embracing the journey of repentance. In shaping the sacred environment, environment ministers participate in a dual ministry of preparing the community to enter Lent with intention and entering more deeply themselves into the rhythm of conversion and renewal.

Living Liturgy: The Entrance Antiphon

The entrance antiphon for Ash Wednesday draws us into a persistent appeal: "You are merciful to all, O Lord, and despise nothing that you have made." This is a continual turning. It is an unceasing reaching toward God amid our brokenness. It expresses the church's lived experience that we are a people aware that life's wounds and failures require constant healing. Yet the prayer does more than acknowledge our frailty; it unveils the very character of God. Lent begins here, in the tension between our vulnerability and God's steadfast love, teaching the assembly that repentance is a courageous trust. The entrance antiphon invites the assembly into a posture of ongoing openness and dependence, reminding us that worship is a living encounter with God's mercy. In this way, the prayer shapes how the community gathers, turning hearts outward in humble trust while also drawing them inward to the transformative presence of Christ. Lent begins not just in words, but in the lived experience of mercy made real in our shared worship.

SPIRITUALITY

GOSPEL ACCLAMATION
Matt 4:4b

One does not live on bread alone,
but on every word that comes forth from the mouth of God.

Gospel

Mark 1:12-15; L23B

The Spirit drove Jesus out into the desert,
and he remained in the desert for forty days, tempted by Satan.
He was among wild beasts,
and the angels ministered to him.

After John had been arrested,
Jesus came to Galilee proclaiming the gospel of God:
"This is the time of fulfillment.
The kingdom of God is at hand.
Repent, and believe in the gospel."

Praying with Gospel Words and Phrases
In the desert for forty days . . . The kingdom of God is at hand . . .

Reflecting on the Gospel
Again, we come face to face with the abrupt terseness of Mark's Gospel. Forty days in the desert, a pivotal time of formation following Jesus's baptism in the Jordan by his cousin, and how long does it take Mark to summarize all of that? Thirty-one words, comprising two sentences. While the other Synoptic Gospels are indeed more verbose, they too lack a lot of detail. Surely Jesus didn't spend every waking hour only in fasting, prayer, and temptation! Think of your last forty days: how many words and sentences would you need to summarize them?

The other Synoptics are clearer that Jesus was tempted by Satan only at the end of his self-imposed exile. I don't know about you, but I don't know if I'd last forty minutes in a hot and dry desert, let alone forty days. Jesus, being human while being divine, experienced everything any other human ever did or will, except sin. Hunger, thirst, weariness, doubt, and more were all present when Satan comes to persuade Jesus to forego his divine mission for one of earthly sin and vices.

It's easy to imagine Satan waiting for just the right moment, when he knew Jesus would be at his weakest. And Satan presents Jesus with versions of sacred power and might that have been twisted and distorted—it takes true eyes and ears of faith sometimes to tell the difference between the true goodness of God and that same goodness warped into something evil.

Persevering though the trial, Jesus begins his earthly mission, Mark tells his readers, by proclaiming the immediacy of the reign of God, that the many covenants of God in former days are coming to fulfillment. Jesus's coming words and deeds over the next three years of his life will make it clear that he is the living embodiment of God and the new and everlasting covenant.

To the Point
Jesus is the immanent expression of God's covenantal love for each of us, calling us to respond with a similar immediacy. Now is the time: repent and believe in the gospel!

Preparing to Proclaim, Preach, and Pray

Making Connections Between the Readings: The creators of the current Lectionary, when putting together the pericopes for Lent Cycle B, obviously had an overarching theme or goal in mind: covenants. Said another way, they seem to have sought to prepare the faithful for the celebration of Easter, that once-and-for-all moment of salvation, by recounting many of the times that God "broke in" to human time and space to offer redemption and sanctification through promise and relationship.

Covenants, at least in the realm of faith, are different than contracts. Covenants are promises that have no particular conditions or consequences. When between God and us, the basic shape is always, "You shall be my people, and I will be your God." Noah's is the first of the covenants in Scripture and the first we encounter this Lenten season: God promises to never again destroy the earth or living things by flood waters. These waters that, in a way, cleansed the earth, prefigure the baptism Jesus received just before this weekend's gospel, and prefigure our baptism and those coming at the Easter Vigil.

Peter writes of this in his epistle. Noah and his family were saved by water, just as Christ is our salvation by his death and resurrection. Christ's bloody sacrifice is the new and everlasting covenant—words we hear in our eucharistic prayers and to which we might want to bring extra attention these next few weeks.

Making Connections to the Responsorial Psalm: Just in case someone in the pew might otherwise "miss the memo," words of divine covenant are put directly on their lips with Psalm 25. What does living a covenant with God mean? How is it done? We disciples ask for God's guidance, truth, and teaching, reminding God of his ancient compassion, love, kindness, and goodness. These, then, are the tangible fruits of love and truth that we are also called to live, in humility and uprightness.

This is one of the longer refrains that the assembly is ever asked to sing during the liturgy. Especially if your congregants attend to the Liturgy of the Word with focused listening and without printed aids, make sure their first hearing of the refrain is clear and easy to follow, that they may fully enter into this moment of prayer without reservation or hesitation.

CONNECTING TO EXPERIENCE: LIVING THE PASCHAL MYSTERY

Noah's obedience to God plays out in the ark, a raft built on faith in the salvation of God and the foundation of the people of God. Jesus's obedience to the Father begins not on a flooded plain, but a desert filled with wild beasts. As our ancestors in faith walked out of the waters onto dry land, Jesus steps out of the desert, into the waters of baptism. Our Lenten season is also a time for practicing obedience and tangling with wild beasts (with sins like pride, self-harm, or jealousy), and ends with the promise of new, fresh creation and the waters of baptism. Jesus emerges from his journey with Spirit and with fire. This Lenten desert prepares us to repent, believe in the gospel, and live out our call to discipleship. Let us prepare our own ark to traverse the desert, kindle in our hearts the fire of Christ's love, and prepare for new life brought to us through his paschal mystery.

PROMPTS FOR FAITH-SHARING

- This Lent, what is God asking of you? Does his request require your obedience in a new way?
- As you consider John the Baptist's call to repentance, what does this mean to you? Do you need to repent? To put on baptism in a new way? To turn away from something?
- How can your Lent be a time of fulfillment? How can you embrace this time of "desert fasting" with joy?

Model Penitential Act

Presider: Jesus calls us to repent and believe in the gospel. Let us call to mind our sins as we prepare our hearts to celebrate these sacred mysteries . . . *[pause]*

Confiteor: I confess . . .

Model Universal Prayer (Prayer of the Faithful)

Presider: We bring our prayers before the Lord, who remembers his faithfulness always.

Response: Lord, hear our prayer.

For the church, especially where our brothers and sisters in Christ are suffering from persecution and oppression, we pray . . .

For nations whose people are afraid for their safety and the safety of their loved ones, we pray . . .

For communities suffering from the effects of climate change with drought, flooding, heat, and cold, we pray . . .

For all who have been entrapped by habits of sin and destruction, we pray . . .

Presider: O God, in your goodness you remember your people. Hear our prayers and petitions this day for ourselves and all the world, and may we work to spread love for your justice. We ask this through Christ our Lord. **Amen.**

Liturgy and Covenant

The Old Testament passage about Noah and his family seeing the rainbow at the end of the great flood is the first of many readings regarding covenant in this cycle of the Lenten readings. "God of the Covenants" (WLP, a division of GIA) by Orin Johnson (this author) speaks directly to these readings and the varied theological concepts of covenant that are so strongly represented these next few weeks.

Another wonderful pairing of text and tune is "Covenant Hymn" (GIA) by Rory Cooney and Gary Daigle. While many perceive this song as a quintessential wedding piece, it was written to accompany the newly initiated on their faith journey, showing to them the support of the Christian community. These relational loves, after all, are ultimately one and the same: husband and wife, Christian brothers and sisters, and God for his people and we for God. The earthly loves reflect the divine love, making it visible and tangible.

Do not neglect your catechumens and candidates when considering music for the season, even at Masses which they are not at, even if your parish has none this year. The church universal always has these each year, and even "cradle Catholics" are called to the same annual Lenten journey of conversion and recommitment.

COLLECT

Let us pray.

Pause for silent prayer

Grant, almighty God,
through the yearly observances of holy Lent,
that we may grow in understanding
of the riches hidden in Christ
and by worthy conduct pursue their effects.
Through our Lord Jesus Christ, your Son,
who lives and reigns with you in the unity of the Holy Spirit,
God, for ever and ever. **Amen.**

FIRST READING

Gen 9:8-15

God said to Noah and to his sons with him:
"See, I am now establishing my covenant with you
and your descendants after you
and with every living creature that was with you:
all the birds, and the various tame and wild animals
that were with you and came out of the ark.
I will establish my covenant with you,
that never again shall all bodily creatures be destroyed
by the waters of a flood;
there shall not be another flood to devastate the earth."
God added:
"This is the sign that I am giving for all ages to come,
of the covenant between me and you
and every living creature with you:
I set my bow in the clouds to serve as a sign
of the covenant between me and the earth.
When I bring clouds over the earth,
and the bow appears in the clouds,
I will recall the covenant I have made
between me and you and all living beings,
so that the waters shall never again become a flood
to destroy all mortal beings."

RESPONSORIAL PSALM
Ps 25:4-5, 6-7, 8-9

℟. (cf. 10) Your ways, O Lord, are love and truth to those who keep your covenant.

Your ways, O LORD, make known to me;
teach me your paths.
Guide me in your truth and teach me,
for you are God my savior.

℟. Your ways, O Lord, are love and truth to those who keep your covenant.

Remember that your compassion, O LORD,
and your love are from of old.
In your kindness remember me,
because of your goodness, O LORD.

℟. Your ways, O Lord, are love and truth to those who keep your covenant.

Good and upright is the LORD,
thus he shows sinners the way.
He guides the humble to justice,
and he teaches the humble his way.

℟. Your ways, O Lord, are love and truth to those who keep your covenant.

SECOND READING
1 Pet 3:18-22

Beloved:
Christ suffered for sins once,
the righteous for the sake of the unrighteous,
that he might lead you to God.
Put to death in the flesh,
he was brought to life in the Spirit.
In it he also went to preach to the spirits in prison,
who had once been disobedient
while God patiently waited in the days of Noah
during the building of the ark,
in which a few persons, eight in all,
were saved through water.
This prefigured baptism, which saves you now.
It is not a removal of dirt from the body
but an appeal to God for a clear conscience,
through the resurrection of Jesus Christ,
who has gone into heaven
and is at the right hand of God,
with angels, authorities, and powers subject to him.

Liturgical Ministry: Music Ministers

In Lent, the music of the liturgy takes on a more restrained tone, yet it remains profoundly communal. For music ministers, this season invites renewed attention to the dialogue between music and assembly, especially in sung refrains, psalms, and acclamations. These are not performances but shared proclamations, where the voice of the church emerges in response to God's word. The responsorial psalm, for example, becomes a conversation. The cantor offers the verse, and the assembly claims it as its own in the refrain. The gospel acclamation, though often brief, is a moment of eager expectation, sung together as the community stands ready to receive Christ's voice. Music ministers serve this dialogue by listening as much as leading and by attending to pacing, clarity, and tone so that all can enter the exchange. In this way, their ministry strengthens not only the prayer of the community, but its unity, trust, and desire to journey together toward renewal.

Living Liturgy: The Gospel Procession

The gospel procession does more than deliver the Book of the Gospels to the ambo. It draws the assembly into the drama of salvation. On this First Sunday of Lent, we hear about Jesus being driven into the wilderness, but we also begin to walk with him. As the procession moves through the assembly, it traces a path not just across the ambo, but across the heart. The liturgy doesn't narrate from afar; it brings the story into our midst. This movement reveals something the church holds true: that the word of God is not static or confined to the page. It is active, close, and personal. It seeks not just to be understood, but to be followed. The assembly's act of standing, turning, and singing reflects a belief that God's word meets us where we are and leads us forward. It does not remain at the margins. It asks something of us. The procession reminds us that the gospel is never an idea alone; it is a presence that compels, moves, and transforms.

FEBRUARY 14, 2027

FIRST SUNDAY OF LENT

SPIRITUALITY

GOSPEL ACCLAMATION
cf. Matt 17:5

From the shining cloud the Father's voice is heard:
This is my beloved Son, listen to him.

Gospel

Mark 9:2-10; L26B

Jesus took Peter, James, and John
and led them up a high mountain
apart by themselves.
And he was transfigured before them,
and his clothes became dazzling white,
such as no fuller on earth could bleach them.
Then Elijah appeared to them along with Moses,
and they were conversing with Jesus.
Then Peter said to Jesus in reply,
"Rabbi, it is good that we are here!
Let us make three tents:
one for you, one for Moses, and one for Elijah."
He hardly knew what to say, they were so terrified.
Then a cloud came, casting a shadow over them;
from the cloud came a voice,
"This is my beloved Son. Listen to him."
Suddenly, looking around, they no longer saw anyone
but Jesus alone with them.

As they were coming down from the mountain,
he charged them not to relate what they had seen to anyone,
except when the Son of Man had risen from the dead.
So they kept the matter to themselves,
questioning what rising from the dead meant.

Praying with Gospel Words and Phrases

Transfigured before them . . . dazzling white . . . not to relate what they had seen . . .

Reflecting on the Gospel

On this Sunday of Lent in each lectionary cycle, we always hear about the transfiguration of the Lord, one of the few passages found in each of the three Synoptic Gospels, and a moment even alluded to in Peter's second epistle. Jesus's clothes become dazzlingly white, Mark tells us, and Luke's Gospel adds that Jesus's face shone brightly like the sun. Light, considered together with darkness, is an always-present sign and symbol of our faith. There is no darkness the light cannot overcome, John's beautiful prologue reminds us.

Some theologically speculate that the transfiguration happened, at least in part, to prepare these select apostles for darker times ahead: Jesus's agony in the garden, arrest, trial, and passion. Jesus, though, also instructs Peter, James, and John to not tell anyone else about the experience, presumably not even the other apostles. Such a "messianic secret" is a frequent motif in Mark's Gospel, and scholars debate the significance of that theme. We, however, are called to be zealous evangelists of the good news, to all lands and peoples.

There is a hopefully familiar line in Eucharistic Prayer III that says, "so that from the rising of the sun to its setting a pure sacrifice may be offered to your name." There is that presence of light and darkness again. At first hearing, one might assume this phrase describes a length of time, the duration that the sun shines in any specific spot on the earth. One can quickly determine this must not be the case, however: otherwise, this would be prescribing that Masses ought not be offered anywhere after sundown.

Instead of a statement of only light and darkness, this phrase is rather a geographical one. The previous English translation of this phrase used the words "so that from east to west . . ." which indicates perhaps more clearly that it is all over the world people are gathered unto the Lord to worship and give thanks. Indeed, somewhere on earth the sun—and the Son—is always shining.

To the Point

The divine light is always piercing the darkness, one way or another. Christ's light fills the earth at all times, even if reflected by the moon, making it impossible for the darkness to ever achieve final victory.

Preparing to Proclaim, Preach, and Pray

Making Connections Between the Readings: The next stop on our Lenten "tour of covenants" is the one between God and Abraham. Because this father of faith—of many faiths—exhibited such obedience to God, even being willing to sacrifice his only son, God promises to reward him abundantly with countless descendants and plentiful blessings. A fuller version of this reading is one of the passages from the coming Easter Vigil liturgy. If perhaps this is one not often used at your vigil liturgy, including it in this year's celebration would be especially meaningful to your elect.

This is understandably a difficult passage for many of the faithful, in various ways. Some, at a minimum, find it confusing and inconsistent with a God of love. Moreso, that God asks a parent to commit the worst atrocity is simply too much for some to bear. Much like the passage from Job just a few weeks ago, the meta message of this passage is simply this: God is God, and Abraham isn't—no human being is. God is inscrutable; God is love.

Paul elaborates: "He who did not spare his own Son . . . acquits us" and that same Son "is at the right hand of God, who indeed intercedes for us." Ultimately, God does not ask Abraham to make of his only son a sacrificial offering, God gives us his only Son instead as that final sacrifice. And how could a God as generous as that not give us "everything else," including eternal life?

Making Connections to the Responsorial Psalm: Echoing Abraham's obedience, the words of the psalmist declare our own servitude. We worship God with sacrifice, grateful for freedom from sin, publicly attesting to our promises to God who is ever faithful and leads us to the "land of the living."

Just as today's Genesis reading is part of the Triduum, so too is Psalm 116, with a slightly differing text, on Holy Thursday, at the Mass of the Lord's Supper. It is a profound mystery of our faith that Jesus's Last Supper is his death on the cross and is a foretaste of the eternal heavenly banquet. Mass is not a recreation of the Last Supper, it *is* Jesus's last supper, which we are present to, just as we are present to his cross and as we ourselves receive that same foretaste as those at the historical Last Supper.

That's an awful lot for a child—or anyone, frankly—to grasp, but this might be a good weekend to lavish some extra attention toward anyone preparing for first Communion, whether adults at the Vigil or youth preparing for a first Communion Mass in a few weeks' time. What does your children's Liturgy of the Word look like this weekend? Is this a good weekend for a first Communion retreat?

CONNECTING TO EXPERIENCE: LIVING THE PASCHAL MYSTERY

When James, John, and Peter accompany Jesus in the gospel today, they are dazzled by what they experience. In their surprise, only Peter could sputter out the inexplicable longing that they should remain in this glorious presence as long as they could: "It is good that we are here!" The "mountaintop experience" of the transfiguration is a glimpse of God's glory, and certainly should dazzle us. But it should not prevent us from moving forward. We are invited to carry these moments with us, and to be reminded of Christ's transforming presence every time we hear it in the gospel and receive the grace of the sacraments. We do not leave Christ behind on the mountaintop. He is here, he is with us, and he goes forth with us as we bring the grace of God we encounter in our worship to those who need to be reminded of God's presence.

PROMPTS FOR FAITH-SHARING

- What does Jesus's transfiguration say to you? How might this miracle teach you something about Jesus?
- Have you ever had a powerful experience, like Peter, that you did not want to move beyond? What did you learn from that experience?
- As you descend into the valley of Lent, to whom is God sending you? Why do you think so?

Model Penitential Act

Presider: Like Abraham, we must be willing to offer God everything we have. Let us offer him repentance for those times that we have strayed from his covenant . . . *[pause]*

Confiteor: I confess . . .

Model Universal Prayer (Prayer of the Faithful)

Presider: Lord God, your light is revealed in the face of Christ, who suffered and died for us. Confident that you are with us and hear us always, we offer you our petitions this day.

Response: Lord, hear our prayer.

For the bishops and pastors of the church: may they always seek to teach the fullness of the law and prophets in Christ crucified, we pray . . .

For the civil leaders of our country and our world: may the law of God inform their judgments and actions, we pray . . .

For those who are persecuted under unjust uses of the law: may they find God's freedom and justice, we pray . . .

For all gathered here: may we embrace the prophetic task of proclaiming truth and mercy in our daily lives, we pray . . .

Presider: Lord, you hear us as a father hears his children. We trust in your justice and mercy as we bring these prayers to you. We ask this through Christ our Lord. **Amen.**

Liturgy and the Altar (Again)

The altar exists with a such a rich history and so many multivalent meanings that only using very few words will not do it justice. Yet let us recall here that "[a]t the Eucharist, the liturgical assembly celebrates the ritual sacrificial meal that recalls and makes present Christ's life, death and resurrection, proclaiming 'the death of the Lord until he comes'" (*Built of Living Stones* 56). The altar is a "both/and" of our faith: it is both an altar of sacrificial offering and a table for a memorial meal. It is not helpful to be mindful of one of these things without holding the other with it—both give the other meaning and vitality they would not have on their own.

Abraham brings Isaac to an altar intending to offer sacrifice, and in fact, eventually does, with a ram in place of his son. In a verse omitted from the Lectionary, we learn that "Abraham named that place Yahweh-yireh; hence people today say, 'On the mountain the Lord will provide'" (Gen 22:14). Thus this altar too became both one of sacrifice and a place where the Lord provided a rich bounty.

Call special attention to the altar today: in preaching, in the universal prayers, in liturgical music, or by a reverence beyond that of a typical Sunday: a longer presidential kiss during the entrance procession, for instance.

COLLECT

Let us pray.

Pause for silent prayer

O God, who have commanded us
to listen to your beloved Son,
be pleased, we pray,
to nourish us inwardly by your word,
that, with spiritual sight made pure,
we may rejoice to behold your glory.
Through our Lord Jesus Christ, your Son,
who lives and reigns with you in the unity
of the Holy Spirit,
God, for ever and ever. **Amen.**

FIRST READING

Gen 22:1-2, 9a, 10-13, 15-18

God put Abraham to the test.
He called to him, "Abraham!"
"Here I am!" he replied.
Then God said:
"Take your son Isaac, your only one,
whom you love,
and go to the land of Moriah.
There you shall offer him up as a holocaust
on a height that I will point out to you."

When they came to the place of which God
had told him,
Abraham built an altar there and
arranged the wood on it.
Then he reached out and took the knife to
slaughter his son.
But the LORD's messenger called to him
from heaven,
"Abraham, Abraham!"
"Here I am!" he answered.
"Do not lay your hand on the boy," said the
messenger.
"Do not do the least thing to him.
I know now how devoted you are to God,
since you did not withhold from me your
own beloved son."
As Abraham looked about,
he spied a ram caught by its horns in
the thicket.
So he went and took the ram
and offered it up as a holocaust in place
of his son.

Again the LORD's messenger called to
Abraham from heaven and said:
"I swear by myself, declares the LORD,
that because you acted as you did
in not withholding from me your
beloved son,
I will bless you abundantly
and make your descendants as countless

as the stars of the sky and the sands of
the seashore;
your descendants shall take possession
of the gates of their enemies,
and in your descendants all the nations
of the earth shall find blessing—
all this because you obeyed my
command."

RESPONSORIAL PSALM

Ps 116:10, 15, 16-17, 18-19

℟. (116:9) I will walk before the Lord, in
the land of the living.

I believed, even when I said,
"I am greatly afflicted."
Precious in the eyes of the LORD
is the death of his faithful ones.

℟. I will walk before the Lord, in the land
of the living.

O LORD, I am your servant;
I am your servant, the son of your
handmaid;
you have loosed my bonds.
To you will I offer sacrifice of
thanksgiving,
and I will call upon the name of the
LORD.

℟. I will walk before the Lord, in the land
of the living.

My vows to the LORD I will pay
in the presence of all his people,
in the courts of the house of the LORD,
in your midst, O Jerusalem.

℟. I will walk before the Lord, in the land
of the living.

SECOND READING

Rom 8:31b-34

Brothers and sisters:
If God is for us, who can be against us?
He who did not spare his own Son
but handed him over for us all,
how will he not also give us everything
else along with him?

Who will bring a charge against God's
chosen ones?
It is God who acquits us. Who will
condemn?
Christ Jesus it is who died—or, rather, was
raised—
who also is at the right hand of God,
who indeed intercedes for us.

Liturgical Ministry: Lectors

On the mountain, Peter, James, and John see Jesus transfigured before them, radiant, startling, and clear. It is a moment they do not fully understand, but one they are commanded to remember. Lectors serve the church by opening such moments week after week. In a world saturated with noise, their task is not only to read, but to still the room long enough for the word to break open and be heard. What often goes unnoticed is the space between words. The pause before a sentence begins, the breath taken after a phrase. These silences are not empty. They allow the word to settle, to echo, to invite. In that pause, the lector mirrors the disciples on the mountain: standing before something greater, unsure, awed. The pause becomes a sign that the word is not ours to master but something entrusted to us and meant to be received, not rushed. It is space made for glory.

Living Liturgy: The Universal Prayer

The universal prayer often feels ordinary, predictable even. But on this Sunday, after hearing of Christ's transfiguration, the church stands as a people who have glimpsed something more. The prayers we offer are shaped by that vision. We don't pray from a place of confusion or fear, but from a growing awareness of who Christ is and what God desires for the world. The intercessions flow from revelation.

When the assembly responds, "Lord, hear our prayer," it does so as those who have been called up the mountain and invited to listen. The prayer is a moment when the church exercises its baptismal role to stand between heaven and earth. Just as Peter wanted to stay in the brightness of glory, we are tempted to hold on to what we've seen. But the universal prayer turns us outward, down the mountain, into the needs of the world so that what we've witnessed in Christ might now shape what we long for together.

SPIRITUALITY

GOSPEL ACCLAMATION
John 3:16

God so loved the world that he gave his only Son,
so that everyone who believes in him might have
eternal life.

Gospel

John 2:13-25; L29B

Since the Passover of the Jews was near,
Jesus went up to Jerusalem.
He found in the temple area those who sold oxen, sheep, and doves,
as well as the money changers seated there.
He made a whip out of cords
and drove them all out of the temple area, with the sheep and oxen,
and spilled the coins of the money changers
and overturned their tables,
and to those who sold doves he said,
"Take these out of here,
and stop making my Father's house a marketplace."
His disciples recalled the words of Scripture,
Zeal for your house will consume me.
At this the Jews answered and said to him,
"What sign can you show us for doing this?"
Jesus answered and said to them,
"Destroy this temple and in three days I will raise it up."
The Jews said,
"This temple has been under construction for forty-six years,
and you will raise it up in three days?"

Continued in Appendix A, p. 274.

Year A readings may be used, see Appendix A, pp. 275–277.

Praying with Gospel Words and Phrases

Zeal for your house will consume me . . . he was speaking about the temple of his body . . .

Reflecting on the Gospel

At the start of each school year at a parish where I once served as music director, we would gather all students—Pre-K through eighth grade—in the church to practice some music for upcoming school Masses. Once, as the Pre-K students arrived early, still learning typical routines and appropriate reverence, I sat next to a little girl. She looked at me and, quite matter-of-factly, asked, "Are you God?"

There was no awe or confusion—just a simple, logical question from someone who'd probably been told by a parent or a teacher, that "church is God's house." And there I was.

"Are you God?"

"No," I eventually answered. "I'm not God."

"Well, where is God?" she continued.

I began, as best my reflexes could muster, to explain how God is everywhere, in everything God ever created. Just then, a boy nearby pointed to the large crucifix on the wall: "That's God, up there!" Their teacher, walking by, added, "Yes, Jesus is God—but we'll get into that later . . ."

Jesus is God. And in today's gospel, we see him filled with righteous anger as he drives out the money changers from the temple. This image—zealous and forceful—can feel jarring when we're used to seeing Jesus as the Good Shepherd or the Prince of Peace. But it's an important reminder: God is more than any one image or role.

It can be refreshing to approach God as that young girl did—without preconceived limits. Yes, we should have awe and reverence in God's presence, especially in sacred spaces. But if we only ever see God as distant Creator or Almighty Judge, we risk missing the fullness of God's identity—also revealed as Parent, Brother, and Friend.

This fullness is made known in Jesus Christ—fully God and fully human, who gave himself to us in love, even to death on a cross. Too often, we emphasize one aspect over the other. Yet it's important to remember that Jesus is both divine and human, always. How do we approach such a God? With awe? With familiarity? With childlike wonder? How do we help others do the same?

To the Point

Reverence is vital to our faith yet can be expressed in so many ways. No image of the divine is complete; all are necessary in striving to know better our limitless God and grow in relationship with him.

Preparing to Proclaim, Preach, and Pray

Making Connections Between the Readings: Divine covenant this week appears in the form of the Ten Commandments, given, of course, to Moses on Mount Sinai and to all the freed slaves of Egypt. They are a concise summation of right relationship with God and with one another. The nascent morality embedded in them were foundational to the Israelites and remain so today, across lands, peoples, and faiths.

God does not ask for all that much to be in right relationship with him. Put no other gods before him, don't use his name carelessly, and keep holy the Sabbath. These commands sound simple, but humanity has been struggling with them ever since. It's so very easy to prioritize our work, our comfort, our pride instead of God. It's so very easy to utter an "Oh my God!" when it's not a moment of prayer or supplication. It's so very easy to neglect the command to rest and renew once a week.

Paul reminds us, as he reminds the Corinthians, that "the foolishness of God is wiser than human wisdom"—a theme we've encountered many times this year already! And the promise of God for giving to him our trust and obedience is spelled out as the assembly joins in the responsorial psalm.

Making Connections to the Responsorial Psalm: It's easy these days, and has been for some time, to misunderstand what freedom is. It's easier to start, though, with what freedom isn't, at least as our faith teaches. Freedom isn't being without laws and rules. Rather, the *Catechism* tells us, "Freedom is the power, rooted in reason and will, to act or not to act, to do this or that, and so to perform deliberate actions on one's own responsibility" (CCC 1731). These choices that one makes, with the help of an informed conscience, build upon one another. "The more one does what is good, the freer one becomes. There is no true freedom except in the service of what is good and just" (CCC 1733).

Psalm 19 then is our hymn of praise for the laws of God that make, or set, us free. Everlasting life is found in following the laws of the Lord, even and perhaps especially when they are challenging and countercultural.

CONNECTING TO EXPERIENCE: LIVING THE PASCHAL MYSTERY

Do not have other gods before me, God tells the Israelites. But God's people will—in a matter of moments—cast a golden calf out of trinkets and call it a god. We may think we don't need to worry about this commandment. But the gods that pry our hearts from Christ are not the ones to whom we pray. Our god is pride; our god is greed; our god is worry. Sin has taken up camp in the temple of our hearts. Jesus, filled with zeal, overturns these tables of sin. Importantly, zeal is not anger but fierce love, passionate fervor, and defense of a person or place or thing. Jesus is ready to do the same to us when our hearts fill with the clutter of sin. His hands are ready to turn us over, to topple sin, and to transform us. Will we let him enter the temple of our hearts and cleanse us with the words of everlasting life?

PROMPTS FOR FAITH-SHARING

- Where do you, your family, or your community most need to set aside false idols?
- Have you ever experienced righteous anger in yourself or others? What was the occasion?
- Where in your life do you have the most zeal? Where in your life would you like to ask Christ for the grace of more zeal?

CELEBRATION and CATECHESIS

Model Penitential Act

Presider: In the gospel today, Jesus enters the temple, spilling the coins of the money changers and overturning their tables. May he enter our hearts this day as we ask for him to dispel our sin with his mercy . . . *[pause]*

Confiteor: I confess . . .

Model Universal Prayer (Prayer of the Faithful)

Presider: The precepts of the Lord are right, rejoicing the heart. Let us trust in the Lord, whose laws are perfect and whose kindness is everlasting

Response: Lord, hear our prayer.

That zeal for our faith might consume the church, drawing us into communion with one another, rather than self-righteousness and division, we pray . . .

That our lawmakers and government officials may seek guidance in the wisdom and justice of God, we pray . . .

That all who feel cast off and divided from their homes, their families, or their communities might find new hope and restoration in their lives, we pray . . .

That we might reject vengeance and violence fed by hatred, and instead fill our hearts with the merciful love of God, we pray . . .

Presider: O God, you alone have the words of everlasting life. May we be filled with zeal for your love and for the care and protection of our neighbors. We ask this through Christ our Lord. **Amen.**

Liturgy and the Hours

Advent and Lent are perfect times to introduce your community to the Liturgy of the Hours, if you haven't already. Perhaps that might mean Sunday night Vespers or Compline, or morning prayer during the upcoming Triduum. When we say that the liturgy is the prayer of the church, that's more than Mass—it includes other sacraments and these liturgies as well.

Quoting *Lumen Gentium*, the *General Instruction of the Liturgy of the Hours* states: "Christ's priesthood is also shared by the whole Body of the Church, so that the baptized are consecrated as a spiritual temple and holy priesthood through the rebirth of baptism and the anointing by the Holy Spirit and are empowered to offer the worship of the New Covenant, a worship that derives not from our own powers but from Christ's merit and gift" (7). Later, when describing who today ought to pray the Liturgy of the Hours, the list leaves no one out, mentioning those in religious life but also being sure to include groups of lay faithful and the domestic church (27).

(continued on next page)

COLLECT

Let us pray.

Pause for silent prayer

O God, author of every mercy and of all
goodness,
who in fasting, prayer and almsgiving
have shown us a remedy for sin,
look graciously on this confession of our
lowliness,
that we, who are bowed down by our
conscience,
may always be lifted up by your mercy.
Through our Lord Jesus Christ, your Son,
who lives and reigns with you in the unity
of the Holy Spirit,
God, for ever and ever. **Amen.**

FIRST READING

Exod 20:1-17

In those days, God delivered all these
commandments:
"I, the LORD, am your God,
who brought you out of the land of
Egypt, that place of slavery.
You shall not have other gods besides me.
You shall not carve idols for yourselves
in the shape of anything in the sky
above
or on the earth below or in the waters
beneath the earth;
you shall not bow down before them or
worship them.
For I, the LORD, your God, am a jealous
God,
inflicting punishment for their fathers'
wickedness
on the children of those who hate me,
down to the third and fourth generation;
but bestowing mercy down to the
thousandth generation
on the children of those who love me
and keep my commandments.

"You shall not take the name of the LORD,
your God, in vain.
For the LORD will not leave unpunished
the one who takes his name in vain.

"Remember to keep holy the sabbath day.
Six days you may labor and do all your
work,
but the seventh day is the sabbath of
the LORD, your God.
No work may be done then either by you,
or your son or daughter,
or your male or female slave, or your
beast,
or by the alien who lives with you.

In six days the LORD made the heavens and
the earth,
the sea and all that is in them;
but on the seventh day he rested.
That is why the LORD has blessed the
sabbath day and made it holy.

"Honor your father and your mother,
that you may have a long life in the land
which the LORD, your God, is giving you.
You shall not kill.
You shall not commit adultery.
You shall not steal.
You shall not bear false witness against
your neighbor.
You shall not covet your neighbor's house.
You shall not covet your neighbor's wife,
nor his male or female slave, nor his ox
or ass,
nor anything else that belongs to him."

or

Exod 20:1-3, 7-8, 12-17

In those days, God delivered all these
commandments:
"I, the LORD, am your God,
who brought you out of the land of
Egypt, that place of slavery.
You shall not have other gods besides me.

"You shall not take the name of the LORD,
your God, in vain.
For the LORD will not leave unpunished
the one who takes his name in vain.

"Remember to keep holy the sabbath day.
Honor your father and your mother,
that you may have a long life in the land
which the LORD, your God, is giving you.
You shall not kill.
You shall not commit adultery.
You shall not steal.
You shall not bear false witness against
your neighbor.
You shall not covet your neighbor's house.
You shall not covet your neighbor's wife,
nor his male or female slave, nor his ox
or ass,
nor anything else that belongs to him."

RESPONSORIAL PSALM
Ps 19:8, 9, 10, 11

SECOND READING
1 Cor 1:22-25

See Appendix A, p. 274.

If we ourselves are a "spiritual temple," our worship of God is sanctification of that temple and ought not be limited to just one hour per week! The resources to support this prayer grow more plentiful constantly—from many publishers and various online resources. If your community already has adoration, public rosaries, devotional Stations of the Cross, it also needs this liturgical prayer as part of its faith life!

Liturgical Ministry: Eucharistic Ministers

On this Third Sunday of Lent, Jesus does not reject the temple but reclaims it. He clears out what distracts so that worship can return to its center. Eucharistic ministers serve in this same reclaimed space, where Christ is not only present on the altar, but moving among the people. Their ministry is not a task to complete but a threshold to hold open. When they offer the body or blood of Christ, they stand at the place where heaven touches earth. They do so not just handing out a host but honoring the mystery of divine self-giving. What often feels routine is, in fact, a fragile moment of encounter. Eyes meet. Hands extend. Grace is given and received. The one who ministers is not above the moment but within it and is called to be present, steady, and attentive to what God is doing in the person before them.

Living Liturgy: The Offertory

The offertory is not a break in the liturgy but shifts our focus. It marks the moment when the assembly does more as they offer themselves up. Bread and wine are carried forward, but they carry with them more than grain and grape. They bear the quiet weight of the lives of the gathered assembly—grief, gratitude, struggle, hope. In this act, the whole church approaches the altar. The collection, too, is not just about money. It is a sign that we place our lives, not just our resources, into God's hands. The offertory signals a deeper truth that worship is not a spectator act. It is shared. The altar is not filled by the presider alone, but by the offerings of the entire people of God. The offertory becomes a mirror of the gospel, inviting us to offer not just what we have but who we are. Each person, in their own way, brings something unseen and real to the foot of the altar.

SPIRITUALITY

GOSPEL ACCLAMATION
John 3:16

God so loved the world that he gave his only Son,
so everyone who believes in him might have
eternal life.

Gospel

John 3:14-21; L32B

Jesus said to Nicodemus:
"Just as Moses lifted up the serpent in the desert,
so must the Son of Man be lifted up,
so that everyone who believes in him may have eternal life."

For God so loved the world that he gave his only Son,
so that everyone who believes in him might not perish
but might have eternal life.
For God did not send his Son into the world to condemn the world,
but that the world might be saved through him.
Whoever believes in him will not be condemned,
but whoever does not believe has already been condemned,
because he has not believed in the name of the only Son of God.
And this is the verdict,
that the light came into the world,
but people preferred darkness to light,
because their works were evil.
For everyone who does wicked things hates the light
and does not come toward the light,
so that his works might not be exposed.
But whoever lives the truth comes to the light,
so that his works may be clearly seen as done in God.

Year A readings may be used, see Appendix A, pp. 278–280.

Praying with Gospel Words and Phrases

For God so loved the world . . . that the world might be saved through him . . .

Reflecting on the Gospel

Readers of a certain age will remember watching Sunday afternoon football games, and, during field goals and extra point kicks, seeing behind the goalposts a fan holding a homemade sign featuring only a Bible verse reference. John 3:16 was likely a familiar passage for most Christians before this fad, but of course it has received extra attention from this unique method of evangelization. One occasionally still sees the practice today, with similar efforts on highway billboards and the like.

What is it about this passage that prompts its ubiquity? Notably, this is the first time in John's Gospel that the phrase "eternal life" is seen. Jesus is teaching Nicodemus during the Passover celebrations, when the Jewish people celebrate their liberation from slavery and the miracle of passing to their new life through the Red Sea. The healing action of Moses raising a serpent on a staff is compared by Jesus to his coming salvific crucifixion—though in opaque language.

And this eternal life *is* offered to us as a gift. It is nothing to be earned or bought; like any gift, it can only be gratefully received. The immensity of God's love for us is represented both in what the gift is—eternal life with God—and by, so to speak, its method of delivery—God sending his Son as the ultimate sacrificial offering. All of this perhaps explains the fame and near omnipresence of this singular Bible verse.

We would do well to add further context to the verse. Beyond that already mentioned, Jesus, in his continuing monologue, explains that not everyone seems to want such an amazing gift from God. Some "people preferred darkness to light," he says, referring back to the prologue of John, heard at Mass on Christmas Day. He also explains what it is we can do to accept the gift. It's not something we can hold very easily in our hands, after all. While such salvation is nothing that can be earned, we do accept the gift by living the truth that leads to the light of Christ. In doing so, we are rescued from the bondage of sin and death.

To the Point

The words of John 3:16 are ever-present to the point of being a cliché. Context and careful attention to them are required that their significance not be unnoticed.

Preparing to Proclaim, Preach, and Pray

Making Connections Between the Readings: The Old Testament passage for today paints a dire picture of the misdeeds of God's people: defiling the temple, mocking prophets, and rousing the anger of a compassionate and loving God. It's worth noting here that the passage says nothing about God bringing retribution directly; rather, it's the "enemies" of God's people who ravage them, their lands, and the holy temple. The Babylonian exile then begins, as the people of God are led away in captivity.

We too are captives—to sin, principally, but with a wide variety of manifestations. Pride, gluttony, sloth, and the other deadly sins are perhaps easy to list, but what really do they mean? How do they appear in our day-to-day lives? We all need a Sabbath rest; do we extend that rest too far, for too long? Or perhaps we never take the rejuvenating rest that God commands.

Freedom from sinfulness, we know, is nothing we can earn, but only accept as gift. Paul teaches that God, "even when we were dead in our transgressions, brought us to life with Christ—by grace [we] have been saved."

Make sure the gospel acclamation verse, the oft-heard John 3:16 text, is not overlooked and is given a clear, attention-commanding presentation today, so that perhaps its profound meaning may be listened to and understood anew, and heard rightly in context in the following gospel proclamation.

Making Connections to the Responsorial Psalm: Today's psalmist decries, "Let my tongue be silenced, if ever I forget you!" The liturgy requires silences from time to time—and it may be the only silence many in your assembly get in any given week. So, we must help our assemblies become proficient in utilizing times of sacred silence. We are in a world that, more and more each passing day, bombards us with a variety of smart phone alerts, breaking news chyrons, and bright flashing billboards demanding our attention and reaction. We are pulled hour by hour, minute by minute, in eighteen different directions. Frequently, the only downtime we get is not by our own choosing, but rather only if the power goes out or our phone battery dies.

The axiom states "you get good at what you practice." That is step one—making sure that silences at liturgy are not an occasional thing, but an every-Mass thing. They should be expected, consistent, and obviously intentional. Give the assembly that time and space.

CONNECTING TO EXPERIENCE: LIVING THE PASCHAL MYSTERY

Jesus is the light sent into the world. He is the one by whom all things were made, and so even the light that we know as the sun, the moon, and the stars came into being through Christ. But we so often prefer darkness to the light. Instead of turning ourselves toward the source of our creation and redemption, we turn inward. But if we refuse to look at the source of all wisdom and redemption, we refuse growth, which is the joy of discovering the power and presence of God in our midst. It is time to remove fears, habits, and obstacles that keep us from opening outward to the source of our health and life. Like Nicodemus, may we have the courage to turn away from only what we already know and to turn toward the light that surprises and perhaps even overwhelms us, always heals and encompasses us in salvation and joy.

PROMPTS FOR FAITH-SHARING

- How can you take on a new life in Christ's light this Lent? Is there something or someone in your life that you are afraid to shed light on?
- Jesus challenges the conventions of the world. Which worldly customs or comforts would you find most difficult to have condemned?
- Do you believe that Jesus brings eternal life? Does anything worry you about your own salvation?

Model Penitential Act

Presider: Today's gospel reminds us that eternal life comes from Christ, and we are called to believe in him. Confident that he is our salvation, we seek Christ's pardon and peace . . . *[pause]*

Confiteor: I confess . . .

Model Universal Prayer (Prayer of the Faithful)

Presider: God, you are the source of our life and salvation. Confident that you hear us and want us in your light, we offer to you our needs and petitions.

Response: Lord, hear our prayer.

For the leaders of our world, especially leaders of international bodies for relief and peacekeeping, that they might be inspired to bring God's light to those places marked by violence and war, we pray . . .

For this nation's leaders, that they might lead, speak, and guide according to the truth, we pray . . .

For those who struggle with the truth of their addictions, harmful actions, and hurtful relationships, we pray . . .

For the members of our community, that they might always find themselves in the healing light of God, we pray . . .

Presider: Living God, you are light unending and truth eternal. We ask you to hear our prayers and to help us to walk in your ways. We ask this though Christ our Lord. **Amen.**

Liturgy and Silence

In addition to allowing silences in the liturgy, we must help assemblies truly use well the sacred time. It can be easy to want to immediately fill such silences with a myriad of quasi-liturgical activities: finding the next hymn in the book, reading a bit of the bulletin, and the like. One might even fill the moment with activities that take one out of *kairos* time: checking a watch, recalling the day's activities that lie ahead, and so many more "human" pursuits.

Consider having a column in the bulletin, perhaps a pre-Mass announcement, or even incorporating catechesis on effectively using silent time into a homily today. Silence is an opportunity to watch and listen, both with our eyes and with our hearts, to the sacred space around us. To begin, it's important that we not bother with questions like "why" or "how," but rather just observe and notice. Most church buildings are so detailed that one could go on for endless Sundays noticing bits of architecture, stained glass windows, or statuary and find details previously overlooked. We can hear the smallest features in the organ playing during the preparation of the gifts: the colors of the tones,

(continued on next page)

COLLECT

Let us pray.

Pause for silent prayer

O God, who through your Word
reconcile the human race to yourself in a
wonderful way,
grant, we pray,
that with prompt devotion and eager faith
the Christian people may hasten
toward the solemn celebrations to come.
Through our Lord Jesus Christ, your Son,
who lives and reigns with you in the unity
of the Holy Spirit,
God, for ever and ever. **Amen.**

FIRST READING

2 Chr 36:14-16, 19-23

In those days, all the princes of Judah, the
priests, and the people
added infidelity to infidelity,
practicing all the abominations of the
nations
and polluting the LORD's temple
which he had consecrated in Jerusalem.

Early and often did the LORD, the God of
their fathers,
send his messengers to them,
for he had compassion on his people and
his dwelling place.
But they mocked the messengers of God,
despised his warnings, and scoffed at
his prophets,
until the anger of the LORD against his
people was so inflamed
that there was no remedy.
Their enemies burnt the house of God,
tore down the walls of Jerusalem,
set all its palaces afire,
and destroyed all its precious objects.
Those who escaped the sword were carried
captive to Babylon,
where they became servants of the king
of the Chaldeans and his sons
until the kingdom of the Persians came
to power.
All this was to fulfill the word of the LORD
spoken by Jeremiah:
"Until the land has retrieved its lost
sabbaths,
during all the time it lies waste it shall
have rest
while seventy years are fulfilled."

In the first year of Cyrus, king of Persia,
in order to fulfill the word of the LORD
spoken by Jeremiah,
the LORD inspired King Cyrus of Persia

to issue this proclamation throughout
his kingdom,
both by word of mouth and in writing:
"Thus says Cyrus, king of Persia:
All the kingdoms of the earth
the LORD, the God of heaven, has given
to me,
and he has also charged me to build him
a house
in Jerusalem, which is in Judah.
Whoever, therefore, among you belongs to
any part of his people,
let him go up, and may his God be with
him!"

RESPONSORIAL PSALM
Ps 137:1-2, 3, 4-5, 6

℟. (6ab) Let my tongue be silenced, if I
ever forget you!

By the streams of Babylon
we sat and wept
when we remembered Zion.
On the aspens of that land
we hung up our harps.

℟. Let my tongue be silenced, if I ever
forget you!

For there our captors asked of us
the lyrics of our songs,
and our despoilers urged us to be joyous:
"Sing for us the songs of Zion!"

℟. Let my tongue be silenced, if I ever
forget you!

How could we sing a song of the LORD
in a foreign land?
If I forget you, Jerusalem,
may my right hand be forgotten!

℟. Let my tongue be silenced, if I ever
forget you!

May my tongue cleave to my palate
if I remember you not,
if I place not Jerusalem
ahead of my joy.

℟. Let my tongue be silenced, if I ever
forget you!

SECOND READING
Eph 2:4-10

See Appendix A, p. 277.

the harmonies shifting, the melody floating toward the heavens. We can begin, after noticing and observing the prayerful environment around us, to contemplate in our hearts what it is that God is speaking to us and how it is we will choose to respond to a loving God, in word and in deeds.

Liturgical Ministry: Altar Servers

When altar servers set the altar, they do more than arrange objects. They prepare the ground where the church will meet the living God. Spreading the corporal, placing the chalice, and arranging the paten are all gestures of reverent anticipation. The altar is not a surface to organize but the table of sacrifice and communion. What happens there changes the world. To set it is to make space for mystery, to ready a place where heaven and earth will meet. This ministry teaches trust in what we cannot yet see. It shows that readiness itself is a kind of offering. The alter server becomes a quiet herald, calling the assembly to recognize that something holy is about to unfold. In this small but weighty act, the church models what every believer is called to do: prepare their heart, clear space, and wait for the Lord who draws near.

Living Liturgy: Orate Fratres

The brief invitation, "Pray, brothers and sisters, that my sacrifice and yours may be acceptable to God, the almighty Father," is a pivotal moment in the Mass often passed over quickly. The *Orate, fratres* is the moment when the presider invites the assembly to unite their prayers with his, transforming the Mass from a private act into a communal offering. The phrase "my sacrifice and yours" expresses the shared nature of the eucharistic celebration as the entire church that offers itself to the Father. This invitation calls the assembly beyond passive attendance to active participation. It acknowledges that the Eucharist is the church's self-offering made present through the priest but owned by all. The prayer that follows relies on the community's response, highlighting that liturgy is a dialogue between the presider and the people. By joining their prayers to the presider's, the faithful recognize their role as co-celebrants who bring their lives, their hopes, failings, and praise into worship. The *Orate, fratres* reveals that the Eucharist is not only about sacrifice but about the church's continual self-giving in communion with Christ.

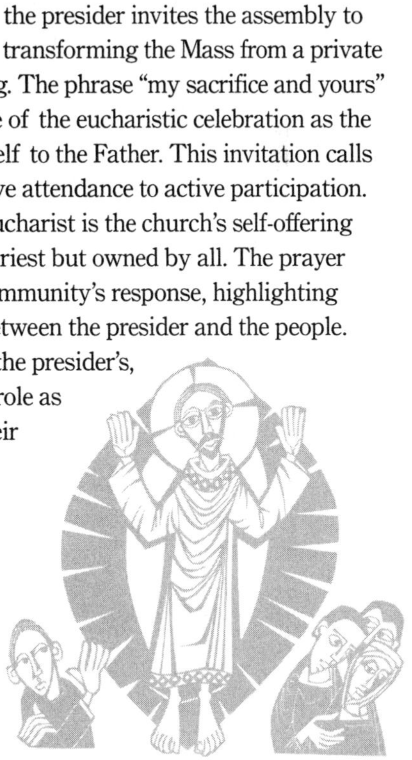

MARCH 7, 2027

FOURTH SUNDAY OF LENT

SPIRITUALITY

GOSPEL ACCLAMATION
John 12:26

Whoever serves me must follow me, says the Lord;
and where I am, there also will my servant be.

Gospel

John 12:20-33; L35B

Some Greeks who had come to worship at the Passover Feast
came to Philip, who was from Bethsaida in Galilee,
and asked him, "Sir, we would like to see Jesus."
Philip went and told Andrew;
then Andrew and Philip went and told Jesus.
Jesus answered them,
"The hour has come for the Son of Man to be glorified.
Amen, amen, I say to you,
unless a grain of wheat falls to the ground and dies,
it remains just a grain of wheat;
but if it dies, it produces much fruit.
Whoever loves his life loses it,
and whoever hates his life in this world
will preserve it for eternal life.
Whoever serves me must follow me,
and where I am, there also will my servant be.
The Father will honor whoever serves me.

"I am troubled now. Yet what should I say?
'Father, save me from this hour'?
But it was for this purpose that I came to this hour.
Father, glorify your name."
Then a voice came from heaven,
"I have glorified it and will glorify it again."

Continued in Appendix A, p. 280.

Year A readings may be used, see Appendix A, pp. 280–283.

Praying with Gospel Words and Phrases

The hour has come . . . if it dies, it produces much fruit . . .

Reflecting on the Gospel

In some ways, today's Lectionary readings bring our Lenten journey, nearing its end once again, back to where the journey began. You will recall that this particular Lenten cycle is one of covenants: first Noah, then Abraham, and others. On this Sunday we hear that there are days coming when God will make a new covenant, where God's laws will not be handed on to us externally, like the Ten Commandments on tablets, but will be written on our hearts. In the gospel, we are told of God's thunderous voice, much like the voice at the transfiguration. Everything seems to return us to where the journey began: Jesus's proclamation that the kingdom of God is at hand.

In life, it can frequently feel like we too are running in circles, sometimes without purpose or goal. A modern-day parable—not an original one—may be helpful in this circumstance. It seems that one day, a man came upon a group of laborers, stone masons. He approached the first to ask what he was doing that day. Barely looking up from his work, the man grumbled, "I'm laying bricks," and with a sigh continued his labors. Approaching a second worker, the man asked him this same question. "I'm making a wall," the worker said, pausing to look left and right at the long expanse already partially created. Then the man walked up to the third worker. "What are you doing today?" he asked him. Putting down his tools, the mason gestured that the man should follow him a few steps away. Turning back around to his work, the laborer spread his arms wide and exclaimed, "I'm building a church!"

So it is for each of us, if we pause a few moments to ponder our labors in the vineyard. What is the expression, if we don't have ten minutes a day during which we can pray, we should pray for twenty minutes? Find some time during these next few weeks—in all the busyness that can at times seem like we are just fortifying a wall or even just moving heavy stones from point A to point B— to contemplate how we are, in fact, building a church, a sacred assembly of God's holy people, the Body of Christ present in the world.

To the Point

While there is more to the Lenten journey ahead, this Sunday is a natural time to look back before continuing forward. Has this season been fruitful for you? What spiritual work remains?

Preparing to Proclaim, Preach, and Pray

Making Connections Between the Readings: Our season of exploring divine covenant draws to a close by coming around full circle. Having prayed with a multiplicity of covenants thus far, we hear a prophecy, one of consolation to the lamentations of Jeremiah, of a new covenant coming. He says that this coming one, though, will be unlike any other God has made with us. God will write the law on our hearts—God will again come to be among us, in a new creation.

We understand this to be the eternal Logos, God's Word, becoming incarnate and dwelling physically among us, the fullest self-revelation of God. The law that God writes on our heart is love, and the fullest expression of that love is self-sacrifice. Suffering, obedience, and fervent prayer, the epistle explains, is embedded in that perfect act of love, and is an example to each of us, striving to exude that same love and show others the presence of God by our words and deeds.

God promises, in all of this, simply to be our God—to be love, forgiveness, healing, renewal, sustenance, salvation, and more. We promise to be people of God—serving, following, and evangelizing. God's Son is the new and everlasting covenant, once and for all. This mystery is embedded in the paschal mystery, soon to be celebrated and experienced anew.

Making Connections to the Responsorial Psalm: Psalm 51 today also brings us full circle to the beginning of the Lenten season. The refrain, the lens through which we experience the rest of the verses, however, has changed. What we sang on Ash Wednesday, "Be merciful, O Lord, for we have sinned," is now replaced by "Create a clean heart in me, O God." The former is a prayer of supplication and perhaps even despondency; the latter is a prayer of trust and confidence.

Make sure the musical setting used today, as well as the singing of it, reflects that change in tone. Seek out settings in major keys, instruct the cantor to share their words with a cheerful disposition, especially in the last lines, "I will teach transgressors your ways, / and sinners shall return to you." Sharing the good news must have as its source and foundation joy and cheerfulness—the method and tone of the evangelization must match the good news that it is!

CONNECTING TO EXPERIENCE: LIVING THE PASCHAL MYSTERY

If the days are coming, they sure can't come soon enough. Whether we are frustrated, brokenhearted, or feeling our bodies clenching with anger, none of these feelings sound like the clean heart and right spirit that God promises us. How can we possibly hear God's voice in the midst of our troubles? In today's gospel, Jesus, Son of God, is troubled for his hour has come. But out of the clouds a voice like thunder rumbles. It is the voice of God. Out of the trouble, out of the angst, hope comes. Out of prayers, tears, and supplication comes Christ, waiting to wash our sorrows and melt our anger. Out of death will come new life. In his death on the cross, Christ crosses through the paschal mystery. We are invited to follow and to invite others through Christ, who calls all people to himself.

PROMPTS FOR FAITH-SHARING

- Do you hear God's voice speaking to you today? What is it saying?
- Has your hour come? Is there something for which you are or are not ready that you feel you must do? How can you be ready for it?
- What does Jesus's courage teach you today? How can you model it in your own life this week?

Model Penitential Act

Presider: In the greatness of his compassion, the Lord wipes out our offense. Let us turn to the Lord as we remember our sinfulness and humbly ask for his mercy . . . *[pause]*

Confiteor: I confess . . .

Model Universal Prayer (Prayer of the Faithful)

Presider: Seeking always to glorify God's name, we offer our prayers and petitions for ourselves and for all the world.

Response: Lord, hear our prayer.

For the church this Lenten season: may it be filled with the Holy Spirit, new life, and hope for the future, we pray . . .

For all who have devoted their lives to serving their communities: may they find abundant blessing in their work and peace in their hearts, we pray . . .

For those who feel directionless and long to know the Lord: may they encounter him in the word, in the sacraments, and in the witness of all the faithful, we pray . . .

For those among us and in our community preparing for baptism, confirmation, and full communion with the Catholic Church: may their prayers and supplications be heard as they approach the sacraments of initiation, we pray . . .

Presider: Merciful God, you draw all people to yourself. Hear our prayers as we offer them to you and help us to grow in perfect obedience to your will. We ask this through Christ our Lord. **Amen.**

Liturgy and Ministry

It doesn't happen just to those in the pews: in our various ministries it can frequently feel like we too are running in circles, especially if we lose sight of the reasons for our ministry, our love of it and the people of God, or if we feel unsupported by our peers, by those in leadership roles, or by the very people we believe we have been called to serve. Particularly as Holy Week approaches, days can grow very long and stressful with the many different preparations demanded of us.

Make sure to take ample time for yourselves in coming days. Identify the people and places that can minister to you as well. Approach the coming days with an awareness that likely not everything will be perfect. Understand that likely not quite everything will get done. Both of these realities, while perhaps disappointing, are not only understandable but human. Liturgy, which is both human and divine, would not be what it is without our humanity present to it and within it.

The work of the people sometimes can feel too much like work. As we've seen here, appropriate rest and renewal is commanded by God and necessary to make the coming liturgies powerful and meaningful for everyone, including those who minister them.

COLLECT

Let us pray.

Pause for silent prayer

By your help, we beseech you, Lord our
God,
may we walk eagerly in that same charity
with which, out of love for the world,
your Son handed himself over to death.
Through our Lord Jesus Christ, your Son,
who lives and reigns with you in the unity
of the Holy Spirit,
God, for ever and ever. **Amen.**

FIRST READING

Jer 31:31-34

The days are coming, says the LORD,
when I will make a new covenant with
the house of Israel
and the house of Judah.
It will not be like the covenant I made with
their fathers
the day I took them by the hand
to lead them forth from the land of
Egypt;
for they broke my covenant,
and I had to show myself their master,
says the LORD.
But this is the covenant that I will make
with the house of Israel after those
days, says the LORD.
I will place my law within them and write
it upon their hearts;
I will be their God, and they shall be my
people.
No longer will they have need to teach
their friends and relatives
how to know the LORD.
All, from least to greatest, shall know me,
says the LORD,
for I will forgive their evildoing and
remember their sin no more.

RESPONSORIAL PSALM
Ps 51:3-4, 12-13, 14-15

℟. (12a) Create a clean heart in me, O God.

Have mercy on me, O God, in your
goodness;
in the greatness of your compassion
wipe out my offense.
Thoroughly wash me from my guilt
and of my sin cleanse me.

℟. Create a clean heart in me, O God.

A clean heart create for me, O God,
and a steadfast spirit renew within me.
Cast me not out from your presence,
and your Holy Spirit take not from me.

℟. Create a clean heart in me, O God.

Give me back the joy of your salvation,
and a willing spirit sustain in me.
I will teach transgressors your ways,
and sinners shall return to you.

℟. Create a clean heart in me, O God.

SECOND READING
Heb 5:7-9

In the days when Christ Jesus was in the
flesh,
he offered prayers and supplications
with loud cries and tears
to the one who was able to save him
from death,
and he was heard because of his
reverence.
Son though he was, he learned obedience
from what he suffered;
and when he was made perfect,
he became the source of eternal
salvation for all who obey him.

Liturgical Ministers: Ushers and Greeters

On the Fifth Sunday of Lent, the parish begins Passiontide. Ushers and greeters exercise a *diakonia* at the door, orienting bodies and hearts to the paschal pattern. They shape silence and pace; they signal reverence without rigidity; they notice the fragile—including catechumens, the bereaved, newcomers—and accompany them. Their ministry is ascetical: relinquishing chatter, urgency, and control; receiving each person as gift; shepherding processions, seating, and the approach to Communion with unhurried clarity. In small gestures they teach the community how to yield, how to make room. As the gospel speaks of the grain of wheat, they model the holy "falling to the ground," letting self-preference die so that others may pray. Practiced week after week, this service forms ministers themselves in their patient attentiveness, a sacramental imagination for thresholds, and a readiness to be unseen so that Christ may be noticed.

Living Liturgy: Communion Antiphon

Today's communion antiphon takes up the Lord's words "unless a grain of wheat falls to the ground and dies, it remains just a grain of wheat; but if it dies, it produces much fruit." Sung as we approach the table, this text interprets our movement. We do not come to take; we come to be taken up into Christ's self-offering. The antiphon situates our Communion within the new covenant promised by Jeremiah. The law inscribed on hearts becomes Christ's life shared in us. Receiving the body and blood is therefore a moment of dying and rising, releasing fears, grudges, and self-protection so that charity may flourish. The assembly answers not only with voices but with a eucharistic "Amen" that pledges a way of life to become bread for others. Fruitfulness comes through paschal loss; the Father glorifies the Son in this offering, and we consent, here and now, to be gathered into that same mystery.

SPIRITUALITY

GOSPEL ACCLAMATION
Ps 84:5

Blessed are those who dwell in your house,
O Lord;
they never cease to praise you.

Gospel

Matt 1:16, 18-21, 24a; L543

Jacob was the father of Joseph, the husband of Mary.
Of her was born Jesus who is called the Christ.

Now this is how the birth of Jesus Christ came about.
When his mother Mary was betrothed to Joseph,
but before they lived together,
she was found with child through the Holy Spirit.
Joseph her husband, since he was a righteous man,
yet unwilling to expose her to shame,
decided to divorce her quietly.
Such was his intention when, behold,
the angel of the Lord appeared to him in a dream and said,
"Joseph, son of David,
do not be afraid to take Mary your wife into your home.
For it is through the Holy Spirit
that this child has been conceived in her.
She will bear a son and you are to name him Jesus,
because he will save his people from their sins."
When Joseph awoke,
he did as the angel of the Lord had commanded him
and took his wife into his home.

or Luke 2:41-51a *in Appendix A, p. 283.*

See Appendix A, p. 284, for the other readings.

Praying with Gospel Words and Phrases

He did as the angel of the Lord had commanded him . . .

Reflecting on the Gospel

We arrive at a bit of a late Lenten oasis, the solemnity of St. Joseph, perhaps made even more of a relief by the date of the celebration falling on a Friday this year. "Solemnities are counted as the principal days in the calendar, whose celebration begins with First Vespers (Evening Prayer I) on the preceding day" (*General Norms for the Liturgical Year and Calendar* 11). Mass is celebrated then as if on a Sunday, with the Gloria and Creed recited. In some parts of the world, Mass attendance on this solemnity is obligatory.

Further, canon law tells us, "Abstinence from meat, or from some other food as determined by the Episcopal Conference, is to be observed on all Fridays, unless a solemnity should fall on a Friday" (c. 1251). Much like the way certain penitential practices are "suspended" on Sundays of Lent, they too are lifted on solemnities, even when falling on a Friday.

Today's gospel—and other bits of today's Scriptures—are heard in fuller forms at the Vigil Mass on Christmas Eve, we will recall. Those many months ago we noted that Joseph, silent in the gospels, is an example of "walking the walk"—being a model of faith by doing more than simply saying words. Certain other celebrations of the church year that are raised to the rank of a solemnity also give examples of saints who share meaning by what they do. The expanded elements of the liturgy testify to the significance of that being celebrated. The suspension of the abstinence requirement similarly attests to the importance of St. Joseph in the liturgical year and indeed the life of the church.

Joseph, the son of David, would have helped Mary teach Jesus about the faith, especially the Scriptures. The law he learned was that which Jesus would come to complete; the prophets he read he would come to fulfill. So take the opportunity, both inside and outside the church building, to celebrate this silent, holy man. St. Joseph, pray for us!

To the Point

St. Joseph brings a "weekday Sunday" to our late Lenten journeys. Make sure to celebrate him well and not lose sight of his presence and example with Palm Sunday just around the corner.

Model Penitential Act

Presider: Turning to the Lord who seeks righteousness, we ask for his forgiveness and mercy . . . *[pause]*

Lord Jesus, you offer hope to the hopeless: Lord, have mercy.
Christ Jesus, you uphold the righteous of heart: Christ, have mercy.
Lord Jesus, you call us to follow you with constancy: Lord, have mercy.

Model Universal Prayer (Prayer of the Faithful)

Presider: Trusting in God's providence as St. Joseph did, we offer our prayers and petitions.

Response: Lord, hear our prayer.

For Pope N.: may the prayerful trust of St. Joseph be a constant guide, we pray . . .

For government officials, politicians, and those in the military: may they find safety in their lives and pursue peace in their labors, we pray . . .

For fathers who are absent from their children's lives: may they find courage to love and support their families, we pray . . .

For all gathered here this day: may we choose to quiet our hearts and minds so that we might hear God's voice, as St. Joseph did, we pray . . .

Presider: God our Father, you gave us the model of St. Joseph, the spouse of the Blessed Virgin Mary, to learn integrity and trust. Hear our prayers this day, and allow us to become bearers and protectors of your word throughout the world. We ask this through Christ our Lord. **Amen.**

COLLECT

Let us pray.

Pause for silent prayer

Grant, we pray, almighty God,
that by Saint Joseph's intercession
your Church may constantly watch over
the unfolding of the mysteries of
human salvation,
whose beginnings you entrusted to his
faithful care.
Through our Lord Jesus Christ, your
Son,
who lives and reigns with you in the
unity of the Holy Spirit,
God, for ever and ever. **Amen.**

Liturgical Ministers: Lectors

On this solemnity, lectors inhabit a unique role as they give voice to a saint renowned for his silence. St. Joseph speaks not by words but through fidelity, trusting in dreams, sheltering the Divine Child, embodying obedience in the ordinary. Lectors proclaim Scripture that gives shape to these silent virtues. As they stand at the ambo, their proclamation invites the assembly to listen attentively, honoring the power of what is not said. In doing so, they teach a different kind of listening. They teach one that leans into stillness, waits for the Spirit's whisper, and values interior attunement. By modeling fluid speech rooted in interior quiet, lectors show that ministry is not only about articulation but about creating a space where the word can echo in hearts, much like Joseph's unspoken fiat formed the household of salvation.

Living Liturgy: Communion Antiphon

As the assembly receives Communion today, the antiphon summons the image of Christ the Bridegroom praising the humble steward. Joseph, a "righteous man," becomes an embodied example of that servant who quietly fulfilled God's purposes, entrusted with Mary and Jesus. This text reframes Communion not only as gift received but as vocation affirmed. The Eucharist empowers each believer to mirror Joseph's faithfulness in the faithful custodianship of everyday love. In doing so we offer kindness without fanfare, embrace vulnerability without complaint, and respond to God's call even when it's hidden in dreams. The body of Christ we eat becomes the food of hidden devotion. The faithful are shaped into just and attentive servants, whose greatest act of discipleship may be to awaken from within.

SPIRITUALITY

GOSPEL ACCLAMATION
Phil 2:8-9

Christ became obedient to the point of death,
even death on a cross.
Because of this, God greatly exalted him
and bestowed on him the name which is above
every name.

Gospel at the procession with palms

Mark 11:1-10; L37B (John 12:12-16 may also be read.)

When Jesus and his disciples drew near to Jerusalem,
to Bethphage and Bethany at the Mount of Olives,
he sent two of his disciples and said to them,
"Go into the village opposite you,
and immediately on entering it,
you will find a colt tethered on which no one has ever sat.
Untie it and bring it here.
If anyone should say to you,
'Why are you doing this?' reply,
'The Master has need of it
and will send it back here at once.'"
So they went off
and found a colt tethered at a gate outside on the street,
and they untied it.

Continued in Appendix A, p. 285.

Gospel at Mass Mark 14:1–15:47; L38B

or Mark 15:1–39; L38B *in Appendix A, pp. 285–288.*

Praying with Gospel Words and Phrases

They went out . . . They . . . led him away . . . [They] led him off to crucify him . . .

Reflecting on the Gospel

Humans, dependent on factors like age, abilities, and more, have lots of different ways of getting around: crawling, walking, skipping, marching, running—and these are just with our bodies alone, without considering bicycles, cars, trains, planes, ships, and so many other modes of transportation.

Palm Sunday has its own unique entrance procession (as an option), though each Sunday Mass has a procession to begin the liturgy. But there are others too: the procession with the Book of the Gospels, the procession with the gifts of bread and wine, the communion procession, and the recessional. These movements are practical to be sure—people and things need to get from one place to another—but they are also symbolic, particularly at this time of year. Our faith is itself a journey, where all the ground is holy, where we pass though valleys and over hills, we the church on the same journey as Christ himself lived. We hear, in part, these words as the liturgy begins: "Today we gather together to herald with the whole Church the beginning of the celebration of our Lord's Paschal Mystery, that is to say, of his Passion and Resurrection. For it was to accomplish this mystery that he entered his own city of Jerusalem" (Roman Missal, Palm Sunday 5).

Within the gospels today, it might be easily overlooked how often Jesus goes, or is led, from place to place: the journey to and entrance into Jerusalem, to the dwelling of the Passover supper, to the agony in the garden, the arrest to the trial, to Pilate, to the stripping and mocking, to the Via Dolorosa and his crucifixion. Each of these is a procession, many forming the devotional traditional processional praying of the Stations of the Cross.

Jesus's many processions—the ones we hear about today and all those before and after—are linked to our own processions, both logistically and spiritually. Our earthly travels mirror his: visiting friends, dining, sharing good news, and more. Our spiritual travels mirror his: pilgrimages through both the joys and sorrows of life, with the goal of eternal unity with God and God's people.

To the Point

The processional/pilgrimage aspects of Palm Sunday can be easily overlooked. Exploring these facets of the day may be a fresh way to engage the assembly—with preaching, music, and more.

Preparing to Proclaim, Preach, and Pray

Making Connections Between the Readings: As a youth, hearing this canticle from Philippians each year, it took me quite some time to have a clear, correct understanding of its first lines. My immature interpretation, especially of the term "grasped," was that Jesus did not *strive* for that equality with God of which the passage speaks. My mind imagined Jesus reaching out, almost physically, for that equality—or rather, not reaching out—to try to grasp it.

Jesus, of course, as God's only Son, is divine, is God. The passage is Paul's teaching that Jesus did not cling to that divinity, that he did not, with unrelenting grip, choose to retain it and its power and authority. Rather, "he emptied himself," and this silent act of kenosis is perhaps the strongest word ever spoken. Jesus, by deeds, spoke of service and humility throughout his ministry; here both come together in the most profound and impactful way imaginable.

The other facet of faith spoken in the passion and death of the Messiah is that of trust. Like the Suffering Servant, Jesus trusts in God (the Father) as his help, such that the disgrace and shame of the cross will be transformed into heavenly, salvific glory.

Making Connections to the Responsorial Psalm: Many psalms take their narrator, and we who sing them now, on spiritual journeys, often from despair and lament to trust and hope. Psalm 22 does so, as its verses progress as does Jesus's passion: mocking, piercing, stripping—but then, at the end, a strong public proclamation of reliance on God.

The refrain of this psalm can be a challenge to this structure, however, as it seems to want to negate that progression by returning the assembly to words of doubtful abandonment. It may be worth considering leaving off that last refrain—its unexpected silence could speak volumes to the faithful.

Depending on how your parish celebrates the end of the coming Holy Thursday liturgy, it may be worth borrowing a musical practice from the pre-conciliar liturgy. Psalm 22 was assigned to the stripping of the altar, with the antiphon "They divide my garments about them; for my clothing they cast lots." This practice could help to unify Holy Week, and by ritual action catechize the faithful on the symbolism of the altar as Christ himself.

CONNECTING TO EXPERIENCE: LIVING THE PASCHAL MYSTERY

Oil appears twice in the gospel today. First, it arrives in the hand of an unnamed woman. Ignoring the indignance of the others around the table, she recognizes Jesus for who he really is, anointing him in preparation for his passion. Days later, Jesus will again be sitting at table, and will again encounter oil—this time, in a dish into which one dips bread. Those gathered at table are flustered by Jesus's words once more: the one who eats bread with me will betray me. They have not recognized who he is; in the coming moments, one will betray, another will deny, and the rest will flee. When we encounter Jesus during his passion this week, what oil will we bring him? Will we also dip our hand in his dish, but deny him by destroying those around us in words and deeds? Or will we honor him by remembering the anointing of our own baptisms, choosing to unite ourselves more profoundly to Christ?

PROMPTS FOR FAITH-SHARING

- Do you identify more with Jesus, who allows his feet to be anointed, or with those who thought that the woman with the oil was wasting Jesus's time?
- Are you willing to sit at the feet of Jesus because his feet are precious? What does this gospel passage teach you about the paschal mystery?
- Is there something in your life for which you need anointing, healing, or prayers? Whom can you invite into your life who might be able to help?

Model Penitential Act

Presider: On this day, we offer our hosannas to the Lord as he enters Jerusalem. May we enter this Holy Week with him, and begin by seeking his mercy . . . *[pause]*

Confiteor: I confess . . .

Model Universal Prayer (Prayer of the Faithful)

Presider: We offer our prayers and petitions to God who hears us in our need (petitions drawn from *Fratelli Tutti* 5, 9-19).

Response: Lord, hear our prayer.

That the church might serve as a light to the nations, calling all to care for our elderly and our young, and honoring the dignity of all human persons, we pray . . .

That nations who are consumed by selfishness and aggressive ideologies might give way to goodness, love, justice, and solidarity, we pray . . .

That those who choose violence and destruction of life might be freed from the snares of evil which entrap them, we pray . . .

That our community and all gathered here may join in caring for creation, remembering that our whole human family dwells in a common home, we pray . . .

Presider: God, creator of all, you have called human beings to live as brothers and sisters. In the sight of the unbounded mercy of your Son's passion, may we bind ourselves in solidarity with all the world. We ask this through Christ our Lord. **Amen.**

Liturgy and Processions

The assembly today ought to be able to tell from the first instant that this week is unlike any other: vibrant reds abound and palm branches greet their arrival. If using the first form, and the procession commemorating the Lord's entrance into Jerusalem is done and done well, the assembly is likely gathering in a spot very separate from the church.

If one is creating this procession for what the missal calls "the principal Mass," it is not worth pursuing unless it is done abundantly well. Simply gathering outside the church front doors won't cut it! Gather somewhere distinctly different, perhaps a school gym, or on an athletic field on campus or at a park or nearby. If the people of God are to process, the journey must be something more than the usual trip from the car in the parking lot to the front doors. Adequate sound reinforcement must be obtained, ministers must be well-prepared, and music must be carefully chosen. Lastly, the congregation should be instructed on not just the logistics of the procession, but the theological and liturgical meanings of processions in general, and of the one that begins the holiest week of the church year.

COLLECT

Let us pray.

Pause for silent prayer

Almighty ever-living God,
who as an example of humility for the human race to follow
caused our Savior to take flesh and submit to the Cross,
graciously grant that we may heed his lesson of patient suffering
and so merit a share in his Resurrection.
Who lives and reigns with you in the unity of the Holy Spirit,
God, for ever and ever. **Amen.**

FIRST READING

Isa 50:4-7

The Lord GOD has given me
a well-trained tongue,
that I might know how to speak to the weary
a word that will rouse them.
Morning after morning
he opens my ear that I may hear;
and I have not rebelled,
have not turned back.
I gave my back to those who beat me,
my cheeks to those who plucked my beard;
my face I did not shield
from buffets and spitting.

The Lord GOD is my help,
therefore I am not disgraced;
I have set my face like flint,
knowing that I shall not be put to shame.

RESPONSORIAL PSALM

Ps 22:8-9, 17-18, 19-20, 23-24

℟. (2a) My God, my God, why have you abandoned me?

All who see me scoff at me;
they mock me with parted lips, they wag their heads:
"He relied on the LORD; let him deliver him,
let him rescue him, if he loves him."

℟. My God, my God, why have you abandoned me?

Indeed, many dogs surround me,
a pack of evildoers closes in upon me;
they have pierced my hands and my feet;
I can count all my bones.

℟. My God, my God, why have you abandoned me?

They divide my garments among them,
and for my vesture they cast lots.
But you, O Lord, be not far from me;
O my help, hasten to aid me.

℟. My God, my God, why have you abandoned me?

I will proclaim your name to my brethren;
in the midst of the assembly I will praise you:
"You who fear the Lord, praise him;
all you descendants of Jacob, give glory to him;
revere him, all you descendants of Israel!"

℟. My God, my God, why have you abandoned me?

SECOND READING
Phil 2:6-11

Christ Jesus, though he was in the form of God,
did not regard equality with God
something to be grasped.
Rather, he emptied himself,
taking the form of a slave,
coming in human likeness;
and found human in appearance,
he humbled himself,
becoming obedient to the point of death,
even death on a cross.
Because of this, God greatly exalted him
and bestowed on him the name
which is above every name,
that at the name of Jesus
every knee should bend,
of those in heaven and on earth and under the earth,
and every tongue confess that
Jesus Christ is Lord,
to the glory of God the Father.

Liturgical Ministers: Music Ministers

Palm Sunday challenges music ministers to carry the community through the extremes of Holy Week's opening drama. From jubilant hosannas in the opening procession to the solemn silence that follows the passion, their ministry models prayerful adaptability. Music is not just embellishment but a guide, helping the assembly feel the liturgy's shifting tone. Leading sung responses during the passion requires sensitivity. The goal is not performance but participation, helping worshippers find their own voice within Christ's story. Music ministers' careful preparation in choosing chant-like refrains and pacing the narrative teaches the community how song can deepen contemplation. By serving this liturgy's contrasts, music ministers witness to the paschal mystery in joy and suffering intertwined, praise and lament in a single breath.

Living Liturgy: Procession with Palms

Palm Sunday begins with movement and song. The blessing of palms and the procession invite us to join Christ's entry into Jerusalem not as spectators but participants. The church steps outside, literally and spiritually, before returning to the sanctuary to hear the passion. This choreography catechizes without words. Discipleship is not static but a walk with Christ toward his cross. The shift from joyful procession to somber gospel reveals the heart of Holy Week, that triumph is inseparable from self-giving love. Palms at home become signs of conversion; we wave them in worship, then watch them dry and fade, teaching us that faith must be renewed daily. The liturgy today shapes us to follow Christ not only in moments of acclaim but through the hard road of surrender.

MARCH 21, 2027

PALM SUNDAY OF THE PASSION OF THE LORD

EASTER TRIDUUM

SPIRITUALITY

GOSPEL ACCLAMATION
John 13:34

I give you a new commandment, says the Lord:
love one another as I have loved you.

Gospel John 13:1-15; L39ABC

Before the feast of Passover, Jesus knew that his hour had come
to pass from this world to the Father.
He loved his own in the world and he loved them to the end.
The devil had already induced Judas, son of Simon the Iscariot, to hand him over.
So, during supper,
fully aware that the Father had put everything into his power
and that he had come from God and was returning to God,
he rose from supper and took off his outer garments.
He took a towel and tied it around his waist.
Then he poured water into a basin
and began to wash the disciples' feet
and dry them with the towel around his waist.
He came to Simon Peter, who said to him,
"Master, are you going to wash my feet?"
Jesus answered and said to him,
"What I am doing, you do not understand now,
but you will understand later."
Peter said to him, "You will never wash my feet."
Jesus answered him,
"Unless I wash you, you will have no inheritance with me."
Simon Peter said to him,
"Master, then not only my feet, but my hands and head as well."

Continued in Appendix A, p. 289.

See Appendix A, p. 289, for the other readings.

Praying with Gospel Words and Phrases

He loved them to the end . . . I have given you a model to follow . . .

Reflecting on the Gospel

One would rightly expect to hear not only a gospel passage from the Last Supper tonight, but one about the meal specifically. Instead, that content is found in the epistle, and John's Gospel famously describes the washing of the feet. The liturgy itself links the eucharistic meal to that which those who partake in it must be and must do. The followers of Christ must be humble servants, giving of themselves as the least among their peers.

This is what it means to be in Christian community: each member in Christ's body should be a humble, generous servant to one another. This is where unity is found—not in any uniformity of language or appearance, but in love, perfectly demonstrated by God's own Son. Elements of unity and community are a part of every eucharistic rite, and in the ritualized washing of the feet during this liturgy. Further, an optional rite at the beginning of the Mass can expand that community and unity more broadly.

It can be effective, as part of the liturgy this evening, to celebrate the rite of reception of oils from the diocesan chrism Mass. Including this rite helps the faithful stay more connected to the bishop and the whole of the diocese. By having the oils processed in by members of the community connected to their use—for instance, those in the OCIA program about to experience the rites of initiation at the Easter Vigil—there comes about an even stronger bond connecting many facets of the life of the church together.

And a bit of liturgical minutiae: while the oil of the catechumens and the oil of the sick were blessed at the chrism Mass, the chrism oil was *consecrated*—set apart for a sacred purpose. We use "consecration" language when we speak of the bread and wine at Mass, when the church's prayer transforms them into the Real Presence of Christ. Some argue that consecrated chrism oil is the real presence of the Holy Spirit, due to the nature of the prayer of consecration, before which "the Bishop, if appropriate, breathes upon the opening of the vessel of the Chrism" (Order of Blessing the Oil of Catechumens and of the Sick and of Consecrating the Chrism 25).

To the Point

Among more familiar significances of this evening, don't neglect what the evening's Scriptures and rituals say about unity and community.

Model Penitential Act

Presider: Coming before the Lord who loves us, we ask for his mercy . . . *[pause]*

Lord Jesus, you wash us from our sins: Lord, have mercy.
Christ Jesus, you ask us to love: Christ, have mercy.
Lord Jesus, you died so that we might live: Lord, have mercy.

Model Universal Prayer (Prayer of the Faithful)

Presider: Turning to the Lord as we enter his paschal mystery, we pray . . .

Response: Lord, hear our prayer.

For our bishops, priests, and deacons: may the Lord who has called them to serve the faithful in word and sacrament be always present in their lives, we pray . . .

For peace among nations: may we who have learned from the model of Christ Jesus be agents of his love in the world, we pray . . .

For those who have turned away from their faith: may they feel the prompting of the Spirit during this holy time, we pray . . .

For all gathered here, especially those awaiting the sacraments of initiation: may they feel the love of the Lord, we pray . . .

Presider: O God, you gave your only Son so that we might have eternal life. Hear our prayers this holy night, and lead us ever closer to your Son, Jesus Christ our Lord, who lives and reigns with you and the Holy Spirit, God forever and ever. **Amen.**

COLLECT

Let us pray.

Pause for silent prayer

O God, who have called us to participate
in this most sacred Supper,
in which your Only Begotten Son,
when about to hand himself over to death,
entrusted to the Church a sacrifice new for all eternity,
the banquet of his love,
grant, we pray,
that we may draw from so great a mystery,
the fullness of charity and of life.
Through our Lord Jesus Christ, your Son,
who lives and reigns with you in the unity of the Holy Spirit,
God, for ever and ever. **Amen.**

Liturgical Ministers: Eucharistic Ministers

Holy Thursday invites those who share the body and blood of Christ to rediscover the deep meaning of their ministry. At this liturgy, we remember not only the institution of the Eucharist but also the heart of Christ who gave himself in humble service. Distributing Communion is more than a practical duty; it is a visible extension of the Lord's own hands, stretched out to wash the feet of his friends. Ministers approach the altar not as functionaries but as disciples who have first been nourished. Each act of offering the consecrated host or chalice is a small homily about God's generosity. Eucharistic ministers are invited to reflect deeply on their gestures, including the care with which they handle the body of Christ and the way their eyes meet those they serve, all of which can either reveal or obscure the mystery they carry. Tonight's liturgy, rich with signs and symbols, calls them to integrate prayer and service. Their ministry is an invitation to the whole assembly to see that Communion is not a private devotion but a gift that forms us as one Body, united for mission.

Living Liturgy: The Mandatum

The washing of feet is one of the church's most striking liturgical actions. It is a catechesis in movement as the Lord and Teacher kneels before his disciples and performs the work of a servant. This is not a quaint gesture or a historical reenactment; it is a sacramental sign that opens a way of life. Those who have been washed are sent to wash others. In this moment the Eucharist is explained without words: love empties itself, stoops down, and becomes tangible. The *mandatum* prepares the faithful to see that the altar and the streets are connected. The same hands that receive Christ's body are sent to carry mercy, justice, and healing to the world. Holy Thursday draws the church into the mystery of a love that humbles itself and transforms everything it touches.

GOSPEL ACCLAMATION
Phil 2:8-9

Christ became obedient to the point of death,
even death on a cross.
Because of this, God greatly exalted him
and bestowed on him the name which is above
every other name.

* The passion narratives are proclaimed in full so that all see vividly the love of Christ for each person. In light of this, the crimes during the Passion of Christ cannot be attributed, in either preaching or catechesis, indiscriminately to all Jews of that time, nor to Jews today. The Jewish people should not be referred to as though rejected or cursed, as if this view followed from Scripture. The Church ever keeps in mind that Jesus, his mother Mary, and the apostles all were Jewish. As the Church has always held, Christ freely suffered his passion and death because of the sins of all, that all might be saved.

Gospel John 18:1–19:42; L40ABC

Jesus went out with his disciples across the Kidron valley
to where there was a garden,
into which he and his disciples entered.
Judas his betrayer also knew the place,
because Jesus had often met there with his disciples.
So Judas got a band of soldiers and guards
from the chief priests and the Pharisees
and went there with lanterns, torches, and weapons.
Jesus, knowing everything that was going to happen to him,
went out and said to them, "Whom are you looking for?"
They answered him, "Jesus the Nazorean."
He said to them, "I AM."
Judas his betrayer was also with them.
When he said to them, "I AM,"
they turned away and fell to the ground.

Continued in Appendix A, pp. 290–292.
See Appendix A, pp. 292–293, for the other readings.

Praying with Gospel Words and Phrases
Carrying the cross himself . . .

Reflecting on the Gospel
It's said that if one were to gather all the relics across the globe that claim to be a splinter from the "true cross" of Christ, the quantity would far exceed what a cross of the time would have actually been. Yet there is something profound in the way that the faithful, across many centuries and lands, revere this instrument of torture and death. Indeed, just as Christ transformed suffering and death, he also transformed the cross into a symbol of hope and joy.

The passion narratives, though, say very little about the cross itself. The authors apparently presume that their readers know what it is without any elaboration. John does take time to observe that Jesus carried the cross himself and makes no reference to Simon of Cyrene as the three Synoptics do. Why is this important? Perhaps it alludes to Isaac, who carried the wood for the holocaust on his own shoulders. The difference may also be to emphasize Jesus's conscious, willing, and intentional fulfillment of prophecy and his divine mission.

It may at first seem like unnecessary semantics, but on this day when the principal rite of the church is adoration, care should be taken that it is a cross which is adored, and not a crucifix. The missal, over and over again, in texts the presider says, in rubrics he and the faithful perform, and in the words that are sung, uses the word "cross" and never "crucifix." For instance, when the cross is processed in (or unveiled), these words are sung: "Behold the wood of the Cross, on which hung the salvation of the world." The assembly responds, "Come, let us adore" (Roman Missal, Good Friday 15).

Growing up, I had the experience of kissing the feet of a corpus on Good Friday, but that's misdirecting the intent of the moment. We are meant to adore and contemplate the cross itself, the instrument of suffering and death. The antiphon the missal offers gives us insight as to why: "We adore your Cross, O Lord, we praise and glorify your holy Resurrection, for behold, because of the wood of a tree joy has come to the whole world" (Roman Missal, Good Friday 20).

To the Point
John's Gospel takes care to present Jesus as the Passover sacrificial lamb. That he carries his own cross is a significant detail within that imagery. That we reverence a cross today—and not a crucifix—is also significant and imbued with meaning.

Liturgical Ministers: Ushers and Greeters

On this day of stark simplicity, those who welcome and guide the assembly take on a ministry that feels different from every other liturgy of the year. There is no entrance procession, no opening song, and no eucharistic prayer, yet the church gathers with a reverence that demands careful attention to space, silence, and movement. Ushers and greeters help shape that reverence. Their role is not simply to provide directions but to model prayerful stillness, gently ushering worshippers into the solemnity of this day. They are the first to invite the faithful to experience Good Friday's profound silence, allowing hearts to settle into awe before the cross. During the veneration, their ministry becomes even more crucial, ensuring a smooth flow so that the assembly's prayer is not disrupted but deepened. Their quiet service embodies what Good Friday teaches. Discipleship often calls us to step back, to guide without drawing attention, and to hold space for others to encounter the mystery of Christ's sacrifice.

Living Liturgy: Solemn Intercessions

The solemn intercessions are among the most ancient prayers of the church, stretching back to the early centuries of Christian worship. They remind us that Christ's sacrifice is for the salvation of all, and they train us to pray with the wide heart of God. On Good Friday, the assembly kneels and rises repeatedly, listening as the deacon or priest names each intention: for the church, for the world, for those who suffer, for those who do not believe. This rhythm of listening, kneeling, and standing enacts our solidarity with all humanity. These prayers shape us into a community that embraces the world's wounds rather than ignores them. By praying for friend and enemy alike, the church reveals the cross as the center of all hope. We are to be intercessors, carrying the cries of the world to the foot of Christ's cross, where love redeems all.

COLLECT

Let us pray.

Pause for silent prayer

Remember your mercies, O Lord,
and with your eternal protection
sanctify your servants,
for whom Christ your Son,
by the shedding of his Blood,
established the Paschal Mystery.
Who lives and reigns for ever and ever.
Amen.

or:

O God, who by the Passion of Christ
your Son, our Lord,
abolished the death inherited from
ancient sin
by every succeeding generation,
grant that just as, being conformed to
him,
we have borne by the law of nature
the image of the man of earth,
so by the sanctification of grace
we may bear the image of the Man of
heaven.
Through Christ our Lord.
Amen.

SPIRITUALITY

Gospel

Mark 16:1-7; L41B

When the sabbath was over,
Mary Magdalene, Mary, the mother of James, and Salome
bought spices so that they might go and anoint him.
Very early when the sun had risen,
on the first day of the week, they came to the tomb.
They were saying to one another,
"Who will roll back the stone for us
from the entrance to the tomb?"
When they looked up,
they saw that the stone had been rolled back;
it was very large.
On entering the tomb they saw a young man
sitting on the right side, clothed in a white robe,
and they were utterly amazed.
He said to them, "Do not be amazed!
You seek Jesus of Nazareth, the crucified.
He has been raised; he is not here.
Behold the place where they laid him.
But go and tell his disciples and Peter,
'He is going before you to Galilee;
there you will see him, as he told you.'"

See Appendix A, pp. 293–299, for the other readings.

Praying with Gospel Words and Phrases

Very early when the sun had risen . . .

Reflecting on the Gospel

There is something quite magical about witnessing a sunrise in its entirety. Being outside before dawn and then experiencing the gradual transition from darkness to light, looking for the first sign of the rising sun appearing on the horizon, seeing how the growing rays paint the sky and clouds hues of oranges and reds—these are moments like no other.

Importantly, it doesn't happen the way that a darkened room in our house is illuminated. When the switch on the wall is flipped, instantly the whole room is filled with light. A sunrise is far from instant: it takes its own time, outside of human control, to achieve its purpose of bringing light and warmth to a waiting world. If we wish, we can look up for any various date what time sunrise will be, but in truth, the sunrise itself is not limited to any precise moment in time.

One of the most ignored rubrics in the whole of the Roman Missal may be part of tonight's liturgy: "Then the Deacon places the paschal candle on a large candlestand prepared next to the ambo or in the middle of the sanctuary. And lights are lit throughout the church, except for the altar candles" (Easter Vigil 17). Liturgy is performative by nature (only to a certain point, of course): why turn on all the lights at that moment when the pillar of fire and its light, which shatters the darkness, has just entered the church, its flame divided but undimmed?

It seems this rubric is a somewhat old one, dating from the time before electricity, when it would take a rather long time to completely illumine a church, going from lantern to lantern one by one, bringing about a gradual lighting to the space. Perhaps there is a lesson here for modern times. If your lighting is sophisticated enough to have faders, consider bringing up the lights gradually during the chanting of the Easter proclamation. Or if not too jarring, individual banks of lights could be turned on every so often to achieve a similar effect.

To the Point

No one knows the exact moment at which Christ rose from the dead. Of course, the precise moment is nowhere near as important as that he did in fact rise, whenever it happened. Just as the Son rose, the sun also rises each day, gradually but without fail, an important image of the risen Christ bringing new life to the world.

Model Universal Prayer (Prayer of the Faithful)

Presider: Coming with confidence before the Lord, we offer our prayers and petitions as we pray . . .

Response: Lord, hear our prayer.

That the church, filled with Easter joy, may be a light for the nations, hope for all people, and home for the homeless, we pray . . .

That our leaders may seek peace, protect the poor, and support family life, we pray . . .

That those who are afraid, lost, or in pain might find freedom from darkness and new hope in Christ, we pray . . .

That we who are gathered here this night might be filled with healing, hope, and the will to bring light to others, we pray . . .

Presider: Loving God, this is the night when darkness was overcome. May your light shine upon us as we lift our prayers to you, and allow us to go forth bringing your light to all the world. We ask this through Christ the Lord. Amen.

COLLECT

Let us pray.

Pause for silent prayer

O God, who make this most sacred night radiant
with the glory of the Lord's Resurrection,
stir up in your Church a spirit of adoption,
so that, renewed in body and mind,
we may render you undivided service.
Through our Lord Jesus Christ, your Son,
who lives and reigns with you in the unity of the Holy Spirit,
God, for ever and ever. **Amen.**

Liturgical Ministers: Sacristans

The Easter Vigil is the Church's most intricate and symbol-filled liturgy, and sacristans carry a large responsibility in bringing its beauty to life. This night begins in stillness and darkness, yet it is carefully orchestrated so that every sign can speak its full meaning. Sacristans prepare the new fire, the paschal candle, oils, holy water, vestments, and vessels, anticipating each movement with prayerful attention. Their ministry is spiritual, forming a space where the church's worship flows without distraction. In preparing the sanctuary, sacristans silently proclaim the mystery of the resurrection, reminding the community that careful preparation is itself an act of love. This Vigil teaches that no gesture is too small to be offered to God. Sacristans learn vigilance through their ministry, embodying the very posture the liturgy celebrates, that we are a people awake, expectant, and ready to welcome the risen Christ. Their work forms them in humility and reverence and offers the assembly a setting where the signs of salvation can shine with clarity and power.

Living Liturgy: The Exsultet

When the *Exsultet* is proclaimed, the church stands at the cusp of Easter joy. The hymn calls all creation to rejoice and unfolds the meaning of every sign that fills this night. The paschal candle becomes a living icon of Christ, the light of the world, conquering the darkness of sin and death. As the single flame spreads from candle to candle, the assembly sees itself reflected in this mystery. The *Exsultet* is both song and proclamation, a meditation on salvation history and a summons to praise. Its poetry reminds us that this night is the heart of Christian faith, when time itself bends before God's saving work. We are not mere observers but participants in Christ's victory, standing within the story we proclaim. The *Exsultet* invites the faithful to let Easter light penetrate every shadow, to carry this flame beyond the church walls, and to live as witnesses of the resurrection in a world still longing for dawn.

SPIRITUALITY

GOSPEL ACCLAMATION
cf. 1 Cor 5:7b-8a

℟. Alleluia, alleluia.
Christ, our paschal lamb, has been sacrificed;
let us then feast with joy in the Lord.
℟. Alleluia, alleluia.

Gospel

John 20:1-9; L42ABC

On the first day of the week,
Mary of Magdala came to the tomb early in the morning,
while it was still dark,
and saw the stone removed from the tomb.
So she ran and went to Simon Peter
and to the other disciple whom Jesus loved, and told them,
"They have taken the Lord from the tomb,
and we don't know where they put him."
So Peter and the other disciple went out and came to the tomb.
They both ran, but the other disciple ran faster than Peter
and arrived at the tomb first;
he bent down and saw the burial cloths there, but did not go in.
When Simon Peter arrived after him,
he went into the tomb and saw the burial cloths there,
and the cloth that had covered his head,
not with the burial cloths but rolled up in a separate place.
Then the other disciple also went in,
the one who had arrived at the tomb first,
and he saw and believed.
For they did not yet understand the Scripture
that he had to rise from the dead.

or Mark 16:1-7; L41B *in Appendix A, p. 300,*

or, at an afternoon or evening Mass,
Luke 24:13-35; L46 *in Appendix A, p. 300.*

See Appendix A, p. 301, for the other readings.

Praying with Gospel Words and Phrases
The other disciple ran faster than Peter . . .

Reflecting on the Gospel
Have you ever noticed that no fewer than three times in John's telling of the discovery of the resurrection he points out that "the other disciple whom Jesus loved" ran faster than Peter to the tomb? Of course, it's commonly believed that John is speaking of himself when speaking of "the one whom Jesus loved," which adds an almost amusing layer. "I'm not going to be so boastful as to name myself here, but it is important that you know I could run faster than Peter."

By including such a specific detail, perhaps John is signaling that this is eyewitness testimony. Perhaps he is trying to contrast his personality and Peter's: while John arrives at the tomb first, he does not enter. Rather, it is the typically impetuous Peter who enters to examine the scene. John's Gospel, at least in written form, came several decades after the resurrection, and might be an appeal to two truths: that John and his love for Christ (and perhaps his age relative to Peter's) allowed him to reach the empty tomb first. But Peter, the rock on which the church was built, was the first to plunge into that resurrection mystery, affirming his role in the early church.

All of this though, happens because Mary of Magdala runs to them first, having been the first to see the stone rolled away. As Apostle to the Apostles, the first kerygma belongs to her, even if her initial understanding of it here in John's Gospel is more practical ("They have taken the Lord from the tomb, and we don't know where they put him") than theological. It is just beyond the conclusion of today's reading where Mary of Magdala is the first (in John's Gospel) to encounter the risen Christ in his glorified body. Upon recognizing him, she again goes to the disciples to announce what she has seen.

Without each of these experiences, especially without Mary and her initial encounters and conversations, our understanding and appreciation of the resurrection might be vastly different, incomplete, and lacking in impact.

To the Point
The good news of the day of resurrection demands of each of us what we are told of John, Peter, and Mary: that we run with haste to the mystery, that we enter into it deeply, and that we continually share the truth of that morning and its impact on our lives with all those we meet.

Model Penitential Act

Presider: We come with joy before the Lord who offers us pardon and peace . . . *[pause]*

Lord Jesus, you are the way, the truth, and the life: Lord, have mercy.

Christ Jesus, you are the light that overcomes the darkness: Christ, have mercy.

Lord Jesus, you alone have the words of everlasting life: Lord, have mercy.

Model Universal Prayer (Prayer of the Faithful)

Presider: Turning with confidence to the Lord we offer our prayers and petitions.

Response: Lord, hear our prayer.

For the church: may the joy of Easter widen our hearts and deepen our love for one another, we pray . . .

For our public servants, health care workers, and first responders: may those charged with caring for their communities receive abundant blessings, we pray . . .

For all who are alone this day: may we who are blessed with community recognize them, we pray . . .

For all who have received sacraments of initiation this Easter: may Easter joy continue to enliven and enrich their lives, we pray . . .

Presider: O God, you are giver of life and source of all things good. Hear our prayers this joyous day, and fill our hearts with trust that you will answer all our needs. We ask this through Christ our Lord. **Amen.**

COLLECT

Let us pray.

Pause for silent prayer

O God, who on this day,
through your Only Begotten Son,
have conquered death
and unlocked for us the path to eternity,
grant, we pray, that we who keep
the solemnity of the Lord's Resurrection
may, through the renewal brought by your Spirit,
rise up in the light of life.
Through our Lord Jesus Christ, your Son,
who lives and reigns with you in the unity of the Holy Spirit,
God, for ever and ever. **Amen.**

Liturgical Ministers: Environment Ministers

Easter morning greets the church with an explosion of color, fragrance, and light. Environment ministers are entrusted with creating a sacred space that reveals the fullness of the resurrection. Their ministry begins long before the liturgy, transforming the bare, stripped sanctuary of Good Friday into a place alive with beauty. Flowers, fabrics, candles, and banners are chosen not simply for decoration but to proclaim the truth of Christ risen. Each arrangement preaches, inviting the community to see God's glory revealed in creation. The paschal candle becomes the centerpiece, a visual sign that all beauty radiates from the light of Christ. Through their prayerful planning, environment ministers teach the assembly to notice how space itself can celebrate mystery. Their work forms them in stewardship and contemplation, reminding them that their labor is not about personal taste but about creating a setting that allows the liturgy to speak. By crafting an environment that stirs awe, these ministers help the faithful experience Easter not only through word and song but through sight, scent, and texture.

Living Liturgy: The Sequence

The Easter Sequence offers a moment of pause before the gospel, slowing the liturgy so the wonder of the resurrection can take root. Its chant connects us to a tradition stretching back nearly a millennium, when believers first sang this hymn to mark Easter morning as the center of all time. The Sequence gives voice to Mary Magdalene, whose testimony becomes a doorway for us to enter the mystery. She saw the tomb, she encountered the risen Lord, and she proclaimed what she witnessed. This ancient hymn is not a relic but a living catechism, shaping our hearts as we sing. It invites the church to savor Easter joy as something intimate and communal, announcing that Christ is alive here and now. Its poetry reminds us that resurrection is not a concept but an event that transforms all creation. Through this moment of stillness and praise, the faithful learn to see Easter light in every shadowed place, carrying its hope into the world.

SEASON OF EASTER

SPIRITUALITY

GOSPEL ACCLAMATION
John 20:29

℟. Alleluia, alleluia.
You believe in me, Thomas, because you have seen me, says the Lord;
blessed are those who have not seen me, but still believe!
℟. Alleluia, alleluia.

Gospel

John 20:19-31; L44B

On the evening of that first day of the week,
when the doors were locked, where the disciples were,
for fear of the Jews,
Jesus came and stood in their midst
and said to them, "Peace be with you."
When he had said this, he showed them his hands and his side.
The disciples rejoiced when they saw the Lord.
Jesus said to them again, "Peace be with you.
As the Father has sent me, so I send you."
And when he had said this, he breathed on them and said to them,
"Receive the Holy Spirit.
Whose sins you forgive are forgiven them,
and whose sins you retain are retained."

Thomas, called Didymus, one of the Twelve,
was not with them when Jesus came.
So the other disciples said to him,
"We have seen the Lord."
But he said to them,
"Unless I see the mark of the nails in his hands
and put my finger into the nailmarks
and put my hand into his side, I will not believe."

Continued in Appendix A, p. 302.

Praying with Gospel Words and Phrases

Put your finger here and see my hands . . . do not be unbelieving, but believe . . . My Lord and my God! . . .

Reflecting on the Gospel

Think for a moment about a scar you have, and a word or two you might pick to describe the circumstances that led to it. Perhaps words like "accident" or "scary" come to mind, or "embarrassed," "foolish," or even "reckless." But I doubt the word "glorious" came to mind.

Yet it is on this Second Sunday of Easter each year when we hear about the apostle Thomas and his first encounter with the risen Lord. Christ's resurrected and glorified body certainly could have been made completely whole again, yet the wounds of the nails and spear persist, and Thomas is able to touch and feel them. "My Lord and My God!" he cries. Here Christ is truly a wounded healer—and beyond that, a teacher, a friend, and a brother.

Liturgically, this attention to the "scars" of Christ should remind us of his humanity and his divinity, which we are invited to share with him one day. We also reflect on our kinship with Christ and the future glory offered and promised to us. Today is also an opportunity to call particular attention to the fraction rite, a ritual moment often lost in most liturgies.

On *M*A*S*H*, Charles Emerson Winchester III once famously said, "I do one thing at a time, I do it very well, and then I move on." Make sure that, at any liturgy, the fraction rite doesn't become a side note to a lingering sign of peace. The *General Instruction of the Roman Missal* tells us, "the gesture of the fraction or breaking of bread . . . was quite simply the term by which the Eucharist was known in apostolic times . . ." (321). It is at this eucharistic table that brings us, in one moment, to Christ broken on the cross and to a foretaste of the eternal and heavenly banquet. We believe, as we sing in the *Agnus Dei* accompanying the rite, that it is Christ broken on the cross which is the ultimate sign of God's mercy, and only with God in paradise will we know that true and divine peace.

To the Point

Christ's glorified body retained its woundedness. This is not only necessary for Thomas's belief, but stands as an example for each of us, called from our own imperfections to minister, teach, and heal.

Preparing to Proclaim, Preach, and Pray

Making Connections Between the Readings: For those who come to Mass only on Sundays, it's remarkable that the church would put this Sunday's first reading before them as the very next Scripture passage proclaimed following the resurrection, at least this year. In each cycle, the reading from Acts on this Second Sunday of Easter emphasizes unity within the nascent church; this pericope from chapter 4 is the strongest declaration of it. No one claiming personal possessions, no one going needy—the end of the passage sounds positively socialist, to use a modern political term.

It's unclear if there is any cause-effect relationship intended, but this reading (and those from the other cycles for today) also emphasizes the powerful proclamation of the resurrection and the quickly growing number of believers. One can imagine, at least, correlation intended by the author: that the love of God, manifest in the paschal mystery of Christ's death and resurrection, brings about both unity of believers and potent witness to that same love.

The epistles of John are preoccupied with both love and unity, like "a dog with a bone," as is sometimes said. The phrasing in our passage today might make a critical point hard to understand. "[T]he victory that conquers the world is our faith . . . the victor over the world [is] . . .the one who believes that Jesus is the Son of God." This victory is apparent in love and unity, bolstered by the Spirit who is truth.

Making Connections to the Responsorial Psalm: Psalm 118 continues today, the end of the Easter octave, though in a different permutation than at the Easter Vigil or Easter Day. While settings with the longer refrain of the Second Sunday of Easter are harder to find in the repertoire, it is worth seeking one out, rather than repeating "This is the day . . ." or using the Alleluia option.

As the refrain is the lens through which the rest of the text is seen, the words of gratitude for God's love are a necessary step beyond the praise from last Sunday. The text of the middle verse is not included in last week's texts either. It may seem inconsequential, but this set of words links more closely the salvation just won for us to our own trials and failings. Moving from kerygma to a deeper theology is an important aspect of these continuing weeks of Eastertide.

Psalm 118 will come to us again, in yet another form, in just a couple weeks—with again a different refrain as another lens.

CONNECTING TO EXPERIENCE: LIVING THE PASCHAL MYSTERY

We may be inclined to think Thomas is a failure. He doubts. He's suspicious. He's pessimistic. What pride must he harbor to ignore the testimony of those who *weren't* late for the party? But we learn a lot from Thomas. We learn that Christ Jesus still bears the wounds of his crucifixion. The passion was real, just as real as the resurrection. We also see God's mercy. Jesus does not respond with scorn to Thomas's skepticism. Jesus invites Thomas to look and feel again—and Thomas responds with a heart broken open. And we learn this: we do not have to see Jesus in order to know and believe in him. Jesus is ready for us to enter his heart just as he was ready for Thomas to place a hand in his side. We need only to believe and proclaim with our lives anointed by the Spirit in our baptism: "My Lord and my God!"

PROMPTS FOR FAITH-SHARING

- Like Thomas, did you ever feel left out or find yourself doubtful about an experience you didn't share?
- Like Thomas, are there times when you need clear evidence of Jesus's presence? If so, where do you find his presence?
- Do you have the faith to believe without seeing? How can you grow your confidence in Jesus's resurrected mercy?

Model Rite for the Blessing and Sprinkling of Water

Presider: In today's gospel, Jesus comes in the midst of his disciples and tells them, "Peace be with you." Let us open the doors of our hearts as we accept his invitation to receive his mercy . . . *[pause]*

[continue with The Roman Missal, *Appendix II]*

Model Universal Prayer (Prayer of the Faithful)

Presider: Believing in the wondrous power of God, we bring our prayers and petitions before him.

Response: Lord, hear our prayer.

For the church: may we become a community of believers of one heart and mind, growing in patience and holiness, we pray . . .

For leaders of nations: may their governing promote the care for the common good and protection of the innocent, we pray . . .

For those who are suffering: may they find comfort in the mystery of Christ and care in the love of their neighbors, we pray . . .

For all gathered here today: may we testify to the love of the Lord through our mercy toward those around us, we pray . . .

Presider: O God, when we love you and obey your commandments, we make you known throughout the world. May we follow you always, filled by your Spirit and testifying to your truth. We ask this through Christ our Lord. Amen.

Liturgy and Eastertide

Well before the arrival of Easter, we should ensure that the joy of Easter Day remains throughout the whole octave, ending today, and that the lengthy season of Easter continues to exude the joy and good news that Christ's resurrection brought to earth.

Hopefully you continued singing the Gloria at weekday Masses this past week! Preface I for Easter continues too, emphasizing the octave as, in essence, one grand (and long) Easter Day.

As the season continues, consider using the option for the sprinkling rite, with care not to conflate the sprinkling itself with the singing of the Gloria. Lest the Easter liturgies become too musically top-heavy—entrance hymn, sprinkling rite, and Gloria within minutes of one another—consider utilizing brief entrance antiphons for the season, paired with a favorite Alleluia of the assembly, or the appropriate *O filii et filiae* refrain.

Are additional flowers ordered for later in the season? If your budget allows, make sure to do so. The vibrant lilies of Easter Day will not last long no matter how well cared for, and the Fifth and Sixth Sundays of Easter (and beyond) should appear just as exuberant as the earliest days of the season.

COLLECT

Let us pray.

Pause for silent prayer

God of everlasting mercy,
who in the very recurrence of the paschal feast
kindle the faith of the people you have made your own,
increase, we pray, the grace you have bestowed,
that all may grasp and rightly understand
in what font they have been washed,
by whose Spirit they have been reborn,
by whose Blood they have been redeemed.
Through our Lord Jesus Christ, your Son,
who lives and reigns with you in the unity of the Holy Spirit,
God, for ever and ever. **Amen.**

FIRST READING

Acts 4:32-35

The community of believers was of one heart and mind,
and no one claimed that any of his possessions was his own,
but they had everything in common.
With great power the apostles bore witness
to the resurrection of the Lord Jesus,
and great favor was accorded them all.
There was no needy person among them,
for those who owned property or houses would sell them,
bring the proceeds of the sale,
and put them at the feet of the apostles,
and they were distributed to each according to need.

RESPONSORIAL PSALM

Ps 118:2-4, 13-15, 22-24

℟. (1) Give thanks to the Lord for he is good, his love is everlasting.
or:
℟. Alleluia.

Let the house of Israel say,
"His mercy endures forever."
Let the house of Aaron say,
"His mercy endures forever."
Let those who fear the LORD say,
"His mercy endures forever."

℟. Give thanks to the Lord for he is good, his love is everlasting.
or:
℟. Alleluia.

I was hard pressed and was falling,
but the LORD helped me.
My strength and my courage is the LORD,
and he has been my savior.
The joyful shout of victory
in the tents of the just.

℟. Give thanks to the Lord for he is good,
his love is everlasting.
or:
℟. Alleluia.

The stone which the builders rejected
has become the cornerstone.
By the LORD has this been done;
it is wonderful in our eyes.
This is the day the LORD has made;
let us be glad and rejoice in it.

℟. Give thanks to the Lord for he is good,
his love is everlasting.
or:
℟. Alleluia.

SECOND READING
1 John 5:1-6

Beloved:
Everyone who believes that Jesus is the
Christ is begotten by God,
and everyone who loves the Father
loves also the one begotten by him.
In this way we know that we love the
children of God
when we love God and obey his
commandments.
For the love of God is this,
that we keep his commandments.
And his commandments are not
burdensome,
for whoever is begotten by God
conquers the world.
And the victory that conquers the world is
our faith.
Who indeed is the victor over the world
but the one who believes that Jesus is
the Son of God?

This is the one who came through water
and blood, Jesus Christ,
not by water alone, but by water and
blood.
The Spirit is the one that testifies,
and the Spirit is truth.

Liturgical Ministers: Lectors

On this Sunday the word resounds with the risen Christ's greeting of peace. Lectors serve as the first heralds of that peace, proclaiming texts that remind the church that the resurrection is not an event locked in the past but a reality breaking into the present. Their ministry is more than reading aloud; it is a work of invitation. They lend their voices so that the word may pierce the assembly's fear and doubt, just as it did for the first disciples gathered in a locked room. Preparation for this ministry calls for prayerful reading, careful pacing, and a deep listening to the Spirit. A lector's posture, tone, and silence between phrases all form the community, helping them enter the word's mystery.
In proclaiming the Acts of the Apostles, lectors also testify to the church's life: a community marked by shared resources, bold witness, and a mission that continues today. Their service embodies synodality, showing that all ministers share in the church's mission to announce Christ risen and present in their midst.

Living Liturgy: The Preface of Easter II

The preface for this Sunday reminds us that Christ is the true Paschal Lamb who takes away the sins of the world and who by dying has destroyed death. These words frame the eucharistic prayer as a proclamation of salvation, connecting the church gathered today with the first believers who touched Christ's wounds and were sent forth in peace. The preface becomes an emphasis of faith, teaching that our worship is not a mere recollection but an encounter. As the priest lifts his hands in prayer, the assembly is drawn into a cosmic mystery that unites heaven and earth. The preface invites the faithful to see the Eucharist as the moment where resurrection power flows into their lives, sending them as witnesses of mercy. By praying these words together, the church learns to live the joy of Easter as a vocation, not just a season.

SPIRITUALITY

GOSPEL ACCLAMATION
John 1:14ab

℟. Alleluia, alleluia.
The Word of God became flesh and made his
dwelling among us;
and we saw his glory.
℟. Alleluia, alleluia.

Gospel

Luke 1:26-38; L545

The angel Gabriel was sent from God
to a town of Galilee called Nazareth,
to a virgin betrothed to a man named Joseph,
of the house of David,
and the virgin's name was Mary.
And coming to her, he said,
"Hail, full of grace! The Lord is with you."
But she was greatly troubled at what was said
and pondered what sort of greeting this might be.
Then the angel said to her,
"Do not be afraid, Mary,
for you have found favor with God.
Behold, you will conceive in your womb and bear a son,
and you shall name him Jesus.
He will be great and will be called Son of the Most High,
and the Lord God will give him the throne of David his father,
and he will rule over the house of Jacob forever,
and of his Kingdom there will be no end."
But Mary said to the angel,
"How can this be,
since I have no relations with a man?"
And the angel said to her in reply,
"The Holy Spirit will come upon you,
and the power of the Most High will overshadow you.

Continued in Appendix A, p. 302.
See Appendix A, p. 302, for the other readings.

Praying with Gospel Words and Phrases

This is the sixth month for her who was called barren . . .

Reflecting on the Gospel

The liturgical calendar and its various celebrations do not, as a rule, place us in a specific historical moment of time. That is, we don't celebrate Good Friday as if we are unaware that Easter Sunday follows closely behind. There is still, sometimes, a beautiful logic and humanness to the calendar, even if this year that logic doesn't quite hold.

March 25 as the usual date for this solemnity might seem a bit arbitrary, though today's gospel passage does indicate that the event happened sometime in the sixth month of the Hebrew calendar. However, let us ponder more of the liturgical year, principally that Christmas falls on December 25, nine months of pregnancy later, which in turn, in our reflection, suddenly can make Mary seem that much more human. Further, we are told that Elizabeth, Mary's elder cousin, is already in her sixth month of carrying John the Baptist in her womb. So it makes sense that the feast of the Nativity of John the Baptist is June 24. Note too that the feast of the Birth of Mary is on September 8, nine months following the Solemnity of the Immaculate Conception (which can be a helpful aid in the annual explaining of what the immaculate conception itself was!).

Of course, this year, the Annunciation is delayed because Holy Thursday landed on March 25 and took liturgical precedence, as did the rest of the Triduum, as well as the days of the octave of Easter. So does that mean all those other celebrations on the calendar have to shift as well? No, no, they will be celebrated when expected to be.

Sharper wits will also notice that this is about the 837th time this gospel passage has appeared at liturgy thus far this year. That which is important is emphasized by repetition, and it's a bit unique that the Annunciation happens within the Easter season, owing to how the date of Easter itself is calculated. Making connections between the two holidays of Christmas and Easter should be especially natural this time around. The annunciation is often seen as the true moment of incarnation, in utero. That God saved us by becoming one like us is a beautiful truth, worthy of contemplation today.

To the Point

Our church calendar is beautiful at times, and quirky at times—and today it's both! Emphasize the humanity of it as well as that of Mary, and the unique, intricate linking of incarnation and resurrection today.

Model Penitential Act

Presider: In today's gospel, Mary is encouraged to not be afraid. Let us dispel fear from our own hearts as we come before the Lord asking for his pardon and peace . . . *[pause]*

Lord Jesus, you are giver of mercy and of life: Lord, have mercy.
Christ Jesus, you reign in the kingdom that has no end: Christ, have mercy.
Lord Jesus, you call us to be your children in baptism and grace: Lord, have mercy.

COLLECT

Let us pray.

Pause for silent prayer

O God, who willed that your Word
should take on the reality of human flesh
in the womb of the Virgin Mary,
grant, we pray,
that we, who confess our Redeemer to be God and man,
may merit to become partakers even in his divine nature.
Who lives and reigns with you in the unity of the Holy Spirit,
God, for ever and ever. **Amen.**

Model Universal Prayer (Prayer of the Faithful)

Presider: Placing our hope in the Lord with whom all things are possible, we present our prayers and petitions.

Response: Lord, hear our prayer.

For Pope N. and for all Christian leaders: may they trust in the Holy Spirit as the Blessed Virgin Mary did, we pray . . .

For our politicians, our policymakers, and our public servants: may they always seek to protect the most poor and vulnerable, we pray . . .

For those who are suffering in mind, body, or spirit: may their hopes for healing be answered with grace, we pray . . .

For us gathered here this day: may we grow and remain steadfast in our life of prayer, we pray . . .

Presider: O God, you sent your angel to your servant Mary to bear glad tidings of your Son. May we who know him through word and sacrament come to trust more deeply in your providence. We ask this through Christ our Lord. **Amen.**

Liturgical Ministers: Music Ministers

This feast reveals that God's plan of salvation unfolds through Mary's consent, and it invites music ministers to consider how their ministry also participates in God's ongoing work. Their service is not simply leading song but helping the assembly listen for the Word that became flesh. Mary's response, offered in humility and trust, models the disposition needed for this ministry: openness to the Spirit and a willingness to serve as an instrument rather than the focus. Music ministers are called to interior formation, growing in contemplation and theological depth so that every note they lead flows from prayer. The annunciation reminds them that God works through willing hearts, often in quiet ways. Their ministry forms the assembly's imagination, teaching that music is a language of faith that reveals mystery. In embracing this calling, music ministers join Mary's song, magnifying the Lord not for their own glory but with lives rooted in obedience and love.

Living Liturgy: The Gospel Proclamation

When the angel's greeting to Mary is proclaimed, the church hears not only a story from the past but a word addressed to us. The liturgy invites believers to receive this announcement with the same openness Mary showed. Her "yes" is a model of discipleship, teaching that salvation is welcomed, not achieved. Every Eucharist echoes this mystery, as the Word becomes flesh among us and dwells within us. The annunciation forms us to approach the altar with the same reverence and trust, ready to carry Christ into the world as Mary did.

SPIRITUALITY

GOSPEL ACCLAMATION
cf. Luke 24:32

℟. Alleluia, alleluia.
Lord Jesus, open the Scriptures to us;
make our hearts burn while you speak to us.
℟. Alleluia, alleluia.

Gospel

Luke 24:35-48; L47B

The two disciples recounted what had taken place on the way,
and how Jesus was made known to them
in the breaking of bread.

While they were still speaking about this,
he stood in their midst and said to them,
"Peace be with you."
But they were startled and terrified
and thought that they were seeing a ghost.
Then he said to them, "Why are you troubled?
And why do questions arise in your hearts?
Look at my hands and my feet, that it is I myself.
Touch me and see, because a ghost does not have flesh and bones
as you can see I have."
And as he said this,
he showed them his hands and his feet.
While they were still incredulous for joy and were amazed,
he asked them, "Have you anything here to eat?"
They gave him a piece of baked fish;
he took it and ate it in front of them.

He said to them,
"These are my words that I spoke to you while I was still with you,
that everything written about me in the law of Moses
and in the prophets and psalms must be fulfilled."

Continued in Appendix A, p. 303.

Praying with Gospel Words and Phrases

You are witnesses of these things . . .

Reflecting on the Gospel

One can employ a variety of words to speak of what liturgy is and how it accomplishes what it does. For instance, the liturgy is catechetical, performative, sacrificial, sustaining, and/or formative (and so much more), depending on which facet one wants to dig deeper into and give closer attention to.

The Scriptures today should remind us to pay attention to how our liturgies are evangelical; that is, how (and how well) our liturgies preach the good news, both to those we see every week in the pew and those we have not seen before. Up until now, the good news of Christ's resurrection was primarily shared among friends and relatives, a very close circle of those who surrounded Jesus himself during his three years of ministry. We are at a "hinge" moment of the narrative, and of our Easter season, when Christ, in the last line of the gospel, reminds the apostles that it is their ministry, foretold by the prophets, to share the joy of the resurrection and forgiveness of sins with all nations. The reading from Acts shows Peter, boldly, doing just that.

We too must consider how we do that ourselves. It is far too simple—some would call it a cop-out—to consider only words, only language when evaluating these efforts. Words, for instance, in homilies and hymns, pale in comparison to *how* it is we preach and *how* it is the music ministry is led. If we wish our assemblies to continue living the faith outside the doors of the church building the other six days and twenty-three hours of their week, the church's ministers must show them in action how to do that during that one hour.

The tone of the preaching and presiding must be joyful, without sacrificing reverence. It must seem as if the celebrant has no choice but to proclaim the risen Christ and the difference that makes in day-to-day living. Music must be led invitingly, by action reminding the congregation that the sung liturgy is their responsibility! Texts of both preaching and music must not only themselves evangelize, but spur others on to that same holy activity in the world—not just among their friends and relatives, their closest circle, but among all those who need to hear good news, every minute of every day.

To the Point

Being witnesses of the risen Lord means that *how* we share the good news must be consistent with the good news itself!

Preparing to Proclaim, Preach, and Pray

Making Connections Between the Readings: As we continue through the Acts of the Apostles, Peter is turning his attention to "the people" and more broadly sharing his witness to the resurrection. "The people," in this case, are Jews in Jerusalem gathering for prayer, who have just witnessed a man, crippled from birth, being healed. Peter, "in the name of Jesus Christ the Nazorean" (Acts 3:6), bids the man rise and walk. The healing power of Christ is present, even if Christ himself is not bodily so: the man is indeed healed. This causes a stir, and as people gather around, Peter addresses them.

He seems to chastise them for their denial of Jesus during his passion; one can imagine that not being well-received. In the continuing passage beyond our pericope, Peter and John are eventually arrested for proclaiming the resurrection—but, at the same time, "many of those who heard the word came to believe and [the] number of men grew to [about] five thousand" (Acts 4:4).

John's epistle today has at its core this truth about Jesus: "He is expiation for our sins, and not for our sins only but for those of the whole world." Peter healing this man in Jesus's name is an initial outward sign of that saving power growing beyond apostles and disciples, beyond Jews and Jerusalem: soon, to the entire world.

Making Connections to the Responsorial Psalm: Psalm 4 isn't seen at the eucharistic liturgy very often. In fact, it's just twice: today (every three years, anyway), and on Tuesday of the Tenth Week of Ordinary Time, Cycle B. On that day, the first reading tells of Elijah asking the widow, short on oil and flour, to make him a cake. The oil and flour last for a year instead of a day, fulfilling the powerful promise of the Lord. Psalm 4 is also sometimes used at Compline (Night Prayer) where its concluding verses are seen as a metaphor for death and trust in God.

In each of these contexts, reliance on the providence of God is apparent. God sustains the widow and her son for a year, God keeps us safe during the night and even in death, and, in the verses that precede today's reading from Acts, God makes whole the crippled man, giving him new and abundant life.

CONNECTING TO EXPERIENCE: LIVING THE PASCHAL MYSTERY

No matter how many times we encounter the Lord, he surprises us when he comes in our midst. Should we be surprised that the disciples who met him along the way, even with his words still ringing in their ears, are startled and terrified? How many times do we need to hear his word and encounter his presence before we simply gaze at him with joy, as the angels might? Jesus invites us to encounter him again and again, beginning in our baptism and every day of our lives, in the Scripture, in the sacraments, and in one another. When we gather together in prayer and sacrament, Jesus comes among us. He opens the Scriptures and breaks the bread. Are we surprised? Will we encounter him today in the word proclaimed and preached? Will we encounter him today in his body and blood, broken and shared for us? Do we believe that we are called to be his body in the world?

PROMPTS FOR FAITH-SHARING

- Has Jesus ever surprised you by meeting you along your way?
- Do you ever have trouble recognizing Jesus in your midst? What prompts you to notice that Jesus is there?
- Have you ever felt your heart burning within you? If you have, what was that feeling about? If you have not, how can you allow God to enkindle that feeling in your life?

Model Rite for the Blessing and Sprinkling of Water

Presider: Today, the risen Lord appears to his disciples to dispel their fears and offer them peace. Let us open our hearts before him asking for his mercy, as we prepare to celebrate these sacred mysteries . . . *[pause]*

[continue with The Roman Missal, *Appendix II]*

Model Universal Prayer (Prayer of the Faithful)

Presider: We trust that the Lord does wonders for his faithful, and hears all who call upon him. Let us come before him with joy and hope as we bring our prayers and petitions.

Response: Lord, hear our prayer.

For the church this Easter season, and for our Orthodox brothers and sisters throughout the world: may we rejoice together in the glory of the Risen Lord, we pray . . .

For nations throughout the world, especially those whose citizens lack security, confidence, and peace: may their leaders reject corruption and seek righteousness, we pray . . .

For refugees and migrants who are afraid for their safety and the safety of their loved ones: may they feel Christ's presence in the support of those who help them, we pray . . .

For all gathered here, especially those who have received the sacraments of initiation during this Easter season: may they find continued strength in their new life in Christ, we pray . . .

Presider: O God, you made your justice known through the paschal mystery of your Son, Jesus Christ. May we rejoice in your love this Easter season, and make your salvation known as we work for justice throughout the world. We ask this through Christ our Lord. Amen.

Liturgy and Music

A gentle melody which perfectly matches its text is "Partners in the Mission" (WLP) by Peter Hesed. It serves today's Scriptures well by inviting those who sing it to loving service, acknowledging the fear we might have, calmed by Christ's easy and light yoke.

The *Psallite* refrain "Shout to the Ends of the Earth" (Liturgical Press) prefigures in a way the ascension commission, with bouncy Alleluias that send us forth, people redeemed by the Lord to proclaim the kingdom of God.

For music that speaks more about the good news being proclaimed, a hymn that might need a reintroduction to your community is "Priestly People" (WLP) by Lucien Deiss. "Out of Darkness" (OCP) by Christopher Walker can also festively speak to both witnessing and being proclaimed, if your performing forces are adequate and well-prepared.

(continued on next page)

COLLECT

Let us pray.

Pause for silent prayer

May your people exult for ever, O God,
in renewed youthfulness of spirit,
so that, rejoicing now in the restored glory
of our adoption,
we may look forward in confident hope
to the rejoicing of the day of resurrection.
Through our Lord Jesus Christ, your Son,
who lives and reigns with you in the unity
of the Holy Spirit,
God, for ever and ever. **Amen.**

FIRST READING

Acts 3:13-15, 17-19

Peter said to the people:
"The God of Abraham,
the God of Isaac, and the God of Jacob,
the God of our fathers, has glorified his
servant Jesus,
whom you handed over and denied in
Pilate's presence
when he had decided to release him.
You denied the Holy and Righteous One
and asked that a murderer be released
to you.
The author of life you put to death,
but God raised him from the dead; of
this we are witnesses.
Now I know, brothers,
that you acted out of ignorance, just as
your leaders did;
but God has thus brought to fulfillment
what he had announced beforehand
through the mouth of all the prophets,
that his Christ would suffer.
Repent, therefore, and be converted, that
your sins may be wiped away."

RESPONSORIAL PSALM

Ps 4:2, 4, 7-8, 9

℟. (7a) Lord, let your face shine on us.
or:
℟. Alleluia.

When I call, answer me, O my just God,
you who relieve me when I am in
distress;
have pity on me, and hear my prayer!

℟. Lord, let your face shine on us.
or:
℟. Alleluia.

Know that the LORD does wonders for his
faithful one;
the LORD will hear me when I call upon
him.

℟. Lord, let your face shine on us.
or:
℟. Alleluia.

O LORD, let the light of your countenance
shine upon us!
You put gladness into my heart.

℟. Lord, let your face shine on us.
or:
℟. Alleluia.

As soon as I lie down, I fall peacefully
asleep,
for you alone, O LORD,
bring security to my dwelling.

℟. Lord, let your face shine on us.
or:
℟. Alleluia.

SECOND READING
1 John 2:1-5a

My children, I am writing this to you
so that you may not commit sin.
But if anyone does sin, we have an
Advocate with the Father,
Jesus Christ the righteous one.
He is expiation for our sins,
and not for our sins only but for those
of the whole world.
The way we may be sure that we know
him is to keep
his commandments.
Those who say, "I know him," but do not
keep his commandments
are liars, and the truth is not in them.
But whoever keeps his word,
the love of God is truly perfected in him.

Some will note that the Liturgy of the Word is only one place we find Scripture at liturgy: the prayers of the liturgy often have scriptural underpinnings ("enter under my roof . . ." [Matt 8:8]) and the various antiphons are almost entirely scriptural as well. For those picking hymnody week to week, much if not sole attention is given to the Scripture proclaimed. Don't forget to also study and pray with the prescribed prayers and antiphons of each celebration. Doing so may provide unexpected insights and point you toward unanticipated musical treasures!

Liturgical Ministers: Music Ministers

The gospel this Sunday recounts the risen Christ opening the Scriptures and breaking bread with his disciples, a moment of recognition that becomes central to Christian worship. Music ministers help the community experience this same encounter, not by drawing attention to themselves but by shaping prayer through sound. Their work begins long before the liturgy: selecting music rooted in Scripture and tradition, rehearsing with care, and praying with the texts they will sing. In the liturgy, their leadership draws the assembly into a deeper participation in the mystery being celebrated. The Easter season calls for music that is jubilant without being hurried, inviting contemplation even in moments of joy. This ministry requires attentiveness, humility, and collaboration with clergy and other ministers, reflecting the synodal vision of a church walking together. Music ministers help the faithful understand that song is a form of proclamation and catechesis, echoing the gospel itself that Christ is recognized in the breaking of bread, and our voices join that witness.

Living Liturgy: The Gloria

On this Sunday, the Gloria resounds again, filling the church with the joy of resurrection. Far from a routine hymn, it is a proclamation of salvation, echoing the angels' song at Christ's birth and the victory over death revealed at Easter. Singing the Gloria after weeks of Lenten silence awakens the community to the transformation wrought by Christ. Its structure itself becomes a form of mystagogy: praise of God's majesty, confession of Christ as Lord and Lamb, and a doxology glorifying the Trinity. As the assembly stands and sings, they enter into the worship of heaven, joining angels and saints in a hymn that transcends time. The Gloria teaches the faithful that Christian joy is not naïve but rooted in the paschal mystery. It is sung even as the wounds of Christ remain visible, a sign that hope is stronger than suffering. Each repetition during the Easter season deepens this lesson, inviting believers to live out what they sing: that glory is given to God in every act of daily life.

SPIRITUALITY

GOSPEL ACCLAMATION
John 10:14

℟. Alleluia, alleluia.
I am the good shepherd, says the Lord;
I know my sheep, and mine know me.
℟. Alleluia, alleluia.

Gospel

John 10:11-18; L50B

Jesus said:
"I am the good shepherd.
A good shepherd lays down his life for the sheep.
A hired man, who is not a shepherd
and whose sheep are not his own,
sees a wolf coming and leaves the sheep and runs away,
and the wolf catches and scatters them.
This is because he works for pay and has no concern for the sheep.
I am the good shepherd,
and I know mine and mine know me,
just as the Father knows me and I know the Father;
and I will lay down my life for the sheep.
I have other sheep that do not belong to this fold.
These also I must lead, and they will hear my voice,
and there will be one flock, one shepherd.
This is why the Father loves me,
because I lay down my life in order to take it up again.
No one takes it from me, but I lay it down on my own.
I have power to lay it down, and power to take it up again.
This command I have received from my Father."

Praying with Gospel Words and Phrases
I am the good shepherd . . . I will lay down my life for the sheep . . .

Reflecting on the Gospel
Though the imagery is not as prevalent in this cycle of readings, it is still Good Shepherd Sunday, the gospel reminds us. While we might wish to imagine the good shepherd as the one who, upon finding the lost sheep, lovingly hoists it over his shoulders to bring it back to the other ninety-nine, this is not the shepherd Jesus speaks of today. This good shepherd has to protect the flock from wolves—and lays down his life to do so.

While at the parish level, the good shepherd is of course the pastor, many who coordinate liturgical ministries have, in a way, a small subset of that community under our care. Perhaps we are choir directors, or coordinate altar servers, lectors, extraordinary ministers, hospitality ministers, or others. Part of how we exercise such leadership should be as a pastor, as a good shepherd does. This can become manifest in at least two ways: by leading through service and by truly knowing those we serve.

If all we do at rehearsal is learn notes, if all we do at our desk is type up schedules, our ministry is hollow and does not truly serve the ministers. Make sure to share with those you coordinate materials that can help them spiritually reflect on their roles and feed their spirits. Plan retreat days for them; recommission them yearly within a Sunday Eucharist. If they have suggestions or concerns, truly listen to them. Don't just respond to what a specific complaint might be, but spend a moment to investigate what motivates the report, what factors into the person coming to you with the issue at hand.

All of that is easier to do if, as Jesus describes himself in today's gospel, we too get to know "our sheep." If the only time you encounter your liturgical ministers is at Mass or at rehearsals or trainings, that too is hollow. In addition to the retreat days mentioned above, also plan social gatherings from time to time. Encourage one another to live the gospel by planning days of service together.

To the Point
Above all, be attentive to the needs of each person individually, and encourage the small community to rally around someone—in turn it will be each of us—who needs the loving support of the Christian community surrounding them. All of this is a small part of truly being a good shepherd here and now.

Preparing to Proclaim, Preach, and Pray

Making Connections Between the Readings: Today's passage from Acts skips ahead a bit from last week's verses. But Peter is still speaking of the miraculous healing from last week, rightly pointing to the One who accomplished the healing. It is not Peter himself, but Christ working through him. Peter quotes the familiar excerpt from Psalm 118 when describing Jesus and his relationship to those who not only rejected him in life but seem also to reject the resurrection and his continuing healing power.

John speaks today of our status as adopted children of God, continuing our slow approach during Eastertide of the gospel message being spread more broadly among a wider diversity of people. Just as sheep are tended to by the good shepherd, here God, as a parent, cares for his children with great love.

Both readings speak of transformational resurrection: Jesus, raised from the dead, gives all the faithful the gift of becoming transformed upon our death and reunification with God, when "we shall be like him, for we shall see him as he is."

Making Connections to the Responsorial Psalm: Psalm 118, as previously promised, is again heard this Sunday as an echo of Peter in the first reading. Make sure to find yet another setting so that the proper refrain is placed on the assembly's lips, reinterpreting these verses heard so many times already.

Does everyone know what a cornerstone is and its importance in construction? Many churches rightly have their cornerstone inscribed with the name of the parish and the date of construction, even if with more modern construction the cornerstone is more symbolic. Perhaps include an image of a cornerstone—your parish's or another—in the weekly bulletin!

CONNECTING TO EXPERIENCE: LIVING THE PASCHAL MYSTERY

Jesus is the Good Shepherd. First of all, this means that he is *good.* He ardently seeks the members of his flock, even when they are smelly, wander, or foolishly run away. Jesus is also a *shepherd.* He has taken upon himself work that is tiring, tedious, and often afforded little respect. But Jesus wants to tend to us; he is not like the hired hand who works only for compensation. Jesus loves us.

He wants to find those who are lost. Like a good shepherd who would lay down in the dirt in front of the sheep's pen to bar the attack of thieves and predators, Jesus lays down his life to lead us out of harm. A good shepherd protects the sheep from becoming an easy meal.

The Good Shepherd protects us from being consumed by sin and death.

The Good Shepherd leads us to new life.

PROMPTS FOR FAITH-SHARING

- What part of you feels lost? How can Jesus help you find it?
- Are you hiding from Christ? Are you hoping he doesn't find you? Why?
- Can you make space for Christ, so that he can protect you? Do others in your life need you, likewise, to protect them?

Model Rite for the Blessing and Sprinkling of Water

Presider: The Lord is the Good Shepherd who lays down his life for his sheep. Let us listen to his voice, coming before him for his pardon and peace . . . *[pause]*

[continue with The Roman Missal, *Appendix II]*

Model Universal Prayer (Prayer of the Faithful)

Presider: The Lord, the rock of our salvation, hears our cries and showers us with his eternal graces. Let us offer our needs and petitions to him this day.

Response: Lord, hear our prayer.

For Pope N. and all the bishops of the church: may they lead with the humility and steadfastness of shepherds, we pray . . .

For the leaders of nations: may they steward their people with loving care, we pray . . .

For local civic officials: may they embrace their office as an opportunity for service, we pray . . .

For those gathered here: may the light of the resurrection inspire us to faithful service of our neighbors, we pray . . .

Presider: Loving God, you care for your flock with tenderness and joy. Hear our prayers, which we humbly offer to you. We ask this through Christ our Lord. Amen.

Liturgy and Psalmody

While at each Mass we of course attend to singing the responsorial psalm, we ought not be afraid to include psalmody elsewhere during the liturgy. The prescribed antiphons in the missal are often themselves psalms, or at least scriptural. Further, these antiphons are intended not to be sung on their own, as seems often to be the current practice. Rather, they are meant to be paired with psalmody and returned to every few verses.

Much of our contemporary hymnody already has that form, of course. Consider the familiar James Moore Jr. setting of Psalm 34, "Taste and See" (OCP), which textually is more or less the equivalent of the prescribed communion antiphon for the Fourteenth Sunday in Ordinary Time. Other parallels exist for the other antiphons of Mass as well.

I mention this here because Good Shepherd Sunday is a good Sunday to sing a lot of psalms! While settings of Psalm 23 abound, don't forget about Psalm 100, "We are his people, the flock he shepherds" (v. 3c). "All People That on Earth Do Dwell" is a paraphrase of the beginning of that psalm and is found in many hymnals. Francis Patrick O'Brien's "Shepherd of My Heart" (GIA) might be a hidden gem waiting to be uncovered, or rediscovered! Note too that the first reading and psalm bring back the imagery of the rejected cornerstone, so don't be afraid to revisit a favorite Psalm 118 setting from the Easter Vigil or Easter Day celebrations.

COLLECT

Let us pray.

Pause for silent prayer

Almighty ever-living God,
lead us to a share in the joys of heaven,
so that the humble flock may reach
where the brave Shepherd has gone before.
Who lives and reigns with you in the unity
of the Holy Spirit,
God, for ever and ever. **Amen.**

FIRST READING

Acts 4:8-12

Peter, filled with the Holy Spirit, said:
"Leaders of the people and elders:
If we are being examined today
about a good deed done to a cripple,
namely, by what means he was saved,
then all of you and all the people of
Israel should know
that it was in the name of Jesus Christ
the Nazorean
whom you crucified, whom God raised
from the dead;
in his name this man stands before you
healed.
He is *the stone rejected by you, the builders,*
which has become the cornerstone.
There is no salvation through anyone else,
nor is there any other name under
heaven
given to the human race by which we
are to be saved."

RESPONSORIAL PSALM

Ps 118:1, 8-9, 21-23, 26, 28, 29

℟. (22) The stone rejected by the builders
has become the cornerstone.
or:
℟. Alleluia.

Give thanks to the LORD, for he is good,
for his mercy endures forever.
It is better to take refuge in the LORD
than to trust in man.
It is better to take refuge in the LORD
than to trust in princes.

℟. The stone rejected by the builders has
become the cornerstone.
or:
℟. Alleluia.

I will give thanks to you, for you have
answered me
and have been my savior.
The stone which the builders rejected
has become the cornerstone.
By the LORD has this been done;
it is wonderful in our eyes.

℟. The stone rejected by the builders has become the cornerstone.
or:
℟. Alleluia.

Blessed is he who comes in the name of the LORD;
we bless you from the house of the LORD.
I will give thanks to you, for you have answered me
and have been my savior.
Give thanks to the LORD, for he is good;
for his kindness endures forever.

℟. The stone rejected by the builders has become the cornerstone.
or:
℟. Alleluia.

SECOND READING
1 John 3:1-2

Beloved:
See what love the Father has bestowed on us
that we may be called the children of God.
Yet so we are.
The reason the world does not know us
is that it did not know him.
Beloved, we are God's children now;
what we shall be has not yet been revealed.
We do know that when it is revealed we shall be like him,
for we shall see him as he is.

Liturgical Ministers: Eucharistic Ministers

On Good Shepherd Sunday, the image of Christ who knows and calls each of his sheep offers a deeper lens for those who serve at the altar. Eucharistic ministers are called not only to serve but to be formed by the mystery they handle. The Eucharist is the church's heartbeat; ministers are entrusted with more than a role. They are invited to cultivate a spirituality of presence, and prayer that radiates beyond the liturgy. Serving at the altar begins in personal prayer with Scripture, allowing the word to shape one's way of seeing others. Eucharistic ministry calls for interior transformation deepening one's humility, patience, and awe before the mystery. Ministers become witnesses to the Eucharist in their daily lives, carrying Christ's presence into workplaces, families, and communities. Formation for this ministry is lifelong, rooted in study of the Mass, theology of Real Presence, and an understanding of the Eucharist as mission. To serve at the altar is to be drawn into Christ's shepherding love, which seeks out and heals the lost. Ministers embody that love not only in ritual moments but in their daily encounters, extending eucharistic hospitality into every sphere of life.

Living Liturgy: The Gospel Acclamation

The Alleluia that precedes the gospel on this Sunday does more than herald the gospel. It is an exclamation of wonder that shapes how we hear God's word. In Eastertide, this simple chant carries the church's entire proclamation that Christ is risen and speaks to his people now. On Good Shepherd Sunday, the Alleluia opens our hearts to hear the voice of the Shepherd who calls us by name. It reminds us that every gospel reading is an encounter with the living Christ, not a historical retelling. Rising and singing Alleluia becomes an act of discipleship, proclaiming our readiness to follow wherever he leads. This acclamation, brief as it is, trains us to approach Scripture with reverence and joy, to listen not as passive hearers but as followers who recognize the Shepherd's voice and respond with faith.

SPIRITUALITY

GOSPEL ACCLAMATION
John 15:4a, 5b

℟. Alleluia, alleluia.
Remain in me as I remain in you, says the Lord.
Whoever remains in me will bear much fruit.
℟. Alleluia, alleluia.

Gospel

John 15:1-8; L53B

Jesus said to his disciples:
"I am the true vine, and my Father is the vine grower.
He takes away every branch in me that does not bear fruit,
and every one that does he prunes so that it bears more fruit.
You are already pruned because of the word that I spoke to you.
Remain in me, as I remain in you.
Just as a branch cannot bear fruit on its own
unless it remains on the vine,
so neither can you unless you remain in me.
I am the vine, you are the branches.
Whoever remains in me and I in him will bear much fruit,
because without me you can do nothing.
Anyone who does not remain in me
will be thrown out like a branch and wither;
people will gather them and throw them into a fire
and they will be burned.
If you remain in me and my words remain in you,
ask for whatever you want and it will be done for you.
By this is my Father glorified,
that you bear much fruit and become my disciples."

Praying with Gospel Words and Phrases

I am the vine, you are the branches . . . he prunes so that it bears more fruit . . .

Reflecting on the Gospel

Is the hectic pace brought about by the continuing Eastertide colliding with the ending months of the academic year starting to take its toll yet? Along with the usual Sunday to Sunday routines, the church asks us to participate in *mystagogia* with the neophytes, and to help our younger parishioners encounter the Lord and complete their own initiations through First Eucharist and confirmation. Your parish school might have you preparing for year-end celebrations, a matrimony rush is just about to begin, and of course there are also three funerals this week. Is that the light at the end of the tunnel, or the train coming to run me over?

Today's gospel offers some lessons for ecclesial ministers, especially those charged with great responsibilities of one sort or another this time of year. First, Jesus reminds us that sometimes his Father prunes the vine, so that it may bear more fruit. If you are feeling particularly stretched this year, it may be time for some pruning. A time of stress and anxiety is not conducive to clearheaded decision-making, so consider starting a list, perhaps on a smartphone or in a little notebook in your pocket or purse, of the various responsibilities and tasks you have to do each day. In a month or two, look at that list and see where opportunities may exist to prune the vine.
A reminder here that perhaps a pruning may not be completely up to you. Be prepared for some initial pain amid the pruning as well, trusting the Lord that more abundant fruit lies ahead.

It may be that it seems impossible in your current context to prune the vine. Perhaps you are in a paid ministerial role that is too demanding of time and resources, yet the job description places all the various responsibilities on your shoulders. Or perhaps you place all the burden on your own shoulders: "When I do it myself, I can do it quicker, and I can do it better." If so, it is likely past time to evaluate your ability to delegate and to make better use of the main resource available to you, that is, God's people in your very community.

To the Point

Sometimes we, the branches, need pruning so that our lives of faith may be more fruitful. Discerning the times and places of pruning demands prayer and reflection. Sometimes the pruning happens unexpectedly—this too demands prayer and reflection.

Preparing to Proclaim, Preach, and Pray

Making Connections Between the Readings: Without warning, Acts has now jumped several chapters ahead. We have, for now, left Peter behind and are jumping into the scene at the tail end of the conversion of Saul. The great persecutor of the early church is soon transformed into its greatest evangelist. The good news of Jesus Christ is about to explode upon the waiting world now that Saul has been grafted onto the true vine and can begin bearing much fruit.

If Paul was the greatest evangelist by his words both spoken and written, John urges us to spread the gospel message of love in "deed and truth." If our actions keep the command of Christ to love one another as he loved (and loves!) us, then like a branch of the vine, we "remain in him, and he in them," and we will know that because of the Spirit. We will hear much more about this in coming weeks.

Recall that just a few weeks ago we pondered that *how* our words are imparted—in homilies, music, and more—is just as important as the words themselves, if not more. Our actions, our deeds indeed show others more obviously and directly that we are branches of the true vine, especially when they reveal that we truly live what we believe. This includes any words about our faith that we speak or sing.

Making Connections to the Responsorial Psalm: While none of the text repeats, it's likely worth pointing out to your psalmist, your choir, and even your congregations that today's verses from Psalm 22 pick up roughly from where the section from Palm Sunday just a few weeks ago left off. You will recall that that portion was a journey from despair and supplication to trust and hope.

Today that trust and hope now become praise and proclamation. God is generous and worthy of adulation, publicly and strongly. Let all coming generations know of God's enduring justice and might! Let the good news be shared across not just space but also time: "May your hearts live forever!"

CONNECTING TO EXPERIENCE: LIVING THE PASCHAL MYSTERY

A branch cut off from the rest of the plant—be it a daffodil or a dogwood—is just a branch. It might serve a decorative function for a few days, but the branch is dead. A cut branch has no way to be fed with food and water and has ceased to gather light. This is who we are when we cut ourselves off from our relationship with Christ. We have no food to feed us, no water to liven us, no light to animate us. After Jesus's glorious resurrection and ascension, the first Christians faced great challenges, from disbelief and fear to attacks and attempts to destroy. They risked being cut off—from life in the synagogue, their communities, or even life itself. Yet they chose to remain in Christ. We are called to do likewise, to come, remain in him, and be filled. To be filled is to remain alive, full of the light, the food, and the love of Christ Jesus.

PROMPTS FOR FAITH-SHARING

- Are you, or someone you know, feeling cut off from Christ? Why so?
- Are you, or someone you know, trying to grow without a vine, without rootedness in God's food?
- How can you, like the branch of an apple tree, seek to be grafted to Christ more completely this week? What can you do to make a stronger bind?

Model Rite for the Blessing and Sprinkling of Water

Presider: Jesus calls us to remain in him as he remains in us. Let us acknowledge our sins, allowing his mercy and love to reign in our hearts . . . *[pause]*

[continue with The Roman Missal, *Appendix II]*

Model Universal Prayer (Prayer of the Faithful)

Presider: Let us have confidence in the Lord as we come before him with our prayers and petitions.

Response: Lord, hear our prayer.

For the church this Easter season: may we be filled with new peace and the unity to which your Son calls us, we pray . . .

For all nations, especially those suffering from conflict and violence: may they find justice and protection in you, we pray . . .

For all who have been baptized, confirmed, and have received their first Eucharist this Easter season: may they be filled with the grace of Christ and find confidence in their new life of faith, we pray . . .

For our community assembled here today: may we find assurance that God is greater than our hearts can imagine, we pray . . .

Presider: God our Father, your Son gave us your command to love one another as he has loved us. May we keep your command to love, and allow the Spirit he gave us to dwell more deeply within us. We ask this through Christ our Lord. Amen.

Liturgy and Delegation

With some amount of "heavy lifting" at the outset, setting in place a networked, trained, and empowered team of ministry coordinators can very much lighten the load on any one person, and help give a sense of ownership and mission to a larger percentage of the parishioners. There are many ways to tackle any responsibility and ensure that an array of ministry goals are met. The path that includes and enlarges the Body of Christ will never be the wrong one to take, if travelled carefully and honestly.

"Newbies" at liturgical coordination especially will often feel all the responsibility for all the things that fall on their shoulders—and that's not wrong. The distinction is that, while the responsibility may be there, the "doing" does not need to be—should not be. You don't have to train and schedule the servers yourself, for instance; you *do* have to ensure that it happens, and you can find a volunteer or two to take care of that for you and for the whole parish. Good communication will be necessary, and formation. The parish as a whole will be stronger and more vibrant the more that parishioners are involved and invested!

COLLECT

Let us pray.

Pause for silent prayer

Almighty ever-living God,
constantly accomplish the Paschal
Mystery within us,
that those you were pleased to make new
in Holy Baptism
may, under your protective care, bear
much fruit
and come to the joys of life eternal.
Through our Lord Jesus Christ, your Son,
who lives and reigns with you in the unity
of the Holy Spirit,
God, for ever and ever. **Amen.**

FIRST READING

Acts 9:26-31

When Saul arrived in Jerusalem he tried to
join the disciples,
but they were all afraid of him,
not believing that he was a disciple.
Then Barnabas took charge of him and
brought him to the apostles,
and he reported to them how he had
seen the Lord,
and that he had spoken to him,
and how in Damascus he had spoken
out boldly in the name of Jesus.
He moved about freely with them in
Jerusalem,
and spoke out boldly in the name of the
Lord.
He also spoke and debated with the
Hellenists,
but they tried to kill him.
And when the brothers learned of this,
they took him down to Caesarea
and sent him on his way to Tarsus.

The church throughout all Judea, Galilee,
and Samaria was at peace.
It was being built up and walked in the
fear of the Lord,
and with the consolation of the Holy
Spirit it grew in numbers.

RESPONSORIAL PSALM

Ps 22:26-27, 28, 30, 31-32

℟. (26a) I will praise you, Lord, in the
assembly of your people.
or: ℟. Alleluia.

I will fulfill my vows before those who fear
the LORD.
The lowly shall eat their fill;

they who seek the LORD shall praise him:
"May your hearts live forever!"

℟. I will praise you, Lord, in the assembly of your people. *or:* ℟. Alleluia.

All the ends of the earth
shall remember and turn to the LORD;
all the families of the nations
shall bow down before him.

℟. I will praise you, Lord, in the assembly of your people. *or:* ℟. Alleluia.

To him alone shall bow down
all who sleep in the earth;
before him shall bend
all who go down into the dust.

℟. I will praise you, Lord, in the assembly of your people. *or:* ℟. Alleluia.

And to him my soul shall live;
my descendants shall serve him.
Let the coming generation be told of the LORD
that they may proclaim to a people yet to be born
the justice he has shown.

℟. I will praise you, Lord, in the assembly of your people. *or:* ℟. Alleluia.

SECOND READING
1 John 3:18-24

Children, let us love not in word or speech
but in deed and truth.
Now this is how we shall know that we belong to the truth
and reassure our hearts before him
in whatever our hearts condemn,
for God is greater than our hearts and knows everything.
Beloved, if our hearts do not condemn us,
we have confidence in God
and receive from him whatever we ask,
because we keep his commandments
and do what pleases him.
And his commandment is this:
we should believe in the name of his Son, Jesus Christ,
and love one another just as he commanded us.
Those who keep his commandments
remain in him, and he in them,
and the way we know that he remains in us
is from the Spirit he gave us.

Liturgical Ministers: Lectors

Today's gospel speaks of Christ as the true vine and the Father as the vine grower, an image that calls lectors to reflect on their own connection to the word they proclaim. Serving as a lector is a participation in this living vine. The Scriptures are not a text simply to be read but a word that carries the life of Christ into the assembly. Lectors are invited to a discipline of prayerful study, reading the Sunday texts slowly, listening for the phrases that speak first to their own hearts. This encounter shapes their proclamation so that when they stand at the ambo, they are not simply announcing words but sharing what has already transformed them. Ministers of the word embody the church's mission to make Christ present in every age. Their ministry teaches that proclamation begins in listening and that the authority of Scripture is made visible in the humble, careful voice of the lector.

Living Liturgy: The Collect

The collect for this Sunday asks God to help the faithful bear fruit that will last. This prayer sets the tone for the whole liturgy, drawing us into the imagery of the gospel and inviting us to see ourselves as branches grafted onto Christ. The collect gathers all the hopes and struggles of the assembly into one voice, offering them to the Father through Christ who is present at the altar.
In this brief prayer, the church learns to see growth in faith as a divine gift and a communal mission. The liturgy is not simply a gathering but an experience of being pruned and nourished so that the life of Christ flows through us. The collect reminds us that worship shapes how we live. Every Mass is an invitation to allow God to cultivate holiness in us, making our lives signs of his presence in the world.

SPIRITUALITY

GOSPEL ACCLAMATION
John 14:23

℟. Alleluia, alleluia.
Whoever loves me will keep my word, says the Lord,
and my Father will love him and we will come to him.
℟. Alleluia, alleluia.

Gospel

John 15:9-17; L56B

Jesus said to his disciples:
"As the Father loves me, so I also love you.
Remain in my love.
If you keep my commandments, you will remain in my love,
just as I have kept my Father's commandments
and remain in his love.

"I have told you this so that my joy may be in you
and your joy might be complete.
This is my commandment: love one another as I love you.
No one has greater love than this,
to lay down one's life for one's friends.
You are my friends if you do what I command you.
I no longer call you slaves,
because a slave does not know what his master is doing.
I have called you friends,
because I have told you everything I have heard from my Father.
It was not you who chose me, but I who chose you
and appointed you to go and bear fruit that will remain,
so that whatever you ask the Father in my name he may give you.
This I command you: love one another."

Praying with Gospel Words and Phrases

Remain in my love . . . your joy might be complete . . .

Reflecting on the Gospel

In today's gospel passage, Jesus speaks some of his most tender and challenging words, inviting his disciples—and by extension, all of us—into the depths of divine friendship. "As the Father loves me, so I also love you. Remain in my love." The love that flows eternally between the Father and the Son is now shared with humanity. The command to "remain" is not a demand of servitude, but a call to mutual relationship, sustained through love and fidelity.

What is most striking in this passage is the transformation of language. Jesus moves from describing his followers as *slaves* to calling them *friends*. This shift marks a profound change in the nature of the relationship between God and humanity. Servants obey without full understanding—they carry out commands because they must. Friends, however, are invited into trust, transparency, and shared purpose. Friendship is rooted in revelation and intimacy; God no longer remains distant or hidden but draws near in honesty and vulnerability.

This transition is not merely linguistic—it is theological and relational. To be called a friend of Jesus is to be drawn into the very heart of divine love. Yet it also carries responsibility. Jesus immediately connects this new friendship with the commandment to love one another as he has loved us. Friendship with Christ is not a private privilege; it is the soil from which self-giving love must grow. We are chosen and appointed to bear fruit—fruit that will last—by living out that same sacrificial love that defined Jesus's life and death.

In calling his disciples friends, Jesus dignifies their humanity. He elevates them from mere participants in a mission to coworkers in divine love. Friendship with God does not erase obedience but transforms it: love becomes both the command and the means of fulfilling it.

To the Point

When we love one another as friends in Christ, we reflect the friendship God has extended to us. This is the deepest meaning of discipleship—not fear-driven service, but love freely given and received, sustained in the abiding presence of Jesus, the Friend who laid down his life for us.

Preparing to Proclaim, Preach, and Pray

Making Connections Between the Readings: The Acts of the Apostles returns us to the words and deeds of Peter this week. In his meeting with Cornelius, Peter, and the Jewish people with him, are greatly surprised—"astounded"—that the Holy Spirit falls upon the Gentiles as well. They speak in tongues, glorifying God, and Peter has them all baptized then and there.

While down the road Peter and Paul have some differences to work out regarding the early church, they both realize that the good news must be brought to all peoples, and that the church must truly be universal and all-encompassing—that is, catholic. All must be brought into relationship with God and with one another, loving, serving, and believing.

God is love, John reminds us—nearly incessantly reminds us—and we must love one another because God is what love is. Love is manifest, Paul teaches elsewhere in the epistles, by patience, kindness, trust, hopefulness, perseverance, and more. God, then, is also all those things. I would add that love is never coercion—or, to express that in positive language, God is invitation. Today God invites us to communion, with one another and with himself, in an ever-expanding union of believers and of love.

Making Connections to the Responsorial Psalm: Here again, scripturally, is another link from Christmas to Easter. Many months ago, on Christmas Day, Psalm 98 sang of the arrival of the Prince of Peace, whom all the world would soon see: first shepherds, followed by the magi, and then an ever-growing circle of humanity. Today's liturgy shows that circle grows wider still, the messianic promise being revealed to the early church as belonging not only to the chosen Jewish people but to Gentiles in far-flung lands as well.

If you'll permit a brief excursion into geometry, the image of a widening circle may be helpful. Because the area of a circle is calculated by the formula $A=\pi r^2$ each time the radius of the circle grows, the area grows significantly more. When our circle of faith grows, when that radius of our community is expanded (and multiplied by itself) just a little bit, the number of people within that circle grows significantly more; the community of God's love and light grows significantly more.

CONNECTING TO EXPERIENCE: LIVING THE PASCHAL MYSTERY

Christ has withheld nothing from his Father and he has withheld nothing from us. He lays down his life for us, yes, but he has also shared with us everything he has learned from his Father. We are called to lay down our lives for our friends, too. And we are called to share everything we have learned from Christ: we must take up the same way of the cross because bearing Christ's load is to carry others in love. This burden laid upon Christ's followers brings true life and service that unleashes God's charity upon the earth. And, we are not alone. Christ assures us that the Father will hear us and will grant us what we need to love, to serve, and to bear much fruit. We have been chosen by Christ to take up this love and to give ourselves fully in the work of love.

PROMPTS FOR FAITH-SHARING

- Are you withholding anything from Christ? Is your church or home community withholding anything from Christ?
- How can you, in a new way, pass on the wisdom of Christ to others? Who in your life needs it most?
- In this moment, for what would you like to ask God's strength and wisdom?

Model Rite for the Blessing and Sprinkling of Water

Presider: Jesus has commanded us to love one another. Let us keep his commandment, seeking his pardon and peace . . . *[pause]*

[continue with The Roman Missal, *Appendix II]*

Model Universal Prayer (Prayer of the Faithful)

Presider: The God of love calls us to follow in his ways. As we journey towards God, we offer the hopes and needs of our community this day.

Response: Lord, hear our prayer.

For the universal church: may it be a sign of God's love from age to age, we pray . . .

For all engaged in global trade: may they treat their partners with justice and dignity, we pray . . .

For those who reside in our own country, especially those who suffer from lack of resources: may they be graced with access to local food sources and a just market, we pray . . .

For all gathered here: may the love of Christ unite us in the work of the Gospel, we pray . . .

Presider: Father of compassion, see our strivings and hear our prayers with mercy. Grant that, from end to end, our world might be touched by your covenantal love. We ask this through Christ our Lord. Amen.

Liturgy and Transferred Feasts

The Lectionary begins this week not with a Scripture passage, but with . . . let's call it a warning: "When the Ascension of the Lord is celebrated the following Sunday, the second reading and Gospel from the Seventh Sunday of Easter (see nos. 59–61) may be read on the Sixth Sunday of Easter" (Lectionary 56B).

If you have any responsibility for lectors over this next score of days, it's imperative that the correct readings for each celebration (Sixth Sunday of Easter, solemnity of the Ascension, Seventh Sunday of Easter, and Pentecost Vigil and Pentecost) be clearly communicated to each. If you give these ministers some sort of preparatory workbook, your communication becomes even more important. Due to the vagaries of the liturgical calendar from diocese to diocese at this time of year, along with the legitimate choices each local parish can make day-by-day, mishaps can and will occur. These preparation books can be confusing to navigate, as they offer every conceivable option for every place and time. Be clear about which date should be used, as well as the exact Scripture reference, which Lectionary number, and which page in the preparation workbook. Perhaps even the first few words of

(continued on next page)

COLLECT

Let us pray.

Pause for silent prayer

Grant, almighty God,
that we may celebrate with heartfelt
devotion these days of joy,
which we keep in honor of the risen Lord,
and that what we relive in remembrance
we may always hold to in what we do.
Through our Lord Jesus Christ, your Son,
who lives and reigns with you in the unity
of the Holy Spirit,
God, for ever and ever. **Amen.**

FIRST READING

Acts 10:25-26, 34-35, 44-48

When Peter entered, Cornelius met him
and, falling at his feet, paid him
homage.
Peter, however, raised him up, saying,
"Get up. I myself am also a human
being."

Then Peter proceeded to speak and said,
"In truth, I see that God shows no
partiality.
Rather, in every nation whoever fears him
and acts uprightly
is acceptable to him."

While Peter was still speaking these
things,
the Holy Spirit fell upon all who were
listening to the word.
The circumcised believers who had
accompanied Peter
were astounded that the gift of the Holy
Spirit
should have been poured out on the
Gentiles also,
for they could hear them speaking in
tongues and glorifying God.
Then Peter responded,
"Can anyone withhold the water for
baptizing these people,
who have received the Holy Spirit even
as we have?"
He ordered them to be baptized in the
name of Jesus Christ.

RESPONSORIAL PSALM

Ps 98:1, 2-3, 3-4

℟. (cf. 2b) The Lord has revealed to the
nations his saving power.
or:
℟. Alleluia.

Sing to the Lord a new song,
for he has done wondrous deeds;
his right hand has won victory for him,
his holy arm.

℟. The Lord has revealed to the nations
his saving power.
or:
℟. Alleluia.

The Lord has made his salvation known:
in the sight of the nations he has
revealed his justice.
He has remembered his kindness and his
faithfulness
toward the house of Israel.

℟. The Lord has revealed to the nations
his saving power.
or:
℟. Alleluia.

All the ends of the earth have seen
the salvation by our God.
Sing joyfully to the Lord, all you lands;
break into song; sing praise.

℟. The Lord has revealed to the nations
his saving power.
or:
℟. Alleluia.

SECOND READING
1 John 4:7-10

Beloved, let us love one another,
because love is of God;
everyone who loves is begotten by God
and knows God.
Whoever is without love does not know
God, for God is love.
In this way the love of God was revealed
to us:
God sent his only Son into the world
so that we might have life through him.
In this is love:
not that we have loved God, but that he
loved us
and sent his Son as expiation for our
sins.

Or, where the Ascension is celebrated on Sunday, the second reading and gospel for the Seventh Sunday of Easter may be used on this Sunday.

1 John 4:11-16, p. 133.

John 17:11b-19, p. 130.

each Scripture reading can be pointed out. Any amount of seemingly redundant communication, with a few words of why you are being so redundant, will help alleviate any possible Sunday morning misadventures.

Liturgical Ministers: Music Ministers

The readings for this Sunday speak of love poured out by God and shared among his people. Music ministers help the assembly experience that love through the very structure of the liturgy. Their work is a ministry of prayer rather than performance, shaping an atmosphere that invites full participation. Each choice of chant or hymn draws on Scripture and tradition, teaching theology through melody and rhythm. This Sunday's focus on God's love challenges musicians to lead with humility and to listen closely to the Spirit who is present in the gathered church. Music ministers form community by helping worshippers pray with one heart and one voice. They are also called to a life of ongoing formation, studying liturgical documents, Scripture, and musical craft so their leadership flows from knowledge and prayer. This ministry is a witness that beauty is an essential language of faith. Music is not decoration but revelation. When led with integrity, it helps the assembly experience God's presence with both mind and heart.

Living Liturgy: The Prayer over the Offerings

This prayer asks that the gifts brought to the altar become a sign of salvation for the whole world. In this moment, bread and wine are not the only offerings. The prayer teaches that the assembly's lives, joys, and sorrows are placed on the altar as well. The eucharistic liturgy transforms these gifts and returns them to us as Christ's own life. This prayer reveals the deeply missionary nature of the Mass. We come not only to receive but to be formed and sent. The prayer over the offerings invites us to see the Eucharist as a mystery of exchange. God takes what we bring and gives it back transformed. Every Sunday this moment trains us to surrender more fully to Christ, allowing his Spirit to change us into instruments of his love.

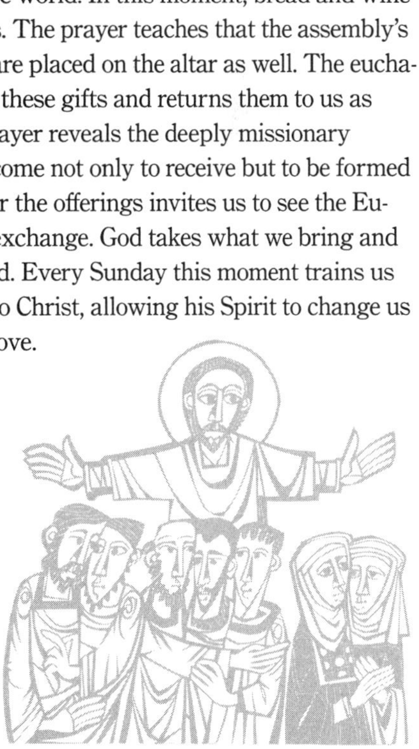

SPIRITUALITY

GOSPEL ACCLAMATION
Matt 28:19a, 20b

℟. Alleluia, alleluia.
Go and teach all nations, says the Lord;
I am with you always, until the end of the world.
℟. Alleluia, alleluia.

Gospel

Mark 16:15-20; L58B

Jesus said to his disciples:
"Go into the whole world
and proclaim the gospel to every creature.
Whoever believes and is baptized will be saved;
whoever does not believe will be condemned.
These signs will accompany those who believe:
in my name they will drive out demons,
they will speak new languages.
They will pick up serpents with their hands,
and if they drink any deadly thing, it will not harm them.
They will lay hands on the sick, and they will recover."

So then the Lord Jesus, after he spoke to them,
was taken up into heaven
and took his seat at the right hand of God.
But they went forth and preached everywhere,
while the Lord worked with them
and confirmed the word through accompanying signs.

Praying with Gospel Words and Phrases

The Lord Jesus, after he spoke to them, was taken up into heaven . . .

Reflecting on the Gospel

A few years ago, my wife and I were getting some landscaping done at our home. The backyard had always been a bit of a jungle—an empty and not-well-maintained rectangle that was not very usable space for us. When we were finally able to put some attention and money into it, we recreated a parking space and a gate off the alley, added a storage shed, a patio area of pavers, had the whole thing leveled, and laid down sod. It seemed like we were then done.

But we weren't. A few years later, a hot tub landed in our yard. And we are still not done: there is need for a shady pergola yet, and other improvements. So while our backyard appeared to be finished a couple different times, it really isn't yet, and won't be, until some unknown time in the future. Life in the church is like that as well—seemingly complete at times, but not really finished yet, and not until some unknown time down the road.

We celebrate Jesus's ascension now and will soon celebrate the coming of the Spirit at Pentecost. Jesus's death and resurrection earned for us a new life and a "new Jerusalem," but we're not there yet. Jesus's ascension and the arrival of the Spirit show us that same thing—where he has gone, we one day hope to follow—but not yet. "Already, not yet" is one of the often overlooked paradoxes of our Christian faith. This odd in-between time is hard to wrap our heads around. To wit: most of us view heaven as the ultimate and final destination of our souls. Your grandparents (or even parents) might have had to memorize this answer from the *Baltimore Catechism* once upon a time: "God made me to know Him, to love Him, and to serve Him in this world, *and* to be happy with Him for ever in heaven" (*Baltimore Catechism* of 1891, Q6, emphasis added). But wait—isn't that ultimate goal, as recited in the Creed every Sunday, the resurrection of the dead *and* the life of the world to come?

To the Point

We live in a strange "in-between" time. Our salvation already has been won but it is not yet fully a part of our existence. How do we live this long-lived mystery of our faith, maintaining an expectation for the Lord to come again?

Preparing to Proclaim, Preach, and Pray

Making Connections Between the Readings: The Acts of the Apostles today not only "rewinds" to the very beginning of its text; it paints a slightly different picture of the ascension than does Mark's Gospel. Notably, Luke's telling here adds the unexplained "two men dressed in white garments" who, in different words, seem to chastise the apostles. "Why are you still here? He's gone, better get busy!" They add that Jesus one day will return in the same way they just saw him depart.

There's a story that one day a journalist asked Pope John XXIII what the people in the Vatican would be advised to do if they heard that Jesus was returning. Known for his sense of humor, he reportedly replied: "Look busy." And so we should! No one knows the day nor the hour. There is probably a cloud up in the sky where you are right now—go ahead, look. Is *that* the one which is bringing Jesus back to earth?

Amidst all the glory and majesty in Paul's epistle today, at the end he reminds the Ephesians, and us, that God has placed Christ as "head over all things to the church, which is his body"—where Jesus has gone, we too, as his body, one day hope to follow.

Making Connections to the Responsorial Psalm: Unlike many psalms that focus on Israel's relationship with God, Psalm 47 proclaims God's rule over *all* the nations. This global vision is a bold declaration in a context where most gods were seen as regional or national deities. The Israelites were of course monotheistic, but there is some debate as to whether, at different times, they believed that YHWH was the only God, or their one God among many other gods.

The final verse offers a profound theological twist: the Gentile nations and peoples are gathered into God's covenant people. It echoes God's promise to Abraham that "all nations will be blessed through you"—a rare moment of inclusivity in the Hebrew Scriptures and one which parallels the expanding church found in the later chapters of the Acts of the Apostles.

CONNECTING TO EXPERIENCE: LIVING THE PASCHAL MYSTERY

Jesus gives his disciples a great commission—proclaiming the gospel to every creature. But one might wonder how the fantastic abilities they are to possess might apply to us who are called to be Christ's disciples by reason of our baptism. We might not touch someone and heal cancer or the effects of a stroke, but we can visit them, pray with them, accompany them, and advocate for them in their distress. We might not pick up venomous snakes, but we can choose to handle the poisonous words and deeds that spear and sting the most vulnerable among us. Yes, Christ is with us, and we, too, have a great commission. This is the promise of the ascension: I am with you always until the end of the world. We have only to grow to the full stature of the gift we have already received. How will we live it?

Model Rite for the Blessing and Sprinkling of Water

Presider: Though Christ Jesus has risen and ascended into heaven, he calls us always to follow him as we first began in our baptism. Calling to mind the times we have failed to live our baptismal calling, we ask for his mercy . . . *[pause]*

[continue with The Roman Missal, *Appendix II]*

Model Universal Prayer (Prayer of the Faithful)

Presider: Trusting in the Lord who calls us to believe in his goodness, we pray . . .

Response: Lord, hear our prayer.

For the church throughout the world: may we grow in greater unity, equipping our ministers, lay and ordained, for the work of building up the Body of Christ, we pray . . .

For all nations, especially for those struggling with religious tensions and persecution: may faith in the living God inspire peace and compromise so that all faiths might live in harmony, we pray . . .

For those serving as missionaries and ministers in dangerous situations: may they be protected in their work of bringing the gospel of peace to the faithful, we pray . . .

For all gathered here: may we reject temptations to divide our hearts from our neighbors who are different than ourselves, we pray . . .

Presider: O God, you are king above all the earth and reign over the nations. Rule over our hearts so that we might always sing your praises, be agents of peace, and draw all peoples to you. We ask this through Christ our Lord. Amen.

Liturgy and the Parousia

It feels, sometimes, as if our church has lost a sense of expectation of "the life of the world to come" after all this time. Do we, like the early apostles might have, glance up at each passing cloud and wonder, is this the one that is bringing Jesus back to us? When will Christ come again? Is it today? Am I ready?

It also feels, sometimes, as if Christ can't return to us soon enough. We notice around us injustices, warfare, and sharp divisions, and yearningly pray, "Please—let this next cloud at last bring Christ's return, and his wholeness, peace, and joy!"

These are the sorts of things we pray over at the end of each church year and into Advent as well—but this is also a perfect time to reexamine our lives and our faith. Are you ready? How can you be more ready? How can we lead our assemblies to more deeply ponder these serious questions?

Said another way, the solemnity of the Ascension is both end and beginning—a paradox embodied as Christ depicted in Revelation, both Alpha and Omega. Be sure to attend to this curious reality in preaching, universal prayers, and hymn selection.

COLLECT

Let us pray.

Pause for silent prayer

Gladden us with holy joys, almighty God,
and make us rejoice with devout
thanksgiving,
for the Ascension of Christ your Son
is our exaltation,
and, where the Head has gone before in
glory,
the Body is called to follow in hope.
Through our Lord Jesus Christ, your Son,
who lives and reigns with you in the unity
of the Holy Spirit,
God, for ever and ever. **Amen.**

or

Grant, we pray, almighty God,
that we, who believe that your Only
Begotten Son, our Redeemer,
ascended this day to the heavens,
may in spirit dwell already in heavenly
realms.
Who lives and reigns with you in the unity
of the Holy Spirit,
God, for ever and ever. **Amen.**

FIRST READING

Acts 1:1-11

In the first book, Theophilus,
I dealt with all that Jesus did and taught
until the day he was taken up,
after giving instructions through the
Holy Spirit
to the apostles whom he had chosen.
He presented himself alive to them
by many proofs after he had suffered,
appearing to them during forty days
and speaking about the kingdom of God.
While meeting with them,
he enjoined them not to depart from
Jerusalem,
but to wait for "the promise of the
Father
about which you have heard me speak;
for John baptized with water,
but in a few days you will be baptized
with the Holy Spirit."

When they had gathered together they
asked him,
"Lord, are you at this time going to
restore the kingdom to Israel?"
He answered them, "It is not for you to
know the times or seasons
that the Father has established by his
own authority.
But you will receive power when the
Holy Spirit comes upon you,

and you will be my witnesses in Jerusalem,
throughout Judea and Samaria,
and to the ends of the earth."
When he had said this, as they were looking on,
he was lifted up, and a cloud took him from their sight.
While they were looking intently at the sky as he was going,
suddenly two men dressed in white garments stood beside them.
They said, "Men of Galilee,
why are you standing there looking at the sky?
This Jesus who has been taken up from you into heaven
will return in the same way as you have seen him going into heaven."

RESPONSORIAL PSALM
Ps 47:2-3, 6-7, 8-9

℟. (6) God mounts his throne to shouts of joy: a blare of trumpets for the Lord.
or: ℟. Alleluia.

All you peoples, clap your hands,
shout to God with cries of gladness.
For the LORD, the Most High, the awesome,
is the great king over all the earth.

℟. God mounts his throne to shouts of joy: a blare of trumpets for the Lord.
or: ℟. Alleluia.

God mounts his throne amid shouts of joy;
the LORD, amid trumpet blasts.
Sing praise to God, sing praise;
sing praise to our king, sing praise.

℟. God mounts his throne to shouts of joy: a blare of trumpets for the Lord.
or: ℟. Alleluia.

For king of all the earth is God;
sing hymns of praise.
God reigns over the nations,
God sits upon his holy throne.

℟. God mounts his throne to shouts of joy: a blare of trumpets for the Lord.
or: ℟. Alleluia.

SECOND READING
Eph 1:17-23

or Eph 4:1-13

or Eph 4:1-7, 11-13

See Appendix A, p. 303.

Liturgical Ministers: Music Ministers

The Ascension reveals Christ's glory and his promise to remain present through the Spirit. For music ministers, this feast is a reminder that their work is not merely about skill or leadership but about shaping a community that learns to hope. The songs chosen for this day invite the assembly to see the liturgy as participation in the heavenly worship Christ has entered. Music ministers are formed through this mystery to become bearers of that hope in their lives. This feast calls them to pray with the texts they lead, to understand their theological depth, and to allow the liturgy itself to form their hearts. When music is offered with humility and reverence, it helps the assembly recognize that Christ's ascension is not an absence but a deeper presence. Their ministry becomes a sign that beauty and truth draw the community closer to God.

Living Liturgy: The Preface of Ascension I

The preface today praises Christ who ascends to the Father yet remains with his church. It teaches that our humanity is now seated in heaven and that the liturgy joins earth and heaven in worship. This prayer draws believers into awe, reminding us that Christ's glory reveals our destiny. In celebrating the ascension, the church is also sent on mission, echoing Christ's command to make disciples of all nations. The liturgy forms us to hold these truths together: worship is not an escape but the source of our witness. The ascension encourages us to see every Eucharist as a moment where Christ draws us upward while also sending us outward. This feast trains us to live with hope, to see the world as already touched by heaven, and to proclaim that Christ is truly present through his Spirit.

SPIRITUALITY

GOSPEL ACCLAMATION
cf. John 14:18

℟. Alleluia, alleluia.
I will not leave you orphans, says the Lord.
I will come back to you, and your hearts will rejoice.
℟. Alleluia, alleluia.

Gospel

John 17:11b-19; L60B

Lifting up his eyes to heaven, Jesus prayed, saying:
"Holy Father, keep them in your name that you have given me,
so that they may be one just as we are one.
When I was with them I protected them in your name that you gave me,
and I guarded them, and none of them was lost
except the son of destruction,
in order that the Scripture might be fulfilled.
But now I am coming to you.
I speak this in the world
so that they may share my joy completely.
I gave them your word, and the world hated them,
because they do not belong to the world
any more than I belong to the world.
I do not ask that you take them out of the world
but that you keep them from the evil one.
They do not belong to the world
any more than I belong to the world.
Consecrate them in the truth. Your word is truth.
As you sent me into the world,
so I sent them into the world.
And I consecrate myself for them,
so that they also may be consecrated in truth."

Praying with Gospel Words and Phrases

So that they may be one . . . they may share my joy completely . . .

Reflecting on the Gospel

The collect for today is a brief encapsulation of the pericope from near the end of John's "Last Supper Discourse," which speaks of the promised divine abiding presence, "as he promised, until the end of the world . . . "

Yet as succinct as it is, it will be difficult for the faithful to grasp its meaning on one hearing alone. This collect, statistically speaking, is one single sentence with forty words, seven commas, and a lot of potential for the assembly to "tune out" due to unintelligible clauses.

Too often these prayers (the collect, prayer over the gifts, and the prayer after Communion) feel a bit like a transitionary hinge, that is, something we need liturgically to turn a corner, but not anything of real substance in the liturgy. This is of course dramatically wrong. One technique to counter this affect, in addition to simply practicing the orations, is to indicate to the congregation that the invitation "let us pray" is in fact sincere. To achieve this, have the missal in place and opened to the proper page before that invitation. Following it but before the oration, bow your head silently for several seconds. In short order, the congregation will learn by this lead what this moment in time is for: their own private prayers, soon to be gathered to one by the celebrant.

The gospel today is indeed Jesus praying, as if a presider over his community. He asks his Father that "they may share my joy completely" and that he "keep them from the evil one." Not invoked by name in this pericope, Jesus had just spoken of the coming Advocate, and we may safely link the Holy Spirit to these prayers for joy, security, and unity.

If we are to pray what we believe and believe what we pray, let us all give these orations the attention and intelligibility they need, and not relegate them to passing moments of overlooked substance.

To the Point

At several different times Jesus teaches us how to pray: sometimes by exact words, sometimes by example. Jesus, in his prayers for us, shows us what to pray for as well. Our prayers should inform both our beliefs and our day-to-day lives.

Preparing to Proclaim, Preach, and Pray

Making Connections Between the Readings: If God is love, and God the Trinity is three persons in one, then love is also by its divine nature meant to be shared among community. In this way John continues his theology of the God who is love, expanding that community and that love to the Body of Christ. The Spirit is the bringer of and the strong evidence of that love and our union with the Trinity.

Sometimes it's helpful to the think of the Spirit as "the gerund" of the Trinity. As a reminder, a gerund is an "-ing" word, a suffix that turns a verb into a noun. If God is love, the Spirit who proceeds from Father and Son could be thought of, titularly, as "Loving"—a title that exemplifies the vibrant, unifying action of this person of the Trinity.

If even one person in the Body of Christ is hurt or is absent, then the whole of the Body of Christ shares that pain or is found incomplete. One of the first literal acts of the apostles seemed to be aware of this theological fact. While still in the first chapter of Acts, Peter exhorts the remaining apostles to find someone to take up the place formerly filled by Judas Iscariot. Two men are nominated, and the casting of lots brings the apostolic ministry to Matthias. With the twelve again complete, the particular ministry trusted to the apostles may again proceed.

Making Connections to the Responsorial Psalm: The psalm for this Seventh Sunday of Easter is a theological continuation of the psalm from Ascension Day (at least if you celebrated Ascension on the preceding Thursday!). Where Psalm 47 presents a hymn of praise to the God who has ascended the throne, this portion of Psalm 103 not only continues that praise, but describes the attributes of such a God: unsurpassed in kindness, vastly merciful, omnipotent in rule. God even commands mighty angels from his throne in heaven.

If the perception of God was this lofty and distant, no wonder then that the promise of the Holy Spirit was so necessary to those who watched Jesus ascend. No wonder then that the Holy Spirit still is that same comforter to us today! The faithful need both visions of God, both transcendent and immanent, and these liturgies at the end of Eastertide give us both.

CONNECTING TO EXPERIENCE: LIVING THE PASCHAL MYSTERY

Jesus has left the earth, but he has not left us alone. He continues to guard us and sends his Spirit to abide with us. We are called to remain in him, filled with the Spirit, and to be one together, just as he and the Father are one. Do we believe the Spirit abides with us? Are we united as a church? As a community? How can we be better bearers of unity in our world, especially among our fellow Christians? As St. John Paul II and Vatican II teach us, we must begin with an interior conversion toward openness and dialogue, and love expressed through common prayer. Common prayers for peace, as well as Christian unity, allow us to begin responding to Christ's command: that all might be one in him (*Ut Unum Sint* 1). He remains with us, and we with him, until the end of the ages when we will all rejoice before the heavenly Father.

PROMPTS FOR FAITH-SHARING

- Do you believe that Christ is really with you? Is it a struggle to believe this?
- Do you believe that you can bring unity into the lives of others? How can you grow in this belief, with Christ and in the Holy Spirit?
- Since we have all been commissioned to bring the gospel to the ends of the earth, to which end have you been called? How can you find unity with Christ even when you do not feel settled?

Model Rite for the Blessing and Sprinkling of Water

Presider: The Lord calls us to come to him and share in his joy. For those times we have forgotten his love for us, we ask for his pardon and peace . . . *[pause]*

[continue with The Roman Missal, *Appendix II]*

Model Universal Prayer (Prayer of the Faithful)

Presider: Jesus came into the world so that the world might be saved. Trusting in his promise, we turn to him with our prayers and petitions.

Response: Lord, hear our prayer.

For the church: may we seek greater unity with our Christian brothers and sisters around the world, we pray . . .

For leaders of nations: may collaboration for the common good and a commitment to protecting all citizens shape their governing, we pray . . .

For the sick and suffering: may their anxieties be relieved as they hope for healing, we pray . . .

For those in our midst experiencing divisions: may they seek and find reconciliation among family and friends, we pray . . .

Presider: Heavenly Father, you sent your Son so that we might come to know and believe in the love you have for us. Hear our prayers this day as we place our trust in you. We ask this through Christ our Lord. Amen.

Liturgy and Lex Orandi, Lex Credendi

There is a Latin axiom, likely familiar to readers of this volume, that quite briefly explains the integral connection that liturgy has to our faith and beliefs, and how that faith and those beliefs shape our communal prayer: "*Lex orandi, lex credendi.*" In English, that is often rendered, "The law of prayer is the law of belief." The axiom operates in either transactional direction, and it can be expressed even more colloquially: we pray what we believe, we believe what we pray.

Some even choose to add a third "lex" to the expression, "*lex vivendi,*" the law of living. Each of the three must be consonant with the other two, and, as if a bit of braided rope, weave in and out of one another and fill the others with meaning and purpose.

Because of this, make sure the prayers of the Mass are not glossed over or rushed through, but rather prayed with intensity of purpose and communicatively, so that their words may be believed and truly lived by all the faithful people of God.

COLLECT

Let us pray.

Pause for silent prayer

Graciously hear our supplications, O Lord,
so that we, who believe that the Savior of the human race
is with you in your glory,
may experience, as he promised,
until the end of the world,
his abiding presence among us.
Who lives and reigns with you in the unity of the Holy Spirit,
God, for ever and ever. **Amen.**

FIRST READING

Acts 1:15-17, 20a, 20c-26

Peter stood up in the midst of the brothers
—there was a group of about one hundred and twenty persons
in the one place—.
He said, "My brothers,
the Scripture had to be fulfilled
which the Holy Spirit spoke beforehand
through the mouth of David, concerning Judas,
who was the guide for those who arrested Jesus.
He was numbered among us
and was allotted a share in this ministry.

"For it is written in the Book of Psalms:
May another take his office.

"Therefore, it is necessary that one of the men
who accompanied us the whole time
the Lord Jesus came and went among us,
beginning from the baptism of John
until the day on which he was taken up from us,
become with us a witness to his resurrection."
So they proposed two, Judas called Barsabbas,
who was also known as Justus, and Matthias.
Then they prayed,
"You, Lord, who know the hearts of all,
show which one of these two you have chosen
to take the place in this apostolic ministry
from which Judas turned away to go to his own place."
Then they gave lots to them, and the lot fell upon Matthias,
and he was counted with the eleven apostles.

RESPONSORIAL PSALM
Ps 103:1-2, 11-12, 19-20

℟. (19a) The Lord has set his throne in heaven.
or:
℟. Alleluia.

Bless the LORD, O my soul;
and all my being, bless his holy name.
Bless the LORD, O my soul,
and forget not all his benefits.

℟. The Lord has set his throne in heaven.
or:
℟. Alleluia.

For as the heavens are high above the earth,
so surpassing is his kindness toward those who fear him.
As far as the east is from the west,
so far has he put our transgressions from us.

℟. The Lord has set his throne in heaven.
or:
℟. Alleluia.

The LORD has established his throne in heaven,
and his kingdom rules over all.
Bless the LORD, all you his angels,
you mighty in strength, who do his bidding.

℟. The Lord has set his throne in heaven.
or:
℟. Alleluia.

SECOND READING
1 John 4:11-16

Beloved, if God so loved us,
we also must love one another.
No one has ever seen God.
Yet, if we love one another, God remains in us,
and his love is brought to perfection in us.

This is how we know that we remain in him and he in us,
that he has given us of his Spirit.
Moreover, we have seen and testify
that the Father sent his Son as savior of the world.
Whoever acknowledges that Jesus is the Son of God,
God remains in him and he in God.
We have come to know and to believe in the love God has for us.

God is love, and whoever remains in love
remains in God and God in him.

Liturgical Ministers: Altar Servers

The altar is the meeting place of heaven and earth, where Christ offers himself for the life of the world. Those who serve closest to this mystery are invited to grow in reverence, not by memorizing roles but by letting the liturgy form their hearts. On this Sunday, the church lingers in prayer between Ascension and Pentecost, a moment of anticipation that mirrors the life of every altar server. Their ministry teaches waiting with attention, watching for Christ in the details of worship, and discovering that silence is as much a part of prayer as movement. Standing near the altar shapes their imagination, helping them see that service in the church is participation in the prayer of Christ himself. This calling also invites maturity and responsibility. When young ministers are trusted with sacred tasks, they learn that God works through them to serve his people. Altar servers remind the assembly that holiness is not reserved for adulthood or for those in leadership; it begins wherever there is faithful service, offered with love and joy.

Living Liturgy: The Collect

The collect for this Sunday asks God to make the church one as Christ and the Father are one. This prayer gathers the tension of this liturgical moment, when the disciples awaited the Spirit in the Upper Room. The church prays in that same posture, learning that unity is not achieved by human effort but is a gift from God. The collect draws us to see the Eucharist as the source of that unity. In this prayer, the assembly learns to turn to God with humility and trust, aware that our divisions and struggles are healed only by grace. The simple structure of the collect as invocation, petition, and conclusion models the Christian life itself: turning to God, offering our needs, and giving praise. As we prepare for Pentecost, this prayer reminds us that the liturgy is both a celebration and a source of faith, shaping us to live in communion with God and one another.

SPIRITUALITY

GOSPEL ACCLAMATION

℟. Alleluia, alleluia.
Come, Holy Spirit, fill the hearts of your faithful and kindle in them the fire of your love.
℟. Alleluia, alleluia.

Gospel

John 7:37-39; L62ABC

On the last and greatest day of the feast,
Jesus stood up and exclaimed,
"Let anyone who thirsts come to me and drink.
As Scripture says:
***Rivers of living water will flow from within him* who believes in me."**
He said this in reference to the Spirit that those who came to believe in him were to receive.
There was, of course, no Spirit yet, because Jesus had not yet been glorified.

Praying with Gospel Words and Phrases

Rivers of living water will flow . . .

Reflecting on the Gospel

Liturgically speaking, it can seem that the Holy Spirit, as a person of the Trinity, gets short shrift. It is almost as if the only time we can hear Scripture regarding the Spirit or pray or sing other Spirit-infused texts is on Pentecost or at confirmation Masses. Certainly, there are hundreds (thousands?) of trinitarian doxologies, but a brief passing mention doesn't really level the balance, ultimately.

Perhaps this is partly behind two relatively unique aspects of the liturgies of this weekend: the optional extended Pentecost Vigil, and the sequence on Pentecost Day. Yes, there are other vigils and sequences, but these two deserve special mention.

The Vigil of Pentecost is not especially well known or practiced, but it is unique, save for the Easter Vigil, in its celebration. It includes four Old Testament readings, each with its own psalm, or a period of silence, to follow. It also delays the Gloria and collect until after the last of these readings, right before the epistle reading. This form of the liturgy creates a natural tie to the Easter Vigil in its form, and like the Easter Vigil readings, which in part trace salvation history, these readings help bring to life the role of the Spirit in the life of the church.

Preachers will perhaps be surprised to examine the gospel passage for the Vigil and find not tongues of flame nor driving winds, but rather "Rivers of living water" as the dominant image for the coming of the Holy Spirit. This could be a refreshing change both for homilist and assembly! The image of flowing water is abundant across our Scriptures: water flows from the rock struck by Moses, water flows from the four corners of the temple, and a spring of life-giving water is promised to the thirsty in the book of Revelation (21:6). Each of these use water as a symbol of new life offered to the faithful. The gift of the Holy Spirit, poured out upon the faithful, brings new life as well, or at least brings to life a new purpose and intensity. Lastly, it's intriguing, isn't it, that seemingly oppositional imagery, fire and water, can be used to embody the same Spirit!

To the Point

No language nor symbol fully expresses or communicates all that God is—and today's gospel imagery is an opportunity to present to the faithful aspects of God the Holy Spirit in new and unique ways.

COLLECT

Let us pray.

Pause for silent prayer

Almighty ever-living God,
who willed the Paschal Mystery
to be encompassed as a sign in fifty days,
grant that from out of the scattered nations
the confusion of many tongues
may be gathered by heavenly grace
into one great confession of your name.
Through our Lord Jesus Christ, your Son,
who lives and reigns with you in the unity of the Holy Spirit,
God, for ever and ever. **Amen.**

or:

Grant, we pray, almighty God,
that the splendor of your glory
may shine forth upon us
and that, by the bright rays of the Holy Spirit,
the light of your light may confirm the hearts
of those born again by your grace.
Through our Lord Jesus Christ, your Son,
who lives and reigns with you in the unity of the Holy Spirit,
God, for ever and ever. **Amen.**

FIRST READING

Gen 11:1-9

The whole world spoke the same language, using the same words.
While the people were migrating in the east,
they came upon a valley in the land of Shinar and settled there.
They said to one another,
"Come, let us mold bricks and harden them with fire."
They used bricks for stone, and bitumen for mortar.
Then they said, "Come, let us build ourselves a city
and a tower with its top in the sky,
and so make a name for ourselves;
otherwise we shall be scattered all over the earth."

The LORD came down to see the city and the tower
that the people had built.
Then the LORD said: "If now, while they are one people,
all speaking the same language,
they have started to do this,
nothing will later stop them from doing whatever they presume to do.
Let us then go down there and confuse their language,
so that one will not understand what another says."
Thus the LORD scattered them from there all over the earth,
and they stopped building the city.
That is why it was called Babel,
because there the LORD confused the speech of all the world.
It was from that place that he scattered them all over the earth.

or Exod 19:3-8a, 16-20b

Moses went up the mountain to God.
Then the LORD called to him and said,
"Thus shall you say to the house of Jacob;
tell the Israelites:
You have seen for yourselves how I treated the Egyptians
and how I bore you up on eagle wings
and brought you here to myself.
Therefore, if you hearken to my voice and keep my covenant,
you shall be my special possession,
dearer to me than all other people,
though all the earth is mine.
You shall be to me a kingdom of priests, a holy nation.
That is what you must tell the Israelites."
So Moses went and summoned the elders of the people.
When he set before them
all that the LORD had ordered him to tell them,
the people all answered together,
"Everything the LORD has said, we will do."

On the morning of the third day
there were peals of thunder and lightning,
and a heavy cloud over the mountain,
and a very loud trumpet blast,
so that all the people in the camp trembled.
But Moses led the people out of the camp to meet God,
and they stationed themselves at the foot of the mountain.
Mount Sinai was all wrapped in smoke,
for the LORD came down upon it in fire.
The smoke rose from it as though from a furnace,
and the whole mountain trembled violently.
The trumpet blast grew louder and louder, while Moses was speaking,
and God answering him with thunder.

When the LORD came down to the top of Mount Sinai,
he summoned Moses to the top of the mountain.

or Ezek 37:1-14

The hand of the LORD came upon me,
and he led me out in the spirit of the LORD
and set me in the center of the plain,
which was now filled with bones.
He made me walk among the bones in every direction
so that I saw how many they were on the surface of the plain.
How dry they were!
He asked me:
Son of man, can these bones come to life?
I answered, "Lord GOD, you alone know that."
Then he said to me:
Prophesy over these bones, and say to them:
Dry bones, hear the word of the LORD!
Thus says the Lord GOD to these bones:
See! I will bring spirit into you, that you may come to life.
I will put sinews upon you, make flesh grow over you,
cover you with skin, and put spirit in you
so that you may come to life and know that I am the LORD.
I, Ezekiel, prophesied as I had been told,
and even as I was prophesying I heard a noise;
it was a rattling as the bones came together, bone joining bone.

Continued in Appendix A, p. 304.
See Appendix A, p. 304, for the other readings.

SPIRITUALITY

GOSPEL ACCLAMATION
℟. Alleluia, alleluia.
Come, Holy Spirit, fill the hearts of your faithful and kindle in them the fire of your love.
℟. Alleluia, alleluia.

Gospel John 20:19-23; L63B

On the evening of that first day of the week,
when the doors were locked, where the disciples were,
for fear of the Jews,
Jesus came and stood in their midst
and said to them, "Peace be with you."
When he had said this, he showed them his hands and his side.
The disciples rejoiced when they saw the Lord.
Jesus said to them again, "Peace be with you.
As the Father has sent me, so I send you."
And when he had said this, he breathed on them and said to them,
"Receive the Holy Spirit.
Whose sins you forgive are forgiven them,
and whose sins you retain are retained."

or John 15:26-27; 16:12-15

Jesus said to his disciples:
"When the Advocate comes whom I will send you from the Father,
the Spirit of truth that proceeds from the Father,
he will testify to me.
And you also testify,
because you have been with me from the beginning.

"I have much more to tell you, but you cannot bear it now.
But when he comes, the Spirit of truth,
he will guide you to all truth.

Continued in Appendix A, p. 305.

Praying with Gospel Words and Phrases

So I send you . . . Receive the Holy Spirit . . . Whose sins you forgive are forgiven them . . .

Reflecting on the Gospel

John's Gospel, when compared with the Synoptics, has some different timetables as it endeavors to present the good news more symbolically. The Synoptics, for instance, place the Last Supper as a Passover seder; John's Gospel has the crucifixion itself on Passover, so that Christ is more clearly present as the sacrificial lamb.

When John describes the coming of the Holy Spirit upon the apostles, this too differs from the other three gospels. John places his Pentecost on resurrection day itself, "the evening of that first day of the week." This too is to place a priority on theology rather than chronology.

One theological component may be a desire to more fully paint the "new creation" that Jesus's resurrection brought to birth. This "eighth day" is not fully complete without Jesus breathing the Spirit onto the disciples, mimicking the breath of life God breathed into Adam. Another impetus for closely linking resurrection and Pentecost is the immediacy of the holy work the faithful are called to. Just before receiving the Spirit, those who have until then been locked, hiding in the Upper Room, are sent on a mission.

The first detail of that mission is truly noteworthy. It's not that death has been destroyed by death itself, as one might rightly guess. Rather, the first specific directive is about the forgiveness of sins—or alternatively, the withholding of that forgiveness. John's narrative describes a resurrection that isn't just a personal victory for Jesus—it's the start of a new way of life for humanity. That new life begins with reconciliation, the healing of broken relationships. The Holy Spirit empowers the disciples to extend resurrection life by offering forgiveness. The same Spirit also allows for an understanding that reconciliation can only take place with true sorrow for sin, a desire to change, and even some sort of penance performed.

Sin is what separates people from God and one another; community cannot exist without forgiveness. Just as Jesus's resurrection overcomes death, the Spirit overcomes sin. The Spirit is the power that enables the church to be a community of grace. For John, forgiveness isn't just a moral act—in John's Gospel, it's a Spirit-filled sign that the world is being made new.

To the Point

Forgiveness is a key way in which resurrection power flows into the world. The disciples were sent as agents of divine reconciliation, and we are ministers of that same reconciliation today.

Preparing to Proclaim, Preach, and Pray

Making Connections Between the Readings: The presentation of the day of Pentecost in Acts, by the evangelist Luke, is not only chronologically different than in John's Gospel but is much richer in symbolism—driving winds, tongues of flame—and more descriptive about the immediate impact the descent of the Spirit has. The mighty acts of God are directly shared by the apostles in a wide variety of languages to a plethora of peoples from lands near and far away. A wise preacher might choose to focus on one telling of Pentecost or the other, given the diversity of imagery, chronology, and theological significance. Time spent detailing these differences, likely, would be too academic and bear little fruit among the faithful generally.

Whichever epistle reading is proclaimed gives the church a description of life in the Spirit from a greater distance of time after the resurrection. Paul sees how the continuing gifts of the Spirit are manifested in day-to-day life and their impact on the unity of the Christian community. These readings may be easiest for the preacher to find connections to modern life and a relevance for the faithful of today: the Spirit empowers us to find unity while not only recognizing but celebrating our diversity. Further, gifts of the Spirit, like patience, kindness, and generosity, build Christ's loving kingdom if we allow ourselves to be aware of the gifts and let the Spirit guide our words and deeds.

Making Connections to the Responsorial Psalm: If John's Gospel gives us resurrection day as the "eighth day," the stupendous day of new creation, and if the breath of the Spirit completes this new creation, Psalm 104 is our hymn of praise and adulation for all these gifts. It's perhaps easy to let the familiar words here be glossed over, so give them a closer look this time around. Especially the middle verses (104:29-30) as the psalm is offered today can be the lens through which to view the whole celebration.

It's God who gives us each breath we have, both our physical breaths and the breath of our spiritual lives. It is the Spirit, proceeding from Father and Son, who completes creation and gives life and indeed all creation a new and more complete meaning and significance. This Spirit, our creed reminds us, is to be adored and glorified—and more than on just this one day a year!

CONNECTING TO EXPERIENCE: LIVING THE PASCHAL MYSTERY

It's hard to feel peaceful when you're hiding. The disciples certainly felt anxiety and guilt mixed with sadness over Jesus's recent death, mixed with literal fear for their own lives that *they* might be next. Yet trembling behind closed doors—or closed hearts—doesn't stop Jesus. In John's Gospel, Jesus walks into the midst of them regardless of their dead bolts. He breathes on them and says, "Receive the Holy Spirit." And they were changed. From that day forward, the disciples may not have been perfect, but they began teaching, leading, defending, converting, and dying for God's people as they proclaimed Christ crucified. While one might guess that huddling quietly behind a closed door afforded more peace, it was not until they were filled with the Spirit, doing God's challenging work in the world, that they received and experienced the peace of Christ. What about us? Are our hearts dead bolted to the challenging peace of the Spirit? Or has Jesus appeared in our midst as well?

PROMPTS FOR FAITH-SHARING

- Whether in real life or symbolically, do you have a room that's locked? Why so?
- Have you ever experienced Jesus showing up even when you didn't want someone else there?
- Like Jesus's first followers, where or in what way do you most need courage?

Model Rite for the Blessing and Sprinkling of Water

Presider: Coming before the risen Lord who breaks down barriers of sin and death, we ask for his mercy . . . *[pause]*

[continue with The Roman Missal, *Appendix II]*

Model Universal Prayer (Prayer of the Faithful)

Presider: We come before the Lord who calls his faithful to pray for one another, as we pray . . .

Response: Lord, hear our prayer.

For the church on this holy day of Pentecost: may we shed our apathy and inaction and feel our hearts on fire with the Spirit, we pray . . .

For our leaders, and all called to watch over and protect their homelands: may the gifts of the Spirit guide them in the way of peace, we pray . . .

For those who are suffering, sick, lonely, and hopeless: may the Spirit of the Lord touch their lives through the people they encounter, we pray . . .

For all of us gathered here today: may no doors and no walls separate us from the love of Christ Jesus who stands in our midst, we pray . . .

Presider: Loving God, throughout time you have called your people to yourself. In these days you have given us your Holy Spirit to guide us ever more closely. Hear our prayers, and unite us in your Spirit through your Son. We ask this through Christ our Lord. Amen.

Liturgy and Sequences

The Pentecost sequence is one of only two that are still mandatory in liturgies today. The name itself is a bit odd and comes from the practice a millennium ago of extending the last syllable of the Alleluia before the gospel to allow time for the deacon to arrive at the ambo. The melisma eventually started taking on prose of its own and became known as the sequence because it followed the Alleluia (at that time). Present practice places it before the gospel acclamation. The sequence should be sung if possible. It can be confusing for an assembly, even following along in a worship aid, so be sure to help them with information, either in print, or announced: "Please remain seated and join with one another in singing the Pentecost sequence . . ." The text of the sequence is an invitation for the Holy Spirit to enter into our lives with practical manifestations of divine power and love.

There are several accessible and effective settings of the Pentecost sequence. Some are especially appropriate to bring the Easter season to a fitting conclusion. One setting uses the Ode to Joy

(continued on next page)

COLLECT

Let us pray.

Pause for silent prayer

O God, who by the mystery of today's great feast
sanctify your whole Church in every people and nation,
pour out, we pray, the gifts of the Holy Spirit
across the face of the earth
and, with the divine grace that was at work
when the Gospel was first proclaimed,
fill now once more the hearts of believers.
Through our Lord Jesus Christ, your Son,
who lives and reigns with you in the unity of the Holy Spirit,
God, for ever and ever. **Amen.**

FIRST READING

Acts 2:1-11

When the time for Pentecost was fulfilled,
they were all in one place together.
And suddenly there came from the sky
a noise like a strong driving wind,
and it filled the entire house in which they were.
Then there appeared to them tongues as of fire,
which parted and came to rest on each one of them.
And they were all filled with the Holy Spirit
and began to speak in different tongues,
as the Spirit enabled them to proclaim.

Now there were devout Jews from every nation under heaven staying in Jerusalem.
At this sound, they gathered in a large crowd,
but they were confused
because each one heard them speaking in his own language.
They were astounded, and in amazement they asked,
"Are not all these people who are speaking Galileans?
Then how does each of us hear them in his native language?
We are Parthians, Medes, and Elamites,
inhabitants of Mesopotamia, Judea and Cappadocia,
Pontus and Asia, Phrygia and Pamphylia,
Egypt and the districts of Libya near Cyrene,

as well as travelers from Rome,
both Jews and converts to Judaism,
Cretans and Arabs,
yet we hear them speaking in our own tongues
of the mighty acts of God."

RESPONSORIAL PSALM

Ps 104:1, 24, 29-30, 31, 34

℟. (cf. 30) Lord, send out your Spirit, and renew the face of the earth.
or:
℟. Alleluia.

Bless the Lord, O my soul!
O Lord, my God, you are great indeed!
How manifold are your works, O Lord!
The earth is full of your creatures.

℟. Lord, send out your Spirit, and renew the face of the earth.
or:
℟. Alleluia.

If you take away their breath, they perish
and return to their dust.
When you send forth your spirit, they are created,
and you renew the face of the earth.

℟. Lord, send out your Spirit, and renew the face of the earth.
or:
℟. Alleluia.

May the glory of the Lord endure forever;
may the Lord be glad in his works!
Pleasing to him be my theme;
I will be glad in the Lord.

℟. Lord, send out your Spirit, and renew the face of the earth.
or:
℟. Alleluia.

SECOND READING

1 Cor 12:3b-7, 12-13

or

Gal 5:16-25

SEQUENCE

See Appendix A, p. 305.

tune and appears in several hymnals; "Come, Holy Spirit, on Us Shine" (GIA) is among a few settings that use the *O Filii et Filiae* tune; Rob Glover has a setting (GIA) that naturally folds into the Celtic Alleluia at its finish as a gospel acclamation.

Liturgical Ministers: Lectors

On Pentecost the proclamation of Scripture takes center stage, recalling the Spirit's descent and the birth of the church's mission. Lectors have a unique role today as they proclaim readings filled with imagery of wind, fire, and unity. Their ministry is not only technical but prophetic, inviting the assembly to hear the Spirit speaking now. Preparation for this day involves more than practicing pronunciation or pacing. It begins in prayer, asking the Spirit to make the lector's own heart receptive. This ministry calls lectors to listen deeply so that their proclamation is not performance but testimony. The Spirit who inspired the Scriptures is the same Spirit who enlivens the proclamation, making it a living word for the gathered church. Lectors on Pentecost also model the church's diversity and unity, showing through their voice that all are called to share in the mission of the gospel.

Living Liturgy: The Sequence Veni Sancte Spiritus

The sequence for Pentecost is a rich prayer that invites the Spirit to renew the church. Sung or recited, it becomes a moment of contemplation within a day of celebration. This ancient hymn names the Spirit as Comforter, Teacher, and Healer, and through its poetry, the assembly is drawn into a posture of trust and openness. The sequence is not a decorative addition but a theological statement, teaching that the Spirit is God's gift to every believer. By pausing the liturgy to sing or recite it, the church shows that the Spirit is central to all Christian life and worship. This text forms us to see Pentecost as an ongoing reality rather than a distant event. Every Mass is a new outpouring of the Spirit, and the sequence invites us to open our lives to that presence. Through this prayer, the liturgy teaches us that God's Spirit continues to guide, comfort, and send us into the world as witnesses of the risen Christ.

ORDINARY TIME II

SPIRITUALITY

GOSPEL ACCLAMATION
Rev 1:8

℟. Alleluia, alleluia.
Glory to the Father, the Son, and the Holy Spirit;
to God who is, who was, and who is to come.
℟. Alleluia, alleluia.

Gospel

Matt 28:16-20; L165B

The eleven disciples went to Galilee,
to the mountain to which Jesus had ordered them.
When they all saw him, they worshiped, but they doubted.
Then Jesus approached and said to them,
"All power in heaven and on earth has been given to me.
Go, therefore, and make disciples of all nations,
baptizing them in the name of the Father,
and of the Son, and of the Holy Spirit,
teaching them to observe all that I have commanded you.
And behold, I am with you always, until the end of the age."

Praying with Gospel Words and Phrases

Go, therefore . . . baptizing them in the name of the Father, and of the Son, and of the Holy Spirit . . .

Reflecting on the Gospel

Today's solemnity, in a way, could be seen as the "Solemnity of Who God Is, Not What God Does." Of course, what God has accomplished for us across salvation history is important, to dramatically understate things. We would be wise, however, to avoid naming God, especially the three persons, by titles of actions or accomplishments. We must rather recall that the persons of the Trinity are not defined by what they do, but only who they are: each God, related to but not the other two persons. Therefore, in preaching, in hymn texts, in intercessions, we ought to avoid texts with words like "Creator, Redeemer, Sanctifier" if possible. Often these sorts of names are offered to avoid any gendered names for God, and understandably so. Changing "God the Father" to "Creator," however, neglects the Word spoken at creation, by the breath of the Spirit—indeed, all three persons of the Trinity are a part of creation, redemption, and sanctification.

The gospel assigned for today is obviously there because the ascension moment described includes the titles of each person of the Trinity. This Great Commission is about more than evangelization, more than increasing membership in the church. Notice that the word "name" here is in the singular, emphasizing the unity and oneness of God.

Of course, this passage is the scriptural warrant for sacramental baptism. Baptism, we believe, isn't just about repentance or washing away sin—it's about entering into communion with God by entering into the communion that is the church. God as Trinity is one divine nature in three persons—God as Trinity is communion. To be baptized in the name of the Trinity is to be:

- Adopted by the Father
- United with the death and resurrection of the Son
- Filled with and sanctified by the Holy Spirit

In short, the trinitarian formula reflects the fullness of God's saving action, present in each person of the Trinity.

Early Christians believed that (adult) baptism was a profession of faith. In modern times, this is seen permeating the Order of Christian Initiation of Adults (OCIA) and the Easter Vigil initiation sacraments. Belief in the Trinity is central to the faith and orthodoxy. To be baptized in the name of the Father, Son, and Holy Spirit is to be immersed not just in water—but in relationship with God who is communion, and church as communion as well.

To the Point

Today celebrates God's identity as Trinity—three persons, one communion—not just divine actions.

Preparing to Proclaim, Preach, and Pray

Making Connections Between the Readings: The epistle today is a succinct encapsulation of trinitarian faith lived by the early church. It is the Spirit who empowers us to be adopted by God the Father and to cry out in prayer. By that adoption we are not only children of God but heirs with Christ to all God has promised us. If we live, as best we can, as Christ did, uniting our sufferings with his, one day we may hope to be glorified with him, in union with the whole of the Trinity and all creation.

Of course, finding explicit references to the Trinity in the Hebrew Scriptures is a bit of a fool's errand, though by the same token the activity of the Trinity is frequently present. Take for instance the previous reflection of the presence of the Trinity at the six days of creation. So we need to look with such eyes of faith into this reading from Deuteronomy. Obviously the compilers of the modern Lectionary placed it as a part of today's celebration for a reason: what is it?

Let us consider the themes of adoption and communion already pondered here. Moses is teaching the Israelites not only of the greatness of God, but of some of the things which prove that greatness: that God, "by signs and wonders . . . with strong hand and outstretched arm" has adopted for himself a holy nation, something no other god has done because there is no other god. And our inheritance as God's children includes prosperity and long life—indeed, eternal life.

Making Connections to the Responsorial Psalm: With similar eyes and ears of faith, we may reflect upon the words of Psalm 33, and especially its refrain: God has chosen—adopted—us to be his own. We, the Christian community, are in communion with each other by being in communion with God, and we are recipients of the benefits of being God's children and heirs: justice, kindness, deliverance, preservation, and hope.

More than some other celebrations today's psalm refrain can serve as a recurrent text to unlock key details in the other Scripture passages. Structured well, the refrain could even remain on the assembly's lips throughout the homily and perhaps even later at Mass—musically during the communion procession or in a time of thanksgiving just after. Rather than spending homily time trying to academically expound on the ineffable mystery of the Trinity, let us preach and sing about a facet of the Trinity's relevance in our day-to-day lives: adoption and communion.

CONNECTING TO EXPERIENCE: LIVING THE PASCHAL MYSTERY

God is three persons who are one God. The Father, the Son, and the Holy Spirit are a divine communion of love. How blessed we are to have a God who cares so much for us that he chooses to dwell among us as Son and as Spirit! God so loves the world that he chooses to be for us and with us always. And here is the good news: when we, too, are united with our brothers and sisters in love; when we serve others in love; and when our communities call upon God in love, it is no wonder that we experience God's life most fully. We are made in the image of the Trinity. When we love we are most like ourselves, how God intended us to be. By forging communities-in-love, we become most fully who were are, we allow God to be most fully in our midst, and we come to know God by being like him.

PROMPTS FOR FAITH-SHARING

- What does the Trinity mean to you and for you? Does anything about it particularly strike you today?
- With which person of the Holy Trinity are you most comfortable? Why so?
- If love is the key expression of trinitarian life, how can you better love in a way that reflects that of the Father, the Son, and the Holy Spirit?

Model Penitential Act

Presider: We have a merciful and triune God who is with us always. Let us recall those times that we have strayed from him . . . *[pause]*

Lord Jesus, you are united to us fully in the power of the Holy Spirit: Lord, have mercy.
Christ Jesus, you are one with the Father: Christ, have mercy.
Lord Jesus, you are ruler of all nations: Lord, have mercy.

Model Universal Prayer (Prayer of the Faithful)

Presider: The Father, Son, and Holy Spirit are always for us and with us. Confident that our God is present, we bring to him our needs.

Response: Lord, hear our prayer.

For our bishops: may they convey the Trinity in their celebration of the sacraments and by opening the Scriptures, we pray . . .

For our elected officials: may they be informed by God's generous love so they might serve our nation with compassion and fidelity, we pray . . .

For the homeless and the hungry: may they find not only material shelter, but also the shelter of God's providence, we pray . . .

For the members of this parish, especially those who are sick: may they find accompaniment, community, and healing, we pray . . .

Presider: Triune God, you restore us to yourself by the gift of your covenant. We know that you are eternally ours and we ask that you hear our prayers with patience, mercy, and wisdom. We ask this through Christ our Lord. **Amen.**

Liturgy and Sacred Gesture

Just as the sign of the cross is at the beginning and end of each prayer we make, so too that same sign of the cross is at the beginning and end of our very lives. It shows to whom we belong: we trace on our bodies and bear in our souls the marks of Jesus's cross. As we speak the names of the persons of the Trinity, we recall that it is not just our prayer, but it is in fact all we do that is dedicated to them: "In the name of . . ."

There is a long and varied history of the sign of the cross. Suffice it to say here that it is both an ancient gesture and one imbued with significance for all Christians across time and space. Of it, St. Athanasius said, "By the signing of the holy and life-giving cross, devils and various scourges are driven away. For it is without price and without cost, and praises him who can say it."

Be more deliberate with the sign of the cross the several times it takes place during Mass, especially at the beginning and end of

(continued on next page)

COLLECT

Let us pray.

Pause for silent prayer

God our Father, who by sending into the world
the Word of truth and the Spirit of sanctification
made known to the human race your wondrous mystery,
grant us, we pray, that in professing the true faith,
we may acknowledge the Trinity of eternal glory
and adore your Unity, powerful in majesty.
Through our Lord Jesus Christ, your Son,
who lives and reigns with you in the unity of the Holy Spirit,
God, for ever and ever. **Amen.**

FIRST READING

Deut 4:32-34, 39-40

Moses said to the people:
"Ask now of the days of old, before your time,
ever since God created man upon the earth;
ask from one end of the sky to the other:
Did anything so great ever happen before?
Was it ever heard of?
Did a people ever hear the voice of God
speaking from the midst of fire, as you did, and live?
Or did any god venture to go and take a nation for himself
from the midst of another nation,
by testings, by signs and wonders, by war,
with strong hand and outstretched arm, and by great terrors,
all of which the LORD, your God,
did for you in Egypt before your very eyes?
This is why you must now know,
and fix in your heart, that the LORD is God
in the heavens above and on earth below,
and that there is no other.
You must keep his statutes and commandments that I enjoin on you today,
that you and your children after you may prosper,
and that you may have long life on the land
which the LORD, your God, is giving you forever."

RESPONSORIAL PSALM
Ps 33:4-5, 6, 9, 18-19, 20, 22

℟. (12b) Blessed the people the Lord has
chosen to be his own.

Upright is the word of the LORD,
and all his works are trustworthy.
He loves justice and right;
of the kindness of the LORD the earth is
full.

℟. Blessed the people the Lord has chosen
to be his own.

By the word of the LORD the heavens were
made;
by the breath of his mouth all their host.
For he spoke, and it was made;
he commanded, and it stood forth.

℟. Blessed the people the Lord has chosen
to be his own.

See, the eyes of the LORD are upon those
who fear him,
upon those who hope for his kindness,
to deliver them from death
and preserve them in spite of famine.

℟. Blessed the people the Lord has chosen
to be his own.

Our soul waits for the LORD,
who is our help and our shield.
May your kindness, O LORD, be upon us
who have put our hope in you.

℟. Blessed the people the Lord has chosen
to be his own.

SECOND READING
Rom 8:14-17

Brothers and sisters:
Those who are led by the Spirit of God are
sons of God.
For you did not receive a spirit of slavery
to fall back into fear,
but you received a Spirit of adoption,
through whom we cry, "Abba, Father!"
The Spirit himself bears witness with our
spirit
that we are children of God,
and if children, then heirs,
heirs of God and joint heirs with Christ,
if only we suffer with him
so that we may also be glorified with
him.

the liturgy with the assembly's participation. Slower recitation and broader gestures would be more appropriate—perhaps even a moment in the homily regarding the threefold gesture on forehead, lips, and heart just prior to the gospel proclamation.

Liturgical Ministers: Eucharistic Ministers

On this feast, the church encounters the mystery of God as relationship, love, and communion. Eucharistic ministers find their spiritual formation here: they become sign and sacrament of Christ's love entering the world. Each experience at the altar reflects the truth that God is communion, and through this ministry, eucharistic ministers grow into that reality. The offering and reception of the Eucharist mirrors the life of the Trinity—that is, self-giving, mutual indwelling, and creative love. When eucharistic ministers approach their calling with prayerfulness, they reflect a church formed by sacrament. Their service invites a deeper identity not as performers but as bearers of communion, shaped by the Trinity's inner life. Over time, this ministry transforms them into people of faith, of encounter, and of divine hospitality.

Living Liturgy: The Preface of Trinity Sunday

The preface for this solemnity is itself a profession of faith. In it, the church praises the Father, the Son, and the Holy Spirit as one God, equal in glory and majesty. These words, prayed at the altar, form the assembly's faith far more powerfully than any explanation. They reveal that our understanding of God comes first through worship as we bow, we listen, we give thanks, and we are drawn into mystery. This preface teaches us that God is not distant but a communion of love, inviting us into relationship. The prayer shapes our vision of Christian life. To believe in the Trinity is to live in communion, to see every person as created in God's image, and to approach the world as a place infused with God's presence. By lifting our hearts in this preface, we are formed in it, learning to live what we pray.

SPIRITUALITY

GOSPEL ACCLAMATION
John 6:51

℟. Alleluia, alleluia.
I am the living bread that came down from heaven,
says the Lord; whoever eats this bread will live forever.
℟. Alleluia, alleluia.

Gospel

Mark 14:12-16, 22-26; L168B

On the first day of the Feast of Unleavened Bread,
when they sacrificed the Passover lamb,
Jesus' disciples said to him,
"Where do you want us to go
and prepare for you to eat the Passover?"
He sent two of his disciples and said to them,
"Go into the city and a man will meet you,
carrying a jar of water.
Follow him.
Wherever he enters, say to the master of the house,
'The Teacher says, "Where is my guest room
where I may eat the Passover with my disciples?"'
Then he will show you a large upper room furnished and ready.
Make the preparations for us there."
The disciples then went off, entered the city,
and found it just as he had told them;
and they prepared the Passover.

While they were eating,
he took bread, said the blessing,
broke it, gave it to them, and said,
"Take it; this is my body."
Then he took a cup, gave thanks, and gave it to them,
and they all drank from it.

Continued in Appendix A, p. 306.

Praying with Gospel Words and Phrases

This is my body . . . This is my blood of the covenant . . .

Reflecting on the Gospel

No one should be surprised that the gospel today is an institution narrative. While a centuries-old solemnity, the celebration of late has taken on renewed significance. Many of us are familiar with the expression "source and summit of our faith." In fact, this expression has blossomed and become widely known among a large number of the faithful, particularly over the last two decades or so. A resurgence in eucharistic devotion has brought about an awareness of what the church says and teaches regarding the Eucharist. For instance, we read in the *Catechism*, "The Eucharist is 'the source and summit of the Christian life'" (CCC 1324). It is drawing from the Vatican II text *Lumen Gentium* as it says this, notably regarding the faithful: "Taking part in the Eucharistic sacrifice, the source and summit of the christian life, they offer the divine victim to God and themselves along with him" (LG 11).

Note that the quote from *Lumen Gentium* refers specifically to taking part in the eucharistic sacrifice—that is, the whole of Mass, not just the consumption of the host, or the host itself and its worship outside of Mass. This is bolstered in meaning by *Sacrosanctum Concilium*, when early on it says, "Nevertheless, the liturgy is the summit toward which the activity of the church is directed; it is also the source from which all its power flows. For the goal of apostolic endeavor is that all who are made children of God by faith and Baptism should come together to praise God in the midst of his church, to take part in the sacrifice and to eat the Lord's Supper" (SC 10).

To the Point

Understanding that it is the liturgy itself, the whole action of the church at prayer, that is source and summit, font and apex, is an integral part of our communal spirituality. It is one that, if it was ever particularly strong, appears to be quickly fading. While we must celebrate our belief in what the eucharistic substances are and what they become (and, in part the mystery of *how* they become), this is another significant example of a faith that might be better expressed in terms of verbs instead of nouns—that is, it's in the doing and activity of our faith that it becomes alive, not in the objects we rightly revere in wonder and awe.

Preparing to Proclaim, Preach, and Pray

Making Connections Between the Readings: It surely is not accidental that the reading from the book of Exodus is about ritual sacrifice, and explicitly, the blood of sacrificed bulls. While we are accustomed to hearing about the first Passover and the blood of lambs smeared upon the lintels, here the blood of the covenant is sprinkled directly on the people! (If you are the lector of this reading, do not shy away from that critical moment. Make sure the proclamation is vivid and evocative.)

While this obviously prefigures the once, final, and for-all sacrifice of Christ, the language can nonetheless be jarring. We will recall the passage in Revelation where the martyrs' robes have become dazzlingly white, washed in the blood of the Lamb. There is a visceral "realness" to blood as a real and tangible sign of the covenant.

The epistle describes how Christ's death on the cross replaced the practice of animal sacrifice as a profoundly more effective act of worship and sanctification. And as much as last Sunday's celebration of the Trinity was, in part, one of adoption, so too we hear here that Christ's sacrifice makes him the mediator of the new and everlasting covenant, that "those who are called may receive the promised eternal inheritance."

Making Connections to the Responsorial Psalm: Just as it ought not surprise anyone that the gospel today is an institution narrative, nor should it surprise anyone that the psalm for today is a reprise of sorts from the Holy Thursday Mass of the Lord's Supper. The refrain is different, we will observe, and again points us toward blood, or at least the cup that the blood is found in.

While it's common in our hymns to sing of bread that we understand to be Christ's body, the "scriptural warrants" for singing similarly of wine are not there. Rather, Scripture uses "cup" instead. The word "cup" carries with it different significance than does "wine." Wine can have connotations of joy and jollity. The word "cup" can bring to mind one's fate in life, as Jesus prayed in the Garden of Gethsemane and as mentioned in Mark 10:38: "Can you drink the cup that I drink . . . ?" A cup is also something shared among those gathered, inasmuch as all participate in Christ's covenantal relationship.

CONNECTING TO EXPERIENCE: LIVING THE PASCHAL MYSTERY

On the first day of Passover, instead of preparing a paschal lamb, Jesus was preparing himself. When his disciples asked, "Where do you want us to go?" to prepare the feast, Jesus might have closed his eyes and thought: to the Garden of Eden—where there is no sin, no sadness, no death or sorrow. But Jesus doesn't wish for Eden. He claims this cup, saying: "This is my blood of the covenant . . . shed for many." And for you. When we come to the Lord's Supper, do we also long for the Garden of Eden? In our world touched by sin, we cannot re-enter the Garden, but we can join Jesus in the paschal feast that never ends. Jesus asks us, filled with his eucharistic feast, to bring about the Garden of Eden here on earth. Let us commit to being his body, bringing healing and offering love. For all.

PROMPTS FOR FAITH-SHARING

- Is there something to which you long to return? How can Christ help you to move forward rather than backward?
- Christ has prepared himself for us, but are you feeling prepared for him this week? If not, what is keeping you from being ready?
- Like Christ, how can you lay down your life for those who need you in a new way?

Model Penitential Act

Presider: Mindful that we often fall short of the self-gift that we witness in Christ, we call upon the mercy of our God . . . *[pause]*

Lord Jesus, your very presence is the fullness of the law: Lord, have mercy.

Christ Jesus, your body and blood give us redemption and life: Christ, have mercy.

Lord Jesus, your mercy and love bring us an eternal inheritance: Lord, have mercy.

Model Universal Prayer (Prayer of the Faithful)

Presider: Trusting that our God is truly for us, we approach him as we seek the well-being of the church and our world.

Response: Lord, hear our prayer.

For our Holy Father N.: that he might continue to gather the nations into Christ's body by his witness to the gospel, we pray . . .

For the leaders of nations: that they might heed the gospel's call for faith and repentance, we pray . . .

For the poorest members of Christ's body: that they might find healing, community, and peace and so find the wealth of our Lord, we pray . . .

For this parish: that its members might grow closer to one another by the observance of prayer and service, becoming more fully Christ's body for one another, we pray . . .

Presider: O God, you gather us into one by the saving body and blood of your Son, Christ Jesus. Confident in our union with him, we offer these petitions for the life of the world. We ask this through Christ our Lord. **Amen.**

Liturgy and Music

Note that while the older and still familiar name for this solemnity is the feast of Corpus Christi, the current and proper name acknowledges both the body *and blood* of Christ. To that end, consider music that focuses on Jesus's blood, and of drinking in his life and love. "At the Lamb's High Feast We Sing" includes the line, "Where the Paschal blood is poured, death's dark angel sheathes his sword . . ." and could be a nice connection to the Easter season just completed. "Come to Me and Drink" (OCP) by Bob Hurd, "Behold the Lamb" (OCP) by Martin Willett, or "Take and Eat" (GIA) by Michael Joncas deserve consideration too.

While we believe that either species on its own is the fullness of body, blood, soul, and divinity, there is a lavish fullness to the sacrament when offered to all under both species. The Covid-19

(continued on next page)

COLLECT

Let us pray.

Pause for silent prayer

O God, who in this wonderful Sacrament
have left us a memorial of your Passion,
grant us, we pray,
so to revere the sacred mysteries of your
Body and Blood
that we may always experience in
ourselves
the fruits of your redemption.
Who live and reign with God the Father
in the unity of the Holy Spirit,
God, for ever and ever. **Amen.**

FIRST READING

Exod 24:3-8

When Moses came to the people
and related all the words and ordinances
of the LORD,
they all answered with one voice,
"We will do everything that the LORD
has told us."
Moses then wrote down all the words of
the LORD and,
rising early the next day,
he erected at the foot of the mountain an
altar
and twelve pillars for the twelve tribes
of Israel.
Then, having sent certain young men of
the Israelites
to offer holocausts and sacrifice young
bulls
as peace offerings to the LORD,
Moses took half of the blood and put it
in large bowls;
the other half he splashed on the altar.
Taking the book of the covenant, he read it
aloud to the people,
who answered, "All that the LORD has
said, we will heed and do."
Then he took the blood and sprinkled it on
the people, saying,
"This is the blood of the covenant
that the LORD has made with you
in accordance with all these words of
his."

RESPONSORIAL PSALM
Ps 116:12-13, 15-16, 17-18

℟. (13) I will take the cup of salvation, and
call on the name of the Lord.
or: ℟. Alleluia.

How shall I make a return to the LORD
for all the good he has done for me?
The cup of salvation I will take up,
and I will call upon the name of the
LORD.

℟. I will take the cup of salvation, and call
on the name of the Lord.
or: ℟. Alleluia.

Precious in the eyes of the LORD
is the death of his faithful ones.
I am your servant, the son of your
handmaid;
you have loosed my bonds.

℟. I will take the cup of salvation, and call
on the name of the Lord.
or: ℟. Alleluia.

To you will I offer sacrifice of
thanksgiving,
and I will call upon the name of the
LORD.
My vows to the LORD I will pay
in the presence of all his people.

℟. I will take the cup of salvation, and call
on the name of the Lord.
or: ℟. Alleluia.

SECOND READING
Heb 9:11-15

OPTIONAL SEQUENCE
See Appendix A, p. 306.

pandemic may seem like a distant and strange memory at this point, but many parishes that had formerly offered Eucharist under both species fell out of that practice as churches began to regather. If any of this describes your parish, it may be time to revisit that discussion. If it is your practice that the assembly only receives the body of Christ, does the music sung during the procession align with that practice? That is, don't musically invite those in the pews, "Come to me and drink" if you don't actually offer them anything to drink.

Liturgical Ministers: Music Ministers

On this solemnity, the church marvels at the gift of Christ's presence in the Eucharist. Music ministers are called to be shaped by that mystery, not only through their song but through their prayer and life. The hymns and chants chosen for this day carry centuries of eucharistic devotion and theology, forming the assembly in awe and thanksgiving. For music ministers, this is a feast to deepen reverence. It is not to impress, but to let music become a channel of worship. Music ministers become students of the liturgy by spending time with these texts and melodies, allowing them to form their hearts. The ministry of music is a participation in Christ's self-giving love, as every sung note serves to draw the church into adoration. In a world that often values sound over silence, this ministry reminds the assembly that beauty and reverence are essential ways of proclaiming the presence of Christ.

*Living Liturgy: The Sequence (*Lauda Sion*)*

The sequence for Corpus Christi is a theological masterpiece, rich with imagery and truth. Its verses proclaim Christ as the true manna, food for the journey, and the fulfillment of ancient promise. In lifting our voices with *Lauda Sion*, we profess that what we receive at the altar is no symbol but Christ himself, given for our salvation. The liturgy becomes a school of belief, shaping how we see and live. Eucharistic faith is learned here: to adore, to receive, and to be sent. The sequence leads us into contemplation, reminding us that this sacrament is at once a banquet of love and a sacrifice of redemption. Corpus Christi invites us to let the words of this ancient hymn take root, forming us into a people who live what they sing, becoming Christ's presence for the world.

SPIRITUALITY

GOSPEL ACCLAMATION
Matt 11:29ab

℟. Alleluia, alleluia.
Take my yoke upon you, says the Lord;
and learn from me, for I am meek and humble of heart.
℟. Alleluia, alleluia.

or 1 John 4:10b

℟. Alleluia, alleluia.
God first loved us
and sent his Son as expiation for our sins.
℟. Alleluia, alleluia.

Gospel

John 19:31-37; L171B

Since it was preparation day,
in order that the bodies might not remain on the cross on the sabbath,
for the sabbath day of that week was a solemn one,
the Jews asked Pilate that their legs be broken
and they be taken down.
So the soldiers came and broke the legs of the first
and then of the other one who was crucified with Jesus.

Continued in Appendix A, p. 307.

See Appendix A, p. 307, for the other readings.

Praying with Gospel Words and Phrases

One soldier thrust his lance into his side, and immediately blood and water flowed out . . .

Reflecting on the Gospel

The typically drawn heart, at least as usually depicted by Hallmark or on elementary school St. Valentine's Day cards, is a rather sanitized expression of the human organ, vital and, yes, bloody. It is also, frankly, a sanitized expression of what "love" is, or at least the way many people live out love for their family, friends, and spouse.

One can of course define "love" many differing ways. "I love pickles!" may be common secular parlance, but that's not what the church means, of course, when speaking of love. Christ himself teaches us that there is no greater love than the one who lays down his life for his friends. Love is literally life. To love someone completely is to give up—or at least to be willing to give up—your life for them. Christ stands as the fullest example of this love, this life-blood, shed for the redemption of the world.

Last Sunday's solemnity considered quite incessantly the bloodiness of Christ's sacrifice and covenant. There is no escaping it: the realness that permeates so much of our faith is present here in raw and palpable form. We all have blood flowing through our arteries and veins, and we've all seen our own and others' blood from wounds both accidental and, unfortunately, sometimes purposeful. Blood is about as real and human as it gets.

Today's devotion is about the heart of Christ, unsanitized and "real," pierced by the soldier's lance while on the cross, and a love expressed by that same torturous and sacrificial death. For those who are preparing this liturgy, take every opportunity to make Christ's heart and Christ's love as "real" as you can. Do the prayers and other texts of liturgy allow for contemplation of Christ and how, in the words of a song by Shannon Cerneka, "love is less about feeling than sacrifice"?

To the Point

Be careful not to shy away from anything liturgically, which, because it is "real" and honest, makes us or those around us uncomfortable. It is likely in this discomfort where Christ is active and speaking to our own sacred hearts.

Model Penitential Act

Presider: Even on the cross, Jesus did not cease to love. Mindful of his mercy, we ask for his pardon and peace . . . *[pause]*

Lord Jesus, you invite us to faith in you: Lord, have mercy.
Christ Jesus, you offer hope to the hopeless: Christ, have mercy.
Lord Jesus, your love is greater than life: Lord, have mercy.

Model Universal Prayer (Prayer of the Faithful)

Presider: Lifting our hearts to the Lord who opens his Most Sacred Heart to us, we offer our prayers and petitions.

Response: Lord, hear our prayer.

For the church throughout the world: may our capacity to love one another inspire the world to go and do likewise, we pray . . .

For our leaders at home and in our nation: may they be guided by wisdom and compassion, we pray . . .

For the suffering, the sick, and the sorrowful: may they receive the healing they desire, we pray . . .

For all who seek greater unity with Christ: may the Spirit set their hearts on fire this day, we pray . . .

Presider: Lord God, you show us your love through the brokenness of your Son, Jesus Christ. Hear our prayers this day, dispel our fears, and allow us to bring love to a world in need of healing. We ask this through Christ our Lord. **Amen.**

COLLECT

Let us pray.

Grant, we pray, almighty God,
that we, who glory in the Heart of your beloved Son
and recall the wonders of his love for us,
may be made worthy to receive
an overflowing measure of grace
from that fount of heavenly gifts.
Through our Lord Jesus Christ, your Son,
who lives and reigns with you in the unity of the Holy Spirit,
God, for ever and ever. **Amen.**

or:

O God, who in the Heart of your Son,
wounded by our sins,
bestow on us in mercy
the boundless treasures of your love,
grant, we pray,
that, in paying him the homage of our devotion,
we may also offer worthy reparation.
Through our Lord Jesus Christ, your Son,
who lives and reigns with you in the unity of the Holy Spirit,
God, for ever and ever. **Amen.**

Liturgical Ministers: Altar Servers

This solemnity reveals the love of Christ poured out for humanity, symbolized by his pierced heart. Altar servers are invited to enter this mystery not only by their service but by letting the liturgy shape their hearts. Serving at the altar places them near the source of grace, where they see firsthand that the Eucharist is the expression of Christ's love. This ministry forms young disciples, teaching that reverence is a language of faith and that love is shown in attention to detail. The Sacred Heart calls servers to see their ministry as a silent witness to God's love at work. Over time, servers become leaders by example, drawing others into deeper participation. Their service nurtures a sense of vocation, showing that the church's future is formed through prayer and devotion. The Sacred Heart invites them to model humility and joy to serve wherever God calls.

Living Liturgy: The Preface of the Sacred Heart

The preface for this feast invites the assembly to contemplate Christ's love made visible in his wounded heart. Every sacrament flows from this love, and the Eucharist is not only nourishment but encounter. Praying these words reveals that belief is formed at the altar, where Christ's sacrifice is made present. This preface calls us to recognize that devotion to the Sacred Heart is not sentiment but participation in God's saving work.

The liturgical experience draws us into this mystery. It is the love that suffers, redeems, and remains with us. The liturgy becomes a place of transformation, shaping believers to reflect this divine love in the world. As we kneel before the altar, we stand before Christ himself, whose heart remains open, inviting us to trust and to serve with that same generosity.

SPIRITUALITY

GOSPEL ACCLAMATION
John 12:31b-32

℟. Alleluia, alleluia.
Now the ruler of this world will be driven out, says the Lord;
and when I am lifted up from the earth, I will draw everyone to myself.
℟. Alleluia, alleluia.

Gospel Mark 3:20-35; L89B

Jesus came home with his disciples.
Again the crowd gathered,
making it impossible for them even to eat.
When his relatives heard of this they set out to seize him,
for they said, "He is out of his mind."
The scribes who had come from Jerusalem said,
"He is possessed by Beelzebul,"
and "By the prince of demons he drives out demons."

Summoning them, he began to speak to them in parables,
"How can Satan drive out Satan?
If a kingdom is divided against itself,
that kingdom cannot stand.
And if a house is divided against itself,
that house will not be able to stand.
And if Satan has risen up against himself
and is divided, he cannot stand;
that is the end of him.
But no one can enter a strong man's house to plunder his property
unless he first ties up the strong man.
Then he can plunder the house.
Amen, I say to you,
all sins and all blasphemies that people utter will be forgiven them.
But whoever blasphemes against the Holy Spirit
will never have forgiveness,
but is guilty of an everlasting sin."
For they had said, "He has an unclean spirit."

Continued in Appendix A, p. 308.

Praying with Gospel Words and Phrases

How can Satan drive out Satan . . . Whoever does the will of God is my brother and sister and mother . . .

Reflecting on the Gospel

Two accusations are leveled against Jesus by the scribes in today's gospel. First, that he is possessed by an unclean spirit, because secondly, that is the only explanation for his power over demons. Jesus responds, as is so commonly seen, with parables. This preferred method of teaching by Jesus likely served multiple purposes. It allowed him to simultaneously reveal and conceal: revealing God's truth to those open to it and concealing it to those closed off. The commonplace imagery of parables also invited contemplation, reflection, and potential conversion. The messiah was also prophesied to teach in parables; see Psalm 78:2: "I will open my mouth in a parable, unfold the puzzling events of the past."

Mark's Gospel often abruptly jumps from scene to scene, and today's pericope is no exception. Coming off of a couple weeks where we could reflect on our adoption by God, it's noteworthy here that Jesus is redefining what it means to be family. Even—and perhaps especially—in our modern context, what constitutes a family continues to evolve, expand, and account for a myriad of circumstances. Jesus teaches that to him, family is "whoever does the will of God."

Would that every parish family be bold enough to embrace that definition! Inasmuch as no follower of Jesus is perfect, this Sunday is a good time for each of us to check ourselves, both as individuals and as part of a Christian community. Are there certain sins, more than others, that you see as "exclusionary" to belonging to the community? Do not all sinners strive to do the will of God? Are there certain aspects of another's life you perceive as sinful that may not actually be so? Did Jesus not teach us elsewhere to rid the plank from our own eye first?

To the Point

The parables of Jesus resist any definitive interpretation, any one-for-one analogizing or meaning. So too with our brothers and sisters in the family of God, our perceptions must be through the lens of God's truth, love, and mercy, always seeking the ways in which others strive to live God's will more than any other attributes that may distract us.

Preparing to Proclaim, Preach, and Pray

Making Connections Between the Readings: This sinfulness we all share is completely universal, an aspect of each person's life from the very first scriptural humans, Adam and Eve. It's noteworthy that, as each of us on the path of discipleship is striving to better know and live the will of God, to better align our will with God's, the original sin of Adam and Eve is, essentially, the desire to fully have the mind of God. The snake's temptation just a few verses before today's pericope: "your eyes will be opened and you will be like gods, who know good and evil" (Gen 3:5). Like most sinfulness, this first sin is an overabundance of something good and holy.

In Ordinary Time, the epistle passages are not part of the Sunday celebration because of any common thematic material. Rather, large chunks of epistles are read and studied in sequential order. Yet almost always there will be connections to be made. Paul speaks of the fragile and temporary earthly condition, our fleshly "tents," in contrast to the glory that awaits those of us who live our faith seeking grace, truth, and alignment with the divine will. The "light affliction" of human weakness is deemed almost necessary for God's glory to be sensed rightly: immense, eternal, and "beyond all comparison."

Making Connections to the Responsorial Psalm: With sinfulness an inborn part of the human condition, mercy and redemption balance the scales as part of who God is and what God does. Psalm 130 is the exemplar of psalms of lament: "Out of the depths . . ." it begins, imploring God to hear our cries before turning our attention to the greatness of God, worthy of our trust, hope, and praise.

Many psalm settings use the same music for each set of verses, regardless of their meaning. And that can function satisfactorily when the psalm's text is monolithic: all praise or thankfulness, for instance. Today's psalm takes the believer on a spiritual journey, and ideally a composer would help paint that journey by setting the verses in differing ways, amplifying the meaning of each verse a bit differently. Even if your chosen setting does not do this, your psalmist can vary their expressive delivery of this beautiful text to effectively communicate the variety of meanings in the verses.

CONNECTING TO EXPERIENCE: LIVING THE PASCHAL MYSTERY

If we say we believe in Christ Jesus, do we show that we believe? Do we show that we love? Does our outreach end with those closest to us—our family and friends, or political allies? In today's gospel, in the midst of gawking crowds and quibbling scribes, Jesus gets word that his family has arrived. In a world where kinship loyalties exerted powerful force, Jesus should have expelled the crowding onlookers immediately and welcomed those known to him instead. But Jesus looks at the crowd of questioning, hungry strangers and says: "Whoever does the will of God is my brother and sister and mother." Jesus teaches that kinship does not triumph over belief in him. The bonds of baptism that forge our relationship as adopted children of God break boundaries of separation forged by humans. Our belief demands that our celebration of the sacraments spill into our proclaiming Christ's word in charity and outreach.

PROMPTS FOR FAITH-SHARING

- Do you love those who need you most? Are those people different from those with whom you are most familiar or comfortable?
- Have you ever chosen to spend your time with your family of faith rather than your family of origin?
- Do you have the courage to go against some of the unnecessary expectations others may have for you? To go against your own unnecessary expectations?

Model Penitential Act

Presider: In our first reading today, we hear how our first parents chose sin and destruction over relationship with God. Let us call to mind the times when we have failed to listen to God, hiding from him instead . . . *[pause]*

Lord Jesus, you bestow grace in abundance on your people: Lord, have mercy.

Christ Jesus, you draw all people to yourself: Christ, have mercy.

Lord Jesus, you heal us from our iniquities and cleanse us from our sin: Lord, have mercy.

Model Universal Prayer (Prayer of the Faithful)

Presider: Trusting in the Lord who listens to our voice, we bring him our prayers and supplications for ourselves and all the world.

Response: Lord, hear our prayer.

For the church fed by the sacraments and led by the word: may we bring Christ's love to life in our works of charity and justice, we pray . . .

For those who lead, teach, and shape the lives of those around them: may they seek to bring about the glory of God in all they do, we pray . . .

For all who suffer from the violence of war and terror: may they find protection and peace in the mercy of Christ and the help of their neighbors, we pray . . .

For the church gathered here today: may we bring hope to those who are discouraged, we pray . . .

Presider: Lord God, you draw all people to yourself. As we lift our prayers to you, may we be raised with the Lord Jesus, and so always dwell in your presence. We ask this through Christ our Lord. **Amen.**

Liturgy and the Sanctoral Cycle

This is the Sunday we're often "welcomed back" to Ordinary Time—usually during the opening greeting or homily. But Ordinary Time actually began two weeks ago, on Trinity Sunday, even though the vestments remained white until today, and only now do we hear the phrase "Sunday in Ordinary Time."

Alongside this welcome, there's often a remark about how green vestments haven't appeared in months, and how—after Easter and the feasts of the Trinity and the Body and Blood of Christ—we're returning to "Ordinary" Time, as though it were somehow dull or insignificant. Others may overcorrect by calling it "extraordinary," emphasizing the weeks of discipleship formation ahead, found, in the upcoming readings.

(continued on next page)

COLLECT

Let us pray.

Pause for silent prayer

O God, from whom all good things come,
grant that we, who call on you in our need,
may at your prompting discern what is right,
and by your guidance do it.
Through our Lord Jesus Christ, your Son,
who lives and reigns with you in the unity of the Holy Spirit,
God, for ever and ever.

FIRST READING

Gen 3:9-15

After the man, Adam, had eaten of the tree,
the LORD God called to the man and asked him, "Where are you?"
He answered, "I heard you in the garden;
but I was afraid, because I was naked,
so I hid myself."
Then he asked, "Who told you that you were naked?
You have eaten, then,
from the tree of which I had forbidden you to eat!"
The man replied, "The woman whom you put here with me—
she gave me fruit from the tree, and so I ate it."
The LORD God then asked the woman,
"Why did you do such a thing?"
The woman answered, "The serpent tricked me into it, so I ate it."

Then the LORD God said to the serpent:
"Because you have done this, you shall be banned
from all the animals
and from all the wild creatures;
on your belly shall you crawl,
and dirt shall you eat
all the days of your life.
I will put enmity between you and the woman,
and between your offspring and hers;
he will strike at your head,
while you strike at his heel."

RESPONSORIAL PSALM

Ps 130:1-2, 3-4, 5-6, 7-8

℟. (7bc) With the Lord there is mercy, and fullness of redemption.

Out of the depths I cry to you, O LORD;
LORD, hear my voice!

Let your ears be attentive
to my voice in supplication.

℟. With the Lord there is mercy, and
fullness of redemption.

If you, O LORD, mark iniquities,
LORD, who can stand?
But with you is forgiveness,
that you may be revered.

℟. With the Lord there is mercy, and
fullness of redemption.

I trust in the LORD;
my soul trusts in his word.
More than sentinels wait for the dawn,
let Israel wait for the LORD.

℟. With the Lord there is mercy, and
fullness of redemption.

For with the LORD is kindness
and with him is plenteous redemption;
and he will redeem Israel
from all their iniquities.

℟. With the Lord there is mercy, and
fullness of redemption.

SECOND READING
2 Cor 4:13–5:1

Brothers and sisters:
Since we have the same spirit of faith,
according to what is written, *I believed, therefore I spoke,*
we too believe and therefore we speak,
knowing that the one who raised the Lord Jesus
will raise us also with Jesus
and place us with you in his presence.
Everything indeed is for you,
so that the grace bestowed in abundance on more and more people
may cause the thanksgiving to overflow for the glory of God.
Therefore, we are not discouraged;
rather, although our outer self is wasting away,
our inner self is being renewed day by day.
For this momentary light affliction
is producing for us an eternal weight of glory
beyond all comparison,
as we look not to what is seen but to what is unseen;
for what is seen is transitory, but what is unseen is eternal.

Continued in Appendix A, p. 308.

While the latter point is true, calling this time "extraordinary" misunderstands the terminology. "Ordinary Time" isn't called that because it's plain or routine—it comes from the use of ordinal numbers (first, second, third . . .) in how these Sundays are counted. Likewise, in church language, "extraordinary" doesn't just mean "amazing" or "special." It typically means "outside the norm"—as in extraordinary ministers of Holy Communion, who assist when ordinary (ordained) ministers are unavailable.

These weeks of Ordinary Time—though not part of Advent, Christmas, Lent, or Easter—are deeply important for the church's life, prayer, and formation. We should be mindful of how we speak about them, recognizing their quiet depth and essential role in shaping us as disciples of Christ.

Liturgical Ministers: Lectors

This Sunday's readings reveal humanity's struggle with sin and God's constant desire to heal and restore. Lectors stand at the center of this drama, lending their voice to God's word that both convicts and consoles. This ministry is not about performance but about being steeped in Scripture so that the word becomes alive when proclaimed. Lectors are called to enter prayerfully into the story, allowing it to transform them before they speak it.
In this way, proclamation becomes an act of witness, not recitation. When they proclaim passages like the account of Adam and Eve or Christ's response to his critics, they model how faith listens to God even in moments of difficulty. The lector's formation is lifelong, rooted in study, prayer, and an ever-deepening love of Scripture. By serving at the ambo, they remind the assembly that God still speaks, and that his word has the power to create, challenge, and heal.

Living Liturgy: The Collect

"O God, from whom all good things come, grant that we . . . discern what is right, and by your guidance do it." This simple plea names God as the source of all goodness and wisdom, shifting our focus away from self-reliance. In this prayer, the church stands like Adam in the garden, aware of weakness yet longing for God's healing guidance. It is a prayer of humility, reminding us that discipleship begins in listening rather than striving.
The words prepare us to hear Christ's teaching in the Gospel of Mark, where those who do the Father's will are named as his family. The collect forms us into this family, shaping a posture of obedience that flows from trust. By praying these words together, the assembly learns that Christian life is not only about choosing good but receiving it as a gift from God. Each time this prayer is lifted, we are drawn back to the truth that holiness begins not with our effort but with God's grace, freely given and faithfully received.

SPIRITUALITY

GOSPEL ACCLAMATION
℟. Alleluia, alleluia.
The seed is the word of God, Christ is the sower.
All who come to him will live for ever.
℟. Alleluia, alleluia.

Gospel

Mark 4:26-34; L92B

Jesus said to the crowds:
"This is how it is with the kingdom of God;
it is as if a man were to scatter seed on the land
and would sleep and rise night and day
and through it all the seed would sprout and grow,
he knows not how.
Of its own accord the land yields fruit,
first the blade, then the ear, then the full grain in the ear.
And when the grain is ripe, he wields the sickle at once,
for the harvest has come."

He said,
"To what shall we compare the kingdom of God,
or what parable can we use for it?
It is like a mustard seed that, when it is sown in the ground,
is the smallest of all the seeds on the earth.
But once it is sown, it springs up and becomes the largest of plants
and puts forth large branches,
so that the birds of the sky can dwell in its shade."
With many such parables
he spoke the word to them as they were able to understand it.
Without parables he did not speak to them,
but to his own disciples he explained everything in private.

Praying with Gospel Words and Phrases

It is like a mustard seed . . . it springs up and becomes the largest of plants . . .

Reflecting on the Gospel

The mustard seed in Jesus's parable today is small, unassuming, and ordinary. Yet it is from exactly this that a sprout grows to become the largest of plants. God can take the ordinary and from it, if hearts are receptive and willing, bring about holiness, devotion, and even saintliness.

Consider the posture of sitting—likely the posture you are in right now, reading this. It is perhaps the most ordinary posture we humans have. Whether at a desk in a workplace or relaxing at home, eating a meal, watching a movie or a play in a theater, sitting is perhaps the posture in which we spend most of our days.

When we consider the postures utilized at liturgy, sitting is typically overlooked, or given short shrift. Sitting may not look like action or power, but it is the posture of growth—the fertile stillness where something begins to take root. Just as the mustard seed holds hidden potential for astonishing growth, sitting attentively before the Word allows the seed of faith to be planted and nurtured in us.

Sitting isn't the full vulnerability of lying down, nor the powerful stature of standing; it hovers somewhere in between, not action, not rest, yet it is calm, watchful, alert. If we let it, it can become a posture of receptivity, of openness, of a willingness to hear and understand. We spend much of the Liturgy of the Word in this posture, listening to Scripture, and that Scripture broken open in a well-crafted homily.

For a presider, the chair has dignity and presidential authority when it is used; for a bishop, that *cathedra* is so important that the building it occupies—a cathedral—is named for it. Let us pray that our servant-leaders are mindful that, when sitting, they too are called to hear and understand the words of Scripture and the needs of the flock they shepherd.

To the Point

Like the birds resting in the shade of the mustard tree's branches, the church becomes a place of shelter and rest—but only if it grows from the quiet, ordinary act of receptivity, often while sitting, attentive and ready.

Preparing to Proclaim, Preach, and Pray

Making Connections Between the Readings: Today's reading from Ezekiel is quite apparently connected to the gospel parable of the mustard seed, as both speak of the reign of God growing from small beginnings into something expansive, sheltering, and full of life. God is the planter, starting with the smallest seed, the smallest shoot, and from that humble beginning there eventually arrives an impressive outcome: not just surprising growth, but growth into a place of shelter, serenity, and strength. Each of these Scripture readings exhibits such hopefulness: that God's reign can and will flourish, even when its beginnings seem fragile.

And just as the mighty cedar or the impressive mustard plant becomes a home, we must come to understand that this earthly existence we live is but a small shoot, a tiny seed. These bodies of flesh are but a temporary home, Paul writes to the Corinthians, while we aspire to our eventual and eternal home with the Lord. We must always be cautious, while wishing to bring God's vision of holiness to birth here on earth, to know that we are but helpers of that mission, and that the goal will only know fullness of life at Christ's second coming. Rather than inducing any frustration, we should find peace and liberation in that, in the words of Bishop Ken Untener's well-known prayer, "Prophets of a Future Not Our Own," which might be a worthy addition to today's preaching or musical offerings.

Making Connections to the Responsorial Psalm: Psalm 92 today links the first reading and the gospel by introducing the holy practice of gratitude and praise to our reflections. The superficial connections are obvious: the flourishing palm tree, the sturdy cedar—yet here we also hear of the mature plants bearing fruit, a detail absent from the other readings, which dwell on shelter and security. This fruit is not only gratitude, but the example of a just life, just as our God is just, and the public declaration of the goodness and strength of God, the "rock, in whom there is no wrong."

This sort of evangelization by example is so needed in our world today, where far too often people "talk the talk" without "walking the walk." Beyond that, we faithful must be attentive to the simple, holy deeds of others, and the ways in which an unassuming Christian life may better build the reign of God than 10,000 fiery and zealous words of faith and conviction.

CONNECTING TO EXPERIENCE: LIVING THE PASCHAL MYSTERY

We hear the word "parable" day in and day out in the synoptic Gospels of Matthew, Mark, and Luke. The word literally means a "throwing alongside." Jesus throws one idea, image, or metaphor, alongside the kingdom of God. He throws many ideas: from seeds and salt to pearls and treasure. Interestingly, Jesus never uses an abstract concept, such as "the kingdom of God is like pure reason"; he almost always sticks with something we can hold in our hands and see with our eyes. Jesus routinely leans on the stuff of the earth—creation—to hear and see the Lord, and allow us to "catch" the meaning of the kingdom of God he throws to us. Jesus, with the Father at the dawn of creation, has come down to earth. He throws his words alongside us. Will we have ears to hear and hearts to listen? Will we let our lives become a parable that we can show and share with those around us?

PROMPTS FOR FAITH-SHARING

- What about Jesus's parables do you find difficult to understand?
- Of the images Jesus uses to explain the kingdom of God, which connects with you most readily?
- Do you feel that you are fertile soil for the word of God? What might be keeping you from receiving the gospel more fully?

Model Penitential Act

Presider: Today, the Scriptures reflect on the smallest of seeds growing to bear good fruit. Remembering the times we have failed to bear good fruit, we ask for his mercy and peace . . . *[pause]*

Lord Jesus, your faithfulness is constant even in our failure: Lord, have mercy.

Christ Jesus, you call us always to return to yourself: Christ, have mercy.

Lord Jesus, in you alone we find mercy and peace: Lord, have mercy.

Model Universal Prayer (Prayer of the Faithful)

Presider: Gathering our prayers and petitions, we offer them before the Lord who comes to dwell in our midst.

Response: Lord, hear our prayer.

For the church, scattered throughout the world: may the word of God take root in the hearts of young people and fill them with zeal for their faith, we pray . . .

For nations struggling against the powers of corruption: may their leaders be filled with courage to withstand political pressures and to protect their people, we pray . . .

For all those suffering in mind, body, and spirit: may they take strength and courage in the Lord's mercy, and find healing at the hands of their caregivers, we pray . . .

For all gathered here this day: may we remember our mission to go forth and witness to the love of Christ through our daily lives, we pray . . .

Presider: Loving God, you gather all people to yourself. Hear our prayers this day and allow us who have heard your word to share the joy of the gospel throughout the earth. We ask this through Christ our Lord. **Amen.**

Liturgy and Sung Parables

The Gospel of Mark is not as laden with parables as other gospels, yet today we hear two, both with seeds playing a pivotal role. "Seed, Scattered and Sown" (International Liturgy Publications [ILP]), is found in several hymnals and would make a thoughtful communion hymn this weekend. A more recent text by Shirley Erena Murray, "A Place at the Table," has settings by multiple composers and further paints what the reign of God ought to look like right here and now.

Parables like today's often begin in the gospels with words to alert us that we are going to learn something about the kingdom of God. We might easily and accidentally overlook that the phrase

(continued on next page)

COLLECT

Let us pray.

Pause for silent prayer

O God, strength of those who hope in you,
graciously hear our pleas,
and, since without you mortal frailty can do nothing,
grant us always the help of your grace,
that in following your commands
we may please you by our resolve and our deeds.
Through our Lord Jesus Christ, your Son,
who lives and reigns with you in the unity of the Holy Spirit,
God, for ever and ever. **Amen.**

FIRST READING

Ezek 17:22-24

Thus says the Lord God:
I, too, will take from the crest of the cedar,
from its topmost branches tear off a tender shoot,
and plant it on a high and lofty mountain;
on the mountain heights of Israel I will plant it.
It shall put forth branches and bear fruit,
and become a majestic cedar.
Birds of every kind shall dwell beneath it,
every winged thing in the shade of its boughs.
And all the trees of the field shall know that I, the Lord,
bring low the high tree,
lift high the lowly tree,
wither up the green tree,
and make the withered tree bloom.
As I, the Lord, have spoken, so will I do.

RESPONSORIAL PSALM
Ps 92:2-3, 13-14, 15-16

℟. (cf. 2a) Lord, it is good to give thanks to you.

It is good to give thanks to the LORD,
to sing praise to your name, Most High,
to proclaim your kindness at dawn
and your faithfulness throughout the night.

℟. Lord, it is good to give thanks to you.

The just one shall flourish like the palm tree,
like a cedar of Lebanon shall he grow.
They that are planted in the house of the LORD
shall flourish in the courts of our God.

℟. Lord, it is good to give thanks to you.

They shall bear fruit even in old age;
vigorous and sturdy shall they be,
declaring how just is the LORD,
my rock, in whom there is no wrong.

℟. Lord, it is good to give thanks to you.

SECOND READING
2 Cor 5:6-10

Brothers and sisters:
We are always courageous,
although we know that while we are at home in the body
we are away from the Lord,
for we walk by faith, not by sight.
Yet we are courageous,
and we would rather leave the body and go home to the Lord.
Therefore, we aspire to please him,
whether we are at home or away.
For we must all appear before the judgment seat of Christ,
so that each may receive recompense,
according to what he did in the body,
whether good or evil.

"kingdom of God" contains gendered language that is ultimately not necessary nor especially helpful. Substituting "reign" for "kingdom" is a simple way to alleviate that issue, when those choices are ours to make (not, for instance, with the missal itself, or with copyrighted music). We have already in this space examined how the title "Father" for that genderless person of the Trinity is not ideal and simultaneously without a suitable substitute that does not resort to "doing" rather than "being." Be mindful in preaching, the universal prayers, and in hymn selection to avoid, when possible, such exclusionary and imprecise language.

Liturgical Ministers: Music Ministers

In this Sunday's gospel, Jesus describes God's kingdom as a seed that grows silently, without human control, and becomes a place of shelter. Music ministers share in this mystery, offering their gifts so the Spirit can work quietly in the hearts of the faithful. Music has the power to make the invisible kingdom audible, inviting worshippers to sense God's nearness and respond in praise. This ministry is an act of trust. Ministers prepare carefully, yet the fruit of their work belongs to God. Music ministers are formed by the very words they sing, learning to proclaim hope even in times of uncertainty. Their service shows that music is not mere ornamentation in the liturgy but what we believe, revealing a God who plants and nurtures seeds of faith. Each hymn, chant, or psalm becomes a vessel of grace, shaping the community's faith and opening space for the Spirit's hidden work.

Living Liturgy: The Collect

The collect this Sunday names God as the strength of those who hope in him. Its brevity and simplicity reflect the parables we hear exalting that God's kingdom grows in mystery, yet with assurance. This prayer teaches that hope is not optimism but trust in the God who works even when we do not see. Praying these words together forms the church's vision, teaching us to expect God's action and to recognize grace at work in small beginnings. The collect itself becomes a seed, planted in our hearts, shaping us to see that every act of worship is a moment of growth. Over time, the liturgy trains us to hope in God's timing, not our own, and to rejoice in the quiet ways his kingdom takes root.

SPIRITUALITY

GOSPEL ACCLAMATION
Luke 7:16

℟. Alleluia, alleluia.
A great prophet has risen in our midst.
God has visited his people.
℟. Alleluia, alleluia.

Gospel

Mark 4:35-41; L95B

On that day, as evening drew on, Jesus said to his disciples:
"Let us cross to the other side."
Leaving the crowd, they took Jesus with them in the boat just as he was.
And other boats were with him.
A violent squall came up and waves were breaking over the boat,
so that it was already filling up.
Jesus was in the stern, asleep on a cushion.
They woke him and said to him,
"Teacher, do you not care that we are perishing?"
He woke up,
rebuked the wind, and said to the sea,
"Quiet! Be still!"
The wind ceased and there was great calm.
Then he asked them, "Why are you terrified?
Do you not yet have faith?"
They were filled with great awe and said to one another,
"Who then is this whom even wind and sea obey?"

Praying with Gospel Words and Phrases

Teacher, do you not care . . . "Quiet! Be still!" . . . Do you not yet have faith?. . .

Reflecting on the Gospel

Very few of us experience God in such an obvious, tangible way as do the disciples in today's gospel pericope. Have you ever seen the divine literally silence a stormy sea? I know I haven't, and likely never will. As a five-year-old, though, I had a different, more subtle, experience of God that was no less powerful.

I saw a sketch of a person with hands raised in prayer in a missalette open in my father's lap. It was accompanied by a caption, which I asked my father to read to me. "Here I am, Lord, I come to do your will," was the caption, quoting Psalm 40 from that Sunday's readings. Without telling anyone, I decided that this image and these words must be teaching me a new way to pray, that by taking this posture and saying these words, I would experience an immediate and clear response from the divine: "Well, today I want you to clean your room, help with the dishes after dinner, and try not to pick on your sister too much . . ."

Monday morning, I went out in the backyard to give it a try. Unsurprisingly, though I had the posture correct and prayed the words with all the fervor any five-year-old could muster, there was no obvious and immediate answer to my declaration. Further, no matter where I stood in the backyard, no matter how often I appealed to God, no answer came. Was I doing something wrong? Why wasn't God answering my earnest prayer the way I thought God would?

Today I know that prayer, especially the gathered liturgical prayer of the church, typically doesn't operate like that. This is not to say God is not communicating with us, trying to answer our prayers in accordance with divine will. Inasmuch as we might experience individually God's voice in communal prayer, the whole of the community also experiences God: Christ sharing himself by his presence in word, Eucharist, the priest-celebrant, and the assembly itself (SC, 7). The answer to our prayers at liturgy then, whatever they are, is always relationship with God (word, sacrifice, meal) and with one another (priest and assembly), all underpinned by faith and trust.

To the Point

While we may not experience God as immediately and dramatically as the disciples did, God still speaks to us—often subtly—through prayer, community, and liturgy. Even when we don't receive clear answers, God's response is always relationship: with Christ in word and sacrament, and with one another in faith.

Preparing to Proclaim, Preach, and Pray

Making Connections Between the Readings: In today's brief Old Testament passage, Job is reminded that only God (the Creator) has power over nature. Yes, the sea represents wildness and untamable chaos—but God is able to set its limits. Jesus, in today's gospel, does what God does in Job's presence. In both instances, the storm reveals (in Job, among the disciples) not just fear, but faith—faith in the One whose Word brings order to chaos, just as it did in the beginning (Gen 1).

One needs to squint a bit more than usual to find in today's epistle some element to bring into conversation with these two other readings. Certainly, Paul's writing here describes divine power in its ultimate manifestation: dying to overcome death and bring the gift of resurrection and new life to all. Christ's resurrection, we have already mentioned, is creation's "eighth day," a new creation in which we all share, as Paul reminds the Corinthains and us. "[T]he old things have passed away; behold, new things have come"—so it should be no surprise that the Son of God, who is himself God, should have such power over all creation. It is he who is the new creation.

We of course are not divine, but are yet a new creation in Christ, and one day destined to know loving union with him and with all the faithful and all of sacred creation.

Making Connections to the Responsorial Psalm: Such storytelling in today's psalm! That aspect of Psalm 107 is truly unique. Psalm 107, in its fullness, is a hymn of praise to God, who rescues us from four dire circumstances: the barren desert, imprisonment in gloom, mortal illness, and in today's gospel, the angry sea. Each episode ends with thanks to God, and each is reminiscent of the activity of God throughout salvation history.

We would be wise to link God's action of lifting the disciples from certain death in the deep waters—as with Job's plight, as with the saga told in Psalm 107—to our baptisms, in which we die with Christ that he may raise us to new life. In baptism we are made new creations, spiritually transformed to enter into a new relationship with God and the Christian community. Each baptized soul is a new creation in Christ, with the old self passing away.

CONNECTING TO EXPERIENCE: LIVING THE PASCHAL MYSTERY

What is it like to be caught in a storm? We might be in our home, hearing thunder crash and hoping the water won't rise. We might be in our car, clinging to taillights in front of us while we're blinded by the rain. Today, God speaks out of the storm; just as God the Father silenced the storm surrounding the suffering Job, Jesus the Son calms the waves crashing around the frightened disciples. In a storm, whether in our sky or in our hearts, we are distressed. The word of God calms the earth. Will we allow the word of God to calm our hearts? We began our life in Christ with our baptism—doused in water with the Holy Spirit. Baptism does not magically end distress. But baptism in the name of the Father, Son, and Holy Spirit promises that God will be with us, will calm our fears, and ask us anew every day to have faith in him.

PROMPTS FOR FAITH-SHARING

- Like Jesus's followers, do you struggle to remain calm when things are turbulent? How can you trust Christ to bring you calm?
- Do you believe that God's word can alter creation? How can God's word alter your life for the better today?
- Can Jesus's command to "be still" bring peace to some part of your life today? Where do you most need stillness?

Model Penitential Act

Presider: In our readings today, the Lord quells a raging storm in order to bring peace and show the greatness of his power. Let us allow the Lord to quiet our own tumultuous hearts and minds as we come before him asking for mercy . . . *[pause]*

Lord Jesus, you see and hear our affliction: Lord, have mercy.

Christ Jesus, you rescue us from our distress: Christ, have mercy.

Lord Jesus, you take away the bonds of sin and death: Lord, have mercy.

Model Universal Prayer (Prayer of the Faithful)

Presider: The Lord hears our distress and our every need. We bring our prayers and petitions before him, trusting in his providence and care.

Response: Lord, hear our prayer.

For the church: may we have greater courage to speak and be God's justice and mercy despite the tumult of the world around us, we pray . . .

For all who serve as leaders in their family, their workplaces, or their communities: may they have the wisdom to offer direction to those who rely upon them, we pray . . .

For those suffering from oppression and violence within their homes: may peace and protection come quickly, we pray . . .

For us who are gathered here today: may the love of Christ compel us to love those who surround us, we pray . . .

Presider: God our Father, just as you ordered the cosmos from chaos into creation, you dispel sin from our lives with your great love. Hear our prayers this day as we long for peace throughout our world. We ask this through Christ our Lord. **Amen.**

Liturgy and the Orans Position

The raising of hands is a most ancient practice of prayer. The USCCB document "Praying with Body, Mind, and Voice" states, "Early Christian art frequently depicts the saints and others standing in this posture, offering their prayers and surrendering themselves, with hands uplifted to the Lord, in a gesture that echoes Christ's outstretched arms as he offered himself on the Cross." The name itself means "prayer," as in the Latin litanic response "*ora pro nobis*."

There is much debate about whether the orans posture is reserved, always and everywhere, for a priest. The introduction of the *Book of Blessings* directs that while the ordained minister speaks words of blessing with arms outstretched, a lay person does so while keeping hands folded (BB 18, together with instructions given in applicable rites). The orans position is prescribed for priests in certain other moments, such as the eucharistic

(continued on next page)

COLLECT

Let us pray

Pause for silent prayer

Grant, O Lord,
that we may always revere and love your holy name,
for you never deprive of your guidance
those you set firm on the foundation of your love.
Through our Lord Jesus Christ, your Son,
who lives and reigns with you in the unity of the Holy Spirit,
God, for ever and ever. **Amen.**

FIRST READING

Job 38:1, 8-11

The Lord addressed Job out of the storm and said:
Who shut within doors the sea,
when it burst forth from the womb;
when I made the clouds its garment
and thick darkness its swaddling bands?
When I set limits for it
and fastened the bar of its door,
and said: Thus far shall you come but no farther,
and here shall your proud waves be stilled!

RESPONSORIAL PSALM

Ps 107:23-24, 25-26, 28-29, 30-31

℟. (1b) Give thanks to the Lord, his love is everlasting.
or: ℟. Alleluia.

They who sailed the sea in ships,
trading on the deep waters,
these saw the works of the LORD
and his wonders in the abyss.

℟. Give thanks to the Lord, his love is everlasting.
or: ℟. Alleluia.

His command raised up a storm wind
which tossed its waves on high.
They mounted up to heaven; they sank to the depths;
their hearts melted away in their plight.

℟. Give thanks to the Lord, his love is everlasting.
or: ℟. Alleluia.

They cried to the LORD in their distress;
from their straits he rescued them,
he hushed the storm to a gentle breeze,

and the billows of the sea were stilled.

℟. Give thanks to the Lord, his love is
everlasting.
or: ℟. Alleluia.

They rejoiced that they were calmed,
and he brought them to their desired
haven.
Let them give thanks to the LORD for his
kindness
and his wondrous deeds to the children
of men.

℟. Give thanks to the Lord, his love is
everlasting.
or: ℟. Alleluia.

SECOND READING
2 Cor 5:14-17

Brothers and sisters:
The love of Christ impels us,
once we have come to the conviction
that one died for all;
therefore, all have died.
He indeed died for all,
so that those who live might no longer
live for themselves
but for him who for their sake died and
was raised.

Consequently, from now on we regard no
one according to the flesh;
even if we once knew Christ according
to the flesh,
yet now we know him so no longer.
So whoever is in Christ is a new creation:
the old things have passed away;
behold, new things have come.

prayer and presidential prayers. It's never mentioned for a deacon, at least at Eucharist. Some take this as evidence that the orans posture is meant for the priest alone. Others, employing a different but valid logic, suggest that at appropriate presidential moments, anyone can utilize the orans posture.

Many liturgical rites may be rightly led by a lay person, who is not, in any liturgical law that I know of, barred from utilizing orans for presidential prayers (collects, for instance). Some go so far as to suggest the orans posture is okay for anyone anywhere, noting the relative silence of the rubrics when it comes to the assembly, compared to the mountains of rubrics for celebrants and other liturgical ministers.

Liturgical Ministers: Eucharistic Ministers

This Sunday's gospel takes us into the boat with the disciples as Jesus stills the storm with his command. The scene is dramatic, yet it mirrors the quiet reality of every eucharistic celebration where Christ himself is present, bringing peace to a restless world. For eucharistic ministers this is an invitation to understand their ministry not only as service but as a participation in Christ's authority over chaos. Each act of offering Communion is a space to rejoice that the risen Lord is here and his presence transforms fear into trust. This calling forms ministers into disciples who embody what they handle. It asks for a eucharistic spirituality rooted in prayer time before the Blessed Sacrament and an intentional awareness of the people they serve. Through this ministry ministers become bridges between the altar and the assembly bearing Christ's presence. The sacredness of this task is not in outward formality but in the humility and love with which it is carried out. Eucharistic ministers become signs of Christ and witnesses to a God who still steps into the storms of human life to calm hearts and strengthen faith.

Living Liturgy: The Prayer after Communion

The prayer after Communion for this Sunday asks that the mystery we have celebrated may profit us for our redemption. These words are a reminder that the Eucharist is not an isolated act of devotion but a gift meant to transform daily life. In praying this petition the church acknowledges that salvation is not only a promise for the future but a reality unfolding here and now through the sacraments. This prayer also reveals that grace is not a vague concept but a power that strengthens and directs us. Each time we conclude the Communion rite the liturgy moves us from receiving to living, sending us out with renewed faith. It teaches that Communion is not a private affair but a sacramental encounter meant to bear fruit in mission. This prayer becomes a lens for the entire Eucharist, where what we have celebrated shapes who we are and how we live.

SPIRITUALITY

GOSPEL ACCLAMATION
cf. Luke 1:76

℟. Alleluia, alleluia.
You, child, will be called prophet of the Most High,
for you will go before the Lord to prepare his way.
℟. Alleluia, alleluia.

Gospel Luke 1:57-66, 80; L587

When the time arrived for Elizabeth to have her child
she gave birth to a son.
Her neighbors and relatives heard
that the Lord had shown his great mercy toward her,
and they rejoiced with her.
When they came on the eighth day to circumcise the child,
they were going to call him Zechariah after his father,
but his mother said in reply,
"No. He will be called John."
But they answered her,
"There is no one among your relatives who has this name."
So they made signs, asking his father what he wished him to be called.
He asked for a tablet and wrote, "John is his name,"
and all were amazed.
Immediately his mouth was opened, his tongue freed,
and he spoke blessing God.
Then fear came upon all their neighbors,
and all these matters were discussed throughout the hill country of Judea.
All who heard these things took them to heart, saying,
"What, then, will this child be?"
For surely the hand of the Lord was with him.

The child grew and became strong in spirit,
and he was in the desert until the day of his manifestation to Israel.

See Appendix A, pp. 308–310 for the other readings.

Praying with Gospel Words and Phrases

Elizabeth . . . gave birth to a son . . . [Zechariah] asked for a tablet and wrote, "John is his name" . . .

Reflecting on the Gospel

Names are important. In today's gospel, everyone is astounded that Elizabeth and Zechariah would name their child John, as it wasn't a name in their family history. Proclaiming "John is his name" in writing is what finally allows Zechariah to regain his speaking voice.

Knowing, using, and teaching others to use liturgical verbiage is important. It's always an altar, not a table. It's always an ambo, not a podium. It's an ambry, not "the thingy with oils in it over there." Names, in our faith tradition, indicate conversion and consecration, being changed and set apart for sacred purposes. Abram becomes Abraham, Simon becomes Peter, Saul becomes Paul. Their lives now are for the Lord and only the Lord.

It seems obvious that the altar ought not be used, for instance, for donut Sunday following Mass. Ponder then the ambo, the "altar of the word"; should it be used for sharing anything but the word of God and the homily that breaks it open for us? Does your worship space have another microphone somewhere, which could be used for important announcements, greetings, and other words for the assembly?

Beyond liturgical furnishings, it is so important that each member of the Christian community know one another by name. Some parishes, for a few weekends each year, go so far as to have "name tag Sundays" and allow a few minutes of greeting and conversation before Mass begins. Knowing someone else by name is a first and elemental sign that you care about them and hope to know them better. It's a recognition that the Body of Christ is incomplete if just one person is absent, unknown.

To the Point

Names carry deep meaning in Scripture and liturgy, signaling identity, purpose, and sacred belonging. Just as Zechariah's naming of John marked a moment of faith and restoration, so too in our worship, using proper names—of people, places, and liturgical objects—honors their sacred role and strengthens our sense of communal identity in the Body of Christ.

Model Penitential Act

Presider: The Lord showed his mercy to Elizabeth and Zechariah, the faithful parents of John the Baptist. Following their example, in faith we seek his mercy . . . *[pause]*

Lord Jesus, you bring new life to those in need: Lord, have mercy.
Christ Jesus, you dispel doubts that crush our hope: Christ, have mercy.
Lord Jesus, you offer forgiveness for all our sins: Lord, have mercy.

Model Universal Prayer (Prayer of the Faithful)

Presider: Coming before the Lord who is ever faithful, we offer our prayers and petitions.

Response: Lord, hear our prayer.

That all who are baptized might find renewed hope and strengthened faith this day, we pray . . .

That our leaders, managers, and all who hold authority will take time to listen to the needs of those they serve, we pray . . .

That all who long for the birth of a child might find reason for joy, we pray . . .

That we may remember and value our loved ones who are among us and who are far from us, we pray . . .

Presider: Loving God, you gave your faithful servants, Zechariah and Elizabeth, their child, John. Increase our faith, so that we might live with joyful hope in the life of your Son, Jesus Christ, who lives and reigns with you in the unity of the Holy Spirit, God forever and ever. **Amen.**

COLLECT

Let us pray.

Pause for silent prayer

O God, who raised up Saint John the
Baptist
to make ready a nation fit for Christ the
Lord,
give your people, we pray,
the grace of spiritual joys
and direct the hearts of all the faithful
into the way of salvation and peace.
Through our Lord Jesus Christ, your Son,
who lives and reigns with you in the
unity of the Holy Spirit,
God, for ever and ever. **Amen.**

Liturgical Ministers: Altar Servers

This solemnity celebrates the birth of the one who prepared the way for Christ, a feast filled with joy and prophetic mission. Altar servers are formed in every liturgical celebration, where every action points to God's plan unfolding in history. Like John, who was chosen from the womb to herald the Lord, altar servers learn through their ministry that God calls each person to go and do likewise. Their closeness to the altar teaches them that holiness is rooted in service and attentiveness. This day is an invitation for servers to reflect on John's humility, his willingness to decrease so Christ could increase. By assisting in the liturgy, they experience how every detail of worship is an act of witness.

The discipline and prayerfulness required for this ministry become a path of mission, shaping servers to listen for God's voice and respond with courage. Through their quiet yet visible service, they embody the mission of John the Baptist, pointing beyond themselves to the presence of Christ in the midst of the assembly.

Living Liturgy: The Preface

The preface for this solemnity praises God for choosing John as a prophet before his birth and filling him with the Spirit to prepare the way for Christ. This prayer reveals that God's call is active even before we are aware of it and that every life is part of his saving plan.

By proclaiming this preface, the church professes that John's role is not only historical but present. The liturgy forms us to see that every celebration of the Eucharist is a participation in God's ongoing work of preparing hearts to receive Christ. The preface reminds us that holiness begins with God's initiative. We are drawn into a story larger than ourselves, a story of promise, preparation, and fulfillment. In praying this text, we are invited to let John's mission become our own, living lives that point others to Christ and preparing the way for his presence in the world today.

SPIRITUALITY

GOSPEL ACCLAMATION
cf. 2 Tim 1:10

℟. Alleluia, alleluia.
Our Savior Jesus Christ destroyed death
and brought life to light through the Gospel.
℟. Alleluia, alleluia.

Gospel

Mark 5:21-43; L98B

When Jesus had crossed again in the boat
to the other side,
a large crowd gathered around him,
and he stayed close to the sea.
One of the synagogue officials, named Jairus, came forward.
Seeing him he fell at his feet and pleaded earnestly with him, saying,
"My daughter is at the point of death.
Please, come lay your hands on her
that she may get well and live."
He went off with him,
and a large crowd followed him and pressed upon him.

There was a woman afflicted with hemorrhages for twelve years.
She had suffered greatly at the hands of many doctors
and had spent all that she had.
Yet she was not helped but only grew worse.
She had heard about Jesus and came up behind him in the crowd
and touched his cloak.
She said, "If I but touch his clothes, I shall be cured."
Immediately her flow of blood dried up.
She felt in her body that she was healed of her affliction.
Jesus, aware at once that power had gone out from him,
turned around in the crowd and asked,
"Who has touched my clothes?"

Continued in Appendix A, p. 311, or
Mark 5:21-24, 35b-43 *in Appendix A, p. 311.*

Praying with Gospel Words and Phrases

The child is not dead but asleep . . . *Talitha koum* . . .

Reflecting on the Gospel

There are very few Aramaic words of Jesus quoted directly in Scripture, untranslated into Greek by the evangelists. So, when we do encounter them—like *"Talitha koum,"* spoken to Jairus's daughter—we should recognize their deep importance, even if some of that meaning is now lost. It's as though without those specific words, the girl might not have risen from what Jesus called her "sleep."

Liturgically, the dialogue between the assembly and the priest, deacon, or lector functions in a similar way. The community listens for a specific "call" that cues their correct "response." These moments are familiar to most of us at Mass. What is noteworthy here, then, is that it's unwise—and often improper—for ministers to improvise or alter these texts.

First, it is no one's right to change nearly any of the liturgical texts. On rare occasions, the rubrics may allow for "these or similar words," but that's the exception. Second, altering the words can disrupt not just the flow of dialogue, but the liturgical moment itself.

For example, I know a celebrant who, after Communion and before the final blessing, often greets the people with, "The Lord *is* with you." While the sentiment may be theologically sound—after receiving Christ intimately in the Eucharist—it disregards the formality, tradition, and communal rhythm of "The Lord be with you." The assembly may not—and anecdotally, often does not—know how to respond. A more obvious example: perhaps you know a priest or deacon who likes to adapt the dismissal to refer back to something from the readings or the homily. One for today might sound like, "Go in peace to bring Christ's healing and hope to all you meet." While well-intentioned, it disrupts the expected cue, leaving the assembly unsure of how or when to reply.

In our call to evangelize, to share the good news, the words we choose are of utmost importance, and we must consider what we wish the response to be when picking them. Each individual will receive our evangelization differently, so we must approach each person with specific care and attention, that our kerygma elicit in them the new life that Jesus's *"Talitha koum"* did for Jairus's daughter.

To the Point

At liturgy, and with faith, specific words are important. They are part of what makes the liturgy prayerful, communal, and effective, and what makes our faith meaningful, engaging, and powerful.

Preparing to Proclaim, Preach, and Pray

Making Connections Between the Readings: Wisdom literature makes relatively few appearances in our Sunday Lectionary. Today's passage serves to set the stage for the raising of Jairus's daughter by sharing with the faithful divine wisdom about what death is—or rather, what death isn't. Death isn't from God but only came into the world because of a fallen angel, envious of God and more envious of God's great love for us, faithful adopted children of God. Rather, God created humankind to be imperishable—an existence regained for us through the incarnation and the sacrifice of Jesus on the cross.

This Word-made-flesh, Paul writes, is God, for our sake, becoming poor so that in that poverty we might become rich. This sort of generous kenosis should be a model for our own living, offering as much of ourselves as we can so that others may be enriched and lifted up. This then is truly a tangible example of living grace, a small-s sacrament. In doing so, all might share in the life God intended for us from the very beginning and reclaimed for us in Christ.

The paradoxical paschal mystery is not ours to fully understand but is also not ours to ignore or shy away from—this is such a simple but fiendishly difficult lesson of discipleship.

Making Connections to the Responsorial Psalm: Today's grand hymn of praise from the psalms offers several signs and symbols of death and new life. For death, images of "enemies," "the netherworld," "the pit," "nightfall," and "mourning" are all counterbalanced by God's actions and presence: "brought me up," "preserved," "the dawn," and "dancing."

The image of dancing is not one utilized very often in hymnody and preaching, though it should be, since it reflects so much about life. Dancing embodies joy, freedom, and harmony. In dance, we move in response to rhythm—just as the Christian life responds to the movement of the Spirit. Scripture speaks of David dancing before the Lord, and here in Psalm 30 of mourning turned into dancing.

Life in Christ is not rigid or solitary but dynamic and communal, like a dance shared with others. In this divine choreography, Christ leads and we follow—not always knowing the steps but trusting the rhythm of grace to guide us.

CONNECTING TO EXPERIENCE: LIVING THE PASCHAL MYSTERY

The twelve-year-old child was born at the same time the woman with the hemorrhage began suffering. For twelve years, the woman suffered, and in her twelfth year, a little girl became dangerously—deathly—ill. Their paths may never have crossed, but on the same day, both encountered Jesus, and both a child and a woman receive a second chance at life. The woman who'd been suffering from loss of blood—and was therefore unclean and prevented from approaching the temple—receives a healed body and an affirmation from Jesus: "your faith has saved you." The little girl, thanks to the faith of her father in seeking out Jesus, is resuscitated—she has a chance to live her life with rejoicing, rather than ending with the tragedy of untimely death. The healing grace of Jesus—whether in an illness overcome or a hardship resolved and eased—offers new life. When we are blessed with such mercy, let us never forget to give thanks.

PROMPTS FOR FAITH-SHARING

- Like the woman who was hemorrhaging, how can you reach out to God in faith for the healing that you need?
- Like the father of the little girl, how can you reach out to Christ on behalf of someone else who needs healing?
- Like Christ, how can you pause your expected journey to attend to someone who needs healing this day?

Model Penitential Act

Presider: Our first reading today from the book of Wisdom reminds us that God did not make death, and God does not rejoice in the destruction of the living. Calling to mind the times we have forged our own destruction through sin, we ask for his pardon and peace . . . *[pause]*

Lord Jesus, you have rescued us from the pit: Lord, have mercy.
Christ Jesus, your justice is undying: Christ, have mercy.
Lord Jesus, you have brought life to light through your gospel: Lord, have mercy.

Model Universal Prayer (Prayer of the Faithful)

Presider: Coming before the Lord who is always our helper, we offer our prayers and petitions.

Response: Lord, hear our prayer.

For Pope N., our Bishop N., and all our priests and deacons: may they be filled with the grace and truth of our Lord Jesus Christ, we pray . . .

For leaders of nations facing the effects of climate change: may their partnership and dialogue find solutions for their people and their futures, we pray . . .

For all who lack resources to sustain their families: may those blessed with abundance be filled with generosity toward those in need, we pray . . .

For us gathered here today to celebrate these sacred mysteries: may we find rich fare in the word of God proclaimed, we pray . . .

Presider: Loving God, your Son, Jesus Christ, destroyed death and brought new hope to life through the gospel. Hear our prayers this day, and draw us closer to you as we seek to make his gospel known throughout the world. We ask this through Christ our Lord. **Amen.**

Liturgy and Music

Note that today's gospel of healings, each featuring people of great faith, will be followed next week by Jesus returning to his native place and experiencing a great lack of faith there. Because of this, music selections this week and next should be attentive not only to the healing power of God but to the hope and trust people of faith place in Christ, healer and teacher. This will help set the stage for next week's spiritual turnabout.

John Angotti's "Arise, O Church, Arise" (GIA), with text by Paul Nienaber, SJ, not only speaks directly to the pivotal gospel narrative but evocatively describes how people of faith live and evangelize. Consider too "I Am the Resurrection" from the *Psallite*

(continued on next page)

COLLECT

Let us pray.

Pause for silent prayer

O God, who through the grace of adoption
chose us to be children of light,
grant, we pray,
that we may not be wrapped in the darkness of error
but always be seen to stand in the bright light of truth.
Through our Lord Jesus Christ, your Son,
who lives and reigns with you in the unity of the Holy Spirit,
God, for ever and ever. **Amen.**

FIRST READING

Wis 1:13-15; 2:23-24

God did not make death,
nor does he rejoice in the destruction of the living.
For he fashioned all things that they might have being;
and the creatures of the world are wholesome,
and there is not a destructive drug among them
nor any domain of the netherworld on earth,
for justice is undying.
For God formed man to be imperishable;
the image of his own nature he made him.
But by the envy of the devil, death entered the world,
and they who belong to his company experience it.

RESPONSORIAL PSALM

Ps 30:2, 4, 5-6, 11, 12, 13

℟. (2a) I will praise you, Lord, for you have rescued me.

I will extol you, O Lord, for you drew me clear
and did not let my enemies rejoice over me.
O Lord, you brought me up from the netherworld;
you preserved me from among those going down into the pit.

℟. I will praise you, Lord, for you have rescued me.

Sing praise to the LORD, you his faithful ones,
and give thanks to his holy name.
For his anger lasts but a moment;
a lifetime, his good will.
At nightfall, weeping enters in,
but with the dawn, rejoicing.

℟. I will praise you, Lord, for you have rescued me.

Hear, O LORD, and have pity on me;
O LORD, be my helper.
You changed my mourning into dancing;
O LORD, my God, forever will I give you thanks.

℟. I will praise you, Lord, for you have rescued me.

SECOND READING
2 Cor 8:7, 9, 13-15

Brothers and sisters:
As you excel in every respect, in faith, discourse,
knowledge, all earnestness, and in the love we have for you,
may you excel in this gracious act also.

For you know the gracious act of our Lord Jesus Christ,
that though he was rich, for your sake he became poor,
so that by his poverty you might become rich.
Not that others should have relief while you are burdened,
but that as a matter of equality
your abundance at the present time should supply their needs,
so that their abundance may also supply your needs,
that there may be equality.
As it is written:
Whoever had much did not have more,
and whoever had little did not have less.

collection (Liturgical Press), which speaks to the ultimate rising our faith directs us toward.

For music that speaks more specifically of hope and trust, consider "The Jesus Song" (OCP) by Tom Booth, with text drawn from the Divine Mercy devotions, or Rory Cooney's "Do Not Fear to Hope" (OCP), an anthem of trust in darkest times. Settings of Psalm 139 and profound prayers of trust, like Bernadette Farrell's sublime "O God, You Search Me" (OCP), or "You Are Near" (OCP) by Dan Schutte, should also be considered.

Liturgical Ministers: Ushers and Greeters

This Sunday's gospel reveals Jesus as one who draws near to human suffering with tenderness, entering Jairus's home to restore life and responding to the woman who reaches out in faith. Ushers and greeters reflect this same pastoral heart at the doors of the church, where the first gestures of welcome set the tone for prayer. Their ministry is a participation in the hospitality of Christ himself, who gathers the church not as strangers but as one body. Through this service, ministers see each person's dignity and are called to notice the quiet needs that often go unspoken. A parent carrying a restless child, someone arriving with sorrow, or a visitor who feels unsure. The ministry of welcome becomes a catechesis in action, teaching the assembly that God receives every person with joy and reverence. Ushers and greeters prepare the assembly for worship not only by offering assistance but by fostering an atmosphere of peace and belonging. Their ministry is a reminder that the liturgy begins before the opening hymn, as soon as the faithful are met with the warmth of Christ's church.

Living Liturgy: The Dismissal

The dismissal is a commissioning that flows naturally from what we have celebrated at the altar. The words "Go in peace" are not a conclusion but a charge, sending the gathered assembly into the world to carry Christ's healing presence. In this Sunday's gospel, Jesus does not remain in one place; he moves toward the needs of his people. The dismissal draws us into that same movement, showing that the Eucharist forms us to become Christ's hands and feet beyond the sanctuary. It is a moment of encounter that, having been fed by the Lord's body and word, we are entrusted with his mission. This Sunday, where Christ restores life and honors faith, the dismissal reminds us that every believer is sent to embody that hope. The liturgy becomes a place of gathering and sending, shaping a church that receives grace at the altar and then carries it into the world with reverence and courage.

SPIRITUALITY

GOSPEL ACCLAMATION
Matt 16:18

℟. Alleluia, alleluia.
You are Peter and upon this rock I will build my
Church,
and the gates of the netherworld shall not prevail
against it.
℟. Alleluia, alleluia.

Gospel

Matt 16:13-19; L591

**When Jesus went into the region of
Caesarea Philippi
he asked his disciples,
"Who do people say that the Son of
Man is?"
They replied, "Some say John the
Baptist, others Elijah,
still others Jeremiah or one of the
prophets."
He said to them, "But who do you say
that I am?"
Simon Peter said in reply,
"You are the Christ, the Son of the
living God."
Jesus said to him in reply, "Blessed are
you, Simon son of Jonah.
For flesh and blood has not revealed
this to you, but my heavenly Father.
And so I say to you, you are Peter,
and upon this rock I will build my
Church,
and the gates of the netherworld
shall not prevail against it.
I will give you the keys to the Kingdom
of heaven.
Whatever you bind on earth shall be
bound in heaven;
and whatever you loose on earth shall
be loosed in heaven."**

See Appendix A, pp. 312–314 for the other readings.

Praying with Gospel Words and Phrases

"But who do you say that I am?" . . . "You are the Christ, the Son of the living God."

Reflecting on the Gospel

Have you ever had one of those moments in which you pause to consider a certain person or a liturgical practice they espouse, and wonder to yourself how it is you and they can coexist in the same church?

We don't know everything there is to know about Ss. Peter and Paul, but a lot of what we do know shows them frequently disagreeing. At times their relationship is argumentative and strained to the point where any one of us might have just given up.

Yet it is divine wisdom that pairs these two, liturgically and otherwise, in the hearts and minds of the faithful. The church as we know it would not exist with only one half of this pair. So too we must keep in mind the church they helped build is broad and deep, vast and nearly immeasurable in every conceivable direction. If devotional practices to Divine Mercy, for instance, aren't your cup of tea, they do appeal and are helpful to someone you know. So too lay-led Liturgy of the Hours, or adoration, or Taizé prayer, and so on.

Peter in today's gospel is his usual honest and immediate self, answering Jesus's "But who do you say that I am?" with typical direct and terse—and correct—language. Where Paul's affirmation of who Christ is, across so many epistles, fills pages and pages, Peter sums it up in ten succinct words. Neither profession of faith is wrong, after all.

Is there someone on the parish staff who just consistently rubs you the wrong way? Someone who has driven you to the comical but perhaps earnest prayer, "May God bless and keep you . . . far away from me"? Rather, Peter and Paul call us—because Christ himself calls us—to look for that which is holy in that person, that which is beautiful, that which is true. They too are part of the Body of Christ, a loved child of God: they too are church. If divine wisdom has paired Peter and Paul, can we be humble enough to allow that same wisdom to pair us with that other "certain person"?

To the Point

It's a big church, Peter and Paul can remind us, if we allow it to be.

Model Penitential Act

Presider: Today we celebrate Ss. Peter and Paul, who go before us marked with Christ's compassion and mercy. Let us follow them in asking for Christ's pardon and peace . . . *[pause]*

Lord Jesus, you break open hearts that are hardened: Lord, have mercy.
Christ Jesus, you transform our fear into faith: Christ, have mercy.
Lord Jesus, you give us strength to follow you: Lord, have mercy.

Model Universal Prayer (Prayer of the Faithful)

Presider: Coming with hope before the Lord, we offer our prayers and petitions.

Response: Lord, hear our prayer.

For the church: may the fervor of Peter and the wisdom of Paul inspire the faithful, we pray . . .

For peace among nations: may leaders seek diplomacy and dialogue instead of violence and oppression, we pray . . .

For those who are alienated from their loved ones: may divisions be healed with courage, we pray . . .

For all gathered here this day: may our daily labors build up the kingdom of God, we pray . . .

Presider: Lord God, you sent your servants Peter and Paul to bring Christ to all the nations. Hear our prayers this day and strengthen us, so that we might be bearers of your good news to all we meet. We ask this through Christ our Lord. **Amen.**

COLLECT

Let us pray.

Pause for silent prayer

O God, who on the Solemnity of the
Apostles Peter and Paul
give us the noble and holy joy of this
day,
grant, we pray, that your Church
may in all things follow the teaching
of those through whom she received
the beginnings of right religion.
Through our Lord Jesus Christ, your
Son,
who lives and reigns with you in the
unity of the Holy Spirit,
God, for ever and ever. **Amen.**

Liturgical Ministers: Lectors

This feast immerses us in the witness of two apostles whose voices shaped the Church's earliest confession of faith. The Scriptures we hear today are not only historical accounts but living testimony, and the lector becomes a herald of this apostolic memory. In proclaiming Peter's confession that Jesus is the Christ and Paul's bold proclamation of the gospel, the lector enters into the liturgy's work of handing on faith. The ambo is not simply a platform but the place where Christ speaks to his people through human voice. Ministers of the word are called to interior formation so that the Scriptures proclaimed are not distant texts but living encounters. In prayerful preparation, the lector steps into Peter's humility and Paul's zeal, allowing the word to take root in their own heart before it is spoken aloud. This ministry becomes rooted in discipleship, forming the lector to love what they proclaim and to trust the Spirit who works through their voice. Each proclamation is an act of tradition, uniting the assembly to the apostolic faith and the church that continues to be built upon their witness.

Living Liturgy: The Preface

The entrance antiphon for this solemnity declares, "These are the ones who, living in the flesh, planted the Church with their blood; they drank the chalice of the Lord and became the friends of God." This chant sets the tone for the celebration, teaching that worship is not a mere remembrance but a participation in the same sacrifice that gave life to the church. Sung or recited, the entrance antiphon gathers the assembly into the mystery of apostolic witness, revealing that the liturgy is always a movement from earth into heaven's praise. In these few lines, theology is proclaimed that friendship with God is the fruit of eucharistic sacrifice, and the church is built upon the courage of martyrs who followed Christ's path. The entrance antiphon becomes a doorway into the feast, inviting us to see that what began with Peter and Paul continues here and now. It reminds us that every liturgy is a joining of voices across time and space, uniting us to the apostles who first confessed and spread the gospel.

SPIRITUALITY

GOSPEL ACCLAMATION
cf. Luke 4:18

℟. Alleluia, alleluia.
The Spirit of the Lord is upon me
for he sent me to bring glad tidings to the poor.
℟. Alleluia, alleluia.

Gospel

Mark 6:1-6; L101B

Jesus departed from there and came to his native place, accompanied by his disciples.
When the sabbath came he began to teach in the synagogue,
and many who heard him were astonished.
They said, "Where did this man get all this?
What kind of wisdom has been given him?
What mighty deeds are wrought by his hands!
Is he not the carpenter, the son of Mary,
and the brother of James and Joses and Judas and Simon?
And are not his sisters here with us?"
And they took offense at him.
Jesus said to them,
"A prophet is not without honor except in his native place
and among his own kin and in his own house."
So he was not able to perform any mighty deed there,
apart from curing a few sick people by laying his hands on them.
He was amazed at their lack of faith.

Praying with Gospel Words and Phrases

Where did this man get all this . . . What kind of wisdom has been given him . . .

Reflecting on the Gospel

Communication always carries risk. No matter the medium—spoken, written, or digital—there's always a chance the message received won't match the message intended. Listeners and readers interpret through their own lens, drawing from tone, context, or cultural background, often mishearing or misunderstanding, even when intentions are good. Perhaps this is a main reason that even Jesus was received in his native place—as we hear in today's gospel—without honor, and even snarkily, to use modern parlance.

This reality is especially important when we consider the intersection of religiosity and patriotism in Catholic liturgy—topics like displaying national flags in sanctuaries or singing patriotic hymns during Mass. While these practices are both common and well-debated, it's worth considering what they might unintentionally communicate, regardless of the intent behind them.

For instance, what message does an American flag in a sanctuary send to a visitor from another country? Might it suggest that this specific church is more American than Catholic—or that being American is somehow spiritually superior? Similarly, do certain prayers or songs for our nation sound as if we're asking God to bless only our country, as though others are less worthy of divine care? Is it possible that one might, between the lines, see or hear "God bless, protect, and guide America—but not those other less worthy lands"?

A parish I know once prayed a "patriotic rosary" using religious quotes from historical American figures—including Confederate general Robert E. Lee. One must ask: how would this feel to a Black parishioner who came to pray that day?

Independence Day is of course an American celebration, and regardless of where one lives around the globe, there is nothing wrong with praying for one's country and homeland, one's civic leaders and citizens. But on civic holidays like this one, we must be mindful of the universal nature of the church and the diverse people gathered in Christ's name. Often, what we don't say or do communicates as much as what we do.

To the Point

Communication is easily misunderstood, especially when shaped by personal and cultural filters. In liturgy, mixing patriotism with prayer—like displaying flags or singing national hymns—can unintentionally suggest exclusion or national superiority, undermining the church's universal identity. Even well-meant gestures may alienate some, so we must remain attentive to what our worship communicates, both explicitly and implicitly.

Preparing to Proclaim, Preach, and Pray

Making Connections Between the Readings: The reading from Ezekiel is one instance in a long tradition of prophets—those who speak God's truth—not being welcome in their native land. This is most often because of the hardness of heart found in the people receiving the prophet, be that Ezekiel, Jesus, or the prophets of modern times: consider those like Sr. Helen Prejean, Fr. James Martin, SJ, Dorothy Day, Bishop Desmond Tutu, and others. People are often resistant to change, especially when their comfort or status is at risk. Prophets today still do what the biblical prophets did: confront power with truth, comfort the afflicted, and afflict the comfortable, always pointing to God's justice and mercy.

Sometimes, though, prophets would do well to consider molding their message—and by this I mean not so much the content but the delivery of it—in ways that might help it be more successfully received, heard, and heeded. God spoke to Elijah, for instance, not in a storm or earthquake but in gentle whispers. The truth (with or without a capital "T") isn't any more true because of its volume.

The thorn in his side that Paul speaks of today is never defined. Some speculate it was some sort of physical ailment, or perhaps a spiritual struggle, or more obliquely the frequently hostile opposition to his evangelization. One intriguing theory shared by some is that perhaps Paul had a speech impediment, as did Moses centuries before. If so, neither he nor Moses let that deter them from the mission imposed on them by God.

Making Connections to the Responsorial Psalm: Like any prophet boldly sharing God's truth, the messenger must not make the endeavor about themselves, but rather, always be pointing to the divine source of the message. Today's psalm puts just such a prayer on all our lips, that we focus our gaze constantly on the Lord. For ourselves and for our community, we seek God's pity, compassion, and mercy.

As the lens that unlocks additional meaning in the other readings, this psalm stands as a subtle call to each of us, showing each faithful citizen the simplicity of being a prophet: speaking truth while fixed on God. This is not to say that such ministry is easy or that it ought to belong to a great number of people much of the time. Rather, each of us, every day, has some circumstance where speaking God's truth—and sometimes more by action than by words—is our divine calling.

CONNECTING TO EXPERIENCE: LIVING THE PASCHAL MYSTERY

What does it mean to have our eyes fixed upon the Lord? As the gospel today reveals, some of those who actually *knew* the Lord when he walked the earth failed to see who he really was. But when the Lord speaks of seeing, he does not always mean our physical eyes that squint, grow tired, and need glasses. In the gospel today, it is knowledge that blinds Jesus's listeners to understanding the reality of his role as Messiah. So when we fix our eyes on Jesus, what do we "see"? A Jesus who makes us feel good? A Jesus who is around when we need him, but quietly sidelined elsewise? Or does seeing him change our perspective? Can we also bring glad tidings to the poor and sight to the blind—bringing knowledge and love of him to all the world?

PROMPTS FOR FAITH-SHARING

- Have you ever failed to see that God was in your midst? When and why so?
- Have you ever underestimated the holiness of someone because of their lack of education or fortune? When and why so?
- Have you ever been so challenged by something good and true that you were made angry? What do you think is the cause of that anger? How can God help?

Model Penitential Act

Presider: Whether in our weakness or in our strength, we are in need of the Lord. Let us recall the times we have failed to follow his will as we ask for his forgiveness . . . *[pause]*

Lord Jesus, you seek the hard of face and obstinate of heart: Lord, have mercy.

Christ Jesus, you have pity on those who turn to you: Christ, have mercy.

Lord Jesus, you fill us with the abundance of your grace: Lord, have mercy.

Model Universal Prayer (Prayer of the Faithful)

Presider: Relying on the Lord's grace, let us offer our prayers for those in need.

Response: Lord, hear our prayer.

For the church scattered throughout the world: may the faithful experience grace and hope, especially in communities suffering from persecution, we pray . . .

For leaders of nations: may they be acutely attentive to the suffering in their midst, we pray . . .

For those who have become refugees due to natural disasters: may they be granted safety and swift return to their homes, we pray . . .

For all who love God, especially amidst our local communities: may the love of God feed our love of our neighbors, we pray . . .

Presider: Loving God, you sent your Spirit out into the world so that we might hear your voice and respond to your call. Hear our prayers this day and allow us to be agents of your love. We ask this through Christ our Lord. **Amen.**

Liturgy and Displays of Flags

Often, communities wonder about displaying flags, especially the American flag, in parishes. On a section of the USCCB website ("Display of Flags in Catholic Churches"), the USCCB reminds us that there are no regulations in the liturgical books or in canon law on this subject, and therefore the question is left to the discretion of the diocesan bishop, who in turn may delegate the decision to the discretion of the pastor. The USCCB website recounts the history of displaying the American flag in parishes during World War II and other wars, and the practice of placing "a book of remembrance near the American flag, requesting prayers for loved ones—especially those serving their country in the armed forces—as a way of keeping before the attention of the faithful the needs of military families." As far as where the American flag itself should be placed, the "Bishops' Committee on the Liturgy has in the past encouraged pastors not to place the flag within

(continued on next page)

COLLECT

Let us pray.

Pause for silent prayer

O God, who in the abasement of your Son
have raised up a fallen world,
fill your faithful with holy joy,
for on those you have rescued from slavery to sin
you bestow eternal gladness.
Through our Lord Jesus Christ, your Son,
who lives and reigns with you in the unity of the Holy Spirit,
God, for ever and ever. **Amen.**

FIRST READING

Ezek 2:2-5

As the LORD spoke to me, the spirit entered into me
and set me on my feet,
and I heard the one who was speaking say to me:
Son of man, I am sending you to the Israelites,
rebels who have rebelled against me;
they and their ancestors have revolted against me to this very day.
Hard of face and obstinate of heart
are they to whom I am sending you.
But you shall say to them: Thus says the Lord GOD!
And whether they heed or resist—for they are a rebellious house—
they shall know that a prophet has been among them.

RESPONSORIAL PSALM
Ps 123:1-2, 2, 3-4

℟. (2cd) Our eyes are fixed on the Lord,
pleading for his mercy.

To you I lift up my eyes
who are enthroned in heaven—
as the eyes of servants
are on the hands of their masters.

℟. Our eyes are fixed on the Lord, pleading
for his mercy.

As the eyes of a maid
are on the hands of her mistress,
so are our eyes on the LORD, our God,
till he have pity on us.

℟. Our eyes are fixed on the Lord, pleading
for his mercy.

Have pity on us, O LORD, have pity on us,
for we are more than sated with
contempt;
our souls are more than sated
with the mockery of the arrogant,
with the contempt of the proud.

℟. Our eyes are fixed on the Lord, pleading
for his mercy.

SECOND READING
2 Cor 12:7-10

Brothers and sisters:
That I, Paul, might not become too elated,
because of the abundance of the
revelations,
a thorn in the flesh was given to me, an
angel of Satan,
to beat me, to keep me from being too
elated.
Three times I begged the Lord about this,
that it might leave me,
but he said to me, "My grace is
sufficient for you,
for power is made perfect in weakness."
I will rather boast most gladly of my
weaknesses,
in order that the power of Christ may
dwell with me.
Therefore, I am content with weaknesses,
insults,
hardships, persecutions, and
constraints,
for the sake of Christ;
for when I am weak, then I am strong.

the sanctuary itself, in order to reserve that space for the altar, the ambo, the presidential chair and the tabernacle. Instead, the suggestion has been made that the American flag be placed outside the sanctuary, or in the vestibule of the Church together with a book of prayer requests." Be sure to consult your diocese for any regulations determined by the diocesan bishop. See more at https://www.usccb.org/prayer-and-worship/sacred-art-and-music/architecture-and-environment/display-of-flags-in-catholic-churches.

Liturgical Ministry: Eucharistic Ministers

The readings this week place us with Ezekiel sent to a stubborn people, with Paul who boasts of weakness, and with Jesus in Nazareth where familiarity causes unbelief. At the altar this pattern becomes a source for those who serve Communion. Here the Lord chooses smallness and nearness, grace given under the sign of ordinary bread. Eucharistic ministers who live close to this mystery learn a eucharistic way of seeing. Strength is received rather than asserted. Holiness appears in neighbors who seem unremarkable. Thanksgiving rises even when results are hidden. This ministry asks for an inner poverty that leaves room for the Presence, a steady patience that lets the rite teach in silence, and a gratitude that remembers the gift comes first to the minister before it is shared with the assembly. The altar forms a people who rely on God more than on acclaim. Week by week these ministers who stand where the bread is broken are schooled in the paradox Paul names. Power is made perfect in weakness. From that flows a gentle authority, not the authority of status, but of mercy learned at close range.

Living Liturgy: The Fraction Rite and the Lamb of God

The breaking of the consecrated bread unveils what we believe. Life is given through a body offered and shared. As the host is broken the church sings "Lamb of God, you take away the sins of the world, have mercy on us. . . . grant us peace." This litany is not commentary. It is the faith of the church prayed aloud. The assembly beholds the sign of brokenness and calls upon mercy, then asks for peace that the world cannot give. The Sunday readings echo within this act. Nazareth stumbles at the ordinary. Paul discovers sufficiency in grace. The rite answers both. God chooses the humble form and fills it with saving power. Praying the Lamb of God trains the heart to trust that reconciliation flows from the crucified who is present here and now. What we sing is what we carry out of the church. Mercy received becomes mercy given. Peace asked for becomes peace shared.

SPIRITUALITY

GOSPEL ACCLAMATION
cf. Eph 1:17-18

℟. Alleluia, alleluia.
May the Father of our Lord Jesus Christ
enlighten the eyes of our hearts,
that we may know what is the hope that
belongs to our call.
℟. Alleluia, alleluia.

Gospel

Mark 6:7-13; L104B

Jesus summoned the Twelve and began to send them out two by two
and gave them authority over unclean spirits.
He instructed them to take nothing for the journey
but a walking stick—
no food, no sack, no money in their belts.
They were, however, to wear sandals but not a second tunic.
He said to them,
"Wherever you enter a house, stay there until you leave.
Whatever place does not welcome you or listen to you,
leave there and shake the dust off your feet
in testimony against them."
So they went off and preached repentance.
The Twelve drove out many demons,
and they anointed with oil many who were sick and cured them.

Praying with Gospel Words and Phrases

Wherever you enter a house, stay there until you leave . . .

Reflecting on the Gospel

As Jesus sends his apostles out in pairs to proclaim the reign of God, one of the very few instructions he offers is that once they have entered a house, to stay there until leave. On the surface, this seems like unnecessary guidance—how can anyone do anything but stay in a house until they leave that house? Likely the teaching was more about remaining in the same house as a guest rather than moving to another offering greater comfort. This would avoid any appearance of seeking personal benefits and showing dishonor to one's host.

To enter a house, of course, one must pass through the door of that house; perhaps this is another reason Christ phrased this instruction in this way. Christ calls himself "the gate" elsewhere in the gospels (John 10:9), the door through which salvation is secured. Think of all the many doors you might pass through on a given day: front or back doors, sliding doors, revolving doors, barn doors, garage doors, car doors, screen doors, wooden doors. . . . Ponder now Jesus as a door, as *the* salvation door.

Doors often figure prominently in church architecture and liturgy for the very same reasons. The door to the church is a gateway to heaven itself, or at least a foretaste of it. Candidates in OCIA are met at those doors, as is a casket, holding the remains of a loved one who in baptism died with Christ, hoping one day to share his glory. "Practically, of course, they [doors] secure the building from the weather and exterior dangers, expressing by their solid strength the safe harbor that lies within" (*Built of Living Stones* 97).

As we enter the church by such a door, "taken" by Christ, we are also sent out, "shared" through it, to be Christ's hands and feet, to in turn bring more people to the church, to the door, to salvation itself. Salvation door, kingdom door, the Jesus door.

To the Point

Jesus's instruction to remain in one house while on mission reflects humility and integrity, avoiding any appearance of seeking comfort or personal gain. Seen more deeply, it evokes the image of Christ as the door—the only true entryway to salvation—inviting us to recognize every church door, every household door, and ultimately, every act of faith as a passage through him into grace, community, and mission.

Preparing to Proclaim, Preach, and Pray

Making Connections Between the Readings: Last week we reflected on how biblical prophets, and prophets of our own time, are seldom accepted in their native lands. Amos this week is another in that long line, with Amaziah trying to cast Amos off from a land that "cannot endure all his words" (Amos 7:10, just prior to today's pericope). Amos appears to make the case that he is not a prophet, but don't be fooled: he is only trying to state that he is not a "prophet-for-hire" yet still called by God to speak truth to Israel. When paired with the gospel for this Sunday, Jesus's sending of the apostles takes on characteristics of God sending prophets, and helps provide context for Jesus offering his instruction to "shake the dust off your feet" when leaving places that are unwelcoming and unresponsive.

Paul, near the beginning of his epistle to the Ephesians, describes his readers as people "who have heard the word of truth, the gospel of your salvation, and have believed in [Christ]." The Ephesians, and we across broad time and space, are the faithful who are the fruits of a Pauline admonition to the Romans: "But how can they call on him in whom they have not believed? And how can they believe in him of whom they have not heard? And how can they hear without someone to preach?" (Rom 10:14). In this way, every evangelist is, at least in some small part, also a prophet, sharing God's truth, which is always the good news.

Making Connections to the Responsorial Psalm: What is the truth of God that a prophet might proclaim? Psalm 85 tells us some of them, at least, as if coming from God's own mouth: "I will hear what God proclaims." In the verses that follow, God proclaims peace, salvation, glory, kindness, truth, and justice.

What these few verses don't make plain is that Psalm 85 as a whole is a prayer of lament, reminding God of past generosity and asking for those same abundant blessings to again return. This places the composition of the psalm in some moment of decline, perhaps of people no longer heeding the word of God, perhaps during exile or just after. These are commonly times when prophets are most bold and most needed—as is prayer to our just and merciful God.

CONNECTING TO EXPERIENCE: LIVING THE PASCHAL MYSTERY

Why would you not listen to one who had the power to drive out demons or cure the sick? Yet Jesus instructs his disciples what to do if they encounter persons who will not listen: shake the dust off your feet in testimony against them and leave. When do we need to "leave" a situation, and "shake the dust" from our feet—or our hearts? Leaving something feels like giving up, something that every inspirational poster tells us not to do. But Jesus gives us permission: when we are not heard, when we are not loved, when our mission fails—we can leave. We are free to pursue a relationship with God. But this freedom is not only our own. As adopted sons and daughters of God, we have the responsibility to ensure others' freedom as well, especially those who cannot easily leave systems of oppression, poverty, and corruption. We are bound as Christians to ensure that all the world might be free as well.

PROMPTS FOR FAITH-SHARING

- Have you ever felt that your life's work needed a decisive change in place or direction? What was God saying in the midst of that change?
- Have you ever chosen to commit or recommit to others, even those who were difficult, because you knew that God was calling you to care for them? How did you know to do so?
- Is there something or someone that God is asking you to leave or re-embrace today?

Model Penitential Act

Presider: Through our baptism in Christ Jesus, we have been sealed with the Holy Spirit, receiving his grace. Mindful of the times that we have failed to fulfill our baptismal call, we ask for his mercy . . . *[pause]*

Lord Jesus, through you we have been adopted by God the Father: Lord, have mercy.

Christ Jesus, in you we have forgiveness for our transgressions: Christ, have mercy.

Lord Jesus, with you we have the fullness of redemption: Lord, have mercy.

Model Universal Prayer (Prayer of the Faithful)

Presider: Coming before the Lord, we place our hope in him as we offer our prayers and petitions.

Response: Lord, hear our prayer.

For the church throughout the world: may the faithful find confidence in Christ in the midst of secularism and worldly powers, we pray . . .

For those who teach, who minister, and who serve in missions: may they find courage in their work and support in their communities, we pray . . .

For all who do not believe in God: may their spirits be moved by the witness of the faithful and their hearts awakened by God's love, we pray . . .

For us gathered here: may we always welcome the stranger in our midst, treating visitors and newcomers with graciousness and dignity, we pray . . .

Presider: Lord God, we seek always to follow you with our whole self. May our hearts, our minds, and our strength be devoted to your love and to the care of our neighbor. We ask this through Christ our Lord. **Amen.**

Liturgy and the Eucharistic Action

The eucharistic liturgy can be summed up in four key actions: take, bless, break, share. These words describe what Jesus did at the feeding of the multitudes, the Last Supper, and the Emmaus meal—and what happens at every Mass. The presider takes the bread and wine offered by the people, blesses (consecrates) them, breaks them, and shares them. Though some symbolic clarity may be lost in modern practice, the pattern remains.

This pattern also reflects what Christ does with us. Though we might think we choose to attend Mass, it is ultimately Christ who takes us, blesses us, and sends us to be shared with a world in need. But to be shared, we must also be broken.

(continued on next page)

COLLECT

Let us pray.

Pause for silent prayer

O God, who show the light of your truth
to those who go astray,
so that they may return to the right path,
give all who for the faith they profess
are accounted Christians
the grace to reject whatever is contrary to
the name of Christ
and to strive after all that does it honor.
Through our Lord Jesus Christ, your Son,
who lives and reigns with you in the unity
of the Holy Spirit,
God, for ever and ever. **Amen.**

FIRST READING

Amos 7:12-15

Amaziah, priest of Bethel, said to Amos,
"Off with you, visionary, flee to the land
of Judah!
There earn your bread by prophesying,
but never again prophesy in Bethel;
for it is the king's sanctuary and a royal
temple."
Amos answered Amaziah, "I was no
prophet,
nor have I belonged to a company of
prophets;
I was a shepherd and a dresser of
sycamores.
The LORD took me from following the flock,
and said to me,
Go, prophesy to my people Israel."

RESPONSORIAL PSALM

Ps 85:9-10, 11-12, 13-14

℟. (8) Lord, let us see your kindness, and
grant us your salvation.

I will hear what God proclaims;
the LORD—for he proclaims peace.
Near indeed is his salvation to those who
fear him,
glory dwelling in our land.

℟. Lord, let us see your kindness, and
grant us your salvation.

Kindness and truth shall meet;
justice and peace shall kiss.
Truth shall spring out of the earth,
and justice shall look down from heaven.

℟. Lord, let us see your kindness, and
grant us your salvation.

The LORD himself will give his benefits;
our land shall yield its increase.

Justice shall walk before him,
and prepare the way of his steps.

℟. Lord, let us see your kindness, and grant us your salvation.

SECOND READING
Eph 1:3-14

Blessed be the God and Father of our Lord Jesus Christ,
who has blessed us in Christ
with every spiritual blessing in the heavens,
as he chose us in him, before the foundation of the world,
to be holy and without blemish before him.
In love he destined us for adoption to himself through Jesus Christ,
in accord with the favor of his will,
for the praise of the glory of his grace
that he granted us in the beloved.

In him we have redemption by his blood,
the forgiveness of transgressions,
in accord with the riches of his grace
that he lavished upon us.
In all wisdom and insight, he has made known to us
the mystery of his will in accord with his favor
that he set forth in him as a plan for the fullness of times,
to sum up all things in Christ, in heaven and on earth.

In him we were also chosen,
destined in accord with the purpose of the One
who accomplishes all things according to the intention of his will,
so that we might exist for the praise of his glory,
we who first hoped in Christ.
In him you also, who have heard the word of truth,
the gospel of your salvation, and have believed in him,
were sealed with the promised Holy Spirit,
which is the first installment of our inheritance
toward redemption as God's possession,
to the praise of his glory.

or Eph 1:3-10

See Appendix A, p. 315.

This "breaking" may seem counterintuitive—aren't we at Mass to be made whole? Yes, but part of holiness is vulnerability. Sometimes we come already broken by life; sometimes the liturgy itself—through prayer, Scripture, music, and Christ's Real Presence—must lovingly break us open so we can be reformed. As the hymn "Led by the Spirit" by Bob Hurd reminds us: "Rend not your garments, rend your hearts" (OCP). Each liturgy becomes a moment of conversion, when we allow ourselves to be taken, blessed, broken, and shared—so that like the apostles, we too may be sent to proclaim the gospel, heal, and help build the reign of God.

Liturgical Ministers: Music Ministers

Today's readings place us in the company of Amos, a prophet sent not from privilege but from the fields, and with the apostles, sent two by two with little more than Christ's authority. This pattern shapes those who lead music in the liturgy. Music ministry is not primarily about artistry or performance but about serving a mission that is older and greater than themselves. Like Amos and the apostles, music ministers are sent to announce God's kingdom, and their work is steeped in humility. They help the gathered assembly to remember that God acts through the voices of his people. Preparing music for worship is a spiritual discipline that invites ministers to pray with Scripture and the texts of the liturgy so what they sing is not only beautiful but true. Music ministers become instruments of communion, uniting the assembly's prayer and forming hearts for mission. Song is a gift the church offers to God, and through it, God strengthens his people for the journey ahead.

Living Liturgy: The Offertory Procession

The procession of bread and wine at this Mass echoes the apostles' journey in the gospel. As they were sent out with little, they return with what Christ will transform. The offertory is not a pause in worship but a sign of participation. The gifts we bring are not only bread and wine but the labor, prayers, and lives of the faithful, placed before God to be changed. This ritual act enables us to see that everything we have and all that we are belong to the Lord. The readings reinforce this truth. Amos was called from tending flocks, and the apostles traveled without excess; yet God made their smallness fruitful. The offertory mirrors this reality. What is ordinary becomes extraordinary through God's action. When the assembly joins in song during the procession, music draws us into this mystery, teaching us that worship is an exchange. We bring what we are, and God returns it transformed. The offertory prepares us not only for the eucharistic prayer but for the transformation of our lives in Christ's service.

SPIRITUALITY

GOSPEL ACCLAMATION
John 10:27

℟. Alleluia, alleluia.
My sheep hear my voice, says the Lord;
I know them, and they follow me.
℟. Alleluia, alleluia.

Gospel

Mark 6:30-34; L107B

The apostles gathered together with Jesus
and reported all they had done and taught.
He said to them,
"Come away by yourselves to a deserted place and rest a while."
People were coming and going in great numbers,
and they had no opportunity even to eat.
So they went off in the boat by themselves to a deserted place.
People saw them leaving and many came to know about it.
They hastened there on foot from all the towns
and arrived at the place before them.

When he disembarked and saw the vast crowd,
his heart was moved with pity for them,
for they were like sheep without a shepherd;
and he began to teach them many things.

Praying with Gospel Words and Phrases

"Come away by yourselves to a deserted place and rest a while" . . .

Reflecting on the Gospel

In the gospel today, Jesus invites the apostles, having apparently returned from the mission we heard of last week, to "Come away by yourselves." Both taking time away from it all on retreat as well as forming smaller Christian communities within a larger whole have immense value—and it seems Jesus, here in this scene and elsewhere, is pursuing both. Small, faith-sharing groups intensify a sense of belonging in a world where the number of close friendships is shrinking, and people yearn for any connection and "fitting in."

Many parishes offer a designated youth Mass in an effort to engage teens and young adults, especially in light of research showing that many people disaffiliate from religion as early as age thirteen. These liturgies are often designed with younger people in mind: contemporary music, peer-led ministries, brief and relevant homilies, and times that suit student schedules. While these efforts are well-intentioned and not inherently problematic, challenges arise in how the liturgy is framed and the community is divided.

Labeling one Mass for a specific age group can unintentionally fragment the parish. The church is meant to be universal and unified; when one demographic is separated, liturgically or otherwise, it risks isolating them from the rest of the Body of Christ. Youth lose out on the wisdom of elders, and older generations are deprived of the passion and vitality of the young. Additionally, differences in musical repertoire and liturgical style may leave some parishioners feeling excluded from a form of worship they may appreciate, despite not belonging to the targeted demographic.

Such divisions can also lead to harmful comparisons: one Mass being seen as more relevant, more spiritual, or more entertaining than another. These unintended consequences undermine the unity of the church. Rather than tailoring a liturgy exclusively for youth, it is more fruitful to make *every* liturgy a place where all feel welcome, valued, and engaged. When all ministers and parishioners alike recognize the diversity of the Body gathered at each Mass, the whole community grows together in holiness and unity.

To the Point

Like most things in life, there is good and bad, pros and cons to small, faith-sharing communities, especially when these overlap with the liturgy. Approaching them with mindfulness and intentionality is key.

Preparing to Proclaim, Preach, and Pray

Making Connections Between the Readings: The concept of God, and of God the Son specifically, permeates the readings this weekend. The image of the shepherd is one of the most powerful and enduring in Scripture because it conveys deep truths about God's relationship with humanity—especially God's guidance, care, protection, and commitment.

In biblical times, shepherds were responsible for guiding, feeding, and defending their sheep from predators and danger. Kings and spiritual leaders were expected to "shepherd" their people—not rule harshly, but rather lead wisely and compassionately. The prophets often criticized corrupt leaders for being bad shepherds (see Ezek 34), while pointing to God as the true shepherd who would rescue and heal the flock.

While the direct quote is absent from today's gospel, elsewhere Jesus adopts this identity explicitly, saying "I am the good shepherd. A good shepherd lays down his life for the sheep" (John 10:11). As the Good Shepherd Jesus knows his sheep and pursues them when they lose their way. This is even echoed in today's epistle—placed on this Sunday not for its content directly, but still cohesive in meaning: "In Christ Jesus you who once were far off have become near by the blood of Christ." Pastors—and each of us, in some way—are called to this same way of living our faith.

Making Connections to the Responsorial Psalm: Something that often goes unnoticed about Psalm 23 is how it quietly transforms our roles in relationship with God—from member of the flock to a beloved guest. The psalm begins with familiar pastoral imagery: God as shepherd, guiding, providing, and protecting. But midway through, the metaphor shifts: "You spread the table before me / in the sight of my foes; / you anoint my head with oil; / my cup overflows." Suddenly, we are no longer sheep led through dark valleys—we are honored guests at God's banquet table, an image of royal hospitality. In ancient Israel, to anoint someone and fill their cup was to show favor, abundance, and welcome. This shift reflects a profound intimacy: not only are we guided by God, but we are celebrated by God. Psalm 23, then, is not just a psalm of comfort, but of dignity and invitation. We are not mere followers; we are cherished, known, and always welcome in the house of the Lord.

CONNECTING TO EXPERIENCE: LIVING THE PASCHAL MYSTERY

Jesus knows when we work hard: when we are so busy we can't even stop to eat. But defying worldly pressures (from outside or from our own hearts), Jesus does not ask us to simply "work harder." Jesus looks at his haggard, overwhelmed disciples and says, "Come away to a deserted place and rest a while." He invites his disciples to leave the crowds, leading them to much needed rest. Jesus himself left the crowds to pray, and to be silent before his Father. Doing so does not mean that Jesus or we are lazy—far from it. To take rest seriously is to take the Lord's transformation of chaos into creation seriously: the Lord rested on the seventh day. If we do not rest and allow space and time for the Lord and for one another, we will let chaos and distraction reign in our hearts. Jesus calls us to rest, to be together, and to be with him, in solidarity and in friendship.

PROMPTS FOR FAITH-SHARING

- Do you feel that you have been working too hard? Are you working on the right things? Do you believe Jesus agrees with you?
- Do you believe that God is inviting you to find more time for prayer and rest? If so, how can you take more time to embrace that invitation?
- Have you ever been afraid to step away from those who surround you, in order to rest and pray? How can you do so in a way that is still generous and loving?

Model Penitential Act

Presider: In today's gospel, the faithful follow Jesus and his disciples, hungry for his healing. Let us come before the Lord as we acknowledge our sins and hunger for his mercy . . . *[pause]*

Lord Jesus, you came preaching peace to all the world: Lord, have mercy.

Christ Jesus, your heart is moved with pity for your people: Christ have mercy.

Lord Jesus, you broke down barriers of sin and death to reconcile us to the Father: Lord, have mercy.

Model Universal Prayer (Prayer of the Faithful)

Presider: We come before the Lord who always hears his people as we offer our prayers and petitions.

Response: Lord, hear our prayer.

For the church, especially all who have suffered from the crisis of abuse: may healing, protection, and the Lord's mercy and justice guide the faithful always, we pray . . .

For our bishops throughout the world: may they exhort the faithful to follow Jesus and find peace with one another, we pray . . .

For those who walk in the darkness of the valley of death: may they fear no evil, and know the presence of the Lord, we pray . . .

For those of us gathered today: may we allow the Good Shepherd to fill our hearts with the food from his table, we pray . . .

Presider: O God, you sent your Son to call us to yourself. Grant that we might hear your voice this day, and heed your call to follow you in justice and righteousness. We ask this through Christ our Lord. **Amen.**

Liturgy and Evaluating It

The next five Sundays (beginning next week) form a kind of mini-liturgical season—a retreat the church offers every three years to reflect deeply on the Eucharist. While the Eucharist is often described as the "source and summit of the Christian life," we have already examined how this phrase applies not only to the consecrated elements themselves (the body and blood of Christ), but also to the eucharistic liturgy—the communal action of sharing in Christ's sacrifice and meal.

As we begin this period of reflection, the readings emphasize not simply the sacred bread and wine, but the generous act of God feeding his people. It's not a matter of choosing between the eucharistic action and the eucharistic presence—which one is truly "source and summit." Both are vital and inseparably connected, much like the refrain from "Love and Marriage," the song made famous by Frank Sinatra, which reminds us: "You can't have one without the other."

(continued on next page)

COLLECT

Let us pray.

Pause for silent prayer

Show favor, O Lord, to your servants
and mercifully increase the gifts of your grace,
that, made fervent in hope, faith, and charity,
they may be ever watchful in keeping your commands.
Through our Lord Jesus Christ, your Son,
who lives and reigns with you in the unity of the Holy Spirit,
God, for ever and ever. **Amen.**

FIRST READING

Jer 23:1-6

Woe to the shepherds
who mislead and scatter the flock of my pasture,
says the LORD.
Therefore, thus says the LORD, the God of Israel,
against the shepherds who shepherd my people:
You have scattered my sheep and driven them away.
You have not cared for them,
but I will take care to punish your evil deeds.
I myself will gather the remnant of my flock
from all the lands to which I have driven them
and bring them back to their meadow;
there they shall increase and multiply.
I will appoint shepherds for them who will shepherd them
so that they need no longer fear and tremble;
and none shall be missing, says the LORD.

Behold, the days are coming, says the LORD,
when I will raise up a righteous shoot to David;
as king he shall reign and govern wisely,
he shall do what is just and right in the land.
In his days Judah shall be saved,
Israel shall dwell in security.
This is the name they give him:
"The LORD our justice."

RESPONSORIAL PSALM
Ps 23:1-3, 3-4, 5, 6

℟. (1) The Lord is my shepherd; there is
nothing I shall want.

The Lord is my shepherd; I shall not want.
In verdant pastures he gives me repose;
beside restful waters he leads me;
he refreshes my soul.

℟. The Lord is my shepherd; there is
nothing I shall want.

He guides me in right paths
for his name's sake.
Even though I walk in the dark valley
I fear no evil; for you are at my side
with your rod and your staff
that give me courage.

℟. The Lord is my shepherd; there is
nothing I shall want.

You spread the table before me
in the sight of my foes;
you anoint my head with oil;
my cup overflows.

℟. The Lord is my shepherd; there is
nothing I shall want.

Only goodness and kindness follow me
all the days of my life;
and I shall dwell in the house of the Lord
for years to come.

℟. The Lord is my shepherd; there is
nothing I shall want.

SECOND READING
Eph 2:13-18

Brothers and sisters:
In Christ Jesus you who once were far off
have become near by the blood of
Christ.

For he is our peace, he who made both one
and broke down the dividing wall of
enmity, through his flesh,
abolishing the law with its
commandments and legal claims,
that he might create in himself one new
person in place of the two,
thus establishing peace,
and might reconcile both with God,
in one body, through the cross,
putting that enmity to death by it.
He came and preached peace to you who
were far off
and peace to those who were near,
for through him we both have access in
one Spirit to the Father.

These coming five weeks offer an invitation to evaluate how we celebrate Eucharist in our communities—whether our practices align with the church's guidance and truly serve the people gathered. Numerous resources and approaches are available for such evaluation, and previous reflections have offered helpful tools. Over the next few weeks, this space will take up that evaluation through the lens of the parable of the cloth and wineskins (Luke 5:36–38), which reminds us that new wine needs fresh wineskins to be poured into. It's a call to consider whether our liturgical structures can hold the grace being poured into them—and if not, how they might need to be renewed.

Liturgical Ministers: Altar Servers

Altar servers lead the entrance procession, carrying the cross and candles before the assembly, embodying the church's movement toward God. This action is theological within our liturgical celebrations. The cross they lift high is the sign of salvation, and the light they carry announces Christ's presence. Today's readings reveal Christ as the shepherd who draws his people together, inviting his disciples to rest even as he cares for the crowds. Servers participate in this shepherding ministry by guiding the assembly's prayer through their visible service. Leading the procession reminds them that the liturgy begins as a journey, God's people moving together to the altar, following the sign of redemption. Altar servers' reverence, attentiveness, and confident movement encourage the assembly to enter prayerfully into the sacred mysteries. Over time, serving in this role teaches that leadership in the church is expressed through humility, preparation, and quiet faithfulness. By standing at the front of the liturgical procession, servers are a reminder that the path of discipleship always follows the cross, leading the church into deeper communion with the Lord.

Living Liturgy: The Communion Antiphon

The communion antiphon this Sunday proclaims, "Behold, I stand at the door and knock, says the Lord. If anyone hears my voice and opens . . . , I will enter . . . and dine with him, and he with me." These words from Revelation bring the gospel to fulfillment. The Lord who welcomed the weary apostles and hungry crowds is the same Christ who comes to us in the Eucharist, seeking to dwell within each believer. Singing or praying this text at Communion turns the procession into a moment of encounter, reminding us that the Lord approaches every heart. The antiphon is a declaration of eucharistic faith that this meal is a true communion with Christ, who longs to share life with his people. By repeating these words week after week, the liturgy teaches us to open ourselves to him more fully, so the mystery of the altar may shape who we are and how we live in the world.

SPIRITUALITY

GOSPEL ACCLAMATION

Luke 7:16

℟. Alleluia, alleluia.
A great prophet has risen in our midst.
God has visited his people.
℟. Alleluia, alleluia.

Gospel

John 6:1-15; L110B

Jesus went across the Sea of Galilee.
A large crowd followed him,
because they saw the signs he was performing on the sick.
Jesus went up on the mountain,
and there he sat down with his disciples.
The Jewish feast of Passover was near.
When Jesus raised his eyes
and saw that a large crowd was coming to him,
he said to Philip,
"Where can we buy enough food for them to eat?"
He said this to test him,
because he himself knew what he was going to do.
Philip answered him,
"Two hundred days' wages worth of food would not be enough
for each of them to have a little."
One of his disciples,
Andrew, the brother of Simon Peter, said to him,
"There is a boy here who has five barley loaves and two fish;
but what good are these for so many?"
Jesus said, "Have the people recline."
Now there was a great deal of grass in that place.
So the men reclined, about five thousand in number.

Continued in Appendix A, p. 315.

Praying with Gospel Words and Phrases

[They] filled twelve wicker baskets with fragments from the five barley loaves that had been more than they could eat . . .

Reflecting on the Gospel

The five-week stretch of the bread of life discourse (interrupted this year by the Solemnity of the Assumption) can be a bit problematic for those responsible for the liturgy week to week. While there is no shortage of eucharistic hymns, many communities know a limited number of them, and when seeking three or four for a given weekend instead of the more typical one, options can run out quickly. While the Eucharist is an inexhaustible mystery, creating preaching each week that isn't repetitive or superficial can be difficult. It is critical then that a close reading of each of the scriptural texts these next few weeks gives distinction and nuance to the liturgy, and that this five-week period be planned as a whole, mindful of the eucharistic journey the readings provide for us every three years.

This first Sunday, the readings of this pilgrimage, especially words of the gospel, speak to us of the miraculous abundance of sustenance the Lord is able to provide for us. What is sometimes seen as an epilogue, almost an afterthought to this miracle, is the people's response to it. Since "Jesus knew that they were going to come and carry him off to make him king," Jesus avoids the people—this is not the response, apparently, that he desired. So what is our immediate response to the Real Presence supposed to be? If not such devotion, then what?

It is seemingly no accident that in our rites the assembly is sent forth almost immediately upon reception of the Eucharist. Within mere moments, the presider pronounces the dismissal: "*Ite, missa est*"—which roughly translates to "Go, you are sent." "Go" is what we're told, not "but wait, adore for a minute what is literally now inside you in an order of magnitude different than what's achieved ocularly." Not even "but wait and sing this recessional hymn first." Our mission work as faithful disciples, the Christian activity we are all called to, begins immediately while we are still literally filled with Christ's Real Presence, which a waiting world sorely needs.

To the Point

Liturgy and devotion, particularly eucharistic liturgy and devotion, must be in right relationship. The presence of Christ calls us both to contemplative prayer and to action as disciples—and the last words of the Mass make clear what is asked of us in that moment.

Preparing to Proclaim, Preach, and Pray

Making Connections Between the Readings: The reading we hear from 2 Kings this weekend again holds no special mystery as to why it's paired with the gospel of the day. It is an abrupt little tale, with no other context nor denouement to be found. Elisha, whose name translates to "God is salvation," was the successor to Elijah. As a prophet, he performed several miracles that demonstrated not only God's power, but God's care for the people of the covenant. Earlier in this same chapter of 2 Kings, Elisha raised a boy from death, among other marvels! The name Jesus translates similarly, to "YHWH saves"—in this case, saving us from sin and death.

Paul's epistle to the Ephesians speaks of another facet of Eucharist and communion, that of unity. The word "one" is repeated over and over, most notably in the expression "one body." At Eucharist, the faithful are united as the Body of Christ, both spiritually and sacramentally. Receiving the same body and blood of the Lord in Communion makes real and visible the unity Paul speaks of. Paul's exhortation to unity (found over and over again across his epistles) mirrors what the Eucharist makes visible and real—the oneness of the church, grounded in shared faith, sacraments, and divine life. The Eucharist is both the sign and the source of this unity.

Making Connections to the Responsorial Psalm: Liturgically speaking, many of us know Psalm 145 with the refrain "I will praise your name, my king and my God." Today's iteration of Psalm 145 is a prime example of why attending to the given psalm of a liturgy with its proper refrain is so vital to the Liturgy of the Word. The refrain here is not a direct scriptural quote but alludes to Psalm 145:16, and reshapes the included verses, many of which will be familiar. What is the "glory of your kingdom" and the might of God we are to speak of? In which ways is the Lord just and holy? How does the Lord show nearness to us? It's all there in today's succinct refrain—meaning which would be lost using a different refrain, or a different seasonal psalm entirely. While it's easier, especially when sung (as it should be), to use a known psalm setting, the value in putting in a bit more effort is usually worth it.

CONNECTING TO EXPERIENCE: LIVING THE PASCHAL MYSTERY

There are obvious human limitations to growing, purchasing, preparing, and distributing food. Philip notes the practical problem of cost and supply. Andrew can't imagine that a mere lunchbox-full of food could ever feed the massive crowd gripped with hunger. But God magnificently exceeds human limitations. In today's gospel, Jesus feeds them all, with an abundance left over. Rather than showing a lack of faith, the concerned questions of Andrew and Philip show us clearly the parameters of impossibility that Jesus shatters. Jesus changes us just as he changes bread. Our miracle today reminds us that we can have faith in the unthinkable, for Christ, whose body was broken and shared for us, breaks all bonds of human expectations.

The presence of Christ fills us with abundance—abundance so massive that we are sent out into the world to share it.

PROMPTS FOR FAITH-SHARING

- Have you ever doubted that God could provide for you? How can you ask Jesus for greater faith?
- When you are confronted with someone's need, do you respond to them? Do you respond with the radical generosity of God?
- Has God ever exceeded your expectations? What does that say to you about God? About yourself?

Model Penitential Act

Presider: In our gospel today, Jesus sees the need of his hungry followers and feeds them with the abundance of his mercy. Recalling our need for his mercy, we ask for his pardon and peace . . . *[pause]*

Lord Jesus, you are the Bread of Life: Lord, have mercy.
Christ Jesus, you fill the hungry with good things: Christ, have mercy.
Lord Jesus, you are the savior of the world: Lord, have mercy.

Model Universal Prayer (Prayer of the Faithful)

Presider: The hand of the Lord feeds us; he answers all our needs. Trusting in him, let us come before the Lord with our prayers and petitions.

Response: Lord, hear our prayer.

For the church, and for Christians throughout the world: may we one day grow closer in communion, and work side by side in charity for the world as we wait, we pray . . .

For our leaders here and throughout our nation: may they support initiatives for sustainable agriculture, and the protection of those who grow and cultivate our food, we pray . . .

For those imprisoned unjustly: may they find release and freedom, and untiring support from their friends, we pray . . .

For all gathered here today: may prejudice be stripped from our hearts, we pray . . .

Presider: O God, you call us to one faith, one baptism, and one hope. Draw us ever closer to Jesus Christ your Son, so that we might all be one in him. We ask this through Christ our Lord. **Amen.**

Liturgy and Wineskins, Old and New

Returning to the parable of the cloth and wineskins, let us use its imagery to help evaluate our eucharistic liturgies. Most are familiar with the second half of the parable—about not putting new wine into old wineskins. But understanding why is key: wineskins were made of animal hides and used to store fermenting wine. As fermentation continued, gases would stretch the skins. Old wineskins, already stretched to their limit, would burst if filled with new wine, wasting both wine and vessel.

This metaphor challenges us to examine longstanding liturgical traditions—not necessarily to discard them, but to ask: are they still flexible and life-giving, or have they become rigid? In church life, especially in a tradition-rich faith like Catholicism, even just a few years of repetition can make a practice feel immovable. Some customs are rooted in wisdom; others persist mainly due to inertia.

(continued on next page)

COLLECT

Let us pray.

Pause for silent prayer

O God, protector of those who hope in you,
without whom nothing has firm
foundation, nothing is holy,
bestow in abundance your mercy upon us
and grant that, with you as our ruler and
guide,
we may use the good things that pass
in such a way as to hold fast even now
to those that ever endure.
Through our Lord Jesus Christ, your Son,
who lives and reigns with you in the unity
of the Holy Spirit,
God, for ever and ever. **Amen.**

FIRST READING

2 Kgs 4:42-44

A man came from Baal-shalishah bringing
to Elisha, the man of God,
twenty barley loaves made from the
firstfruits,
and fresh grain in the ear.
Elisha said, "Give it to the people to eat."
But his servant objected,
"How can I set this before a hundred
people?"
Elisha insisted, "Give it to the people to
eat.
For thus says the LORD,
'They shall eat and there shall be some
left over.'"
And when they had eaten, there was some
left over,
as the LORD had said.

RESPONSORIAL PSALM

Ps 145:10-11, 15-16, 17-18

℟. (cf. 16) The hand of the Lord feeds us;
he answers all our needs.

Let all your works give you thanks,
O LORD,
and let your faithful ones bless you.
Let them discourse of the glory of your
kingdom
and speak of your might.

℟. The hand of the Lord feeds us; he
answers all our needs.

The eyes of all look hopefully to you,
and you give them their food in due season;
you open your hand
and satisfy the desire of every living thing.

℟. The hand of the Lord feeds us; he answers all our needs.

The Lord is just in all his ways
and holy in all his works.
The Lord is near to all who call upon him,
to all who call upon him in truth.

℟. The hand of the Lord feeds us; he answers all our needs.

SECOND READING
Eph 4:1-6

Brothers and sisters:
I, a prisoner for the Lord,
urge you to live in a manner worthy of the call you have received,
with all humility and gentleness, with patience,
bearing with one another through love,
striving to preserve the unity of the spirit through the bond of peace:
one body and one Spirit,
as you were also called to the one hope of your call;
one Lord, one faith, one baptism;
one God and Father of all,
who is over all and through all and in all.

So, let us ask: Are our current "wineskins"—our liturgical forms, habits, and assumptions—still capable of holding new wine, the fresh movement of the Spirit? Are they nurturing the eucharistic life of our communities, or do they need renewal? Some may need refreshing or repurposing; others, replacing entirely. And for new wine, new wineskins—adaptable, responsive structures—must be found or formed. This process of evaluation helps ensure our liturgies remain authentic, dynamic, and open to grace.

Liturgical Ministers: Ushers and Greeters

The miracle of the loaves and fishes reminds us that God's abundance is revealed through ordinary things offered in faith. Ushers and greeters live this mystery in simple gestures that open worship to the assembly. The act of handing out a worship aid or hymnal is not a small courtesy but a liturgical moment. It invites each person to full, conscious participation and signals that they belong to this prayer. Offering a worship aid is a quiet sign: here is the prayer of the church; come and take part. This ministry becomes catechetical because it shows that the liturgy is not a performance but the work of the whole people of God. Ushers and greeters are also stewards of the sacred space, guiding and welcoming so that the liturgy begins with a sense of peace and attentiveness. Over time, this role shapes ministers to see their service as a reflection of Christ's hospitality. Like the disciples who passed bread among the crowds, they extend what the church has prepared so that all may be nourished. The offering of something as simple as a worship aid becomes an act of evangelization, drawing people deeper into the mystery of the Mass.

Living Liturgy: The Preparation of the Gifts

The bringing forward of bread and wine mirrors the story of the gospel, where a few loaves become a feast for thousands. This procession is a sacramental sign. The gifts carried forward represent not only food and drink but the lives of the faithful, placed before God to be transformed. The quietness of this ritual invites us to see how God works through what is ordinary, blessing and multiplying it. The liturgy forms us to live this mystery beyond Mass, teaching that nothing offered to God is too small to bear fruit. As the bread and wine are prepared for consecration, the assembly is reminded that God receives our offerings and returns them as Christ's body and blood, giving life to the world.

SPIRITUALITY

GOSPEL ACCLAMATION
Matt 4:4b

℟. Alleluia, alleluia.
One does not live on bread alone, but by every word that comes forth from the mouth of God.
℟. Alleluia, alleluia.

Gospel

John 6:24-35; L113B

When the crowd saw that neither Jesus nor his disciples were there,
they themselves got into boats
and came to Capernaum looking for Jesus.
And when they found him across the sea they said to him,
"Rabbi, when did you get here?"
Jesus answered them and said,
"Amen, amen, I say to you,
you are looking for me not because you saw signs
but because you ate the loaves and were filled.
Do not work for food that perishes
but for the food that endures for eternal life,
which the Son of Man will give you.
For on him the Father, God, has set his seal."
So they said to him,
"What can we do to accomplish the works of God?"
Jesus answered and said to them,
"This is the work of God, that you believe in the one he sent."
So they said to him,
"What sign can you do, that we may see and believe in you?
What can you do?
Our ancestors ate manna in the desert, as it is written:
He gave them bread from heaven to eat."

Continued in Appendix A, p. 315.

Praying with Gospel Words and Phrases

[M]y Father gives you the true bread from heaven . . . I am the bread of life . . .

Reflecting on the Gospel

The distinctiveness of today's readings is one of dependence, relying on God completely for sustenance. This is elaborated in the words of the Lord's Prayer: "Give us this day our daily bread." This prayer asks for only what is needed today and no more, and petitions the Lord, no one else, to provide it. This sort of complete dependence is something most of us are not well versed in, or typically, willing to accept. Dependence isn't something that can be faked; it isn't something that speech alone can prove. It must be lived by example, by prayer into action, or even inaction, if you will.

There is a heightened use these days of the phrase, "the holy sacrifice of the Mass." The phrase itself isn't wrong, though it's incomplete. Similarly, speaking of Mass as if solely a banquet feast is also lacking. Mass, importantly and significantly, is both, and loses meaning and impact when it isn't both. "[A]s we share in Christ / the feast that frees us," we sing in Marty Haugen's hymn "All Are Welcome" (GIA). Some look down on this hymn as one that treats the Eucharist as a common meal, apparently ignoring that eloquent turn of phrase.

Indeed, many people who spend their time seeking out what they might call "inadequate hymnody" in our common pew books also frequently take issue with the word "bread" used a bit too haphazardly. There are surely instances of the word "bread" being used in hymns, in prayers, and in preaching that serve to confuse belief in the unique Real Presence of Christ in the Eucharist. Today's gospel shows us that the phrase "Bread of Life" or even the word "bread" alone, depending on the context surrounding it, need not be shunned. I know one of my compositional peers had a diocesan worship office take issue with the text of one of his hymns—until he pointed out he was merely (and directly) quoting Scripture. Does the phrase "the bread of God . . . which comes down from heaven and gives life to the world" (John 6:33) speak of Real Presence? Does it speak of Eucharist as both meal and sacrifice?

To the Point

Dependence on God extends to how we understand the Eucharist—not merely as sacrifice or as meal, but as both. Terms like "bread of life" or "bread from heaven," when rooted in Scripture, affirm the Eucharist's richness, including the Real Presence of Christ.

Preparing to Proclaim, Preach, and Pray

Making Connections Between the Readings: In the gospel, Jesus is asked by the crowd for a sign that he has come from God, even though he had just multiplied the loaves and fishes. Even more strangely, they ask for something like their ancestors experienced, manna from heaven. Jesus points out that Moses didn't feed the Israelites; rather, God (the Father) did.

Manna prefigures the Eucharist in profound ways. Just as manna sustained the physical lives of God's people on their journey to the Promised Land, the Eucharist nourishes the spiritual lives of Christians as they journey toward eternal life. Manna was a daily gift that required trust in God's providence—paralleling the petition of the Lord's Prayer, "Give us this day our daily bread." The Eucharist is also a daily, ongoing gift of Christ's own body and blood, fulfilling and surpassing the manna as the true bread from heaven. Where manna sustained for a day, the Eucharist sustains for eternity.

This week's pericope from Paul's epistle to the Ephesians notes the renewal and continuing conversion Christ calls us to. Each day, sustained in faith, we are renewed and recreated. By this, we join ourselves more completely to the Body of Christ and the holy unity found there.

Making Connections to the Responsorial Psalm: Much like a particular refrain can instill on psalm verses a particular interpretation, today's verses from Psalm 78 show that selectively picking a few verses from here and there can change our perception of the whole text. The selected refrain and verses today would lead one to believe Psalm 78 is a hymn of praise. It really is, however, a long psalm that recounts the story of God's relationship with the people of Israel, emphasizing God's faithfulness and Israel's repeated unfaithfulness. It serves as both a warning and a teaching tool, calling the people to remember and learn from the past. Specifically, it recounts how Israel repeatedly forgot God's miracles—especially the exodus and manna from the sky—and turned to sin.

In short, Psalm 78 is about remembering God's works, learning from past failures, and trusting in God's chosen leaders. It challenges us to remain faithful and to teach God's ways to future generations. May we faithful of today heed this call, especially regarding our belief in Christ and his presence in Eucharist, both banquet and sacrifice.

CONNECTING TO EXPERIENCE: LIVING THE PASCHAL MYSTERY

The Israelites escaped hardship, dehumanization, and even death at the hands of their captors. Now they long for the ease of knowing what tasks would fill their days and what scraps of food might fill them for a few moments. It is easy to long for the place we were—even if that place breaks us down and causes us to die. We have been saved by Christ through the waters of our baptism. Yet do we continue to choose those things that bring us—and those around us—hardship, dehumanization, and even death? Would we look at Jesus and ask "What can you do?" to make us more certain that he was the Son of God? When we pray, do we make bargains with Jesus to prove himself? Or do we acknowledge that we know who he is and what he does: *You are the Bread of Life—you take away the sins of the world. Have mercy on me.*

PROMPTS FOR FAITH-SHARING

- When was the last time you really went looking for Jesus?
- Do you struggle to believe Jesus's words? What about him is hardest for you to believe at this moment?
- Have you accepted Jesus's offer of himself? What might be keeping you from accepting him more completely?

Model Penitential Act

Presider: Coming before the Lord with humility and hope, we call to mind our sins . . . *[pause]*

Lord Jesus, you are the true bread that came down from heaven: Lord, have mercy.

Christ Jesus, whoever comes to you will never hunger: Christ, have mercy.

Lord Jesus, you gave your life so we might know that you are the Son of God: Lord, have mercy.

Model Universal Prayer (Prayer of the Faithful)

Presider: We turn to the Lord who gives forth words of life, offering our prayers for ourselves and all the world.

Response: Lord, hear our prayer.

For the church: may the faithful throughout the world draw more deeply from the life of the Eucharist, finding nourishment that sustains them, we pray . . .

For leaders in our communities, our cities, and our nation: may they not succumb to corruption through deceitful desires, but follow God's ways of righteousness and truth, we pray . . .

For refugees and migrants: may they find safe passage in their journeys and new life in their destinations, we pray . . .

For those of us gathered here today: may our fears and anxieties be released by the Lord who reigns over all, we pray . . .

Presider: Lord God, you fill your people with good things and feed us with abundance. Hear our prayers this day as we hope for all the world to be filled with your goodness and truth. We ask this through Christ our Lord. **Amen.**

Liturgy and Wine, Old and New

As we continue exploring the parable of new wine and old wineskins in light of our eucharistic liturgies, we now turn our focus to wine itself. At Mass, wine is described as "fruit of the vine and work of human hands"—a gift from God, transformed by human labor, and returned in sacrifice and thanksgiving. Symbolically, wine represents joy, vitality, and communal celebration.

If our liturgical traditions are like the old wineskins, then we must ask: what is the wine they hold? Is the "new wine" in our communities the younger generations, changing cultural expressions, shifting demographics, or aging parishioners? Each parish may (will) answer differently. What's new may not be inherently young—it may simply be unfamiliar or emerging.

Sometimes, the "new wine" reflects a pastoral call to minister to diverse groups—multilingual, multicultural, or subcultural communities—whose desired liturgical expressions may not

(continued on next page)

COLLECT

Let us pray.

Pause for silent prayer

Draw near to your servants, O Lord,
and answer their prayers with unceasing kindness,
that, for those who glory in you as their Creator and guide,
you may restore what you have created
and keep safe what you have restored.
Through our Lord Jesus Christ, your Son,
who lives and reigns with you in the unity of the Holy Spirit,
God, for ever and ever. **Amen.**

FIRST READING

Exod 16:2-4, 12-15

The whole Israelite community grumbled against Moses and Aaron.
The Israelites said to them,
"Would that we had died at the LORD's hand in the land of Egypt,
as we sat by our fleshpots and ate our fill of bread!
But you had to lead us into this desert
to make the whole community die of famine!"

Then the LORD said to Moses,
"I will now rain down bread from heaven for you.
Each day the people are to go out and gather their daily portion;
thus will I test them,
to see whether they follow my instructions or not.

"I have heard the grumbling of the Israelites.
Tell them: In the evening twilight you shall eat flesh,
and in the morning you shall have your fill of bread,
so that you may know that I, the LORD, am your God."

In the evening quail came up and covered the camp.
In the morning a dew lay all about the camp,
and when the dew evaporated, there on the surface of the desert
were fine flakes like hoarfrost on the ground.
On seeing it, the Israelites asked one another, "What is this?"
for they did not know what it was.

But Moses told them,
"This is the bread that the LORD has given you to eat."

RESPONSORIAL PSALM
Ps 78:3-4, 23-24, 25, 54

℟. (24b) The Lord gave them bread from heaven.

What we have heard and know,
and what our fathers have declared to us,
we will declare to the generation to come
the glorious deeds of the LORD and his strength
and the wonders that he wrought.

℟. The Lord gave them bread from heaven.

He commanded the skies above
and opened the doors of heaven;
he rained manna upon them for food
and gave them heavenly bread.

℟. The Lord gave them bread from heaven.

Man ate the bread of angels,
food he sent them in abundance.
And he brought them to his holy land,
to the mountains his right hand had won.

℟. The Lord gave them bread from heaven.

SECOND READING
Eph 4:17, 20-24

Brothers and sisters:
I declare and testify in the Lord
that you must no longer live as the Gentiles do,
in the futility of their minds;
that is not how you learned Christ,
assuming that you have heard of him and were taught in him,
as truth is in Jesus,
that you should put away the old self of your former way of life,
corrupted through deceitful desires,
and be renewed in the spirit of your minds,
and put on the new self,
created in God's way in righteousness and holiness of truth.

easily align with existing rubrics. In such cases, we are challenged to discern: Are our current liturgical "wineskins" flexible enough to hold and support this new wine? Or do they need to be reshaped—or replaced entirely?

We also might ask whether the wine is truly new or just new to us. Further, are any old wineskins to be discarded, or could their material be repurposed? As we evaluate, the central task remains: ensuring our liturgical structures are adaptable enough to nourish and welcome the people they serve, while staying faithful to the spirit and structure of the liturgy itself.

Liturgical Ministers: Lectors

The lector's role begins before the procession or their proclamation at the ambo. At home, opening up the Lectionary readings days in advance is a simple act of devotion. It is a way to pray with Scripture before announcing it to the church. The word shapes the lector first, then the assembly. This Sunday's readings highlight God's gift of bread from heaven, pointing to Christ as the true food that endures. By preparing prayerfully, the lector becomes a sign of that nourishment. Carrying the Book of the Gospels in procession is itself catechesis. The elevated book is a visual reminder that God's word leads the church. When lectors arrive early to prepare and pray before reading at Mass, they enter into an understanding that this ministry is an encounter with God. The lector becomes a living bridge between the written word and the hearts of the faithful, embodying the church's reverence for Scripture.

Living Liturgy: The Responsorial Psalm

The psalm this Sunday repeats, "The Lord gave them bread from heaven." Sung after the first reading, it is not an interlude but the assembly's voice responding to God's action. The psalm forms us to see salvation history as a gift. God provides, God feeds, and God fulfills this promise in Christ, the Bread of Life. When the psalmist proclaims the verses and the community responds, the church practices listening and answering. This liturgical dialogue is a foundation of prayer. Over time, the faithful learn that the Eucharist is not a private devotion but God's initiative, a covenant of love sung back to him. The psalm teaches us to interpret our lives in light of God's faithfulness, making every liturgy a thanksgiving for daily bread that points toward eternal life.

AUGUST 1, 2027

EIGHTEENTH SUNDAY IN ORDINARY TIME

SPIRITUALITY

GOSPEL ACCLAMATION
John 6:51

℟. Alleluia, alleluia.
I am the living bread that came down from heaven, says the Lord;
whoever eats this bread will live forever.
℟. Alleluia, alleluia.

Gospel

John 6:41-51; L116B

The Jews murmured about Jesus
because he said,
"I am the bread that came down from heaven,"
and they said,
"Is this not Jesus, the son of Joseph?
Do we not know his father and mother?
Then how can he say,
'I have come down from heaven'?"
Jesus answered and said to them,
"Stop murmuring among yourselves.
No one can come to me unless the Father who sent me draw him,
and I will raise him on the last day.
It is written in the prophets:
They shall all be taught by God.
Everyone who listens to my Father and learns from him comes to me.
Not that anyone has seen the Father
except the one who is from God;
he has seen the Father.
Amen, amen, I say to you,
whoever believes has eternal life.
I am the bread of life.
Your ancestors ate the manna in the desert, but they died;
this is the bread that comes down from heaven
so that one may eat it and not die.
I am the living bread that came down from heaven;
whoever eats this bread will live forever;
and the bread that I will give is my flesh for the life of the world."

Praying with Gospel Words and Phrases

I am the living bread that came down from heaven; whoever eats this bread will live forever . . .

Reflecting on the Gospel

As we seek for something within the readings for this Sunday that will distinguish them from the surrounding Sundays, let us note the emphasis on the Bread of Life sustaining us, and in a way different than other foods—like the manna we pondered a week ago. This bread not only sustains us physically until tomorrow, but "whoever eats this bread will live forever."

Some choose to attend Mass daily to partake in such sustenance. Some choose to attend a period of quiet adoration that their parish offers. Neither approach is, on the surface, better or worse: they are different though, and sometimes those differences are not explained to the faithful, or perhaps worse, they are explained poorly or incorrectly. Oftentimes, the faithful are poorly catechized on liturgy and devotions and on the Eucharist, often by catechists who themselves are poorly catechized.

The church's liturgy is our prescribed, corporate prayer; as mentioned earlier on these pages, the liturgy is our source and summit. And we must quickly note here that Eucharist is but one liturgical practice, among the other sacraments, rites, and the Liturgy of the Hours. Devotions are not prescribed and may tend to personal piety, even when prayed in a group setting. The right relationship between these two is drifting, slowly but surely, out of whack, colloquially. To wit: Someone once told a room full of teens on a pilgrimage after morning Mass, "and later today we'll have the highlight of the day: adoration." This was literally right after celebrating the source and summit of our faith lives!

To ensure I'm distinguishing well here: I'm not decrying adoration wholesale, just noting a growing imbalance between devotion and liturgical practice. An issue with adoration immediately following Mass is that it seems to contradict what the liturgy has accomplished and told us to do, to be. There's a layer too, of the meta-message, of something like "Mass just wasn't enough on its own—let's add adoration, or the St. Michael prayer, or . . ." Perhaps the time has come to look anew at the foundational documents and texts of the liturgy and let them plainly and literally tell us what to do.

To the Point

Devotions, especially eucharistic ones, must flow from and lead back to the liturgy, not contradict, diminish, or distract.

Preparing to Proclaim, Preach, and Pray

Making Connections Between the Readings: Sometimes when one is particularly irritable, the true cause of that sensation is called being "hangry"—a portmanteau of "hungry" and "angry." Usually one is "hangry" without realizing it, until someone else points it out. Perhaps Elijah in today's Old Testament reading was hangry, or perhaps he just needed a little nap—or both? The angel orders him, in his misery, to eat a hearth cake that has miraculously appeared, after which he lays down again—perhaps in a moment of rest—upon which the angel commands him to finish eating. Fortified, he is able to walk for forty days and nights. His destination, as it happens, is Horeb, where he hears God speaking, we will recall, not in storm or earthquake but in a whispering breeze.

Perhaps at times we find ourselves spiritually "hangry" and need sustenance in the Eucharist, our spiritual food. Especially when the days ahead seem long and arduous, make sure to include restful, peaceful time for prayer and liturgy every day, every hour. Jesus feeds us through his body, yes, but also admonished the tempter in the desert: "One does not live by bread alone, but by every word that comes forth from the mouth of God" (Matt 4:4, referencing Deut 8:3). Along with frequent reception of the Eucharist, attend to the Sacred Scriptures as well—through Bible study, *lectio divina*, or a favorite podcast.

Making Connections to the Responsorial Psalm: Psalm 34 connects deeply to the Eucharist, especially through today's refrain, drawn from verse 9, "Taste and see the goodness of the Lord." The faithful at each Mass process forward to "taste and see"—not just symbolically, but sacramentally—receiving Christ's body and blood under the appearance of bread and wine.

The psalm also expresses trust in God's providence and nearness: "When the afflicted man called out, the Lord heard, / and from all his distress he saved him." This mirrors the Eucharist as both sacrifice and meal, where Christ is present to the suffering and lowly, offering healing and communion. Lastly, Psalm 34 connects to the Eucharist by inviting praise, reverence, and reliance on God—all essential attitudes as we approach the table of the Lord.

CONNECTING TO EXPERIENCE: LIVING THE PASCHAL MYSTERY

Eyes and ears often stick out as the most important senses for Jesus. He seems to like healing the deaf and the blind, and we are certainly supposed to hear Jesus and to keep our eyes upon him. But Jesus also frequently focuses on our mouths. What comes from them? What do we put in them? And how do we feed upon him? Jesus knows well the wounding and bitter words that pour forth from the mouths of human beings: murmuring, muttering, complaining, grousing. Bitter words may seem more acceptable when they're about our frustrations with family members, our dissatisfaction with work, or discontentment with how we are recognized for our accomplishments. But murmuring about these things does something else; it stokes bitterness, anger, and even fury. Festering hotly enough, murmuring can foment from violent words to violent actions. Seeking justice and exhorting others to righteousness is good; but quietly stoking the fires of discontent breaks down our ability to speak and act with love.

PROMPTS FOR FAITH-SHARING

- Have you ever doubted someone's gifts because you think you know who they are? Have others ever placed limitations on you because of their presumptions?

- Jesus is food for life, but what kind of nourishment do you most need from him today? Where do you need refreshment?

- Do you believe that you have eternal life? Have you allowed yourself to dwell on the amazing consequences of that reality?

Model Penitential Act

Presider: In the gospel today, Jesus tells us that he is the bread of heaven who has come for the life of the world. Though we eat of this bread, we still fall to sin. Remembering the times we have failed to live as Christ calls us, we ask for his pardon and peace . . . *[pause]*

Lord Jesus, you are the Bread of Life come down from heaven: Lord, have mercy.

Christ Jesus, you gave your flesh for the life of the world: Christ, have mercy.

Lord Jesus, whoever believes in you will have eternal life: Lord, have mercy.

Model Universal Prayer (Prayer of the Faithful)

Presider: God our Father listens to his children who come to him. Let us approach him now with our prayers and petitions for ourselves and all the world.

Response: Lord, hear our prayer.

For the faithful throughout the world: may they find food for their spirits at the table of God's word and the table of the Eucharist, we pray . . .

For our leaders: may they reject bitter rhetoric that clenches hearts, responding to the needs of their people with compassion and patience, we pray . . .

For all who lack access to adequate food and to healthy food: may those blessed with abundance recognize their need, we pray . . .

For the faithful gathered here: may we practice compassion with those closest to us, especially our parents, spouses, children, and families, we pray . . .

Presider: O God, you have prepared your people for your kingdom with the seal of baptism. Hear us in our need and draw us closer to you as your faithful children. We ask this through Christ our Lord. **Amen.**

Liturgy and Patching Rips and Tears, Part I

Returning yet again to the parable of the cloth and wineskins, sharp readers will note that as we have used this text as a lens to evaluate our liturgies, we have completely ignored half of the pericope—that of the cloth used to patch a cloak.

As we have given our liturgies a closer examination, we have thus far used only the imagery of the new wine and old wineskins. What, in our liturgical practices, do these represent? What should our next effort be, given any new insights and revelations?

An example of a common use of this phrase in ministry was recently discussed in this space, the "new wineskin" of a youth

(continued on next page)

COLLECT

Let us pray.

Pause for silent prayer

Almighty ever-living God,
whom, taught by the Holy Spirit,
we dare to call our Father,
bring, we pray, to perfection in our hearts
the spirit of adoption as your sons and daughters,
that we may merit to enter into the inheritance
which you have promised.
Through our Lord Jesus Christ, your Son,
who lives and reigns with you in the unity of the Holy Spirit,
God, for ever and ever. **Amen.**

FIRST READING

1 Kgs 19:4-8

Elijah went a day's journey into the desert,
until he came to a broom tree and sat beneath it.
He prayed for death, saying:
"This is enough, O LORD!
Take my life, for I am no better than my fathers."
He lay down and fell asleep under the broom tree,
but then an angel touched him and ordered him to get up and eat.
Elijah looked and there at his head was a hearth cake
and a jug of water.
After he ate and drank, he lay down again,
but the angel of the LORD came back a second time,
touched him, and ordered,
"Get up and eat, else the journey will be too long for you!"
He got up, ate, and drank;
then strengthened by that food,
he walked forty days and forty nights to the mountain of God, Horeb.

RESPONSORIAL PSALM
Ps 34:2-3, 4-5, 6-7, 8-9

℟. (9a) Taste and see the goodness of the Lord.

I will bless the Lord at all times;
his praise shall be ever in my mouth.
Let my soul glory in the Lord;
the lowly will hear me and be glad.

℟. Taste and see the goodness of the Lord.

Glorify the Lord with me,
let us together extol his name.
I sought the Lord, and he answered me
and delivered me from all my fears.

℟. Taste and see the goodness of the Lord.

Look to him that you may be radiant with joy,
and your faces may not blush with shame.
When the afflicted man called out, the Lord heard,
and from all his distress he saved him.

℟. Taste and see the goodness of the Lord.

The angel of the Lord encamps
around those who fear him and delivers them.
Taste and see how good the Lord is;
blessed the man who takes refuge in him.

℟. Taste and see the goodness of the Lord.

SECOND READING
Eph 4:30–5:2

Brothers and sisters:
Do not grieve the Holy Spirit of God,
with which you were sealed for the day of redemption.
All bitterness, fury, anger, shouting, and reviling
must be removed from you, along with all malice.
And be kind to one another, compassionate,
forgiving one another as God has forgiven you in Christ.

So be imitators of God, as beloved children, and live in love,
as Christ loved us and handed himself over for us
as a sacrificial offering to God for a fragrant aroma.

Mass created for the "new wine" of the up-and-coming younger generation. The writings there expounded a bit upon the values and missteps in pursuing such a liturgy.

Consider the first half of the parable now. If one uses a new piece of fabric to patch a hole, that new fabric will have not yet shrunk. If it shrinks after patching a rip or hole, it is likely to reopen that tear and make it worse. So, while it is true that new wine needs new wineskins, it is simultaneously true that rips and holes in fabric should not necessarily be repaired with something new but rather, a piece of fabric that is more aged and has had a chance to shrink first.

More on this imagery—and the conclusion of this diversion toward evaluating our liturgies—in two weeks' time!

Liturgical Ministers: Eucharistic Ministers

This Sunday Elijah is strengthened for his journey by bread from heaven, and Jesus proclaims himself the Bread of Life. Eucharistic ministers are stewards of this mystery. Holding the body and blood of Christ is an act of trust, reminding them that they themselves are first fed before they serve. The way a minister handles the chalice or ciborium with careful, deliberate movement is a visible sign of the church's faith in the Real Presence. This ministry holds a pastoral dimension. When a minister looks into the eyes of a communicant and says, "The body of Christ," it is a moment of reaching out, a reminder that Christ is near. Eucharistic ministers should allow time in adoration and prayer with Scripture, so that they might become deeply aware of what they offer. Their ministry extends beyond the liturgy when Communion is taken to the sick or dying, carrying the love of the parish to those who cannot be present.

Living Liturgy: The Prayer after Communion

This Sunday's prayer after Communion asks that the mystery we receive will bring us salvation and strengthen our faith. This prayer is not a closing comment but a final moment of mystagogy. It reveals that the Eucharist is a living reality, forming the church into Christ's Body. We pray that the sacrament we consume will transform us, not only for our own benefit but for the salvation of the world. In this prayer, we are reminded that every Mass is preparation for mission. We leave the liturgy carrying Christ within us, strengthened to live the gospel in the ordinary events of life.

AUGUST 8, 2027

NINETEENTH SUNDAY IN ORDINARY TIME

SPIRITUALITY

GOSPEL ACCLAMATION
℟. Alleluia, alleluia.
Mary is taken up to heaven;
a chorus of angels exults.
℟. Alleluia, alleluia.

Gospel Luke 1:39-56; L622

Mary set out
and traveled to the hill country in haste
to a town of Judah,
where she entered the house of Zechariah
and greeted Elizabeth.
When Elizabeth heard Mary's greeting,
the infant leaped in her womb,
and Elizabeth, filled with the Holy Spirit,
cried out in a loud voice and said,
"Blessed are you among women,
and blessed is the fruit of your womb.
And how does this happen to me,
that the mother of my Lord should come to me?
For at the moment the sound of your greeting reached my ears,
the infant in my womb leaped for joy.
Blessed are you who believed
that what was spoken to you by the Lord
would be fulfilled."

And Mary said:
"My soul proclaims the greatness of the Lord;
my spirit rejoices in God my Savior
for he has looked with favor on his lowly servant.
From this day all generations will call me blessed:
the Almighty has done great things for me,
and holy is his Name.
He has mercy on those who fear him
in every generation.

Continued in Appendix A, p. 317.
See Appendix A., p. 316–317, for the other readings.

Praying with Gospel Words and Phrases

My soul proclaims the greatness of the Lord . . . holy is his Name . . .

Reflecting on the Gospel

The bread of life discourse is liturgically interrupted this Sunday by the solemnity of the Assumption. A continuing discussion in liturgical circles is the appropriateness of including Marian hymns at Eucharist. Many see no issue with the practice, especially on Marian feasts, while others decry any Marian hymns at a liturgy focused on Christ and the paschal mystery.

In practice, there are three judgments—liturgical, pastoral, and musical—which, taken together in one evaluation, answer the question: "Is this particular piece of music appropriate for use in this particular liturgy?" (*Sing to the Lord* 126). The pastoral judgment considers the needs and culture of the community, and the musical judgment considers the quality and form of the piece itself. The liturgical judgment evaluates how well the piece matches the rite being celebrated.

Turning to the *General Instruction of the Roman Missal* (GIRM) and *Sing to the Lord* (STL) helps clarify the purpose of music in the liturgy. The entrance chant is meant to "open the celebration, foster the unity of those who have been gathered, introduce their thoughts to the mystery of the liturgical season or festivity, and accompany the procession of the priest and ministers" (STL 142; GIRM 47). STL also says the norms for singing during the preparation of gifts mirror those of the entrance (173). The communion song expresses unity, joy, and the communal nature of the procession (STL 189; GIRM 86). After Communion, if a hymn is sung, it should focus the assembly on the mystery of Holy Communion (STL 196). Though not formally part of the liturgy, the recessional hymn may serve to send the assembly forth (STL 199).

On the solemnity of the Assumption, we encounter the *Magnificat* (Luke 1:46-55), Mary's own canticle of praise. Her words are deeply Christocentric, proclaiming the greatness of God, his mercy, and his justice. In singing Mary's song, the church echoes not just her devotion, but her prophetic joy in the saving power of God. The *Magnificat* isn't only Mary's hymn, it is ours as well. Far from detracting from the eucharistic celebration, music rooted in the *Magnificat* can focus us more fully on the mystery of Christ's presence, as Mary herself always does.

To the Point

On the solemnity of the Assumption, we should make sure that all the "changeable" aspects of the liturgy—preaching, hymns, petitions, etc.—are liturgically appropriate and can deepen our focus on Christ, as Mary's song magnifies God's saving work.

Preparing to Proclaim, Preach, and Pray

Making Connections Between the Readings: Today's solemnity is one of the few times outside of Eastertide that a reading from the New Testament appears as the first reading. Compared to much other imagery in Revelation, the significance of the symbolism within today's pericope is relatively straightforward. John's text here depicts the power of evil, represented by a dragon, in opposition to God and his people. The dragon attacks the woman about to give birth, but her son is saved and "caught up to God and his throne." That son is our salvation, the "loud voice" proclaiming him so, the "Anointed One."

John makes sure, even in such vivid and intense writing, to portray Mary as ultimately not the focus but rather Jesus. Mary flees to the desert, leaving the final victory to Christ and God's angels. This is not to say that Mary was not a strong woman, worthy of attention and worthy of tackling conflict. Mary as our model teaches us time and again to trust in a God of mercy and justice, to point to God and specifically the Messiah as redemption, promise, and hope.

Paul's epistle today expounds on that hope as coming from Christ, both God and man. Since our Fall, which is death, came through the flesh (Adam and Eve), so ought our redemption and life come through Christ, the son of Mary. Paul's logic here is that Jesus's resurrection must necessarily involve ours as well.

Making Connections to the Responsorial Psalm: Psalm 45, in time and space, is a wedding psalm, written for King David's marriage to a foreign princess. While the text extols the beauty and opulence of the queen and the proceedings of the court, it also, by extension, speaks of Mary and of the church. With Christ the King, the queen, arrayed in splendor, is Mary, exalted beside him. As the mother of the King, Mary shares in his glory—not by her own merit, but through her unique role in salvation history. Her exalted position fulfills the psalm's imagery of royal dignity, beauty, and divine favor.

There too is the New Testament vision of the church as the spotless bride of Christ (Eph 5:25–27; Rev 21:2). Just as the bride in Psalm 45 leaves her people to cleave to the king, so the church is called to leave behind worldly attachments and live in faithful union with Christ.

CONNECTING TO EXPERIENCE: LIVING THE PASCHAL MYSTERY

If anyone asks you where Mary, the Mother of God, is buried, rest assured that it is a trick question. Mary, who does not know sin, also does not know the dust to which all humans were destined from the Fall in the Garden of Eden. Like Jesus, her tomb is empty. Upon Mary's death, she was assumed into heaven. She is the first to know the promise of Christ's resurrection: the resurrection of the body as well as her soul. This is what awaits us. We will die, but our baptism begins our long journey to everlasting life—a life so unimaginable it is hard to believe. Yet this is our faith. Mary awaits us in heaven, urging us to continually shed the cloak of sin so that we will be prepared, when her son comes again, to join her with all the angels in unending rejoicing before the living God.

PROMPTS FOR FAITH-SHARING

- How well do you feel you know Mary? Can you read more about her? Can you pray with Mary?
- What does Mary's death teach you about your own? About those close to you?
- Do you believe that baptism gives you eternal life with Mary and the saints? If not, what stands in the way?

Model Penitential Act

Presider: Today, we celebrate the assumption of Mary, the Mother of God, into heaven. Calling to mind the times we have failed to follow her son, we ask for his mercy . . . *[pause]*

Lord Jesus, you are Son of God and son of Mary: Lord, have mercy.

Christ Jesus, you show us the way to the Father: Christ, have mercy.

Lord Jesus, you have broken down the walls of sin and death: Lord, have mercy.

Model Universal Prayer (Prayer of the Faithful)

Presider: Turning in trust to the Lord who hears all our needs, we offer our prayers this day.

Response: Lord, hear our prayer.

For the church: with Mary, may we offer hope for the hopeless and lift up all who are bowed down, we pray . . .

For all those in power: may they use their might to fill the hungry with good things, we pray . . .

For those longing for guidance in their lives: may they feel the prompting and direction of the Spirit in their prayer, we pray . . .

For all of us gathered here today: may we recognize those who need encouragement, kindness, or patience, and find the courage to offer it, we pray . . .

Presider: O God, your servant, Mary, full of grace, responded to your word with joyful hope. Increase our faith, free us from our fears, and fill us with the fire of your love. We ask this through Christ our Lord. **Amen.**

Liturgy and Marian Music

Given the broad guidance offered earlier, it seems that the only time where most Marian hymns would not be a good fit at today's liturgy would be at Communion and perhaps the song after Communion. There surely, though, is wide leeway given to scriptural Marian texts, like settings of the *Magnificat*, or content from Psalm 45 (the prescribed psalm for Assumption) or from the book of Revelation.

It would also be wise to ensure that the texts of any Marian music utilized at liturgy point to Christ, the Trinity, or to some facet of the paschal mystery. "On This Day, O Beautiful Mother," for instance, in most iterations, is only focused on the Blessed Mother. Even "Immaculate Mary," in many versions, gives only a passing reference to Christ and our redemption. Newer hymns often do a better job of allowing Mary to magnify the Lord: "I Sing a Maid" (GIA), with text by M. D. Ridge, allows Mary to watch Christ's life and for us to honor her as his mother.

(continued on next page)

COLLECT

Let us pray.

Pause for silent prayer

Almighty ever-living God,
who assumed the Immaculate Virgin Mary,
the Mother of your Son,
body and soul into heavenly glory,
grant, we pray,
that, always attentive to the things that are above,
we may merit to be sharers of her glory.
Through our Lord Jesus Christ, your Son,
who lives and reigns with you in the unity of the Holy Spirit,
God, for ever and ever. **Amen.**

FIRST READING

Rev 11:19a; 12:1-6a, 10ab

God's temple in heaven was opened,
and the ark of his covenant could be seen in the temple.

A great sign appeared in the sky, a woman clothed with the sun,
with the moon under her feet,
and on her head a crown of twelve stars.
She was with child and wailed aloud in pain as she labored to give birth.
Then another sign appeared in the sky;
it was a huge red dragon, with seven heads and ten horns,
and on its heads were seven diadems.
Its tail swept away a third of the stars in the sky
and hurled them down to the earth.
Then the dragon stood before the woman about to give birth,
to devour her child when she gave birth.
She gave birth to a son, a male child,
destined to rule all the nations with an iron rod.
Her child was caught up to God and his throne.
The woman herself fled into the desert
where she had a place prepared by God.

Then I heard a loud voice in heaven say:
"Now have salvation and power come,
and the Kingdom of our God
and the authority of his Anointed One."

RESPONSORIAL PSALM
Ps 45:10, 11, 12, 16

℟. (10bc) The queen stands at your right hand, arrayed in gold.

The queen takes her place at your right hand in gold of Ophir.

℟. The queen stands at your right hand, arrayed in gold.

Hear, O daughter, and see; turn your ear,
forget your people and your father's house.

℟. The queen stands at your right hand, arrayed in gold.

So shall the king desire your beauty;
for he is your lord.

℟. The queen stands at your right hand, arrayed in gold.

They are borne in with gladness and joy;
they enter the palace of the king.

℟. The queen stands at your right hand, arrayed in gold.

SECOND READING
1 Cor 15:20-27

Brothers and sisters:
Christ has been raised from the dead,
the firstfruits of those who have fallen asleep.
For since death came through man,
the resurrection of the dead came also through man.
For just as in Adam all die,
so too in Christ shall all be brought to life,
but each one in proper order:
Christ the firstfruits;
then, at his coming, those who belong to Christ;
then comes the end,
when he hands over the Kingdom to his God and Father,
when he has destroyed every sovereignty
and every authority and power.
For he must reign until he has put all his enemies under his feet.
The last enemy to be destroyed is death,
for "he subjected everything under his feet."

It must also be noted that it is almost never appropriate to bring Marian music to liturgical celebrations outside of Marian feasts. So too prayers which, even if scriptural, are principally devotional, such as the Hail Mary, should typically never be included in any liturgy, either spoken or sung.

Liturgical Ministers: Music Ministers

Mary's assumption is a message of hope. God's promise of resurrection is already fulfilled in her. Music for this feast should be chosen to reflect both its solemnity and its joy. Music ministers become catechists when they sing of Mary as Ark of the Covenant, Queen assumed into heaven, and first disciple. This feast invites musicians to pray with the *Magnificat*, Mary's song of praise, which becomes a pattern for the church's own voice. Leading the assembly in this feast is not about adding grandeur but about helping the faithful contemplate the mystery of Mary's destiny, which is also ours. Music ministers can lift hearts beyond earthly concerns, reminding the church that we worship with the saints and angels in heaven.

Living Liturgy: The Preface of the Assumption

The preface declares that Mary was raised body and soul into the glory of heaven, a statement of faith in God's victory over death. This liturgical text teaches that Mary's life is not distant from ours; she is a sign of what God desires for every disciple. The preface invites the assembly to see in Mary's assumption the fruit of Christ's paschal mystery. Her life is a mirror of the church's future. This preface reveals that the Eucharist is already a foretaste of that glory: as Mary shares fully in her son's life, we too are drawn toward heaven every time we gather at the altar.

SPIRITUALITY

GOSPEL ACCLAMATION
John 6:63c, 68c

℟. Alleluia, alleluia.
Your words, Lord, are Spirit and life;
you have the words of everlasting life.
℟. Alleluia, alleluia.

Gospel

John 6:60-69; L122B

Many of Jesus' disciples who were listening said,
"This saying is hard; who can accept it?"
Since Jesus knew that his disciples were murmuring about this,
he said to them, "Does this shock you?
What if you were to see the Son of Man ascending
to where he was before?
It is the spirit that gives life,
while the flesh is of no avail.
The words I have spoken to you are Spirit and life.
But there are some of you who do not believe."
Jesus knew from the beginning the ones who would not believe
and the one who would betray him.
And he said,
"For this reason I have told you that no one can come to me
unless it is granted him by my Father."

As a result of this,
many of his disciples returned to their former way of life
and no longer accompanied him.
Jesus then said to the Twelve, "Do you also want to leave?"
Simon Peter answered him, "Master, to whom shall we go?
You have the words of eternal life.
We have come to believe
and are convinced that you are the Holy One of God."

Praying with Gospel Words and Phrases

"This saying is hard; who can accept it?" . . . "Master, to whom shall we go?" . . .

Reflecting on the Gospel

Missing the Twentieth Sunday in Ordinary Time this year means we also miss the crux of the bread of life discourse. The quarreling crowd seems unsure whether to take Jesus literally. He becomes more explicit, saying, "Unless you eat the flesh of the Son of Man and drink his blood, you do not have life within you" (John 6:53).

This shocking catechesis sets up today's passage, the conclusion of our weeks-long retreat on Jesus, the Bread of Life. Today's readings present our response to Christ's difficult teachings and the abundance, reliance, sustenance, and union given to us: belief. "Master, to whom shall we go? You have the words of eternal life."

We should remember that the Christ present in the proclamation of the gospel, in the presider, in the gathered assembly, and in the eucharistic host, is the same Christ present at adoration, Benediction, and eucharistic processions. Having noted here before the renewed emphasis on eucharistic devotions, let us also note that those who champion these practices are not wrong. Yet their praise of these devotions and their energy for improving those experiences ought to be applied equally—if not more so—to the eucharistic liturgy itself.

Is adoration a useful means for deepening relationship, awareness of divine presence, and entry into mystery? Absolutely. But our ministerial efforts should first and foremost enrich the celebration of the liturgy, not only its related devotions.

Recall that the Constitution on the Sacred Liturgy, Vatican II's foundational document, calls the liturgy the "source" and "summit" of the Christian life (SC 10). *Sacrosanctum Concilium* uses the word "liturgy" seventy-seven times—more than "Eucharist" and "Mass" combined—while "adoration" never appears once. The council's liturgical reform aimed to restore full participation by the whole assembly in Christ's paschal mystery through the liturgy's action. In doing so, it sought to correct an earlier overemphasis on Christ's static presence in the consecrated elements and on devotional practices surrounding them.

After the council, attention shifted away from eucharistic adoration and processions toward the Sunday Eucharist itself. Perhaps today's renewed enthusiasm for devotions reflects a rebalancing of priorities—or perhaps it risks missing the continuing point of the reform.

To the Point

Today's readings conclude the bread of life discourse with a call to belief in Christ's Real Presence, especially in the Eucharist. While devotions are valuable, the Mass remains the church's primary place of encounter with Christ—the source and summit of our faith.

Preparing to Proclaim, Preach, and Pray

Making Connections Between the Readings: Joshua, at the end of his life, gathered all Israel to offer his final wisdom and admonitions. After recounting the powerful deeds of God (excised from today's pericope), he proclaims that he and his descendants will serve the Lord, and challenges those gathered to do likewise. They respond to his call as did Peter in today's gospel: their "Far be it from us to forsake the Lord for the service of other gods" is Peter's "Master, to whom shall we go? You have the words of eternal life."

Far from being words of despondency or desperation, these are profound and succinct professions of faith in a God who is eternally faithful to those who keep his covenant. Whereas the Nicene Creed is lengthy and detailed, Christian faith, at its core, is relatively simple: trusting in God and believing in Jesus Christ as the Son of God, who saves us through his life, death, and resurrection.

As did the Israelites of Joshua's time, as did the apostles, so now do we place our hope in God's promises and try to live according to Jesus's teachings.

Making Connections to the Responsorial Psalm: Psalm 34 returns this week, with slightly different verses than before. Eyes and ears of faith may be drawn to verse 21, which says, "he watches over all his bones; / not one of them shall be broken." Where have we heard these words before?

These lines are quoted in John's passion narrative (John 19:31-33) as prophetic of Jesus's death on the cross. Often, to speed their coming death, soldiers would break the legs of those hanging on crosses. Unable to support themselves from below any longer, suffocation would quickly follow. Christ, having died relatively quickly that Good Friday, did not suffer that further torture.

Christ's sacrifice on the cross, the blood of the new and everlasting covenant, is that same blood from the shared chalice of the Last Supper, and is the same drink of the eternal heavenly banquet—and is what we receive a foretaste of from every altar at every Mass. This is the goodness we "taste and see" each time we celebrate Eucharist together.

CONNECTING TO EXPERIENCE: LIVING THE PASCHAL MYSTERY

Moments ago, Jesus concluded his bread of life sermon, chock-full of outlandish claims (I am the Bread of Life; whoever eats of me shall never hunger). After such a speech, it is no wonder that many of his disciples began to doubt their fidelity to this once-interesting prophet. Hearing their murmuring, Jesus questions, "What if you were to see the Son of Man ascending to where he was before?" The shaken disciples hear him, or rather they stop hearing him, and many leave him that day. These followers of Jesus were asked to think and feel and believe in a new way: they did not perceive it, but closed their ears and hearts. Today, we are asked the same question: will the bread that we eat which is his body fill us with the grace to love as he did? Will we be changed today? Or will we walk away, murmuring about what the Messiah should *really* be like?

PROMPTS FOR FAITH-SHARING

- Do you ever find yourself doubting Jesus's identity? Why so?
- Have you ever wanted to walk away from someone who disagreed with you? Was there something you learned from their disagreement?
- When you challenge others, is it to be right? To control or win? Or is it out of love for them and for God's vision for all of us? How can you improve?

Model Penitential Act

Presider: In our first reading today, Joshua reminds us that we can choose to say yes to serving the Lord. Remembering the times we have failed to follow the Lord and have chosen sin instead, let us ask for his pardon and peace . . . *[pause]*

Lord Jesus, you have eyes for the just and hear the cry of the suffering: Lord, have mercy.

Christ Jesus, you confront evildoers and destroy sin and death: Christ, have mercy.

Lord Jesus, you deliver us from all our troubles: Lord, have mercy.

Model Universal Prayer (Prayer of the Faithful)

Presider: The Lord hears the cries of the just and remains close to the brokenhearted. Let us remember to trust in the Lord, bringing before him our prayers and petitions.

Response: Lord, hear our prayer.

For the faithful throughout the world, especially those undergoing persecution: may they find safety in their distress and hope for their future, we pray . . .

For families throughout the world: may the value of the smallest human communities be preserved and protected, we pray . . .

For husbands and wives experiencing hardship in their relationships and in their lives: may they find counsel and hope, we pray . . .

For all of us gathered here today: may we choose always to serve the Lord through our words, our actions, and our love for one another, we pray . . .

Presider: O God, you call us to serve you without ceasing. Fill us with fortitude and strength to always follow your will and to encourage all around us to live in your love. We ask this through Christ our Lord. **Amen.**

Liturgy and Patching Rips and Tears, Part II

When we think of our liturgies, and our communities that gather in prayer, we must not only be mindful of where the new wine and old wineskins are, but also where the holes are, where the gaps in our communities and practices are, and what bit of time-tested fabric we might use to mend the tear. That is, sometimes something new is the necessary solution, but sometimes something new might only make matters worse.

The trick, then, is to discern though prayer, conversations, careful observation, and prudent discernment what the right ministerial course of action is. Is it a reinvigoration of priest-led adoration and Benediction, or is it youth-led Liturgy of the Hours?

(continued on next page)

COLLECT

Let us pray.

Pause for silent prayer

O God, who cause the minds of the faithful
to unite in a single purpose,
grant your people to love what you
command
and to desire what you promise,
that, amid the uncertainties of this world,
our hearts may be fixed on that place
where true gladness is found.
Through our Lord Jesus Christ, your Son,
who lives and reigns with you in the unity
of the Holy Spirit,
God, for ever and ever. **Amen.**

FIRST READING

Josh 24:1-2a, 15-17, 18b

Joshua gathered together all the tribes of
Israel at Shechem,
summoning their elders, their leaders,
their judges, and their officers.
When they stood in ranks before God,
Joshua addressed all the people:
"If it does not please you to serve the
LORD,
decide today whom you will serve,
the gods your fathers served beyond the
River
or the gods of the Amorites in whose
country you are now dwelling.
As for me and my household, we will serve
the LORD."

But the people answered,
"Far be it from us to forsake the LORD
for the service of other gods.
For it was the LORD, our God,
who brought us and our fathers up out
of the land of Egypt,
out of a state of slavery.
He performed those great miracles before
our very eyes
and protected us along our entire
journey
and among the peoples through whom
we passed.
Therefore we also will serve the LORD, for
he is our God."

RESPONSORIAL PSALM
Ps 34:2-3, 16-17, 18-19, 20-21

℟. (9a) Taste and see the goodness of the Lord.

I will bless the LORD at all times;
his praise shall be ever in my mouth.
Let my soul glory in the LORD;
the lowly will hear me and be glad.

℟. Taste and see the goodness of the Lord.

The LORD has eyes for the just,
and ears for their cry.
The LORD confronts the evildoers,
to destroy remembrance of them from the earth.

℟. Taste and see the goodness of the Lord.

When the just cry out, the LORD hears them,
and from all their distress he rescues them.
The LORD is close to the brokenhearted;
and those who are crushed in spirit he saves.

℟. Taste and see the goodness of the Lord.

Many are the troubles of the just one,
but out of them all the LORD delivers him;
he watches over all his bones;
not one of them shall be broken.

℟. Taste and see the goodness of the Lord.

SECOND READING
Eph 5:21-32

Brothers and sisters:
Be subordinate to one another out of reverence for Christ.
Wives should be subordinate to their husbands as to the Lord.
For the husband is head of his wife
just as Christ is head of the church,
he himself the savior of the body.
As the church is subordinate to Christ,
so wives should be subordinate to their husbands in everything.
Husbands, love your wives,
even as Christ loved the church
and handed himself over for her to sanctify her,
cleansing her by the bath of water with the word,
that he might present to himself the church in splendor,

Continued in Appendix A, p. 317.

Is it incorporating more Latin text and chant into Mass, or is it investing in more contemporary musical resources?

Once again, we must realize that ours is a "both/and" faith. Just like in the parable of the cloth and wineskins, most often our answers too must be held together: both adoration and Vespers (perhaps at the same time!), both chant and Christian contemporary music (perhaps at the same Mass!).

In this way, finally, let us also evaluate our evaluations. It's sometimes simple but incorrect to label everything liturgical as either a "right" or a "wrong"—and to be sure, some things are certainty either right or wrong. But if our evaluations only utilize this binary choice, we should learn a lesson from this parable. Our faith, with liturgy and Eucharist as source and summit, is too important not to.

Liturgical Ministers: Altar Servers

In some churches, one of the most striking actions an altar server performs is ringing the bells during the consecration. This sound has served for centuries as a summons to attention, a joyful alarm announcing the mystery unfolding at the altar. For servers, this act is an invitation to faith. The bells also form the assembly as their clear tones pierce distractions, drawing every heart to adoration. In preparing for this task, servers are taught that sound can be sacramental. The bells proclaim what words cannot fully express, that Christ is here. Servers learn to listen closely, to act with dignity, and to sense the flow of the liturgy. Over time, these practices shape an inner devotion that extends beyond the sanctuary. The simple act of ringing the bells becomes a moment of catechesis and prayer, helping young ministers discover that the smallest symbols can reveal the majesty of God.

Living Liturgy: The Book of the Gospels

This Sunday's gospel features Peter's confession of faith, as he witnesses to who Christ is. In every liturgy, the Book of the Gospels is itself a sign of that same witness. The ornate cover, the way it is carried high in procession, and its placement upon the altar before being proclaimed teaches that the gospel is an important part of the celebration of the liturgy. Placing the book on the altar links the word with the sacrifice, showing that Christ speaks and offers himself in the same act. When the deacon or priest lifts the book and processes with it, the church visually confesses its faith that Christ is present in his word. The reverence for the gospel is a natural extension of reverence for the Eucharist. The book is kissed, elevated, and honored because it contains the living voice of the Lord.

SPIRITUALITY

GOSPEL ACCLAMATION
James 1:18

℟. Alleluia, alleluia.
The Father willed to give us birth by the word of truth
that we may be a kind of firstfruits of his creatures.
℟. Alleluia, alleluia.

Gospel

Mark 7:1-8, 14-15, 21-23; L125B

When the Pharisees with some scribes who had come from Jerusalem
gathered around Jesus,
they observed that some of his disciples ate their meals
with unclean, that is, unwashed, hands.
—For the Pharisees and, in fact, all Jews,
do not eat without carefully washing their hands,
keeping the tradition of the elders.
And on coming from the marketplace
they do not eat without purifying themselves.
And there are many other things that they have traditionally observed,
the purification of cups and jugs and kettles and beds.—
So the Pharisees and scribes questioned him,
"Why do your disciples not follow the tradition of the elders
but instead eat a meal with unclean hands?"
He responded,
"Well did Isaiah prophesy about you hypocrites, as it is written:
This people honors me with their lips,
but their hearts are far from me;
in vain do they worship me,
teaching as doctrines human precepts.
You disregard God's commandment but cling to human tradition."

Continued in Appendix A, p. 318.

Praying with Gospel Words and Phrases

[I]n vain do they worship me, teaching as doctrines human precepts . . .

Reflecting on the Gospel

An old joke goes:

A priest, a minister, and a rabbi want to see who's best at their job. So each one goes into the woods, finds a bear, and attempts to convert it. Later, they all get together to report how things had gone.

The priest begins: "When I found the bear, I read to him from the catechism and sprinkled him with holy water. Next week is his first Communion."

"I found a bear by the stream," says the minister, "and preached God's holy Word. The bear was so mesmerized that he let me baptize him."

These two both look down at the rabbi, who is lying on a gurney in a body cast. "Looking back," he says, "maybe I shouldn't have started with the circumcision."

A good joke, yes, but it also has a relevant point to make for those of us who evangelize, especially via the liturgy. From the very beginning, our missionary efforts recognized that step one was always to enter into a human relationship with the people and culture being visited, and to make sure first that their human needs were being met. If those with whom we hope to share the good news don't know us and trust us as friends, any words we share will be hollow and distrusted. If those with whom we hope to share the good news are hungry, poorly clothed, or need shelter, these basic human needs will preclude them from hearing any other message.

I wouldn't say that the priest or the minister of the joke start from a place of relationship and trust, but the rabbi (in this case) seems to have just jumped in with the rules and rituals of his faith. The gospel this Sunday is focused on observances of laws, and we liturgists can frequently get caught up in ensuring that the minutiae of each rubric are followed as closely as possible. How much time do we spend, as liturgists, meeting needs and building relationship? It's likely that the "needs" of those many of us meet are not needs relating to hunger or housing insecurity, but rather needs of relationship: belonging, being understood, sensing one's own belonging.

To the Point

People won't care what you know until they know you care. This remains true for any of us in the church, but especially for those with visible leadership roles.

Preparing to Proclaim, Preach, and Pray

Making Connections Between the Readings: We should be careful here to note that laws in and of themselves are not bad things. Much like water is necessary for life yet potentially can be fatal, laws, rules, and precepts are a double-edged sword. They may set us spiritually free, to live a holy and truth-filled life; lived more scrupulously, they become a hinderance to the mercy of God and sometimes to right relationship with God and one another.

In the Hebraic covenants, the Mosaic laws were deemed more precious than gold, a gift from God who led the Israelites to freedom and a land flowing with milk and honey. By Jesus's time, the Pharisees made God's law burdensome, a hinderance to knowing God's mercy and even an impenetrable wall between humans and God. Jesus's issue with the Pharisees wasn't their devotion to the law, but their inconsistent, prideful, and often unjust application of it. He called for a deeper, more authentic holiness that flowed from love of God and neighbor.

The epistle of James this week eloquently describes what following God's law, the word (really, the capital-W Word), planted in our hearts, should look like: "Religion that is pure and undefiled before God and the Father is this: to care for orphans and widows in their affliction and to keep oneself unstained by the world."

Making Connections to the Responsorial Psalm: The words of Psalm 15 also succinctly clarify what following God's law ought to look like, as if our day-to-day lives were observed by a complete stranger, with no knowledge of our faith or even of God. Justice, to the psalmist, is a one-word definition of what God's laws impel us to do: to think truth, to speak truth, to avoid harming others, to deal with money fairly. This kind of life, of living, places us firmly in the presence of the Lord.

Psalm 15 today tweaks verse 1 for its refrain; the actual text of verse 1 is: "Lord, who may abide in your tent? / Who may dwell on your holy mountain?" Abiding in the Lord's tent is a reference to admittance to worship of the time—and note the answers are all about right relationship with one's neighbor as evidence of being in right relationship with God.

CONNECTING TO EXPERIENCE: LIVING THE PASCHAL MYSTERY

Jesus tells the Pharisees and scribes today—traditional authorities and elders respected in the community—that no amount of cup, jug, or kettle-washing will get them into the kingdom of God. "You hypocrites," Jesus says, slyly quoting one of the very prophets in whom these authorities should be well-versed, "You disregard God's commandment but cling to human tradition." Can't you just feel the rage swelling up in the hearts of the adversaries? Angry at Jesus for questioning their habits, angry at Jesus for not honoring their authority, and angry at Jesus for besting them at their own game of law and prophet-quoting. Their anger, power, and pride swell their hearts and strangle their ability to behold the Messiah. But we cannot sit back and gleefully judge. Jesus has asked the question to us: Do our hearts harden in annoyance, resentment, or judgment about our aesthetic choices in our worship? Or are our hearts touched by the living God made manifest in these sacred mysteries—and changed?

PROMPTS FOR FAITH-SHARING

- Do you spend too much time on appearance, on outer things that do not matter? How can you, like Christ advises, work on the purity of what is inside you?
- When someone challenges your deeply held values or traditions, do you hear them out? Do you feel enraged? How can you moderate your reaction, in case they really have something to teach you?
- Do you have deeply held beliefs about particular forms of prayer or liturgy? How can you open your mind and heart to consider other valid ways of seeing them?

Model Penitential Act

Presider: For the times we have failed in our call to do justice and follow the command of Christ, we pray . . . *[pause]*

Lord Jesus, you alone see the human heart: Lord, have mercy.

Christ Jesus, you planted the word within us that might save our souls: Christ, have mercy.

Lord Jesus, you call us to do justice and to walk in your presence: Lord, have mercy.

Model Universal Prayer (Prayer of the Faithful)

Presider: Humbly coming before the Lord who calls all to holiness, we offer our prayers and petitions.

Response: Lord, hear our prayer.

That the faithful support one another in solidarity and unceasingly defend the human dignity of all, we pray . . .

That nations acting with aggression might be transformed by peace, and those they are persecuting be protected, we pray . . .

That the poor and vulnerable who have been forced to pay bribes for their protection may find new freedom from fear, we pray . . .

That we might allow the wisdom of God to enlighten our hearts and minds as we seek always to do God's will, we pray . . .

Presider: Lord God, you call us to be not only hearers but doers of the word. May we welcome your word always and live fully in your presence. We ask this through Christ our Lord. **Amen.**

Liturgy and the Sign of Peace

The *General Instruction of the Roman Missal* tells us, "There follows the Rite of Peace, by which the Church entreats peace and unity for herself and for the whole human family, and the faithful express to each other their ecclesial communion and mutual charity before communicating in the Sacrament" (82). There is a restlessness within, and sometimes a reluctance to the rite, but Christ always breaks through, strangers bonded by touch and word in divine peace.

The sign of peace, practically speaking, is about creating or restoring relationship before approaching the altar, with at least two profound scriptural roots. In Matthew 5:23-24 Jesus teaches that we should reconcile with our brother before approaching the altar. In other scriptural places a greeting of peace is offered: Jesus just after his resurrection, and many times in the Pauline epistles, just for starters.

The sign of peace is not just a polite gesture, a friendly wave across the pew—it's a liturgical and theological expression of Christ's peace, rooted in Scripture. It reflects Jesus's call to reconciliation and relationship, his own peace-giving in the resurrection, and the early church's practice of greeting others in love.

COLLECT

Let us pray.

Pause for silent prayer

God of might, giver of every good gift,
put into our hearts the love of your name,
so that, by deepening our sense of
reverence,
you may nurture in us what is good
and, by your watchful care,
keep safe what you have nurtured.
Through our Lord Jesus Christ, your Son,
who lives and reigns with you in the unity
of the Holy Spirit,
God, for ever and ever. **Amen.**

FIRST READING

Deut 4:1-2, 6-8

Moses said to the people:
"Now, Israel, hear the statutes and
decrees
which I am teaching you to observe,
that you may live, and may enter in and
take possession of the land
which the LORD, the God of your fathers,
is giving you.
In your observance of the commandments
of the LORD, your God,
which I enjoin upon you,
you shall not add to what I command
you nor subtract from it.
Observe them carefully,
for thus will you give evidence
of your wisdom and intelligence to the
nations,
who will hear of all these statutes and
say,
'This great nation is truly a wise and
intelligent people.'
For what great nation is there
that has gods so close to it as the LORD,
our God, is to us
whenever we call upon him?
Or what great nation has statutes and
decrees
that are as just as this whole law
which I am setting before you today?"

RESPONSORIAL PSALM
Ps 15:2-3, 3-4, 4-5

℟. (1a) The one who does justice will live in the presence of the Lord.

Whoever walks blamelessly and does justice;
who thinks the truth in his heart
and slanders not with his tongue.

℟. The one who does justice will live in the presence of the Lord.

Who harms not his fellow man,
nor takes up a reproach against his neighbor;
by whom the reprobate is despised,
while he honors those who fear the Lord.

℟. The one who does justice will live in the presence of the Lord.

Who lends not his money at usury
and accepts no bribe against the innocent.
Whoever does these things
shall never be disturbed.

℟. The one who does justice will live in the presence of the Lord.

SECOND READING
Jas 1:17-18, 21b-22, 27

Dearest brothers and sisters:
All good giving and every perfect gift is from above,
coming down from the Father of lights,
with whom there is no alteration or shadow caused by change.
He willed to give us birth by the word of truth
that we may be a kind of firstfruits of his creatures.

Humbly welcome the word that has been planted in you
and is able to save your souls.

Be doers of the word and not hearers only, deluding yourselves.

Religion that is pure and undefiled before God and the Father is this:
to care for orphans and widows in their affliction
and to keep oneself unstained by the world.

Liturgical Ministers: Ushers and Greeters
James urges the church to be doers of the word, and Jesus points from outward custom to the conversion of the heart. Ushers and greeters can pray this Sunday with a very specific practice in mind. They receive the community's shared offering. The baskets they carry are not solely about fundraising. They are a sign that lives and labor are placed before God. This moment can form ministers in a spirituality of mercy. When the gifts are gathered, the poor are remembered and the mission of the parish is sustained. Treating the collection with prayerful care teaches the assembly that generosity is worship. Discreet attentiveness to those who have nothing to give models dignity. Inviting a family or a newcomer to join the procession of gifts reveals that every person brings a gift. In these simple actions ministers become witnesses that true religion visits the orphan and the widow, and keeps the heart free for God. The collection becomes a place where the whole parish learns to offer itself.

Living Liturgy: Liturgy and Synodality
Mark asks for interior honesty. Synodality asks for the same. A listening church is not a strategy meeting. It is a people who pray, hear the word, and then speak and listen within that light. Parish listening can be scheduled like any gathering, yet its form is learned at the ambo and the altar. Reverent silence makes room for truth. Scripture sets the measure for desire and decision. The prayer of the faithful becomes a habit of carrying real needs together. This Sunday invites communities to examine whether our conversations sound like disciples around the Lord or like arguments at the edges. Synodal listening is a place of conversion. We learn to receive one another as gifts and to seek what the Spirit is saying in this time and place.

AUGUST 29, 2027

TWENTY-SECOND SUNDAY IN ORDINARY TIME

SPIRITUALITY

GOSPEL ACCLAMATION
cf. Matt 4:23

℟. Alleluia, alleluia.
Jesus proclaimed the Gospel of the kingdom
and cured every disease among the people.
℟. Alleluia, alleluia.

Gospel

Mark 7:31-37; L128B

Again Jesus left the district of Tyre
and went by way of Sidon to the Sea of Galilee,
into the district of the Decapolis.
And people brought to him a deaf man who had a speech impediment
and begged him to lay his hand on him.
He took him off by himself away from the crowd.
He put his finger into the man's ears
and, spitting, touched his tongue;
then he looked up to heaven and groaned, and said to him,
***"Ephphatha!"*—that is, "Be opened!"—**
And immediately the man's ears were opened,
his speech impediment was removed,
and he spoke plainly.
He ordered them not to tell anyone.
But the more he ordered them not to,
the more they proclaimed it.
They were exceedingly astonished and they said,
"He has done all things well.
He makes the deaf hear and the mute speak."

Praying with Gospel Words and Phrases

"Ephphatha!" . . . "Be opened!"

Reflecting on the Gospel

Today's gospel, as did one earlier this year, includes Aramaic words: *"Ephphatha!"* "Be opened!" We will recall that the inclusion of the original language is rare, likely indicating a certain importance or reverence to these specific utterances from either the evangelist or the community.

Today, the church continues to wrestle with questions of openness, especially around the Eucharist. Pope Francis, in *Evangelii Gaudium*, reminded us that the Eucharist is "not a prize for the perfect but a powerful medicine and nourishment for the weak" (EG 47). This echoes St. Ambrose, who said, "I who sin often should receive it often: I need a frequent remedy." Pope Francis concludes (again, EG 47) that "the Church is not a tollhouse," but "the house of the Father, where there is a place for everyone, with all their problems."

St. Paul, in 1 Corinthians 11:27-29, warns that one must receive the Eucharist worthily, discerning the body of Christ. Yet he places the responsibility of discernment not on others, but on each individual before God. Still, in practice, we often set up barriers for others—judging their worthiness, enforcing unwritten rules, or excluding those who differ only slightly from us in belief or expression.

Too often, we limit who is welcome in our churches and ministries, passing judgment based on appearances, backgrounds, or imperfect conformity. This contradicts the heart of Christ's mission, which was always directed toward the sinner, the outsider, the forgotten. Sometimes the most painful divisions arise not from stark differences but from near-agreements laced with misunderstanding or mistrust.

We must resist the urge to create these fractures. As the hymn *Ubi Caritas* urges, "Lest we be divided in mind, let us beware. / Let cease malicious quarrels, let strife give way. / And in the midst of us be Christ our God." We are on the same team in ministry, in worship, and in love. Jesus said, "Whoever is not against us is for us" (Mark 9:40). Let us be vigilant in being open to all who seek Christ—especially in the liturgy—without placing artificial restrictions on who may pray, serve, or be nourished by grace.

To the Point

The early church chose inclusion over strict legalism, opening the way for Gentiles to follow Christ without full adherence to the Mosaic Law—a spirit echoed today in calls to welcome all to the Eucharist and ministry. Rather than placing human made barriers around God's grace, we are called to recognize that all who seek Christ belong at the table.

Preparing to Proclaim, Preach, and Pray

Making Connections Between the Readings: Today's pericope from Isaiah speaks of transformation, healing, and new life—all images that deeply resonate with the sacrament of baptism. There is a promise of salvation and courage; in baptism, God comes near to us in a definitive way, claiming the baptized person as beloved, washing away sin, and offering the courage of divine presence. It is their entrance into salvation, a fulfillment of this promise to the frightened and weary. The healing, the opening of our eyes and ears Isaiah speaks of, reminds us that baptism is about spiritual awakening, that the baptized are given new eyes to see Christ, new ears to hear the word, and a heart opened to grace. The streams breaking forth in the desert evoke the life-giving water of baptism. Just as the desert blooms from time to time with unexpected streams, baptism brings life to a soul previously dry, desolate, or lost.

As the epistle of James continues this week, he reminds us: "Did not God choose those who are poor in the world to be rich in faith and heirs of the kingdom that he promised to those who love him?" In baptism, we are God's adopted children, made spiritually rich and inheritors of the kingdom of Christ, achieved through his death and resurrection, in which we also share.

Making Connections to the Responsorial Psalm: The miracle of giving sight to the blind, like many miracles, is an outward sign of interior grace—and in Jesus's case, his divine nature. If eyes opened are obvious to a bystander, perhaps less obvious are other works of the Lord, enumerated in Psalm 146: feeding the hungry, setting captives free, raising the lowly, protecting the alien, sustaining the orphan and the widow. These too are miracles, seen with opened eyes of faith.

Psalm 146 is a hymn of someone who has learned there is no other source of strength except the merciful God. Only God, not mortal human beings (verses 3-4, omitted from today's liturgy), can help vulnerable and oppressed people. It is the first of the last five psalms in the Bible, sometimes known as the "hallelujah psalms." Each of these psalms begins and ends with the Hebrew word "Hallelujah," which translates to "praise the Lord." These psalms serve as a grand finale to the book of Psalms, culminating in a powerful call to praise God for divine greatness and mighty deeds.

CONNECTING TO EXPERIENCE: LIVING THE PASCHAL MYSTERY

Today, Jesus radically changes a man who could not speak or hear. If we were to see such bodily transformation before our eyes—or to experience it ourselves—would we recognize God's gift? Would we be changed ourselves? Jesus initiates this man into his new life in a very specific way by touching the very instruments that have been out of tune: ears and tongue. How does this gospel speak to us today? We might not ask Jesus to touch our ears or tongues, but we do say, "Only say the word and we shall be healed." We ask Jesus to transform our hearts so that we might be changed, so that when we hear his word we might proclaim it in all we do and say. The man in our gospel today experienced new life at the word of Jesus: *Ephphatha!* Be opened! May we have open hearts to receive the mystery of his transformative grace.

PROMPTS FOR FAITH-SHARING

- Do you need to see or hear differently today? How can Christ bring you healing?
- Do you ever feel astonished by God's work? If so, when? If not, how can you look for God's work anew?
- Can Christ, who opens ears, mouths, and hearts, open something new for you this week?

Model Penitential Act

Presider: In today's gospel, Jesus says "Be opened!," opening the ears of the deaf man and freeing his mouth to speak. We turn to the Lord as we ask for his mercy, opening our ears to hear and obey his word and inviting our mouths to speak of his love . . . *[pause]*

Lord Jesus, you cure every disease among your people: Lord, have mercy.

Christ Jesus, you give sight to the blind and raise up those who are bowed down: Christ, have mercy.

Lord Jesus, you are the Word of everlasting life: Lord, have mercy.

Model Universal Prayer (Prayer of the Faithful)

Presider: Coming before the Lord who heals the oppressed and sustains those who are broken in body and spirit, we offer our prayers and petitions.

Response: Lord, hear our prayer.

For the church: may the faithful throughout the world work for the protection and care of the most vulnerable in our midst, we pray . . .

For nations experiencing drought, heat, torrential rain, and excessive cold: may the suffering find relief, and may communities find long-term solutions, we pray . . .

For all those struggling with pain, weakness, and fatigue: may they find relief for their bodies and sustenance for their spirits, we pray . . .

For all of us gathered here today: may we remember to care for our bodies as well as our souls, pursuing healthy habits and lifestyles, we pray . . .

Presider: O God, you give life to all creation and sustain it in your love. Hear our prayers this day, and may we find healing and hope in your sustaining care. We ask this through Christ, our Lord. **Amen.**

Liturgy and Music of Openness

Many readers are familiar with Jesse Manibusan's song "Open My Eyes" (OCP), and of course, "Amazing Grace," found in nearly all hymnals. A lesser-known hymn choice would include "O Christ, the Healer, We Have Come" (Hope Publishing), which pairs nicely with "Erhalt uns, Herr," available in a number of different hymnals.

For music that speaks more of the Christian community being an open and welcoming place, consider "All Are Welcome (All Belong)" by Jesse and Jennah Manibusan (OCP), or

(continued on next page)

COLLECT

Let us pray.

Pause for silent prayer

O God, by whom we are redeemed and
receive adoption,
look graciously upon your beloved sons
and daughters,
that those who believe in Christ
may receive true freedom
and an everlasting inheritance.
Through our Lord Jesus Christ, your Son,
who lives and reigns with you in the unity
of the Holy Spirit,
God, for ever and ever. **Amen.**

FIRST READING

Isa 35:4-7a

Thus says the LORD:
Say to those whose hearts are
frightened:
Be strong, fear not!
Here is your God,
he comes with vindication;
with divine recompense
he comes to save you.
Then will the eyes of the blind be
opened,
the ears of the deaf be cleared;
then will the lame leap like a stag,
then the tongue of the mute will sing.
Streams will burst forth in the desert,
and rivers in the steppe.
The burning sands will become pools,
and the thirsty ground, springs of
water.

RESPONSORIAL PSALM

Ps 146:6-7, 8-9a, 9bc-10

℟. (1b) Praise the Lord, my soul!
or: ℟. Alleluia.

The God of Jacob keeps faith forever,
secures justice for the oppressed,
gives food to the hungry.
The LORD sets captives free.

℟. Praise the Lord, my soul!
or: ℟. Alleluia.

The LORD gives sight to the blind;
the LORD raises up those who were bowed down.
The LORD loves the just;
the LORD protects strangers.

R/. Praise the Lord, my soul!
or: R/. Alleluia.

The fatherless and the widow the LORD sustains,
but the way of the wicked he thwarts.
The LORD shall reign forever;
your God, O Zion, through all generations.
Alleluia.

R/. Praise the Lord, my soul!
or: R/. Alleluia.

SECOND READING

Jas 2:1-5

My brothers and sisters, show no partiality
as you adhere to the faith in our glorious Lord Jesus Christ.
For if a man with gold rings and fine clothes
comes into your assembly,
and a poor person in shabby clothes also comes in,
and you pay attention to the one wearing the fine clothes
and say, "Sit here, please,"
while you say to the poor one, "Stand there," or "Sit at my feet,"
have you not made distinctions among yourselves
and become judges with evil designs?

Listen, my beloved brothers and sisters.
Did not God choose those who are poor in the world
to be rich in faith and heirs of the kingdom
that he promised to those who love him?

"Come to Me, O Weary Traveler" (text by Sylvia Dustan), or "There's a Wideness in God's Mercy" (text by Frederick William Faber), the latter two found in a variety of hymnals with varying familiar tunes.

This could be a good weekend to celebrate baptisms within Mass, especially if the varying aspects of the liturgy are crafted around the community being open and welcoming—likely many hymns from the Christian initiation section of your hymnals would then also fit in nicely.

Liturgical Ministers: Lectors

The gospel tells of *Ephphatha*, "Be opened." One concrete practice can shape lectors for this day. Carry the Book of the Gospels as if the whole church rests upon it. At home let the word rest upon you. Open the text days before the liturgy and let the phrases open your own hearing. Mark breaths on the page not as performance but as consent to the Spirit's voice. When the procession begins, lift the book high with a quiet heart. At the ambo, pause before the holy words and allow the assembly to lean in. The lector's body teaches the community that the gospel is living and active. It is an opening of ears and hearts by the One who speaks.

Living Liturgy: Baptismal Ephphatha

The *Ephphatha* gesture in baptism touches ears and lips with a prayer for hearing and speaking. Many never witness it, yet it belongs to the church's memory. This Sunday is an invitation to retrieve that memory. The gospel heals deafness and loosens tongues. The baptismal gesture explains how that healing continues in us. A parish can catechize around this sign in the homily, bulletin, or catechumenate. The rite shows what discipleship is meant to be. We receive the word and we speak the word. We are opened for God and opened for the world.

SPIRITUALITY

GOSPEL ACCLAMATION
Gal 6:14

℟. Alleluia, alleluia.
May I never boast except in the cross of our Lord
through which the world has been crucified to me
and I to the world.
℟. Alleluia, alleluia.

Gospel

Mark 8:27-35; L131B

Jesus and his disciples set out
for the villages of Caesarea Philippi.
Along the way he asked his disciples,
"Who do people say that I am?"
They said in reply,
"John the Baptist, others Elijah,
still others one of the prophets."
And he asked them,
"But who do you say that I am?"
Peter said to him in reply,
"You are the Christ."
Then he warned them not to tell anyone about him.

He began to teach them
that the Son of Man must suffer greatly
and be rejected by the elders, the chief priests, and the scribes,
and be killed, and rise after three days.
He spoke this openly.
Then Peter took him aside and began to rebuke him.
At this he turned around and, looking at his disciples,
rebuked Peter and said, "Get behind me, Satan.
You are thinking not as God does, but as human beings do."

He summoned the crowd with his disciples and said to them,
"Whoever wishes to come after me must deny himself,
take up his cross, and follow me.
For whoever wishes to save his life will lose it,
but whoever loses his life for my sake
and that of the gospel will save it."

Praying with Gospel Words and Phrases

"But who do you say that I am?" . . . "You are the Christ" . . .

Reflecting on the Gospel

In today's gospel, Jesus asks his disciples, "But who do you say that I am?" Liturgically, we might imagine today a parallel question from Christ: "Where do you say that I am?"—a prompt to reflect on his presence in the liturgy, the assembly, the altar, the ministers, and the ritual actions of the Mass.

Ever since *Summorum Pontificum,* a mutual influence between the Tridentine Rite and the Novus Ordo has emerged. One result is the occasional reintroduction of the priest facing *ad orientem* ("to the East") during presidential prayers. Though often misunderstood as the priest turning his back to the people, the intent is for the whole assembly and presider to face God together, facing East, or at least to what has been coined "liturgical east." This practice is sometimes justified as ancient and universal, though liturgical history reveals a much more diverse tradition.

Interestingly, "liturgical east" is often not aligned with actual geographic east in our churches, which in turn raises questions in a church that values the real over the symbolic. Does facing a particular direction imply God is only "over there" and not everywhere? And can we not also encounter God by facing each other—especially when each person is made in God's image and is a temple of the Holy Spirit?

While Christ is not bound by time or space, *Sacrosanctum Concilium* (SC 7) teaches us that Christ is truly present in the liturgy in four ways: in the assembly, the word, the presiding minister, and uniquely so in the Eucharist. The altar itself, central in worship, is a symbol of Christ. This is affirmed in both the US bishops' document *Built of Living Stones* and the Roman Missal's Preface V of Easter: Christ is the "priest, altar, and lamb" of his sacrifice.

So, when we gather around the altar—assembly and priest alike—we are already facing Christ: in each other, in the altar, and in the Eucharist we share. The last verse of "In Christ There is No East or West" by John Oxenham (1908) puts it quite succinctly:

In Christ now meet both east and west;
in him meet south and north.
All Christly souls are one in him
throughout the whole wide earth.

To the Point

In the liturgy, we encounter Christ not in a single direction, but all around us—in the altar, the Eucharist, the word, the presiding minister, and in one another.

Preparing to Proclaim, Preach, and Pray

Making Connections Between the Readings: The Suffering Servant today in the first reading may remind some in the assembly of Palm Sunday of the Lord's Passion, whose first reading overlaps significantly with today's. With the Lord's passion as the culmination of his suffering as God's servant, today's gospel is the first time (in Mark) that Jesus prophesies those coming days. Indeed, it's a turning point in the gospel narrative, with Jesus being identified as Messiah for the first time.

Popular, contemporary ideas of what a Messiah would be did not match at all with the vision Christ had for such a role. People in that time and place, largely, were looking for a political or military leader who would serve to free Israel from the outside Roman (and pagan) rule. Christ's vision aligned more with Isaiah's Suffering Servant, who would take the abuse of his people while finding strength in God, a constant and sure help in times of distress. This version of the Messiah would indeed set people free, not politically but spiritually, lifting us from the yokes of sin and death. Christ as Messiah accomplishes this by embodying the prophesied Suffering Servant most completely and fully.

Where the words from James the last two weeks easily found a path of integration with the other readings, one may need to squint a bit more today, but the veiled connection is in fact strong. James calls for a faith visible through acts, and the Suffering Servant is the ultimate example of such faith. Just as James challenges believers to show their faith through works, the Suffering Servant shows God's redemptive power through action—a life poured out for others. Both texts point to the same truth: faith is most real when it is lived, especially in love, sacrifice, and service.

Making Connections to the Responsorial Psalm: Whichever Suffering Servant we turn our attention to—that of Isaiah's writings, Jesus during his passion, or any of a myriad of current-day prophets—the surety of the God who protects, upholds, and ultimately saves is our constant hope. Psalm 116, with wholly different words from the other times we have encountered it at liturgy this year, speaks strongly of that God of redemption. The phrase "the land of the living" may refer to the temple, or God's living presence in that temple.

The thanksgiving in the psalm today is a setup of sorts to the words from the same psalm on Holy Thursday. Today, God rescues from despair and mortal danger; later in the psalm, verses we sing on Holy Thursday, we ask how to repay God for such goodness. The answer is a sacrifice of praise—in the psalmist's time that would be a burnt offering. Today we offer our very selves, in worship and service to God and the church.

CONNECTING TO EXPERIENCE: LIVING THE PASCHAL MYSTERY

To deny oneself is not human nature. From the original sin of our first parents, we are hardwired for greed. We avoid duties and difficulties, and push them off at others. Instead, we grasp at power, pride, and the best-looking piece of fruit we can reach, and we're ready to push others out of the way. We're even prepared to destroy—relationships, hearts, or life itself—to get what we want. Human beings seem destined for a miserable future. Yet Jesus offers a surprising antidote: Deny thyself. Pick up your cross, whatever size it may be. Follow me. Follow the One who will suffer, be rejected, and be killed. This is not in human nature to embrace. Yet grafted to Christ and filled with his grace, we surprise human nature by seeking the perfection God designed for us: love of him, love of neighbor, and love for ourselves. Jesus invites us to walk with him, let go of sin and death, and find life.

PROMPTS FOR FAITH-SHARING

- What burdens do you bear? Are they from Christ? If not, can you dispense with them?
- What cross might Christ be asking you to take up? How can you see it as a path to freedom?
- How can you embrace the mystery of Christ's suffering with new joy and wisdom today?

Model Penitential Act

Presider: In the gospel today, Jesus calls his disciples to take up their cross and follow him. For the times we have failed to be faithful disciples of Jesus, we come before him to ask for his mercy . . . *[pause]*

Lord Jesus, you are gracious and just, the protector of the lowly: Lord, have mercy.

Christ Jesus, you are the crucified one, who gave his life for the world: Christ, have mercy.

Lord Jesus, you are the Christ, the Son of the living God: Lord, have mercy.

Model Universal Prayer (Prayer of the Faithful)

Presider: The Lord calls us to follow him in love and justice. Having heard his word, we begin by offering our prayers for the world.

Response: Lord, hear our prayer.

That all Christians who are persecuted, especially among our Eastern Orthodox brothers and sisters, find mercy and refuge, we pray . . .

That we might work to support the most poor and vulnerable among the nations, especially where civil unrest has disrupted lives, we pray . . .

That first responders might be protected in their labors to stop and heal suffering, we pray . . .

That all gathered here might recognize signs of distress and sorrow in our loved ones and seek to help them, we pray . . .

Presider: Lord God, you free our eyes from tears, our feet from stumbling, and our souls from death. Hear us this day as we seek always to walk with joy in your everlasting mercy. We ask this through Christ our Lord. **Amen.**

Liturgy and Music

In addition to the hymn "In Christ There is No East or West," the theme of discipleship is so strong in today's readings it in turn prompts two hymns that share the title "Take Up Your Cross." The first has text by Charles W. Everest and is found in many hymnals with a variety of tunes ("Waly, Waly" is particularly nice with these words). A newer song of the same title mentioned earlier this year is by Jaime Cortez (OCP), and draws lyrics more directly from today's gospel.

If you are looking for a more christological text, especially one of praise, look no further than Bernadette Farrell's triumphant "Praise to You, O Christ Our Savior" (OCP), particularly effective as either a gathering or sending hymn today.

COLLECT

Let us pray.

Pause for silent prayer

Look upon us, O God,
Creator and ruler of all things,
and, that we may feel the working of your mercy,
grant that we may serve you with all our heart.
Through our Lord Jesus Christ, your Son,
who lives and reigns with you in the unity of the Holy Spirit,
God, for ever and ever. **Amen.**

FIRST READING

Isa 50:4c-9a

The Lord GOD opens my ear that I may hear;
and I have not rebelled,
have not turned back.
I gave my back to those who beat me,
my cheeks to those who plucked my beard;
my face I did not shield
from buffets and spitting.

The Lord GOD is my help,
therefore I am not disgraced;
I have set my face like flint,
knowing that I shall not be put to shame.
He is near who upholds my right;
if anyone wishes to oppose me,
let us appear together.
Who disputes my right?
Let that man confront me.
See, the Lord GOD is my help;
who will prove me wrong?

RESPONSORIAL PSALM

Ps 116:1-2, 3-4, 5-6, 8-9

℟. (9) I will walk before the Lord, in the land of the living.
or: ℟. Alleluia.

I love the LORD because he has heard
my voice in supplication,
because he has inclined his ear to me
the day I called.

℟. I will walk before the Lord, in the land of the living.
or: ℟. Alleluia.

The cords of death encompassed me;
the snares of the netherworld seized upon me;
I fell into distress and sorrow,
and I called upon the name of the LORD,
"O LORD, save my life!"

℟. I will walk before the Lord, in the land of the living.
or: ℟. Alleluia.

Gracious is the LORD and just;
yes, our God is merciful.
The LORD keeps the little ones;
I was brought low, and he saved me.

℟. I will walk before the Lord, in the land of the living.
or: ℟. Alleluia.

For he has freed my soul from death,
my eyes from tears, my feet from stumbling.
I shall walk before the LORD
in the land of the living.

℟. I will walk before the Lord, in the land of the living.
or: ℟. Alleluia.

SECOND READING
Jas 2:14-18

What good is it, my brothers and sisters,
if someone says he has faith but does not have works?
Can that faith save him?
If a brother or sister has nothing to wear
and has no food for the day,
and one of you says to them,
"Go in peace, keep warm, and eat well,"
but you do not give them the necessities of the body,
what good is it?
So also faith of itself,
if it does not have works, is dead.

Indeed someone might say,
"You have faith and I have works."
Demonstrate your faith to me without works,
and I will demonstrate my faith to you from my works.

Liturgical Ministers: Eucharistic Ministers

Jesus speaks of taking up the cross and following. One expression of this call is the Sunday sending of Communion to the sick. Ministers who carry the Eucharist from the altar to homes or hospitals extend the assembly's prayer across distance. The pyx they hold becomes a small tabernacle and a pledge that the suffering are not forgotten. This practice forms a eucharistic imagination. The body received is the body sought out in the lonely and the ill. A brief parish sending after Communion can sustain this link. The assembly prays, the minister departs, and love travels with the sacrament. In this pattern ministers learn to read the world through the altar. Christ given here is Christ carried there.

Living Liturgy: Co-responsibility in Care for the Sick

The church's prayer for the sick flows from the altar and reaches into every home and hospital room. The intercessions at Mass do more than list needs; they teach us that every suffering member belongs at the heart of the assembly's prayer. When Communion is brought to the homebound, the procession does not end at the church doors but extends the eucharistic celebration, making the sick present at the same sacrifice offered for their healing and hope. The rite of Communion to the sick draws directly from the liturgy of the Mass. Scripture is proclaimed, the prayers of the faithful are offered, and the body of Christ is received with reverence. Blessings for caregivers within Mass and celebrations of the anointing of the sick make visible that this is not private devotion but the church's worship poured into moments of suffering. Co-responsibility in this aspect means the entire parish recognizes that Christ's healing presence belongs to all. These rites teach that to care for the sick is to share in the church's priestly prayer, where mercy and solidarity are as much an offering as the bread and wine placed on the altar.

SPIRITUALITY

GOSPEL ACCLAMATION
cf. 2 Thess 2:14

℟. Alleluia, alleluia.
God has called us through the Gospel
to possess the glory of our Lord Jesus Christ.
℟. Alleluia, alleluia.

Gospel

Mark 9:30-37; L134B

Jesus and his disciples left from there
and began a journey through Galilee,
but he did not wish anyone to know about it.
He was teaching his disciples and telling them,
"The Son of Man is to be handed over to men
and they will kill him,
and three days after his death the Son of Man will rise."
But they did not understand the saying,
and they were afraid to question him.

They came to Capernaum and, once inside the house,
he began to ask them,
"What were you arguing about on the way?"
But they remained silent.
They had been discussing among themselves on the way
who was the greatest.
Then he sat down, called the Twelve, and said to them,
"If anyone wishes to be first,
he shall be the last of all and the servant of all."
Taking a child, he placed it in their midst,
and putting his arms around it, he said to them,
"Whoever receives one child such as this in my name, receives me;
and whoever receives me,
receives not me but the One who sent me."

Praying with Gospel Words and Phrases

"What were you arguing about on the way?" . . .

Reflecting on the Gospel

Disorder, wars, conflict, envy, passions: all words from the epistle this Sunday, with similar words from the book of Wisdom, all of them culminating in the gospel, with disciples arguing with one another. Where do these troubles come from, why do they seem so persistent? Perhaps a quick case study might be useful here.

Have you ever noticed how, at the Holy Thursday Mass of the Lord's Supper, the gospel reading is not what it seems like it ought to be? One would think that we would hear one of the evangelists describe the Passover meal, the last supper Christ shared with his apostles. Rather, in the epistle that night Paul explains how the tradition of that meal was handed down to him. Then in the gospel, we hear a narrative unique to John—Christ's humble washing of the apostle's feet.

John's Gospel doesn't include a narrative about the Last Supper meal the way the Synoptics do. Some see the significance of this—that the description of the meal is, essentially, replaced with this story of the foot washing—as one that instructs the early Christian community to live eucharistically, in lives of solidarity and service, both important tenets of contemporary Catholic social teaching.

Many have often wondered why foot washing didn't "make the cut," so to speak, as the church finally focused in on the seven "big S" sacraments. It seems like it would meet the usual requirements and definitions of a sacrament. For instance, St. Augustine's primal and simple definition, "a visible sign of an invisible grace," paired with the typical sacramental need for form and matter do seem to describe foot washing well.

Pause for a moment and imagine if, when preparing for first Communion, young people also learned about and prepared for foot washing alongside the usual catechetical and spiritual pursuits. How much more linked, then, would we as a church find our reception of Eucharist to the command we are given just a few minutes later: "Go in peace, glorifying the Lord by your life." As much as it is thanksgiving, Eucharist is also service, solidarity, and our freedom.

To the Point

This Sunday's readings, especially when viewed through the lens of the Last Supper, remind us that the Eucharist is not only a meal of thanksgiving but a call to service and solidarity—where true worship leads to justice, humility, and peace.

Preparing to Proclaim, Preach, and Pray

Making Connections Between the Readings: As already noted, the readings all work in consort this weekend, including the epistle, which only does so by coincidence. Just ponder the litany of antagonistic words across all the pericopes today: beset, obnoxious, reproaches, transgressions, violations, revilement, torture, condemn, jealousy, disorder, foul, wars, conflicts, covet, kill, envy, fight, passions, arguing . . .

Of course, the readings aren't only these words, but also speak of the antidote: Jesus teaches that whoever receives a child is his name receives Christ himself. That is, one must welcome the teachings of Christ, the love of Christ, all things that are Christ, the way one would welcome a child. Mark probably places this exchange in his gospel quite intentionally, as a commentary on the disciples' lack of understanding his teaching on the paschal mystery just prior. Their role in Jesus's ministry is supposed to be one of service, especially to the poor and lowly. Children were often the symbol Jesus used for the lowest of the Christian community.

James asks, "Where do the wars and where do the conflicts among you come from?" He then quickly answers his own question: misdirected passions, love of worldly things over things divine. It's not that pleasures are innately evil, but rather, that the motivation for any action can be sinful, especially if selfishness is at the heart of desire.

Making Connections to the Responsorial Psalm: Where the reading from Wisdom today describes a scene where wicked people choose, from their malice, to punish a just person, Psalm 54 is the prayer of such a one beset by reproaches and opposition. The strongest prophecy one can make often is not in words but by deeds: living a just life and by that good example proving the wickedness found in some others.

Living from a profound trust in God is almost never easy, hoping that one's own righteousness will be known by God and that divine power will shield, save, and uphold. Today's psalm is then a profound prayer that probably should be better known, that should find a place in our liturgical prayers more often. As such psalms typically do, the psalmist pledges thanks and praise for such a God, eternally watchful and loving.

CONNECTING TO EXPERIENCE: LIVING THE PASCHAL MYSTERY

Indulging in an argument with your siblings about which one of you is loved *best* by your parents does no one any good. Yet the disciples find themselves in a similar situation, arguing with one another about who is the greatest. When Jesus asks what they are discussing, and they are silent, he does not indulge them further. Calling a child—who is also silent—to himself with an embrace, Jesus reminds them that humility, trust, and care for the most vulnerable among them reveal power, strength, and understanding of God's will. Unlike comparisons and competition, which lead to division, humility leads to love. An argument among a few followers and the presence of a small child seem insignificant. But in these everyday signs, Jesus reminds us that power corrupts human hearts. Humility invites peace.

PROMPTS FOR FAITH-SHARING

- Have you ever found yourself locked into endless competition, which goes nowhere? How does the gospel's challenge help you to change such situations?
- With Christ, do you see children as a vessel of divine wisdom? How can you take time to appreciate childlike wisdom all the more?
- Is there some aspect of human achievement or power that occupies too much of your concerns? Or those of someone you love? How can Christ help?

Model Penitential Act

Presider: Our psalm today reminds us that the Lord upholds and sustains us, even in our distress. We are to love even when we are hurting. Recalling the times we have let darkness overwhelm our hearts, we come to the Lord asking for his mercy . . . *[pause]*

Lord Jesus, you save us and defend us: Lord, have mercy.

Christ Jesus, you wipe away jealousy and selfishness with your peace: Christ, have mercy.

Lord Jesus, you call us to conversion by the word of your gospel: Lord, have mercy.

Model Universal Prayer (Prayer of the Faithful)

Presider: Turning to the Lord who made heaven and earth, we offer our prayers and our petitions.

Response: Lord, hear our prayer.

For the faithful throughout the world and of every generation: may divisions among us come to an end as we seek to love one another in unity and charity, we pray . . .

For leaders of nations, especially those embroiled by conflict: may powers of destruction be overtaken by peace, we pray . . .

For all suffering from wounds inflicted by pride, hate, and the stripping away of rights: may justice and freedom be found for the oppressed, we pray . . .

For us gathered here today: may we welcome the children in our midst, be they our neighbors' or our own, we pray . . .

Presider: Loving God, you have called us through your gospel to possess the glory of your Son, Jesus Christ. Hear our prayers this day as we follow your call to serve one another in faith and charity. We ask this through Christ our Lord. **Amen.**

Liturgy and Reconciliation

On a weekend when the Scriptures urge us to pursue peace with one another, it is useful to examine a bit of the etymology of the word "reconciliation." The typical current practice of the sacrament—individual confession and absolution (and penance)—obscures a bit that a coequal thrust of the sacrament is reconciliation with the whole Christian community, alongside repairing our relationship with God.

Have you ever shared "butterfly kisses" with a loved one? Such a sweet, affectionate gesture, where one person flutters their eyelashes against another person's skin—usually on the cheek or near the eye—creates a light, tickling sensation like a butterfly's wings. They're often shared between parents and children, romantic partners, or close loved ones as a tender, playful sign of love and closeness.

(continued on next page)

COLLECT

Let us pray.

Pause for silent prayer

O God, who founded all the commands of
your sacred Law
upon love of you and of our neighbor,
grant that, by keeping your precepts,
we may merit to attain eternal life.
Through our Lord Jesus Christ, your Son,
who lives and reigns with you in the unity
of the Holy Spirit,
God, for ever and ever. **Amen.**

FIRST READING

Wis 2:12, 17-20

The wicked say:
Let us beset the just one, because he is obnoxious to us;
he sets himself against our doings,
reproaches us for transgressions of the law
and charges us with violations of our training.
Let us see whether his words be true;
let us find out what will happen to him.
For if the just one be the son of God, God will defend him
and deliver him from the hand of his foes.
With revilement and torture let us put the just one to the test
that we may have proof of his gentleness
and try his patience.
Let us condemn him to a shameful death;
for according to his own words, God will take care of him.

RESPONSORIAL PSALM
Ps 54:3-4, 5, 6-8

℟. (6b) The Lord upholds my life.

O God, by your name save me,
and by your might defend my cause.
O God, hear my prayer;
hearken to the words of my mouth.

℟. The Lord upholds my life.

For the haughty have risen up against me,
the ruthless seek my life;
they set not God before their eyes.

℟. The Lord upholds my life.

Behold, God is my helper;
the Lord sustains my life.
Freely will I offer you sacrifice;
I will praise your name, O LORD, for its goodness.

℟. The Lord upholds my life.

SECOND READING
Jas 3:16–4:3

Beloved:
Where jealousy and selfish ambition exist,
there is disorder and every foul practice.
But the wisdom from above is first of all pure,
then peaceable, gentle, compliant,
full of mercy and good fruits,
without inconstancy or insincerity.
And the fruit of righteousness is sown in peace
for those who cultivate peace.

Where do the wars
and where do the conflicts among you come from?
Is it not from your passions
that make war within your members?
You covet but do not possess.
You kill and envy but you cannot obtain;
you fight and wage war.
You do not possess because you do not ask.
You ask but do not receive,
because you ask wrongly, to spend it on your passions.

Taking reconciliation to its Latin roots syllable by syllable, "re" means "again," "con" means "with," and "cilia" is the Latin word for "eyelash." So then "re-con-cilia-tion" is a posture, "to again be eyelash to eyelash with [someone]." What a beautiful image of the invisible grace found in this sacrament! This would be a good weekend to present this image to the assembly and invite them to partake in a celebration of the sacrament that restores and makes whole.

Liturgical Ministers: Music Ministers

Music ministry is often seen as leading the congregation in song, but the deeper reality is that musicians stand at the intersection of Scripture and prayer. The church's ancient tradition of psalmody reveals that music is not an ornament to the liturgy but one of its primary voices. The cantor or choir does not simply "start the singing" but acts as a herald of the word, especially in the responsorial psalm, which is Scripture itself proclaimed through melody. In fact, the *General Instruction of the Roman Missal* names the psalm as a proclamation equal in dignity to the readings. This perspective calls music ministers to approach their service as doers of the word and to cultivate a spirituality of listening. A musician's preparation is *lectio divina* with notes, prayerfully entering the text so that the church's voice can rise in unity. This ministry also has a mystical dimension. When the church sings together, heaven and earth touch; this is why Augustine wrote, "He who sings prays twice." Music ministers, then, are keepers of a theological treasure, helping the church hear the word not only with ears but with the heart.

Living Liturgy: The Penitential Act

This Sunday's readings highlight humility and service. The penitential act embodies this disposition and sets the tone for every liturgy. This brief rite draws us together as sinners seeking mercy, reminding us that we are equal before God. The ancient *Kyrie* connects us to the earliest Christian assemblies, showing that worship is always a plea for God's saving love. When the church bows its head and voices "Lord, have mercy," it rehearses the very posture of our destiny. The liturgy forms us through this act, teaching that forgiveness comes before praise and that God's love is always first.

SPIRITUALITY

GOSPEL ACCLAMATION
cf. John 17:17b, 17a

℟. Alleluia, alleluia.
Your word, O Lord, is truth;
consecrate us in the truth.
℟. Alleluia, alleluia.

Gospel

Mark 9:38-43, 45, 47-48; L137B

At that time, John said to Jesus,
"Teacher, we saw someone driving out demons in your name,
and we tried to prevent him because he does not follow us."
Jesus replied, "Do not prevent him.
There is no one who performs a mighty deed in my name
who can at the same time speak ill of me.
For whoever is not against us is for us.
Anyone who gives you a cup of water to drink
because you belong to Christ,
amen, I say to you, will surely not lose his reward.

"Whoever causes one of these little ones who believe in me to sin,
it would be better for him if a great millstone
were put around his neck
and he were thrown into the sea.
If your hand causes you to sin, cut it off.
It is better for you to enter into life maimed
than with two hands to go into Gehenna,
into the unquenchable fire.
And if your foot causes you to sin, cut it off.
It is better for you to enter into life crippled
than with two feet to be thrown into Gehenna.

Continued in Appendix A, p. 318.

Praying with Gospel Words and Phrases
Do not prevent him . . . whoever is not against us is for us . . .

Reflecting on the Gospel
As a child, I often played lawn darts (back when they were actually quite dangerous) with my neighbor Wade, who was famously terrible at it. One day, after an especially bad throw that veered wildly off target, Wade's mom hugged him and said, "Oh, but honey—look how deep it went into the ground!" Her words, though kind, reframed success by praising something irrelevant. No longer was getting the dart in the target the fundamental measure of achievement; that was diminished and placed next to something really rather unimportant, how deeply the dart burrowed into the ground.

In today's readings, we hear of people preaching, healing, and leading, even without formal authorization. In the gospel, Jesus tells John to let a stranger continue driving out demons in his name because "whoever is not against us is for us." This openness contrasts with the church's current liturgical norms, where preaching during Mass is reserved for the ordained. The *Catechism* teaches that ordination confers a unique grace and identity, configuring the minister to "Christ as Priest, Teacher, and Pastor" (CCC 1585). The church points to this as indication that the charism for preaching is given at ordination and part of the ontological change that occurs there.

At the same time, the church affirms that by baptism, all are priest, prophet, and king. Laypeople lead, teach, and evangelize in many important ways. Yet for many Catholics, the only time they encounter the church's teaching and leadership is during the eucharistic liturgy. When lay voices are limited to preaching outside the Mass, and when this is presented as a sufficient alternative, it can feel like Wade's mom insisting his throw was great because it went deep into the dirt—even when it missed the target entirely.

This isn't a call to disregard church law or demand immediate change. It is an invitation to imagine what our liturgy could be if it included a broader range of voices—especially those that have been historically silenced or marginalized. Opportunities like the Liturgy of the Hours already allow lay preaching. Could we find more ways to amplify diverse voices at the eucharistic table?

To the Point
Jesus's teaching and Moses's prayer remain a challenge for us today: "Would that all the people of the Lord were prophets!" How might we better honor the Spirit at work in the whole Body of Christ, especially in our worship?

Preparing to Proclaim, Preach, and Pray

Making Connections Between the Readings: Imagine a world, if you can, that fulfilled Moses's dream, where all "people of the Lord" spoke God's truth, in word and deed. Moses's exhortation continues, "Would that the Lord might bestow his spirit on them all!" Of course we Christians believe the gifts of the Holy Spirit come upon us at baptism and are sealed and strengthened at confirmation. Truly, what is there that prevents each of us from fulfilling Moses's vision?

James gives us a hint, a continuation of his admonitions from last week, that we must guard against improper motivations behind our desires, especially any selfishness for worldly pleasures. Today's pericope paints a vivid picture of what will ultimately transpire: a life of earthly wealth and gratification culminates in condemnation—and not just any condemnation. "[Y]ou have murdered the righteous one"—the poor, the lowly, Christ himself, ultimately. Earthly riches will fade and decay and become worthless in time; a life of love, mercy, justice, and holiness reaps infinitely valuable and eternal rewards.

This is one of the main thrusts of discipleship, of disciplining ourselves in the way of Christ and his example and teachings, aligning our will to the divine will, one facet of which is speaking and living truth in all times and places. If only it could be so!

Making Connections to the Responsorial Psalm: Laws, precepts, ordinances, decrees—today's psalmist must have had a thesaurus open when setting to work on this hymn of praise. As the Israelites sought to learn God's wisdom and live in God's love, one way that these were most accessible to them was through God's laws.

Laws, we've already pondered on these pages (see February 28, p. 75), can seem rigid or constricting, but properly understood and lived, can set us free to do what is good and live in God's love. Misunderstood, lived scrupulously, they serve only to inflict spiritual harm rather than aid growth. Instead of leading to freedom and communion with God, the faith experience becomes marked by fear, anxiety, and self-focus. Burdens replace grace, fear replaces relationship, legalism replaces conversion: in short, a true image of God becomes distorted.

We must be watchful, guarding against obsessing over minor faults or imagined sins, forgetting that God's mercy is greater than our weaknesses. "For my yoke is easy, and my burden light" (Matt 11:30), Christ tells us. Scrupulosity turns that yoke into something heavy and oppressive.

CONNECTING TO EXPERIENCE: LIVING THE PASCHAL MYSTERY

Jesus's metaphor today is stark: if you cause a little one who believes to sin, it is better that you are thrown into the sea. With a millstone around your neck, which weighed probably in excess of 3,000 pounds, you would quickly find yourself at the *bottom* of the sea. We may think that we would never lead anyone to sin purposely. But our lack of commitment to caring for the poor and vulnerable invites similar conditions, opening the path for exploitation, greed, corruption, and violence. Our inaction—or our apathy—enables evil to continue. Far from a body that is cut apart by sin, we are called by Christ to unity. As Pope Francis taught us, "All of us have a responsibility for the wounded, those of our own people and all the peoples of the earth" (*Fratelli Tutti* 78). Let us embrace the poor and vulnerable as Jesus did, living as agents of justice and peace.

PROMPTS FOR FAITH-SHARING

- Have you been hurt by someone who refused to see your vulnerability? How have you sought forgiveness in this matter?
- Have you ever hurt someone whom you have refused to see as vulnerable? How can you bring about reconciliation in this matter?
- What can you, or your community, do to promote greater justice and peace today, especially for those on the margins?

Model Penitential Act

Presider: The precepts of the Lord are true, all of them just. Calling to mind the times we have sinned, we ask for God's mercy and peace . . . *[pause]*

Lord Jesus, you call us through the waters of baptism to be your people: Lord, have mercy.

Christ Jesus, you bear our sins and cleanse us from all our faults: Christ, have mercy.

Lord Jesus, you bring us healing and hope with the very food of life: Lord, have mercy.

Model Universal Prayer (Prayer of the Faithful)

Presider: Coming before the Lord who watches always over his people, we offer our prayers and petitions.

Response: Lord, hear our prayer.

That the church throughout the world might grow in faith and vibrancy, especially in those places suffering from secularism and atheism, we pray . . .

That our teachers, mentors, and all who lead young people might be granted wisdom as they pass on their knowledge to others, we pray . . .

That all who are unemployed or underemployed might find steady work with livable wages, we pray . . .

That the faithful gathered here might recognize the gifts of others around them as well as their own, we pray . . .

Presider: Lord God, your law is perfect and refreshes the soul. May we become ever more perfect in your law as we strive to follow you. We ask this through Christ our Lord. **Amen.**

Liturgy and Preaching

For more on what the church legislates regarding preaching, turn to the *Code of Canon Law*, 762–772. Here are a few notable excerpts:

C. 766. Lay persons can be permitted to preach in a church or oratory, if necessity requires it in certain circumstances or it seems advantageous in particular cases, according to the prescripts of the conference of bishops and without prejudice to c. 767 §1.

C. 767 §1. Among the forms of preaching, the homily, which is part of the liturgy itself and is reserved to a priest or deacon, is preeminent; in the homily the mysteries of faith and the norms of Christian life are to be explained from the sacred text during the course of the liturgical year.

C. 770. At certain times according to the prescripts of the diocesan bishop, pastors are to arrange for those types of

(continued on next page)

COLLECT

Let us pray.

Pause for silent prayer

O God, who manifest your almighty power
above all by pardoning and showing
mercy,
bestow, we pray, your grace abundantly
upon us
and make those hastening to attain your
promises
heirs to the treasures of heaven.
Through our Lord Jesus Christ, your Son,
who lives and reigns with you in the unity
of the Holy Spirit,
God, for ever and ever. **Amen.**

FIRST READING

Num 11:25-29

The LORD came down in the cloud and
spoke to Moses.
Taking some of the spirit that was on
Moses,
the LORD bestowed it on the seventy
elders;
and as the spirit came to rest on them,
they prophesied.

Now two men, one named Eldad and the
other Medad,
were not in the gathering but had been
left in the camp.
They too had been on the list, but had not
gone out to the tent;
yet the spirit came to rest on them also,
and they prophesied in the camp.
So, when a young man quickly told Moses,
"Eldad and Medad are prophesying in
the camp,"
Joshua, son of Nun, who from his youth
had been Moses' aide, said,
"Moses, my lord, stop them."
But Moses answered him,
"Are you jealous for my sake?
Would that all the people of the LORD were
prophets!
Would that the LORD might bestow his
spirit on them all!"

RESPONSORIAL PSALM

Ps 19:8, 10, 12-13, 14

℟. (9a) The precepts of the Lord give joy
to the heart.

The law of the LORD is perfect,
refreshing the soul;

the decree of the LORD is trustworthy,
giving wisdom to the simple.

℟. The precepts of the Lord give joy to the heart.

The fear of the LORD is pure,
enduring forever;
the ordinances of the LORD are true,
all of them just.

℟. The precepts of the Lord give joy to the heart.

Though your servant is careful of them,
very diligent in keeping them,
yet who can detect failings?
Cleanse me from my unknown faults!

℟. The precepts of the Lord give joy to the heart.

From wanton sin especially, restrain your servant;
let it not rule over me.
Then shall I be blameless and innocent
of serious sin.

℟. The precepts of the Lord give joy to the heart.

SECOND READING

Jas 5:1-6

Come now, you rich, weep and wail over your impending miseries.
Your wealth has rotted away, your clothes have become moth-eaten,
your gold and silver have corroded,
and that corrosion will be a testimony against you;
it will devour your flesh like a fire.
You have stored up treasure for the last days.
Behold, the wages you withheld from the workers
who harvested your fields are crying aloud;
and the cries of the harvesters
have reached the ears of the Lord of hosts.
You have lived on earth in luxury and pleasure;
you have fattened your hearts for the day of slaughter.
You have condemned;
you have murdered the righteous one;
he offers you no resistance.

preaching which are called spiritual exercises and sacred missions or for other forms of preaching adapted to needs.

C. 771 §2. They are also to make provision that the message of the gospel reaches non-believers living in the territory since the care of souls must also extend to them no less than to the faithful.

Liturgical Ministers: Altar Servers

Altar servers hold a unique role as they are among the few lay ministers who physically handle the vessels and linens closest to the altar. This ministry is an apprenticeship in eucharistic spirituality. Preparing the chalice, handling the cruets, and arranging the corporal is not housekeeping but a participation in the church's deepest prayer. The corporal itself is a sign of reverence for the Real Presence. Its careful unfolding and refolding reflect centuries of tradition. Servers are stewards of these sacred objects, and through this responsibility, they gain a sense of the altar as both table and place of sacrifice. These acts form their imagination, teaching that ordinary elements such as bread, wine, fabric, and flame are transformed by grace. Serving at the altar gives these ministers a tactile theology where they learn through their hands that holiness is embodied, that God meets us in material reality, and that care for these small details is an act of worship.

Living Liturgy: Blessings of Ministries

The Spirit's gifts are not confined to clergy; every baptized person is equipped for service. The church's *Book of Blessings* offers rites to commission catechists, lectors, pastoral leaders, and ministers of charity, showing that all ministry flows from baptism. Incorporating these blessings into Sunday Mass makes visible the co-responsibility of the entire parish. The community sees that ministry is not a volunteer task but a participation in Christ's priestly mission. These blessings remind us that the Spirit's gifts are for the whole church and for the sake of the world.

SEPTEMBER 26, 2027

TWENTY-SIXTH SUNDAY IN ORDINARY TIME

SPIRITUALITY

GOSPEL ACCLAMATION
1 John 4:12

℟. Alleluia, alleluia.
If we love one another, God remains in us
and his love is brought to perfection in us.
℟. Alleluia, alleluia.

Gospel

Mark 10:2-16; L140B

The Pharisees approached Jesus and asked,
"Is it lawful for a husband to divorce his wife?"
They were testing him.
He said to them in reply, "What did Moses command you?"
They replied,
"Moses permitted a husband to write a bill of divorce
and dismiss her."
But Jesus told them,
"Because of the hardness of your hearts
he wrote you this commandment.
But from the beginning of creation, *God made them male and female.*
For this reason a man shall leave his father and mother
and be joined to his wife,
and the two shall become one flesh.
So they are no longer two but one flesh.
Therefore what God has joined together,
no human being must separate."
In the house the disciples again questioned Jesus about this.
He said to them,
"Whoever divorces his wife and marries another
commits adultery against her;
and if she divorces her husband and marries another,
she commits adultery."

Continued in Appendix A, p. 318, or Mark 10:2-12 *in Appendix A, p. 318.*

Praying with Gospel Words and Phrases

They were testing him . . . the kingdom of God belongs to such as these . . .

Reflecting on the Gospel

Fr. Godfrey Diekmann, OSB, wrote these words, originally in Latin, in his 1964 diary:

O God, who through the Order of Rubricists has impeded the way to heaven,
we pray that you give to us who have been buried under this sea of red,
another way to eternal life.

He wrote these words (a "Prayer Against Rubricists") while at Vatican II, considering the ancient Tridentine Rite and looking forward to the liturgical reforms that were to come. In this Sunday's gospel, the Pharisees try to trap Jesus by asking his opinion on Judaic laws of divorce and marriage, much like it seems Fr. Diekmann felt trapped by the red rubrics of the missal of the time, themselves liturgical laws to be followed and obeyed.

"Say the black, do the red" is a frequent mantra among some liturgists: remain true to the missal and only the words and rubrics within, and with that, good liturgy will simply come to be. While we ought to be most reluctant to change these words and rubrics, it is also true that to create a rite that the faithful can truly enter into, participate in fully, and by which they can be sanctified, much more needs to be planned and created than is contained in any missal.

The second portion of today's gospel offers wisdom here. Many long for their children to be touched by Jesus, and he welcomes them, embraces them, saying that the kingdom of God belongs to such as these. Jesus here is probably not speaking about children who are pure or simplistic, but rather children who are powerless and rely on their parents for everything—shelter, food, love, and more. So too the kingdom of God belongs to those who rely on God, our adopted Father, for everything. If we place our reliance both on black and red words in a missal but more so on God who always, as a loving parent, reaches out to embrace us, then our liturgies might reach out and embrace all the faithful with shelter, sustenance, and love.

To the Point

Fr. Diekmann's satirical prayer and this Sunday's gospel both highlight the danger of rigid legalism—whether in liturgical rubrics or religious law—and call us instead to rely fully on God's mercy and love. One facet of that may be creating liturgies that embrace the faithful like children were embraced by Christ.

Preparing to Proclaim, Preach, and Pray

Making Connections Between the Readings: The Pharisees tested Jesus often, trying to trip him up in a mingling of Judaic laws and, sometimes, unlikely circumstances. Jesus today explains that the Mosaic Law on divorce was only given because of hardness of heart. He continues with a proclamation that permanence is God's desire, from the very beginning. Of course, we know the church has a remedy for marriages deemed invalid from the onset—lack of free consent, lack of maturity, lack of proper judgment, excluding a true vow of fidelity, permanence, or the willingness to have and raise children. There are many circumstances under which a marriage ought not continue, just like there are circumstances where a couple gives up too easily on their sacred vows.

In the letter to the Hebrews, the author speaks of God's desire for closeness with us differently, reminding us that from that desire God took on human flesh (lower than the angels) and suffered—because it's fitting that our redemption be made perfect in such a way. Christ, today's pericope concludes, is not afraid to call us "brothers" (siblings, truly), the divine desire for closeness being that sincere, that profound.

Making Connections to the Responsorial Psalm: Today's Psalm 128 is likely familiar to us from countless wedding ceremonies, and rightly so. It is a reflective statement that our steadfast God will bless the reverent, and that God's blessing may be tangible: satisfaction and prosperity, a fertile spouse, and many children. The concluding verses extend the blessing to all the people for generations to come.

We do well to remind ourselves that a married couple, in the ideal, reflects for us the love shared between God and the church. Specially, a married person loves their spouse in such a way that they desire only the sacred best for them, to the point of, God forbid, dying for them. The expression "die to self" exemplifies the married life then, reflecting Christ's redemptive death and resurrection, that all may be made one again, united with God and one another.

CONNECTING TO EXPERIENCE: LIVING THE PASCHAL MYSTERY

In movies, advertisements, or when we're looking at *other* people's kids, children are cute, kind, and charming. In our *own* families, children bring different realities. Children can be defiant, cranky, confusing, or self-centered. When Jesus says to let the children come to him, perhaps it's not because they're fluffy little lambs of compliance. Perhaps it's precisely because their growing and changing emotions, their insatiable need for love and belonging, and their ability to trust (and to be naughty) provide an image for all of us. We are all imperfect, learning, changing, children of God. It's not children's beauty alone that causes Jesus to call them to himself—but their ability to utterly depend upon him in their vulnerability. God has emptied himself with love for his children throughout the world. God cares for us in our hunger, our thirst, our fatigue, our loneliness, and our peril. God always loves. Can we do likewise, starting with the small worlds of our own families?

PROMPTS FOR FAITH-SHARING

- As Jesus asks, can you embrace life in a way that is childlike? What stands in the way?
- As the disciples did, have you ever rebuked someone for approaching Jesus in a childlike way, or for putting children first? Why so?
- How can you learn from the children and childlike whom God has put before you today?

Model Penitential Act

Presider: Today, we hear of the love found among human families and the love God has for the smallest among us. Remembering the times we have failed to love and have forgotten God's care, we ask for his mercy . . . *[pause]*

Lord Jesus, you call us to love one another: Lord, have mercy.
Christ Jesus, you offer healing and peace to broken hearts:
Christ, have mercy.
Lord Jesus, your love calls us to perfection: Lord, have mercy.

Model Universal Prayer (Prayer of the Faithful)

Presider: Coming before the Lord with our prayers and petitions, we offer our hopes for ourselves and all the world.

Response: Lord, hear our prayer.

For the church: may the faithful who have experienced divorce and broken relationships find new life and healing in their lives, we pray . . .

For leaders in our communities and in our nations: may they seek always to protect and advocate for the most vulnerable among us, especially children and our elderly, we pray . . .

For families suffering from estrangement and strained relationships: may the grace of Christ Jesus touch their lives and offer them healing and new hope, we pray . . .

For all of us gathered here: that we may learn to honor those who care for us and cherish those who rely on us, we pray . . .

Presider: Loving God, you call little children to come to you. Help us to be like children, trusting in you and relying on your care. We ask this through Christ our Lord. **Amen.**

Liturgy and Touch

Human beings were created to be in community, in relationship with one another. That is one important facet of what it means to be created in the image and likeness of God, God who is Trinity community, and relationship. Yet especially since the days of Covid-19, human proximity and closeness have given way to distance and detachment at times.

An especially important component of human relationship is that of touch. In her book *The Blind Assassin*, author Margaret Atwood tells us, "Touch comes before sight, before speech. It is the first language and the last, and it always tells the truth." Laura Guerrero, who cowrote *Close Encounters: Communication in Relationships*, states, "We feel more connected to someone if they touch us."

This is why touch is an integral part to many of our sacraments: the anointings within baptism, confirmation, holy orders,

(continued on next page)

COLLECT

Let us pray.

Pause for silent prayer

Almighty ever-living God,
who in the abundance of your kindness
surpass the merits and the desires of those
who entreat you,
pour out your mercy upon us
to pardon what conscience dreads
and to give what prayer does not dare to
ask.
Through our Lord Jesus Christ, your Son,
who lives and reigns with you in the unity
of the Holy Spirit,
God, for ever and ever. **Amen.**

FIRST READING

Gen 2:18-24

The LORD God said: "It is not good for the
man to be alone.
I will make a suitable partner for him."
So the LORD God formed out of the ground
various wild animals and various birds
of the air,
and he brought them to the man to see
what he would call them;
whatever the man called each of them
would be its name.
The man gave names to all the cattle,
all the birds of the air, and all wild
animals;
but none proved to be the suitable
partner for the man.

So the LORD God cast a deep sleep on the
man,
and while he was asleep,
he took out one of his ribs and closed up
its place with flesh.
The LORD God then built up into a woman
the rib
that he had taken from the man.
When he brought her to the man, the man
said:
"This one, at last, is bone of my bones
and flesh of my flesh;
this one shall be called 'woman,'
for out of 'her man' this one has been
taken."
That is why a man leaves his father and
mother
and clings to his wife,
and the two of them become one flesh.

RESPONSORIAL PSALM
Ps 128:1-2, 3, 4-5, 6

℟. (cf. 5) May the Lord bless us all the days of our lives.

Blessed are you who fear the LORD,
who walk in his ways!
For you shall eat the fruit of your handiwork;
blessed shall you be, and favored.

℟. May the Lord bless us all the days of our lives.

Your wife shall be like a fruitful vine
in the recesses of your home;
your children like olive plants
around your table.

℟. May the Lord bless us all the days of our lives.

Behold, thus is the man blessed
who fears the LORD.
The LORD bless you from Zion:
may you see the prosperity of Jerusalem
all the days of your life.

℟. May the Lord bless us all the days of our lives.

May you see your children's children.
Peace be upon Israel!

℟. May the Lord bless us all the days of our lives.

SECOND READING
Heb 2:9-11

Brothers and sisters:
He "for a little while" was made "lower than the angels,"
that by the grace of God he might taste death for everyone.

For it was fitting that he,
for whom and through whom all things exist,
in bringing many children to glory,
should make the leader to their salvation perfect through suffering.
He who consecrates and those who are being consecrated
all have one origin.
Therefore, he is not ashamed to call them "brothers."

and anointing of the sick, for instance. In the sacrament of matrimony, the celebrant instructs the two to be married to join their right hands while pronouncing the vows. More than just a handshake, this human touch is a symbol of connection, trust, and the truth of what is being expressed: that the love being witnessed at a marriage is reflective of the self-sacrificial love that Christ has for the church.

Liturgical Ministers: Ushers and Greeters

The Scriptures this Sunday proclaim marriage and family as part of God's covenant plan, and Jesus's welcome of children reveals the kingdom's heart. Ushers and greeters participate in this catechesis through their ministry of hospitality. They make visible the church's identity as a family gathered at the Father's table. Welcoming a family into the assembly shows that all are members of Christ's Body, no matter their age or circumstance. The simple act of handing a worship aid to a child or guiding parents to a seat is a form of liturgical teaching. It shows that the liturgy is a prayer of the whole church, where children and parents are integral participants. Ushers and greeters should understand their role as part of the church's sacramental life. The door they stand by is not only an entrance to a building but an image of Christ, who calls all into communion. This vision transforms their ministry from service alone to catechesis in action, forming the assembly to see itself as a family gathered by grace.

Living Liturgy: Blessing of Families

The liturgy reveals that family life is a vocation lived within God's saving plan. Celebrating a blessing of families during Mass can catechize the entire parish, showing that holiness is cultivated not only in monasteries or parishes but around the dinner table and in the patterns of daily life. This blessing links the altar and the home, teaching that the Eucharist strengthens families to become domestic churches, places where Scripture is heard, forgiveness is practiced, and love is nurtured. By lifting up family life in worship, the church teaches that every household is part of its mission. Liturgy forms us to see that family is not a private reality but a witness to Christ's covenantal love, and blessing families at Mass makes that theology visible.

SPIRITUALITY

GOSPEL ACCLAMATION
Matt 5:3

℟. Alleluia, alleluia.
Blessed are the poor in spirit,
for theirs is the kingdom of heaven.
℟. Alleluia, alleluia.

Gospel

Mark 10:17-30; L143B

As Jesus was setting out on a journey,
a man ran up,
knelt down before him, and asked him,
"Good teacher, what must I do to inherit eternal life?"
Jesus answered him, "Why do you call me good?
No one is good but God alone.
You know the commandments:
You shall not kill;
you shall not commit adultery;
you shall not steal;
you shall not bear false witness;
you shall not defraud;
honor your father and your mother."
He replied and said to him,
"Teacher, all of these I have observed from my youth."
Jesus, looking at him, loved him and said to him,
"You are lacking in one thing.
Go, sell what you have, and give to the poor
and you will have treasure in heaven;
then come, follow me."
At that statement his face fell,
and he went away sad, for he had many possessions.

Jesus looked around and said to his disciples,
"How hard it is for those who have wealth
to enter the kingdom of God!"
The disciples were amazed at his words.

Continued in Appendix A, p. 319, or
Mark 10:17-27 *in Appendix A, p. 319.*

Praying with Gospel Words and Phrases

[H]e went away sad, for he had many possessions . . . All things are possible for God . . .

Reflecting on the Gospel

There is a fable told about a king who needed to choose among his three sons which would be the next ruler of the land. His two older sons had roles in the government as minister of war and minister of finance; the youngest son eschewed that life and instead lived a life of solitude and prayer as a hermit far from home.

The king could not decide among the three, so he devised a test: each in turn would have from sundown to sunrise to fill a dungeon room in the castle completely, from floor to ceiling, with whatever and however they chose.

The eldest son, the minister of war, began by ordering the many military troops of the land to bring every rock and boulder that they could find to the castle. By morning, the room appeared to be completely full; the king, though, noted he could place his fingers, and sometimes his whole hand, in various crevices and gaps between the stones. This son would not be the next king.

The next son, the minister of finance, knew the country had grown prosperous under his father's rule, so he had those under his command gather all of the paper money, the coins, the jewels, and precious metals of the land to bring to the dungeon. But by sunrise, even all of the affluence of the land only filled the room halfway. He too would not be the next king.

The last son, when it came his turn, did not know how to proceed. He didn't have authority to command thousands of troops, nor any amount of money or riches of his own. So, at sundown, as the door shut behind him, leaving him in complete darkness, he did what he knew: he pulled a candle from his knapsack and lit it, and then a prayer book, and he began to pray. He prayed with such fervor that before he knew it, it was sunrise, and his father was opening the door.

"Father, I'm sorry," the son said. "My son, whatever for?" the father replied. "Your two brothers tried to fill this room with power, with wealth—and they failed. You, however, succeeded—by filling this room with light."

To the Point

Jesus teaches in the gospel about the trappings of wealth, security, and influence. Desiring these too much, relying on them too much, is not the way of the gospel. As we learned last week and are reminded this week, full reliance on God—powerlessness—is instead what we are called to.

Preparing to Proclaim, Preach, and Pray

Making Connections Between the Readings: Wisdom, as a concept, is often personified in the Hebrew Scriptures, as it is today. In Hebrew, the word for wisdom is grammatically feminine. Like many languages, Hebrew assigns grammatical gender to nouns, and we might quickly note that this doesn't necessarily imply biological sex. Wisdom is not just described as feminine but often more specifically as a woman of great beauty, strength, and spiritual depth. Today, she brings great wealth to those who seek her, "countless riches"—though not a worldly wealth, but rather a spiritual one.

Some early Christian thinkers saw connections between Lady Wisdom and Christ, especially in his role as the *Logos* (Word) of God. While Jesus is male, the pre-incarnate Word has no gender or sex and shares many characteristics with the feminine Wisdom of the Old Testament.

The epistle to the Hebrews today also speaks of the physical human body as insignificant when it comes to the piercing word of God. Seeing into the heart, God knows all, and we must one day stand before that divine omnipotence and account for our life on this earth. Lest this eventual moment seem too daunting, next week we will study the following few verses of this epistle and in gratitude thank the Word, our heavenly High Priest, who gains for us mercy and grace.

Making Connections to the Responsorial Psalm: Where the book of Wisdom invites us to welcome her spiritual riches, the psalmist today petitions God that divine love and kindness fill our hearts. Psalm 90 is likely familiar to many of us from its earlier verses, a lament on the brevity of life, especially compared to an eternal God: the familiar hymn "O God, Our Help in Ages Past" is a familiar paraphrase of these verses, and Bernadette Farrell's striking "Restless is the Heart" (OCP), pairs those words with the familiar St. Augustine aphorism.

Yet today's verses have moved beyond lament into petition and praise. We end today's passage by asking God not for any wealth of our own but that the work of our hands be prosperous. We ask God that our lives, our work, be meaningful, lasting, and fruitful. It's not just about material success—it's about giving lasting significance and consequence to all we do.

CONNECTING TO EXPERIENCE: LIVING THE PASCHAL MYSTERY

If the word of God is the source of life, why is it sharper than a two-edged sword (one that can strike no matter in which direction it is swung), cutting between soul and spirit, joints and marrow? This word cuts us apart, exposes us, and renders us vulnerable. Perhaps this is what Jesus's word is meant to do: to open hearts of stone, to break apart fetters that bind us, to free souls tangled in tendrils of sadness and suffering. To cut something down invites it to change and grow. In the gospel today, a young man approaches Jesus, asking what he must do to gain eternal life. Jesus names God's commandments and adds one more: Give away all you have, then come, follow me. And the young man becomes sad. Jesus's word cuts to his heart—and he turns away, unwilling to follow. When are we cut to the heart by the word of God? Do we change? Or do we walk away?

PROMPTS FOR FAITH-SHARING

- What possessions are holding you back from following God completely?
- What people or expectations are holding you back from following God completely?
- Have you ever felt the sadness of saying no to Christ's invitation? How can you reverse that sadness with the joy of faith?

Model Penitential Act

Presider: The word of God is living and effective, knowing us more than we know ourselves. Turning to God whose wisdom sees all things, we ask for his mercy and peace . . . *[pause]*

Lord Jesus, your word penetrates our soul and spirit: Lord, have mercy.

Christ Jesus, we can conceal nothing from you: Christ, have mercy.

Lord, Jesus, you have pity on your servants: Lord, have mercy.

Model Universal Prayer (Prayer of the Faithful)

Presider: Seeking the Lord who teaches us wisdom of heart, we offer our prayers and petitions.

Response: Lord, hear our prayer.

That the church throughout the world might be fed and transformed by a renewed love for reading God's word, we pray . . .

That political leaders may relinquish temptation for power and instead seek the prospering of their peoples, we pray . . .

That women who are denied access to education might be protected and defended in their human flourishing, we pray . . .

That those among us experiencing loss will feel hope in God's mercy and peace, we pray . . .

Presider: Lord God, with you, all things are possible. Grant us greater trust in your wisdom so that we might share the joy of your salvation with all the world. We ask this through Christ our Lord. **Amen.**

Liturgy and the Community

We can sometimes be tempted to make our liturgies better through use of authority and power, be that from whatever position we hold at the parish or by appealing to the liturgical documents and the weight they have. Sometimes we might try to buy our way to better liturgies, be that through hiring professional musicians or being especially lavish with spending toward art and environment. May I suggest today we ponder the fable above, and today's gospel, and reimagine how our liturgies, in our various contexts, might be improved instead by bringing God's light to the study, preparation, and execution of divine worship?

Better than power and riches would be leading by humble example: offering trainings to liturgical ministers as the servant of those who serve the liturgy; showing reverence in worship by studying and practicing its *ars celebrandi*; and not relying on wealth to create profound corporate prayer but relying instead on true community peer ministry. Enable and welcome the giftedness already present in the pews! Offer opportunities for

(continued on next page)

COLLECT

Let us pray.

Pause for silent prayer

May your grace, O Lord, we pray,
at all times go before us and follow after
and make us always determined
to carry out good works.
Through our Lord Jesus Christ, your Son,
who lives and reigns with you in the unity
of the Holy Spirit,
God, for ever and ever. **Amen.**

FIRST READING

Wis 7:7-11

I prayed, and prudence was given me;
I pleaded, and the spirit of wisdom
came to me.
I preferred her to scepter and throne,
and deemed riches nothing in comparison
with her,
nor did I liken any priceless gem to her;
because all gold, in view of her, is a little
sand,
and before her, silver is to be accounted
mire.
Beyond health and comeliness I loved her,
and I chose to have her rather than the
light,
because the splendor of her never yields
to sleep.
Yet all good things together came to me in
her company,
and countless riches at her hands.

RESPONSORIAL PSALM
Ps 90:12-13, 14-15, 16-17

℟. (14) Fill us with your love, O Lord, and we will sing for joy!

Teach us to number our days aright,
that we may gain wisdom of heart.
Return, O LORD! How long?
Have pity on your servants!

℟. Fill us with your love, O Lord, and we will sing for joy!

Fill us at daybreak with your kindness,
that we may shout for joy and gladness all our days.
Make us glad, for the days when you afflicted us,
for the years when we saw evil.

℟. Fill us with your love, O Lord, and we will sing for joy!

Let your work be seen by your servants
and your glory by their children;
and may the gracious care of the LORD our God be ours;
prosper the work of our hands for us!
Prosper the work of our hands!

℟. Fill us with your love, O Lord, and we will sing for joy!

SECOND READING
Heb 4:12-13

Brothers and sisters:
Indeed the word of God is living and effective,
sharper than any two-edged sword,
penetrating even between soul and spirit, joints and marrow,
and able to discern reflections and thoughts of the heart.
No creature is concealed from him,
but everything is naked and exposed to the eyes of him
to whom we must render an account.

formation and catechesis. Do not be afraid of delegating tasks and responsibilities—and some level of ownership—to the implementation of the source and summit of the faith, our liturgical worship, which not only glorifies God but, after all, is about the sanctification of the faithful community.

Liturgical Ministers: Lectors

This Sunday's reading from the book of Wisdom reveals a dimension of Scripture that speaks not only in commands or narratives but in contemplation. Wisdom literature draws us into God, offering insight into creation, virtue, and the heart's longing for God's friendship. Lectors participate in this mystery whenever they give voice to these texts. Their ministry is a moment where divine wisdom is offered to the assembly as a living reality. These books often speak in imagery through light, treasure, and the pursuit of holiness that invites listeners to prayer and discernment. When lectors proclaim such passages, they become instruments through which the Spirit breathes wisdom into the church, teaching that God's word is not abstract but transformative. Their ministry becomes a window into God's eternal wisdom, revealing that Scripture forms the church's heart and guides its path. In this way, the lector is a herald of divine insight, helping the assembly experience the Scriptures as an encounter with Christ, who is Wisdom incarnate.

Living Liturgy: Enthronement of the Scriptures

The gospel is not merely a text to be read; it is Christ himself speaking to his church. The Book of the Gospels, elevated and placed on the altar, expresses this truth before a word is proclaimed. This ritual action shows that the word of God belongs to the eucharistic mystery. Christ who speaks is the same Christ who offers himself in sacrifice. The practice of enthroning the Scriptures, often surrounded with candles or incense, is a visible catechesis, reminding the church that God's word is at the heart of worship. To honor the Scriptures this way is to confess that listening is an act of faith. Each Sunday, when the deacon or priest lifts the gospel book high, the church is drawn into reverence, recognizing that Christ is present in both word and sacrament.

SPIRITUALITY

GOSPEL ACCLAMATION
Mark 10:45

℟. Alleluia, alleluia.
The Son of Man came to serve
and to give his life as a ransom for many.
℟. Alleluia, alleluia.

Gospel

Mark 10:35-45; L146B

James and John, the sons of Zebedee,
came to Jesus and said to him,
"Teacher, we want you to do for us
whatever we ask of you."
He replied, "What do you wish me to do
for you?"
They answered him, "Grant that in your
glory
we may sit one at your right and the
other at your left."
Jesus said to them, "You do not know
what you are asking.
Can you drink the cup that I drink
or be baptized with the baptism with
which I am baptized?"
They said to him, "We can."
Jesus said to them, "The cup that
I drink, you will drink,
and with the baptism with which I am
baptized, you will be baptized;
but to sit at my right or at my left is
not mine to give
but is for those for whom it has been
prepared."
When the ten heard this, they became
indignant at James and John.
Jesus summoned them and said to
them,
"You know that those who are
recognized as rulers over the
Gentiles
lord it over them,
and their great ones make their
authority over them felt.
But it shall not be so among you.

Continued in Appendix A, p. 320.

Praying with Gospel Words and Phrases

Grant that in your glory we may sit one at your right and the other at your left . . . Whoever wishes to be great among you will be your servant . . .

Reflecting on the Gospel

Two Sundays in a row regarding powerlessness, full reliance on God, and yet here we are in today's gospel, with James and John not even being coy about what they seek: to sit on either side of Christ when he enters into glory. Do they not yet get it? How can they be so unabashed about pursuing exactly the wrong thing?

The Christian virtue of temperance is "the moral virtue that moderates the attraction of pleasures and provides balance in the use of created goods. It ensures the will's mastery over instincts and keeps desires within the limits of what is honorable. The temperate person directs the sensitive appetites toward what is good and maintains a healthy discretion" (CCC 1809).

In fact, CCC 1809 goes on to quote St. Augustine in that regard: "To live well is nothing other than to love God with all one's heart, with all one's soul and with all one's efforts; from this it comes about that love is kept whole and uncorrupted (through temperance). No misfortune can disturb it (and this is fortitude). It obeys only (God) (and this is justice), and is careful in discerning things, so as not to be surprised by deceit or trickery (and this is prudence)."

This particular cardinal virtue can—and should—impact how we approach all we say and do. One way of living temperance, balance, and moderation is (more secularly) embodied in the "Virtue Continuum," as created by Jim Lanctot in 2007. Temperance is one of seven virtues on the continuum, which has for each virtue listed extremes of "deficiency" and "excess." A deficiency of temperance leads to licentiousness; an excess of temperance leads to strictness. Neither is healthy or good, and shows us a clear example of the saying, "everything in moderation, including moderation."

One of the goals of any liturgical ministry is to better create, form, and hold together the Christian community, which is almost always best served neither by extremism nor zealotry, but by love, mercy, temperance, and communion.

To the Point

Despite the disciples' misguided pursuit of glory in today's gospel, we are reminded that true Christian living—and effective ministry—requires the virtue of temperance, a balanced self-mastery that avoids both excess and deficiency, and instead fosters love, mercy, and unity in all we do.

Preparing to Proclaim, Preach, and Pray

Making Connections Between the Readings: We return yet again to Isaiah's Suffering Servant, who in his suffering and affliction justifies many. It is no wonder that early theologians saw fulfillment of these words in the Christ, crucified for our salvation. Jesus knew these words, we can presume, and as often as the gospels report his prophesies of his own coming passion and death, would have connected these ancient words to himself, in the flesh. This is "the cup" he warned James and John about, the same cup he prayed about in the Garden of Gethsemane, before eventually aligning his will to that of the Father.

As we continue in the letter to the Hebrews from last week, we remind ourselves that it is exactly because God took on flesh that Jesus Christ has become our high priest, and through his sacrifice—not of burnt animal offerings but of his own body and blood—we may "approach the throne of grace to receive mercy" when we at last come before God to account for our days on this earth. God's Son took on all of our humanity except sin; he even took on humiliation, suffering, and death that we might be redeemed. When we are invited at times to "unite our sufferings to Christ," these distresses and pains are transformed and even given redemptive purpose.

Making Connections to the Responsorial Psalm: One of the core paradoxes of our faith that we looked at nearly a year ago, last Advent, is that the greatest shall be as the servant, that the first shall be last. Christ's teaching of this paradox in today's gospel is a frame for his upcoming passion and death, prophesied often in the Old Testament, most notably in the Suffering Servant sections in Isaiah.

Today's Psalm 33 bridges these passages by observing that true strength and security come not from self-reliance, but from complete dependence on God. God is trustworthy, just, and loving—far more so than any human power or plans. The humble heart recognizes this and stops striving for control, trusting instead in the goodness and stability of God's will. Christian humility is not weakness, but a posture of confident surrender. Those who admit their vulnerability become the ones God watches over and rescues. By acknowledging our limits and placing our trust in God, we receive protection, purpose, and peace that human effort alone can never achieve.

CONNECTING TO EXPERIENCE: LIVING THE PASCHAL MYSTERY

We are created in the image of God and have innate dignity. God wants us to flourish. So why should our happiness be so fragile, able to be crushed by brokenhearted worry in an instant? Why are we so flawed? Why are there tasks we can't do well? Why are there things (or people) that make us lose our patience? Why can't we be perfect? Aside from remembering that God alone is perfect, God has granted us weaknesses for another reason: so that we might have compassion upon the weaknesses of others. We are flawed so that we might show others compassion, mindful of our own challenges. When we are disappointed or we suffer, we might remember that God is merciful and we learn to hope. And perhaps we are imperfect so that we can increase in strength and perfection, until one day, we might grow to the full stature of Christ.

PROMPTS FOR FAITH-SHARING

- Are you ready for the cross, or are you hoping for a kind of human exaltation, like James and John?
- Do you feel that there are elements of baptism that you want to enact more boldly and with risk?
- How can you be more ready for Christ's demands on you? What presumptions might you need to set aside?

Model Penitential Act

Presider: Today, Jesus tells us that he came not to be served but to serve, giving his life as a ransom for many. Remembering the times we have failed to follow Jesus in humility, we come before him asking for his mercy and peace . . . *[pause]*

Lord Jesus, you love justice and righteousness: Lord, have mercy.

Christ Jesus, you bear our guilt and deliver us from death: Christ, have mercy.

Lord Jesus, you offer mercy and grace to those who come to you: Lord, have mercy.

Model Universal Prayer (Prayer of the Faithful)

Presider: We come before the Lord in hope and confidence as we bring our prayers for ourselves and all the world.

Response: Lord, hear our prayer.

For all the baptized in churches throughout the world: may the faithful who believe in Christ Jesus grow in confidence in his mercy and in collaboration with one another, we pray . . .

For leaders of our nations and for those running for election: may those seeking positions do so in order to serve their constituents, never to gain power or to secure their own interests, we pray . . .

For all who are suffering in mind, body, and spirit: may they trust in the Lord and find healing in his mercy, we pray . . .

For all gathered here and for our families and friends: may we encourage each other in love and make time to be present for one another, we pray . . .

Presider: Lord God, we come to you with confidence in your grace and wonder at the wideness of your mercy. Hear our prayers this day as we offer them for ourselves and for all the world. We ask this through Christ our Lord. **Amen.**

Liturgy and Kneeling

Our kneeling at prayer, be it at church, at our bedside, or by a small child, can communicate many different affects and values. Piety, penance, adoration, and supplication are but a few, and kneeling might mean any one or several of these, depending on context.

Notably, at Eucharist, the postures of those gathered at prayer have varied broadly over time and space, sometimes with the assembly and the presider sharing a common posture, and in more recent times a dissimilar posture. At least partly because of this, in some ways, kneeling has also come to represent theologies of humility and differentiation.

(continued on next page)

COLLECT

Let us pray.

Pause for silent prayer

Almighty ever-living God,
grant that we may always conform our will to yours
and serve your majesty in sincerity of heart.
Through our Lord Jesus Christ, your Son,
who lives and reigns with you in the unity of the Holy Spirit,
God, for ever and ever. **Amen.**

FIRST READING

Isa 53:10-11

The LORD was pleased
to crush him in infirmity.

If he gives his life as an offering for sin,
he shall see his descendants in a long life,
and the will of the LORD shall be accomplished through him.

Because of his affliction
he shall see the light in fullness of days;
through his suffering, my servant shall justify many,
and their guilt he shall bear.

RESPONSORIAL PSALM
Ps 33:4-5, 18-19, 20, 22

℟. (22) Lord, let your mercy be on us, as
we place our trust in you.

Upright is the word of the LORD,
and all his works are trustworthy.
He loves justice and right;
of the kindness of the LORD the earth is
full.

℟. Lord, let your mercy be on us, as we
place our trust in you.

See, the eyes of the LORD are upon those
who fear him,
upon those who hope for his kindness,
to deliver them from death
and preserve them in spite of famine.

℟. Lord, let your mercy be on us, as we
place our trust in you.

Our soul waits for the LORD,
who is our help and our shield.
May your kindness, O LORD, be upon us
who have put our hope in you.

℟. Lord, let your mercy be on us, as we
place our trust in you.

SECOND READING
Heb 4:14-16

Brothers and sisters:
Since we have a great high priest who has
passed through the heavens,
Jesus, the Son of God,
let us hold fast to our confession.
For we do not have a high priest
who is unable to sympathize with our
weaknesses,
but one who has similarly been tested in
every way,
yet without sin.
So let us confidently approach the throne
of grace
to receive mercy and to find grace for
timely help.

When kneeling in humility, we can recognize, rightly, that God is God and that we are not. Yet St. Augustine's thought that God does not need any outward sign of gesture or posture for our hearts to be open to God is reflected in the many diverse postures the assembly enacts during any given liturgy.

While our bodily postures and gestures can (and will) be communicative, we might be mindful that unity need not always demand uniformity. Indeed, many physical bodies are simply incapable of the variety of postures called for at Mass. We mustn't let such differences then be necessarily seen as disruptive or disorderly.

Liturgical Ministers: Eucharistic Ministers

The church treats every fragment of the consecrated host and every drop of the precious blood with care, expressing our faith in Christ's Real Presence. This act of reverence is an extension of worship. For eucharistic ministers, participating in or witnessing this purification shapes a eucharistic spirituality. It teaches that what has been consecrated is holy and that Christ's presence endures beyond the moment of reception. The ablution of fingers after distributing Communion reminds ministers that their service has touched the mystery of Christ himself. This action forms a deeper reverence, training eucharistic ministers to handle sacred vessels and the sacrament with love and awe. The silence that often accompanies these gestures allows the assembly to enter contemplation, recognizing that the Eucharist is not only received but adored. Through this ritual care, ministers are drawn into a theology of stewardship, learning that the holiness they reverence in the sacrament is the same holiness God desires for each person they serve.

Living Liturgy: Genuflecting to the Tabernacle

Each time we bend the knee before the reserved sacrament, we confess that Christ remains present among his people, even outside the celebration of the Mass. This act is a witness of faith that shapes how we live. To bow before Christ in the tabernacle is to acknowledge that all creation belongs to him and that every person we meet carries dignity rooted in him. The church's posture before the tabernacle teaches us a posture that we should have toward the world. In this way, a brief movement before entering a pew becomes a mode of discipleship. It reminds us that each act of prayer before the Eucharist sends us out to recognize Christ's presence wherever we go, especially in those who are poor, vulnerable, or forgotten. Genuflection is not only a liturgical act; it is a daily way of seeing.

OCTOBER 17, 2027

TWENTY-NINTH SUNDAY IN ORDINARY TIME

SPIRITUALITY

GOSPEL ACCLAMATION
cf. 2 Tim 1:10

℟. Alleluia, alleluia.
Our Savior Jesus Christ destroyed death
and brought life to light through the Gospel.
℟. Alleluia, alleluia.

Gospel

Mark 10:46-52; L149B

As Jesus was leaving Jericho with his disciples and a sizable crowd,
Bartimaeus, a blind man, the son of Timaeus,
sat by the roadside begging.
On hearing that it was Jesus of Nazareth,
he began to cry out and say,
"Jesus, son of David, have pity on me."
And many rebuked him, telling him to be silent.
But he kept calling out all the more,
"Son of David, have pity on me."
Jesus stopped and said, "Call him."
So they called the blind man, saying to him,
"Take courage; get up, Jesus is calling you."
He threw aside his cloak, sprang up, and came to Jesus.
Jesus said to him in reply, "What do you want me to do for you?"
The blind man replied to him, "Master, I want to see."
Jesus told him, "Go your way; your faith has saved you."
Immediately he received his sight and followed him on the way.

Praying with Gospel Words and Phrases

Master, I want to see . . . Go your way; your faith has saved you . . .

Reflecting on the Gospel

"Master, I want to see." So often we wish we could help our assemblies see themselves for who they actually are: the Body of Christ, the full and consciously engaged and active people of God. We do have some opportunity to tell them these things, in preaching or in careful music selection. What is even more powerful, though, is when we have the ability to *show* them.

I'm reminded of the lesson I learned a while back, most useful typically in a rehearsal or classroom setting, which seems appropriate for those of us with any sort of platform from which we are called to speak truth. If folks are being too loud or noisy and not listening to you, sometimes speaking softer is the solution. Whisper. Make people have to be quiet to hear you. As a conductor, if your choir isn't following your tempo, conduct smaller, down to your pointer finger keeping time an inch from your chest. Make people watch you and pay attention. Jesus was at his most strong when silent in front of the Sanhedrin and Pilate.

As we continue pondering divine justice and how our liturgies embody that facet of who God is, we must hold as true that brash voices are needed sometimes, and sometimes kinder voices are needed. We also are not in any position to dictate to other people how they speak truth, but we can decide for ourselves, in any given context, what manner of speaking the truth might be best received, might best achieve a desired result. Those whose hearts and minds are most in need of change, from our perspective, are often also the folks we think might need to be spoken to most forcefully, and they are also most likely to walk away from—to be blind to—the subject matter *because* they feel they are being yelled at, at the same time. Remember, volume doesn't make a truth any more true. Similarly, those who might need most to hear bold, sustained voices of justice ought not tune out the message because it is bold and sustained.

To the Point

It is important for us all to hear and understand all voices, perhaps only to recognize and affirm the humanity and dignity that has not always (or rarely) been recognized and affirmed; perhaps someday—or sooner—that's so we can all together be part of building a just world, the reign of God.

Preparing to Proclaim, Preach, and Pray

Making Connections Between the Readings: When in Sacred Scriptures we see the word "Behold," like we do today, it's a call to pay close attention. It's like God is saying, "This is important!" It often signals that something significant is being revealed or about to happen. In modern language, we don't often say "behold," but such biblical uses demonstrate urgency, importance, and revelation: "Look at this carefully—it matters."

In the gospel, Jesus restores a man's sight, and in doing so also restores his place in the community. Jeremiah describes God reuniting the scattered and exiled people of Israel as if his children are being brought back together, not just for a family reunion but permanently, in joy and gladness. "Behold," we are told, what the power of our loving God can accomplish.

As God's adopted children, we also know such unity in Christ, the high priest of the epistle to the Hebrews. Christ, the begotten of God, is our brother as well as redeemer. He took on human flesh, becoming like us and dying for us that one day we may become more like him. Behold, the saving power of God!

Making Connections to the Responsorial Psalm: Psalm 126 was likely written just after Israel's return from the Babylonian exile. There is rejoicing in being once again home in the Promised Land, yet there is still work, sowing, to be done. There can be no reaping without sowing, after all.

On a weekend where we contemplate restoration—and being more aware of God's power within both—the psalm reminds us of the necessity of our participation in bringing the reign of God to fruition. We must not wait and watch for God to get to work; God's work is ours too. The solemnity of the Ascension all those months ago reminded us that God has no hands, feet, or voice on earth now but ours.

If God's faithful are to "behold" a new reality, a world of transformation and hope, we must align our will with God's and discern what it is God wishes of our discipleship—and ask for perseverance and strength to accomplish it.

CONNECTING TO EXPERIENCE: LIVING THE PASCHAL MYSTERY

When Jesus comes upon Bartimaeus sitting by the roadside, Jesus not only sees him, but hears him and asks: "What do you want me to do for you?" Bartimaeus may not have been able to see Jesus, but his faith compelled him to believe without seeing. He believed, and so he saw.

What about us, sitting at our own crossroads of busyness and worry? Would we see Jesus? If Jesus were to stand in front of us and say, "What do you want me to do for you?," would we know what to say? Would we even hear him? Let us perfect our senses and attune our hearts to hear and see even if our imperfect bodies cannot. Let us be changed. Let us long for that change. And not only that—let us do as Bartimaeus did. He was healed. He began to follow Christ Jesus who had brought light into his world. Let us go and do likewise.

PROMPTS FOR FAITH-SHARING

- If Jesus asked you what you wanted from him, what would you say?
- Do you have faith that Christ hears your concerns? Why or why not?
- What does Christ's light mean to you? How can it help you to see better?

Model Penitential Act

Presider: In the gospel today, Bartimaeus comes to Jesus in faith to ask for healing. Remembering our own need to come before the Lord, we ask for his healing mercy . . . *[pause]*

Lord Jesus, you know our ignorance and our erring: Lord, have mercy.

Christ Jesus, you heal the sinner and bind up the broken-hearted: Christ, have mercy.

Lord Jesus, you destroyed sin and death and brought life through the gospel: Lord have mercy.

Model Universal Prayer (Prayer of the Faithful)

Presider: The Lord gathers all from the ends of the earth and draws them into one. Drawing our hearts together before the Lord, we pray for the needs of the world.

Response: Lord, hear our prayer.

That our Holy Father, Pope N., might encourage all nations to seek unity and peace, rejecting the darkness of war, we pray . . .

That our leaders will advance policies that protect families, offer support to parents, and ensure safety and security for both the young and the old, we pray . . .

That refugees and migrants, especially those with infants and children, find deliverance from their oppressors, we pray . . .

That we might find greater patience and mercy for our own families and the ones we love most, we pray . . .

Presider: Lord God, you gather your people from the ends of the world and draw them to yourself. Hear our prayers this day, and may we grow in solidarity and love with all the people of God. We ask this through Christ our Lord. **Amen.**

Liturgy and Watching

Silence and stillness often don't get much attention in liturgy preparations, yet the liturgy is likely one of the few places the faithful might experience it. Our lives are full of work and when coupled with our digital devices and social media, it's no wonder the difficulty we have, more and more with each passing day, of simply being still. A critical skill to develop or maintain in pursuit of stillness is that of watching—not just seeing but watching.

Within stillness, if we allow time for observation and contemplation, we begin to recognize the activity and interconnectedness of the world—and the liturgy—around us. We are not ourselves responsible for every action, yet we are, even in observant stillness, a part of all that lives and moves and has being. The external prayer informs and illumines our internal prayer. As if looking into a mirror, the movements of others reflect our own inner

(continued on next page)

COLLECT

Let us pray.

Pause for silent prayer

Almighty ever-living God,
increase our faith, hope, and charity,
and make us love what you command,
so that we may merit what you promise.
Through our Lord Jesus Christ, your Son,
who lives and reigns with you in the unity
of the Holy Spirit,
God, for ever and ever. **Amen.**

FIRST READING

Jer 31:7-9

Thus says the LORD:
Shout with joy for Jacob,
exult at the head of the nations;
proclaim your praise and say:
The LORD has delivered his people,
the remnant of Israel.
Behold, I will bring them back
from the land of the north;
I will gather them from the ends of the
world,
with the blind and the lame in their
midst,
the mothers and those with child;
they shall return as an immense throng.
They departed in tears,
but I will console them and guide them;
I will lead them to brooks of water,
on a level road, so that none shall
stumble.
For I am a father to Israel,
Ephraim is my first-born.

RESPONSORIAL PSALM

Ps 126:1-2, 2-3, 4-5, 6

℟. (3) The Lord has done great things for us; we are filled with joy.

When the LORD brought back the captives
of Zion,
we were like men dreaming.
Then our mouth was filled with laughter,
and our tongue with rejoicing.

℟. The Lord has done great things for us;
we are filled with joy.

Then they said among the nations,
"The LORD has done great things for
them."
The LORD has done great things for us;
we are glad indeed.

℟. The Lord has done great things for us;
we are filled with joy.

Restore our fortunes, O LORD,
like the torrents in the southern desert.
Those that sow in tears
shall reap rejoicing.

℟. The Lord has done great things for us;
we are filled with joy.

Although they go forth weeping,
carrying the seed to be sown,
they shall come back rejoicing,
carrying their sheaves.

℟. The Lord has done great things for us;
we are filled with joy.

SECOND READING
Heb 5:1-6

Brothers and sisters:
Every high priest is taken from among men
and made their representative before God,
to offer gifts and sacrifices for sins.
He is able to deal patiently with the ignorant and erring,
for he himself is beset by weakness
and so, for this reason, must make sin offerings for himself
as well as for the people.
No one takes this honor upon himself
but only when called by God,
just as Aaron was.
In the same way,
it was not Christ who glorified himself in becoming high priest,
but rather the one who said to him:
You are my son:
this day I have begotten you;
just as he says in another place:
You are a priest forever
according to the order of Melchizedek.

stirrings, and the liturgy reflects all of life. The living liturgy becomes life itself.

It may be a good time to include in a homily or a bulletin column some words or some moment of the liturgy the assembly may easily watch but may have overlooked lately. Perhaps the priest's washing of hands at the offertory, or the significance of the fraction rite and the breaking of the one bread that it might be shared and transform us all.

Liturgical Ministers: Music Ministers
The *Kyrie* is one of the church's oldest prayers, a simple cry for mercy that has been on the lips of Christians for centuries. For music ministers, leading this prayer is a path of formation. Singing the *Kyrie* teaches humility. It reminds ministers that their role is not to perform but to voice the longing of the whole assembly for God's compassion. This ancient chant also forms a sense of continuity with the church across time, linking today's liturgy with the earliest gatherings where Christians prayed these very words in Greek. Practicing and praying with the *Kyrie* draws ministers deeper into the mystery of sin and redemption, helping them internalize the posture of discipleship. In this way, music ministry becomes a vehicle of prayer. The repetition of this chant shapes the minister's spiritual life, cultivating reverence and a heart that listens before it sings. Music ministers grow into their vocation not just through skill but through this constant immersion in prayer that both humbles and emboldens the church.

Living Liturgy: Silence in the Liturgy
Silence is one of the church's greatest teachers. After the readings, after the homily, and especially after Communion, silence allows the word to take root and the sacrament to be received with reverence. In these pauses, the liturgy draws us into contemplation, forming us to listen for God in a world filled with noise. Silence is not emptiness but presence. It trains us to encounter Christ beyond words or song. The church places silence alongside spoken prayer, teaching that the liturgy speaks through stillness as much as sound. Embracing these moments prepares us to carry that attentiveness into daily life, recognizing God's presence in ordinary encounters and in the lives of those often overlooked.

SPIRITUALITY

GOSPEL ACCLAMATION
John 14:23

℟. Alleluia, alleluia.
Whoever loves me will keep my word,
says the Lord; and my Father will love him
and we will come to him.
℟. Alleluia, alleluia.

Gospel

Mark 12:28b-34; L152B

One of the scribes came to Jesus and asked him,
"Which is the first of all the commandments?"
Jesus replied, "The first is this:
Hear, O Israel!
The Lord our God is Lord alone!
You shall love the Lord your God with all your heart,
with all your soul,
with all your mind,
and with all your strength.
The second is this:
You shall love your neighbor as yourself.
There is no other commandment greater than these."
The scribe said to him, "Well said, teacher.
You are right in saying,
'He is One and there is no other than he.'
And 'to love him with all your heart,
with all your understanding,
with all your strength,
and to love your neighbor as yourself'
is worth more than all burnt offerings and sacrifices."
And when Jesus saw that he answered with understanding,
he said to him,
"You are not far from the kingdom of God."
And no one dared to ask him any more questions.

Praying with Gospel Words and Phrases
Hear, O Israel! The Lord our God is Lord alone! . . .

Reflecting on the Gospel
The Sh'ma, "Hear, O Israel . . ." is a central Jewish prayer akin to the Lord's Prayer in Christianity. It proclaims God's unity and singularity, reminding us of our relationship with the one true God.

If you're a music director choosing liturgical songs each week, or a preacher preparing weekly homilies, the tasks can sometimes feel repetitive. You may find yourself wondering what you did the last time these readings came up. But both we and our communities change over time—our needs, experiences, and perspectives shift. These changes should shape how we engage with Scripture and how we prepare for worship.

One way to re-engage creatively and prayerfully is through the following reflective method inspired by *lectio divina*—a tradition of reading Scripture not just for study but for transformation. This adapted practice can be used by anyone looking to listen more deeply to God's word, alone or in a group, in one sitting or over several days.

Begin by inviting yourself to look for a single word or phrase in the passage that "clings" to you—something that stirs your heart. It doesn't matter what the word is; what matters is that it speaks to you. Afterward, keep silence for ten seconds, and repeat this chosen word to yourself three times.

Then read the Scripture passage a second time. This time, imagine an image involving your word—this could be a painting, a scene, a moment from real life, or something more abstract. It need not relate directly to the Scripture, only to that "clingy" word. If you have time, you may even sketch it out.

The Scripture is read a third time. After silence and repeating your word, you can at last connect your image to the reading. Allow ample time for this final reflection. Then invite yourself, internally, to share any insights or movements of the Spirit you experienced. Some may emerge right away, others may take some time. Resist any urge to fill the silence or abandon the process. Trust that prayerful fruitfulness will eventually emerge.

This process not only deepens engagement with Scripture but can also spark creative choices for music or homiletic themes, rooted in genuine spiritual encounter. You might be amazed at the deep level of faith and holiness this simple form of reflection can offer!

To the Point
Just as last week we were urged to "behold"—to look carefully and not just see—this week we are urged to listen carefully and understand, not just hear.

Preparing to Proclaim, Preach, and Pray

Making Connections Between the Readings: Today's passage from Deuteronomy expands the first commandment (found with the other nine one chapter earlier), and in its brevity contains the whole Mosaic Law. Jesus cites these words as "the greatest and the first commandment" (Matt 22:38), embracing in itself the whole law of God.

Yet the translation of the Sh'ma is a bit tricky, or at least multifaceted, and perhaps purposely so. According to the USCCB Bible website, one version could be "The Lord is our God, the Lord alone." Other possibilities include "The Lord our God is one Lord"; "The Lord our God, the Lord is one"; "The Lord is our God, the Lord is one." Each of these is similar but in minute differences exist a broad profundity of meanings.

From the Christian perspective, these definitions are even more profound when pondering God the Trinity, one God in three persons, God who is, by definition, sacred community. The unity of the faithful community is often on the minds of Jews, Christians, and most any follower of any faith tradition. For us, eyes of faith strive to see God's unity and ours as one and the same.

Making Connections to the Responsorial Psalm: Where the Sh'ma proclaims God's unity and calls for our devotion, Psalm 18 today responds with a personal testimony of someone who has experienced God's saving power and replies with deep, intimate love and trust. The psalmist not only affirms God's greatness and faithfulness (just as the Sh'ma does), but expresses it through vivid images: rock, fortress, deliverer.

There is a lot more to Psalm 18 than the few verses our liturgy gives us today. Note well in the citation, we skip from verse 4 all the way to verse 47! This is a great pity, as the omitted texts are full of thanksgiving for rescue and vivid, mythic language of victory in battle. In its entirety, Psalm 18 reveals God's consistency and strength in action. The God who is "One" is also unshakably faithful, the source of strength and salvation. The Sh'ma proclaims who God is and how we should respond; Psalm 18 is the voice of someone who has lived that truth—and now sings it in gratitude.

CONNECTING TO EXPERIENCE: LIVING THE PASCHAL MYSTERY

Why does the scribe come up to Jesus with a quiz? Jesus (of course) answers rightly. The scribe is satisfied and praises Jesus for getting the answer. Then Jesus, seeing that the scribe "answered with understanding," tells him he is not far from the kingdom of God. Unlike other scribes who appear in the gospels, this scribe isn't asking Jesus to trip him up. The scribe's motives are not malicious, but spring from a desire to know Jesus more. Jesus sees this. We also are free to ask questions of Jesus, who wants us to seek understanding. He longs for us to ponder the word of God so that we might hear it, live it, and be changed. It is in our desiring to conform ourselves to the living God, seeking to understand, seeking to hear God's voice, that we come closest to being the children of God we have been called to be in our baptism.

PROMPTS FOR FAITH-SHARING

- Do you ever want Jesus to prove himself to you just a little more? What makes you want that proof?
- Like the scribe, have you ever brought a question to Jesus that allowed him to talk to you more deeply? What may be preventing you from bringing your deepest questions to Christ?
- Like the scribe, is Jesus challenging you to widen your sense of what it means to love your neighbors, both the ones you know and those you do not know?

Model Penitential Act

Presider: In our readings today, we hear God's call to love him with all our heart, all our soul, and all our strength. For the times we have failed to be steadfast in our love for God and neighbor we ask for his pardon and peace . . . *[pause]*

Lord Jesus, you lift up the lowly and show kindness to your anointed: Lord, have mercy.

Christ Jesus, you rescue us from our enemies and free us from our sin: Christ, have mercy.

Lord Jesus, you deliver us from evil and offer us salvation: Lord, have mercy.

Model Universal Prayer (Prayer of the Faithful)

Presider: Coming before the Lord, who is our rock and our redeemer, we offer our prayers and petitions.

Response: Lord, hear our prayer.

For the church: may the faithful of all ages grow in strength of fervor for Christ and in mercy for their neighbors, we pray . . .

For all who serve their countries, their regions, and their cities: may their work be guided by love and respect for their colleagues and their constituents, we pray . . .

For those who have suffered at the hands of their neighbors: may a renewed and right spirit reign, and reconciliation be found, we pray . . .

For all gathered here before the Living One: may we remember always to pray for our loved ones and our enemies, we pray . . .

Presider: O God, to love you and to love our neighbor is worth more than all burnt offerings and sacrifices. Hear the prayers which we offer you today for the love of all the world. We ask this through Christ our Lord. **Amen.**

Liturgy and Music

"Eye Has Not Seen" by Marty Haugen (GIA) has the beautiful line, "To those who see with eyes of faith, / the Lord is ever near . . ." and would be a beautiful text for an assembly this weekend. The *Psallite* (Liturgical Press) refrain "I Know I Shall See the Goodness of the Lord" effectively quotes Psalm 27 for a simple and beautiful sung prayer.

For more adventuresome choirs, the Sh'ma prayer is one that is often sung for Shabbat services at synagogues, and many accessible settings are easily available online. Some are in Hebrew only, some are also in English; there are a variety of settings in a wide range of musical styles and sounds as well, and surely one would blend in with your sung prayer this weekend. Look for settings by Sulzer, Powers, Friedman, Pik, and others.

(continued on next page)

COLLECT

Let us pray.

Pause for silent prayer

Almighty and merciful God,
by whose gift your faithful offer you
right and praiseworthy service,
grant, we pray,
that we may hasten without stumbling
to receive the things you have promised.
Through our Lord Jesus Christ, your Son,
who lives and reigns with you in the unity
of the Holy Spirit,
God, for ever and ever. **Amen.**

FIRST READING

Deut 6:2-6

Moses spoke to the people, saying:
"Fear the LORD, your God,
and keep, throughout the days of your lives,
all his statutes and commandments
which I enjoin on you,
and thus have long life.
Hear then, Israel, and be careful to observe them,
that you may grow and prosper the more,
in keeping with the promise of the LORD,
the God of your fathers,
to give you a land flowing with milk and honey.

"Hear, O Israel! The LORD is our God, the LORD alone!
Therefore, you shall love the LORD, your God,
with all your heart,
and with all your soul,
and with all your strength.
Take to heart these words which I enjoin on you today."

RESPONSORIAL PSALM
Ps 18:2-3, 3-4, 47, 51

℟. (2) I love you, Lord, my strength.

I love you, O Lord, my strength,
O Lord, my rock, my fortress, my deliverer.

℟. I love you, Lord, my strength.

My God, my rock of refuge,
my shield, the horn of my salvation, my stronghold!
Praised be the Lord, I exclaim,
and I am safe from my enemies.

℟. I love you, Lord, my strength.

The Lord lives! And blessed be my rock!
Extolled be God my savior,
you who gave great victories to your king
and showed kindness to your anointed.

℟. I love you, Lord, my strength.

SECOND READING
Heb 7:23-28

Brothers and sisters:
The levitical priests were many
because they were prevented by death from remaining in office,
but Jesus, because he remains forever,
has a priesthood that does not pass away.
Therefore, he is always able to save those who approach God through him,
since he lives forever to make intercession for them.

It was fitting that we should have such a high priest:
holy, innocent, undefiled, separated from sinners,
higher than the heavens.
He has no need, as did the high priests,
to offer sacrifice day after day,
first for his own sins and then for those of the people;
he did that once for all when he offered himself.
For the law appoints men subject to weakness to be high priests,
but the word of the oath, which was taken after the law,
appoints a son,
who has been made perfect forever.

Especially if sung only in Hebrew, the assembly may need a moment of introduction and catechesis. The "one God" of the Hebrew Scriptures is also our one Christian God (albeit in three persons), after all. Lastly, none of these settings are beyond expectation of an assembly's participation as well! Take time before Mass to educate, instruct, and inspire.

Liturgical Ministers: Altar Servers
Carrying the processional cross is an act of mission and witness. It is the first image the assembly sees as the liturgy begins: Christ leading his church. For the server, it is personal encounter with the mystery of salvation. Holding the cross high shapes the heart, reminding the server that every procession symbolizes the pilgrimage of the church toward the altar, where heaven and earth meet. They learn to see the liturgy as a journey guided by Christ and to recognize the cross as both burden and victory. Standing so close to the altar each week gives servers a privileged experience of the sacred, forming a reverence that extends beyond the sanctuary. Worship is a walk with the crucified and risen Lord. Carrying the cross out of the church at the dismissal is a visible reminder that the liturgy sends us forth to follow Christ in daily life, bearing his sign into the world. In this way, altar servers are not only assistants but living witnesses to the mystery we celebrate each Sunday.

Living Liturgy: Processions as Pilgrimage
The entrance and concluding processions at Mass are ritual expressions of the church's pilgrimage toward God. When the assembly rises to sing as the cross leads the ministers to the altar, this movement embodies our baptismal journey as a people called and gathered, walking together toward the heavenly banquet. The closing procession reverses this dynamic, sending the community forth to live what they have celebrated. These ritual actions draw us into the paschal mystery so that we can carry it into the world. Every procession becomes a foretaste of the heavenly liturgy, where Christ himself leads his people into the fullness of life with God.

OCTOBER 31, 2027

THIRTY-FIRST SUNDAY IN ORDINARY TIME

SPIRITUALITY

GOSPEL ACCLAMATION
Matt 11:28

℟. Alleluia, alleluia.
Come to me, all you who labor and are burdened,
and I will give you rest, says the Lord.
℟. Alleluia, alleluia.

Gospel

Matt 5:1-12a; L667

When Jesus saw the crowds, he went up the mountain,
and after he had sat down, his disciples came to him.
He began to teach them, saying:

"Blessed are the poor in spirit,
for theirs is the Kingdom of heaven.
Blessed are they who mourn,
for they will be comforted.
Blessed are the meek,
for they will inherit the land.
Blessed are they who hunger and thirst for righteousness,
for they will be satisfied.
Blessed are the merciful,
for they will be shown mercy.
Blessed are the clean of heart,
for they will see God.

Continued in Appendix A, p. 320.
See Appendix A., p. 321, for the other readings.

Praying with Gospel Words and Phrases

Blessed are they . . . your reward will be great in heaven . . .

Reflecting on the Gospel

Who is the holiest person you ever met face to face? Describe them. What is it about them that causes you to see their holiness? Take just a minute too, and call to mind this person's face: their smile, their eyes, their wrinkles perhaps, their hair . . .

The Ten Commandments include a prohibition on making graven images, both so that idol worship could be avoided and so that an image of God might not be created that limits who God is. How striking then, that while today's psalm implores God, "this is the people that longs to see your face," that if we want to see holiness, we must turn our gaze elsewhere? In the Sermon on the Mount, Jesus tells us where to look: to the poor in spirit, to the peacemakers, to those who hunger and thirst for righteousness. Seeing people such as these are the closest we will, during our earthly days, come to seeing the face of God.

When phrases like "what would Jesus do (WWJD)?" or "love like Christ loved" are inserted into conversation, usually the meaning inferred is along the lines of "Stop judging, that you may not be judged" (Matt 7:1), or that one should love in a self-giving, sacrificial way. While both of these are reasonable and possible, it's difficult and impossible for most of us to completely love as Christ loves us. God is God, and we are not—all of us are but sinners on the path to sainthood.

While we must always stand with and support those harmed by sinful people, we too must hope for, if not work for, the repentance and conversion of the sinners. If such are exiled from community, they may struggle to learn, grow, express sorrow and regret, and ultimately may never fully—or even partially—rejoin the Christian community. Sinners and those they have wronged, depending on context, will likely find difficulty remaining in relationship; it may even not be advisable in many circumstances. Saints and sinners, broadly speaking, must remain in conversation, and even in communion with one another.

To the Point

Holiness is most clearly seen not in perfect images or lofty ideals, but in the faces and lives of real people—saints and sinners alike—who strive to love, repent, and reflect God's presence in a broken world, reminding us that the path to sainthood is one of persistent, imperfect effort.

Model Rite for the Blessing and Sprinkling of Water

Presider: Today we join in praising all the saints who have gone before us marked with the sign of Christ. Remembering our own baptism, we come before the Lord who offers us his mercy . . . *[pause]*

[continue with The Roman Missal*, Appendix II]*

Model Universal Prayer (Prayer of the Faithful)

Presider: The Lord hears the prayers of his faithful ones. In confidence we pray to the Lord.

Response: Lord, hear our prayer.

For the church: may we rejoice in all the saints, and follow their example as we seek to love and serve the Lord, we pray . . .

For leaders of nations: may they seek wisdom, virtue, and holiness in their daily labors, we pray . . .

For all who are burdened: may they not lose hope, but find confidence and care, we pray . . .

For us gathered here: may we invite the joy of the saints into our daily lives, enriching our families, schools, and workplaces with love for Christ, we pray . . .

Presider: O God, you have called us all to be your children in our baptism. Hear our prayers this day and strengthen our resolve to live as your saints did, conforming to the will of your Son, Jesus Christ, our Lord, who lives and reigns with you in the Holy Spirit, God forever and ever. Amen.

COLLECT

Let us pray.

Pause for silent prayer

Almighty ever-living God,
by whose gift we venerate in one
celebration
the merits of all the Saints,
bestow on us, we pray,
through the prayers of so many
intercessors,
an abundance of the reconciliation with
you
for which we earnestly long.
Through our Lord Jesus Christ, your
Son,
who lives and reigns with you in the
unity of the Holy Spirit,
God, for ever and ever. **Amen.**

Liturgical Ministers: Lectors

On this feast of All Saints, the lector proclaims Scripture that unveils who the church truly is: a communion of disciples made holy by God's grace. When they give voice to the vision in Revelation, the lector is not simply reading words but serving as a bridge between the heavenly liturgy and the earthly assembly. This ministry teaches that every time Scripture is read, it is a participation in the communion of saints, for these texts are not distant history but the living memory of God's saving work. The lector becomes a catechist in holiness as they show that the word is a gift that transforms. Through this ministry, the faithful encounter their own call to sanctity, not as an ideal for a few but as the shared vocation of all the baptized. The lector's ministry helps the church recognize that the saints are not merely figures in stained glass but companions and intercessors. By lifting Scripture high, the lector embodies the church's mission to announce God's word so that holiness takes root in every heart.

Living Liturgy: The Preface of Saints I

The Preface of Saints I is a mystical doorway into the heart of the feast. It praises God who crowned the merits of the saints and offers us their example, fellowship, and intercession, revealing that holiness is God's work before it is ours. This preface shows that every saint is a sign of God's transforming grace, and that the Eucharist is a foretaste of the heavenly banquet they now enjoy. When the priest chants or recites these words, heaven and earth are drawn together and the voices of the faithful join those of angels and saints in a single hymn of praise. The preface reminds us that the eucharistic prayer is never a private act but a participation in the worship of heaven. Each time we lift our hearts to join in the *Sanctus*, we step into that eternal praise, united with those who have gone before us. The saints are present and active, interceding for us as we strive for holiness. This preface forms the assembly to see their own lives as a path to sainthood, shaped by grace and nourished by the sacrament of Christ's body and blood.

SPIRITUALITY

GOSPEL ACCLAMATION
See John 6:40

℟. Alleluia, alleluia.
This is the will of my Father, says the Lord,
that everyone who sees the Son and believes
in him
may have eternal life.
℟. Alleluia, alleluia.

Gospel

John 6:37-40; L668

Jesus said to the crowds:
"Everything that the Father gives me
will come to me,
and I will not reject anyone who
comes to me,
because I came down from heaven not
to do my own will
but the will of the one who sent me.
And this is the will of the one who
sent me,
that I should not lose anything of
what he gave me,
but that I should raise it on the
last day.
For this is the will of my Father,
that everyone who sees the Son and
believes in him
may have eternal life,
and I shall raise him on the last day."

See Appendix A, p. 322, for the other readings, or any other readings from L668 or any readings from the Masses for the Dead (L1011–1016).

Praying with Gospel Words and Phrases
[E]veryone who sees the Son and believes in him may have eternal life . . .

Reflecting on the Gospel
We are all familiar with the expression "true colors," when someone lets their "real selves" finally show through their usual outward expressions of self, revealing more of their heart and soul to the community. Sometimes someone's true colors show them to be a much more caring and warmer person than what was seen as their usual hard and cold exterior; sometimes those true colors show someone to be much more judgmental, and angrier than their calm exterior.

The liturgy itself has true colors too, which reveal something of the inner character of the celebration or season. White is used as a color of resurrection and new life; violet for penitence; red for the blood of martyrs or the fire of the Spirit; green that in Ordinary Time symbolizes growth and hope.

Yet the symbolism of colors can sometimes be problematic, especially in a global church with cultures and peoples who have customs and practices very different than the Roman/European ones that became foundational in our liturgical practice. In China, Korea, and some other Asian countries, white represents death, mourning, and bad luck, and is traditionally worn at funerals—not as a symbol of resurrection, but in the same way that mourners in America wear black at funerals.

There are two lesser-used liturgical colors too, rose and black. Black especially had been nearly forgotten for many years, but is, in some instances, returning, at least to vestments. As already noted, black is symbolic of death and mourning. It may be used at funeral Masses, the feast of All Souls, or the anniversary of the death of a loved one. Following Vatican II norms, however, white is the preferred color since it reminds us of the resurrection and our baptism.

In the suggested gospel from John (one of many options) for this year's Masses on All Souls' Day, Jesus teaches that it is his Father's will "that everyone who sees the Son and believes in him may have eternal life." When planning your All Souls' liturgy, consider carefully what your community will see and how they will see it—especially when crafting the art and environment, and picking which vestment to wear.

To the Point
When we use and talk about liturgical colors and symbolism, let us be mindful of the intended representations, the potential difficulty of other meanings, and all the options available to more fully celebrate liturgy Sunday by Sunday, feast by feast, season by season.

Model Penitential Act

Presider: Coming before the Lord who frees us from our sin, we ask for his pardon and peace . . . *[pause]*

Lord Jesus, you call all people to yourself: Lord, have mercy.
Christ Jesus, you offer us yourself, the Bread of Life: Christ, have mercy.
Lord Jesus, whoever believes in you has eternal life: Lord, have mercy.

Model Universal Prayer (Prayer of the Faithful)

Presider: The Lord listens to all those who come to him in faith. Let us offer our prayers and petitions.

Response: Lord, hear our prayer.

For the church: may we encourage vocations to the priestly and religious life, and to the permanent diaconate, we pray . . .

For our parents, teachers, and mentors: may those who guide us now, and those who have gone before us, be guided with God's grace, we pray . . .

For families who have lost loved ones: may they rest in confidence that their loved ones rest in the arms of Christ Jesus, we pray . . .

For all gathered here: may we never cease to follow Christ Jesus who shows us the way to eternal life, we pray . . .

Presider: Lord God, you have given us the gift of your Son so that we might learn to follow you. Hear our prayers this day, and strengthen our commitment to live as your Son has shown us. We ask this through Christ our Lord. **Amen.**

COLLECT (from the first Mass)
Let us pray.

Pause for silent prayer

Listen kindly to our prayers, O Lord,
and, as our faith in your Son,
raised from the dead, is deepened,
so may our hope of resurrection for
your departed servants
also find new strength.
Through our Lord Jesus Christ, your
Son,
who lives and reigns with you in the
unity of the Holy Spirit,
God, for ever and ever. **Amen.**

Liturgical Ministers: Eucharistic Ministers

On All Souls' Day, the church gathers to intercede for those who have died, entrusting them to God's mercy. For eucharistic ministers, this day reveals a dimension of their service. Eucharistic ministers hold in their hands the very mystery that brings life out of death. Distributing the body and blood of Christ is always a ministry of hope, but on this day, that hope becomes especially visible. Every communicant who approaches the altar carries memories of loved ones, griefs, and prayers for those who have gone before them. Ministers become signs of the church's faith in the resurrection, offering the sacrament as both nourishment for the living and a pledge of eternal life. The Eucharist is a foretaste of the heavenly banquet promised to all the faithful departed. For the eucharistic minister, each moment of liturgy is a meditation on Christ's victory over death, forming a heart that sees beyond the grave and believes in the communion of saints.

Living Liturgy: The Preface of All Souls

The preface of this day offers a striking message of Christian hope: "[F]or your faithful, Lord, life is changed not ended." Death does not sever communion but renews it. In the liturgy, the church stands between time and eternity, interceding for the departed and proclaiming Christ's triumph over death. The preface reveals that those who have died remain united with the living through Christ's sacrifice. When the assembly sings the *Sanctus*, it joins its voice with those who now behold God face to face. The preface invites us to see the Eucharist as the meeting place of heaven and earth. At this table, the church's love for her dead is united to Christ's own offering, and the living are strengthened to live in hope. All Souls' Day is not only remembrance but formation, teaching that every Eucharist is a pledge of resurrection and communion without end.

SPIRITUALITY

GOSPEL ACCLAMATION
Matt 5:3

℟. Alleluia, alleluia.
Blessed are the poor in spirit,
for theirs is the kingdom of heaven.
℟. Alleluia, alleluia.

Gospel

Mark 12:38-44; L155B

In the course of his teaching Jesus said to the crowds,
"Beware of the scribes, who like to go around in long robes
and accept greetings in the marketplaces,
seats of honor in synagogues,
and places of honor at banquets.
They devour the houses of widows and, as a pretext,
recite lengthy prayers.
They will receive a very severe condemnation."

He sat down opposite the treasury
and observed how the crowd put money into the treasury.
Many rich people put in large sums.
A poor widow also came and put in two small coins worth a few cents.
Calling his disciples to himself, he said to them,
"Amen, I say to you, this poor widow put in more
than all the other contributors to the treasury.
For they have all contributed from their surplus wealth,
but she, from her poverty, has contributed all she had,
her whole livelihood."

or Mark 12:41-44 *in Appendix A, p. 323.*

Praying with Gospel Words and Phrases

They devour the houses of widows and, as a pretext, recite lengthy prayers . . .

Reflecting on the Gospel

Jesus warns the crowds in today's gospel to beware of the scribes who "as a pretext, recite lengthy prayers." Some of us, especially in moments of improvised prayer, tend to ramble on and on. Likely this is because moments of prayer like these lack structure; sometimes it's because we're nervous as well. To be clear: there is no wrong way to pray. However, the liturgy offers us a pattern to follow, found in most of the presidential prayers, an easy way to create spur-of-the-moment prayers:

YOU—WHO—DO—THROUGH

YOU: *Name God.* That can be as simple as "Lord" or "God" or something more elaborate, like "God of wisdom and understanding." Think about what you want to pray for and how that connects with God. If you are going to pray broadly about love, for example, you might simply use "loving God."

WHO: *Name something that God has already done for us.* What can you say to thank and praise God, or offer God a compliment? What has God already done, or what is God doing? Your answer to that question becomes your "who"—"Loving God, who answers all our needs."

DO: *This is the point in the prayer where we ask or petition God to do something for us.* At meals, we ask a blessing on our food. We can ask that God bless hungry people and bring an end to world famine. Often, the WHO relates to the DO. "Loving God, who answers all our needs, we ask you to guide and strengthen us as we care for all those who are in need."

THROUGH: *Typically, we ask our prayers through Jesus Christ, because he is our connection to God.* Some familiar ways to express this relationship are "We ask this through Christ our Lord" or more simply, "Through Christ our Lord." Or use your creativity, but be sure that you pray "through Jesus Christ," who is Lord forever and ever. Amen.

To the Point

Collects at Mass are easily overlooked by the assembly. Perhaps call them and their structure to the attention of your congregations this weekend. Look and listen for the YOU—WHO—DO—THROUGH format in the presidential prayers at Mass and remember it when it is next your turn to publicly improvise prayer.

Preparing to Proclaim, Preach, and Pray

Making Connections Between the Readings: The story of Elijah and the widow of Zarephath foreshadows the Eucharist through its themes of faith, divine provision, and the miraculous abundance that follows sacrificial trust. In the midst of drought and famine, Elijah asks a poor widow for water and bread. She replies she only has a handful of flour and a little oil—just enough for one final meal for her and her son before they die. Yet, at Elijah's word, she gives what little she has. In return, "the jar of flour did not go empty, nor the jug of oil run dry"—a miracle of sustaining nourishment.

Christ too is for us an inexhaustible source of spiritual nourishment. Just as the widow's flour and oil never run out, so too does the Eucharist nourish us without bounds. The unending supply of flour and oil is a sign of God's generous, sustaining love—a love fully revealed in Christ, who gives himself completely and endlessly in the Eucharist.

We must be mindful that Mass is both banquet and sacrifice, and today's epistle makes that abundantly clear. Jesus Christ is not only the priest of the sacrifice, but he himself is the offering, made "once to take away the sins of many" and bring salvation to all believers.

Making Connections to the Responsorial Psalm: Our last visit with Psalm 146 was not so very long ago—see the Twenty-Third Sunday in Ordinary Time (September 5, p. 209). At that time, we reflected on how the mighty deeds of God described by the psalmist are, essentially, sacramental, though that word was not used. Sacraments are, of course, outward, visible signs of invisible grace. The tremendous, merciful divine activity described is our calling as well. More than just being nice, we are called to be holy, to show to those most in need a healing and uplifting presence.

And for this calling to be sacrificial, it can't stop if it only comes from our excess. Why should anyone be lacking in food, shelter, and security if any one of us has more of that than we need? To be sacrificial, our giving must come not from our surplus but, like the widow's mite, from our livelihood if not from our poverty.

CONNECTING TO EXPERIENCE: LIVING THE PASCHAL MYSTERY

We hear of two widows today, both of whom have great courage. One offers not only her own but her child's last mouthful to the prophet Elijah. Another offers two small coins to the temple treasury, choosing to honor God rather than care for herself. In the Bible, widows and orphans represent the most vulnerable in society—lacking community, livelihoods, protection, and hope for their future. And yet these lowly ones are the ones who become signs for us. For God, the lowly are blessed in spirit. From a small token of love in the shape of a few coins, or a bit of bread given freely, the choice to love God and love neighbor brings life. What will happen in our Eucharist today, where a small token of great love begins with a bit of bread? Will we love our neighbor? Will we grow in faith in God? Will we have new life with Jesus who sustains us?

PROMPTS FOR FAITH-SHARING

- Like the widow, how do you, or your parish, practice giving to those in need of food?
- Like Elijah, how do you, or your parish, practice receiving the generosity of others?
- As God's child, how can you receive the sacraments with greater love? How can you pass on that love generously this week?

Model Penitential Act

Presider: In our gospel today, Jesus sees into the heart of the poor and the rich in spirit alike. We invite him to examine our hearts as we call to mind our sins . . . *[pause]*

Lord Jesus, you offered your life to take away our sin: Lord, have mercy.

Christ Jesus, you set captives free and raise up those who are bowed down: Christ, have mercy.

Lord Jesus, you bring salvation to those who fear you: Lord, have mercy.

Model Universal Prayer (Prayer of the Faithful)

Presider: Placing our trust in the God who gives life, we offer our prayers and petitions.

Response: Lord, hear our prayer.

For Pope N., and for our bishops, priests, deacons, and lay ministers who serve the church: may they always find food for their faith in their lives of service, we pray . . .

For peoples experiencing upheaval due to climate change: may their leaders be granted wisdom as they seek humanitarian aid and long-term solutions, we pray . . .

For all who lack access to healthy food, especially young children: may their communities work to alleviate their hunger and enable their flourishing, we pray . . .

For all gathered here today: may we find joy in doing small things for the sake of others and for God, we pray . . .

Presider: Loving God, you fill the hungry with good things and send the rich away empty. Hear our prayers this day and fill us with the desire to always do your will. We ask this through Christ our Lord. **Amen.**

Liturgy and Music

Today's gospel offers an image of a woman who gives not of her surplus wealth, but sacrificially from "her whole livelihood." Connecting that kind of giving to our gifts offered at Mass—monetary, yes, but also spiritual—is imperative. An obscure text with a delightful tune, "What You Gave Us for Our Taking," prays well that linking of sacrifices. Some GIA hymnals contain "The Temple Rang with Golden Coins," which retells the gospel in music and poetry.

Songs that more obliquely align with today's Scriptures as a whole include "Where Charity and Love Prevail" by Omer Westendorf (found in many hymnals), other settings of the *Ubi Caritas*, and "A Generous Heart" (GIA) by Chris de Silva.

The epistle, on the other hand, is more explicitly about Christ's redemptive sacrifice. Possible referent hymns would include

(continued on next page)

COLLECT

Let us pray.

Pause for silent prayer

Almighty and merciful God,
graciously keep from us all adversity,
so that, unhindered in mind and body alike,
we may pursue in freedom of heart
the things that are yours.
Through our Lord Jesus Christ, your Son,
who lives and reigns with you in the unity of the Holy Spirit,
God, for ever and ever. **Amen.**

FIRST READING

1 Kgs 17:10-16

In those days, Elijah the prophet went to Zarephath.
As he arrived at the entrance of the city,
a widow was gathering sticks there; he called out to her,
"Please bring me a small cupful of water to drink."
She left to get it, and he called out after her,
"Please bring along a bit of bread."
She answered, "As the LORD, your God, lives,
I have nothing baked; there is only a handful of flour in my jar
and a little oil in my jug.
Just now I was collecting a couple of sticks,
to go in and prepare something for myself and my son;
when we have eaten it, we shall die."
Elijah said to her, "Do not be afraid.
Go and do as you propose.
But first make me a little cake and bring it to me.
Then you can prepare something for yourself and your son.
For the LORD, the God of Israel, says,
'The jar of flour shall not go empty,
nor the jug of oil run dry,
until the day when the LORD sends rain upon the earth.'"
She left and did as Elijah had said.
She was able to eat for a year, and he and her son as well;
the jar of flour did not go empty,
nor the jug of oil run dry,
as the LORD had foretold through Elijah.

RESPONSORIAL PSALM
Ps 146:7, 8-9, 9-10

℟. (1b) Praise the Lord, my soul!
or: ℟. Alleluia.

The LORD keeps faith forever,
secures justice for the oppressed,
gives food to the hungry.
The LORD sets captives free.

℟. Praise the Lord, my soul!
or: ℟. Alleluia.

The LORD gives sight to the blind;
the LORD raises up those who were bowed down.
The LORD loves the just;
the LORD protects strangers.

℟. Praise the Lord, my soul!
or: ℟. Alleluia.

The fatherless and the widow he sustains,
but the way of the wicked he thwarts.
The LORD shall reign forever;
your God, O Zion, through all generations. Alleluia.

℟. Praise the Lord, my soul!
or: ℟. Alleluia.

SECOND READING
Heb 9:24-28

Christ did not enter into a sanctuary made by hands,
a copy of the true one, but heaven itself,
that he might now appear before God on our behalf.
Not that he might offer himself repeatedly,
as the high priest enters each year into the sanctuary
with blood that is not his own;
if that were so, he would have had to suffer repeatedly
from the foundation of the world.
But now once for all he has appeared at the end of the ages
to take away sin by his sacrifice.
Just as it is appointed that human beings die once,
and after this the judgment, so also Christ,
offered once to take away the sins of many,
will appear a second time, not to take away sin
but to bring salvation to those who eagerly await him.

"One Sacrifice of Christ" (OCP) by Rick Modlin and Robert Feduccia, or "Sent Forth by God's Blessing," again by Omer Westendorf and found in several songbooks.

Liturgical Ministers: Ushers and Greeters

The unseen ministry of tidying the church after Mass, straightening books, and ensuring a prayerful space for the next assembly is itself a form of prayer. Ushers and greeters who quietly serve in this way share a reverence for the sacred space and for the community that gathers there. It is a sign of stewardship that teaches the dignity of every person who will soon kneel or sit in that place. This ministry forms ministers to see the church not as a building but as a dwelling of Christ's presence. In caring for the space of worship, they also cultivate an interior reverence. It reveals that preparing a place for prayer is itself an act of love. The one who wipes a pew or places a hymnal neatly on a rack proclaims silently that the liturgy is a gift worthy of preparation. By serving in this hidden way, ushers and greeters become keepers of sacred hospitality.

Living Liturgy: Walking Together in Synodality

The church's call to synodality is a reminder that every baptized person has a voice in discerning God's will. Today's readings, which highlight humility and trust, challenge us to listen deeply to Scripture, to the Spirit, and to one another. The liturgy itself models this "walking together." Ministers process side by side, readers proclaim the word for all, and the assembly responds with one voice. The prayers we speak are not individual but communal, shaping us as a people of dialogue and discernment. Synodality begins in worship, where we learn to listen to God together and to see each person's gifts as essential to the church's mission. When we leave the liturgy, this shared vision becomes a way of life. Communities that practice true listening in prayer are equipped to listen well in conversation, to notice the needs of their neighbors, and to act as one Body in service of the world. The Eucharist forms us to be a synodal church: a people walking humbly with God and with one another.

NOVEMBER 7, 2027

THIRTY-SECOND SUNDAY IN ORDINARY TIME

SPIRITUALITY

GOSPEL ACCLAMATION
Luke 21:36

℟. Alleluia, alleluia.
Be vigilant at all times
and pray that you have the strength to stand
before the Son of Man.
℟. Alleluia, alleluia.

Gospel

Mark 13:24-32; L158B

Jesus said to his disciples:
"In those days after that tribulation
the sun will be darkened,
and the moon will not give its light,
and the stars will be falling from the sky,
and the powers in the heavens will be shaken.

"And then they will see 'the Son of Man coming in the clouds'
with great power and glory,
and then he will send out the angels
and gather his elect from the four winds,
from the end of the earth to the end of the sky.

"Learn a lesson from the fig tree.
When its branch becomes tender and sprouts leaves,
you know that summer is near.
In the same way, when you see these things happening,
know that he is near, at the gates.
Amen, I say to you,
this generation will not pass away
until all these things have taken place.
Heaven and earth will pass away,
but my words will not pass away.

"But of that day or hour, no one knows,
neither the angels in heaven, nor the Son, but only the Father."

Praying with Gospel Words and Phrases

Learn a lesson from the fig tree . . .

Reflecting on the Gospel

Speaking of the end times, as is typical for mid-November liturgies, Jesus points our attention to the budding fig tree. When its outward appearance changes and its tender branches sprout leaves, one knows what that signifies: summer is near.

In the Rite of Baptism, those gathered hear the celebrant speak of the white garment, and the candle lit from the Easter candle just after the baptismal washing and anointing. The dignity and purity the white garment represents is inextricably linked to what the light of the candle represents: a burning and zealous faith, the light of Christ for all to see. The dignity of our baptism must be lived in an obvious and public way. This is what our Scriptures this weekend call us to as well. Just as the budding fig tree indicates summer is coming, the passage from Daniel reminds us that "the wise shall shine brightly like the splendor of the firmament, and those who lead the many to justice shall be like the stars forever."

The alb particularly is a wonderful way to present the dignity given us at baptism in a public way. Some see it as only a priestly garment, meaning the ordained priesthood to them, but it is in fact a garment of the "priesthood of the baptized" and the public faith we are all called to by our initiation into the church.

Some are bothered when laypeople wear an alb in some liturgical ministry, be it as a lector, a choir member, or as a presider at an appropriate moment. To those people, that vexation arises because they believe a layperson is "pretending" to be an ordained minister, for whatever reason. It's worth noting that at nearly any Sunday Mass we see altar servers in albs, and rarely if ever are complaints raised about their liturgical attire.

Properly catechized, there can be something wonderful (and itself catechetical) about a lay liturgical minister wearing an alb, public showing their Christian dignity, to the whole of the Christian community at prayer.

To the Point

Just as the budding fig tree signals the nearness of summer, Christians are called to live out the dignity of their baptism in visible, public ways so that their faith, like the light of Christ, may shine clearly for all to see.

Preparing to Proclaim, Preach, and Pray

Making Connections Between the Readings: Our Old Testament reading today from the book of Daniel is a dramatic and hopeful prophecy about the end times, focusing on deliverance, resurrection, and eternal destiny. It speaks of a great tribulation, a period of intense suffering and upheaval. It echoes other apocalyptic literature and sets the stage for divine intervention. God promises liberation to those "written in the book," often interpreted as the "book of life." It's a promise of hope in the midst of chaos.

The line, "Many of those who sleep in the dust of the earth shall awake . . ." may be one of the clearest references to resurrection in the Old Testament. Some will rise to eternal life, others to shame and everlasting disgrace. It also introduces the idea of individual judgment and eternal consequence: those who live wisely and guide others toward righteousness will receive eternal glory, compared to stars that shine forever—an image of Godly radiance and reward.

The epistle ends the portions of the epistle to the Hebrews included in the Sunday Lectionary, and speaks of the victory of Christ, once and for all. It is Jesus and his redemptive death and resurrection that adds us all to that "book of life," if we in turn choose to accept the precious, divine gift.

Making Connections to the Responsorial Psalm: Though it is principally the Johannine epistles that give us our "adopted children of God" language, there are other references throughout the Bible, even back to the Old Testament, as evidenced by today's Psalm 16. The chosen verses clearly link our relationship with God, that of heirs to God's promises, to the most significant of those promises, that of immortality and incorruptibility.

Christians believe that our resurrected bodies, at the Parousia, will be glorified and something very different than the flesh we have now. We will no longer suffer pain or death; we will radiate purity and beauty; we will be perfected and whole again. Our glorified bodies will be modeled after Christ's resurrected body, allowing us eternal communion with God and others in the fullness of life.

We may recall from the Second Sunday of Easter that Christ's glorified body retained its woundedness, which Thomas examined, bolstering his faith. We are then reminded that God often doesn't take away our sufferings, doesn't completely heal us of our ills but does abide with us through them, and dwells even within our trials and pains.

CONNECTING TO EXPERIENCE: LIVING THE PASCHAL MYSTERY

The end of a year is a mysterious time. The church's year does not follow our civic calendar but falls right before the hustle and bustle of far more attractive events, like holiday turkeys or bright Christmas lights and sales. It is difficult to take warnings about the sun ceasing to shine and stars falling from the sky seriously. Yet we're being prepared for the coming of Christ: Christ came, yes, as an infant child, and there was much rejoicing. Christ will come again, however, and he will gather all people to himself at the end of time (if they choose it). Christ also *is.* In the midst of busyness and bustle, Christ reminds us that heaven and earth will pass away—as will the busy days that distract us. In the meantime, we are to live as Christ asked us to live: in him, with him, and through him. We are to live in love, awaiting with joyful hope the coming of Christ.

PROMPTS FOR FAITH-SHARING

- Are you ready for Christ? Do you believe that he was there before creation and will judge all?
- What distractions are keeping you from right relationship with God and others this day?
- What in your life would you like Christ to help you to complete?

Model Penitential Act

Presider: We are called to be vigilant at all times for the coming of Christ. Let us pray that we have the strength to stand before the Son of Man as we bring before him our need for mercy . . . *[pause]*

Lord Jesus, you sit at the right hand of the Father: Lord, have mercy.

Christ Jesus, you offer mercy to those who seek you: Christ, have mercy.

Lord Jesus, you will show us the path of life: Lord, have mercy.

Model Universal Prayer (Prayer of the Faithful)

Presider: Coming before the Lord who reigns over heaven and earth, we offer our petitions as we hope for all the world to be restored to him.

Response: Lord, hear our prayer.

For the faithful scattered throughout the world: may the church grow in strength and mission, especially in places where secularism and apathy reign, we pray . . .

For our politicians, our government officials, and our nation's leaders: may their policies and programs unceasingly promote the dignity of all human beings and care for all creation, we pray . . .

For those burdened with loss, regret, and shame: may the mercy of Christ offer them hope for healing and restoration, we pray . . .

For all gathered together in this place: may we free our hearts from the snares of jealousy and pride, becoming better disciples of Christ, we pray . . .

Presider: God our Father, as the days of your Son's coming draw near, draw our hearts closer to you and fill us with the strength to stand before you and rejoice in your presence. We ask this through Christ our Lord. **Amen.**

Liturgy and Candles

Even on the brightest Sunday morning, when the church is bathed in light, we light candles. In the lifeless, taciturn darkness of night, we light candles. Burning brightly, they remind us that we too bear the light of Christ, given us at our baptism, shining brightly on a pedestal, not hidden under a basket. Light helps us to see: Christ, the light of the nations and the glory of our people.

In the days before electricity, candles were necessary for illumination during worship, especially in early morning or evening liturgies. Over time, like many practical elements of our liturgies, their use took on symbolic meaning as well. Candles at Mass, those at the altar and ambo—and the Easter Candle at the font, if there is a baptism during Mass—fulfill many functions. They remind us of Christ's light, honor sacred actions, symbolize prayer, and connect us to our baptismal call to be lights in the world.

COLLECT

Let us pray.

Pause for silent prayer

Grant us, we pray, O Lord our God,
the constant gladness of being devoted to you,
for it is full and lasting happiness
to serve with constancy
the author of all that is good.
Through our Lord Jesus Christ, your Son,
who lives and reigns with you in the unity of the Holy Spirit,
God, for ever and ever. **Amen.**

FIRST READING

Dan 12:1-3

In those days, I, Daniel,
heard this word of the Lord:
"At that time there shall arise
Michael, the great prince,
guardian of your people;
it shall be a time unsurpassed in distress
since nations began until that time.
At that time your people shall escape,
everyone who is found written in the book.

"Many of those who sleep in the dust of the earth shall awake;
some shall live forever,
others shall be an everlasting horror and disgrace.

"But the wise shall shine brightly
like the splendor of the firmament,
and those who lead the many to justice
shall be like the stars forever."

RESPONSORIAL PSALM
Ps 16:5, 8, 9-10, 11

℟. (1) You are my inheritance, O Lord!

O LORD, my allotted portion and my cup,
you it is who hold fast my lot.
I set the LORD ever before me;
with him at my right hand I shall not be disturbed.

℟. You are my inheritance, O Lord!

Therefore my heart is glad and my soul rejoices,
my body, too, abides in confidence;
because you will not abandon my soul to the netherworld,
nor will you suffer your faithful one to undergo corruption.

℟. You are my inheritance, O Lord!

You will show me the path to life,
fullness of joys in your presence,
the delights at your right hand forever.

℟. You are my inheritance, O Lord!

SECOND READING
Heb 10:11-14, 18

Brothers and sisters:
Every priest stands daily at his ministry,
offering frequently those same sacrifices
that can never take away sins.
But this one offered one sacrifice for sins,
and took his seat forever at the right hand of God;
now he waits until his enemies are made his footstool.
For by one offering
he has made perfect forever those who are being consecrated.

Where there is forgiveness of these,
there is no longer offering for sin.

Liturgical Ministers: Lectors

The readings this Sunday draw us into apocalyptic visions, revealing a world being remade by God's promise. Lectors who stand at the ambo become icons of this hope. They do not simply read aloud but lend their bodies and voices so that God's word can shake and console his people. To carry these words is to feel their weight: Daniel's prophecy of deliverance, the letter to the Hebrews' assurance of Christ's priesthood, and Jesus's own warning to stay alert. These passages form lectors to be both heralds and intercessors. By immersing themselves in Scripture, they allow the word to echo within them first, so that it is not merely heard but felt. In the stillness of the assembly, the lector becomes a kind of watchman, sounding the promise of salvation and judgment, calling the church to wakefulness. This ministry reminds the whole community that every time the word is proclaimed, Christ himself speaks, summoning us to holiness and trust.

Living Liturgy: Listening as a Synodal Church

As the liturgical year draws toward its close, the church hears readings about Christ's coming in glory and the call to remain faithful. These passages challenge us to see that listening is central to our call as the people of God. The liturgy is a place for listening. We rise for the gospel, pause in silence after readings, and respond with psalms and acclamations. This pattern in our liturgy teaches us that faith grows in a posture of receptivity.
In a synodal church, this listening extends beyond the sanctuary. The reverence we show for Scripture forms us to hear Christ's voice in the poor, in those at the margins, and in our fellow disciples. The liturgy trains us to discern together, to hold God's promises with hope, and to be watchful for his presence in unexpected places. In this way, the readings for these final weeks of the liturgical year become a formation in patience and trust, shaping us to be a people ready for the Lord's coming by listening deeply to him now.

NOVEMBER 14, 2027

THIRTY-THIRD SUNDAY IN ORDINARY TIME

SPIRITUALITY

GOSPEL ACCLAMATION
Mark 11:9, 10

℟. Alleluia, alleluia.
Blessed is he who comes in the name of the Lord!
Blessed is the kingdom of our father David that
is to come!
℟. Alleluia, alleluia.

Gospel

John 18:33b-37; L161B

Pilate said to Jesus,
"Are you the King of the Jews?"
Jesus answered, "Do you say this on your own
or have others told you about me?"
Pilate answered, "I am not a Jew, am I?
Your own nation and the chief priests handed you over to me.
What have you done?"
Jesus answered, "My kingdom does not belong to this world.
If my kingdom did belong to this world,
my attendants would be fighting
to keep me from being handed over to the Jews.
But as it is, my kingdom is not here."
So Pilate said to him, "Then you are a king?"
Jesus answered, "You say I am a king.
For this I was born and for this I came into the world,
to testify to the truth.
Everyone who belongs to the truth listens to my voice."

Praying with Gospel Words and Phrases

My kingdom does not belong to this world . . .

Reflecting on the Gospel

For at least a dozen years now, Americans—and many others around the globe—have hotly debated which political candidates could best lead their citizens according to the Constitution, values, and beliefs we hold dear. The aftermath of many election days has left heads spinning, hearts broken, and lives unsettled. This solemnity should remind us of two things.

First, before his passion and crucifixion, Christ reminds Pilate, "My kingdom does not belong to this world," and, "For this I was born and for this I came into the world, to testify to the truth." Jesus shows us through his passion that his kingship is upside down from what most expect: one who is sneered at and reviled yet serves the repentant—and indeed, everyone—with love and compassion, giving himself in humility to the point of death on a cross.

Many today feel angry, scared, and isolated. But just as Christ's kingdom is not of this world, neither is his peace. Anyone who believes a political candidate alone can bring God's peace to earth is mistaken. Christ is the source of peace and needs his whole body on earth to make it real for all creation.

Second, the book of Revelation reminds us that "Jesus Christ . . . the firstborn of the dead and ruler of the kings of the earth. To him who loves us and has freed us from our sins by his blood . . . to him be glory and power forever" (1:5-6).

What does this mean for us today? It means we belong only to Christ, who is eternal. Our identity is far greater than any world leader can bestow, and our lives are owed to Christ alone. It is his kingdom we strive to build and his peace we work to bring. No matter who wins any election, we all have work to do. In our liturgies and in the world, we must strive—in the words attributed to a few different saints—to pray as if it all depends on God, and act as if it all depends on us.

To the Point

Christians are called to remember that their true identity and hope lie not in worldly leaders but in Christ the King, whose kingdom is built on truth, humility, and sacrificial love—and that we are charged with making that kingdom visible through prayer and action.

Preparing to Proclaim, Preach, and Pray

Making Connections Between the Readings: Our liturgical year, as it has come to us in the 2,000 years since Jesus's time physically with us, is cyclical, as we are likely already aware. This should not be surprising to us. Our very lives, owing to the rotations and revolutions of the earth, hurtling through space, return us to each season—spring, summer, fall, and winter—in due course. As the sun rises and falls, as the earth, tilted on its axis, gives certain portions of our planet more or less sun at certain times of year, so too our human activities change. By close observation of the sun, moon, and stars, humankind has for many centuries marked the cyclical passing of time.

Instead of the sun rising and falling, Daniel speaks instead of a "Son of man" arising in glory. Of course, the celestial sun is an evocative natural image of the Son of God, who too has, in Daniel's words, "an everlasting dominion" and a kingship that "shall not be destroyed."

Rather than from an epistle, the second reading is from Revelation, itself a repository of fantastical imagery and symbolism. Very little of that, however, is in today's pericope, which is much more direct: "'I am the Alpha and the Omega,' says the Lord God, 'the one who is and who was and who is to come, the almighty.'"

Making Connections to the Responsorial Psalm: Psalm 93, along with Psalm 47, utilized on the solemnity of the Ascension, are sometimes called "enthronement psalms." It's possible that either may have been used in some unique, ancient liturgy where God's ascent to the throne was ritually reenacted.

They can also be, with post-messianic eyes, interpreted eschatologically, pointing to the coming of God as king at the end of human time. The reign of God, like God, is eternal, without beginning or end—as Revelation puts it, God reigns from Alpha to Omega, God's infinite *kairos* unfathomable to human intellect and understanding.

So too is the peace of Christ beyond all human logic and power, something only God can give to us. Psalm 93 extols this God as majestic, clothed with might, with ancient throne and an everlasting reign. May it all be so!

CONNECTING TO EXPERIENCE: LIVING THE PASCHAL MYSTERY

Wherever we go in the world, we see humans battling for power. It may be on a massive scale of destruction with weapons and drones, where humans plot to kill as many of one another as possible. It may be in the most mundane of local turf wars, where gossip and backbiting arrange opposing camps. Division is not power in God's eyes. In celebrating Christ the King, we remember that Jesus does not battle for power. Jesus relinquishes it. Far from securing loyal subjects who will garner favors, or arranging political alliances, Jesus warns his disciples that it will be difficult to drink from the cup of which he drinks. Christ, the living God, laid down his life so that our sins might be forgiven. In whatever our place may be, we are asked to lay down our thirst for power. It is from the evil one. Only God is all in all.

PROMPTS FOR FAITH-SHARING

- What can Jesus, the King of the Universe, do for you today?
- Are you distracted by power, politics, or turbulence in your life? Why so?
- Like Pilate, have you wanted to help Jesus, but have not had the courage to do so? How can Christ the King help you to change?

Model Penitential Act

Presider: Today, we honor Christ the King, the one who frees us from our sins. We empty our hearts before him as we ask for his mercy . . . *[pause]*

Lord Jesus, you are the Alpha and the Omega: Lord, have mercy.

Christ Jesus, you are the one who is, who was, and who is to come: Christ, have mercy.

Lord Jesus, you call all to listen to your voice: Lord, have mercy.

Model Universal Prayer (Prayer of the Faithful)

Presider: Coming before the Lord who reigns over heaven and earth, we offer our prayers for ourselves and all the world.

Response: Lord, hear our prayer.

For the faithful throughout the church: may we live truly as Jesus's disciples, serving in charity and truth and defending the poor and lowly, we pray . . .

For all nations: may the rights of all peoples be protected, respected, and valued, we pray . . .

For people throughout the world who have had their freedoms removed: may their dignity be restored, we pray . . .

For all of us gathered today: may we refuse to become addicted to technology, social media, and self-focused practices that attempt to rule our lives, we pray . . .

Presider: Lord God, your dominion is an everlasting dominion that will never be taken away. May all the world come to know you, who alone reigns for ever and ever. We ask this through Christ our Lord. **Amen.**

Liturgy and Music

There certainly is no shortage of music appropriate for today's solemnity! When choosing selections, a particular mindfulness must be present to ensure that the texts speak not only of Christ, reigning in heavenly splendor, but also of Christ who chose no such title for himself on earth but rather chose a crown of thorns. So, while perhaps utilizing traditional favorites like "Crown Him with Many Crowns" or "To Jesus Christ, Our Sovereign King," both found in many hymnals, ensure too that hymns like "Amazing Love" (Hillsong), or perhaps "At the Name of Jesus" in either the traditional setting or the gospel music-like version by Christopher Walker (OCP), are part of your assembly's sung prayer this weekend.

As our Scriptures this time of year call us to contemplate the end times and the second coming of Christ, our music could reflect these too. There is a certain "doom and gloom" that must

(continued on next page)

COLLECT

Let us pray.

Pause for silent prayer

Almighty ever-living God,
whose will is to restore all things
in your beloved Son, the King of the
universe,
grant, we pray,
that the whole creation, set free from
slavery,
may render your majesty service
and ceaselessly proclaim your praise.
Through our Lord Jesus Christ, your Son,
who lives and reigns with you in the unity
of the Holy Spirit,
God, for ever and ever. **Amen.**

FIRST READING

Dan 7:13-14

As the visions during the night continued,
I saw
one like a Son of man coming,
on the clouds of heaven;
when he reached the Ancient One
and was presented before him,
the one like a Son of man received
dominion, glory, and kingship;
all peoples, nations, and languages
serve him.
His dominion is an everlasting dominion
that shall not be taken away,
his kingship shall not be destroyed.

RESPONSORIAL PSALM
Ps 93:1, 1-2, 5

℟. (1a) The Lord is king; he is robed in
majesty.

The LORD is king, in splendor robed;
robed is the LORD and girt about with
strength.

℟. The Lord is king; he is robed in majesty.

And he has made the world firm,
not to be moved.
Your throne stands firm from of old;
from everlasting you are, O LORD.

℟. The Lord is king; he is robed in majesty.

Your decrees are worthy of trust indeed;
holiness befits your house,
O LORD, for length of days.

℟. The Lord is king; he is robed in majesty.

SECOND READING
Rev 1:5-8

Jesus Christ is the faithful witness,
the firstborn of the dead and ruler of
the kings of the earth.
To him who loves us and has freed us from
our sins by his blood,
who has made us into a kingdom,
priests for his God and Father,
to him be glory and power forever and
ever. Amen.

Behold, he is coming amid the clouds,
and every eye will see him,
even those who pierced him.
All the peoples of the earth will lament
him.
Yes. Amen.

"I am the Alpha and the Omega," says the
Lord God,
"the one who is and who was and who is
to come, the almighty."

be tempered by hope and promise as well. This might bring to mind Rory Cooney's "Canticle of the Turning" (GIA), an Irish melody with a wonderful paraphrase of Mary's *Magnificat*. Look too at "The King Shall Come When Morning Dawns," in either its traditional setting or with a more contemporary setting from either Joe Mattingly or Christian Cosas (both GIA).

Liturgical Ministers: Music Ministers

On this solemnity, the church proclaims that Christ's reign is unlike any other. It is a kingdom of service, mercy, and love. Music ministers become living witnesses of this reign, offering not only music but nourishment for the soul. Their ministry is shaping a spiritual environment where the word of God takes root. In every psalm, hymn, and acclamation, the assembly is fed with beauty and truth, drawn into a deeper encounter with Christ the King. This is why the church calls music integral to liturgy because it does not decorate worship but becomes a form of prayer that strengthens faith. Music ministers themselves are formed by this reality. Their service draws them into contemplation, teaching them that what they sing is not for applause but for transformation, firstly of their own, then that of the assembly. Their work is a participation in Christ's own mission to gather his people, heal hearts, and proclaim the gospel. In this way, they not only proclaim Christ as king but also mirror his way of ruling by feeding his people with love.

Living Liturgy: The Collect of Christ the King

The collect of this feast prays to God, "whose will it is to restore all things in your beloved Son," showing us that the kingship of Christ is not imposed by force but revealed in love. This prayer teaches the church about the meaning of power in God's kingdom that Christ reigns from the cross, inviting all creation into communion with him. When we pray these words, we learn that the goal of history is restoration, not domination. The liturgy today is a mirror of that future. At the altar, heaven and earth are drawn together, and Christ is enthroned not in majesty apart from us but in the humble gifts of bread and wine. The collect forms us to see this kingship as a mission. Those who kneel before the king are sent to embody his reign, which is mercy, truth, and peace. As the liturgical year ends, this prayer sends the church forward with renewed purpose: to proclaim by word and action that Christ is Lord, and his kingdom has already begun.

Readings *(continued)*

Second Sunday of Advent, December 6, 2026

SECOND READING *(cont.)*
2 Pet 3:8-14

Since everything is to be dissolved in
this way,
what sort of persons ought you to be,
conducting yourselves in holiness
and devotion,
waiting for and hastening the
coming of the day of God,
because of which the heavens will be
dissolved in flames
and the elements melted by fire.
But according to his promise
we await new heavens and a new
earth
in which righteousness dwells.
Therefore, beloved, since you await
these things,
be eager to be found without spot or
blemish before him, at peace.

The Immaculate Conception of the Blessed Virgin Mary, December 8, 2026

Gospel (cont.)
Luke 1:26-38; L689

He will be great and will be called Son of the Most High,
and the Lord God will give him the throne of David his
father,
and he will rule over the house of Jacob forever,
and of his Kingdom there will be no end."
But Mary said to the angel,
"How can this be,
since I have no relations with a man?"
And the angel said to her in reply,
"The Holy Spirit will come upon you,
and the power of the Most High will overshadow you.
Therefore the child to be born
will be called holy, the Son of God.
And behold, Elizabeth, your relative,
has also conceived a son in her old age,
and this is the sixth month for her who was called barren;
for nothing will be impossible for God."
Mary said, "Behold, I am the handmaid of the Lord.
May it be done to me according to your word."
Then the angel departed from her.

Other readings on next page.

FIRST READING
Gen 3:9-15, 20

After the man, Adam, had eaten of the tree,
the LORD God called to the man and asked him, "Where are you?"
He answered, "I heard you in the garden;
but I was afraid, because I was naked,
so I hid myself."
Then he asked, "Who told you that you were naked?
You have eaten, then,
from the tree of which I had forbidden you to eat!"
The man replied, "The woman whom you put here with me—
she gave me fruit from the tree, and so I ate it."
The LORD God then asked the woman,
"Why did you do such a thing?"
The woman answered, "The serpent tricked me into it, so I ate it."

Then the LORD God said to the serpent:
"Because you have done this, you shall be banned
from all the animals
and from all the wild creatures;
on your belly shall you crawl,
and dirt shall you eat
all the days of your life.
I will put enmity between you and the woman,
and between your offspring and hers;
he will strike at your head,
while you strike at his heel."

The man called his wife Eve,
because she became the mother of all the living.

RESPONSORIAL PSALM
Ps 98:1, 2-3ab, 3cd-4

℟. (1a) Sing to the Lord a new song, for he has done marvelous deeds.

Sing to the LORD a new song,
for he has done wondrous deeds;
His right hand has won victory for him,
his holy arm.

℟. Sing to the Lord a new song, for he has done marvelous deeds.

The LORD has made his salvation known:
in the sight of the nations he has revealed his justice.
He has remembered his kindness and his faithfulness
toward the house of Israel.

℟. Sing to the Lord a new song, for he has done marvelous deeds.

All the ends of the earth have seen
the salvation by our God.
Sing joyfully to the LORD, all you lands;
break into song; sing praise.

℟. Sing to the Lord a new song, for he has done marvelous deeds.

SECOND READING
Eph 1:3-6, 11-12

Brothers and sisters:
Blessed be the God and Father of our Lord Jesus Christ,
who has blessed us in Christ
with every spiritual blessing in the heavens,
as he chose us in him, before the foundation of the world,
to be holy and without blemish before him.
In love he destined us for adoption to himself through Jesus Christ,
in accord with the favor of his will,
for the praise of the glory of his grace
that he granted us in the beloved.

In him we were also chosen,
destined in accord with the purpose of the One
who accomplishes all things according to the intention of his will,
so that we might exist for the praise of his glory,
we who first hoped in Christ.

Gospel (cont.)

Luke 1:26-38; L690A

He will be great and will be called Son of the Most High,
and the Lord God will give him the throne of David his father,
and he will rule over the house of Jacob forever,
and of his Kingdom there will be no end."
But Mary said to the angel,
"How can this be,
since I have no relations with a man?"
And the angel said to her in reply,
"The Holy Spirit will come upon you,
and the power of the Most High will overshadow you.
Therefore the child to be born
will be called holy, the Son of God.
And behold, Elizabeth, your relative,
has also conceived a son in her old age,
and this is the sixth month for her who was called barren;
for nothing will be impossible for God."
Mary said, "Behold, I am the handmaid of the Lord.
May it be done to me according to your word."
Then the angel departed from her.

or

Luke 1:39-47

Mary set out
and traveled to the hill country in haste
to a town of Judah,
where she entered the house of Zechariah
and greeted Elizabeth.
When Elizabeth heard Mary's greeting,
the infant leaped in her womb,
and Elizabeth, filled with the Holy Spirit,
cried out in a loud voice and said,
"Most blessed are you among women,
and blessed is the fruit of your womb.
And how does this happen to me,
that the mother of my Lord should come to me?
For at the moment the sound of your greeting reached my ears,
the infant in my womb leaped for joy.
Blessed are you who believed
that what was spoken to you by the Lord
would be fulfilled."

And Mary said:

"My soul proclaims the greatness of the Lord;
my spirit rejoices in God my savior."

FIRST READING

Rev 11:19a; 12:1-6a, 10ab

God's temple in heaven was opened,
and the ark of his covenant could be seen in the temple.

A great sign appeared in the sky, a woman clothed with the sun,
with the moon under her feet,
and on her head a crown of twelve stars.
She was with child and wailed aloud in pain as she labored to give birth.
Then another sign appeared in the sky;
it was a huge red dragon, with seven heads and ten horns,
and on its heads were seven diadems.
Its tail swept away a third of the stars in the sky
and hurled them down to the earth.
Then the dragon stood before the woman about to give birth,
to devour her child when she gave birth.
She gave birth to a son, a male child,
destined to rule all the nations with an iron rod.
Her child was caught up to God and his throne.
The woman herself fled into the desert
where she had a place prepared by God.

Then I heard a loud voice in heaven say:
"Now have salvation and power come,
and the Kingdom of our God
and the authority of his Anointed."

or

Zech 2:14-17

Sing and rejoice, O daughter Zion!
See, I am coming to dwell among you, says the LORD.
Many nations shall join themselves to the LORD on that day,
and they shall be his people,
and he will dwell among you,
and you shall know that the LORD of hosts has sent me to you.
The LORD will possess Judah as his portion in the holy land,
and he will again choose Jerusalem.
Silence, all mankind, in the presence of the LORD!
For he stirs forth from his holy dwelling.

RESPONSORIAL PSALM

Jdt 13:18bcde, 19

℟. (15:9d) You are the highest honor of our race.

Blessed are you, daughter, by the Most High God,
above all the women on earth;
and blessed be the LORD God,
the creator of heaven and earth.

℟. You are the highest honor of our race.

Your deed of hope will never be forgotten
by those who tell of the might of God.

℟. You are the highest honor of our race.

Third Sunday of Advent, *December 13, 2026*

Gospel (cont.)

John 1:6-8, 19-28; L8B

John answered them,
"I baptize with water;
but there is one among you whom you do not recognize,
the one who is coming after me,
whose sandal strap I am not worthy to untie."
This happened in Bethany across the Jordan,
where John was baptizing.

Fourth Sunday of Advent, *December 20, 2026*

Gospel (cont.)

Luke 1:26-38; L11B

Therefore the child to be born
will be called holy, the Son of God.
And behold, Elizabeth, your relative,
has also conceived a son in her old age,
and this is the sixth month for her who was called barren;
for nothing will be impossible for God."
Mary said, "Behold, I am the handmaid of the Lord.
May it be done to me according to your word."
Then the angel departed from her.

The Nativity of the Lord, *December 25, 2026 (Vigil Mass)*

Gospel (cont.)

Matt 1:1-25; L13ABC

Asaph became the father of Jehoshaphat,
Jehoshaphat the father of Joram,
Joram the father of Uzziah.
Uzziah became the father of Jotham,
Jotham the father of Ahaz,
Ahaz the father of Hezekiah.
Hezekiah became the father of Manasseh,
Manasseh the father of Amos,
Amos the father of Josiah.
Josiah became the father of Jechoniah and his brothers
at the time of the Babylonian exile.

After the Babylonian exile,
Jechoniah became the father of Shealtiel,
Shealtiel the father of Zerubbabel,
Zerubbabel the father of Abiud.
Abiud became the father of Eliakim,
Eliakim the father of Azor,
Azor the father of Zadok.
Zadok became the father of Achim,
Achim the father of Eliud,
Eliud the father of Eleazar.
Eleazar became the father of Matthan,
Matthan the father of Jacob,
Jacob the father of Joseph, the husband of Mary.
Of her was born Jesus who is called the Christ.

Thus the total number of generations
from Abraham to David
is fourteen generations;
from David to the Babylonian exile,
fourteen generations;
from the Babylonian exile to the Christ,
fourteen generations.

Now this is how the birth of Jesus Christ came about.
When his mother Mary was betrothed to Joseph,
but before they lived together,
she was found with child through the Holy Spirit.
Joseph her husband, since he was a righteous man,
yet unwilling to expose her to shame,
decided to divorce her quietly.
Such was his intention when, behold,
the angel of the Lord appeared to him in a dream and said,
"Joseph, son of David,
do not be afraid to take Mary your wife into your home.
For it is through the Holy Spirit
that this child has been conceived in her.
She will bear a son and you are to name him Jesus,
because he will save his people from their sins."
All this took place to fulfill
what the Lord had said through the prophet:
Behold, the virgin shall conceive and bear a son,
and they shall name him Emmanuel,
which means "God is with us."
When Joseph awoke,
he did as the angel of the Lord had commanded him
and took his wife into his home.
He had no relations with her until she bore a son,
and he named him Jesus.

or

Matt 1:18-25

This is how the birth of Jesus Christ came about.
When his mother Mary was betrothed to Joseph,
but before they lived together,
she was found with child through the Holy Spirit.
Joseph her husband, since he was a righteous man,
yet unwilling to expose her to shame,
decided to divorce her quietly.
Such was his intention when, behold,
the angel of the Lord appeared to him in a dream and said,
"Joseph, son of David,
do not be afraid to take Mary your wife into your home.

For it is through the Holy Spirit
that this child has been conceived in her.
She will bear a son and you are to name him Jesus,
because he will save his people from their sins."
All this took place to fulfill
what the Lord had said through the prophet:
Behold, the virgin shall conceive and bear a son,
and they shall name him Emmanuel,
which means "God is with us."
When Joseph awoke,
he did as the angel of the Lord had commanded him
and took his wife into his home.
He had no relations with her until she bore a son,
and he named him Jesus.

FIRST READING
Isa 62:1-5

For Zion's sake I will not be silent,
for Jerusalem's sake I will not be quiet,
until her vindication shines forth like the dawn
and her victory like a burning torch.

Nations shall behold your vindication,
and all the kings your glory;
you shall be called by a new name
pronounced by the mouth of the LORD.
You shall be a glorious crown in the hand of the LORD,
a royal diadem held by your God.
No more shall people call you "Forsaken,"
or your land "Desolate,"
but you shall be called "My Delight,"
and your land "Espoused."
For the LORD delights in you
and makes your land his spouse.
As a young man marries a virgin,
your Builder shall marry you;
and as a bridegroom rejoices in his bride
so shall your God rejoice in you.

RESPONSORIAL PSALM
Ps 89:4-5, 16-17, 27, 29

℟. (2a) For ever I will sing the goodness of the Lord.

I have made a covenant with my chosen one,
I have sworn to David my servant:
forever will I confirm your posterity
and establish your throne for all generations.

℟. For ever I will sing the goodness of the Lord.

Blessed the people who know the joyful shout;
in the light of your countenance,
O LORD, they walk.
At your name they rejoice all the day,
and through your justice they are exalted.

℟. For ever I will sing the goodness of the Lord.

He shall say of me, "You are my father,
my God, the rock, my savior."
Forever I will maintain my kindness toward him,
and my covenant with him stands firm.

℟. For ever I will sing the goodness of the Lord.

SECOND READING
Acts 13:16-17, 22-25

When Paul reached Antioch in Pisidia
and entered the synagogue,
he stood up, motioned with his hand,
and said,
"Fellow Israelites and you others
who are God-fearing, listen.
The God of this people Israel chose our ancestors
and exalted the people during their sojourn in the land of Egypt.
With uplifted arm he led them out of it.
Then he removed Saul and raised up David as king;
of him he testified,
'I have found David, son of Jesse, a man after my own heart;
he will carry out my every wish.'
From this man's descendants God,
according to his promise,
has brought to Israel a savior, Jesus.
John heralded his coming by proclaiming a baptism of repentance
to all the people of Israel;
and as John was completing his course, he would say,
'What do you suppose that I am?
I am not he.
Behold, one is coming after me;
I am not worthy to unfasten the sandals of his feet.'"

Gospel (cont.)
Luke 2:1-14; L14ABC

Now there were shepherds in that region living in the fields
and keeping the night watch over their flock.
The angel of the Lord appeared to them
and the glory of the Lord shone around them,
and they were struck with great fear.
The angel said to them,
"Do not be afraid;
for behold, I proclaim to you good news of great joy
that will be for all the people.
For today in the city of David
a savior has been born for you who is Christ and Lord.
And this will be a sign for you:
you will find an infant wrapped in swaddling clothes
and lying in a manger."
And suddenly there was a multitude of the heavenly host
with the angel,
praising God and saying:
"Glory to God in the highest
and on earth peace to those on whom his favor rests."

FIRST READING
Isa 9:1-6

The people who walked in darkness
have seen a great light;
upon those who dwelt in the land of gloom
a light has shone.
You have brought them abundant joy
and great rejoicing,
as they rejoice before you as at the harvest,
as people make merry when dividing spoils.
For the yoke that burdened them,
the pole on their shoulder,
and the rod of their taskmaster
you have smashed, as on the day of Midian.
For every boot that tramped in battle,
every cloak rolled in blood,
will be burned as fuel for flames.
For a child is born to us, a son is given us;
upon his shoulder dominion rests.
They name him Wonder-Counselor, God-Hero,
Father-Forever, Prince of Peace.
His dominion is vast
and forever peaceful,
from David's throne, and over his kingdom,
which he confirms and sustains
by judgment and justice,
both now and forever.
The zeal of the LORD of hosts will do this!

RESPONSORIAL PSALM
Ps 96:1-2, 2-3, 11-12, 13

℟. (Luke 2:11) Today is born our Savior, Christ the Lord.

Sing to the LORD a new song;
sing to the LORD, all you lands.
Sing to the LORD; bless his name.

℟. Today is born our Savior, Christ the Lord.

Announce his salvation, day after day.
Tell his glory among the nations;
among all peoples, his wondrous deeds.

℟. Today is born our Savior, Christ the Lord.

Let the heavens be glad and the earth rejoice;
let the sea and what fills it resound;
let the plains be joyful and all that is in them!
Then shall all the trees of the forest exult.

℟. Today is born our Savior, Christ the Lord.

They shall exult before the LORD, for he comes;
for he comes to rule the earth.
He shall rule the world with justice
and the peoples with his constancy.

℟. Today is born our Savior, Christ the Lord.

SECOND READING
Titus 2:11-14

Beloved:
The grace of God has appeared, saving all
and training us to reject godless ways and worldly desires
and to live temperately, justly, and devoutly in this age,
as we await the blessed hope,
the appearance of the glory of our great God
and savior Jesus Christ,
who gave himself for us to deliver us from all lawlessness
and to cleanse for himself a people as his own,
eager to do what is good.

The Nativity of the Lord, *December 25, 2026 (Mass at Dawn)*

FIRST READING
Isa 62:11-12

See, the LORD proclaims
to the ends of the earth:
say to daughter Zion,
your savior comes!
Here is his reward with him,
his recompense before him.
They shall be called the holy people,
the redeemed of the LORD,
and you shall be called "Frequented,"
a city that is not forsaken.

RESPONSORIAL PSALM
Ps 97:1, 6, 11-12

℟. A light will shine on us this day: the Lord is born for us.

The LORD is king; let the earth rejoice;
let the many isles be glad.
The heavens proclaim his justice,
and all peoples see his glory.

℟. A light will shine on us this day: the Lord is born for us.

Light dawns for the just;
and gladness, for the upright of heart.
Be glad in the LORD, you just,
and give thanks to his holy name.

℟. A light will shine on us this day: the Lord is born for us.

SECOND READING
Titus 3:4-7

Beloved:
When the kindness and generous love
of God our savior appeared,
not because of any righteous deeds we had done
but because of his mercy,
he saved us through the bath of rebirth
and renewal by the Holy Spirit,
whom he richly poured out on us
through Jesus Christ our savior,
so that we might be justified by his grace
and become heirs in hope of eternal life.

The Nativity of the Lord, *December 25, 2026 (Mass during the Day)*

Gospel (cont.)
John 1:1-18; L16ABC

But to those who did accept him
he gave power to become children of God,
to those who believe in his name,
who were born not by natural generation
nor by human choice nor by a man's decision
but of God.

And the Word became flesh
and made his dwelling among us,
and we saw his glory,
the glory as of the Father's only Son,
full of grace and truth.

John testified to him and cried out, saying,
"This was he of whom I said,
'The one who is coming after me ranks ahead of me
because he existed before me.' "
From his fullness we have all received,
grace in place of grace,
because while the law was given through Moses,
grace and truth came through Jesus Christ.
No one has ever seen God.
The only Son, God, who is at the Father's side,
has revealed him.

or
John 1:1-5, 9-14

In the beginning was the Word,
and the Word was with God,
and the Word was God.
He was in the beginning with God.
All things came to be through him,
and without him nothing came to be.
What came to be through him was life,
and this life was the light of the human race;
the light shines in the darkness,
and the darkness has not overcome it.
The true light, which enlightens everyone, was coming into the world.

He was in the world,
and the world came to be through him,
but the world did not know him.
He came to what was his own,
but his own people did not accept him.

But to those who did accept him
he gave power to become children of God,
to those who believe in his name,
who were born not by natural generation
nor by human choice nor by a man's decision
but of God.

And the Word became flesh
and made his dwelling among us,
and we saw his glory,
the glory as of the Father's only Son,
full of grace and truth.

Other readings on next page.

FIRST READING
Isa 52:7-10

How beautiful upon the mountains
are the feet of him who brings glad tidings,
announcing peace, bearing good news,
announcing salvation, and saying to Zion,
"Your God is King!"

Hark! Your sentinels raise a cry,
together they shout for joy,
for they see directly, before their eyes,
the LORD restoring Zion.
Break out together in song,
O ruins of Jerusalem!
For the LORD comforts his people,
he redeems Jerusalem.
The LORD has bared his holy arm
in the sight of all the nations;
all the ends of the earth will behold
the salvation of our God.

RESPONSORIAL PSALM
Ps 98:1, 2-3, 3-4, 5-6

℟. (3c) All the ends of the earth have seen the saving power of God.

Sing to the LORD a new song,
for he has done wondrous deeds;
his right hand has won victory for him,
his holy arm.

℟. All the ends of the earth have seen the saving power of God.

The LORD has made his salvation known:
in the sight of the nations he has revealed his justice.
He has remembered his kindness and his faithfulness
toward the house of Israel.

℟. All the ends of the earth have seen the saving power of God.

All the ends of the earth have seen
the salvation by our God.
Sing joyfully to the LORD, all you lands;
break into song; sing praise.

℟. All the ends of the earth have seen the saving power of God.

Sing praise to the LORD with the harp,
with the harp and melodious song.
With trumpets and the sound of the horn
sing joyfully before the King, the LORD.

℟. All the ends of the earth have seen the saving power of God.

SECOND READING
Heb 1:1-6

Brothers and sisters:
In times past, God spoke in partial and various ways
to our ancestors through the prophets;
in these last days, he has spoken to us through the Son,
whom he made heir of all things
and through whom he created the universe,
who is the refulgence of his glory,
the very imprint of his being,
and who sustains all things by his mighty word.
When he had accomplished purification from sins,
he took his seat at the right hand of the Majesty on high,
as far superior to the angels
as the name he has inherited is more excellent than theirs.

For to which of the angels did God ever say:
You are my son; this day I have begotten you?
Or again:
I will be a father to him, and he shall be a son to me?
And again, when he leads the firstborn into the world, he says:
Let all the angels of God worship him.

Gospel (cont.)

Luke 2:22-40; L17B

He came in the Spirit into the temple;
and when the parents brought in the child Jesus
to perform the custom of the law in regard to him,
he took him into his arms and blessed God, saying:
"Now, Master, you may let your servant go
in peace, according to your word,
for my eyes have seen your salvation,
which you prepared in sight of all the peoples,
a light for revelation to the Gentiles,
and glory for your people Israel."
The child's father and mother were amazed at what was said about him;
and Simeon blessed them and said to Mary his mother,
"Behold, this child is destined
for the fall and rise of many in Israel,
and to be a sign that will be contradicted
—and you yourself a sword will pierce—
so that the thoughts of many hearts may be revealed."
There was also a prophetess, Anna,
the daughter of Phanuel, of the tribe of Asher.
She was advanced in years,
having lived seven years with her husband after her marriage,
and then as a widow until she was eighty-four.
She never left the temple,
but worshiped night and day with fasting and prayer.
And coming forward at that very time,
she gave thanks to God and spoke about the child
to all who were awaiting the redemption of Jerusalem.

When they had fulfilled all the prescriptions
of the law of the Lord,
they returned to Galilee,
to their own town of Nazareth.
The child grew and became strong, filled with wisdom;
and the favor of God was upon him.

or

Luke 2:22, 39-40

When the days were completed for their purification
according to the law of Moses,
they took him up to Jerusalem
to present him to the Lord.

When they had fulfilled all the prescriptions
of the law of the Lord,
they returned to Galilee,
to their own town of Nazareth.
The child grew and became strong, filled with wisdom;
and the favor of God was upon him.

FIRST READING

or

Gen 15:1-6; 21:1-3

The word of the LORD came to Abram
in a vision, saying:
"Fear not, Abram!
I am your shield;
I will make your reward very great."
But Abram said,
"O Lord GOD, what good will your gifts be,
if I keep on being childless
and have as my heir the steward of my house, Eliezer?"
Abram continued,
"See, you have given me no offspring,
and so one of my servants will be my heir."
Then the word of the LORD came to him:
"No, that one shall not be your heir;
your own issue shall be your heir."
The Lord took Abram outside and said,
"Look up at the sky and count the stars, if you can.
Just so," he added, "shall your descendants be."
Abram put his faith in the LORD,
who credited it to him as an act of righteousness.

The LORD took note of Sarah as he had said he would;
he did for her as he had promised.
Sarah became pregnant and bore Abraham a son in his old age,
at the set time that God had stated.
Abraham gave the name Isaac to this son of his
whom Sarah bore him.

RESPONSORIAL PSALM

or

Ps 105:1-2, 3-4, 6-7, 8-9

℟. (7a, 8a) The Lord remembers his covenant for ever.

Give thanks to the LORD, invoke his name;
make known among the nations his deeds.
Sing to him, sing his praise,
proclaim all his wondrous deeds.

℟. The Lord remembers his covenant for ever.

Glory in his holy name;
rejoice, O hearts that seek the LORD!
Look to the LORD in his strength;
constantly seek his face.

℟. The Lord remembers his covenant for ever.

You descendants of Abraham, his servants,
sons of Jacob, his chosen ones!
He, the LORD, is our God;
throughout the earth his judgments prevail.

℟. The Lord remembers his covenant for ever.

He remembers forever his covenant
which he made binding for a thousand generations
which he entered into with Abraham
and by his oath to Isaac.

℟. The Lord remembers his covenant for ever.

Continue on next page.

SECOND READING *(cont.)*

or
Col 3:12-17

Brothers and sisters:
Put on, as God's chosen ones, holy and beloved,
heartfelt compassion, kindness, humility, gentleness, and patience,
bearing with one another and forgiving one another,
if one has a grievance against another;
as the Lord has forgiven you, so must you also do.
And over all these put on love,
that is, the bond of perfection.
And let the peace of Christ control your hearts,
the peace into which you were also called in one body.
And be thankful.
Let the word of Christ dwell in you richly,
as in all wisdom you teach and admonish one another,
singing psalms, hymns, and spiritual songs
with gratitude in your hearts to God.
And whatever you do, in word or in deed,
do everything in the name of the Lord Jesus,
giving thanks to God the Father through him.

or
Heb 11:8, 11-12, 17-19

Brothers and sisters:
By faith Abraham obeyed when he was called to go out to a place
that he was to receive as an inheritance;
he went out, not knowing where he was to go.
By faith he received power to generate,
even though he was past the normal age
—and Sarah herself was sterile—
for he thought that the one who had made the promise was trustworthy.
So it was that there came forth from one man,
himself as good as dead,
descendants as numerous as the stars in the sky
and as countless as the sands on the seashore.
By faith Abraham, when put to the test, offered up Isaac,
and he who had received the promises was ready to offer
his only son,
of whom it was said,
"Through Isaac descendants shall bear your name."
He reasoned that God was able to raise even from the dead,
and he received Isaac back as a symbol.

Solemnity of Mary, the Holy Mother of God, January 1, 2027

FIRST READING
Num 6:22-27

The LORD said to Moses:
"Speak to Aaron and his sons and tell them:
This is how you shall bless the Israelites.
Say to them:
The LORD bless you and keep you!
The LORD let his face shine upon you, and be gracious to you!
The LORD look upon you kindly and give you peace!
So shall they invoke my name upon the Israelites,
and I will bless them."

RESPONSORIAL PSALM
Ps 67:2-3, 5, 6, 8

℟. (2a) May God bless us in his mercy.

May God have pity on us and bless us;
may he let his face shine upon us.
So may your way be known upon earth;
among all nations, your salvation.

℟. May God bless us in his mercy.

May the nations be glad and exult
because you rule the peoples in equity;
the nations on the earth you guide.

℟. May God bless us in his mercy.

May the peoples praise you, O God;
may all the peoples praise you!
May God bless us,
and may all the ends of the earth fear him!

℟. May God bless us in his mercy.

SECOND READING
Gal 4:4-7

Brothers and sisters:
When the fullness of time had come,
God sent his Son,
born of a woman, born under the law,
to ransom those under the law,
so that we might receive adoption as sons.
As proof that you are sons,
God sent the Spirit of his Son into our hearts,
crying out, "Abba, Father!"
So you are no longer a slave but a son,
and if a son then also an heir,
through God.

The Epiphany of the Lord, January 3, 2027

Gospel (cont.)
Matt 2:1-12; L20ABC

After their audience with the king they set out.
And behold, the star that they had seen at its rising preceded them,
until it came and stopped over the place where the child was.
They were overjoyed at seeing the star,
and on entering the house
they saw the child with Mary his mother.
They prostrated themselves and did him homage.
Then they opened their treasures
and offered him gifts of gold, frankincense, and myrrh.
And having been warned in a dream not to return to Herod,
they departed for their country by another way.

Baptism of the Lord, January 10, 2027

FIRST READING
Isa 55:1-11

Thus says the LORD:
All you who are thirsty,
come to the water!
You who have no money,
come, receive grain and eat;
come, without paying and without cost,
drink wine and milk!
Why spend your money for what is not bread,
your wages for what fails to satisfy?
Heed me, and you shall eat well,
you shall delight in rich fare.
Come to me heedfully,
listen, that you may have life.
I will renew with you the everlasting covenant,
the benefits assured to David.
As I made him a witness to the peoples,
a leader and commander of nations,
so shall you summon a nation you knew not,
and nations that knew you not shall run to you,
because of the LORD, your God,
the Holy One of Israel, who has glorified you.

Seek the LORD while he may be found,
call him while he is near.
Let the scoundrel forsake his way,
and the wicked man his thoughts;
let him turn to the LORD for mercy;
to our God, who is generous in forgiving.
For my thoughts are not your thoughts,
nor are your ways my ways, says the LORD.
As high as the heavens are above the earth
so high are my ways above your ways
and my thoughts above your thoughts.

For just as from the heavens
the rain and snow come down
and do not return there
till they have watered the earth,
making it fertile and fruitful,
giving seed to the one who sows
and bread to the one who eats,
so shall my word be
that goes forth from my mouth;
my word shall not return to me void,
but shall do my will,
achieving the end for which I sent it.

RESPONSORIAL PSALM
Isa 12:2-3, 4bcd, 5-6

℟. (3) You will draw water joyfully from the springs of salvation.

God indeed is my savior;
I am confident and unafraid.
My strength and my courage is the LORD,
and he has been my savior.
With joy you will draw water
at the fountain of salvation.

℟. You will draw water joyfully from the springs of salvation.

Give thanks to the LORD, acclaim his name;
among the nations make known his deeds,
proclaim how exalted is his name.

℟. You will draw water joyfully from the springs of salvation.

Sing praise to the LORD for his glorious achievement;
let this be known throughout all the earth.
Shout with exultation, O city of Zion,
for great in your midst
is the Holy One of Israel!

℟. You will draw water joyfully from the springs of salvation.

SECOND READING
1 John 5:1-9

Beloved:
Everyone who believes that Jesus is the Christ is begotten by God,
and everyone who loves the Father
loves also the one begotten by him.
In this way we know that we love the children of God
when we love God and obey his commandments.
For the love of God is this,
that we keep his commandments.
And his commandments are not burdensome,
for whoever is begotten by God conquers the world.
And the victory that conquers the world is our faith.
Who indeed is the victor over the world
but the one who believes that Jesus is the Son of God?

This is the one who came through water and blood, Jesus Christ,
not by water alone, but by water and blood.
The Spirit is the one who testifies,
and the Spirit is truth.
So there are three that testify,
the Spirit, the water, and the blood,
and the three are of one accord.
If we accept human testimony,
the testimony of God is surely greater.
Now the testimony of God is this,
that he has testified on behalf of his Son.

Gospel (cont.)

Matt 6:1-6, 16-18; L219

"When you fast,
  do not look gloomy like the hypocrites.
They neglect their appearance,
  so that they may appear to others to be fasting.
Amen, I say to you, they have received their reward.
But when you fast,
  anoint your head and wash your face,
  so that you may not appear to be fasting,
  except to your Father who is hidden.
And your Father who sees what is hidden will repay you."

FIRST READING

Joel 2:12-18

Even now, says the LORD,
  return to me with your whole heart,
  with fasting, and weeping, and mourning;
Rend your hearts, not your garments,
  and return to the LORD, your God.
For gracious and merciful is he,
  slow to anger, rich in kindness,
  and relenting in punishment.
Perhaps he will again relent
  and leave behind him a blessing,
Offerings and libations
  for the LORD, your God.

Blow the trumpet in Zion!
  proclaim a fast,
  call an assembly;
Gather the people,
  notify the congregation;
Assemble the elders,
  gather the children
  and the infants at the breast;
Let the bridegroom quit his room
  and the bride her chamber.
Between the porch and the altar
  let the priests, the ministers of the LORD, weep,
And say, "Spare, O LORD, your people,
  and make not your heritage a reproach,
  with the nations ruling over them!
Why should they say among the peoples,
  'Where is their God?' "

Then the LORD was stirred to concern for his land
  and took pity on his people.

RESPONSORIAL PSALM

Ps 51:3-4, 5-6ab, 12-13, 14, and 17

℟. (see 3a) Be merciful, O Lord, for we have sinned.

Have mercy on me, O God, in your goodness;
  in the greatness of your compassion wipe out my offense.
Thoroughly wash me from my guilt
  and of my sin cleanse me.

℟. Be merciful, O Lord, for we have sinned.

For I acknowledge my offense,
  and my sin is before me always:
"Against you only have I sinned,
  and done what is evil in your sight."

℟. Be merciful, O Lord, for we have sinned.

A clean heart create for me, O God,
  and a steadfast spirit renew within me.
Cast me not out from your presence,
  and your Holy Spirit take not from me.

℟. Be merciful, O Lord, for we have sinned.

Give me back the joy of your salvation,
  and a willing spirit sustain in me.
O Lord, open my lips,
  and my mouth shall proclaim your praise.

℟. Be merciful, O Lord, for we have sinned.

SECOND READING

2 Cor 5:20–6:2

Brothers and sisters:
We are ambassadors for Christ,
  as if God were appealing through us.
We implore you on behalf of Christ,
  be reconciled to God.
For our sake he made him to be sin who did not know sin,
  so that we might become the righteousness of God in him.

Working together, then,
  we appeal to you not to receive the grace of God in vain.
For he says:

In an acceptable time I heard you,
and on the day of salvation I helped you.

Behold, now is a very acceptable time;
  behold, now is the day of salvation.

Gospel (cont.)

John 2:13-25; L29B

But he was speaking about the temple of his body.
Therefore, when he was raised from the dead,
his disciples remembered that he had said this,
and they came to believe the Scripture
and the word Jesus had spoken.

While he was in Jerusalem for the feast of Passover,
many began to believe in his name
when they saw the signs he was doing.
But Jesus would not trust himself to them because he knew them all,
and did not need anyone to testify about human nature.
He himself understood it well.

RESPONSORIAL PSALM

Ps 19:8, 9, 10, 11

℟. (John 6:68c) Lord, you have the words of everlasting life.

The law of the LORD is perfect,
refreshing the soul;
the decree of the LORD is trustworthy,
giving wisdom to the simple.

℟. Lord, you have the words of everlasting life.

The precepts of the LORD are right,
rejoicing the heart;
the command of the LORD is clear,
enlightening the eye.

℟. Lord, you have the words of everlasting life.

The fear of the LORD is pure,
enduring forever;
the ordinances of the LORD are true,
all of them just.

℟. Lord, you have the words of everlasting life.

They are more precious than gold,
than a heap of purest gold;
sweeter also than syrup
or honey from the comb.

℟. Lord, you have the words of everlasting life.

SECOND READING

1 Cor 1:22-25

Brothers and sisters:
Jews demand signs and Greeks look for wisdom,
but we proclaim Christ crucified,
a stumbling block to Jews and foolishness to Gentiles,
but to those who are called, Jews and Greeks alike,
Christ the power of God and the wisdom of God.
For the foolishness of God is wiser than human wisdom,
and the weakness of God is stronger than human strength.

Other readings on next page.

Third Sunday of Lent, *February 28, 2027 (cont.)*

These Year A readings may be used in place of Year B readings.
They are always used for assemblies celebrating the Scrutinies for the OCIA.

FIRST READING
Exod 17:3-7

In those days, in their thirst for water,
the people grumbled against Moses,
saying, "Why did you ever make us
leave Egypt?
Was it just to have us die here of thirst
with our children and our livestock?"
So Moses cried out to the LORD,
"What shall I do with this people?
A little more and they will stone me!"
The LORD answered Moses,
"Go over there in front of the people,
along with some of the elders of
Israel,
holding in your hand, as you go,
the staff with which you struck the
river.
I will be standing there in front of you
on the rock in Horeb.
Strike the rock, and the water will flow
from it
for the people to drink."
This Moses did, in the presence of the
elders of Israel.
The place was called Massah and
Meribah,
because the Israelites quarreled there
and tested the LORD, saying,
"Is the LORD in our midst or not?"

RESPONSORIAL PSALM
Ps 95:1-2, 6-7, 8-9

℟. (8) If today you hear his voice,
harden not your hearts.

Come, let us sing joyfully to the LORD;
let us acclaim the Rock of our
salvation.
Let us come into his presence with
thanksgiving;
let us joyfully sing psalms to him.

℟. If today you hear his voice, harden
not your hearts.

Come, let us bow down in worship;
let us kneel before the LORD who
made us.
For he is our God,
and we are the people he shepherds,
the flock he guides.

℟. If today you hear his voice, harden
not your hearts.

Oh, that today you would hear his
voice:
"Harden not your hearts as at
Meribah,
as in the day of Massah in the
desert,
Where your fathers tempted me;
they tested me though they had seen
my works."

℟. If today you hear his voice, harden
not your hearts.

SECOND READING
Rom 5:1-2, 5-8

Brothers and sisters:
Since we have been justified by faith,
we have peace with God through our
Lord Jesus Christ,
through whom we have gained
access by faith
to this grace in which we stand,
and we boast in hope of the glory of
God.

And hope does not disappoint,
because the love of God has been
poured out into our hearts
through the Holy Spirit who has
been given to us.
For Christ, while we were still helpless,
died at the appointed time for the
ungodly.
Indeed, only with difficulty does one
die for a just person,
though perhaps for a good person
one might even find courage to
die.
But God proves his love for us
in that while we were still sinners
Christ died for us.

Gospel
John 4:5-42; L28A

Jesus came to a town of Samaria called Sychar,
near the plot of land that Jacob had given to his son
Joseph.
Jacob's well was there.
Jesus, tired from his journey, sat down there at the well.
It was about noon.

A woman of Samaria came to draw water.
Jesus said to her,
"Give me a drink."
His disciples had gone into the town to buy food.
The Samaritan woman said to him,
"How can you, a Jew, ask me, a Samaritan woman, for a
drink?"
—For Jews use nothing in common with Samaritans.—
Jesus answered and said to her,
"If you knew the gift of God
and who is saying to you, 'Give me a drink,'
you would have asked him
and he would have given you living water."

The woman said to him,
"Sir, you do not even have a bucket and the cistern is
deep;
where then can you get this living water?
Are you greater than our father Jacob,
who gave us this cistern and drank from it himself
with his children and his flocks?"
Jesus answered and said to her,
"Everyone who drinks this water will be thirsty again;
but whoever drinks the water I shall give will never thirst;
the water I shall give will become in him
a spring of water welling up to eternal life."
The woman said to him,
"Sir, give me this water, so that I may not be thirsty
or have to keep coming here to draw water."

Jesus said to her,
"Go call your husband and come back."
The woman answered and said to him,
"I do not have a husband."

Jesus answered her,
"You are right in saying, 'I do not have a husband.'
For you have had five husbands,
and the one you have now is not your husband.
What you have said is true."
The woman said to him,
"Sir, I can see that you are a prophet.
Our ancestors worshiped on this mountain;
but you people say that the place to worship is in Jerusalem."
Jesus said to her,
"Believe me, woman, the hour is coming
when you will worship the Father
neither on this mountain nor in Jerusalem.
You people worship what you do not understand;
we worship what we understand,
because salvation is from the Jews.
But the hour is coming, and is now here,
when true worshipers will worship the Father in Spirit and truth;
and indeed the Father seeks such people to worship him.
God is Spirit, and those who worship him
must worship in Spirit and truth."
The woman said to him,
"I know that the Messiah is coming, the one called the Christ;
when he comes, he will tell us everything."
Jesus said to her,
"I am he, the one speaking with you."

At that moment his disciples returned,
and were amazed that he was talking with a woman,
but still no one said, "What are you looking for?"
or "Why are you talking with her?"
The woman left her water jar
and went into the town and said to the people,
"Come see a man who told me everything I have done.
Could he possibly be the Christ?"
They went out of the town and came to him.
Meanwhile, the disciples urged him, "Rabbi, eat."
But he said to them,
"I have food to eat of which you do not know."
So the disciples said to one another,
"Could someone have brought him something to eat?"
Jesus said to them,
"My food is to do the will of the one who sent me
and to finish his work.
Do you not say, 'In four months the harvest will be here'?
I tell you, look up and see the fields ripe for the harvest.
The reaper is already receiving payment
and gathering crops for eternal life,
so that the sower and reaper can rejoice together.
For here the saying is verified that 'One sows and another reaps.'
I sent you to reap what you have not worked for;
others have done the work,
and you are sharing the fruits of their work."

Many of the Samaritans of that town began to believe in him
because of the word of the woman who testified,
"He told me everything I have done."
When the Samaritans came to him,
they invited him to stay with them;
and he stayed there two days.
Many more began to believe in him because of his word,
and they said to the woman,
"We no longer believe because of your word;
for we have heard for ourselves,
and we know that this is truly the savior of the world."

or

John 4:5-15, 19b-26, 39a, 40-42; L28A

Jesus came to a town of Samaria called Sychar,
near the plot of land that Jacob had given to his son Joseph.
Jacob's well was there.
Jesus, tired from his journey, sat down there at the well.
It was about noon.

A woman of Samaria came to draw water.
Jesus said to her,
"Give me a drink."
His disciples had gone into the town to buy food.
The Samaritan woman said to him,
"How can you, a Jew, ask me, a Samaritan woman, for a drink?"
—For Jews use nothing in common with Samaritans.—
Jesus answered and said to her,
"If you knew the gift of God
and who is saying to you, 'Give me a drink,'
you would have asked him
and he would have given you living water."
The woman said to him,
"Sir, you do not even have a bucket and the cistern is deep;
where then can you get this living water?
Are you greater than our father Jacob,
who gave us this cistern and drank from it himself
with his children and his flocks?"
Jesus answered and said to her,
"Everyone who drinks this water will be thirsty again;
but whoever drinks the water I shall give will never thirst;
the water I shall give will become in him
a spring of water welling up to eternal life."
The woman said to him,
"Sir, give me this water, so that I may not be thirsty
or have to keep coming here to draw water.

"I can see that you are a prophet.
Our ancestors worshiped on this mountain;
but you people say that the place to worship is in Jerusalem."
Jesus said to her,
"Believe me, woman, the hour is coming
when you will worship the Father
neither on this mountain nor in Jerusalem.
You people worship what you do not understand;
we worship what we understand,
because salvation is from the Jews.

***Third Sunday of Lent,** February 28, 2027 (cont.)*

Gospel (cont.)

John 4:5-15, 19b-26, 39a, 40-42; L28A

But the hour is coming, and is now here,
when true worshipers will worship the Father in Spirit and truth;
and indeed the Father seeks such people to worship him.
God is Spirit, and those who worship him
must worship in Spirit and truth."
The woman said to him,
"I know that the Messiah is coming, the one called the Christ;
when he comes, he will tell us everything."
Jesus said to her,
"I am he, the one who is speaking with you."

Many of the Samaritans of that town began to believe in him.
When the Samaritans came to him,
they invited him to stay with them;
and he stayed there two days.
Many more began to believe in him because of his word,
and they said to the woman,
"We no longer believe because of your word;
for we have heard for ourselves,
and we know that this is truly the savior of the world."

***Fourth Sunday of Lent,** March 7, 2027*

SECOND READING

Eph 2:4-10

Brothers and sisters:
God, who is rich in mercy,
because of the great love he had for us,
even when we were dead in our transgressions,
brought us to life with Christ—by grace you have been saved—,
raised us up with him,
and seated us with him in the heavens in Christ Jesus,
that in the ages to come
he might show the immeasurable riches of his grace
in his kindness to us in Christ Jesus.
For by grace you have been saved through faith,
and this is not from you; it is the gift of God;
it is not from works, so no one may boast.
For we are his handiwork, created in Christ Jesus for the good works
that God has prepared in advance,
that we should live in them.

Other readings on next page.

Fourth Sunday of Lent, *March 7, 2027 (cont.)*

These Year A readings may be used in place of Year B readings.
They are always used for assemblies celebrating the Scrutinies for the OCIA.

FIRST READING
1 Sam 16:1b, 6-7, 10-13a

The LORD said to Samuel:
"Fill your horn with oil, and be on your way.
I am sending you to Jesse of Bethlehem,
for I have chosen my king from among his sons."

As Jesse and his sons came to the sacrifice,
Samuel looked at Eliab and thought,
"Surely the LORD's anointed is here before him."
But the LORD said to Samuel:
"Do not judge from his appearance or from his lofty stature,
because I have rejected him.
Not as man sees does God see,
because man sees the appearance
but the LORD looks into the heart."
In the same way Jesse presented seven sons before Samuel,
but Samuel said to Jesse,
"The LORD has not chosen any one of these."
Then Samuel asked Jesse,
"Are these all the sons you have?"
Jesse replied,
"There is still the youngest, who is tending the sheep."
Samuel said to Jesse,
"Send for him;
we will not begin the sacrificial banquet until he arrives here."
Jesse sent and had the young man brought to them.
He was ruddy, a youth handsome to behold
and making a splendid appearance.
The LORD said,
"There—anoint him, for this is the one!"
Then Samuel, with the horn of oil in hand,
anointed David in the presence of his brothers;
and from that day on, the spirit of the LORD rushed upon David.

RESPONSORIAL PSALM
Ps 23:1-3a, 3b-4, 5, 6

℟. (1) The Lord is my shepherd; there is nothing I shall want.

The LORD is my shepherd; I shall not want.
In verdant pastures he gives me repose;
beside restful waters he leads me;
he refreshes my soul.

℟. The Lord is my shepherd; there is nothing I shall want.

He guides me in right paths
for his name's sake.
Even though I walk in the dark valley
I fear no evil; for you are at my side
with your rod and your staff
that give me courage.

℟. The Lord is my shepherd; there is nothing I shall want.

You spread the table before me
in the sight of my foes;
you anoint my head with oil;
my cup overflows.

℟. The Lord is my shepherd; there is nothing I shall want.

Only goodness and kindness follow me
all the days of my life;
and I shall dwell in the house of the LORD
for years to come.

℟. The Lord is my shepherd; there is nothing I shall want.

SECOND READING
Eph 5:8-14

Brothers and sisters:
You were once darkness,
but now you are light in the Lord.
Live as children of light,
for light produces every kind of goodness
and righteousness and truth.
Try to learn what is pleasing to the Lord.
Take no part in the fruitless works of darkness;
rather expose them, for it is shameful even to mention
the things done by them in secret;
but everything exposed by the light becomes visible,
for everything that becomes visible is light.
Therefore, it says:
"Awake, O sleeper,
and arise from the dead,
and Christ will give you light."

Gospel reading on next page.

Gospel

John 9:1-41; L31A

As Jesus passed by he saw a man blind from birth.
His disciples asked him,
"Rabbi, who sinned, this man or his parents,
that he was born blind?"
Jesus answered,
"Neither he nor his parents sinned;
it is so that the works of God might be made visible through him.
We have to do the works of the one who sent me while it is day.
Night is coming when no one can work.
While I am in the world, I am the light of the world."
When he had said this, he spat on the ground
and made clay with the saliva,
and smeared the clay on his eyes, and said to him,
"Go wash in the Pool of Siloam"—which means Sent—.
So he went and washed, and came back able to see.

His neighbors and those who had seen him earlier as a beggar said,
"Isn't this the one who used to sit and beg?"
Some said, "It is,"
but others said, "No, he just looks like him."
He said, "I am."
So they said to him, "How were your eyes opened?"
He replied,
"The man called Jesus made clay and anointed my eyes
and told me, 'Go to Siloam and wash.'
So I went there and washed and was able to see."
And they said to him, "Where is he?"
He said, "I don't know."

They brought the one who was once blind to the Pharisees.
Now Jesus had made clay and opened his eyes on a sabbath.
So then the Pharisees also asked him how he was able to see.
He said to them,
"He put clay on my eyes, and I washed, and now I can see."
So some of the Pharisees said,
"This man is not from God,
because he does not keep the sabbath."
But others said,
"How can a sinful man do such signs?"
And there was a division among them.
So they said to the blind man again,
"What do you have to say about him,
since he opened your eyes?"
He said, "He is a prophet."

Now the Jews did not believe
that he had been blind and gained his sight
until they summoned the parents of the one who had gained his sight.
They asked them,
"Is this your son, who you say was born blind?
How does he now see?"
His parents answered and said,
"We know that this is our son and that he was born blind.
We do not know how he sees now,
nor do we know who opened his eyes.
Ask him, he is of age;
he can speak for himself."
His parents said this because they were afraid of the Jews,
for the Jews had already agreed
that if anyone acknowledged him as the Christ,
he would be expelled from the synagogue.
For this reason his parents said,
"He is of age; question him."

So a second time they called the man who had been blind
and said to him, "Give God the praise!
We know that this man is a sinner."
He replied,
"If he is a sinner, I do not know.
One thing I do know is that I was blind and now I see."
So they said to him,
"What did he do to you?
How did he open your eyes?"
He answered them,
"I told you already and you did not listen.
Why do you want to hear it again?
Do you want to become his disciples, too?"
They ridiculed him and said,
"You are that man's disciple;
we are disciples of Moses!
We know that God spoke to Moses,
but we do not know where this one is from."
The man answered and said to them,
"This is what is so amazing,
that you do not know where he is from, yet he opened my eyes.
We know that God does not listen to sinners,
but if one is devout and does his will, he listens to him.
It is unheard of that anyone ever opened the eyes of a person born blind.
If this man were not from God,
he would not be able to do anything."
They answered and said to him,
"You were born totally in sin,
and are you trying to teach us?"
Then they threw him out.

When Jesus heard that they had thrown him out,
he found him and said, "Do you believe in the Son of Man?"
He answered and said,
"Who is he, sir, that I may believe in him?"
Jesus said to him,
"You have seen him,
and the one speaking with you is he."
He said,
"I do believe, Lord," and he worshiped him.
Then Jesus said,
"I came into this world for judgment,
so that those who do not see might see,
and those who do see might become blind."

Fourth Sunday of Lent, March 7, 2027 (cont.)

Gospel (cont.)

John 9:1-41; L31A

Some of the Pharisees who were with him heard this
 and said to him, "Surely we are not also blind, are we?"
Jesus said to them,
 "If you were blind, you would have no sin;
 but now you are saying, 'We see,' so your sin remains."

or

John 9:1, 6-9, 13-17, 34-38; L31A

As Jesus passed by he saw a man blind from birth.
He spat on the ground and made clay with the saliva,
 and smeared the clay on his eyes, and said to him,
 "Go wash in the Pool of Siloam"—which means Sent—.
So he went and washed, and came back able to see.

His neighbors and those who had seen him earlier as a beggar said,
 "Isn't this the one who used to sit and beg?"
Some said, "It is,"
 but others said, "No, he just looks like him."
He said, "I am."

They brought the one who was once blind to the Pharisees.
Now Jesus had made clay and opened his eyes on a sabbath.
So then the Pharisees also asked him how he was able to see.
He said to them,
 "He put clay on my eyes, and I washed, and now I can see."

So some of the Pharisees said,
 "This man is not from God,
 because he does not keep the sabbath."
But others said,
 "How can a sinful man do such signs?"
And there was a division among them.
So they said to the blind man again,
 "What do you have to say about him,
 since he opened your eyes?"
He said, "He is a prophet."

They answered and said to him,
 "You were born totally in sin,
 and are you trying to teach us?"
Then they threw him out.

When Jesus heard that they had thrown him out,
 he found him and said, "Do you believe in the Son of Man?"
He answered and said,
 "Who is he, sir, that I may believe in him?"
Jesus said to him,
 "You have seen him,
 and the one speaking with you is he."
He said,
 "I do believe, Lord," and he worshiped him.

Fifth Sunday of Lent, March 8, 2027

Gospel (cont.)

John 12:20-33; L35B

The crowd there heard it and said it was thunder;
 but others said, "An angel has spoken to him."
Jesus answered and said,
 "This voice did not come for my sake but for yours.
Now is the time of judgment on this world;
 now the ruler of this world will be driven out.
And when I am lifted up from the earth,
 I will draw everyone to myself."
He said this indicating the kind of death he would die.

These Year A readings may be used in place of Year B readings. They are always used for assemblies celebrating the Scrutinies for the OCIA.

FIRST READING

Ezek 37:12-14

Thus says the Lord GOD:
 O my people, I will open your graves
 and have you rise from them,
 and bring you back to the land of Israel.
Then you shall know that I am the LORD,
 when I open your graves and have you rise from them,
 O my people!
I will put my spirit in you that you may live,
 and I will settle you upon your land;
 thus you shall know that I am the LORD.
I have promised, and I will do it, says the LORD.

Other readings on next page.

RESPONSORIAL PSALM
Ps 130:1-2, 3-4, 5-6, 7-8

℟. (7) With the Lord there is mercy and
fullness of redemption.

Out of the depths I cry to you, O Lord;
Lord, hear my voice!
Let your ears be attentive
to my voice in supplication.

℟. With the Lord there is mercy and
fullness of redemption.

If you, O Lord, mark iniquities,
Lord, who can stand?
But with you is forgiveness,
that you may be revered.

℟. With the Lord there is mercy and
fullness of redemption.

I trust in the Lord;
my soul trusts in his word.
More than sentinels wait for the dawn,
let Israel wait for the Lord.

℟. With the Lord there is mercy and
fullness of redemption.

For with the Lord is kindness
and with him is plenteous
redemption;
and he will redeem Israel
from all their iniquities.

℟. With the Lord there is mercy and
fullness of redemption.

SECOND READING
Rom 8:8-11

Brothers and sisters:
Those who are in the flesh cannot
please God.
But you are not in the flesh;
on the contrary, you are in the spirit,
if only the Spirit of God dwells in
you.
Whoever does not have the Spirit of
Christ does not belong to him.
But if Christ is in you,
although the body is dead because
of sin,
the spirit is alive because of
righteousness.
If the Spirit of the One who raised
Jesus from the dead dwells in you,
the One who raised Christ from the
dead
will give life to your mortal bodies
also,
through his Spirit dwelling in you.

Gospel
John 11:1-45; L34A

Now a man was ill, Lazarus from Bethany,
the village of Mary and her sister Martha.
Mary was the one who had anointed the Lord with perfumed
oil
and dried his feet with her hair;
it was her brother Lazarus who was ill.
So the sisters sent word to Jesus saying,
"Master, the one you love is ill."
When Jesus heard this he said,
"This illness is not to end in death,
but is for the glory of God,
that the Son of God may be glorified through it."
Now Jesus loved Martha and her sister and Lazarus.
So when he heard that he was ill,
he remained for two days in the place where he was.
Then after this he said to his disciples,
"Let us go back to Judea."
The disciples said to him,
"Rabbi, the Jews were just trying to stone you,
and you want to go back there?"
Jesus answered,
"Are there not twelve hours in a day?
If one walks during the day, he does not stumble,
because he sees the light of this world.
But if one walks at night, he stumbles,
because the light is not in him."
He said this, and then told them,
"Our friend Lazarus is asleep,
but I am going to awaken him."
So the disciples said to him,
"Master, if he is asleep, he will be saved."
But Jesus was talking about his death,
while they thought that he meant ordinary sleep.
So then Jesus said to them clearly,
"Lazarus has died.
And I am glad for you that I was not there,
that you may believe.
Let us go to him."
So Thomas, called Didymus, said to his fellow disciples,
"Let us also go to die with him."

When Jesus arrived, he found that Lazarus
had already been in the tomb for four days.
Now Bethany was near Jerusalem, only about two miles
away.
And many of the Jews had come to Martha and Mary
to comfort them about their brother.
When Martha heard that Jesus was coming,
she went to meet him;
but Mary sat at home.
Martha said to Jesus,
"Lord, if you had been here,
my brother would not have died.
But even now I know that whatever you ask of God,
God will give you."
Jesus said to her,
"Your brother will rise."
Martha said to him,
"I know he will rise,
in the resurrection on the last day."
Jesus told her,
"I am the resurrection and the life;
whoever believes in me, even if he dies, will live,

and everyone who lives and believes in me will never die.
Do you believe this?"
She said to him, "Yes, Lord.
I have come to believe that you are the Christ, the Son of God,
the one who is coming into the world."

When she had said this,
she went and called her sister Mary secretly, saying,
"The teacher is here and is asking for you."
As soon as she heard this,
she rose quickly and went to him.
For Jesus had not yet come into the village,
but was still where Martha had met him.
So when the Jews who were with her in the house comforting her
saw Mary get up quickly and go out,
they followed her,
presuming that she was going to the tomb to weep there.
When Mary came to where Jesus was and saw him,
she fell at his feet and said to him,
"Lord, if you had been here,
my brother would not have died."
When Jesus saw her weeping and the Jews who had come with her weeping,
he became perturbed and deeply troubled, and said,
"Where have you laid him?"
They said to him, "Sir, come and see."
And Jesus wept.
So the Jews said, "See how he loved him."
But some of them said,
"Could not the one who opened the eyes of the blind man
have done something so that this man would not have died?"

So Jesus, perturbed again, came to the tomb.
It was a cave, and a stone lay across it.
Jesus said, "Take away the stone."
Martha, the dead man's sister, said to him,
"Lord, by now there will be a stench;
he has been dead for four days."
Jesus said to her,
"Did I not tell you that if you believe
you will see the glory of God?"
So they took away the stone.
And Jesus raised his eyes and said,
"Father, I thank you for hearing me.
I know that you always hear me;
but because of the crowd here I have said this,
that they may believe that you sent me."
And when he had said this,
he cried out in a loud voice,
"Lazarus, come out!"
The dead man came out,
tied hand and foot with burial bands,
and his face was wrapped in a cloth.
So Jesus said to them,
"Untie him and let him go."

Now many of the Jews who had come to Mary
and seen what he had done began to believe in him.

or

Gospel

John 11:3-7, 17, 20-27, 33b-45; L34A

The sisters of Lazarus sent word to Jesus saying,
"Master, the one you love is ill."
When Jesus heard this he said,
"This illness is not to end in death,
but is for the glory of God,
that the Son of God may be glorified through it."
Now Jesus loved Martha and her sister and Lazarus.
So when he heard that he was ill,
he remained for two days in the place where he was.
Then after this he said to his disciples,
"Let us go back to Judea."

When Jesus arrived, he found that Lazarus
had already been in the tomb for four days.
When Martha heard that Jesus was coming,
she went to meet him;
but Mary sat at home.
Martha said to Jesus,
"Lord, if you had been here,
my brother would not have died.
But even now I know that whatever you ask of God,
God will give you."
Jesus said to her,
"Your brother will rise."
Martha said,
"I know he will rise,
in the resurrection on the last day."
Jesus told her,
"I am the resurrection and the life;
whoever believes in me, even if he dies, will live,
and everyone who lives and believes in me will never die.
Do you believe this?"
She said to him, "Yes, Lord.
I have come to believe that you are the Christ, the Son of God,
the one who is coming into the world."

He became perturbed and deeply troubled, and said,
"Where have you laid him?"
They said to him, "Sir, come and see."
And Jesus wept.
So the Jews said, "See how he loved him."
But some of them said,
"Could not the one who opened the eyes of the blind man
have done something so that this man would not have died?"

So Jesus, perturbed again, came to the tomb.
It was a cave, and a stone lay across it.
Jesus said, "Take away the stone."
Martha, the dead man's sister, said to him,
"Lord, by now there will be a stench;
he has been dead for four days."
Jesus said to her,
"Did I not tell you that if you believe
you will see the glory of God?"
So they took away the stone.

And Jesus raised his eyes and said,
"Father, I thank you for hearing me.
I know that you always hear me;
but because of the crowd here I have said this,
that they may believe that you sent me."
And when he had said this,
he cried out in a loud voice,
"Lazarus, come out!"
The dead man came out,
tied hand and foot with burial bands,
and his face was wrapped in a cloth.
So Jesus said to them,
"Untie him and let him go."

Now many of the Jews who had come to Mary
and seen what he had done began to believe in him.

Saint Joseph, Spouse of the Blessed Virgin Mary, *March 19, 2027*

Gospel

Luke 2:41-51a; L543

Each year Jesus' parents went to Jerusalem for the feast of Passover,
and when he was twelve years old,
they went up according to festival custom.
After they had completed its days, as they were returning,
the boy Jesus remained behind in Jerusalem,
but his parents did not know it.
Thinking that he was in the caravan,
they journeyed for a day
and looked for him among their relatives and acquaintances,
but not finding him,
they returned to Jerusalem to look for him.
After three days they found him in the temple,
sitting in the midst of the teachers,
listening to them and asking them questions,
and all who heard him were astounded
at his understanding and his answers.
When his parents saw him,
they were astonished,
and his mother said to him,
"Son, why have you done this to us?
Your father and I have been looking for you with great anxiety."
And he said to them,
"Why were you looking for me?
Did you not know that I must be in my Father's house?"
But they did not understand what he said to them.
He went down with them and came to Nazareth,
and was obedient to them.

FIRST READING
2 Sam 7:4-5a, 12-14a, 16

The LORD spoke to Nathan and said:
"Go, tell my servant David,
'When your time comes and you rest with your ancestors,
I will raise up your heir after you, sprung from your loins,
and I will make his kingdom firm.
It is he who shall build a house for my name.
And I will make his royal throne firm forever.
I will be a father to him,
and he shall be a son to me.
Your house and your kingdom shall endure forever before me;
your throne shall stand firm forever.' "

RESPONSORIAL PSALM
Ps 89:2-3, 4-5, 27 and 29

℟. (37) The son of David will live for ever.

The promises of the LORD I will sing forever,
through all generations my mouth will proclaim your faithfulness,
For you have said, "My kindness is established forever";
in heaven you have confirmed your faithfulness.

℟. The son of David will live for ever.

"I have made a covenant with my chosen one,
I have sworn to David my servant:
Forever will I confirm your posterity
and establish your throne for all generations."

℟. The son of David will live for ever.

"He shall say of me, 'You are my father,
my God, the Rock, my savior.'
Forever I will maintain my kindness toward him,
and my covenant with him stands firm."

℟. The son of David will live for ever.

SECOND READING
Rom 4:13, 16-18, 22

Brothers and sisters:
It was not through the law
that the promise was made to Abraham and his descendants
that he would inherit the world,
but through the righteousness that comes from faith.
For this reason, it depends on faith,
so that it may be a gift,
and the promise may be guaranteed to all his descendants,
not to those who only adhere to the law
but to those who follow the faith of Abraham,
who is the father of all of us, as it is written,
I have made you father of many nations.
He is our father in the sight of God,
in whom he believed, who gives life to the dead
and calls into being what does not exist.
He believed, hoping against hope,
that he would become *the father of many nations,*
according to what was said, *Thus shall your descendants be.*
That is why *it was credited to him as righteousness.*

Gospel (cont.) at the procession with palms

Some of the bystanders said to them,
"What are you doing, untying the colt?"
They answered them just as Jesus had told them to,
and they permitted them to do it.
So they brought the colt to Jesus
and put their cloaks over it.
And he sat on it.
Many people spread their cloaks on the road,
and others spread leafy branches
that they had cut from the fields.
Those preceding him as well as those following kept crying out:
"Hosanna!
Blessed is he who comes in the name of the Lord!
Blessed is the kingdom of our father David that is to come!
Hosanna in the highest!"

Gospel at Mass
Mark 14:1–15:47; L38B

The Passover and the Feast of Unleavened Bread
were to take place in two days' time.
So the chief priests and the scribes were seeking a way
to arrest him by treachery and put him to death.
They said, "Not during the festival,
for fear that there may be a riot among the people."

When he was in Bethany reclining at table
in the house of Simon the leper,
a woman came with an alabaster jar of perfumed oil,
costly genuine spikenard.
She broke the alabaster jar and poured it on his head.
There were some who were indignant.
"Why has there been this waste of perfumed oil?
It could have been sold for more than three hundred days' wages
and the money given to the poor."
They were infuriated with her.
Jesus said, "Let her alone.
Why do you make trouble for her?
She has done a good thing for me.
The poor you will always have with you,
and whenever you wish you can do good to them,
but you will not always have me.
She has done what she could.
She has anticipated anointing my body for burial.
Amen, I say to you,
wherever the gospel is proclaimed to the whole world,
what she has done will be told in memory of her."

Then Judas Iscariot, one of the Twelve,
went off to the chief priests to hand him over to them.
When they heard him they were pleased and promised to pay him money.
Then he looked for an opportunity to hand him over.

On the first day of the Feast of Unleavened Bread,
when they sacrificed the Passover lamb,
his disciples said to him,
"Where do you want us to go
and prepare for you to eat the Passover?"
He sent two of his disciples and said to them,
"Go into the city and a man will meet you,
carrying a jar of water.
Follow him.
Wherever he enters, say to the master of the house,
'The Teacher says, "Where is my guest room
where I may eat the Passover with my disciples?"'
Then he will show you a large upper room furnished and ready.
Make the preparations for us there."
The disciples then went off, entered the city,
and found it just as he had told them;
and they prepared the Passover.

When it was evening, he came with the Twelve.
And as they reclined at table and were eating, Jesus said,
"Amen, I say to you, one of you will betray me,
one who is eating with me."
They began to be distressed and to say to him, one by one,
"Surely it is not I?"
He said to them,
"One of the Twelve, the one who dips with me into the dish.
For the Son of Man indeed goes, as it is written of him,
but woe to that man by whom the Son of Man is betrayed.
It would be better for that man if he had never been born."

While they were eating,
he took bread, said the blessing,
broke it, and gave it to them, and said,
"Take it; this is my body."
Then he took a cup, gave thanks, and gave it to them,
and they all drank from it.
He said to them,
"This is my blood of the covenant,
which will be shed for many.
Amen, I say to you,
I shall not drink again the fruit of the vine
until the day when I drink it new in the kingdom of God."
Then, after singing a hymn,
they went out to the Mount of Olives.

Then Jesus said to them,
"All of you will have your faith shaken, for it is written:
I will strike the shepherd,
and the sheep will be dispersed.
But after I have been raised up,
I shall go before you to Galilee."
Peter said to him,
"Even though all should have their faith shaken,
mine will not be."
Then Jesus said to him,
"Amen, I say to you,
this very night before the cock crows twice
you will deny me three times."
But he vehemently replied,
"Even though I should have to die with you,
I will not deny you."
And they all spoke similarly.

Then they came to a place named Gethsemane,
and he said to his disciples,
"Sit here while I pray."
He took with him Peter, James, and John,
and began to be troubled and distressed.
Then he said to them, "My soul is sorrowful even to death.
Remain here and keep watch."
He advanced a little and fell to the ground and prayed
that if it were possible the hour might pass by him;
he said, "Abba, Father, all things are possible to you.
Take this cup away from me,
but not what I will but what you will."
When he returned he found them asleep.
He said to Peter, "Simon, are you asleep?
Could you not keep watch for one hour?
Watch and pray that you may not undergo the test.
The spirit is willing but the flesh is weak."
Withdrawing again, he prayed, saying the same thing.
Then he returned once more and found them asleep,
for they could not keep their eyes open
and did not know what to answer him.
He returned a third time and said to them,
"Are you still sleeping and taking your rest?
It is enough. The hour has come.
Behold, the Son of Man is to be handed over to sinners.
Get up, let us go.
See, my betrayer is at hand."

Then, while he was still speaking,
Judas, one of the Twelve, arrived,
accompanied by a crowd with swords and clubs
who had come from the chief priests,
the scribes, and the elders.
His betrayer had arranged a signal with them, saying,
"The man I shall kiss is the one;
arrest him and lead him away securely."
He came and immediately went over to him and said,
"Rabbi." And he kissed him.
At this they laid hands on him and arrested him.
One of the bystanders drew his sword,
struck the high priest's servant, and cut off his ear.
Jesus said to them in reply,
"Have you come out as against a robber,
with swords and clubs, to seize me?
Day after day I was with you teaching in the temple area,
yet you did not arrest me;
but that the Scriptures may be fulfilled."
And they all left him and fled.
Now a young man followed him
wearing nothing but a linen cloth about his body.
They seized him,
but he left the cloth behind and ran off naked.

They led Jesus away to the high priest,
and all the chief priests and the elders and the scribes came together.
Peter followed him at a distance into the high priest's courtyard
and was seated with the guards, warming himself at the fire.
The chief priests and the entire Sanhedrin
kept trying to obtain testimony against Jesus
in order to put him to death, but they found none.
Many gave false witness against him,
but their testimony did not agree.
Some took the stand and testified falsely against him,
alleging, "We heard him say,
'I will destroy this temple made with hands
and within three days I will build another
not made with hands.' "
Even so their testimony did not agree.
The high priest rose before the assembly and questioned Jesus,
saying, "Have you no answer?
What are these men testifying against you?"
But he was silent and answered nothing.
Again the high priest asked him and said to him,
"Are you the Christ, the son of the Blessed One?"
Then Jesus answered, "I am;
and 'you will see the Son of Man
seated at the right hand of the Power
and coming with the clouds of heaven.' "
At that the high priest tore his garments and said,
"What further need have we of witnesses?
You have heard the blasphemy.
What do you think?"
They all condemned him as deserving to die.
Some began to spit on him.
They blindfolded him and struck him and said to him, "Prophesy!"
And the guards greeted him with blows.

While Peter was below in the courtyard,
one of the high priest's maids came along.
Seeing Peter warming himself,
she looked intently at him and said,
"You too were with the Nazarene, Jesus."
But he denied it saying,
"I neither know nor understand what you are talking about."
So he went out into the outer court.
Then the cock crowed.
The maid saw him and began again to say to the bystanders,
"This man is one of them."
Once again he denied it.
A little later the bystanders said to Peter once more,
"Surely you are one of them; for you too are a Galilean."
He began to curse and to swear,
"I do not know this man about whom you are talking."
And immediately a cock crowed a second time.
Then Peter remembered the word that Jesus had said to him,
"Before the cock crows twice you will deny me three times."
He broke down and wept.

As soon as morning came,
the chief priests with the elders and the scribes,
that is, the whole Sanhedrin, held a council.
They bound Jesus, led him away, and handed him over to Pilate.

Pilate questioned him,
"Are you the king of the Jews?"
He said to him in reply, "You say so."
The chief priests accused him of many things.
Again Pilate questioned him,
"Have you no answer?
See how many things they accuse you of."
Jesus gave him no further answer, so that Pilate was amazed.

Now on the occasion of the feast he used to release to them one prisoner whom they requested.
A man called Barabbas was then in prison
along with the rebels who had committed murder in a rebellion.
The crowd came forward and began to ask him
to do for them as he was accustomed.
Pilate answered,
"Do you want me to release to you the king of the Jews?"
For he knew that it was out of envy
that the chief priests had handed him over.
But the chief priests stirred up the crowd
to have him release Barabbas for them instead.
Pilate again said to them in reply,
"Then what do you want me to do
with the man you call the king of the Jews?"
They shouted again, "Crucify him."
Pilate said to them, "Why? What evil has he done?"
They only shouted the louder, "Crucify him."
So Pilate, wishing to satisfy the crowd,
released Barabbas to them and, after he had Jesus scourged,
handed him over to be crucified.

The soldiers led him away inside the palace,
that is, the praetorium, and assembled the whole cohort.
They clothed him in purple and,
weaving a crown of thorns, placed it on him.
They began to salute him with, "Hail, King of the Jews!"
and kept striking his head with a reed and spitting upon him.
They knelt before him in homage.
And when they had mocked him,
they stripped him of the purple cloak,
dressed him in his own clothes,
and led him out to crucify him.

They pressed into service a passer-by, Simon,
a Cyrenian, who was coming in from the country,
the father of Alexander and Rufus,
to carry his cross.

They brought him to the place of Golgotha
—which is translated Place of the Skull—.
They gave him wine drugged with myrrh,
but he did not take it.
Then they crucified him and divided his garments
by casting lots for them to see what each should take.
It was nine o'clock in the morning when they crucified him.
The inscription of the charge against him read,
"The King of the Jews."
With him they crucified two revolutionaries,
one on his right and one on his left.
Those passing by reviled him,
shaking their heads and saying,
"Aha! You who would destroy the temple
and rebuild it in three days,
save yourself by coming down from the cross."
Likewise the chief priests, with the scribes,
mocked him among themselves and said,
"He saved others; he cannot save himself.
Let the Christ, the King of Israel,
come down now from the cross
that we may see and believe."
Those who were crucified with him also kept abusing him.

At noon darkness came over the whole land
until three in the afternoon.
And at three o'clock Jesus cried out in a loud voice,
"Eloi, Eloi, lema sabachthani?"
which is translated,
"My God, my God, why have you forsaken me?"
Some of the bystanders who heard it said,
"Look, he is calling Elijah."
One of them ran, soaked a sponge with wine, put it on a reed
and gave it to him to drink saying,
"Wait, let us see if Elijah comes to take him down."
Jesus gave a loud cry and breathed his last.

Here all kneel and pause for a short time.

The veil of the sanctuary was torn in two from top to bottom.
When the centurion who stood facing him
saw how he breathed his last he said,
"Truly this man was the Son of God!"
There were also women looking on from a distance.
Among them were Mary Magdalene,
Mary the mother of the younger James and of Joses, and Salome.
These women had followed him when he was in Galilee
and ministered to him.
There were also many other women
who had come up with him to Jerusalem.

When it was already evening,
since it was the day of preparation,
the day before the sabbath, Joseph of Arimathea,
a distinguished member of the council,
who was himself awaiting the kingdom of God,
came and courageously went to Pilate
and asked for the body of Jesus.
Pilate was amazed that he was already dead.
He summoned the centurion
and asked him if Jesus had already died.
And when he learned of it from the centurion,
he gave the body to Joseph.
Having bought a linen cloth, he took him down,
wrapped him in the linen cloth,
and laid him in a tomb that had been hewn out of the rock.

Then he rolled a stone against the entrance to the tomb.
Mary Magdalene and Mary the mother of Joses
watched where he was laid.

or

Mark 15:1-39; L38B

As soon as morning came,
the chief priests with the elders and the scribes,
that is, the whole Sanhedrin, held a council.
They bound Jesus, led him away, and handed him over to Pilate.
Pilate questioned him,
"Are you the king of the Jews?"
He said to him in reply, "You say so."
The chief priests accused him of many things.
Again Pilate questioned him,
"Have you no answer?
See how many things they accuse you of."
Jesus gave him no further answer, so that Pilate was amazed.

Now on the occasion of the feast he used to release to them
one prisoner whom they requested.
A man called Barabbas was then in prison
along with the rebels who had committed murder in a rebellion.
The crowd came forward and began to ask him
to do for them as he was accustomed.
Pilate answered,
"Do you want me to release to you the king of the Jews?"
For he knew that it was out of envy
that the chief priests had handed him over.
But the chief priests stirred up the crowd
to have him release Barabbas for them instead.
Pilate again said to them in reply,
"Then what do you want me to do
with the man you call the king of the Jews?"
They shouted again, "Crucify him."
Pilate said to them, "Why? What evil has he done?"
They only shouted the louder, "Crucify him."
So Pilate, wishing to satisfy the crowd,
released Barabbas to them and, after he had Jesus scourged,
handed him over to be crucified.

The soldiers led him away inside the palace,
that is, the praetorium, and assembled the whole cohort.
They clothed him in purple and,
weaving a crown of thorns, placed it on him.
They began to salute him with, "Hail, King of the Jews!"
and kept striking his head with a reed and spitting upon him.
They knelt before him in homage.
And when they had mocked him,
they stripped him of the purple cloak,
dressed him in his own clothes,
and led him out to crucify him.

They pressed into service a passer-by, Simon,
a Cyrenian, who was coming in from the country,
the father of Alexander and Rufus,
to carry his cross.

They brought him to the place of Golgotha
—which is translated Place of the Skull—.
They gave him wine drugged with myrrh,
but he did not take it.
Then they crucified him and divided his garments
by casting lots for them to see what each should take.
It was nine o'clock in the morning when they crucified him.
The inscription of the charge against him read,
"The King of the Jews."
With him they crucified two revolutionaries,
one on his right and one on his left.
Those passing by reviled him,
shaking their heads and saying,
"Aha! You who would destroy the temple
and rebuild it in three days,
save yourself by coming down from the cross."
Likewise the chief priests, with the scribes,
mocked him among themselves and said,
"He saved others; he cannot save himself.
Let the Christ, the King of Israel,
come down now from the cross
that we may see and believe."
Those who were crucified with him also kept abusing him.

At noon darkness came over the whole land
until three in the afternoon.
And at three o'clock Jesus cried out in a loud voice,
"Eloi, Eloi, lema sabachthani?"
which is translated,
"My God, my God, why have you forsaken me?"
Some of the bystanders who heard it said,
"Look, he is calling Elijah."
One of them ran, soaked a sponge with wine, put it on a reed
and gave it to him to drink saying,
"Wait, let us see if Elijah comes to take him down."
Jesus gave a loud cry and breathed his last.

Here all kneel and pause for a short time.

The veil of the sanctuary was torn in two from top to bottom.
When the centurion who stood facing him
saw how he breathed his last he said,
"Truly this man was the Son of God!"

Gospel (cont.)

John 13:1-15; L39ABC

Jesus said to him,
"Whoever has bathed has no need except to have his feet washed,
for he is clean all over;
so you are clean, but not all."
For he knew who would betray him;
for this reason, he said, "Not all of you are clean."

So when he had washed their feet
and put his garments back on and reclined at table again,
he said to them, "Do you realize what I have done for you?
You call me 'teacher' and 'master,' and rightly so, for indeed I am.
If I, therefore, the master and teacher, have washed your feet,
you ought to wash one another's feet.
I have given you a model to follow,
so that as I have done for you, you should also do."

FIRST READING

Exod 12:1-8, 11-14

The LORD said to Moses and Aaron in the land of Egypt,
"This month shall stand at the head of your calendar;
you shall reckon it the first month of the year.
Tell the whole community of Israel:
On the tenth of this month every one of your families
must procure for itself a lamb, one apiece for each household.
If a family is too small for a whole lamb,
it shall join the nearest household in procuring one
and shall share in the lamb
in proportion to the number of persons who partake of it.
The lamb must be a year-old male and without blemish.
You may take it from either the sheep or the goats.
You shall keep it until the fourteenth day of this month,
and then, with the whole assembly of Israel present,
it shall be slaughtered during the evening twilight.
They shall take some of its blood
and apply it to the two doorposts and the lintel
of every house in which they partake of the lamb.
That same night they shall eat its roasted flesh
with unleavened bread and bitter herbs.

"This is how you are to eat it:
with your loins girt, sandals on your feet and your staff in hand,
you shall eat like those who are in flight.
It is the Passover of the LORD.
For on this same night I will go through Egypt,
striking down every firstborn of the land, both man and beast,
and executing judgment on all the gods of Egypt—I, the LORD!
But the blood will mark the houses where you are.
Seeing the blood, I will pass over you;
thus, when I strike the land of Egypt,
no destructive blow will come upon you.

"This day shall be a memorial feast for you,
which all your generations shall celebrate
with pilgrimage to the LORD, as a perpetual institution."

RESPONSORIAL PSALM

Ps 116:12-13, 15-16bc, 17-18

℟. (cf. 1 Cor 10:16) Our blessing-cup is a communion with the Blood of Christ.

How shall I make a return to the LORD
for all the good he has done for me?
The cup of salvation I will take up,
and I will call upon the name of the LORD.

℟. Our blessing-cup is a communion with the Blood of Christ.

Precious in the eyes of the LORD
is the death of his faithful ones.
I am your servant, the son of your handmaid;
you have loosed my bonds.

℟. Our blessing-cup is a communion with the Blood of Christ.

To you will I offer sacrifice of thanksgiving,
and I will call upon the name of the LORD.
My vows to the LORD I will pay
in the presence of all his people.

℟. Our blessing-cup is a communion with the Blood of Christ.

SECOND READING

1 Cor 11:23-26

Brothers and sisters:
I received from the Lord what I also handed on to you,
that the Lord Jesus, on the night he was handed over,
took bread, and, after he had given thanks,
broke it and said, "This is my body that is for you.
Do this in remembrance of me."
In the same way also the cup, after supper, saying,
"This cup is the new covenant in my blood.
Do this, as often as you drink it, in remembrance of me."
For as often as you eat this bread and drink the cup,
you proclaim the death of the Lord until he comes.

Gospel (cont.)

John 18:1–19:42; L40ABC

So he again asked them,
"Whom are you looking for?"
They said, "Jesus the Nazorean."
Jesus answered,
"I told you that I AM.
So if you are looking for me, let these men go."
This was to fulfill what he had said,
"I have not lost any of those you gave me."
Then Simon Peter, who had a sword, drew it,
struck the high priest's slave, and cut off his right ear.
The slave's name was Malchus.
Jesus said to Peter,
"Put your sword into its scabbard.
Shall I not drink the cup that the Father gave me?"

So the band of soldiers, the tribune, and the Jewish guards seized Jesus,
bound him, and brought him to Annas first.
He was the father-in-law of Caiaphas,
who was high priest that year.
It was Caiaphas who had counseled the Jews
that it was better that one man should die rather than the people.

Simon Peter and another disciple followed Jesus.
Now the other disciple was known to the high priest,
and he entered the courtyard of the high priest with Jesus.
But Peter stood at the gate outside.
So the other disciple, the acquaintance of the high priest,
went out and spoke to the gatekeeper and brought Peter in.
Then the maid who was the gatekeeper said to Peter,
"You are not one of this man's disciples, are you?"
He said, "I am not."
Now the slaves and the guards were standing around a charcoal fire
that they had made, because it was cold,
and were warming themselves.
Peter was also standing there keeping warm.

The high priest questioned Jesus
about his disciples and about his doctrine.
Jesus answered him,
"I have spoken publicly to the world.
I have always taught in a synagogue
or in the temple area where all the Jews gather,
and in secret I have said nothing. Why ask me?
Ask those who heard me what I said to them.
They know what I said."
When he had said this,
one of the temple guards standing there struck Jesus and said,
"Is this the way you answer the high priest?"
Jesus answered him,
"If I have spoken wrongly, testify to the wrong;
but if I have spoken rightly, why do you strike me?"
Then Annas sent him bound to Caiaphas the high priest.

Now Simon Peter was standing there keeping warm.
And they said to him,
"You are not one of his disciples, are you?"
He denied it and said,
"I am not."
One of the slaves of the high priest,
a relative of the one whose ear Peter had cut off, said,
"Didn't I see you in the garden with him?"
Again Peter denied it.
And immediately the cock crowed.

Then they brought Jesus from Caiaphas to the praetorium.
It was morning.
And they themselves did not enter the praetorium,
in order not to be defiled so that they could eat the Passover.
So Pilate came out to them and said,
"What charge do you bring against this man?"
They answered and said to him,
"If he were not a criminal,
we would not have handed him over to you."
At this, Pilate said to them,
"Take him yourselves, and judge him according to your law."
The Jews answered him,
"We do not have the right to execute anyone,"
in order that the word of Jesus might be fulfilled
that he said indicating the kind of death he would die.
So Pilate went back into the praetorium
and summoned Jesus and said to him,
"Are you the King of the Jews?"
Jesus answered,
"Do you say this on your own
or have others told you about me?"
Pilate answered,
"I am not a Jew, am I?
Your own nation and the chief priests handed you over to me.
What have you done?"
Jesus answered,
"My kingdom does not belong to this world.
If my kingdom did belong to this world,
my attendants would be fighting
to keep me from being handed over to the Jews.
But as it is, my kingdom is not here."
So Pilate said to him,
"Then you are a king?"
Jesus answered,
"You say I am a king.
For this I was born and for this I came into the world,
to testify to the truth.
Everyone who belongs to the truth listens to my voice."
Pilate said to him, "What is truth?"

When he had said this,
he again went out to the Jews and said to them,
"I find no guilt in him.
But you have a custom that I release one prisoner to you at Passover.
Do you want me to release to you the King of the Jews?"
They cried out again,
"Not this one but Barabbas!"
Now Barabbas was a revolutionary.

Then Pilate took Jesus and had him scourged.
And the soldiers wove a crown out of thorns and placed it on his head,

and clothed him in a purple cloak,
and they came to him and said,
"Hail, King of the Jews!"
And they struck him repeatedly.
Once more Pilate went out and said to them,
"Look, I am bringing him out to you,
so that you may know that I find no guilt in him."
So Jesus came out,
wearing the crown of thorns and the purple cloak.
And he said to them, "Behold, the man!"
When the chief priests and the guards saw him they cried out,
"Crucify him, crucify him!"
Pilate said to them,
"Take him yourselves and crucify him.
I find no guilt in him."
The Jews answered,
"We have a law, and according to that law he ought to die,
because he made himself the Son of God."
Now when Pilate heard this statement,
he became even more afraid,
and went back into the praetorium and said to Jesus,
"Where are you from?"
Jesus did not answer him.
So Pilate said to him,
"Do you not speak to me?
Do you not know that I have power to release you
and I have power to crucify you?"
Jesus answered him,
"You would have no power over me
if it had not been given to you from above.
For this reason the one who handed me over to you
has the greater sin."
Consequently, Pilate tried to release him; but the Jews cried out,
"If you release him, you are not a Friend of Caesar.
Everyone who makes himself a king opposes Caesar."

When Pilate heard these words he brought Jesus out
and seated him on the judge's bench
in the place called Stone Pavement, in Hebrew, Gabbatha.
It was preparation day for Passover, and it was about noon.
And he said to the Jews,
"Behold, your king!"
They cried out,
"Take him away, take him away! Crucify him!"
Pilate said to them,
"Shall I crucify your king?"
The chief priests answered,
"We have no king but Caesar."
Then he handed him over to them to be crucified.

So they took Jesus, and, carrying the cross himself,
he went out to what is called the Place of the Skull,
in Hebrew, Golgotha.
There they crucified him, and with him two others,
one on either side, with Jesus in the middle.
Pilate also had an inscription written and put on the cross.
It read,
"Jesus the Nazorean, the King of the Jews."
Now many of the Jews read this inscription,
because the place where Jesus was crucified was near the city;
and it was written in Hebrew, Latin, and Greek.
So the chief priests of the Jews said to Pilate,
"Do not write 'The King of the Jews,'
but that he said, 'I am the King of the Jews.'"
Pilate answered,
"What I have written, I have written."

When the soldiers had crucified Jesus,
they took his clothes and divided them into four shares,
a share for each soldier.
They also took his tunic, but the tunic was seamless,
woven in one piece from the top down.
So they said to one another,
"Let's not tear it, but cast lots for it to see whose it will be,"
in order that the passage of Scripture might be fulfilled that says:
They divided my garments among them,
and for my vesture they cast lots.
This is what the soldiers did.
Standing by the cross of Jesus were his mother
and his mother's sister, Mary the wife of Clopas,
and Mary of Magdala.
When Jesus saw his mother and the disciple there whom he loved
he said to his mother, "Woman, behold, your son."
Then he said to the disciple,
"Behold, your mother."
And from that hour the disciple took her into his home.

After this, aware that everything was now finished,
in order that the Scripture might be fulfilled,
Jesus said, "I thirst."
There was a vessel filled with common wine.
So they put a sponge soaked in wine on a sprig of hyssop
and put it up to his mouth.
When Jesus had taken the wine, he said,
"It is finished."
And bowing his head, he handed over the spirit.

Here all kneel and pause for a short time.

Now since it was preparation day,
in order that the bodies might not remain
on the cross on the sabbath,
for the sabbath day of that week was a solemn one,
the Jews asked Pilate that their legs be broken
and that they be taken down.
So the soldiers came and broke the legs of the first
and then of the other one who was crucified with Jesus.
But when they came to Jesus and saw that he was already dead,
they did not break his legs,
but one soldier thrust his lance into his side,
and immediately blood and water flowed out.
An eyewitness has testified, and his testimony is true;
he knows that he is speaking the truth,
so that you also may come to believe.
For this happened so that the Scripture passage might be fulfilled:
Not a bone of it will be broken.

And again another passage says:
They will look upon him whom they have pierced.

After this, Joseph of Arimathea,
secretly a disciple of Jesus for fear of the Jews,
asked Pilate if he could remove the body of Jesus.
And Pilate permitted it.
So he came and took his body.
Nicodemus, the one who had first come to him at night,
also came bringing a mixture of myrrh and aloes
weighing about one hundred pounds.

They took the body of Jesus
and bound it with burial cloths along with the spices,
according to the Jewish burial custom.
Now in the place where he had been crucified there was a garden,
and in the garden a new tomb, in which no one had yet been buried.
So they laid Jesus there because of the Jewish preparation day;
for the tomb was close by.

FIRST READING
Isa 52:13–53:12

See, my servant shall prosper,
he shall be raised high and greatly exalted.
Even as many were amazed at him—
so marred was his look beyond human semblance
and his appearance beyond that of the sons of man—
so shall he startle many nations,
because of him kings shall stand speechless;
for those who have not been told shall see,
those who have not heard shall ponder it.

Who would believe what we have heard?
To whom has the arm of the LORD been revealed?
He grew up like a sapling before him,
like a shoot from the parched earth;
there was in him no stately bearing to make us look at him,
nor appearance that would attract us to him.
He was spurned and avoided by people,
a man of suffering, accustomed to infirmity,
one of those from whom people hide their faces,
spurned, and we held him in no esteem.

Yet it was our infirmities that he bore,
our sufferings that he endured,
while we thought of him as stricken,
as one smitten by God and afflicted.
But he was pierced for our offenses,
crushed for our sins;
upon him was the chastisement that makes us whole,
by his stripes we were healed.
We had all gone astray like sheep,
each following his own way;
but the LORD laid upon him
the guilt of us all.

Though he was harshly treated, he submitted
and opened not his mouth;
like a lamb led to the slaughter
or a sheep before the shearers,
he was silent and opened not his mouth.
Oppressed and condemned, he was taken away,
and who would have thought any more of his destiny?
When he was cut off from the land of the living,
and smitten for the sin of his people,
a grave was assigned him among the wicked
and a burial place with evildoers,
though he had done no wrong
nor spoken any falsehood.
But the LORD was pleased
to crush him in infirmity.

If he gives his life as an offering for sin,
he shall see his descendants in a long life,
and the will of the LORD shall be accomplished through him.

Because of his affliction
he shall see the light
in fullness of days;
through his suffering, my servant shall justify many,
and their guilt he shall bear.
Therefore I will give him his portion among the great,
and he shall divide the spoils with the mighty,
because he surrendered himself to death
and was counted among the wicked;
and he shall take away the sins of many,
and win pardon for their offenses.

RESPONSORIAL PSALM
Ps 31:2, 6, 12-13, 15-16, 17, 25

℟. (Luke 23:46) Father, into your hands I commend my spirit.

In you, O LORD, I take refuge;
let me never be put to shame.
In your justice rescue me.
Into your hands I commend my spirit;
you will redeem me, O LORD, O faithful God.

℟. Father, into your hands I commend my spirit.

For all my foes I am an object of reproach,
a laughingstock to my neighbors,
and a dread to my friends;
they who see me abroad flee from me.
I am forgotten like the unremembered dead;
I am like a dish that is broken.

℟. Father, into your hands I commend my spirit.

But my trust is in you, O LORD;
I say, "You are my God.
In your hands is my destiny; rescue me
from the clutches of my enemies and my persecutors."

℟. Father, into your hands I commend my spirit.

Let your face shine upon your servant;
save me in your kindness.
Take courage and be stouthearted,
all you who hope in the LORD.

℟. Father, into your hands I commend my spirit.

Continue on next page.

Friday of the Passion of the Lord (Good Friday), March 26, 2027 (cont.)

SECOND READING
Heb 4:14-16; 5:7-9

Brothers and sisters:
Since we have a great high priest who has passed through the heavens,
Jesus, the Son of God,
let us hold fast to our confession.
For we do not have a high priest
who is unable to sympathize with our weaknesses,
but one who has similarly been tested in every way,
yet without sin.
So let us confidently approach the throne of grace
to receive mercy and to find grace for timely help.

In the days when Christ was in the flesh,
he offered prayers and supplications with loud cries and tears
to the one who was able to save him from death,
and he was heard because of his reverence.
Son though he was, he learned obedience from what he suffered;
and when he was made perfect,
he became the source of eternal salvation for all who obey him.

At the Easter Vigil in the Holy Night of Easter, March 27, 2027

FIRST READING
Gen 1:1–2:2

In the beginning, when God created the heavens and the earth,
the earth was a formless wasteland, and darkness covered the abyss,
while a mighty wind swept over the waters.

Then God said,
"Let there be light," and there was light.
God saw how good the light was.
God then separated the light from the darkness.
God called the light "day," and the darkness he called "night."
Thus evening came, and morning followed—the first day.

Then God said,
"Let there be a dome in the middle of the waters,
to separate one body of water from the other."
And so it happened:
God made the dome,
and it separated the water above the dome from the water below it.
God called the dome "the sky."
Evening came, and morning followed—the second day.

Then God said,
"Let the water under the sky be gathered into a single basin,
so that the dry land may appear."
And so it happened:
the water under the sky was gathered into its basin,
and the dry land appeared.
God called the dry land "the earth,"
and the basin of the water he called "the sea."
God saw how good it was.
Then God said,
"Let the earth bring forth vegetation:
every kind of plant that bears seed
and every kind of fruit tree on earth
that bears fruit with its seed in it."
And so it happened:
the earth brought forth every kind of plant that bears seed
and every kind of fruit tree on earth
that bears fruit with its seed in it.
God saw how good it was.
Evening came, and morning followed—the third day.

Then God said:
"Let there be lights in the dome of the sky,
to separate day from night.
Let them mark the fixed times, the days and the years,
and serve as luminaries in the dome of the sky,
to shed light upon the earth."
And so it happened:
God made the two great lights,
the greater one to govern the day,
and the lesser one to govern the night;
and he made the stars.
God set them in the dome of the sky,
to shed light upon the earth,
to govern the day and the night,
and to separate the light from the darkness.
God saw how good it was.
Evening came, and morning followed—the fourth day.

Then God said,
"Let the water teem with an abundance of living creatures,
and on the earth let birds fly beneath the dome of the sky."
And so it happened:
God created the great sea monsters
and all kinds of swimming creatures with which the water teems,
and all kinds of winged birds.
God saw how good it was, and God blessed them, saying,
"Be fertile, multiply, and fill the water of the seas;
and let the birds multiply on the earth."
Evening came, and morning followed—the fifth day.

Then God said,
"Let the earth bring forth all kinds of living creatures:
cattle, creeping things, and wild animals of all kinds."
And so it happened:
God made all kinds of wild animals,
all kinds of cattle,
and all kinds of creeping things of the earth.

God saw how good it was.
Then God said:
"Let us make man in our image, after our likeness.
Let them have dominion over the fish of the sea,
the birds of the air, and the cattle,
and over all the wild animals
and all the creatures that crawl on the ground."
God created man in his image;
in the image of God he created him;
male and female he created them.
God blessed them, saying:
"Be fertile and multiply;
fill the earth and subdue it.
Have dominion over the fish of the sea,
the birds of the air,
and all the living things that move on the earth."
God also said:
"See, I give you every seed-bearing plant all over the earth
and every tree that has seed-bearing fruit on it to be your food;
and to all the animals of the land, all the birds of the air,
and all the living creatures that crawl on the ground,
I give all the green plants for food."
And so it happened.
God looked at everything he had made,
and he found it very good.
Evening came, and morning followed—
the sixth day.

Thus the heavens and the earth and all their array were completed.
Since on the seventh day God was finished
with the work he had been doing,
he rested on the seventh day from all the work he had undertaken.

or

Gen 1:1, 26-31a

In the beginning, when God created the heavens and the earth,
God said: "Let us make man in our image, after our likeness.
Let them have dominion over the fish of the sea,
the birds of the air, and the cattle,
and over all the wild animals
and all the creatures that crawl on the ground."
God created man in his image;
in the image of God he created him;
male and female he created them.
God blessed them, saying:
"Be fertile and multiply;
fill the earth and subdue it.
Have dominion over the fish of the sea,
the birds of the air,
and all the living things that move on the earth."
God also said:
"See, I give you every seed-bearing plant all over the earth
and every tree that has seed-bearing fruit on it to be your food;
and to all the animals of the land, all the birds of the air,
and all the living creatures that crawl on the ground,
I give all the green plants for food."
And so it happened.
God looked at everything he had made,
and found it very good.

RESPONSORIAL PSALM
Ps 104:1-2, 5-6, 10, 12, 13-14, 24, 35

℟. (30) Lord, send out your Spirit, and renew the face of the earth.

Bless the LORD, O my soul!
O LORD, my God, you are great indeed!
You are clothed with majesty and glory,
robed in light as with a cloak.

℟. Lord, send out your Spirit, and renew the face of the earth.

You fixed the earth upon its foundation,
not to be moved forever;
with the ocean, as with a garment, you covered it;
above the mountains the waters stood.

℟. Lord, send out your Spirit, and renew the face of the earth.

You send forth springs into the watercourses
that wind among the mountains.
Beside them the birds of heaven dwell;
from among the branches they send forth their song.

℟. Lord, send out your Spirit, and renew the face of the earth.

You water the mountains from your palace;
the earth is replete with the fruit of your works.
You raise grass for the cattle,
and vegetation for man's use,
producing bread from the earth.

℟. Lord, send out your Spirit, and renew the face of the earth.

How manifold are your works, O LORD!
In wisdom you have wrought them all—
the earth is full of your creatures.
Bless the LORD, O my soul!

℟. Lord, send out your Spirit, and renew the face of the earth.

or

Ps 33:4-5, 6-7, 12-13, 20 and 22

℟. (5b) The earth is full of the goodness of the Lord.

Upright is the word of the LORD,
and all his works are trustworthy.
He loves justice and right;
of the kindness of the LORD the earth is full.

℟. The earth is full of the goodness of the Lord.

By the word of the LORD the heavens were made;
by the breath of his mouth all their host.
He gathers the waters of the sea as in a flask;
in cellars he confines the deep.

℟. The earth is full of the goodness of the Lord.

Blessed the nation whose God is the LORD,
the people he has chosen for his own inheritance.
From heaven the LORD looks down;
he sees all mankind.

℟. The earth is full of the goodness of the Lord.

Our soul waits for the LORD,
who is our help and our shield.
May your kindness, O LORD, be upon us
who have put our hope in you.

℟. The earth is full of the goodness of the Lord.

SECOND READING
Gen 22:1-18

God put Abraham to the test.
He called to him, "Abraham!"
"Here I am," he replied.
Then God said:
"Take your son Isaac, your only one, whom you love,
and go to the land of Moriah.
There you shall offer him up as a holocaust
on a height that I will point out to you."
Early the next morning Abraham saddled his donkey,
took with him his son Isaac and two of his servants as well,
and with the wood that he had cut for the holocaust,
set out for the place of which God had told him.

On the third day Abraham got sight of the place from afar.
Then he said to his servants:
"Both of you stay here with the donkey,
while the boy and I go on over yonder.
We will worship and then come back to you."
Thereupon Abraham took the wood for the holocaust
and laid it on his son Isaac's shoulders,
while he himself carried the fire and the knife.
As the two walked on together, Isaac spoke to his father Abraham:
"Father!" Isaac said.
"Yes, son," he replied.
Isaac continued, "Here are the fire and the wood,
but where is the sheep for the holocaust?"
"Son," Abraham answered,
"God himself will provide the sheep for the holocaust."
Then the two continued going forward.

When they came to the place of which God had told him,
Abraham built an altar there and arranged the wood on it.
Next he tied up his son Isaac,
and put him on top of the wood on the altar.
Then he reached out and took the knife to slaughter his son.
But the LORD's messenger called to him from heaven,
"Abraham, Abraham!"
"Here I am," he answered.
"Do not lay your hand on the boy," said the messenger.
"Do not do the least thing to him.
I know now how devoted you are to God,
since you did not withhold from me your own beloved son."
As Abraham looked about,
he spied a ram caught by its horns in the thicket.
So he went and took the ram
and offered it up as a holocaust in place of his son.
Abraham named the site Yahweh-yireh;
hence people now say, "On the mountain the LORD will see."

Again the LORD's messenger called to Abraham from heaven and said:
"I swear by myself, declares the LORD,
that because you acted as you did
in not withholding from me your beloved son,
I will bless you abundantly
and make your descendants as countless
as the stars of the sky and the sands of the seashore;
your descendants shall take possession
of the gates of their enemies,
and in your descendants all the nations of the earth
shall find blessing—
all this because you obeyed my command."

or

Gen 22:1-2, 9a, 10-13, 15-18

God put Abraham to the test.
He called to him, "Abraham!"
"Here I am," he replied.
Then God said:
"Take your son Isaac, your only one, whom you love,
and go to the land of Moriah.
There you shall offer him up as a holocaust
on a height that I will point out to you."

When they came to the place of which God had told him,
Abraham built an altar there and arranged the wood on it.
Then he reached out and took the knife to slaughter his son.
But the LORD's messenger called to him from heaven,
"Abraham, Abraham!"
"Here I am," he answered.
"Do not lay your hand on the boy," said the messenger.
"Do not do the least thing to him.
I know now how devoted you are to God,
since you did not withhold from me your own beloved son."
As Abraham looked about,
he spied a ram caught by its horns in the thicket.
So he went and took the ram
and offered it up as a holocaust in place of his son.

Again the LORD's messenger called to Abraham from heaven and said:
"I swear by myself, declares the LORD,
that because you acted as you did
in not withholding from me your beloved son,
I will bless you abundantly
and make your descendants as countless
as the stars of the sky and the sands of the seashore;
your descendants shall take possession
of the gates of their enemies,
and in your descendants all the nations of the earth
shall find blessing—
all this because you obeyed my command."

RESPONSORIAL PSALM
Ps 16:5, 8, 9-10, 11

℟. (1) You are my inheritance, O Lord.

O LORD, my allotted portion and my cup,
you it is who hold fast my lot.
I set the LORD ever before me;
with him at my right hand I shall not be disturbed.

℟. You are my inheritance, O Lord.

Therefore my heart is glad and my soul rejoices,
my body, too, abides in confidence;
because you will not abandon my soul to the netherworld,
nor will you suffer your faithful one to undergo corruption.

℟. You are my inheritance, O Lord.

You will show me the path to life,
fullness of joys in your presence,
the delights at your right hand
forever.

℟. You are my inheritance, O Lord.

THIRD READING

Exod 14:15–15:1

The LORD said to Moses, "Why are you
crying out to me?
Tell the Israelites to go forward.
And you, lift up your staff and, with
hand outstretched over the sea,
split the sea in two,
that the Israelites may pass through
it on dry land.
But I will make the Egyptians so
obstinate
that they will go in after them.
Then I will receive glory through
Pharaoh and all his army,
his chariots and charioteers.
The Egyptians shall know that I am
the LORD,
when I receive glory through
Pharaoh
and his chariots and charioteers."

The angel of God, who had been
leading Israel's camp,
now moved and went around behind
them.
The column of cloud also, leaving the
front,
took up its place behind them,
so that it came between the camp of
the Egyptians
and that of Israel.
But the cloud now became dark, and
thus the night passed
without the rival camps coming any
closer together all night long.
Then Moses stretched out his hand
over the sea,
and the LORD swept the sea
with a strong east wind throughout
the night
and so turned it into dry land.
When the water was thus divided,
the Israelites marched into the midst
of the sea on dry land,
with the water like a wall to their
right and to their left.

The Egyptians followed in pursuit;
all Pharaoh's horses and chariots and
charioteers went after them
right into the midst of the sea.
In the night watch just before dawn
the LORD cast through the column of
the fiery cloud
upon the Egyptian force a glance
that threw it into a panic;
and he so clogged their chariot
wheels
that they could hardly drive.
With that the Egyptians sounded the
retreat before Israel,
because the LORD was fighting for
them against the Egyptians.

Then the LORD told Moses, "Stretch out
your hand over the sea,
that the water may flow back upon
the Egyptians,
upon their chariots and their
charioteers."
So Moses stretched out his hand over
the sea,
and at dawn the sea flowed back to
its normal depth.
The Egyptians were fleeing head on
toward the sea,
when the LORD hurled them into its
midst.
As the water flowed back,
it covered the chariots and the
charioteers of Pharaoh's whole
army
which had followed the Israelites
into the sea.
Not a single one of them escaped.
But the Israelites had marched on dry
land
through the midst of the sea,
with the water like a wall to their
right and to their left.
Thus the LORD saved Israel on that day
from the power of the Egyptians.
When Israel saw the Egyptians lying
dead on the seashore
and beheld the great power that the
LORD
had shown against the Egyptians,
they feared the LORD and believed in
him and in his servant Moses.

Then Moses and the Israelites sang this
song to the LORD:
I will sing to the LORD, for he is
gloriously triumphant;
horse and chariot he has cast into the
sea.

RESPONSORIAL PSALM

Exod 15:1-2, 3-4, 5-6, 17-18

℟. (1b) Let us sing to the Lord; he has
covered himself in glory.

I will sing to the LORD, for he is
gloriously triumphant;
horse and chariot he has cast into the
sea.
My strength and my courage is the
LORD,
and he has been my savior.
He is my God, I praise him;
the God of my father, I extol him.

℟. Let us sing to the Lord; he has
covered himself in glory.

The LORD is a warrior,
LORD is his name!
Pharaoh's chariots and army he hurled
into the sea;
the elite of his officers were
submerged in the Red Sea.

℟. Let us sing to the Lord; he has
covered himself in glory.

The flood waters covered them,
they sank into the depths like a
stone.
Your right hand, O LORD, magnificent in
power,
your right hand, O LORD, has
shattered the enemy.

℟. Let us sing to the Lord; he has
covered himself in glory.

You brought in the people you
redeemed
and planted them on the mountain
of your inheritance—
the place where you made your seat,
O LORD,
the sanctuary, LORD, which your
hands established.
The LORD shall reign forever and ever.

℟. Let us sing to the Lord; he has
covered himself in glory.

FOURTH READING
Isa 54:5-14

The One who has become your
husband is your Maker;
his name is the LORD of hosts;
your redeemer is the Holy One of
Israel,
called God of all the earth.
The LORD calls you back,
like a wife forsaken and grieved in
spirit,
a wife married in youth and then cast
off,
says your God.
For a brief moment I abandoned you,
but with great tenderness I will take
you back.
In an outburst of wrath, for a moment
I hid my face from you;
but with enduring love I take pity on
you,
says the LORD, your redeemer.
This is for me like the days of Noah,
when I swore that the waters of Noah
should never again deluge the earth;
so I have sworn not to be angry with
you,
or to rebuke you.
Though the mountains leave their place
and the hills be shaken,
my love shall never leave you
nor my covenant of peace be shaken,
says the LORD, who has mercy on you.
O afflicted one, storm-battered and
unconsoled,
I lay your pavements in carnelians,
and your foundations in sapphires;
I will make your battlements of rubies,
your gates of carbuncles,
and all your walls of precious stones.
All your children shall be taught by the
LORD,
and great shall be the peace of your
children.
In justice shall you be established,
far from the fear of oppression,
where destruction cannot come near
you.

RESPONSORIAL PSALM
Ps 30:2, 4, 5-6, 11-12, 13

℟. (2a) I will praise you, Lord, for you
have rescued me.

I will extol you, O LORD, for you drew
me clear
and did not let my enemies rejoice
over me.
O LORD, you brought me up from the
netherworld;
you preserved me from among those
going down into the pit.

℟. I will praise you, Lord, for you have
rescued me.

Sing praise to the LORD, you his faithful
ones,
and give thanks to his holy name.
For his anger lasts but a moment;
a lifetime, his good will.
At nightfall, weeping enters in,
but with the dawn, rejoicing.

℟. I will praise you, Lord, for you have
rescued me.

Hear, O LORD, and have pity on me;
O LORD, be my helper.
You changed my mourning into
dancing;
O LORD, my God, forever will I give
you thanks.

℟. I will praise you, Lord, for you have
rescued me.

FIFTH READING
Isa 55:1-11

Thus says the LORD:
All you who are thirsty,
come to the water!
You who have no money,
come, receive grain and eat;
come, without paying and without cost,
drink wine and milk!
Why spend your money for what is not
bread,
your wages for what fails to satisfy?
Heed me, and you shall eat well,
you shall delight in rich fare.
Come to me heedfully,
listen, that you may have life.
I will renew with you the everlasting
covenant,
the benefits assured to David.
As I made him a witness to the peoples,
a leader and commander of nations,
so shall you summon a nation you
knew not,
and nations that knew you not shall
run to you,
because of the LORD, your God,
the Holy One of Israel, who has
glorified you.

Seek the LORD while he may be found,
call him while he is near.
Let the scoundrel forsake his way,
and the wicked man his thoughts;
let him turn to the LORD for mercy;
to our God, who is generous in
forgiving.
For my thoughts are not your thoughts,
nor are your ways my ways, says the
LORD.
As high as the heavens are above the
earth,
so high are my ways above your
ways
and my thoughts above your
thoughts.

For just as from the heavens
the rain and snow come down
and do not return there
till they have watered the earth,
making it fertile and fruitful,
giving seed to the one who sows
and bread to the one who eats,
so shall my word be
that goes forth from my mouth;
my word shall not return to me void,
but shall do my will,
achieving the end for which I sent it.

RESPONSORIAL PSALM
Isa 12:2-3, 4, 5-6

℟. (3) You will draw water joyfully
from the springs of salvation.

God indeed is my savior;
I am confident and unafraid.
My strength and my courage is the
LORD,
and he has been my savior.
With joy you will draw water
at the fountain of salvation.

℟. You will draw water joyfully from
the springs of salvation.

Give thanks to the LORD, acclaim his
name;
among the nations make known his
deeds,
proclaim how exalted is his name.

℟. You will draw water joyfully from
the springs of salvation.

Sing praise to the LORD for his glorious achievement;
let this be known throughout all the earth.
Shout with exultation, O city of Zion,
for great in your midst
is the Holy One of Israel!

℟. You will draw water joyfully from the springs of salvation.

SIXTH READING
Bar 3:9-15, 32–4:4

Hear, O Israel, the commandments of life:
listen, and know prudence!
How is it, Israel,
that you are in the land of your foes,
grown old in a foreign land,
defiled with the dead,
accounted with those destined for the netherworld?
You have forsaken the fountain of wisdom!
Had you walked in the way of God,
you would have dwelt in enduring peace.
Learn where prudence is,
where strength, where understanding;
that you may know also
where are length of days, and life,
where light of the eyes, and peace.
Who has found the place of wisdom,
who has entered into her treasuries?

The One who knows all things knows her;
he has probed her by his knowledge—
the One who established the earth for all time,
and filled it with four-footed beasts;
he who dismisses the light, and it departs,
calls it, and it obeys him trembling;
before whom the stars at their posts
shine and rejoice;
when he calls them, they answer, "Here we are!"
shining with joy for their Maker.
Such is our God;
no other is to be compared to him:
he has traced out the whole way of understanding,
and has given her to Jacob, his servant,
to Israel, his beloved son.

Since then she has appeared on earth,
and moved among people.
She is the book of the precepts of God,
the law that endures forever;
all who cling to her will live,
but those will die who forsake her.
Turn, O Jacob, and receive her:
walk by her light toward splendor.
Give not your glory to another,
your privileges to an alien race.
Blessed are we, O Israel;
for what pleases God is known to us!

RESPONSORIAL PSALM
Ps 19:8, 9, 10, 11

℟. (John 6:68c) Lord, you have the words of everlasting life.

The law of the LORD is perfect,
refreshing the soul;
the decree of the LORD is trustworthy,
giving wisdom to the simple.

℟. Lord, you have the words of everlasting life.

The precepts of the LORD are right,
rejoicing the heart;
the command of the LORD is clear,
enlightening the eye.

℟. Lord, you have the words of everlasting life.

The fear of the LORD is pure,
enduring forever;
the ordinances of the LORD are true,
all of them just.

℟. Lord, you have the words of everlasting life.

They are more precious than gold,
than a heap of purest gold;
sweeter also than syrup
or honey from the comb.

℟. Lord, you have the words of everlasting life.

SEVENTH READING
Ezek 36:16-17a, 18-28

The word of the LORD came to me, saying:
Son of man, when the house of Israel lived in their land,
they defiled it by their conduct and deeds.
Therefore I poured out my fury upon them
because of the blood that they poured out on the ground,
and because they defiled it with idols.
I scattered them among the nations,
dispersing them over foreign lands;
according to their conduct and deeds I judged them.
But when they came among the nations wherever they came,
they served to profane my holy name,
because it was said of them: "These are the people of the LORD,
yet they had to leave their land."
So I have relented because of my holy name
which the house of Israel profaned
among the nations where they came.
Therefore say to the house of Israel:
Thus says the Lord GOD:
Not for your sakes do I act, house of Israel,
but for the sake of my holy name,
which you profaned among the nations to which you came.
I will prove the holiness of my great name, profaned among the nations,
in whose midst you have profaned it.
Thus the nations shall know that I am the LORD, says the Lord GOD,
when in their sight I prove my holiness through you.
For I will take you away from among the nations,
gather you from all the foreign lands,
and bring you back to your own land.
I will sprinkle clean water upon you
to cleanse you from all your impurities,
and from all your idols I will cleanse you.
I will give you a new heart and place a new spirit within you,
taking from your bodies your stony hearts
and giving you natural hearts.
I will put my spirit within you and make you live by my statutes,
careful to observe my decrees.
You shall live in the land I gave your fathers;
you shall be my people, and I will be your God.

RESPONSORIAL PSALM
Ps 42:3, 5; 43:3, 4

℟. (42:2) Like a deer that longs for running streams, my soul longs for you, my God.

Athirst is my soul for God, the living God.
When shall I go and behold the face of God?

℟. Like a deer that longs for running streams, my soul longs for you, my God.

I went with the throng
and led them in procession to the house of God,
amid loud cries of joy and thanksgiving,
with the multitude keeping festival.

℟. Like a deer that longs for running streams, my soul longs for you, my God.

Send forth your light and your fidelity;
they shall lead me on
and bring me to your holy mountain,
to your dwelling-place.

℟. Like a deer that longs for running streams, my soul longs for you, my God.

Then will I go in to the altar of God,
the God of my gladness and joy;
then will I give you thanks upon the harp,
O God, my God!

℟. Like a deer that longs for running streams, my soul longs for you, my God.

or
Isa 12:2-3, 4bcd, 5-6

℟. (3) You will draw water joyfully from the springs of salvation.

God indeed is my savior;
I am confident and unafraid.
My strength and my courage is the LORD,
and he has been my savior.
With joy you will draw water
at the fountain of salvation.

℟. You will draw water joyfully from the springs of salvation.

Give thanks to the LORD, acclaim his name;
among the nations make known his deeds,
proclaim how exalted is his name.

℟. You will draw water joyfully from the springs of salvation.

Sing praise to the LORD for his glorious achievement;
let this be known throughout all the earth.
Shout with exultation, O city of Zion,
for great in your midst
is the Holy One of Israel!

℟. You will draw water joyfully from the springs of salvation.

or
Ps 51:12-13, 14-15, 18-19

℟. (12a) Create a clean heart in me, O God.

A clean heart create for me, O God,
and a steadfast spirit renew within me.
Cast me not out from your presence,
and your Holy Spirit take not from me.

℟. Create a clean heart in me, O God.

Give me back the joy of your salvation,
and a willing spirit sustain in me.
I will teach transgressors your ways,
and sinners shall return to you.

℟. Create a clean heart in me, O God.

For you are not pleased with sacrifices;
should I offer a holocaust, you would not accept it.
My sacrifice, O God, is a contrite spirit;
a heart contrite and humbled, O God, you will not spurn.

℟. Create a clean heart in me, O God.

EPISTLE
Rom 6:3-11

Brothers and sisters:
Are you unaware that we who were baptized into Christ Jesus
were baptized into his death?
We were indeed buried with him through baptism into death,
so that, just as Christ was raised from the dead
by the glory of the Father,
we too might live in newness of life.
For if we have grown into union with him through a death like his,
we shall also be united with him in the resurrection.
We know that our old self was crucified with him,
so that our sinful body might be done away with,
that we might no longer be in slavery to sin.
For a dead person has been absolved from sin.
If, then, we have died with Christ,
we believe that we shall also live with him.
We know that Christ, raised from the dead, dies no more;
death no longer has power over him.
As to his death, he died to sin once and for all;
as to his life, he lives for God.
Consequently, you too must think of yourselves as being dead to sin
and living for God in Christ Jesus.

RESPONSORIAL PSALM
Ps 118:1-2, 16-17, 22-23

℟. Alleluia, alleluia, alleluia.

Give thanks to the LORD, for he is good,
for his mercy endures forever.
Let the house of Israel say,
"His mercy endures forever."

℟. Alleluia, alleluia, alleluia.

The right hand of the LORD has struck with power;
the right hand of the LORD is exalted.
I shall not die, but live,
and declare the works of the LORD.

℟. Alleluia, alleluia, alleluia.

The stone which the builders rejected
has become the cornerstone.
By the LORD has this been done;
it is wonderful in our eyes.

℟. Alleluia, alleluia, alleluia.

Easter Sunday, *March 28, 2027*

Gospel

Mark 16:1-7; L41B

When the sabbath was over,
Mary Magdalene, Mary, the mother of James, and Salome
bought spices so that they might go and anoint him.
Very early when the sun had risen,
on the first day of the week, they came to the tomb.
They were saying to one another,
"Who will roll back the stone for us
from the entrance to the tomb?"
When they looked up,
they saw that the stone had been rolled back;
it was very large.
On entering the tomb they saw a young man
sitting on the right side, clothed in a white robe,
and they were utterly amazed.
He said to them, "Do not be amazed!
You seek Jesus of Nazareth, the crucified.
He has been raised; he is not here.
Behold the place where they laid him.
But go and tell his disciples and Peter,
'He is going before you to Galilee;
there you will see him, as he told you.'"

or, at an afternoon or evening Mass

Gospel

Luke 24:13-35; L46

That very day, the first day of the week,
two of Jesus' disciples were going
to a village seven miles from Jerusalem called Emmaus,
and they were conversing about all the things that had occurred.
And it happened that while they were conversing and debating,
Jesus himself drew near and walked with them,
but their eyes were prevented from recognizing him.
He asked them,
"What are you discussing as you walk along?"
They stopped, looking downcast.
One of them, named Cleopas, said to him in reply,
"Are you the only visitor to Jerusalem
who does not know of the things
that have taken place there in these days?"
And he replied to them, "What sort of things?"
They said to him,
"The things that happened to Jesus the Nazarene,
who was a prophet mighty in deed and word
before God and all the people,
how our chief priests and rulers both handed him over
to a sentence of death and crucified him.
But we were hoping that he would be the one to redeem Israel;
and besides all this,
it is now the third day since this took place.
Some women from our group, however, have astounded us:
they were at the tomb early in the morning
and did not find his body;
they came back and reported
that they had indeed seen a vision of angels
who announced that he was alive.
Then some of those with us went to the tomb
and found things just as the women had described,
but him they did not see."
And he said to them, "Oh, how foolish you are!
How slow of heart to believe all that the prophets spoke!
Was it not necessary that the Christ should suffer these things
and enter into his glory?"
Then beginning with Moses and all the prophets,
he interpreted to them what referred to him
in all the Scriptures.
As they approached the village to which they were going,
he gave the impression that he was going on farther.
But they urged him, "Stay with us,
for it is nearly evening and the day is almost over."
So he went in to stay with them.
And it happened that, while he was with them at table,
he took bread, said the blessing,
broke it, and gave it to them.
With that their eyes were opened and they recognized him,
but he vanished from their sight.
Then they said to each other,
"Were not our hearts burning within us
while he spoke to us on the way and opened the Scriptures to us?"
So they set out at once and returned to Jerusalem
where they found gathered together
the eleven and those with them who were saying,
"The Lord has truly been raised and has appeared to Simon!"
Then the two recounted
what had taken place on the way
and how he was made known to them in the breaking of the bread.

Other readings on next page.

FIRST READING
Acts 10:34a, 37-43

Peter proceeded to speak and said:
"You know what has happened all over Judea,
beginning in Galilee after the baptism that John preached,
how God anointed Jesus of Nazareth with the Holy Spirit and power.
He went about doing good
and healing all those oppressed by the devil,
for God was with him.
We are witnesses of all that he did
both in the country of the Jews and in Jerusalem.
They put him to death by hanging him on a tree.
This man God raised on the third day
and granted that he be visible,
not to all the people, but to us,
the witnesses chosen by God in advance,
who ate and drank with him after he rose from the dead.
He commissioned us to preach to the people
and testify that he is the one appointed by God
as judge of the living and the dead.
To him all the prophets bear witness,
that everyone who believes in him
will receive forgiveness of sins through his name."

RESPONSORIAL PSALM
Ps 118:1-2, 16-17, 22-23

℟. (24) This is the day the Lord has made; let us rejoice and be glad.
or: ℟. Alleluia.

Give thanks to the LORD, for he is good,
for his mercy endures forever.
Let the house of Israel say,
"His mercy endures forever."

℟. This is the day the Lord has made;
let us rejoice and be glad.
or: ℟. Alleluia.

"The right hand of the LORD has struck with power;
the right hand of the LORD is exalted.
I shall not die, but live,
and declare the works of the LORD."

℟. This is the day the Lord has made;
let us rejoice and be glad.
or: ℟. Alleluia.

The stone which the builders rejected
has become the cornerstone.
By the LORD has this been done;
it is wonderful in our eyes.

℟. This is the day the Lord has made;
let us rejoice and be glad.
or: ℟. Alleluia.

SECOND READING
1 Cor 5:6b-8

Brothers and sisters:
Do you not know that a little yeast leavens all the dough?
Clear out the old yeast,
so that you may become a fresh batch of dough,
inasmuch as you are unleavened.
For our paschal lamb, Christ, has been sacrificed.
Therefore, let us celebrate the feast,
not with the old yeast, the yeast of malice and wickedness,
but with the unleavened bread of sincerity and truth.

or
Col 3:1-4

Brothers and sisters:
If then you were raised with Christ, seek what is above,
where Christ is seated at the right hand of God.
Think of what is above, not of what is on earth.
For you have died, and your life is hidden with Christ in God.
When Christ your life appears,
then you too will appear with him in glory.

SEQUENCE

Victimae paschali laudes
Christians, to the Paschal Victim
Offer your thankful praises!
A Lamb the sheep redeems;
Christ, who only is sinless,
Reconciles sinners to the Father.
Death and life have contended in that combat stupendous:
The Prince of life, who died, reigns immortal.
Speak, Mary, declaring
What you saw, wayfaring.
"The tomb of Christ, who is living,
The glory of Jesus' resurrection;
Bright angels attesting,
The shroud and napkin resting.
Yes, Christ my hope is arisen;
To Galilee he goes before you."
Christ indeed from death is risen, our new life obtaining.
Have mercy, victor King, ever reigning!
Amen. Alleluia.

Second Sunday of Easter (or of Divine Mercy), *April 4, 2027*

Gospel (cont.)

John 20:19-31; L44B

Now a week later his disciples were again inside
and Thomas was with them.
Jesus came, although the doors were locked,
and stood in their midst and said, "Peace be with you."
Then he said to Thomas, "Put your finger here and see my hands,
and bring your hand and put it into my side,
and do not be unbelieving, but believe."
Thomas answered and said to him, "My Lord and my God!"
Jesus said to him, "Have you come to believe because you have seen me?
Blessed are those who have not seen and have believed."

Now Jesus did many other signs in the presence of his disciples
that are not written in this book.
But these are written that you may come to believe
that Jesus is the Christ, the Son of God,
and that through this belief you may have life in his name.

The Annunciation of the Lord, *April 5, 2027*

Gospel (cont.)

Luke 1:26-38; L545

Therefore the child to be born
will be called holy, the Son of God.
And behold, Elizabeth, your relative,
has also conceived a son in her old age,
and this is the sixth month for her who was called barren;
for nothing will be impossible for God."
Mary said, "Behold, I am the handmaid of the Lord.
May it be done to me according to your word."
Then the angel departed from her.

FIRST READING

Isa 7:10-14; 8:10

The LORD spoke to Ahaz, saying:
Ask for a sign from the LORD, your God;
let it be deep as the nether world, or high as the sky!
But Ahaz answered,
"I will not ask! I will not tempt the LORD!"
Then Isaiah said:
Listen, O house of David!
Is it not enough for you to weary people,
must you also weary my God?
Therefore the Lord himself will give you this sign:
the virgin shall be with child, and bear a son,
and shall name him Emmanuel,
which means "God is with us!"

RESPONSORIAL PSALM

Ps 40:7-8a, 8b-9, 10, 11

℟. (8a and 9a) Here I am, Lord; I come to do your will.

Sacrifice or offering you wished not,
but ears open to obedience you gave me.
Holocausts and sin-offerings you sought not;
then said I, "Behold, I come."

℟. Here I am, Lord; I come to do your will.

"In the written scroll it is prescribed for me,
To do your will, O my God, is my delight,
and your law is within my heart!"

℟. Here I am, Lord; I come to do your will.

I announced your justice in the vast assembly;
I did not restrain my lips, as you, O LORD, know.

℟. Here I am, Lord; I come to do your will.

Your justice I kept not hid within my heart;
your faithfulness and your salvation I have spoken of;
I have made no secret of your kindness and your truth
in the vast assembly.

℟. Here I am, Lord; I come to do your will.

SECOND READING

Heb 10:4-10

Brothers and sisters:
It is impossible that the blood of bulls and goats
takes away sins.
For this reason, when Christ came into the world, he said:

"Sacrifice and offering you did not desire,
but a body you prepared for me;
in holocausts and sin offerings you took no delight.
Then I said, 'As is written of me in the scroll,
behold, I come to do your will, O God.'"

First Christ says, "Sacrifices and offerings,
holocausts and sin offerings,
you neither desired nor delighted in."
These are offered according to the law.
Then he says, "Behold, I come to do your will."
He takes away the first to establish the second.
By this "will," we have been consecrated
through the offering of the Body of Jesus Christ once for all.

Third Sunday of Easter, April 11, 2027

Gospel (cont.)

Luke 24:35-48; L47B

Then he opened their minds to understand the Scriptures.
And he said to them,
"Thus it is written that the Christ would suffer
and rise from the dead on the third day
and that repentance, for the forgiveness of sins,
would be preached in his name
to all the nations, beginning from Jerusalem.
You are witnesses of these things."

The Ascension of the Lord, May 6 or 9, 2027

SECOND READING

Eph 1:17-23

Brothers and sisters:
May the God of our Lord Jesus Christ,
the Father of glory,
give you a Spirit of wisdom and revelation
resulting in knowledge of him.
May the eyes of your hearts be enlightened,
that you may know what is the hope that belongs to his call,
what are the riches of glory
in his inheritance among the holy ones,
and what is the surpassing greatness of his power
for us who believe,
in accord with the exercise of his great might,
which he worked in Christ,
raising him from the dead
and seating him at his right hand in the heavens,
far above every principality,
authority, power, and dominion,
and every name that is named
not only in this age but also in the one to come.
And he put all things beneath his feet
and gave him as head over all things to the church,
which is his body,
the fullness of the one who fills all things in every way.

or

Eph 4:1-13

Brothers and sisters,
I, a prisoner for the Lord,
urge you to live in a manner worthy of the call you have received,
with all humility and gentleness,
with patience,
bearing with one another through love,
striving to preserve the unity of the Spirit
through the bond of peace:
one body and one Spirit,
as you were also called to the one hope of your call;
one Lord, one faith, one baptism;
one God and Father of all,
who is over all and through all and in all.

But grace was given to each of us
according to the measure of Christ's gift.
Therefore, it says:
He ascended on high and took prisoners captive;
he gave gifts to men.
What does "he ascended" mean except that he also descended
into the lower regions of the earth?
The one who descended is also the one who ascended
far above all the heavens,
that he might fill all things.

And he gave some as apostles, others as prophets,
others as evangelists, others as pastors and teachers,
to equip the holy ones for the work of ministry,
for building up the body of Christ,
until we all attain the unity of faith
and knowledge of the Son of God, to mature to manhood,
to the extent of the full stature of Christ.

or

Eph 4:1-7, 11-13

Brothers and sisters,
I, a prisoner for the Lord,
urge you to live in a manner worthy of the call you have received,
with all humility and gentleness,
with patience,
bearing with one another through love,
striving to preserve the unity of the Spirit
through the bond of peace:
one body and one Spirit,
as you were also called to the one hope of your call;
one Lord, one faith, one baptism;
one God and Father of all,
who is over all and through all and in all.

But grace was given to each of us
according to the measure of Christ's gift.

And he gave some as apostles, others as prophets,
others as evangelists, others as pastors and teachers,
to equip the holy ones for the work of ministry,
for building up the body of Christ,
until we all attain the unity of faith
and knowledge of the Son of God,
to mature to manhood,
to the extent of the full stature of Christ.

FIRST READING *(cont.)*

or
Ezek 37:1-14

I saw the sinews and the flesh come upon them,
and the skin cover them, but there was no spirit in them.
Then the LORD said to me:
Prophesy to the spirit, prophesy, son of man,
and say to the spirit: Thus says the Lord GOD:
From the four winds come, O spirit,
and breathe into these slain that they may come to life.
I prophesied as he told me, and the spirit came into them;
they came alive and stood upright, a vast army.
Then he said to me:
Son of man, these bones are the whole house of Israel.
They have been saying,
"Our bones are dried up,
our hope is lost, and we are cut off."
Therefore, prophesy and say to them:
Thus says the Lord GOD:
O my people, I will open your graves
and have you rise from them,
and bring you back to the land of Israel.
Then you shall know that I am the LORD,
when I open your graves and have you rise from them,
O my people!
I will put my spirit in you that you may live,
and I will settle you upon your land;
thus you shall know that I am the LORD.
I have promised, and I will do it, says the LORD.

Other readings below.

FIRST READING
Joel 3:1-5

Thus says the LORD:
I will pour out my spirit upon all flesh.
Your sons and daughters shall prophesy,
your old men shall dream dreams,
your young men shall see visions;
even upon the servants and the handmaids,
in those days, I will pour out my spirit.
And I will work wonders in the heavens and on the earth,
blood, fire, and columns of smoke;
the sun will be turned to darkness,
and the moon to blood,
at the coming of the day of the LORD,
the great and terrible day.
Then everyone shall be rescued
who calls on the name of the LORD;
for on Mount Zion there shall be a remnant,
as the LORD has said,
and in Jerusalem survivors
whom the LORD shall call.

RESPONSORIAL PSALM
Ps 104:1-2, 24, 35, 27-28, 29, 30

℟. (cf. 30) Lord, send out your Spirit, and renew the face of the earth.
or: ℟. Alleluia.

Bless the LORD, O my soul!
O LORD, my God, you are great indeed!
You are clothed with majesty and glory,
robed in light as with a cloak.

℟. Lord, send out your Spirit, and renew the face of the earth.
or: ℟. Alleluia.

How manifold are your works, O LORD!
In wisdom you have wrought them all—
the earth is full of your creatures;
bless the LORD, O my soul! Alleluia.

℟. Lord, send out your Spirit, and renew the face of the earth.
or: ℟. Alleluia.

Creatures all look to you
to give them food in due time.
When you give it to them, they gather it;
when you open your hand, they are filled with good things.

℟. Lord, send out your Spirit, and renew the face of the earth.
or: ℟. Alleluia.

If you take away their breath, they perish
and return to their dust.
When you send forth your spirit, they are created,
and you renew the face of the earth.

℟. Lord, send out your Spirit, and renew the face of the earth.
or: ℟. Alleluia.

SECOND READING
Rom 8:22-27

Brothers and sisters:
We know that all creation is groaning in labor pains even until now;
and not only that, but we ourselves,
who have the firstfruits of the Spirit,
we also groan within ourselves
as we wait for adoption, the redemption of our bodies.
For in hope we were saved.
Now hope that sees is not hope.
For who hopes for what one sees?
But if we hope for what we do not see,
we wait with endurance.

In the same way, the Spirit too comes to the aid of our weakness;
for we do not know how to pray as we ought,
but the Spirit himself intercedes with inexpressible groanings.
And the one who searches hearts
knows what is the intention of the Spirit,
because he intercedes for the holy ones
according to God's will.

Gospel (cont.)
John 20:19-23; L63B

He will not speak on his own,
but he will speak what he hears,
and will declare to you the things that are coming.
He will glorify me,
because he will take from what is mine and declare it to you.
Everything that the Father has is mine;
for this reason I told you that he will take from what is mine
and declare it to you."

SECOND READING
1 Cor 12:3b-7, 12-13

Brothers and sisters:
No one can say, "Jesus is Lord," except by the Holy Spirit.

There are different kinds of spiritual gifts but the same Spirit;
there are different forms of service but the same Lord;
there are different workings but the same God
who produces all of them in everyone.
To each individual the manifestation of the Spirit
is given for some benefit.

As a body is one though it has many parts,
and all the parts of the body, though many, are one body,
so also Christ.
For in one Spirit we were all baptized into one body,
whether Jews or Greeks, slaves or free persons,
and we were all given to drink of one Spirit.

or
Gal 5:16-25

Brothers and sisters, live by the Spirit
and you will certainly not gratify the desire of the flesh.
For the flesh has desires against the Spirit,
and the Spirit against the flesh;
these are opposed to each other,
so that you may not do what you want.
But if you are guided by the Spirit, you are not under the law.
Now the works of the flesh are obvious:
immorality, impurity, lust, idolatry,
sorcery, hatreds, rivalry, jealousy,
outbursts of fury, acts of selfishness,
dissensions, factions, occasions of envy,
drinking bouts, orgies, and the like.
I warn you, as I warned you before,
that those who do such things will not inherit the kingdom of God.
In contrast, the fruit of the Spirit is love, joy, peace,
patience, kindness, generosity,
faithfulness, gentleness, self-control.
Against such there is no law.
Now those who belong to Christ Jesus have crucified their flesh
with its passions and desires.
If we live in the Spirit, let us also follow the Spirit.

SEQUENCE

Veni, Sancte Spiritus
Come, Holy Spirit, come!
And from your celestial home
Shed a ray of light divine!
Come, Father of the poor!
Come, source of all our store!
Come, within our bosoms shine.
You, of comforters the best;
You, the soul's most welcome guest;
Sweet refreshment here below;
In our labor, rest most sweet;
Grateful coolness in the heat;
Solace in the midst of woe.
O most blessed Light divine,
Shine within these hearts of yours,
And our inmost being fill!
Where you are not, we have naught,
Nothing good in deed or thought,
Nothing free from taint of ill.
Heal our wounds, our strength renew;
On our dryness pour your dew;
Wash the stains of guilt away:
Bend the stubborn heart and will;
Melt the frozen, warm the chill;
Guide the steps that go astray.
On the faithful, who adore
And confess you, evermore
In your sevenfold gift descend;
Give them virtue's sure reward;
Give them your salvation, Lord;
Give them joys that never end.
Amen.
Alleluia.

Gospel (cont.)

Mark 14:12-16, 22-26; L168B

He said to them,
"This is my blood of the covenant,
which will be shed for many.

Amen, I say to you,
I shall not drink again the fruit of the vine
until the day when I drink it new in the kingdom of God."
Then, after singing a hymn,
they went out to the Mount of Olives.

SECOND READING

Heb 9:11-15

Brothers and sisters:
When Christ came as high priest
of the good things that have come to be,
passing through the greater and more perfect tabernacle
not made by hands, that is, not belonging to this creation,
he entered once for all into the sanctuary,
not with the blood of goats and calves
but with his own blood, thus obtaining eternal redemption.
For if the blood of goats and bulls
and the sprinkling of a heifer's ashes
can sanctify those who are defiled
so that their flesh is cleansed,
how much more will the blood of Christ,
who through the eternal Spirit offered himself unblemished to God,
cleanse our consciences from dead works
to worship the living God.

For this reason he is mediator of a new covenant:
since a death has taken place for deliverance
from transgressions under the first covenant,
those who are called may receive the promised eternal inheritance.

OPTIONAL SEQUENCE

Lauda Sion

Laud, O Zion, your salvation,
Laud with hymns of exultation,
Christ, your king and shepherd true:

Bring him all the praise you know,
He is more than you bestow.
Never can you reach his due.

Special theme for glad thanksgiving
Is the quick'ning and the living
Bread today before you set:

From his hands of old partaken,
As we know, by faith unshaken,
Where the Twelve at supper met.

Full and clear ring out your chanting,
Joy nor sweetest grace be wanting,
From your heart let praises burst:

For today the feast is holden,
When the institution olden
Of that supper was rehearsed.

Here the new law's new oblation,
By the new king's revelation,
Ends the form of ancient rite:

Now the new the old effaces,
Truth away the shadow chases,
Light dispels the gloom of night.

What he did at supper seated,
Christ ordained to be repeated,
His memorial ne'er to cease:

And his rule for guidance taking,
Bread and wine we hallow, making
Thus our sacrifice of peace.

This the truth each Christian learns,
Bread into his flesh he turns,
To his precious blood the wine:

Sight has fail'd, nor thought conceives,
But a dauntless faith believes,
Resting on a pow'r divine.

Here beneath these signs are hidden
Priceless things to sense forbidden;
Signs, not things are all we see:

Blood is poured and flesh is broken,
Yet in either wondrous token
Christ entire we know to be.

Whoso of this food partakes,
Does not rend the Lord nor breaks;
Christ is whole to all that taste:

Thousands are, as one, receivers,
One, as thousands of believers,
Eats of him who cannot waste.

Bad and good the feast are sharing,
Of what divers dooms preparing,
Endless death, or endless life.

Life to these, to those damnation,
See how like participation
Is with unlike issues rife.

When the sacrament is broken,
Doubt not, but believe 'tis spoken,
That each sever'd outward token
doth the very whole contain.

Nought the precious gift divides,
Breaking but the sign betides
Jesus still the same abides,
still unbroken does remain.

The shorter form of the sequence begins here.

Lo! the angel's food is given
To the pilgrim who has striven;
See the children's bread from heaven,
which on dogs may not be spent.

Truth the ancient types fulfilling,
Isaac bound, a victim willing,
Paschal lamb, its lifeblood spilling,
manna to the fathers sent.

Very bread, good shepherd, tend us,
Jesu, of your love befriend us,
You refresh us, you defend us,
Your eternal goodness send us
In the land of life to see.

You who all things can and know,
Who on earth such food bestow,
Grant us with your saints, though lowest,
Where the heav'nly feast you show,
Fellow heirs and guests to be. Amen.
Alleluia.

Gospel (cont.)

John 19:31-37; L171B

But when they came to Jesus and saw that he was already dead,
they did not break his legs,
but one soldier thrust his lance into his side,
and immediately blood and water flowed out.
An eyewitness has testified, and his testimony is true;
he knows that he is speaking the truth,
so that you also may come to believe.
For this happened so that the Scripture passage might be fulfilled:
Not a bone of it will be broken.
And again another passage says:
They will look upon him whom they have pierced.

FIRST READING

Hos 11:1, 3-4, 8c-9

Thus says the LORD:
When Israel was a child I loved him,
out of Egypt I called my son.
Yet it was I who taught Ephraim to walk,
who took them in my arms;
I drew them with human cords,
with bands of love;
I fostered them like one
who raises an infant to his cheeks;
Yet, though I stooped to feed my child,
they did not know that I was their healer.

My heart is overwhelmed,
my pity is stirred.
I will not give vent to my blazing anger,
I will not destroy Ephraim again;
For I am God and not a man,
the Holy One present among you;
I will not let the flames consume you.

RESPONSORIAL PSALM

Isa 12:2-3, 4, 5-6

℟. (3)You will draw water joyfully from the springs of salvation.

God indeed is my savior;
I am confident and unafraid.
My strength and my courage is the LORD,
and he has been my savior.
With joy you will draw water
at the fountain of salvation.

℟. You will draw water joyfully from the springs of salvation.

Give thanks to the LORD, acclaim his name;
among the nations make known his deeds,
proclaim how exalted is his name.

℟. You will draw water joyfully from the springs of salvation.

Sing praise to the LORD for his glorious achievement;
let this be known throughout all the earth.
Shout with exultation, O city of Zion,
for great in your midst
is the Holy One of Israel!

℟. You will draw water joyfully from the springs of salvation.

SECOND READING

Eph 3:8-12, 14-19

Brothers and sisters:
To me, the very least of all the holy ones, this grace was given,
to preach to the Gentiles the inscrutable riches of Christ,
and to bring to light for all what is the plan of the mystery
hidden from ages past in God who created all things,
so that the manifold wisdom of God
might now be made known through the church
to the principalities and authorities in the heavens.
This was according to the eternal purpose
that he accomplished in Christ Jesus our Lord,
in whom we have boldness of speech
and confidence of access through faith in him.

For this reason I kneel before the Father,
from whom every family in heaven and on earth is named,
that he may grant you in accord with the riches of his glory
to be strengthened with power through his Spirit in the inner self,
and that Christ may dwell in your hearts through faith;
that you, rooted and grounded in love,
may have strength to comprehend with all the holy ones
what is the breadth and length and height and depth,
and to know the love of Christ which surpasses knowledge,
so that you may be filled with all the fullness of God.

Tenth Sunday in Ordinary Time, June 6, 2027

Gospel (cont.)
Mark 3:20-35; L89B

His mother and his brothers arrived.
Standing outside they sent word to him and called him.
A crowd seated around him told him,
"Your mother and your brothers and your sisters
are outside asking for you."
But he said to them in reply,
"Who are my mother and my brothers?"
And looking around at those seated in the circle he said,
"Here are my mother and my brothers.
For whoever does the will of God
is my brother and sister and mother."

SECOND READING *(cont.)*
2 Cor 4:13–5:1

For we know that if our earthly dwelling, a tent,
should be destroyed,
we have a building from God,
a dwelling not made with hands, eternal in heaven.

The Nativity of Saint John the Baptist, June 24, 2027 (Vigil Mass)

FIRST READING
Jer 1:4-10

In the days of King Josiah, the word of the LORD came to me, saying:

Before I formed you in the womb
I knew you,
before you were born I dedicated you,
a prophet to the nations I appointed you.

"Ah, Lord GOD!" I said,
"I know not how to speak; I am too young."
But the LORD answered me,
Say not, "I am too young."
To whomever I send you, you shall go;
whatever I command you, you shall speak.
Have no fear before them,
because I am with you to deliver you, says the LORD.

Then the LORD extended his hand and touched my mouth, saying,

See, I place my words in your mouth!
This day I set you
over nations and over kingdoms,
to root up and to tear down,
to destroy and to demolish,
to build and to plant.

RESPONSORIAL PSALM
Psalm 71:1-2, 3-4a, 5-6ab, 15ab and 17

℟. (6) Since my mother's womb, you have been my strength.

In you, O LORD, I take refuge;
let me never be put to shame.
In your justice rescue me, and deliver me;
incline your ear to me, and save me.

℟. Since my mother's womb, you have been my strength.

Be my rock of refuge,
a stronghold to give me safety,
for you are my rock and my fortress.
O my God, rescue me from the hand of the wicked.

℟. Since my mother's womb, you have been my strength.

For you are my hope, O LORD;
my trust, O LORD, from my youth.
On you I depend from birth;
from my mother's womb you are my strength.

℟. Since my mother's womb, you have been my strength.

My mouth shall declare your justice,
day by day your salvation.
O God, you have taught me from my youth,
and till the present I proclaim your wondrous deeds.

℟. Since my mother's womb, you have been my strength.

SECOND READING
1 Pet 1:8-12

Beloved:
Although you have not seen Jesus Christ you love him;
even though you do not see him now yet believe in him,
you rejoice with an indescribable and glorious joy,
as you attain the goal of your faith,
the salvation of your souls.

Concerning this salvation,
prophets who prophesied about the grace that was to be yours
searched and investigated it,
investigating the time and circumstances
that the Spirit of Christ within them indicated
when he testified in advance
to the sufferings destined for Christ
and the glories to follow them.
It was revealed to them that they were serving not themselves but you
with regard to the things that have now been announced to you
by those who preached the Good News to you
through the Holy Spirit sent from heaven,
things into which angels longed to look.

GOSPEL ACCLAMATION
cf. John 1:7; Luke 1:17

℟. Alleluia, alleluia.
He came to testify to the light,
to prepare a people fit for the Lord.
℟. Alleluia, alleluia.

Gospel
Luke 1:5-17

In the days of Herod, King of Judea,
there was a priest named Zechariah
of the priestly division of Abijah;
his wife was from the daughters of Aaron,
and her name was Elizabeth.
Both were righteous in the eyes of God,
observing all the commandments
and ordinances of the Lord blamelessly.
But they had no child, because Elizabeth was barren
and both were advanced in years.
Once when he was serving
as priest in his division's turn before God,
according to the practice of the priestly service,
he was chosen by lot
to enter the sanctuary of the Lord to burn incense.
Then, when the whole assembly of the people was praying outside
at the hour of the incense offering,
the angel of the Lord appeared to him,
standing at the right of the altar of incense.
Zechariah was troubled by what he saw, and fear came upon him.
But the angel said to him, "Do not be afraid, Zechariah,
because your prayer has been heard.
Your wife Elizabeth will bear you a son,
and you shall name him John.
And you will have joy and gladness,
and many will rejoice at his birth,
for he will be great in the sight of the Lord.
John will drink neither wine nor strong drink.
He will be filled with the Holy Spirit even from his mother's womb,
and he will turn many of the children of Israel
to the Lord their God.
He will go before him in the spirit and power of Elijah
to turn their hearts toward their children
and the disobedient to the understanding of the righteous,
to prepare a people fit for the Lord."

The Nativity of Saint John the Baptist, *June 24, 2027 (Mass during the Day)*

FIRST READING
Isa 49:1-6

Hear me, O coastlands,
listen, O distant peoples.
The LORD called me from birth,
from my mother's womb he gave me my name.
He made of me a sharp-edged sword
and concealed me in the shadow of his arm.
He made me a polished arrow,
in his quiver he hid me.
You are my servant, he said to me,
Israel, through whom I show my glory.

Though I thought I had toiled in vain,
and for nothing, uselessly, spent my strength,
yet my reward is with the LORD,
my recompense is with my God.
For now the LORD has spoken
who formed me as his servant from the womb,
that Jacob may be brought back to him
and Israel gathered to him;
and I am made glorious in the sight of the LORD,
and my God is now my strength!
It is too little, he says, for you to be my servant,
to raise up the tribes of Jacob,
and restore the survivors of Israel;
I will make you a light to the nations,
that my salvation may reach to the ends of the earth.

RESPONSORIAL PSALM
Ps 139:1b-3, 13-14ab, 14c-15

℟. (14a) I praise you, for I am wonderfully made.

O LORD, you have probed me, you know me;
you know when I sit and when I stand;
you understand my thoughts from afar.
My journeys and my rest you scrutinize,
with all my ways you are familiar.

℟. I praise you, for I am wonderfully made.

Truly you have formed my inmost being;
you knit me in my mother's womb.
I give you thanks that I am fearfully, wonderfully made;
wonderful are your works.

℟. I praise you, for I am wonderfully made.

My soul also you knew full well;
nor was my frame unknown to you
When I was made in secret,
when I was fashioned in the depths of the earth.

℟. I praise you, for I am wonderfully made.

SECOND READING
Acts 13:22-26

In those days, Paul said:
"God raised up David as their king;
of him God testified,
I have found David, son of Jesse,
a man after my own heart;
he will carry out my every wish.
From this man's descendants God,
according to his promise,
has brought to Israel a savior, Jesus.
John heralded his coming by proclaiming a baptism of repentance
to all the people of Israel;
and as John was completing his course, he would say,
'What do you suppose that I am?
I am not he.
Behold, one is coming after me;
I am not worthy to unfasten the sandals of his feet.'

"My brothers, sons of the family of Abraham,
and those others among you who are God-fearing,
to us this word of salvation has been sent."

Gospel (cont.)

Mark 5:21-43; L98B

But his disciples said to Jesus,
"You see how the crowd is pressing upon you,
and yet you ask, 'Who touched me?' "
And he looked around to see who had done it.
The woman, realizing what had happened to her,
approached in fear and trembling.
She fell down before Jesus and told him the whole truth.
He said to her, "Daughter, your faith has saved you.
Go in peace and be cured of your affliction."

While he was still speaking,
people from the synagogue official's house arrived and said,
"Your daughter has died; why trouble the teacher any longer?"
Disregarding the message that was reported,
Jesus said to the synagogue official,
"Do not be afraid; just have faith."
He did not allow anyone to accompany him inside
except Peter, James, and John, the brother of James.
When they arrived at the house of the synagogue official,
he caught sight of a commotion,
people weeping and wailing loudly.
So he went in and said to them,
"Why this commotion and weeping?
The child is not dead but asleep."
And they ridiculed him.
Then he put them all out.
He took along the child's father and mother
and those who were with him
and entered the room where the child was.
He took the child by the hand and said to her, *"Talitha koum,"*
which means, "Little girl, I say to you, arise!"
The girl, a child of twelve, arose immediately and walked around.
At that they were utterly astounded.
He gave strict orders that no one should know this
and said that she should be given something to eat.

or

Mark 5:21-24, 35b-43

When Jesus had crossed again in the boat
to the other side,
a large crowd gathered around him, and he stayed close to the sea.
One of the synagogue officials, named Jairus, came forward.
Seeing him he fell at his feet and pleaded earnestly with him, saying,
"My daughter is at the point of death.
Please, come lay your hands on her
that she may get well and live."
He went off with him,
and a large crowd followed him and pressed upon him.

While he was still speaking, people from the synagogue official's house arrived and said,
"Your daughter has died; why trouble the teacher any longer?"
Disregarding the message that was reported,
Jesus said to the synagogue official,
"Do not be afraid; just have faith."
He did not allow anyone to accompany him inside
except Peter, James, and John, the brother of James.
When they arrived at the house of the synagogue official,
he caught sight of a commotion,
people weeping and wailing loudly.
So he went in and said to them,
"Why this commotion and weeping?
The child is not dead but asleep."
And they ridiculed him.
Then he put them all out.
He took along the child's father and mother
and those who were with him
and entered the room where the child was.
He took the child by the hand and said to her, *"Talitha koum,"*
which means, "Little girl, I say to you, arise!"
The girl, a child of twelve, arose immediately and walked around.
At that they were utterly astounded.
He gave strict orders that no one should know this
and said that she should be given something to eat.

Saints Peter and Paul, Apostles, *June 29, 2027 (Vigil Mass)*

FIRST READING
Acts 3:1-10

Peter and John were going up to the temple area
for the three o'clock hour of prayer.
And a man crippled from birth was carried
and placed at the gate of the temple called "the Beautiful Gate"
every day to beg for alms from the people who entered the temple.
When he saw Peter and John about to go into the temple,
he asked for alms.
But Peter looked intently at him, as did John,
and said, "Look at us."
He paid attention to them, expecting to receive something from them.
Peter said, "I have neither silver nor gold,
but what I do have I give you:
in the name of Jesus Christ the Nazorean, rise and walk."
Then Peter took him by the right hand and raised him up,
and immediately his feet and ankles grew strong.
He leaped up, stood, and walked around,
and went into the temple with them,
walking and jumping and praising God.
When all the people saw the man walking and praising God,
they recognized him as the one who used to sit begging
at the Beautiful Gate of the temple,
and they were filled with amazement and astonishment
at what had happened to him.

RESPONSORIAL PSALM
Ps 19:2-3, 4-5

℟. (5) Their message goes out through all the earth.

The heavens declare the glory of God;
and the firmament proclaims his handiwork.
Day pours out the word to day;
and night to night imparts knowledge.

℟. Their message goes out through all the earth.

Not a word nor a discourse
whose voice is not heard;
through all the earth their voice resounds,
and to the ends of the world, their message.

℟. Their message goes out through all the earth.

SECOND READING
Gal 1:11-20

I want you to know, brothers and sisters,
that the Gospel preached by me is not of human origin.
For I did not receive it from a human being, nor was I taught it,
but it came through a revelation of Jesus Christ.

For you heard of my former way of life in Judaism,
how I persecuted the Church of God beyond measure
and tried to destroy it, and progressed in Judaism
beyond many of my contemporaries among my race,
since I was even more a zealot for my ancestral traditions.
But when God, who from my mother's womb had set me apart
and called me through his grace,
was pleased to reveal his Son to me,
so that I might proclaim him to the Gentiles,
I did not immediately consult flesh and blood,
nor did I go up to Jerusalem
to those who were Apostles before me;
rather, I went into Arabia and then returned to Damascus.

Then after three years I went up to Jerusalem
to confer with Cephas and remained with him for fifteen days.
But I did not see any other of the Apostles,
only James the brother of the Lord.
—As to what I am writing to you, behold,
before God, I am not lying.

GOSPEL ACCLAMATION
John 21:17

℟. Alleluia, alleluia.
Lord, you know everything;
you know that I love you.
℟. Alleluia, alleluia.

Gospel
John 21:15-19

Jesus had revealed himself to his disciples and,
when they had finished breakfast, said to Simon Peter,
"Simon, son of John, do you love me more than these?"
Simon Peter answered him, "Yes, Lord, you know that I love you."
Jesus said to him, "Feed my lambs."
He then said to Simon Peter a second time,
"Simon, son of John, do you love me?"
Simon Peter answered him, "Yes, Lord, you know that I love you."
He said to him, "Tend my sheep."
He said to him the third time,
"Simon, son of John, do you love me?"
Peter was distressed that he had said to him a third time,
"Do you love me?" and he said to him,
"Lord, you know everything; you know that I love you."
Jesus said to him, "Feed my sheep.
Amen, amen, I say to you, when you were younger,
you used to dress yourself and go where you wanted;
but when you grow old, you will stretch out your hands,
and someone else will dress you
and lead you where you do not want to go."
He said this signifying by what kind of death he would glorify God.
And when he had said this, he said to him, "Follow me."

Saints Peter and Paul, Apostles, *June 29, 2027 (Mass during the Day)*

FIRST READING
Acts 12:1-11

In those days, King Herod laid hands upon some members of the Church to harm them.
He had James, the brother of John, killed by the sword,
and when he saw that this was pleasing to the Jews
he proceeded to arrest Peter also.
—It was the feast of Unleavened Bread.—
He had him taken into custody and put in prison
under the guard of four squads of four soldiers each.
He intended to bring him before the people after Passover.
Peter thus was being kept in prison,
but prayer by the Church was fervently being made
to God on his behalf.

On the very night before Herod was to bring him to trial,
Peter, secured by double chains,
was sleeping between two soldiers,
while outside the door guards kept watch on the prison.
Suddenly the angel of the Lord stood by him,
and a light shone in the cell.
He tapped Peter on the side and awakened him, saying,
"Get up quickly."
The chains fell from his wrists.
The angel said to him, "Put on your belt and your sandals."
He did so.
Then he said to him, "Put on your cloak and follow me."
So he followed him out,
not realizing that what was happening through the angel was real;
he thought he was seeing a vision.
They passed the first guard, then the second,
and came to the iron gate leading out to the city,
which opened for them by itself.
They emerged and made their way down an alley,
and suddenly the angel left him.
Then Peter recovered his senses and said,
"Now I know for certain
that the Lord sent his angel
and rescued me from the hand of Herod
and from all that the Jewish people had been expecting."

RESPONSORIAL PSALM
Ps 34:2-3, 4-5, 6-7, 8-9

℟. (8) The angel of the Lord will rescue those who fear him.

I will bless the LORD at all times;
his praise shall be ever in my mouth.
Let my soul glory in the LORD;
the lowly will hear me and be glad.

℟. The angel of the Lord will rescue those who fear him.

Glorify the LORD with me,
let us together extol his name.
I sought the LORD, and he answered me
and delivered me from all my fears.

℟. The angel of the Lord will rescue those who fear him.

Look to him that you may be radiant with joy,
and your faces may not blush with shame.
When the poor one called out, the LORD heard,
and from all his distress he saved him.

℟. The angel of the Lord will rescue those who fear him.

The angel of the LORD encamps
around those who fear him, and delivers them.
Taste and see how good the LORD is;
blessed the man who takes refuge in him.

℟. The angel of the Lord will rescue those who fear him.

SECOND READING
2 Tim 4:6-8, 17-18

I, Paul, am already being poured out like a libation,
and the time of my departure is at hand.
I have competed well; I have finished the race;
I have kept the faith.
From now on the crown of righteousness awaits me,
which the Lord, the just judge,
will award to me on that day, and not only to me,
but to all who have longed for his appearance.

The Lord stood by me and gave me strength,
so that through me the proclamation might be completed
and all the Gentiles might hear it.
And I was rescued from the lion's mouth.
The Lord will rescue me from every evil threat
and will bring me safe to his heavenly Kingdom.
To him be glory forever and ever. Amen.

Fifteenth Sunday in Ordinary Time, July 11, 2027

SECOND READING

or
Eph 1:3-10

Blessed be the God and Father of our Lord Jesus Christ,
who has blessed us in Christ
with every spiritual blessing in the heavens,
as he chose us in him, before the foundation of the world,
to be holy and without blemish before him.
In love he destined us for adoption to himself through Jesus Christ,
in accord with the favor of his will,
for the praise of the glory of his grace
that he granted us in the beloved.

In him we have redemption by his blood,
the forgiveness of transgressions,
in accord with the riches of his grace that he lavished upon us.
In all wisdom and insight, he has made known to us
the mystery of his will in accord with his favor
that he set forth in him as a plan for the fullness of times,
to sum up all things in Christ, in heaven and on earth.

Eighteenth Sunday in Ordinary Time, August 1, 2027

Gospel (cont.)
John 6:24-35; L113B

So Jesus said to them,
"Amen, amen, I say to you,
it was not Moses who gave the bread from heaven;
my Father gives you the true bread from heaven.
For the bread of God is that which comes down from heaven
and gives life to the world."

So they said to him,
"Sir, give us this bread always."
Jesus said to them,
"I am the bread of life;
whoever comes to me will never hunger,
and whoever believes in me will never thirst."

Seventeenth Sunday in Ordinary Time, July 25, 2027

Gospel (cont.)
John 6:1-15; L110B

Then Jesus took the loaves, gave thanks,
and distributed them to those who were reclining,
and also as much of the fish as they wanted.
When they had had their fill, he said to his disciples,
"Gather the fragments left over,
so that nothing will be wasted."
So they collected them,
and filled twelve wicker baskets with fragments
from the five barley loaves
that had been more than they could eat.
When the people saw the sign he had done, they said,
"This is truly the Prophet, the one who is to come into the world."
Since Jesus knew that they were going to come and carry him off
to make him king,
he withdrew again to the mountain alone.

The Assumption of the Blessed Virgin Mary, *August 15, 2027 (Vigil Mass)*

FIRST READING
1 Chr 15:3-4, 15-16; 16:1-2)

David assembled all Israel in Jerusalem
to bring the ark of the LORD
to the place which he had prepared for it.
David also called together the sons of Aaron and the Levites.

The Levites bore the ark of God on their shoulders with poles,
as Moses had ordained according to the word of the LORD.

David commanded the chiefs of the Levites
to appoint their kinsmen as chanters,
to play on musical instruments,
harps, lyres, and cymbals,
to make a loud sound of rejoicing.

They brought in the ark of God and set it within the tent
which David had pitched for it.
Then they offered up burnt offerings and peace offerings to God.
When David had finished offering up the burnt offerings and peace offerings,
he blessed the people in the name of the LORD.

RESPONSORIAL PSALM
Ps 132:6-7, 9-10, 13-14

℟. (8) Lord, go up to the place of your rest, you and the ark of your holiness.

Behold, we heard of it in Ephrathah;
we found it in the fields of Jaar.
Let us enter into his dwelling,
let us worship at his footstool.

℟. Lord, go up to the place of your rest,
you and the ark of your holiness.

May your priests be clothed with justice;
let your faithful ones shout merrily for joy.
For the sake of David your servant,
reject not the plea of your anointed.

℟. Lord, go up to the place of your rest,
you and the ark of your holiness.

For the LORD has chosen Zion;
he prefers her for his dwelling.
"Zion is my resting place forever;
in her will I dwell, for I prefer her."

℟. Lord, go up to the place of your rest,
you and the ark of your holiness.

SECOND READING
1 Cor 15:54b-57

Brothers and sisters:
When that which is mortal clothes itself with immortality,
then the word that is written shall come about:

Death is swallowed up in victory.
Where, O death, is your victory?
Where, O death, is your sting?

The sting of death is sin,
and the power of sin is the law.
But thanks be to God who gives us the victory
through our Lord Jesus Christ.

GOSPEL ACCLAMATION
Luke 11:28

℟. Alleluia, alleluia.
Blessed are they who hear the word of God
and observe it.
℟. Alleluia, alleluia.

Gospel
Luke 11:27-28

While Jesus was speaking,
a woman from the crowd called out and said to him,
"Blessed is the womb that carried you
and the breasts at which you nursed."
He replied,
"Rather, blessed are those
who hear the word of God and observe it."

The Assumption of the Blessed Virgin Mary, *August 15, 2027 (Mass during the Day)*

Gospel (cont.)

Luke 1:39-56; L622

He has shown the strength of his arm,
and has scattered the proud in their conceit.
He has cast down the mighty from their thrones,
and has lifted up the lowly.
He has filled the hungry with good things,
and the rich he has sent away empty.
He has come to the help of his servant Israel
for he has remembered his promise of mercy,
the promise he made to our fathers,
to Abraham and his children forever."

Mary remained with her about three months
and then returned to her home.

Twenty-First Sunday in Ordinary Time, *August 22, 2027*

SECOND READING *(cont.)*

Eph 5:21-32

without spot or wrinkle or any such thing,
that she might be holy and without blemish.
So also husbands should love their wives as their own bodies.
He who loves his wife loves himself.
For no one hates his own flesh
but rather nourishes and cherishes it,
even as Christ does the church,
because we are members of his body.
For this reason a man shall leave his father and his mother
and be joined to his wife,
and the two shall become one flesh.
This is a great mystery,
but I speak in reference to Christ and the church.

or

Eph 5:2a, 25-32

Brothers and sisters:
Live in love, as Christ loved us.
Husbands, love your wives,
even as Christ loved the church
and handed himself over for her to sanctify her,
cleansing her by the bath of water with the word,
that he might present to himself the church in splendor,
without spot or wrinkle or any such thing,
that she might be holy and without blemish.
So also husbands should love their wives as their own bodies.
He who loves his wife loves himself.
For no one hates his own flesh
but rather nourishes and cherishes it,
even as Christ does the church,
because we are members of his body.
For this reason a man shall leave his father and his mother and be joined to his wife,
and the two shall become one flesh.
This is a great mystery,
but I speak in reference to Christ and the church.

Twenty-Second Sunday in Ordinary Time, *August 29, 2027*

Gospel (cont.)

Mark 7:1-8, 14-15, 21-23; L125B

He summoned the crowd again and said to them,
"Hear me, all of you, and understand.
Nothing that enters one from outside can defile that person;
but the things that come out from within are what defile.

"From within people, from their hearts,
come evil thoughts, unchastity, theft, murder,
adultery, greed, malice, deceit,
licentiousness, envy, blasphemy, arrogance, folly.
All these evils come from within and they defile."

Twenty-Sixth Sunday in Ordinary Time, *September 26, 2027*

Gospel (cont.)

Mark 9:38-43, 45, 47-48; L137B

And if your eye causes you to sin, pluck it out.
Better for you to enter into the kingdom of God with one eye
than with two eyes to be thrown into Gehenna,
where 'their worm does not die, and the fire is not quenched.'"

Twenty-Seventh Sunday in Ordinary Time, *October 3, 2027*

Gospel (cont.)

Mark 10:2-16; L140B

And people were bringing children to him that he might touch them,
but the disciples rebuked them.
When Jesus saw this he became indignant and said to them,
"Let the children come to me;
do not prevent them, for the kingdom of God belongs to such as these.
Amen, I say to you,
whoever does not accept the kingdom of God like a child
will not enter it."
Then he embraced them and blessed them,
placing his hands on them.

or

Mark 10:2-12; L140B

The Pharisees approached Jesus and asked,
"Is it lawful for a husband to divorce his wife?"
They were testing him.
He said to them in reply, "What did Moses command you?"
They replied,
"Moses permitted a husband to write a bill of divorce
and dismiss her."
But Jesus told them,
"Because of the hardness of your hearts
he wrote you this commandment.
But from the beginning of creation, *God made them male and female.*
For this reason a man shall leave his father and mother
and be joined to his wife,
and the two shall become one flesh.
So they are no longer two but one flesh.
Therefore what God has joined together,
no human being must separate."
In the house the disciples again questioned Jesus about this.
He said to them,
"Whoever divorces his wife and marries another
commits adultery against her;
and if she divorces her husband and marries another,
she commits adultery."

Gospel (cont.)

Mark 10:17-30; L143B

So Jesus again said to them in reply,
"Children, how hard it is to enter the kingdom of God!
It is easier for a camel to pass through the eye of a needle
than for one who is rich to enter the kingdom of God."
They were exceedingly astonished and said among themselves,
"Then who can be saved?"
Jesus looked at them and said,
"For human beings it is impossible, but not for God.
All things are possible for God."
Peter began to say to him,
"We have given up everything and followed you."
Jesus said, "Amen, I say to you,
there is no one who has given up house or brothers or sisters
or mother or father or children or lands
for my sake and for the sake of the gospel
who will not receive a hundred times more now in this present age:
houses and brothers and sisters
and mothers and children and lands,
with persecutions, and eternal life in the age to come."

or

Mark 10:17-27

As Jesus was setting out on a journey, a man ran up,
knelt down before him, and asked him,
"Good teacher, what must I do to inherit eternal life?"
Jesus answered him, "Why do you call me good?
No one is good but God alone.
You know the commandments: *You shall not kill;*
you shall not commit adultery;
you shall not steal;
you shall not bear false witness;
you shall not defraud;
honor your father and your mother."
He replied and said to him,
"Teacher, all of these I have observed from my youth."
Jesus, looking at him, loved him and said to him,
"You are lacking in one thing.
Go, sell what you have, and give to the poor
and you will have treasure in heaven; then come, follow me."
At that statement his face fell,
and he went away sad, for he had many possessions.

Jesus looked around and said to his disciples,
"How hard it is for those who have wealth
to enter the kingdom of God!"
The disciples were amazed at his words.
So Jesus again said to them in reply,
"Children, how hard it is to enter the kingdom of God!
It is easier for a camel to pass through the eye of a needle
than for one who is rich to enter the kingdom of God."
They were exceedingly astonished and said among themselves,
"Then who can be saved?"
Jesus looked at them and said,
"For human beings it is impossible, but not for God.
All things are possible for God."

Twenty-Ninth Sunday in Ordinary Time, *October 17, 2027*

Gospel (cont.)
Mark 10:35-45; L146B

Rather, whoever wishes to be great among you will be your servant;
whoever wishes to be first among you will be the slave of all.
For the Son of Man did not come to be served
but to serve and to give his life as a ransom for many."

or
Mark 10:42-45

Jesus summoned the Twelve and said to them,
"You know that those who are recognized as rulers over the Gentiles
lord it over them,
and their great ones make their authority over them felt.
But it shall not be so among you.
Rather, whoever wishes to be great among you will be your servant;
whoever wishes to be first among you will be the slave of all.
For the Son of Man did not come to be served
but to serve and to give his life as a ransom for many."

All Saints, *November 1, 2027*

Gospel (cont.)
Matt 5:1-12a; L667

Blessed are the peacemakers,
for they will be called children of God.
Blessed are they who are persecuted for the sake of righteousness,
for theirs is the Kingdom of heaven.
Blessed are you when they insult you and persecute you
and utter every kind of evil against you falsely because of me.
Rejoice and be glad,
for your reward will be great in heaven."

Other readings on next page.

FIRST READING
Rev 7:2-4, 9-14

I, John, saw another angel come up
from the East,
holding the seal of the living God.
He cried out in a loud voice to the four
angels
who were given power to damage the
land and the sea,
"Do not damage the land or the sea
or the trees
until we put the seal on the foreheads
of the servants of our God."
I heard the number of those who had
been marked with the seal,
one hundred and forty-four thousand
marked
from every tribe of the children of
Israel.

After this I had a vision of a great
multitude,
which no one could count,
from every nation, race, people, and
tongue.
They stood before the throne and
before the Lamb,
wearing white robes and holding
palm branches in their hands.
They cried out in a loud voice:

"Salvation comes from our God, who
is seated on the throne,
and from the Lamb."

All the angels stood around the throne
and around the elders and the four
living creatures.
They prostrated themselves before the
throne,
worshiped God, and exclaimed:

"Amen. Blessing and glory, wisdom
and thanksgiving,
honor, power, and might
be to our God forever and ever.
Amen."

Then one of the elders spoke up and
said to me,
"Who are these wearing white robes,
and where did they come from?"
I said to him, "My lord, you are the one
who knows."
He said to me,
"These are the ones who have
survived the time of great
distress;
they have washed their robes
and made them white in the Blood of
the Lamb."

RESPONSORIAL PSALM
Ps 24:1bc-2, 3-4ab, 5-6

℟. (cf. 6) Lord, this is the people that
longs to see your face.

The LORD's are the earth and its
fullness;
the world and those who dwell in it.
For he founded it upon the seas
and established it upon the rivers.

℟. Lord, this is the people that longs to
see your face.

Who can ascend the mountain of the
LORD?
or who may stand in his holy place?
One whose hands are sinless, whose
heart is clean,
who desires not what is vain.

℟. Lord, this is the people that longs to
see your face.

He shall receive a blessing from the
LORD,
a reward from God his savior.
Such is the race that seeks him,
that seeks the face of the God of
Jacob.

℟. Lord, this is the people that longs to
see your face.

SECOND READING
1 John 3:1-3

Beloved:
See what love the Father has bestowed
on us
that we may be called the children of
God.
Yet so we are.
The reason the world does not know us
is that it did not know him.
Beloved, we are God's children now;
what we shall be has not yet been
revealed.
We do know that when it is revealed we
shall be like him,
for we shall see him as he is.
Everyone who has this hope based on
him makes himself pure,
as he is pure.

All Souls, *November 2, 2027*

FIRST READING
Dan 12:1-3; L1011.7

In those days, I, Daniel, mourned
and heard this word of the Lord:
At that time there shall arise
Michael, the great prince,
guardian of your people;
It shall be a time unsurpassed in distress
since nations began until that time.
At that time your people shall escape,
everyone who is found written in the book.

Many of those who sleep in the dust of the earth shall awake;
Some shall live forever,
others shall be an everlasting horror and disgrace.
But the wise shall shine brightly
like the splendor of the firmament,
And those who lead the many to justice
shall be like the stars forever.

RESPONSORIAL PSALM
Ps 27:1, 4, 7, and 8b, and 9a, 13-14; L1013.3

℟. (1a) The Lord is my light and my salvation.
or:
℟. (13) I believe that I shall see the good things of the Lord in the land of the living.

The LORD is my light and my salvation;
whom should I fear?
The LORD is my life's refuge;
of whom should I be afraid?

℟. The Lord is my light and my salvation.
or:
℟. I believe that I shall see the good things of the Lord in the land of the living.

One thing I ask of the LORD;
this I seek:
To dwell in the house of the LORD
all the days of my life,
That I may gaze on the loveliness of the LORD
and contemplate his temple.

℟. The Lord is my light and my salvation.
or:
℟. I believe that I shall see the good things of the Lord in the land of the living.

Hear, O LORD, the sound of my call;
have pity on me and answer me.
Your presence, O LORD, I seek.
Hide not your face from me.

℟. The Lord is my light and my salvation.
or:
℟. I believe that I shall see the good things of the Lord in the land of the living.

I believe that I shall see the bounty of the LORD
in the land of the living.
Wait for the LORD with courage;
be stouthearted, and wait for the LORD.

℟. The Lord is my light and my salvation.
or:
℟. I believe that I shall see the good things of the Lord in the land of the living.

SECOND READING
Rom 6:3-9; L1014.3

Brothers and sisters:
Are you unaware that we who were baptized into Christ Jesus
were baptized into his death?
We were indeed buried with him
through baptism into death,
so that, just as Christ was raised from the dead
by the glory of the Father,
we too might live in newness of life.

For if we have grown into union with him through a death like his,
we shall also be united with him in the resurrection.
We know that our old self was crucified with him,
so that our sinful body might be done away with,
that we might no longer be in slavery to sin.
For a dead person has been absolved from sin.
If, then, we have died with Christ,
we believe that we shall also live with him.
We know that Christ, raised from the dead, dies no more;
death no longer has power over him.

Gospel (cont.)

or
Mark 12:41-44

Jesus sat down opposite the treasury
and observed how the crowd put money into the treasury.
Many rich people put in large sums.
A poor widow also came and put in two small coins worth a few cents.
Calling his disciples to himself, he said to them,
"Amen, I say to you, this poor widow put in more
than all the other contributors to the treasury.
For they have all contributed from their surplus wealth,
but she, from her poverty, has contributed all she had,
her whole livelihood."

APPENDIX B

Lectionary Pronunciation Guide

Lectionary Word	Pronunciation
Aaron	EHR-uhn
Abana	AB-uh-nuh
Abednego	uh-BEHD-nee-go
Abel-Keramin	AY-b'l-KEHR-uh-mihn
Abel-meholah	AY-b'l-mee-HO-lah
Abiathar	uh-BAI-uh-ther
Abiel	AY-bee-ehl
Abiezrite	ay-bai-EHZ-rait
Abijah	uh-BAI-juh
Abilene	ab-uh-LEE-neh
Abishai	uh-BIHSH-ay-ai
Abiud	uh-BAI-uhd
Abner	AHB-ner
Abraham	AY-bruh-ham
Abram	AY-br'm
Achaia	uh-KAY-yuh
Achim	AY-kihm
Aeneas	uh-NEE-uhs
Aenon	AY-nuhn
Agrippa	uh-GRIH-puh
Ahaz	AY-haz
Ahijah	uh-HAI-juh
Ai	AY-ee
Alexandria	al-ehg-ZAN-dree-uh
Alexandrian	al-ehg-ZAN-dree-uhn
Alpha	AHL-fuh
Alphaeus	AL-fee-uhs
Amalek	AM-uh-lehk
Amaziah	am-uh-ZAI-uh
Amminadab	ah-MIHN-uh-dab
Ammonites	AM-uh-naitz
Amorites	AM-uh-raits
Amos	AY-muhs
Amoz	AY-muhz
Ampliatus	am-plee-AY-tuhs
Ananias	an-uh-NAI-uhs
Andronicus	an-draw-NAI-kuhs
Annas	AN-uhs
Antioch	AN-tih-ahk
Antiochus	an-TAI-uh-kuhs
Aphiah	uh-FAI-uh
Apollos	uh-PAH-luhs
Appius	AP-ee-uhs
Aquila	uh-KWIHL-uh
Arabah	EHR-uh-buh
Aram	AY-ram
Arameans	ehr-uh-MEE-uhnz
Areopagus	ehr-ee-AH-puh-guhs
Arimathea	ehr-uh-muh-THEE-uh
Aroer	uh-RO-er
Asaph	AY-saf
Asher	ASH-er
Ashpenaz	ASH-pee-naz
Assyria	a-SIHR-ee-uh
Astarte	as-TAHR-tee
Attalia	at-TAH-lee-uh
Augustus	uh-GUHS-tuhs
Azariah	az-uh-RAI-uh
Azor	AY-sawr
Azotus	uh-ZO-tus
Baal-shalishah	BAY-uhl-shuh-LAI-shuh
Baal-Zephon	BAY-uhl-ZEE-fuhn
Babel	BAY-bl
Babylon	BAB-ih-luhn
Babylonian	bab-ih-LO-nih-uhn
Balaam	BAY-lm
Barabbas	beh-REH-buhs
Barak	BEHR-ak
Barnabas	BAHR-nuh-buhs
Barsabbas	BAHR-suh-buhs
Bartholomew	bar-THAHL-uh-myoo
Bartimaeus	bar-tih-MEE-uhs
Baruch	BEHR-ook
Bashan	BAY-shan
Becorath	bee-KO-rath
Beelzebul	bee-EHL-zee-buhl
Beer-sheba	BEE-er-SHEE-buh
Belshazzar	behl-SHAZ-er
Benjamin	BEHN-juh-mihn
Beor	BEE-awr
Bethany	BEHTH-uh-nee
Bethel	BETH-el
Bethesda	beh-THEHZ-duh
Bethlehem	BEHTH-leh-hehm
Bethphage	BEHTH-fuh-jee
Bethsaida	behth-SAY-ih-duh
Beth-zur	behth-ZER
Bildad	BIHL-dad
Bithynia	bih-THIHN-ih-uh
Boanerges	bo-uh-NER-jeez
Boaz	BO-az
Caesar	SEE-zer
Caesarea	zeh-suh-REE-uh
Caiaphas	KAY-uh-fuhs
Cain	kayn
Cana	KAY-nuh
Canaan	KAY-nuhn
Canaanite	KAY-nuh-nait
Canaanites	KAY-nuh-naits
Candace	kan-DAY-see
Capernaum	kuh-PERR-nay-uhm
Cappadocia	kap-ih-DO-shee-u
Carmel	KAHR-muhl
carnelians	kahr-NEEL-yuhnz
Cenchreae	SEHN-kree-ay
Cephas	SEE-fuhs
Chaldeans	kal-DEE-uhnz
Chemosh	KEE-mahsh
Cherubim	TSHEHR-oo-bihm
Chislev	KIHS-lehv
Chloe	KLO-ee
Chorazin	kor-AY-sihn
Cilicia	sih-LIHSH-ee-uh
Cleopas	KLEE-o-pas
Clopas	KLO-pas
Corinth	KAWR-ihnth
Corinthians	kawr-IHN-thee-uhnz
Cornelius	kawr-NEE-lee-uhs
Crete	kreet
Crispus	KRIHS-puhs
Cushite	CUHSH-ait
Cypriot	SIH-pree-at
Cyrene	sai-REE-nee
Cyreneans	sai-REE-nih-uhnz
Cyrenian	sai-REE-nih-uhn
Cyrenians	sai-REE-nih-uhnz
Cyrus	SAI-ruhs
Damaris	DAM-uh-rihs
Damascus	duh-MAS-kuhs
Danites	DAN-aits
Decapolis	duh-KAP-o-lis
Derbe	DER-bee
Deuteronomy	dyoo-ter-AH-num-mee
Didymus	DID-I-mus
Dionysius	dai-o-NIHSH-ih-uhs
Dioscuri	dai-O-sky-ri
Dorcas	DAWR-kuhs
Dothan	DO-thuhn
dromedaries	DRAH-muh-dher-eez
Ebed-melech	EE-behd-MEE-lehk
Eden	EE-dn
Edom	EE-duhm
Elamites	EE-luh-maitz
Eldad	EHL-dad
Eleazar	ehl-ee-AY-zer
Eli	EE-lai
Eli Eli Lema Sabachthani	AY-lee AY-lee luh-MAH sah-BAHK-tah-nee
Eliab	ee-LAI-ab

Lectionary Word	Pronunciation
Eliakim	ee-LAI-uh-kihm
Eliezer	ehl-ih-EE-zer
Elihu	ee-LAI-hyoo
Elijah	ee-LAI-juh
Elim	EE-lihm
Elimelech	ee-LIHM-eh-lehk
Elisha	ee-LAI-shuh
Eliud	ee-LAI-uhd
Elizabeth	ee-LIHZ-uh-bth
Elkanah	el-KAY-nuh
Eloi Eloi Lama Sabechthani	AY-lo-ee AY-lo-ee LAH-mah sah-BAHK-tah-nee
Elymais	ehl-ih-MAY-ihs
Emmanuel	eh-MAN-yoo-ehl
Emmaus	eh-MAY-uhs
Epaenetus	ee-PEE-nee-tuhs
Epaphras	EH-puh-fras
ephah	EE-fuh
Ephah	EE-fuh
Ephesians	eh-FEE-zhuhnz
Ephesus	EH-fuh-suhs
Ephphatha	EHF-uh-thuh
Ephraim	EE-fray-ihm
Ephrathah	EHF-ruh-thuh
Ephron	EE-frawn
Epiphanes	eh-PIHF-uh-neez
Erastus	ee-RAS-tuhs
Esau	EE-saw
Esther	EHS-ter
Ethanim	EHTH-uh-nihm
Ethiopian	ee-thee-O-pee-uhn
Euphrates	yoo-FRAY-teez
Exodus	EHK-so-duhs
Ezekiel	eh-ZEE-kee-uhl
Ezra	EHZ-ruh
frankincense	FRANGK-ihn-sehns
Gabbatha	GAB-uh-thuh
Gabriel	GAY-bree-ul
Gadarenes	GAD-uh-reenz
Galatian	guh-LAY-shih-uhn
Galatians	guh-LAY-shih-uhnz
Galilee	GAL-ih-lee
Gallio	GAL-ih-o
Gamaliel	guh-MAY-lih-ehl
Gaza	GAH-zuh
Gehazi	gee-HAY-zai
Gehenna	geh-HEHN-uh
Genesis	JEHN-uh-sihs
Gennesaret	gehn-NEHS-uh-reht
Gentiles	JEHN-tailz
Gerasenes	JEHR-uh-seenz
Gethsemane	gehth-SEHM-uh-ne
Gideon	GIHD-ee-uhn
Gilead	GIHL-ee-uhd
Gilgal	GIHL-gal
Golgotha	GAHL-guh-thuh
Gomorrah	guh-MAWR-uh
Goshen	GO-shuhn
Habakkuk	huh-BAK-uhk
Hadadrimmon	hay-dad-RIHM-uhn
Hades	HAY-deez
Hagar	HAH-gar
Hananiah	han-uh-NAI-uh
Hannah	HAN-uh
Haran	HAY-ruhn
Hebron	HEE-bruhn
Hermes	HER-meez
Herod	HEHR-uhd
Herodians	hehr-O-dee-uhnz
Herodias	hehr-O-dee-uhs
Hezekiah	heh-zeh-KAI-uh
Hezron	HEHZ-ruhn
Hilkiah	hihl-KAI-uh
Hittite	HIH-tait
Hivites	HAI-vaitz
Hophni	HAHF-nai
Hor	hawr
Horeb	HAWR-ehb
Hosea	ho-ZEE-uh
Hur	her
hyssop	HIH-suhp
Iconium	ai-KO-nih-uhm
Isaac	AI-zuhk
Isaiah	ai-ZAY-uh
Iscariot	ihs-KEHR-ee-uht
Ishmael	ISH-may-ehl
Ishmaelites	ISH-mayehl-aits
Israel	IHZ-ray-ehl
Ituraea	ih-TSHOOR-ree-uh
Jaar	JAY-ahr
Jabbok	JAB-uhk
Jacob	JAY-kuhb
Jairus	J-hr-uhs
Javan	JAY-van
Jebusites	JEHB-oo-zaits
Jechoniah	jehk-o-NAI-uh
Jehoiakim	jee-HOI-uh-kihm
Jehoshaphat	jee-HAHSH-uh-fat
Jephthah	JEHF-thuh
Jeremiah	jehr-eh-MAI-uh
Jericho	JEHR-ih-ko
Jeroham	jehr-RO-ham
Jerusalem	jeh-ROU-suh-lehm
Jesse	JEH-see
Jethro	JEHTH-ro
Joakim	JO-uh-kihm
Job	job
Jonah	JO-nuh
Joppa	JAH-puh
Joram	JO-ram
Jordan	JAWR-dn
Joseph	JO-zf
Joses	JO-seez
Joshua	JAH-shou-ah
Josiah	jo-SAI-uh
Jotham	JO-thuhm
Judah	JOU-duh
Judas	JOU-duhs
Judea	jou-DEE-uh
Judean	jou-DEE-uhn
Junia	JOU-nih-uh
Justus	JUHS-tuhs
Kephas	KEF-uhs
Kidron	KIHD-ruhn
Kiriatharba	kihr-ee-ath-AHR-buh
Kish	kihsh
Laodicea	lay-o-dih-SEE-uh
Lateran	LAT-er-uhn
Lazarus	LAZ-er-uhs
Leah	LEE-uh
Lebanon	LEH-buh-nuhn
Levi	LEE-vai
Levite	LEE-vait
Levites	LEE-vaits
Leviticus	leh-VIH-tih-kous
Lucius	LOO-shih-uhs
Lud	luhd
Luke	look
Luz	luhz
Lycaonian	lihk-ay-O-nih-uhn
Lydda	LIH-duh
Lydia	LIH-dih-uh
Lysanias	lai-SAY-nih-uhs
Lystra	LIHS-truh
Maccabees	MAK-uh-beez
Macedonia	mas-eh-DO-nih-uh
Macedonian	mas-eh-DO-nih-uhn
Machir	MAY-kihr
Machpelah	mak-PEE-luh
Magdala	MAG-duh-luh
Magdalene	MAG-duh-lehn
magi	MAY-jai
Malachi	MAL-uh-kai
Malchiah	mal-KAI-uh
Malchus	MAL-kuhz
Mamre	MAM-ree
Manaen	MAN-uh-ehn
Manasseh	man-AS-eh
Manoah	muh-NO-uh
Mark	mahrk
Mary	MEHR-ee
Massah	MAH-suh
Mattathias	mat-uh-THAI-uhs
Matthan	MAT-than

Lectionary Word	Pronunciation
Matthew	MATH-yoo
Matthias	muh-THAI-uhs
Medad	MEE-dad
Mede	meed
Medes	meedz
Megiddo	mee-GIH-do
Melchizedek	mehl-KIHZ-eh-dehk
Mene	MEE-nee
Meribah	MEHR-ih-bah
Meshach	MEE-shak
Mespotamia	mehs-o-po-TAY-mih-uh
Micah	MAI-kuh
Midian	MIH-dih-uhn
Milcom	MIHL-kahm
Miletus	mai-LEE-tuhs
Minnith	MIHN-ihth
Mishael	MIHSH-ay-ehl
Mizpah	MIHZ-puh
Moreh	MO-reh
Moriah	maw-RAI-uh
Mosoch	MAH-sahk
myrrh	mer
Mysia	MIH-shih-uh
Naaman	NAY-uh-muhn
Nahshon	NAY-shuhn
Naomi	NAY-o-mai
Naphtali	NAF-tuh-lai
Nathan	NAY-thuhn
Nathanael	nuh-THAN-ay-ehl
Nazarene	NAZ-awr-een
Nazareth	NAZ-uh-rehth
nazirite	NAZ-uh-rait
Nazorean	naz-aw-REE-uhn
Neapolis	nee-AP-o-lihs
Nebuchadnezzar	neh-byoo-kuhd-NEHZ-er
Negeb	NEH-gehb
Nehemiah	nee-hee-MAI-uh
Ner	ner
Nicanor	nai-KAY-nawr
Nicodemus	nih-ko-DEE-muhs
Niger	NAI-jer
Nineveh	NIHN-eh-veh
Noah	NO-uh
Nun	nuhn
Obed	O-behd
Olivet	AH-lih-veht
Omega	o-MEE-guh
Onesimus	o-NEH-sih-muhs
Ophir	O-fer
Orpah	AWR-puh
Pamphylia	pam-FIHL-ih-uh
Paphos	PAY-fuhs
Parmenas	PAHR-mee-nas
Parthians	PAHR-thee-uhnz
Patmos	PAT-mos
Peninnah	pee-NIHN-uh
Pentecost	PEHN-tee-kawst
Penuel	pee-NYOO-ehl
Perez	PEE-rehz
Perga	PER-guh
Perizzites	PEHR-ih-zaits
Persia	PER-zhuh
Peter	PEE-ter
Phanuel	FAN-yoo-ehl
Pharaoh	FEHR-o
Pharisees	FEHR-ih-seez
Pharpar	FAHR-pahr
Philemon	fih-LEE-muhn
Philippi	fil-LIH-pai
Philippians	fih-LIHP-ih-uhnz
Philistines	fih-LIHS-tihnz
Phinehas	FEHN-ee-uhs
Phoenicia	fee-NIHSH-ih-uh
Phrygia	FRIH-jih-uh
Phrygian	FRIH-jih-uhn
phylacteries	fih-LAK-ter-eez
Pi-Hahiroth	pai-huh-HAI-rahth
Pilate	PAI-luht
Pisidia	pih-SIH-dih-uh
Pithom	PAI-thahm
Pontius	PAHN-shus
Pontus	PAHN-tus
Praetorium	pray-TAWR-ih-uhm
Priscilla	PRIHS-kill-uh
Prochorus	PRAH-kaw-ruhs
Psalm	sahm
Put	puht
Puteoli	pyoo-TEE-o-lai
Qoheleth	ko-HEHL-ehth
qorban	KAWR-bahn
Quartus	KWAR-tuhs
Quirinius	kwai-RIHN-ih-uhs
Raamses	ray-AM-seez
Rabbi	RAB-ai
Rabbouni	ra-BO-nai
Rahab	RAY-hab
Ram	ram
Ramah	RAY-muh
Ramathaim	ray-muh-THAY-ihm
Raqa	RA-kuh
Rebekah	ree-BEHK-uh
Rehoboam	ree-ho-BO-am
Rephidim	REHF-ih-dihm
Reuben	ROO-b'n
Revelation	reh-veh-LAY-shuhn
Rhegium	REE-jee-uhm
Rufus	ROO-fuhs
Sabbath	SAB-uhth
Sadducees	SAD-joo-seez
Salem	SAY-lehm
Salim	SAY-lim
Salmon	SAL-muhn
Salome	suh-LO-mee
Salu	SAYL-yoo
Samaria	suh-MEHR-ih-uh
Samaritan	suh-MEHR-ih-tuhn
Samothrace	SAM-o-thrays
Samson	SAM-s'n
Samuel	SAM-yoo-uhl
Sanhedrin	san-HEE-drihn
Sarah	SEHR-uh
Sarai	SAY-rai
saraph	SAY-raf
Sardis	SAHR-dihs
Saul	sawl
Scythian	SIH-thee-uihn
Seba	SEE-buh
Seth	sehth
Shaalim	SHAY-uh-lihm
Shadrach	SHAY-drak
Shalishah	shuh-LEE-shuh
Shaphat	shay-FAT
Sharon	SHEHR-uhn
Shealtiel	shee-AL-tih-ehl
Sheba	SHEE-buh
Shebna	SHEB-nuh
Shechem	SHEE-kehm
shekel	SHEHK-uhl
Shiloh	SHAI-lo
Shinar	SHAI-nahr
Shittim	sheh-TEEM
Shuhite	SHOO-ait
Shunammite	SHOO-nam-ait
Shunem	SHOO-nehm
Sidon	SAI-duhn
Silas	SAI-luhs
Siloam	sih-LO-uhm
Silvanus	sihl-VAY-nuhs
Simeon	SIHM-ee-uhn
Simon	SAI-muhn
Sin *(desert)*	sihn
Sinai	SAI-nai
Sirach	SAI-rak
Sodom	SAH-duhm
Solomon	SAH-lo-muhn
Sosthenes	SAHS-thee-neez
Stachys	STAY-kihs
Succoth	SUHK-ahth
Sychar	SI-kar
Syene	sai-EE-nee
Symeon	SIHM-ee-uhn
synagogues	SIHN-uh-gahgz
Syrophoenician	SIHR-o fee-NIHSH-ih-uhn

Lectionary Word	Pronunciation
Tabitha	TAB-ih-thuh
Talitha koum	TAL-ih-thuh-KOOM
Tamar	TAY-mer
Tarshish	TAHR-shihsh
Tarsus	TAHR-suhs
Tekel	TEH-keel
Terebinth	TEHR-ee-bihnth
Thaddeus	THAD-dee-uhs
Theophilus	thee-AH-fih-luhs
Thessalonians	theh-suh-LO-nih-uhnz
Theudas	THU-duhs
Thyatira	thai-uh-TAI-ruh
Tiberias	tai-BIHR-ih-uhs
Timaeus	tai-MEE-uhs
Timon	TAI-muhn
Titus	TAI-tuhs
Tohu	TO-hyoo
Trachonitis	trak-o-NAI-tis
Troas	TRO-ahs
Tubal	TYOO-b'l
Tyre	TAI-er
Ur	er
Urbanus	er-BAY-nuhs
Uriah	you-RAI-uh
Uzziah	yoo-ZAI-uh
Wadi	WAH-dee
Yahweh-yireh	YAH-weh-yer-AY
Zacchaeus	zak-KEE-uhs
Zadok	ZAY-dahk
Zarephath	ZEHR-ee-fath
Zebedee	ZEH-beh-dee
Zebulun	ZEH-byoo-luhn
Zechariah	zeh-kuh-RAI-uh
Zedekiah	zeh-duh-KAI-uh
Zephaniah	zeh-fuh-NAI-uh
Zerah	ZEE-ruh
Zeror	ZEE-rawr
Zerubbabel	zeh-RUH-buh-behl
Zeus	zyoos
Zimri	ZIHM-rai
Zion	ZAI-uhn
Ziph	zihf
Zoar	ZO-er
Zorah	ZAWR-uh
Zuphite	ZUHF-ait

CONTRIBUTORS

Martin Erspamer, OSB, is a monk and a hermit of Saint Meinrad Archabbey in southern Indiana. He is a well-known liturgical artist and liturgical consultant. Erspamer works in a wide range of media, including pottery, stained glass, and wood, and is nationally known for his illustration of sacred themes.

Katharine E. Harmon is a pastoral liturgist and American Catholic historian serving as the project director for the Obsculta Preaching Initiative at Saint John's School of Theology and Seminary in Collegeville, Minnesota. A graduate of the University of Notre Dame's liturgical studies program, Harmon has contributed both scholarly and pastoral pieces on topics of liturgical renewal and American Catholic faith and practice, including *There Were Also Many Women There: Lay Women in the Liturgical Movement in the United States, 1926–59* (Liturgical Press, 2013) and the award-winning *Mary and the Liturgical Year: A Pastoral Resource* (Liturgy Training Publications, 2023). She has served as a church musician for more than 25 years, and resides in St. Joseph, Minnesota, with her husband and two children.

Orin E. Johnson has held professional music and liturgy positions for 25 years, currently at St. Margaret of Scotland Catholic Church in St. Louis, Missouri. He holds degrees in music and theology from Harvard University, Radford University, and Aquinas Institute of Theology. His liturgical music is published with OCP and GIA; he is the author of *Incarnate in Word and Song: Exploring Music in Liturgy and Life* (Liturgical Press, 2023), and has other writings published by Liturgical Press, Liguori, and Twenty-Third Publications. He is active nationally as a speaker, performer, catechist, and retreat and workshop leader.

Rámond Mitchell serves as director of liturgy for Our Lady of Grace Church and School in Edina, Minnesota. Previously he served as assistant director of liturgy at the Basilica of Saint Mary in Minneapolis, and parish liturgist and then as director of liturgy at Saint George-in-the-East Church in London, UK. Originally from the Bahamas, he earned a bachelor of arts in theology from Saint John's University (Collegeville, Minnesota) and a master of arts in theology and ministry from Boston College. He has been a dedicated cantor and psalmist at Westminster Cathedral in London and enjoys music making and cooking outside of his professional work.

Matthew Sherman serves as the director of lifelong learning and educational effectiveness at Saint John's School of Theology and Seminary in Collegeville, Minnesota. His writing and teaching involve the intersection of theology and ministry, the role of ethics in historical theology, and connections between sacramental and moral thought. He teaches courses in fundamental morals, historical theology, bioethics, marriage and family, and Catholic social teaching.